# ANOINTED WITH OIL

ALSO BY DARREN DOCHUK

*From Bible Belt to Sunbelt:*
*Plain-Folk Religion, Grassroots Politics,*
*and the Rise of Evangelical Conservatism*

Published in cooperation with the William P. Clements Center
for Southwest Studies, Southern Methodist University

# ANOINTED
# WITH OIL

## HOW CHRISTIANITY AND CRUDE
## MADE MODERN AMERICA

## DARREN DOCHUK

BASIC BOOKS

*New York*

Basic Books
Hachette Book Group
1290 Avenue of the Americas, New York, NY 10104
www.basicbooks.com

Printed in the United States of America

First Edition: June 2019

Published by Basic Books, an imprint of Perseus Books, LLC, a subsidiary of Hachette Book Group, Inc. The Basic Books name and logo is a trademark of the Hachette Book Group.

The Hachette Speakers Bureau provides a wide range of authors for speaking events. To find out more, go to www.hachettespeakersbureau.com or call (866) 376-6591.

The publisher is not responsible for websites (or their content) that are not owned by the publisher.

Print book interior design by Jeff Williams.

Library of Congress Cataloging-in-Publication Data
Names: Dochuk, Darren, author.
Title: Anointed with oil: how Christianity and crude made modern America / Darren Dochuk.
Description: First edition. | New York: Basic Books, 2019. | Includes bibliographical references and index.
Identifiers: LCCN 2018057051| ISBN 9780465060863 (hardcover) | ISBN 9781541673946 (ebook)
Subjects: LCSH: United States—Church history. | Business—Religious aspects—Christianity. | Petroleum—United States—History. | Petroleum industry and trade—United States—History. | Oil industries—United States—History.
Classification: LCC BR517 .D55 2019 | DDC 261.8/5—dc23
LC record available at https://lccn.loc.gov/2018057051

ISBNs: 978-0-465-06086-3 (hardcover), 978-1-5416-7394-6 (ebook)

LSC-C

10 9 8 7 6 5 4 3 2 1

*For Debra*

# Contents

# CONTENTS

## PART FOUR: CRUDE RECKONINGS

# The Strange Career of Patillo Higgins

P atillo Higgins sensed oil's arrival before setting eyes on it. Tired after a day of trading timber and fighting a January wind, he prodded his old horse along, eager to settle into the ease of home. As the weary duo made their way through the Gulf Coast town of Beaumont, Texas, Patillo heard someone frantically calling his name. "Mr. Higgins!" Jim Collier, a former business partner, hollered from across the street. "Mr. Higgins—did you know you [are] the wisest man in the world?" Perplexed, the rider appealed for details. The "Lucas 1" oil well had come in—and spectacularly so—at Spindletop, a hill just south of town. It was the exact spot of soil Higgins had long predicted would someday spew liquid gold and make Beaumont forever rich.[1]

Higgins resumed his journey, anxious to get a look. As he drew closer he began to smell the noxious fumes wafting overhead; their pungency overpowered the wood smoke—especially dense this wintery day—fanning out of Beaumont's chimneys. Then he heard the roar and finally caught a glimpse of the column rising in the distance, off the natural earth mound and high into the sky. Arriving at the heart of the action, he stood alongside Beaumont's rapt denizens, tilted his head to take in the full view of the eruption, and froze, staggered by the scene, deafened by the sound. He had always believed Spindletop's yield could be big—perhaps thousands of barrels per day—but Lucas 1 streamed at a rate of *tens* of thousands per day. Just as striking was the picture of black-faced men scrambling to bring the uncontrollable under control. A team of roughnecks, led by chief driller Anthony Lucas, worked feverishly to support a fragile derrick, out of which a deluge six inches in diameter jetted 180 feet into the air. Witnesses compared the geyser to a tornado; others said it was like "a giant black ostrich plume sticking out of the earth's hatband." The blinded toilers trapped under its downpour saw little other than the pool of ebony fluid at their feet, which was rapidly turning into a sea.[2]

Awed by the spectacle, Patillo Higgins nevertheless experienced a range of other emotions. The Lucas gusher of January 10, 1901, had proved him right: pools of oil did indeed rest beneath Beaumont. Yet his self-satisfaction dimmed as he saw the praise heaped upon Anthony Lucas, whose persistence would now yield riches. The multitudes who descended on Spindletop to witness history, Higgins thought, should have been there because of him.[3]

His jealousy must have been disorienting, for a sense of divine certainty had accompanied his every move for quite some time. Such assurance had not come easily, though. Born in 1863, at the height of the Civil War, in a rough coastal section of Southeast Texas, Higgins matched the tumult of his moment and place. When he was six, his family moved north to the lumber town of Beaumont, where townsfolk came to know him simply as "Bud," a prankster who loved to gamble, drink, and brawl. Higgins's delinquency culminated in a violent encounter with a sheriff, who had been called in to stop the armed ruffian from harassing a black church. In the ensuing gunfire, both hit their mark, but only Higgins survived, albeit with his left arm so mangled that it had to be amputated. A jury deemed the killing "self-defense." Having narrowly escaped conviction for murder, Higgins soon changed his ways—dramatically.[4]

His new direction came by way of the cross. In 1885, the one-armed renegade attended a fire-and-brimstone revival at Beaumont's opera house, conducted by Reverend William Penn. A towering, 250-pound Confederate veteran, Penn was a Christian warrior known for his black frock coat, tumbling gray beard, and imposing style. The burly evangelist convinced the twenty-two-year-old Higgins, consumed by guilt over his past transgressions, that only the Bible could help. Higgins committed to Jesus Christ. "I used to put my trust in pistols," he confessed to Penn. "Now my trust is in God." When Higgins walked the aisle toward the altar, his mother almost fainted from surprise; others shared her disbelief that Bud "done got religion." Most doubted it would last. But after converting, Higgins set out to prove everyone wrong and make something of himself. He would become a businessman and use material wealth to build a spiritual kingdom in anticipation of Christ's return.[5]

Higgins tried several vocations before discovering oil. He dabbled in lumber, then brick making. After forming the Higgins Manufacturing Company, he traveled north to gain expertise in his new trade. His visits to industrial compounds with brick-making activity took him to the tucked-away oil region of western Pennsylvania. There, in Titusville three decades earlier, another enterprising sojourner named Edwin Drake had first proved that subterranean crude could be summoned to the surface. Ingratiating himself with locals and embracing the exhilaration of an oil-flush region that journalists came to refer to as "Petrolia," Higgins apprenticed himself in the art of reading the land. Once sure he knew how to survey any topography for signs of rich loam, Higgins returned to Southeast Texas and started seeking his fortune, with Jesus, he liked to think, by his side.[6]

The sequence of events that followed consecrated his marriage to God and black gold. Initially Higgins hunted oil as efficient fuel for his kilns, but it quickly became the endgame. Not for the last time, his Christian commitments complemented his evolving financial priorities. After resettling in Beaumont in 1891, he joined First Baptist, the town's leading church. Deep conviction and desire for acceptance compelled him to serve this congregation in whatever capacity possible, even if it meant teaching a Sunday school class of unruly eight-year-old girls. On one fortuitous Sunday, Higgins took his charges out of town to show them an "everyday application of religion" in the appreciation of nature. With a dozen pupils in tow, he made his way to a quiet spot on Spindletop where springs of water bubbled enchantingly. Higgins had been to the springs before, but this time he noticed clouds of a gaseous substance and hints of an auspicious rock formation. Excited about the possibility of oil, he decided he had to purchase the plot on which the springs sat. For help with financing he contacted his church elder and mentor, George Carroll, the corporate leader who had sponsored the revival at which Higgins found release from his sin.[7]

Together the two formed in 1892 what Higgins insisted be titled the Gladys City Oil, Gas, and Manufacturing Company. The company's namesake drew frowns of disapproval around Beaumont. Higgins, by then a thirty-year-old bachelor, had become infatuated with a Sunday school pupil, Gladys Bingham. He promised to marry her one day. For the time being, he placed her image on the company's official emblem. Over the course of the next two years, with the backing of Carroll and local Methodist businessman George O'Brien, Higgins devised a bold plan. Based on its anticipated lucrative finds of oil and gas, the Gladys City corporation would construct a utopian town—a model "industrial city on the Texas Gulf Coast" replete with a refinery, pipelines, harbor, and thriving business sector and communal life. Higgins exclaimed that "zones [would be] designated for schools and churches, and provision . . . made for numerous city parks, a town hall, and a handsome public square." Higgins did not simply want to find oil. Like an apostle, he wanted to channel it toward realization of human perfection and heavenly splendor.[8]

Higgins's gut sense that something big simmered beneath Beaumont convinced Carroll and O'Brien but failed to attract other investors. Discouraged but undeterred, Higgins busied himself with prayer and study in geological and biblical texts. "If I read anything in the Bible, I know just what it means," he liked to boast. His tiny kerosene lamp, which barely illuminated his books, allowed him to study late into the night. The whistle of a nearby mill blew at four o'clock each morning, signaling the scholar to bed. But Higgins never rested fully. During the day he aggressively pursued financiers, courting local bankers at a barbershop one moment, pleading with faraway corporate czars the next. Even Standard Oil king John D. Rockefeller heard his plea. By then Standard's US monopoly was absolute. Thanks to its grip on Pennsylvania, it saw little need to locate new sources west of the Mississippi River. Nor did it feel such a pursuit could succeed. Standard executive John D. Archbold bragged he would drink every gallon of crude produced west of the Mississippi, so sure was he that the West was dry. Unfazed,

Higgins wrote Archbold's boss directly. Rockefeller declined to invest in Gladys City, citing Archbold's "adverse geological judgment."[9]

Higgins pressed on, determined to prove the critics wrong. As the nineteenth century drew to a close, though, he found it harder to withstand his neighbors' ridicule. Jokes about the "one-armed madman" hurt. More problematic was that his partners began to dismiss him as well. By 1896, his eccentricities had frayed his relationships with Gladys City's other investors. O'Brien, highly respected in the community, could barely handle the embarrassment of his association with Higgins's failing dream. Things only grew worse when a state geologist warned locals "not to fritter away their dollars in the vain outlook for oil in the Beaumont area." Easing O'Brien's stress, the perennially impatient Higgins sold his own interests in Gladys City to Carroll.[10]

But even as he turned his attention to ventures in lumber and real estate, Higgins remained obsessed with locating Beaumont's hidden treasure. He forged a friendship with "Captain" Anthony Lucas, a mechanical engineer and veteran of the Austrian navy, who was exploring the Gulf Coast's salt domes, convinced that minerals lay beneath. In 1899 Higgins and Lucas agreed to partner and lease Spindletop acreage from Gladys City: the captain contributed the capital; Higgins, the prospecting hunches. Promised 10 percent of the profits, Higgins interpreted the deal with his old company as redemptive, even retributive. Yet his good feelings did not last. While Lucas's drilling operation on Spindletop proceeded at a fast pace (penetrating the salt dome was easy), it did not produce quick results; the team would have to drill much deeper, requiring expensive tools. In a quest for funds Lucas looked to industrialist and banker Andrew Mellon in Pittsburgh. Mellon agreed to invest but demanded that Lucas proceed on his own and cut off communications with the rube Higgins. Lucas did so, if regretfully. Hurt by his friend and bitter about how "big oil" people back east had stolen his opportunity, Higgins again found himself elbowed to the margins. On New Year's Day 1901, the Lucas drill team punctured the earth in a new spot, a mere fifty feet away from one of Higgins's original targets. Ten days later, Lucas hit the geyser that blackened the very ground on which Gladys Bingham had once walked.[11]

Spindletop was struck, announcing Texas's oil age and America's era of unrivaled power. Referencing an old hymn, Higgins marveled that "the rocks broke their silence." Grappling with the stabbing truth that he had not been the one to coax the wonders out of the ground, yet never one to wallow in self-pity for long, he did what he would always do: started chasing the next thing, with Jesus by his side. He incorporated the Higgins Oil and Fuel Company and by day began drilling on land he had managed to retain. By night, he privately started work on a theological treatise he hoped would correct his church's teachings on sin and salvation. Then, in April 1901, Higgins No. 1 came in, with a spectacular display that rivaled Lucas 1. Soon Higgins's company became one of the largest in operation on Spindletop, a rival of the Gulf Oil Company, the Mellon-Lucas enterprise. The "Prophet of Spindletop," as Higgins was branded, finally found acceptance in his own land.[12]

# Introduction

*And the rock poured me out rivers of oil.*

—JOB 29:6

The Prophet of Spindletop certainly thought he was special. When poking at the soil for subterranean riches, quoting scripture along the way, he fancied himself a mediator of sorts, connecting the grit of hard labor to a cosmic calling, primordial matter to fantasies of a new age. He also believed history had no hold on him—that his extrasensory perceptions and ability to command the future freed him from the usual constraints of time. With a complete lack of self-doubt, the Bible-toting driller deemed himself a blessing to his people, and with oil in his sights he determined to prove the point. Even when times got tough and biting criticisms of his character mounted, he pressed on, armed with an assurance that God and black gold favored him.

Cordoned off in his own mind as exceptional, Higgins had an unwavering faith in oil—and its role in his destiny—that was orthodox to the core. Higgins himself was as American as they came. Far from unusual, his seamless interchange of sacred and material goals, and his utter conviction that petroleum was his providence, evinced a convulsive combination that has long defined not only the personal lives and communities affected by crude but the United States' very own identity.

Consider the generations of oil hunters who preceded Higgins in Pennsylvania's Petrolia, the petroleum-rich zone nestled up against the Allegheny Mountains in the state's remote northwest corner, and who subsequently followed his lead in the southwestern oil patch. Countless numbers of them chased the black stuff as if it was *their* divine calling and drew on their biblical studies and understandings of the spirit world to engineer better methods of tapping the earth's bounty and claiming dominion over the soil. Driven by the same profit-mindedness of the Christian steward, they embraced a high-risk, high-reward entrepreneurialism in hopes of achieving a prosperity that could signal their blessedness and allow them to save society in anticipation of the end times. Like Higgins, they tenaciously weathered the manifold disruptions of a brutal corporate climate predicated on boom-bust cycles and the mercurial prerogatives of chance. And, also like him, they did so by drawing closer to Christ.

That same faith extended beyond individual oilers to the villages and towns they helped transform. As much as crude held sacred meaning for those who chased it, it was also deemed hallowed by residents of oil patches like Beaumont, Texas, where the chasing occurred. There, people like Higgins's acquaintance Jim Collier waited prayerfully for liquid gold to appear and marveled at the utopian possibilities it would offer were it to actually do so. When oil was finally struck, stargazers and cynics alike reacted with awe at their cascading fortunes, rejoicing that God's favor was now upon them. Enlivened by that notion, God-fearing citizens with the mind-set of George Carroll set out to make their boomtowns puritan "cities on a hill." Oil's attendant nightmares of booming immorality made them all the more determined to turn their communities into crucibles of celestial hope, their towns into models of industry and governance and harbingers of God's kingdom.

Such strong belief in the sacred power of crude also enveloped American society itself. First discovered during the Civil War (1861–1865) in the very Pennsylvania hills Higgins would navigate decades later, petroleum registered as a mystical fount that might ease America out of bloodshed and into a new age of peace and prosperity. Oil was to be a healing balm for the body politic. Yet during the century and a half that unfolded after war's end, it became a catalyst as well, a propellant of America's coming of age. The crude extracted across time from

South Texas and similar locales not only fired the economic engine of the United States as it pursued ever-widening markets at home and overseas but also greased the mechanisms of political and philanthropic empires set on imposing their moral imperatives. Seeing themselves much like Higgins saw himself—as anointed—and eager to act on oil's seemingly transcendent potential, petroleum families such as the Rockefellers carved out creases of unrivaled authority through which they could sell their dreams (and dogmas) for modernity. Equipped with oil's stunning wealth, pious citizens who attended churches like Beaumont's First Baptist in turn constructed enormous ministries with boundless reach. There, as well as in Tulsa, Houston, and countless other nodes of the production nexus, petroleum bankrolled colossal cathedrals, schools, missionary organizations, and foundations, all determined to fashion the United States into a resplendent Christian commonwealth.

Far from an outlier in history, then, Patillo Higgins actually acted at the center of a perpetual fury that saw ideas and institutions of faith spark the discovery and appropriation of oil and the economic weight of crude stir up churchly devotion and cosmic expectations among oil country's people of God. No mere liquid form, gushing petroleum was a life stream to the heavens; no mere escape from difficult times, oil-refined religion promised to turn the earth's bounty into a better tomorrow. Such was the give-and-take that facilitated Higgins's rise from obscurity and stoked America's preponderance in an advancing age.

WHAT FOLLOWS IS the religious biography of a natural resource with outsized—and seemingly otherworldly—importance. Glimpsed from the vantage of the Prophet of Spindletop, it is the story of the dynamic reciprocity that Christianity and crude shared in the making of modern America. Just as importantly, it is a story about the making of America's *ascendant moment*. The same unqualified confidence in the mastery of crude that drove Higgins and fellow oil hunters forward on domestic turf also furnished the United States with the indomitable spirit that made the century inaugurated by the Spindletop strike its epoch of supremacy. Such sanction was justified by this nation's physical and fiscal control of oil, which for most of the nineteenth and twentieth centuries went unmatched. True, and as the chapters that follow will lightly sketch out, the development of the oil industry was global from the start, the impact of crude on the basic functions of daily life as well as the political and economic functions of nation-states universal in degree. Petroleum was never America's to possess alone. Yet, in the decades immediately following oil's discovery—first in Pennsylvania, then with emphasis after Spindletop—Americans could rightly assume that their nation enjoyed sovereignty over the black stuff and that this dominion placed it in an advantageous, even hegemonic position on an international stage. That power, real and imagined, was not simply a natural outgrowth of America's fortuitous proximity to oil or prowess in its handling, however. It was also generated by the US oil industry's ideological prerogatives and self-interests, as well as by its fierce internal clashes, all of which blended religious, economic, and political concerns into one combustive fuel for America's global march.

As a whole, the business world that Higgins fought so hard to join was populated by corporate entities that projected his same faith in crude. Gladys City Oil, Gas, and Manufacturing Company was far from the only petroleum firm to shroud itself in an apostolic aura. To a remarkable degree, many other oil companies—some exceptionally large, most modest and small—openly embraced the theological imperatives that informed their chief executives, aligned their boardrooms with biblical logics, and sacralized their operations as modes of witness and outreach. Once attached to US ambitions abroad, those enterprises provided vital energy and institutional structures for the nation's imperial project. Partnered with visionary politicians and philanthropists, oil's corporate giants articulated ownership of petroleum as the essence of American exceptionalism. The allegories of deistic favor they deployed, the manifest destiny in which they enveloped society: oil's elite wielded these sacred discourses in a quest to conquer, but their words also stemmed from sincere conviction that America's guardianship of crude meant it was responsible for elevating all humanity. Even when their vocabulary was drained of the explicit God talk of earlier generations, late twentieth-century oil's prime movers remained tethered to a language that accentuated the oil-rich nation's special moment in the sun.

Forty years after Spindletop, in February 1941, magazine publisher Henry Luce would give that moment an enduring name: the

"American Century." Luce, the son of foreign missionaries sponsored by the Rockefeller family, used the pages of his *Life* magazine to compel his fellow citizens to "create the first great American Century." He had actually tested that charge a month earlier before the American Petroleum Institute in Oklahoma. In his keynote address, Luce heralded oilmen as the vanguard of pure American values, praising their "dynamic spirit of freedom and enterprise" and "sense of illimitable roundness of the world." When harnessed by God-fearing patriots, he intimated, oil had the capacity to transform the world into something godlier and better. America's special blessing was, in his mind, also its peculiar burden, the source of its prophetic mission. Like so many powerbrokers at the time, he drew on grand metaphors to underscore the need for the United States to use its oil to illumine the world, fuel progress, and power international advancement. Higgins could not have stated it better himself.[1]

These were inspiring sentiments, indeed; yet their open-ended nature made them grounds for fierce debate: Exactly who in the oil guild retained the rights and means to lead Luce's charge? As taken as they were with Luce's lofty vision, oilers only rarely spoke with one voice. Most often, they engaged in unabated cutthroat competition. Such was the by-product of the "rule of capture," a legal canon unique in its application to US mineral rights that guaranteed the right of each driller who had access to a common pool to drain as much crude as he could, at dizzying rates and on his terms. That competition spilled over into the churchly realm, where oil's constituents waged war for the right to define the core beliefs and moral composition of America at home and abroad. Far from presenting the united front imagined in Luce's address, then, the oil fraternity was marked by bitter infighting and fits of righteous rage, which in turn raised the intensity and stakes of the industry's—and, by extension, the nation's—quest for dominance.

The most lasting and important of these contests—and the one that drives this book—was the rivalry between "major" and "independent" oil companies. Patillo Higgins's bitterness toward the "big oil" people in the East—men like John D. Rockefeller and Standard Oil executive John Archbold, who had elbowed him aside—and subsequent determination to make his fledgling oil company competitive against the likes of Andrew Mellon's Gulf Oil were emblematic of the emotionally charged chasm that separated oil's main combatants. At the heart of the rift were perennially opposed market principles and moral economies—in essence, two sparring spirits of capitalism.[2]

As manifested in the workings of Standard Oil and its subsidiaries—and of its founding clan, the Rockefellers—major oil's prerogatives were transparent. It sought to dull the excesses of the rule of capture, centralize authority over its dizzying operational scales, and rationalize the industry. While he espoused oil's core ideals of free enterprise, major oil's architect John D. Rockefeller also saw them as wasteful; his was a bureaucratic outlook in keeping with the Protestant ethic Max Weber would famously write about, which assumed godly capitalists would honor the principles of efficiency and control. And so he proceeded to rein the industry in by conquering and consolidating. That ethic naturally fused with his efforts as a churchman. A refiner of the tallest order, Rockefeller was also a towering reformer who propagated a social gospel that called on Christians to construct a better society by way of their economic and political clout. Over time, that gospel inspired him and particularly his son to pursue a revamped philanthropy. Frustrated with charity that focused on personal matters of the soul, John D. Rockefeller Jr. built a foundation that stressed scientific modernization on a massive scale. Though not as outspokenly religious as their grandfather and father, the third-generation Rockefellers were every bit as eager to use the family's petropower to enhance America's Judeo-Christian values and ensure the nation's place at the head of a new international order of capitalist and humanitarian exchange. These forerunners of major oil may not have worn biblical convictions on their sleeves, but they went about their business with an eye to a higher being and a higher sense of being. Oil's global topographies in this way became their theological planes, on and through which they could envision human accord.[3]

This "civil religion of crude," as major oil's imperatives are labeled in these pages, was countered by another force within US oil: the ethic of "wildcat Christianity." Oil's industrious rank-and-file producers and independent companies embodied the latter spirit. Imbued with the "charismatic" and "heroic" qualities classical thinkers identified with preindustrial capitalists (Weber designated them "warrior heroes," a dying breed), these wildcatters considered the rule of capture sacrosanct.

Their modus operandi was to drill discovery wells on untapped land; their prevailing wish, to act alone, be it on the oil field or before their God. Whether overseeing a single team of oil hunters or managing larger, partially integrated corporations that oversaw refining and marketing as well as production, they took risks and pursued profits as if there were no tomorrow. Beaten into submission by Standard in oil's first frontier of Pennsylvania, they relocated west, beyond the Rockefeller reach. Amid the boom-bust cycles that settled over the western oil patches, they held ever more tightly to a theology premised on the power of personal encounter with an active Creator, the mysteries of an earth whose hidden riches enchanted and eluded reason, and the need to labor tirelessly—be it drilling or evangelizing—before time ran out. The Stewarts of Union Oil and the Pews of Sun Oil, two prominent families in this sector, epitomized wildcat Christianity's intensely other-worldly belief that an immutable God, not a calculating or cunning humanity, was in control. Their species of providentialism embraced (in degrees) the speculative dimensions of oiling and accepted the suffering that they often spawned. Godly people, they believed, were to ride the whims of oil rather than try to discipline them. Likewise, they were to spend more energy on saving people with their simple gospel than on rebuilding society with complex man-made rationales.[4]

As the chapters that follow will show, the collision of major oil's civil religion of crude with independent oil's wildcat Christianity would drive a great deal of America's global expansion—be it to Saudi Arabia or Canada, China or Israel—but also trigger some of the most profound conflicts in our national life, the most conspicuous of which played out in partisan politics. Over time, majors and independents would fight for pro-petroleum policies and against antipetroleum publicity as a united bloc, increasingly within the confines of the Republican Party. But their internecine squabbles persisted, profoundly shaping policies, elections, and culture as a whole. Major oil's proximity to Washington and Wall Street always placed it in a favorable position, allowing it to leverage alliances with powerbrokers to expand productive capacities and profits, as well as its cachet on an international stage. Meanwhile, from oil towns like Dallas, Tulsa, and Beaumont emerged activists and politicians, Protestant and Catholic oilers, beholden to the wildcat doctrine. Zealous in their fuel and family values and prosperity gospel, distrustful of petroleum conglomerates and their willingness to compromise on the rule of capture, and anxious to re-enfranchise their sector and their country in a fierce global arena, they fashioned a radical—and potent—political alternative.[5]

As PROFOUNDLY AS these two absolutes—oil and religion—have shaped modern America and its ascendant moment, scholars and social commentators have tended to analyze them separately, as if they are organically discrete or naturally antagonistic toward each other. While a flourishing field of oil studies has been populated with talented scholars who typically look past the holy to the nitty-gritty of oil economics and diplomacy, experts in American religion have not yet pondered the relevance of a base material to spheres of belief and practice, congregational life and the pulpit. A few journalists have offered commentary—usually biting—on what they consider the occasional intersections of these two entities, but with almost predictable fixation on "big oil" conspiracies and dark political outcomes.[6]

Popular culture has not been any more eager to entertain faith and crude's deepest entanglements. Consider, for instance, Paul Anderson's classic 2008 movie *There Will Be Blood* (based loosely on Upton Sinclair's 1927 novel *Oil!*). The film tackles both subjects, but only in dialectical fashion. In the film viewers encounter parallel subcultures, one commanded by a brutally ambitious oil hunter named Daniel Plainview, the other by a hypocritical Holy Roller preacher called Eli Sunday. Throughout the film, the two antagonists occupy the distinct realms of petroleum and the Pentecostal parish, truly interacting only occasionally (Sunday's prayers over the drill site, Plainview's public confession). The tension between them rises steadily, culminating in the oilman's deadly bludgeoning of the evangelist. Yet, in real life, their two spheres have rarely been held separate or in tension. The Plainviews and Sundays of US history have frequently shared vocational ambitions as well as character traits. Often they have even been one and the same, their conquering spirit and shared sins far more formidable than Anderson allows.[7]

That thick connectivity is on full display in the rich, largely untapped archival sources that buttress *Anointed with Oil*. Drawing on extensive research in numerous archives on both sides of the Atlantic, the book charts the generations-long workings of established oil corporations like Standard, Union, and Sun, whose calculations for crude dominance mirrored their chiefs' theological aspirations, while also accounting for tinier firms whose names—Christian Oil Company, Providential Oil, Zion Oil—betrayed an overreliance on supposition and prayer. *Anointed with Oil* also crosses between California and China, the US Southwest and the Canadian prairies, New York and Saudi Arabia, Oklahoma and Ghana, leaning on the records of philanthropists, missionaries, statesmen, pastors, and engineers to map out US petroleum's and religion's global extensions. What come to light are the expansive, joint efforts of oilmen and churchmen, such as Arabist William Eddy and African American activist Jake Simmons, American evangelist Billy Graham and Alberta premier Ernest Manning, to create projects of immense international importance, ranging from Aramco to the Athabasca Oil Sands and from civil rights in the US South to human rights in the Middle East. And it looks at political operatives in new light. Oklahoma senator Robert Kerr's lobbying on behalf of Baptists and independent oilmen, Nelson and David Rockefeller's attempts to spur on schemes of global development and liberal internationalism, and H. L. Hunt's and J. Howard Pew's efforts to turn the GOP into the party of Barry Goldwater, Ronald Reagan, George W. Bush—and the home of wildcat ideology—all come into clearer focus once glimpsed through the lens of Christianity and crude's arresting, shared power.

Yet, as *Anointed with Oil* will show, these critical trajectories in US politics and culture are not the only ones illuminated anew when broached in the context of God and black gold's co-constituted power. If the dual authority of oil and religion rests at the heart of America's modern moment, it also stands as the fulcrum for so much schism in modern American life, rooted divisions that extend beyond the internal workings of the petroleum industry and its quest for world reign. The very notion that "modernity" has meant the same thing for all Americans is itself a fallacy, exposed in full relief by the historical machinations of Christianity and crude.

As much as these two entities have inspired hopes of progress for American society, for instance, their joint workings have also stirred up passionate dissent and a conviction that oil's inscrutable power leads to barbarism rather than godly civilization. Countless Americans across time have viewed oil's anointing as a threat rather than a grace, a scourge rather than a gift. Deadly conflagrations, energy crises, and ecological disasters—oil-produced calamities sketched in the pages that follow—consistently reminded oil-dependent citizens that petroleum could be as hellacious as it was sublime. "Whenever you punch a hole so deep into the ground that oil pops out, Hades comes with it," one oil-patch resident rued in the 1930s. "And the more oil the more Hades." Amid steady outbreaks of such calamity, the industry was repeatedly forced to confront its naysayers, whose voices got louder with each disastrous turn. Ida Tarbell, Upton Sinclair, Rachel Carson, Bill McKibben—the names of outspoken muckrakers would change with time, even as their message struck a familiar chord: America's dependency on black gold was too heavy a burden, economically, environmentally, politically, and spiritually. Convinced that crude was detrimental to society's well-being, they prayed for relief from the threat and, armed with their theology, demanded that government peel back petroleum's grip.[8]

Other facets of oil's religious biography further underscore how America's anointing has divided the nation. Witnessed in the battle between wildcat Christianity and the civil religion of crude are divergent conceptions of land and labor that continue to flare in our day. Animated by their very personal contact with soil, wildcatters like Patillo Higgins and the Stewarts and Pews conveyed a sense of wonder about the earth and a desire to know it well—this, even as they attacked it with raw determination to drain its hidden riches and fight off anyone preventing them that right. Enjoying the luxury of large-scale operations and the ability to weather the heavy losses they allowed, major oil welcomed greater oversight of the industry's management of its natural resource and embraced the costs of conservation. Yet, with scale also came numbing distance from environmental crises it created in spectacular degrees. The "workscapes" these rivals promoted differed as well. Even as they joined forces to ward off unionization of their industry and to protect its white racial privilege, they tackled the labor question differently. Nearer grassroots action, practitioners of wildcat religion met the roughneck and roustabout at their level and through rigorous propagandizing championed their independence and stoked their populist urge to protect that independence at any cost. In their mammoth operations, meanwhile, practitioners of the civil religion of crude constructed sprawling systems of social welfare to bring the roughneck and roustabout up to their level of cosmopolitan concern and immerse them in a capitalist enterprise far greater than any one part. At the very center of oil's contests over natural and human ecology, in other words, rests a question of fundamental importance to modern American society writ large: Just who controls the levers of democracy?[9]

Also evidenced in the clash of crude gospels are contrasting notions of time and technology. Imbued with a confidence afforded by their integrated capacities, major oilmen were technocrats who readily adopted modern science to map frontier landscapes, design machinery to extract and refine crude on massive scales, and construct corporate domains with stunning breadth. Reinforcing that obsession was a millennial theology that said humanity could (and should) improve its condition in advance of the Lord's final reign. In the Rockefeller mindset, Christians were to command boardrooms, legislatures, and foundations to apply oil's gifts to the construction of a godly society. From their corporate headquarters in city centers, major oilmen envisioned global dominions of their making. The wildcatters and rank and file who populated America's oil patches saw things differently. Their proximity to the planet's subterranean mysteries nurtured wonderment with a resource that could not be completely possessed and with a cosmos that could not be completely explained. They too exploited technologies to engineer better outcomes, yet only insofar as they were applied to the acquisition of earth's profits or exegesis of God's word, not to the questioning of one's origins or the other's authenticity. The unknowables of crude's terrain and impending depletion spurred them on to action—be it drilling or spreading their gospel at a faster clip. Attuned to a messianic time that defied human progress and promised instead cycles of societal rupture in advance of Christ's sudden, salvific return, wildcatters chased petroleum with an end-times feel. Amid jungles of derricks and refining fires, risk-filled labor and violent swings of fortune, their boom-bust existence fed a cataclysmic view of the here and now and of life beyond, as well as a dependency on an all-powerful being who gives and takes and tests his people but is always there.[10]

Considering their contrasting takes on these human universals, it is no wonder that in the tussles between major oil and independent oil—between the civil religion of crude and wildcat Christianity—we are also privy to a final tension that still defines the nation: that which concerns the politics of geography and place. On one hand, the wide-angled vision of outreach that proponents of major oil and its gospel of global development and uplift celebrated in the mid-twentieth century has dimmed. Once bolstered by an indomitable spirit that Luce proclaimed for his carbon-rich country, oil's civil religion of crude is no longer operable as a US imperative or America's to enjoy alone. The cosmopolitan ambassadors of major oil who went out into the world to educate peoples in the fantastic possibilities of the black stuff helped spur other theologies of oil's blessedness and other oil-fueled societies whose religiously sanctioned political classes are now fighting back. Even as America's global standing continues to change, with diminishing returns for the legacies of Luce, its domestic grid has become increasingly segmented along territorial lines. Shaped by the existential realities of life in America's oil-producing heartland, the wildcatters and oil-patch citizens that Patillo Higgins gave new life to in 1901 continue to assert their own christened authority. While they are eager to assist the country in its global quests, their proximity to crude has enabled them to frame their future through proud regional eyes, with their Texas-sized desires and dreams for the nation always at the forefront. Now more than ever, Washington and the American people feel the effects.

Regardless of which side Americans fall on in their proximity to petroleum, its power through time has been virtually impossible to resist, its grip on the human condition total, its latitude to define America's very sense of self, purpose, and world standing wide and profound. Much more than a material form, a commodity around which the US economy circles and politicians rally, oil is an imprint on America's soul.

*part one*

---

# CRUDE AWAKENINGS

Oil derricks occupy the slope at Pioneer Run, near Titusville, Pennsylvania, 1865.

# CHAPTER ONE

# Rules of Capture

The etching of oil onto the nation's psyche began during the Civil War period, with western Pennsylvania's founding generation of hard-driving oil hunters. Among them was Lyman Stewart. He was born in 1840 to a family of tanners and Scots-Irish Presbyterians and grew up in a community—the Venango Valley—newly awakened by curiosity about crude. As a teen, while riding horseback to purchase hides for his father, Stewart liked to pinpoint seeps of a gooey substance he knew as rock oil. This hobby was then merely a brief respite from hard work—hard work and the cultural revolutions of his day. In the late 1850s, a steady flow of revivalistic services and antislavery rallies garnered his commitment. Inspired by the abolitionists who aided the Underground Railroad in his home region and stirred by the intensity of Christian fervor sweeping the area, Stewart dedicated himself to "higher" service as a missionary.[1]

At that very juncture, in 1859, just ten miles from his home, journeying prospector Edwin Drake used his makeshift derrick to prove that crude—rock oil—could be drawn to the earth's surface profitably. Almost instantaneously Stewart caught the oil fever that overtook the land and headed to Titusville, Drake's epicenter of production. Crude's quick cash, he thought, would get him to the mission field sooner. But

Stewart's enthusiasm was immediately tested as his first attempt to drill left him broke. Drake's luck, he learned, was tough to replicate. Before Stewart could act again with more gusto, he was caught in another tumult.[2]

The Civil War shook him to the core. In June 1863 he and his unit, the 16th Pennsylvania Cavalry, headed to Gettysburg for the battle that would redefine America. On the way there, Stewart contracted typhoid and was forced to spend several months in the care of medics. Quarantines in a medical wagon and hospital did not shield him from the horrors of war; quite the opposite—they exposed him to the starkest human atrocities, to the sights and sounds of cadaverous men, which would never leave him. Almost two years later, shortly after his Union brigade, without his presence, accepted General Robert E. Lee's surrender at Appomattox, the weary twenty-five-year-old made his way back to western Pennsylvania. Once there he pooled together what little money he had saved during the war and, with his brother Milton, began to invest in a series of oil wells, this time near an emerging site called Pithole. Once again he hoped petroleum would allow him to further Christ's Kingdom. While by day he scoured for promising spots of earth, in the evenings and on Sundays he preached to the area's multitude of sojourners. As a veteran of carnage, he wanted to usher his society into an epoch of peace and godly expectation.[3]

Five years after Lyman escaped one war, he entered another. By 1870 his work in oil had paid huge dividends. Earning $1,000 per week with $300,000 of cash in the bank, married, and respected in his community, he was truly at the top. His own missteps and petroleum's cutthroat climate, however, undermined that attainment. During the late 1860s, Stewart unwisely invested in a chancy corporate venture, which almost immediately failed, saddling him with enormous debt. At that very moment of financial woe, a battle broke out in Pennsylvania oil country—"Petrolia"—that would shade his future. Standing in his way was John D. Rockefeller, who set in motion schemes to impose order on the speculative—and, in his mind, wasteful—petroleum business. Stewart, though emasculated by bankruptcy, saw things differently. To him, the wastes of his industry were unfortunate by-products of oil's underlying embrace of free enterprise. Ceaseless and uncontrolled drilling, nonstop pumping and stockpiling, ferocious competition, and the reckless abandon that accompanied oilmen's quest to drain a vulnerable land: these extravagancies certainly deserved attention, he believed, and on that count he determined to make his church a marshaling zone for attacking the profligacies of his region. The prodigalities of his profession and of Petrolia would diminish, he believed, once oilmen had Christ in their hearts. Yet the laissez-faire principles and, in his sincere belief, Christian impulses that defined the industry still had merit and needed protection from the slightest threat. And so even as he struggled to rise from the ashes of his demise, Stewart joined an army of small oil producers to slay the Rockefeller leviathan. Illness had kept him from Gettysburg; wounds were not going to prevent him from battling on this next front.[4]

On that score, and in his journey through the epic disruptions of his time, Stewart personified the first phase of petroleum's development. He shared with a rising class of conquering men an unassailable belief that God was guiding him toward earth's bounty and an ordained future. For two decades after liquid gold's 1859 discovery in Pennsylvania, countless profit-minded impresarios went hunting for it with unbending resolve, leaning on spiritualist methods such as divining rods and charismatic prayer to help them read the land for subsurface abundance. Believing that God prospered the inquisitive and strong—those who tapped nature on their terms—oil's first stalkers came to define a wildcat ethic that would imprint oil culture for good.

In doing so, they also laid bare the dark side of the oiler's contract: the inescapable violence that made the pursuit of earth's blood itself a bloody affair. Oil's first frontier wrestled with the repeated tragedies that petroleum's headlong rush engendered and the cycles of death it exacted. There, geological mysteries and crude materialism coexisted, as did prophecies of redemption and damnation. Into this milieu stepped men and women of reformist sensibilities who sought to quell such extremes. Dismayed by the diabolical features of Petrolia, fretting over the damage done to a humanity engulfed by crude's dark fantasies, and armed with righteous indignation, they attempted to clean up the mess. Mirroring their commitment to curb excess was John D. Rockefeller. The pious petroleum refiner from Cleveland shared Stewart's sense of oil as his divine lot but not his patience for the unbridled capitalism that cut against the efficiencies of a bureaucratized industrial economy and what he considered a truer Protestant work ethic. Whereas Stewart placed his full trust in a creed of personal piety and self-help that conceded space for the speculative and supernatural dynamics of his business, Rockefeller leaned on the logics of a social gospel that said good Christians were endowed with an ability to do more than save themselves—they held in their hands the capacity to save their society through the application of a pragmatic and prudent (and earthbound) faith. And so he endeavored to clean up the mess by extending his authority, monopolizing his economic sector, and imposing his own will on it. His zealousness precipitated an internecine struggle between oilmen and their diverging convictions of crude and Christianity, one that would last for generations.

However troublesome, petroleum's many inflictions only served to heighten its profile among Americans. Scarred by war and the brutalities of society's entry into modern times and anxious to usher the body politic out of brokenness into a prosperous carbon age, they were enamored of oil's fate as the emergent nation's elixir. In oil, secular and sacred ambitions were melded into one vexing yet pervasive mandate of progress, one that Americans as a whole would internalize and, with the same unquenchable drive as Lyman Stewart, feverishly enact.

TIMING PUNCTUATED OIL's high-stakes potential. Americans faced several critical junctures in the 1850s, not the least of which involved a flaring sectional divide over slavery. Angst-producing, these discords caused them to assign urgency to crude, as if it were a cure-all for their ills. Their urge to embrace the enchantments of oil only intensified as war widened and casualties mounted, and Petrolia became an escape for businessmen and bedraggled soldiers seeking a fresh start.

The tenuousness of existing oil sources in the 1850s contributed to this anxious energy. By then, the whaling industry, which had long supplied North Americans with the liquid essence for illumination, was dying. Like Captain Ahab, whose fictional plight author Herman Melville released to a reading public in 1851, America seemed to be succumbing to its obsession with a creature it could no longer afford to pursue. As the Atlantic's whale populations dwindled, whalers were forced into much longer and less profitable journeys into faraway ocean waters. Eager to solve the crisis, several trailblazers stepped up with potential replacements for whale products. These included innovations such as the distillation of turpentine into flammable camphene or of coal into burnable illuminant; another alternative was natural gas. Canadian geologist Abraham Gesner's inventive process of extracting oil from bitumen (asphalt) and refining it into brilliant light proved particularly appealing. In 1854, Gesner obtained a patent for his "new liquid hydrocarbon," which he denominated "kerosene." By 1859, his kerosene works in New York City was a US staple, outputting 5,000 gallons a day. Still, in America's dawning industrial order, the demand for an abundant, affordable oil source for illumination *and* machinery lubrication remained great, the door for enterprising pioneers wide open.[5]

That demand was increasingly met with an elevated supply of entrepreneurial initiative. Rapid demographic change set the backdrop for that renaissance. In the 1840s alone, the US population grew nearly 36 percent (to 23,191,876 residents), with most of the surge filling cities. With burgeoning, centralized habitation emerged burgeoning, centralized manufacturing, consumer markets, and corporate restructuring. Almost inevitably, American business underwent a revolution during the 1850s, one that would accelerate after war's end. Moving off their fathers' farms into the Northeast's financial hubs, a host of restless young men, born in the two decades after 1815, entered commerce eager to pursue bigger profit margins and jettison antiquated family-run business models in order to do so. Out of their labor emerged multiunit enterprises of immense scale run by elaborate hierarchies of executives, managers, and investors who envisioned their commercial domains on national and international levels.[6]

Spiritual zeal sparked by the so-called Businessmen's Revival helped fuel the commercial surge. By early 1858, cities along the East Coast began to experience an unusually intense outpouring of religiosity. Sensationalist journalists relayed accounts of "wonderful manifestations of penitence and piety" by famous people, which underscored the unfolding of something massive and profound. However trumped up they were to sell copy, grassroots demonstrations of religious fervor were substantial. Between 1857 and 1859, urban churches grew exponentially. Statistics were one marker of the phenomenon, but stunning to observers was the optic of finely dressed executives walking briskly to church in Manhattan for noonday prayer, singing, and altar calls. While the rise of media-savvy ministry styles contributed to the spectacle, contemporary critics attributed the awakening to the capitalist ferment of the day, which drove financiers to seek forgiveness for their failed speculations and pray for further success. Whatever the root cause, the outcome was clear: the revival lent an already roused class of corporate types more reason to feel empowered to initiate an epoch of societal advance.[7]

Aware of society's pressing need for new sources of oil and the tremendous profit that awaited those who found a way to meet it, and spurred on by the regenerative disruptions of their day, impatient opportunists approached the end of the 1850s with aspirations for discovery on untested frontiers. George Bissell followed that path, with a heralded result for everyone enamored of oil.

Born in 1821 to a two-century-old New Hampshire Yankee family, Bissell embodied the heritage and nervous vim of his generation. After graduating from Dartmouth College in 1845, he dabbled in different careers, starting with a professorship in Greek and Latin before settling on business and law. Despite a heavy workload, the lawyer-entrepreneur maintained close ties with his alma mater. While conversing with a Dartmouth chemistry professor on one occasion, Bissell noticed a bottle of "dark, greenish liquid" that F. B. Brewer of Titusville, Pennsylvania, had sent to the scientist. Brewer's sample had been skimmed off a spring connected to Oil Creek. Intrigued with the fluid's properties, Bissell recruited the professor's son to survey the land near the Allegheny fount. Upon receiving a report about more greenish slicks, Bissell journeyed to western Pennsylvania and, with a business partner, purchased two hundred acres along Oil Creek, then in 1855 founded the Pennsylvania Rock Oil Company, the first petroleum firm to organize in the United States. That same year Bissell reached out to chemist Benjamin Silliman Jr. of Yale University for an early verdict: Was he onto something or chasing folly?[8]

Silliman's study confirmed Bissell was courting success. In his report Silliman surveyed the resinous substances found in "tar springs" and along lake shorelines in other parts of the ancient and contemporary world: Baku, Persia, Parma, the Dead Sea, the "Bitumen Lake of Trinidad." The "crude oil" he collected on Bissell's lands retained a consistency that made it similar to variations found in these other locales. But in its absence of a "crust or deposit," Bissell's liquid was unique, sure to burn brightly. "This difference," Silliman explained, "will be . . . of considerable importance [since] this product exists in great abundance upon your property . . . [and] can be gathered wherever a well is sunk," promising unfailing yields for years to come. "In conclusion," he wrote, "your Company have in their possession a raw material from which, by simple and not expensive process, they may manufacture very valuable products." Bissell was elated and reveled in the prospect of competing against kerosene for control of the highly contested market of illuminants. If he could mine and refine rock oil—petroleum—in large, inexhaustible quantities, his cheaper and purer product would outdo lesser alternatives.[9]

The puzzle was how to acquire it. Skimming and digging methods that oil hunters had long employed around the world would not suffice. While walking a New York street in 1856, Bissell passed a pharmacy that displayed an advertisement for rock oil as a panacea for the age. Pictured on the ad was a derrick of the type used to drill for salt. Since the 1840s, salesmen like local legend Samuel Kier had been boring for western Pennsylvania salt and struggling to find a use for the rock oil that inevitably fouled their wells. Eventually Kier began selling the bothersome discharge as medicine for "burns, bruises, and old sores," as well as "'rheumatick' complaints." A confidence man with a poetic flair, he advertised his product thusly: "The healthful balm, from nature's secret spring, the bloom of health and life to man will bring." Bissell had an epiphany: he would follow the legend's example by erecting a derrick and endeavoring to drill not for salt but for the very crude that Kier originally deemed a nuisance.[10]

Throughout 1858, as his dealings in Pennsylvania multiplied, Bissell maintained a dizzying routine. Even Sundays, like the one his diary dated January 3, busily unfolded:

In the morning I go with O. [Ophelia, his wife] and Mrs. G [his mother-in-law] to the Methodist Church of Dr. McClintock at the corner of Fourth Avenue and 22nd Street. Sermon from Genesis "The Struggle of Jacob." In the afternoon to the Union Place Hotel to see my friend Day. Introduces me to Misters Purvis and Lee. Upon my return, I find Madam Wilson and Miss Gertrude at my place. I translate the first chapter of "Acts of the Apostles" from Greek. Nervous, this evening.

Bissell was uptight because the coming day entailed work on a key case and the election of new directors for his company. The disquiet that accompanied these activities defined most days, which is why the last task of this January Sunday was his favorite. Bissell read ten languages, including Hebrew and Greek, essential to his great passion of translating scripture. He leaned on this hobby to get him through the upheaval of the year, which culminated in a split in his company and—with his blessing and investment—his partners' subsequent formation of another: Seneca Oil Company. Working and worshipping amid the tumult of late-1850s Manhattan, with financial and religious eruptions all around him, Bissell could not help but feel a bit on edge.[11]

But in 1859, Edwin Drake eased Bissell's anxiety by accomplishing what he had imagined possible. Sponsored by Seneca Oil (of which Bissell remained a minor owner and "ruling spirit"), Drake enlisted a local blacksmith to help construct a derrick and drill on the land that had supplied the oil sent by F.B. Brewer to Bissell's Dartmouth acquaintance in 1855. Armed with technology used by Kier's fellow salt borers, on August 27, 1859, the two punctured to a depth of seventy feet. Drake's partner returned the next day—Sunday, August 28—to check on the rig. Peering through the tube he noticed a viscous fluid sitting atop the water: petroleum. Word quickly spread to farmers and backwoodsmen, many of whom were exiting local churches in their Sunday best. Rushing from all points along Oil Creek to Titusville, they shouted, "The Yankee has struck oil."[12]

Within days, word of the monumental strike had spread back to the East Coast, arousing an outsized sense of awe. Of Drake's exploits, one New York reporter offered, "The excitement attendant on the discovery of this vast source of oil was fully equal to what I ever saw in California, when a large lump of gold was accidentally turned out." Other witnesses said the magnitude of the discovery exceeded anything beheld in California. Drake's rock oil, local Thomas Gale wrote, represented a new "light of the age" for all of humanity. Gale paused to ponder his isolated region's new role in hallowed history. In "compensation for privation and poverty, our Kind Father in Heaven has caused the rock to pour us out rivers of oil and thus given us at once magnificent light for our dwellings and a source of honest wealth.... [T]his benefaction on our social order, will be happy, powerful and lasting." George Bissell, meanwhile, had far less to say—he was too busy. At first word of Drake's hit, he boarded a train for Titusville. Upon arrival he wrote his wife, "The whole population are crazy almost.... I never saw such excitement. Our prospects are most brilliant that's certain.... We ought to make an immense fortune."[13]

Even as Bissell made his way to Titusville and word of the oil strike trickled through the dailies, news of radical, armed abolitionist John Brown's raid on the federal armory at Harpers Ferry also spread. The sectional fighting that followed hurled the country into civil war. While petroleum exited the headlines, its economic and political standing grew during the conflict. War was a boon for Pennsylvania oil. It killed shipments of southern turpentine (camphene) to the North, making Allegheny crude and its by-products more necessary. It also dried up one of the North's primary revenue streams: cotton, exported to Europe. For the first time, black gold assumed white gold's privileged standing on Wall Street and in Washington. As of 1864, the federal treasury was collecting substantial tax revenues from the oil sector (nearly $8 million in total) and using the income to buy essential war materials. The White House itself acknowledged the shift in national consciousness. After Methodist bishop Matthew Simpson delivered an inspirational sermon to Washington brass that same year, his friend, Abraham Lincoln, playfully chided him for omitting one critical element: "Bishop, you didn't strike the 'ile." "Mr. President," Simpson conceded, "I am surprised at myself to see that, while I have thought so much about the great resources of our country, I should have entirely overlooked our great oil interests. I shall not do so again."[14]

Previously incentivized by the economic and cultural foment of the late 1850s and now prompted by crude's necessity to the national struggle, oil hunters from all walks of life deluged the hills and valleys Bissell traversed. "There's lawyers and doctors, and men of all grades," a Kentucky minstrel chimed at the time. "Men that live by their wits, and men that have trades; through old Pennsylvania they've trudged many a mile, with their forty-foot auger, they're going to 'strike ile.'"

Geography favored them. In contrast to the California gold rush, no 3,000-mile trek was necessary. Oil's heartland, one chronicler quipped, was "right there at the back door for them to visit." And the place itself enticed them. Titusville sat at the heart of a tucked-away region that was a perennial hothouse of independence. Generations earlier it had unleashed the "Whiskey Rebellion," an insurrection against George Washington's revenue-generating tax on distilled spirits. During the 1830s, as another flow of people inundated the area, western Pennsylvania's radicalism took religious form. With sectarian fervor, this region's Scots-Irish settlers fueled the fires of revivalism that traveled the corridor running across upstate New York into Pennsylvania and Ohio, generating growth of the area's Baptist, Methodist, and Presbyterian churches. During the 1840s and 1850s, this "burned-over" region of religious enthusiasm turned into a center of antislavery activism and radical republicanism. In the 1860s it was oil's turn to fan the trailblazing aura of self-discovery and self-sufficiency.[15]

The trailblazers were an eclectic lot, driven by a mix of pieties and profit seeking. One of them, John Wilkes Booth, was a struggling actor who joined a few friends in the arts to form the appropriately named Dramatic Oil Company. For several weeks in 1864 Booth tried to coax crude out of his land, all the while entertaining locals. Like his father, Junius Brutus Booth, London's leading tragedian, the young man could bring an audience to its knees with a recital of the Sermon on the Mount. At the Methodist church in the new oil town of Franklin, Booth listened attentively to biblical messages and took in the gospel. But by the end of 1864, Booth's oil well was dry. His next steps took him to Washington, where he carried out a task vastly more audacious than anything he had attempted in business or on the stage. Shocked when they learned of Lincoln's murder by an assassin who had once lived among them, the denizens of oil country would for years wonder just how this man could perform such a dastardly act. Although they agreed that he was both saint and sinner, Booth, they noted, had blended in.[16]

Booth's species of scrappy amateur oilmen was joined by buttoned-down investors of Bissell's ilk, who used the war years to lay the foundations for sprawling business empires. Shaped by the outpouring of revival during the late 1850s, they were friendly toward red-hot religiosity but also guided by principles of temperance. Though sharing Petrolia's streets and even its pews with their rambunctious counterparts, they preferred steadier means to the same ends. After his momentous strike, Bissell, for instance, labored diligently, supervising his drill sites from an office in Franklin, then from New York. All the while he drew strength from his Methodism, which he practiced at Franklin Methodist, Booth's parish. Outside church Bissell increased his company's expenditures on land and oil drilling to the tune of $250 million. Hopeful for personal gains, Bissell was also mindful that his success depended on the viability of oil's entire operation. So in 1864 he agreed to join the Petroleum Board of New York City, on behalf of which he petitioned Congress to refrain from imposing heavier taxes on crude producers, an act many credited with saving the vulnerable industry. For the sober Bissell, petroleum's promise was something to safeguard as well as chase.[17]

Caught in the rush of outsiders, the locals of Petrolia did their best to manage the exigencies of their unprecedented epoch. Not unlike Lyman Stewart, the area's young men who were forced to leave for war dreamed of the day they would return to carry on the work that was transforming their hometowns. One Union recruit wrote to his girlfriend during any moment of respite from his soldiering at Antietam, Fredericksburg, and Gettysburg. He doted on her ("Next to my Lord, I love you best," he insisted) and described his battalion's ills. And he wrote about oil. "My heart is not here. . . . [O]ften I find myself thinking of the friends I have left away north and wondering what they are doing and . . . if they ever think of anything except oil lands, greenbacks, and their fortunes in perspective." In July 1865, the veteran made his way back to Pennsylvania's petroleum hub. "I think there is a chance for something to be made," he predicted to his now fiancée. Soon he was telling her about the latest oil finds and his service to his church. Two months later they married, life in oil country now routine.[18]

However much locals sought to remain sober, it was nearly impossible for them not to get swept up in the allegories of wondrous progress that grew out of their newly industrialized landscape. This was all the more the case as the war drew to a close and well-spoken wordsmiths began to extol the region's role in hallowed history, first spoken of by

Thomas Gale, in even grander terms. Petrolia was not simply a parochial phenomenon, they waxed eloquent, but now the pivot and gener-
ator of the nation's quickening strides toward a blessed unity and fate.

Petrolia's visionaries asserted their new narratives first by teth-
ering America to oil's anointed peoples of the past. From "Bakoo
[Baku] . . . the holy city of the ancient fire worshippers," to Persia's
lighted temples and Babylon's hallowed grounds, to the "bituminous
springs" along the Dead Sea, petroleum had long been associated with
the work of the gods. Americans were now custodians of this history.
There to help them connect with the remote, exotic past, oil chroniclers
explained, were Indians, especially the Seneca tribe, which for centuries had handled oil in Pennsylvania's glens. Legends of early missionary and military encounters with the Seneca were now drawn upon
in highly romanticized fashion to convey the indispensable role indigenous peoples played in passing oil's bewitching virtues on to white
civilization. One oilman-turned-poet blended history with nostalgia
in a poem that captured that transference. "In religious worship saw
I the children of the forest," he divined, borrowing from the diary of
an eighteenth-century French commander who had witnessed Indian
worship along a shrouded creek bed. "Seneca Oil, as if by magic, arose
to the surface of the stream. As the torch-bearer dipped his light amid
the oleaginous fluid, the great fire in a golden, lambent glow of flame
shot above their bending forms, while they chanted forth in unison:
'Oh, Great Spirit! Mighty art Thou!'"[19]

Oil's narrators then tied Indian spirituality to modern sensibil-
ity, tales of oil's Edenic past to notions of divine destiny. Such practice was not out of keeping with a wider pattern among modernizing
Americans to ascribe cosmic intent to the minerals upon which society
could be reconstituted. By virtue of its centrality to industrialization,
coal especially carried weight at the time as a substance and symbol
encapsulating ideals of American progress. Yet, from the outset, oil's
stature as a suprahuman force seemed special. It was summoned from
the terra firma, not scraped out in a brute manner. Spectacular in its
earth-shattering arrival and seemingly democratic promise, it seemed
to forecast a new era in humanity's march forward. "We have ascended
another [rung] in the Ladder of Progress," one enthusiast declared,

after outlining petroleum's "more brilliant" light (real and metaphorical) compared to coal's.[20]

Few could weave all these fanciful strands together in a new American consciousness like Reverend S. J. Eaton of Franklin. In his prolific writings about the local oil industry, he highlighted the role indigenous peoples and Christian missionaries who roamed the hills and hollows of western Pennsylvania during the eighteenth century had played in transferring curiosities about crude to modern man. Yet, while their legwork had helped prepare the way for commercial oil's arrival in the nineteenth century, Eaton attributed that outpouring almost entirely to God. "It has always been a feature of the economy of Providence," he wrote, "that the stores of his bounty are brought to light just as they are needed. The minerals of earth have lain hid in its bosom until absolutely needed." Despite millennia of men roaming "Venango valleys ignorant of the precious treasure that flowed beneath, even though it was suggested by a thousand bubbling springs," he declared, hidden riches were now being called up with God's blessing. Now, in this "day of sore trial," "not only blood but treasure" was "to be poured out like water in the nation's cause, and in the cause of civil and religious liberty." For Eaton, petroleum's appearance was truly salvific, its soppy fluid a salve for a society rent asunder by war. As "fountains of petroleum gush[ed] forth in wondrous exuberance," American enterprise and government would all be saved, and so too the psychological well-being of a people battered by conflict. "Who can doubt but that in the wise operations of God's Providence, the immense oil resources of the country have been developed at this particular time, to aid in the solution of the mighty problem of the nation's destiny?" Despite a deep sense of northern superiority, Eaton believed the time had come for his fellow citizens—north and south of the Dixie line—to bathe in oil's sacramental splendor, as Indians once did on quiet shores.[21]

AFTER THE WAR, prospectors of all stripes intensified their quest to bathe in the splendor of which Eaton spoke. Thousands of war veterans arrived, often cloaked in threadbare military uniforms, ready to use their terminal pay to invest in a wellhead or patch of land. Meanwhile, hundreds of oil companies were legally christened in New York City, making office space in Manhattan and elbow room on Wall Street difficult to find. One banker from Europe was utterly perplexed by the "hundreds of thousands of provident working men, who prefer the profits of petroleum to the small rates of interest afforded by savings banks." The upshot of the movement on both fronts was unprecedented wildcat mania, in which the hunt itself assumed metaphysical weight. Oil transfixed precisely because it could not easily be possessed. Rather, it did the possessing.[22]

During the late 1860s, the rising demand for oil and steady enlargement of its domestic and international markets drove speculative fury into an inaugural boom-bust phase. In 1864 alone, the price of oil climbed from $3.00 to $13.75 per forty-two-gallon barrel; by mid-year, well owners could count on profits anywhere from $3 to $7 per barrel, a significant leap from more modest prices earlier in the decade. The momentum accelerated in the postwar years. Men feverishly bored fresh wells in old terrains and set down exploratory ones on untrammeled turf. On one slope of discovery called Cherry Run, a cluster of four wells netted profits of $2 million over a two-year blitz. Another well nearby recorded a phenomenal two-year production span during which it converted every dollar invested into $15,000 of profit. The effect of this maelstrom was startling. One oil chronicler later mused that "the American public disgorged so much money for stocks that the Federal Revenue Commission estimated in 1866 that more than one hundred million dollars had been applied to the purchase and development of oil lands."[23]

But in a pattern that would forever repeat itself, bust quickly followed boom. The ephemeral nature of oiling soon proved trying for Petrolia. In their scramble to drill, its oilers sensed that nature's wellspring might dry up at any moment or explode in anger at their infiltration. Most of the communities that grew up around drill sites were, accordingly, makeshift in their appearance and attitudes, calibrated to expectations of an abbreviated lifespan. Even established hamlets, the places for which homegrown soldiers had fought during the Civil War, now succumbed to an outlook attuned to depletion and devastation.

The threats to sustainability were numerous, starting with fire, petroleum's worst plague. The abundant fuel available in the area made it inevitable. Gaseous fumes from overtaxed derricks and storage tanks filled the atmosphere and on foggier days floated through the valleys as if natural to the cloud canopy. Hastily assembled wells and porous barges allowed gallons of black goop to leak into Oil Creek. "Oil dipping"became a pastime. Standing along the shore with buckets in hand, children skimmed oil waste off the top of the water, poured it into containers, and looked for ready buyers. From the very outset, then, explosions were common, death by burn a regular phenomenon. One of the first incidents happened in 1861, at a flowing well near Rouseville, just south of Edwin Drake's old well (itself a casualty of fire a short time before), and resulted in the loss of nineteen lives, including that of Henry Rouse, a former Pennsylvania legislator and oil lobbyist. Over the course of the next two decades, the oil region suffered numerous conflagrations on this scale, some sparked by thunderstorms, others by carelessly discarded cigars. Natural or man-made, the destruction was often total. One hellhole left behind a charcoaled canvas of ruin that became redundant in Petrolia. "Flames . . . leaped thirty meters high," reports offered, "and for two weeks the fire raged, consuming ten acres. The fire could be seen for kilometers, and vegetation was scorched in all directions. When the inferno exhausted itself, it left ashes and charred earth two-thirds of a meter deep."[24]

The collateral damage of oil fires was far-flung. When, in 1865, a Philadelphia refinery filled with Pennsylvania crude erupted, killing dozens of people, reporters painted a picture right out of Dante's *Inferno*. "The blazing oil that escaped from the burning barrels poured over into Ninth Street . . . filling the entire street with a lake of fire"; "men, women, and children were literally roasted alive in the streets," their abodes "licked up by the red, fiery tongues of the demon of Destruction." Hades's horror, it seemed, was everyone's to endure. Yet Petrolia suffered the most. Burned trees contributed to the deforestation of the slopes that lined Oil Creek, making it prone to flooding. In 1865, sustained rains caused a deluge that unfastened oil barges and lodged them against a bridge, forming a dam that rerouted the stream down one town's main street. One hundred buildings were destroyed and $2 million in damage incurred. More consistently painful to residents was the mud. Runoff from barren hills and crude blended into a corrosive sludge that blanketed the earth. On passageways where oil was transported, locals encountered menacing holes four to eight feet deep, and a year-round slick of petroleum prevented roads from drying in the summer or freezing in the winter.[25]

Such environmental devastation left Petrolia cut off from healthy sustenance. "Everything you see is black," one journeyman noted. "The soil is black, being saturated with waste petroleum. The shanties . . . are black. The men that work among the barrels, machinery, tanks, and teams are white men blackened." Man, animal, earth—all wore "somber . . . sooty clothing," except Oil Creek itself, which "glittered" like "one vast moving string of opal." No simple thread of silver like most creeks glistening under the noonday sun, it enjoyed a "brilliancy of rainbow hues" created from its surface coating of crude. The area's animal population offered further proof of oil's ghastliness. At the peak of production, solid lines of horse teams proceeded along the creek from dawn to dusk, carrying containers of crude or tugging barges. One resident "counted 2,000 teams crossing the bridge on the main road of Titusville in one day." The beasts suffered unimaginably. The toxic clay mixtures that lined roads ate away their hair, leaving their hides raw and bloody. Hauling often forced them into frigid waters, where their bellies iced over, and if the cold creek did not punish them, the whips of their merciless drivers did. All in all, the entire operation amounted to murder of Petrolia's least cared for. "We are unmistakeably [sic] in Oildom!," another traveler rued when witnessing these sights. "The more I see of it, the more I am convinced of the great risk of this oil business."[26]

No one community epitomized the totalizing effect of such risk as Pithole. Established on a remote farm after an oil find in January 1865, the boomtown grew rapidly as a stampede of speculators descended on it. By September of that year, it was home to 16,000 inhabitants, sixty-five hotels, a daily newspaper, the third-largest post office in Pennsylvania, and five theaters. What it lacked in essential infrastructure it made up for in bars and brothels and a dark reputation that extended far and wide. "Pithole" referred to nearby pits that emanated sulfur gases, which residents came to view as portals to hell. Some simply referred to Pithole as "Hell." Offering justification for the label were the town's regular fires and poor waste disposal. One visitor thought Pithole smelled "like a camp full of soldiers with diarrhea." The town was not long for this world. Thriving in the fall of 1865, it met its demise months later. By January 1866, its wells had stopped flowing, and drillers hit only dry holes. By that spring, five hundred days after its founding, Pithole was left to rot as nature reclaimed it.[27]

While extreme in its brevity, Pithole illustrated the cruel fluctuations that awaited those who lived on petroleum's schedule. Even the assiduously prepared fell victim to oil's routine. George Bissell was among the victims. In 1864, amid his efforts to lobby Washington on behalf of oil producers, he and his company founded the town of Petroleum Centre on a two-hundred-acre farm located eight miles south of Titusville. Situated in the middle of rich oil-producing farms, the town soon housed 3,000 people, twelve stores, six hotels, two churches, a theater, and a bank, along with scores of saloons, boarding houses, and gambling dens. Like its larger contemporary, Pithole, Petroleum Centre devolved into a madness that disturbed those associated with it. In the estimation of many locals, the town "eclipsed all others in wickedness." A modest micromanager with a heart for order, Bissell could only watch as his creation self-destructed.[28]

Additional stresses related to the manic timetable of crude characterized Bissell's last years. In 1867, his wife, Ophelia, died suddenly at the family's Fifth Avenue home in New York. This "hour of affliction" hurt him profoundly. Writing to a friend, he admitted, "The death of my dear wife, occurring as it did, with scarcely any premonition, has deeply prostrated my energies." During the "long season of his oil experiments," he told another, no one encouraged him but his wife and mother. "All others asserted his folly," his confidants later recalled. Bissell plowed ahead, but soon his own body—always frail because of overwork and little sleep—failed. In the 1870s, he suffered several illnesses and a stroke that rendered him incapable of leaving home; he died in 1884 following an extended period of steady decline. At the time of his death, Petroleum Centre was itself deteriorating. Abandoned by most residents in 1873 after a sharp drop-off in production, by 1884 it was a ghost town.[29]

Such was the eschatology of America's new energy source: life producing for a time, the extent of which no one could guess, yet certain to disappear in some dark instant, annihilating those who once hoped to govern it. Oil offered a promise that mixed blessed hope with bloody sacrifice. Going forward, its only predictability would be its profound disruptiveness. Stark as the jarring fluctuations were, they made sense to oil's first generation. Having escaped the hells of civil war, scarred with remembrances of suffering and lives snuffed out, petroleum's wild-cat warriors did not expect much else in the days ahead. Even if theirs was a Faustian bargain, they accepted the risk as a way for humanity to thrive, if for a passing moment.

One poetic observer of oil asked his contemporaries to accept this existential arrangement with cheerful resignation. Many of them, he noted, were trapped in fatalistic fear, rooted in ancient prophecies and scripture that said petroleum's "immense influx" would "facilitate [the world's] burning." Oil would be "preparatory to the arrival of the great and notable day, when the elements shall melt with fervent heat, and the earth, and all the things that are therein shall be burned up." Even so, the poet surmised, "the world might as well burn quickly as to be long about it," for what use was it to live long in darkness, shivering in the cold? "Quickly" and brightly, he preferred, with sparkling light and sustenance for all.[30]

Petrolia's oil hunters and residents came to accept the tumult of their industry, but not simply out of resignation or a rush to ravage the earth. Spurring them on amid glances into the metaphoric bowels of hell were other portals of the business that seemed to offer glimpses into heaven. The earth they worked was no cold, demystified blank slate in need of pillaging, they believed, but rather a living, tempestuous partner as well. Respectful of the Spirit's mysterious workings in creation, early oilers were inspired with the notion that the land they tapped would talk back. Reinforcing this mentality was the fact that the early oil industry operated in a haze of geological uncertainty. While chemists such as Benjamin Silliman Jr., who advised Bissell in 1855, were prepared to assess seepages and the properties of the fluid drawn from them, they could not tell oilers precisely where underground reservoirs existed. Unlike natural resources such as coal, iron ore, and timber—usually located with the naked eye and then extracted by sheer human will—the bulk of oil reserves lay hidden from human sight, defying easy retrieval. Scientific systems for finding them were still decades away. In the meantime, oil's discovery remained a matter of trust as much as method, of theology as much as science—of communing with, not just subduing, the land.[31]

Oildom's devout embraced that fact on slightly different grounds. For Christian clerics and scholars such as Silliman, a student of natural theology, reading the land for this oil was ultimately an exercise in deciphering the work of God on earth. As Edward Hitchcock, a former Congregational minister and student of Silliman's father, an esteemed chemist and theologian at Yale, indicated in his 1851 treatise *The Religion of Geology*, earth's very structure bore a complexity that deserved special treatment. In its dirt and liquids, organic matter and uneven surfaces, believers could in gritty fashion grasp "proofs of the Divine Benevolence." Silliman's mind-set was shared by his peers in the pulpits of western Pennsylvania, clerics who sought to educate people in the exigencies of oil. No one was more eager to do so than Reverend Eaton of Franklin. With Hitchcock's text as a guide, Eaton published a book on the technicalities of oil exploration and production. Ever the humanist, he couched the driest mechanical details of oil's functions in testimony, as if they had turned him on to deeper theological truths. One of those truths was that for all the science that gave oilers greater access to black gold, exciting secrets still awaited them. "The hidden path yet remains unexplored," he mused. "It may always remain so; but we have the great fact of Divine Providence, in the rich and copious supply, that is nevertheless valuable because it flows from an unknown source, and comes to us through unexplored channels." "The practical fact," he surmised, was that oil still provoked more questions than answers, requiring steps of blind faith as much as erudition.[32]

Mindful of that, rank-and-file oilers leaned on their own vernaculars of faith to find oil—vernaculars rooted in their cloistered lands where folk traditions and fervent belief enjoyed deep traction. The competition among them was fierce, but it also compelled them to pause to interact with the environment in hopes of earning its favor. One visitor to the region marveled at the way its "keenly inquisitive" people relied on their faculties of touch, smell, and taste, diviners and divination, to guide them. Eaton himself admitted grudgingly that "doodlebugs," primitive devices for identifying underground minerals, were widespread, with the divining rod enjoying huge popularity. Borrowing from an ancient procedure for locating water, oilers grasped the Y-shaped stick in both hands while surveying an entire plot. "If the loose end happened to be pulled toward the ground by an unseen force," it was explained, "this was the spot on which to drill a well." Dozens of other techniques complemented the divining rod. "Guessing tricks, superstitious devices, and spiritualistic means everywhere flourished," one skeptic bemoaned. "Other owners relied more heavily upon dreams to locate a site." And then there was prayer—a mainstay among oilers—which often transpired while the entranced individual trembled, ears and hands plastered to the ground, waiting for a spirit to channel assurance that oil was there.[33]

Although these extrasensory tools served as unscrupulous tactics to lure investors in some instances, in most others the prospectors who utilized them did so with absolute sincerity. That is why they endured. However much scholars and skeptics voiced disdain for doodlebugs, theirs was a difficult job of disproving one tenuous science by asserting the supremacy of another.

The challenges were compounded when the charismatic practitioner in question came through with results. No one fit this bill more than Abraham James. Like other spiritualists who populated the metaphysical movement that flourished during the latter half of the 1800s, James was convinced that the material world was in harmony with—and an access point to—the spirit realm and, with it, the laws of energy that organized the cosmos. Inspired by Edwin Drake's discovery, James traveled to Pennsylvania in October 1866. While looking at farmland east of Titusville, he was (in his biographer's description) thrown to the ground into a "psychometrical condition" in which "Indian spirits controlled his body mechanically, while wisdom spirits induced the trance condition." While in this state James gained the valuable wisdom that he and his friends were standing on top of oil; so they started to drill. In August 1867, "Harmonial No. 1" was sunk, and in February 1868 it started producing one hundred barrels per day. James and his team bored three more wells, raising their intake exponentially. His psychometrics proved the key to unlocking Pennsylvania's next big find; in its wake, hundreds of other oil hunters made their way to the erupting field with their wands and premonitions in tow.[34]

Such was Petrolia's power to elicit dreams of personal and societal empowerment as well as real-life horrors. Nightmare or fantasy, oil inspired its pursuers to visualize history and the end of the world in one bundle of exaggerated anticipation. Through their workings in the Pennsylvania fields, oil's original entrepreneurs sacralized the rhapsodic expectations driving their quest to drill, as well as the volatilities of their new age. As much as that faith inspired the laissez-faire free-for-all that drove men forward, spellbound, into untapped fields, by 1870 it also seemed primed to shape the next stages of nation building.[35]

BY ITS SECOND decade, a bustling Petrolia seemed poised to serve as America's guide toward its fate. But it was also growing increasingly vulnerable to the gluts of its founding generation. Amid the rush to quell extremes in community life along Oil Creek, there emerged within oil's corporate sector reformers who sought to force their prerogatives on the wildcatter. Even while under oil's spell, they recognized the perils of the free-for-all impulses witnessed in John Wilkes Booth, Abraham James, and their like. And so they attacked their industry with the intention to reorder it, commencing an industry battle that would permanently alter oil's future.

John D. Rockefeller headed the charge. Born in 1839, Rockefeller grew up in a family troubled by his absentee father yet grounded by his ardent and disciplined Baptist mother. His contemporaries described him in terms that reflected these maternal imperatives. He was, they said, "reserved, earnest, religious, methodical, and discreet." During his teens, his family moved from Owego, New York, to Cleveland. There, Rockefeller acquired a job as a bookkeeper. Then, at the age of twenty, he moved into the wholesale foodstuffs business with Maurice B. Clark and Samuel Andrews, the latter of whom was a member of Erie Street Baptist Mission Church, which Rockefeller also attended. The three began dabbling in oil refining as well. They did so under the influence of Andrews, a chemist fascinated by the inventions of Abraham Gesner (father of kerosene) and—like Rockefeller (but in striking contrast to the cautious Clark)—a man who chased innovation.[36]

As civil war waged, Rockefeller headed to Oil Creek to survey its potential payoffs. Already wealthy, he hired substitute soldiers to fight in his stead; he contributed to the war effort by way of major financial donations to the Union cause. Rockefeller took a train to the oil region's depot, then made his way by stagecoach into the wooded hills of Oil

Creek. His journey forced him through black muck and treacherous terrain, an experience he found exhilarating. Having seen enough of the bustle to anticipate oil's bright future, he returned to Cleveland determined to commit entirely. In 1863 he and his partners assumed ownership of their first oil refinery in Cleveland for the processing of Petrolia crude. By entering the refining business, Rockefeller signaled that he wanted to operate at the top of petroleum's pecking order. While producers struggled to eke out financial existences in the unpredictable "upstream" sector of petroleum, Rockefeller and wealthier peers saw the "downstream" sector and its greater controlling interests over the refinement, pricing, and marketing of crude as the real prize. But Rockefeller was not yet done sending the message that he had arrived. A short time later, in February 1865, while Union soldiers continued to penetrate the South and peace talks began, he bought out Clark and established the firm of Rockefeller & Andrews. He would describe embarking on this partnership with a man who shared his vision as the day that determined his career.[37]

The young oiler climbed rapidly to the top of his profession. Like so many of his contemporaries, he framed his newfound vocation as providential. Mirroring Lyman Stewart, he saw tangible evidence of this special calling in the unique properties of petroleum itself, whose oozing and gushing registered with him as canonical. The vast stores of oil wealth that he sought "were the bountiful gifts of the great Creator," a "blessing . . . to mankind" waiting to be employed for His Kingdom on this earth. "The whole process seems a miracle," he would add. The economic operandi associated with this "miracle" further convinced him that petrocapitalism was sanctified. Later in his career, he would unabashedly state his opinions about the wealth of his oil work. "I believe the power to make money is a gift from God," he insisted. "Having been endowed with the gifts I possess, I believe it is my duty to make money and still more money, and to use the money I make for the good of my fellow man according to the dictates of my conscience." Rockefeller was not the only budding robber baron to justify his boundless ambitions in such discourse. Yet his exacting piety set him apart from the Carnegies and Goulds of his day, signaling the special traction his hard-shell Baptist confidence in the preeminence of oil enjoyed throughout his life.[38]

Such zest informed the way he organized his faith as well. Never absent from his pew or negligent in his six-decade tenure as a Sunday school instructor, Rockefeller was unwavering in his dedication to a gospel that stressed the importance of salvation in Christ, the New Testament commission to share that faith, and the timelessness of scripture as God's guide to life. He also embraced a communal dimension of his faith, which said good Christians needed to be good citizens. His commitment to a credo of self-realization and social reform grew stronger in the mid-1860s when he married Laura "Cettie" Spelman, the product of one of Cleveland's established Congregational churches. Her religiosity equaled her husband's in sternness. Eventually the couple moved into a mansion on Euclid Avenue, Cleveland's "millionaire's row." While boasting an address envied by all, the Rockefellers demonstrated constant devotion to Christian charity. They poured money into several causes, ranging from the Young Men's Christian Association to the Women's Christian Temperance Union.[39]

As Rockefeller extended his presence into Petrolia during the late 1860s and early 1870s, he extended his ethical predilections as well. Always put off by the heavy drinking and cavorting that accompanied labor in Petrolia, he endorsed the shuttering of pubs and prostitution rings. His employees in Petrolia saw firsthand that his was no wishy-washy moralism. Nothing would dislodge Rockefeller from his Sabbatarian routine. One Sunday his men alerted him to pressing danger: Oil Creek was rising, and the company's barrels of crude were sure to be swept away. Could he help? On other occasions he was known to don scruffy clothes and do just that, but on this one he donned a top hat and headed for church. Prayer came first; petroleum would have to wait. As it happened, his barrels did not budge, and the floodwaters receded—an outcome he surely interpreted in providential terms.[40]

Rockefeller contrived his entire business enterprise to accentuate its godliness. The crucial choices he made in 1870 illustrated the move. After enjoying a fiscal year that saw his company achieve record revenues and establish itself as a standard-bearer in the business, he decided to create a new entity: the Standard Oil Company. The joint-stock trust comprised a centralized management structure overseeing several state-based corporations—an octopus with tentacles covering the map. Owning by far the most shares, Rockefeller was elected president. His brother William was named vice president, while Samuel Andrews was designated superintendent, and Henry M. Flagler became secretary. Flagler emerged as Rockefeller's new right-hand man. For the next several years, the two men would oversee the company's most important decisions. The partnership seemed natural, based on both complementary temperaments and shared religious values. Raised by a Presbyterian minister, Flagler personified the hard-driving entrepreneurialism and exactness of the Protestant generation—Rockefeller's generation—that came of age at mid-century.[41]

Before anyone could fully comprehend what they were up to, the two thrust Standard into a series of bold maneuvers that in a matter of fifteen years resulted in its complete hold on the entire industry. The first steps in that headlong stride transpired between 1870 and 1872 and featured Standard's ruthless takeover of competing Cleveland refiners, whose initial strivings for success had mirrored Rockefeller's. Generally small and scattered, with limited capacity to weather the fluctuations in oil's supply, demand, and pricing, Cleveland's dozens of refineries approached 1870 with trepidation. Making matters worse, expanding rail systems eliminated the geographical advantages they had over larger refineries based farther east. Fully aware of the power railroads now wielded over his industry and wary of the big rail companies' purported plans to solidify links to Pittsburgh and Philadelphia refining centers, Rockefeller clandestinely hammered out a deal with them, formalized under an official-sounding corporate rubric: the South Improvement Company (SIC). Enticed by Standard's potential, the rail companies agreed to raise freight charges for all refiners but then quietly offer SIC substantial rebates that would allow it to increase its profit margins over its rivals. Rockefeller and Flagler then pounced on their competitors and forced them to sell their assets to the Standard machine at rock-bottom prices or enter bankruptcy. Within a few months Standard had swallowed up twenty-two of Cleveland's twenty-six refineries. Many vanquished refiners griped that for all their outward polish, Standard men were predatory at their core. Rockefeller saw things differently, of course. It should have been clear to his competitors, he claimed, that their world was collapsing. Refiners were losing money yet continuing to indulge in "dreadful and ruinous competition," meaning that "collective salvation" was needed.

It was time for someone to reach out and, as if with a visible hand, draw the players in the market together and impose corporate principles on the business. Besides, he later pleaded, "all these purchases of refineries were conducted with the utmost fairness and good faith on our part."[42]

Fairness, good faith, *and* Christian virtue, he believed. Through all his dealings with Cleveland refiners, Rockefeller exhibited a political realism that saw "survival of the fittest" as the rule and gave credence to Herbert Spencer's reading of the times. Business was brutal because it could not help but be. Yet, in their delivery of answers, the oilman and his accomplice leaned on a logic of corporate recovery gleaned from Rockefeller's Baptist ethic of uplift. He was a refiner in that other sense—a man charged by God with cleaning up an industrial sector with transcendent promise yet devoid of coherent purpose and design. No mere rhetorical weapon, his constant referencing of scriptural metaphors when describing his actions during the "Cleveland Massacre" (as some dubbed it) grew out of his sincere conviction—messianic in proportion—that he was a "godsend" to his community. "The Standard was an angel of mercy," he declared, "reaching down from the sky, and saying 'Get into the ark. Put in your old junk. We'll take all the risks!'" Standard was also "the Moses who delivered them [the refiners] from their folly which had wrought such havoc in their fortunes." "It was not a process of destruction and waste," Rockefeller implored in reference to the takeover, but "a process of upbuilding and conservation of all the interests . . . in our efforts most heroic, well meant—and I would almost say, reverently, Godlike—to pull this broken-down industry out of the Slough of Despond." "Faith and work were the rocks upon which Standard Oil was built," he announced, its executives "missionaries of light" whose actions were "the salvation of the oil business."[43]

"Salvation" of the refining sector complete, Standard turned to Petrolia's production zone. Starting in 1872 and with rising intensity during subsequent years, Rockefeller set his reformist sights on the region's vulgarities, which he attributed to the absence of a "law of economy." By then, ghost towns like Pithole served as monuments to the self-destruction. Having taken in the visuals firsthand, Standard's deacon pledged to prod small producers into the security of his "ark" and point everyone in a new direction.[44]

At the heart of the issue for Rockefeller was the legal code that underpinned his business. Unlike divergent patterns of public ownership that gradually centralized and regulated mineral extraction in Europe, the US oil system fortified private interests through fierce and sustained protection of the rule of capture, a doctrine passed down from English common law. Under this rule, the courts equated oil with wildlife, property subject to capture, in this case by an oil well. This part of the equation drew easy comparison between oil extraction and English hunting precedents, which allowed for the owner of one estate to kill any game on his land, even if the bird or animal in question had migrated from a neighboring estate. Yet, unlike wild game, oil instantly brought multiple hunters—not simply two neighbors—into the mix, magnifying the ferocity of the pursuit. In short, the legal code granted all oilmen access to subsurface pools regardless of surface-level property boundaries. Oil belonged to the individual who captured it, meaning it was best to erect as many derricks as possible, as quickly and as close to your neighbor as feasible, and drill aggressively. The architects of the emerging US economy saw oil's governing statute as a healthy way to stimulate capitalist activity and development. For the people most directly affected by the edict—those working the oil patch—the rule justified an abandon that empowered everyone but also set in motion raging cycles of surplus and scarcity.[45]

For Rockefeller, the rule created a troubling conundrum. An independent-minded oilman himself, he certainly embraced the philosophical underpinnings of US oil law, which justified his own aggressive workings in the market. Yet the good Baptist also saw the virtue of bureaucratic order. He assumed that Christian capitalists would not only celebrate market freedom but also embrace systems of control that softened its Darwinian blows. Rushing pell-mell ahead in a futile quest to make quick and big profits was not the godly way, he insisted; cautious accumulation and application of cash reserves, investment in infrastructure, and expectations and output were. Rockefeller's was not a prosperity gospel that augured instant, spectacular blessings from God. It was the calculating steward, according to his faith, who would pass through heaven's pearly gates. When he surveyed Petrolia, he saw a mass of reckless adventurers acting "like silly children" and lacking the "business ability" to count the costs and succeed. And so he and his men started to rein in oil's workings and tamp down the anarchy. "All kinds of men were going into oil production," he later recalled. "So many wells were flowing that the prices of oil kept falling, yet they went right on drilling. We had the capital, and we built tanks to store thousands of gallons of crude oil and thus partly save the situation."[46]

By contrast, Rockefeller's small competitors saw the rule of capture as protecting their very right to compete in the industry. By 1872, Lyman Stewart and his class of wildcatters were well aware of the instability that plagued their sector, including the heavy price paid by those men who carelessly overreached. Yet, while anxious to correct the system, they continued to lean heavily in favor of convention. For them, however problematic, crude's founding principle represented an absolute essence of pure capitalism that desperately needed protection, as did the notion of unlimited personal freedom it engendered. They insisted that the ideals of individualism needed at most to be fortified by small-scale association and local, voluntary controls and should in no way be suppressed or stamped out by bigger businesses or the state.

Stewart's life testified to the totalizing power of that ethic. In the immediate aftermath of war, the serious, missionary-minded young man had slowly redirected his call to Christian service away from foreign fields to his region's oil patch. Petroleum would now be an end rather than a means in fulfillment of God's plan. By the fall of 1867, he could boast some victories. Key to his shifting fortunes was the vernacular knowledge he internalized about how to locate petroleum in the soil. Over time he honed the innate talent for identifying oil seeps and smelling petroleum's presence that he had first tested in his youth while riding horseback with his father's furs. A literalist in his view of scripture and firm in his Presbyterian orthodoxies, Stewart nevertheless accepted his sensory—spiritualist—abilities as a gift from God, a talent to use for the Kingdom. His war-battered body—especially his nose—became the very device that could lead him to gold. Results followed. Along with his brother Milton and investors from his church, Stewart bought interests in farmland located near Abraham James's Harmonial No. 1. Purchased for $40,000, the land soon started producing at a staggering rate—750,000 barrels of oil total. After draining the pool, the corporate team sold the farm for $1.75 million. Even as he cashed in on one investment, he looked for another. The next one, though, which

involved his chancy commitment of funds to an upstart machine manufacturing company, failed mightily. Stewart lost everything and was
forced into arrears. He would long pay for this "dead horse." The payments so hampered him, he would later admit, that he had "been con-
tinuously, and [was] still, a large borrower." His mistake had hurt other
people as well, including his two sisters, a close friend, and his pastor, all
minor partners in the Stewart oil firm. That fact greatly pained him.[47]

Yet, even as he looked out on the tumultuous oil landscape of
the early 1870s, on which he wanted to regain his footing, Stewart
remained steadfastly pledged to the high-risk and, as he saw it, highly
spiritual formula ensconced in oil's rule of capture. Teachings of sin,
sacrifice, and punishment informed his view. Willing to weather the
hazards of petrocapitalism if it meant protecting his right to exercise
his faith and labor in his own way, he was also prepared to shoulder all
the blame for failure. Writing to his children years later, he attributed
his financial collapse to the fact that he had stopped tithing and thus
stopped honoring a contract he had with his Lord, a promise of personal fulfillment in exchange for trust in the Almighty. "I started out in
my business career as a tither," and "the Lord prospered me," he noted,
before conceding, "I began investing faster than my income would warrant, satisfying my conscience by saying 'If I make this investment I will
have so much more to give to the Lord's work' and my tithes were not
paid . . . and at the end of the six years referred to I was 'dead broke.'"
In Stewart's estimation, his lesson was painful but necessary: a good
Christian capitalist had to be willing to take chances in order to strike
it rich and garner opportunities to translate oil wealth into "living gospel truth" that extended the reach of the church. But at no point was
God to be left out of this transaction. In much the same way as Rockefeller, he viewed his vocation as all encompassing, with the mundane
handling of crude directly linked to the prerogatives of the divine. Yet
much more so than his counterpart, who attacked structural inefficien-
cies as the root of petroleum's problems, Stewart held firm to the belief
that the fluctuations of his business were to be expected as part of the
mysterious workings of the Creator in men, in markets, and, most of all,
in the magical realm of oil. Whereas Rockefeller rationalized industrial
capitalism, Stewart reenchanted it.[48]

The fight between Rockefeller, on the one hand, and Stewart's fellow producers, on the other, unfolded at a high pitch during the 1870s. The first phase of combat occurred in early 1872 as word of Rockefeller's role in the formation of the SIC spread across the region. In late February of that year, a local newspaper published the names of the oilmen associated with the SIC; Rockefeller was on the blacklist. Petrolia's small producers, left out in the cold by the SIC, responded with rage and immediately organized a counterrevolution that would become known as the "Oil War." Stewart took the lead. Upon hearing of the SIC plan and reading the blacklist, he recruited a fellow oiler and elder at First Presbyterian Church to help him "call for a mass meeting to combat the South Improvement Company . . . and [make] out a slate for its organization." As both were entering a "trying time" in their careers, Stewart and his accomplice saw the fight with SIC as a life-or-death matter. So did the 3,000 oilmen who answered the call and filled the Titusville opera house with their boisterous protests.[49]

What followed was a two-month blitz by Oil Creek's independent producers to stymie the SIC. As one antiquarian reported, their actions were frenetic: "Mass meetings, parades, speeches exhorting to burn the enemy refiners' oil, to tap the enemy tanks, to lynch the 'conspirators.'" They also formed an association, which "bound its members by fiery oaths and ritual to 'unite against the common enemy,' to stop all oil production, to sell no more to the refiners who were members of the Combination." Standard felt the pressure of their boycott. In its Cleveland refineries, where 1,200 men usually worked, only 70 were now needed to handle the limited supplies. Rockefeller, however, refused to adjust. "It is not the business of the public to change our private contracts," he wrote his wife, adamant that his enemies were out of line. But his enemies, armed with widespread support, won the day. In addition to holding widely publicized protests, they petitioned the Pennsylvania legislature to revoke the SIC's charter. By April, under the weight of scrutiny and diminishing profits, the SIC disbanded. The Oil War appeared over.[50]

But it was not. Rockefeller retained authority over Cleveland's refining sector and thus had the resources to wage a longer war of attrition, which transpired much more surreptitiously during the remaining years of the decade. As the 1870s unfolded, production continued to rise at untenable rates; oil overflowed from storage tanks, oozing into streams and pooling on land, and prices dropped precipitously to under fifty cents a barrel, less than locals at that time were paying for drinking water. With some 16,000 producers populating Oil Creek, the vast majority of them running shoestring operations, the coordination of interests witnessed during the Oil War's opening salvos of 1872 remained a difficult proposition. Associations were attempted and collaboration tried, and in some cases collective action against Standard's Cleveland refineries resurfaced as a way to right the ship. But as conditions continued to decline, the number of faltering companies steadily increased, as did the number of bankrupted oilmen. Seizing the opportunity he had envisioned, Rockefeller slyly spread his influence. First, he bought up more refineries in the area. Then, with the help of Standard spies he had hired to scout potential allies, he approached Oil Creek's more successful small producers with offers they could not refuse. Sell to Standard, he promised, and watch anxieties shrink and pocketbooks swell.[51]

Two of Rockefeller's sellers were Henry Rogers and John Archbold. The product of a Yankee family with ties to the Pilgrims, Rogers was one of the many budding New England entrepreneurs who followed George Bissell to Oil Creek right after petroleum was discovered. In 1861 he and a partner started a refinery near Oil City, just south of Titusville. Over the course of the next decade, Rogers expanded his operations but began to struggle as the market turned sour. Impressed with his skills as a manager, Rockefeller approached him in 1874 and struck a deal: Rogers became a Standard man and quickly ascended the ranks. Yet another Protestant Yankee to whom Rockefeller was naturally drawn, Archbold was a Methodist minister's son raised in the Protestant stronghold of Leesburg, Ohio. The hard-driving fifteen-year-old had made his way to Titusville in early 1864, where he became a proud independent oiler. Archbold's impassioned speech to the independents at Titusville's opera house in February 1872 had galvanized their revolt. "We have been approached by the great anaconda, but do not desire to yield," he shouted indignantly. Of their God-given right to their oil, he proclaimed, "We believe this is the natural point of the business. This is the last desperate struggle of desperate men." By 1875 the firebrand had changed his tune. Facing another economic downturn, he accepted

Rockefeller's offer to join the Standard team. He was not the only independent to succumb to the anaconda's pressure. But his betrayal of the independents' cause was particularly difficult for locals to digest.[52]

Those small producers who did not follow Rogers and Archbold into the Standard empire faced increasingly tenuous prospects. Besides losing their autonomy and dignity, the wildcatters who gave in to their enormous competitor could at least look forward to a settled existence; their fight was over. Their peers who scrapped a bit longer truly felt the wrath of the titan. Rockefeller showed no compunction in having company spies monitor competitors, craft fake deals, and spread damaging misinformation about them—or simply blackmail them. Well into the 1880s a handful of small producers and refiners would fight back, successfully making their cases to the courts and an increasingly angry public, outraged by Standard's monopoly. There would be economic victories as well. In 1879, independents used an innovation, the pipeline, as well as their own deceptive tactics (conducting fake surveys, for example, to prevent Standard from anticipating its route) to escape Rockefeller's grasp. Stretching 110 miles east from the oil region to a major railroad hub, the Tidewater Pipeline started conveying oil in May of that year, marking a key victory for the anti-Standard camp. Standard would catch up to the new technology and find ways to dominate it too, but not for a while. And in the 1890s, a few of the last Pennsylvania independents would combine to form the Pure Oil Company. Advertising itself as the purer company and commodity, which customers could trust, Pure Oil would, by 1905, boast a fully integrated corporate structure, able to withstand any Standard onslaught.[53]

Whatever success awaited Pure Oil's crusading few, by 1880 it was clear to the majority of western Pennsylvania's wildcatters that their rule of capture, their privilege to work the land and drain its riches, was virtually extinct. By the time the second phase of the Oil War played itself out, Standard controlled 90 percent of the entire country's refining capacity. Lyman Stewart and his cohort would have to find another way to slay the giant.[54]

AT THE SAME time that oilmen fought for supremacy in the fields, an army of pastors and their flocks fought for it on Main Street, ultimately raising the stakes of the industry's grasp on society. Dismayed by the hellish side of oil's influence, unwilling to despair, reformers began crafting programs of uplift that could reverse oil's debauchery. Having inspired a potent entrepreneurial verve, oil became equally empowering as an impetus for ardent dissent.

During the initial chaos of the oil boom, the potential for church-borne protest only gradually took shape. As contemporary pundits liked to stress, early on the most notable feature of oil's communal life seemed to be the triumph of "Spartan Law" over "God's Law." Critic William Wright complained how "little respect was shown to the first day of the week." "The people pumped, and barreled, and drove, and shipped petroleum on Sunday as well as Saturday." As Wright subsequently acknowledged, though, church inaction during the Civil War gave way to action once peace returned. "A change has been gradually taking place, giving man and beast the advantage of a septennial day of rest." Penning his thoughts in 1865, he wrote, "Sunday work seldom takes place," and along Oil Creek, "small buildings have been erected, to serve for chapels on Sunday and school-houses during the week." As far as Wright was concerned, Petrolia's church boom was real, yet another arresting sign of a land gripped by change.[55]

Oil country's ecclesiastical bustle was a striking feature of its development in the two decades that followed the Civil War. In boomtowns such as Oil City, church construction was staggering, with congregational memberships expanding exponentially. Statistics were but one measure of expanding church influence; in a very concrete way, parishes of all theological persuasions also became the nerve centers of their communities. Even in notorious Pithole, they quickly emerged as bastions of enforced civility where displaced oil workers could go to escape the harshness of their world. When one oil prospector arrived in town on January 3, 1866, he noted in his diary, "There are but few who attend church, and [there is] the lowest of morals in this part of the country." He immediately sought out a house of worship. By late January he was attending the Methodist church for Sunday sermons. As winter turned to spring, he noted how pleased he was to see that revivals had led to populated pews. And money was pouring in too, making a church bell possible; such was the benefit of running a church with instant riches. By May, as his business—like so many others in Pithole—began to wind down, he found added comfort in the routines of church. On May 19 he admitted anxiety about the untrustworthiness of fellow oilers. "Companions who have proved staunch and true, may betray you for their own interest, fortune may prove fickle after lavishing favor upon you for years," he wrote, "but so long as life remains, Hope will ever be the same kind of encouraging angel to all." On May 20, he attended church and found "Hope" inside. Nine days later, tools and land sold off, with a greater sense of calm, he boarded a train and left town.[56]

Besides sustaining men as they weathered the tempests of oil, churches served as brokers of rich land. As was typical in most American towns, a church's place on the grid was a gauge of its influence; to be located on a downtown corner lot was to seize a cultural import that no one could assail. Yet, along Oil Creek, hilltops held special allure as vistas from which to oversee the shady valley of production. It was no accident that all three of Pithole's original churches clustered together on the town's highest mound, as if to declare that theirs was the region's most important venture. Churches were also sites of extraction. In petroleum's early days, logic held that mounds could be signs that oil was present. The thinking, not without merit, was that hills such as those lining Oil Creek were anticlines or salt domes, geological pockets of oil. Well-established churches that occupied these spaces frequently oversaw graveyards now earmarked for potential profits. They routinely leased their burial grounds to drillers, monitored the derricks towering over their gravestones, and waited for the black stuff to flow. Oilmen zealously drilled, convinced that the dead's resting spots augured huge pools. In some cases, the grave drilling yielded thousands of barrels of crude. In both symbol and substance, Petrolia's parishes, in other words, wished to operate at the heart of the action.[57]

A good number of Petrolia's parishioners did not see themselves as everyday oilers, however. In their eyes, they had been called to Christianize their surroundings. Out of the tumult of post–Civil War crude extraction emerged a band of revolutionaries determined to roll back its negative effects. Subversives in the pulpits railed against the moral dangers of the cutthroat systems that surrounded them, while those in the pews drank in messages of empowerment and strategized ways to reverse the trends. Wildcatters in their own right, these men and women risked whatever was necessary to gain a foothold on uncharted frontier terrain.

One minister, Darius Steadman, provided an early blueprint for Petrolia's spiritual counteroffensive. Steadman pastored Pithole's Methodist church during the town's brief existence between 1865 and 1866; he was the preacher from whom the reflective and financially imperiled oil prospector drew inspiration. Heralded by some as "the man with 'a severe faith but a tender heart,'" by others as "a sentinel who could make a sinner look like thirty cents," Steadman was well equipped for a bruising clash with the demons of oil. He had earned his stripes as Civil War chaplain of the 105th Regiment of the Pennsylvania Volunteers, a unit known as "The Wildcats." After the war he made his way to the overwhelmed Methodist congregation in booming Pithole. "His first sermon, in this town of brothels and saloons, casinos and dance houses, of flowing wells and veterans seeking their fortunes," one chronicler wrote of the divine's arrival, was delivered "in an eighty-foot unfinished building with a dry goods box as a pulpit." Through his skillful management of the church's expanding coffers and membership ranks, Pithole Methodist quickly completed a posh edifice. It was Reverend Steadman who insisted a bell be installed to summon oil's ragtag hordes and stressed speculators.[58]

Yet summoning was not enough for Steadman; he preferred to assault the lost with his legendary tenacity. Shortly after taking over the Pithole pulpit, he began recruiting local residents to his moral campaign: he held revival meetings in the town's largest ballroom, started a choir for roughnecks, and rallied denizens of the iniquitous town to his law-and-order sentiments. Bearded, with a penetrating gaze, he worked the streets as well and took pleasure in frequenting Pithole's saloons to pester its occupants about their backsliding. In the midst of this crusade, he came up with a plan to ensure that Oil Creek's children received an adequate education. He took advantage of a legal stipulation that the fines of lawbreakers be split between court and informant. Walking the city, he cited sixty men selling liquor without licenses. The next day he trekked to the county seat and submitted his report, forcing all sixty to appear before a judge. Steadman calmly collected his share of the fines, bought school equipment, and started classes in the church basement. When funds dried up, he repeated the routine. By far his most daring venture, however, involved the town's most notorious hustler, who recruited Pithole's prostitutes. When one frantic mother sought to extricate her daughter from the pimp's clutches, Steadman stepped forward, infiltrated the flesh peddler's den, and held him at gunpoint until he released his sex slave. The pastor was proclaimed a hero.[59]

Following Pithole's collapse in 1866 and Steadman's departure, other crusaders quickly filled the vacuum of aggressive reform he left behind. Within this fighting force, women especially found their voice. On the hypermasculine oil-patch terrain, their numbers at first paled in comparison to men's, as did their ability to impose their proprieties. But even amid the earliest disruptions to their existences and family economies, women fought back.[60]

The town of Rouseville provided a compelling example of female activism. Distressed by the deadly effects of oil in their area, as well as by the loose morals it seemed to promote, Rouseville's female militants banded together to civilize their society. They went about their task with all the daring illustrated in Steadman's raids on brothels and bars. One night, they helped unmoor a gambling and prostitution "joy boat" called *Floating Palace* from its dock on Oil Creek and set it adrift. Its drunken passengers wound up far downstream. Amid discord, women became moral gatekeepers, celebrated by clerics as partners in justice, held up by many in the pews as saints, and feared by the wayward as more than worthy foes. In private, meanwhile, they sternly exhorted their husbands and children to avoid the wickedness of their environs and, where possible, to shine as examples of how to do right.[61]

One Rouseville mother, Esther Tarbell, diligently practiced the latter strategy. In the fall of 1860, after a brief attempt at farming in Iowa, Esther and her husband, Franklin, moved back to their home in western Pennsylvania, where Franklin entered the oil business. Esther immediately fretted: What had she come to? "A place of perils," she surmised, "a creek rushing wildly at the side of the house, great oil pits sunken in the earth not far away, a derrick inviting to adventurous climbing at the door." The massive Rouseville blaze of 1861, whose horrors Franklin witnessed firsthand, confirmed to the Tarbells that danger lurked everywhere. After using all her resolve and her cherished quilts to treat the fire's victims, Esther was spent; she would never escape the "relics of the tragedy," her daughter would later explain. Meanwhile, just a short walk away, "orgies" of the kind seen in "Monte Carlo and the Latin Quarter combined" were playing out in Petroleum Centre, with a conspicuousness that made Esther shudder. "I indured [*sic*] enough at Rouseville for all the rest of my life," she would admit. Yet, in those years she also showed her daughter moral steadfastness. While lending a hand to the Rouseville mothers' revolt, at every step, with switch in hand and an urgent tone, she scolded and dogged her family to stay true to a righteousness that would only triumph if the devout remained vigilant.[62]

In the 1870s, Esther Tarbell and her sisters in oil drew sustenance from a new institution. In 1874, just fifty miles north of Titusville—merely a daylong buggy trip or morning train ride over a verdant plateau—two prominent Methodist leaders created the Chautauqua Institution as an interdenominational summer school for laity. Its inaugural two-week gathering that summer drew five hundred participants. Within months, families began scheduling annual visits; lodged in cottages that grew more elaborately rustic over time, thronging along Chautauqua Lake, they learned from some of the country's great orators and instructors in faith, science, and the arts. Chautauqua's adult attendees signed up for activities geared to "intellectual and moral self-improvement and civic involvement." Their children, meanwhile, saw learning linked to fun. "What they wanted us to have there was the excellent training given in the Bible with all the sorts of inviting accessories," a girl remembered. "I shall never forget a relief map of Palestine that ran for many rods along the lakefront. We used to romp from Baalbec to Beersheba, shouting out the points of interest, and, when we dared, wading in the Dead Sea. No youngster who knew that map was ever wanting in a Biblical geography examination." Such was the subtle but enduring effect of Chautauqua on a multigenerational phenomenon of cultural improvement that quickly spilled over the New York state line into far-beyond cities and villages.[63]

The Tarbells were among the upright families of Petrolia caught up in the Chautauqua phenomenon. Franklin immediately enlisted in the growing colony and started journeying north via train and lake steamer with his wife and children for annual festivities. By the 1870s, he had achieved some success as an oil producer, leading to a change in status that sat well with his wife. The clan moved from Rouseville to the much larger Titusville and into a Victorian mansion replete with "French windows, a veranda, balconies, and a tower room," which had formerly functioned as a hotel in Pithole. Built for $60,000, the former "Bonta House" was purchased by Franklin for $600, dismantled, then reconstructed in Titusville. Although the town was still scarred by oil's devastation, Esther could now send her kids to fine schools, walk to the opera house on gaslit, graded streets, and baptize her brood in respectability.[64]

Her grassroots fervor remained intact, however, enabled by the learning Chautauqua provided. She and her peers in Titusville's emerging middle-class churches bought books, grappled with the most recent teachings of science—especially Herbert Spencer's social Darwinism, which Esther rejected—and looked for ways to inculcate their communities with their knowledge. In an indirect way, they also came to embrace a nascent feminist movement, which drew momentum from the Chautauqua scene. Tarbell's move out of the isolation of Rouseville allowed her to connect with literature and lecturers flowing through Chautauqua networks into Titusville. During the 1870s, her home played host to speakers such as Mary Livermore and Frances Willard, who spoke openly about the need to fight politically for women's freedom. Esther's cohort was, in a word, engaged—with evolving biblical and scientific truths and with the social and political affairs that defined their culture. As they continued to look at the state of such affairs locally, with sharpened intellect and opinions, their desire to bring Petrolia under control naturally grew. In years to come, Petrolia's oil culture would feel the weight of this fusion of female empowerment. If often working behind the scenes of the furious petroleum production carried out by men, oil-patch women would carve out key niches within the church and civil society to roll back Petrolia's blight. They would do so as activists, as mothers, and as philanthropists, leveraging for social reform the oil fortunes they accrued and managed. And they would do so as writers, the pen their sharpest weapon.[65]

Esther's most important contribution to this rising force came through her daughter, Ida, who would be every bit as important to the future of the American oil patch as John D. Rockefeller. A childhood passed largely at the Chautauqua Institution (it was she who loved to romp from Baalbec to Beersheba and dip in the Dead Sea) and countless hours spent with female liberationists in her mother's parlor had awakened the young Ida Tarbell's conscience. Further exposure to ideas of faith, science, and reform promulgated at Titusville's Methodist church, her home congregation, warmed her to a vocation of teaching and activism. Always prone to serious questioning, Tarbell forayed deeply into the new ideas of the day (especially Herbert Spencer's), at one point wondering whether she should leave the church and her faith behind. But "it was hard to give up heaven," she later mused, and the scientific theories in which she was beginning to indulge did not yet give her anything "to take the place of what had always been the unwritten law of the Tarbell household"—"the teachings of the Bible" and its "guide ... in human relations." Still, enamored of evolutionary theory, she was determined to intuit some truth from it and harness its insights for Christian action.[66]

Ida Tarbell's training at Allegheny College provided her the opportunity to assume that religious and political posture. In 1876, she enrolled at the Methodist school in Meadeville, thirty miles to the west of Titusville. For the next four years she embraced every opportunity to train widely in languages and history, art and literature, and especially natural sciences, which upon graduation she intended to teach. After Tarbell concluded her studies, Methodist elders pleaded for her to enlist in foreign missionary work, insisting she had a "calling to serve God." But she accepted a different service—a professorship at Poland Union Seminary in Ohio. There, she learned as much as she taught. For two years she weathered a heavy teaching load, as well as rejection from male colleagues as she tried to crack the ranks of biological research. Digesting the reality that academia remained a male domain, she also encountered an eastern Ohio countryside under extreme economic transformation. The encroachment of new coalmines and ironworks on the once bucolic farmland circling Youngstown haunted her. Once workers on their land, farmers were now pawns of industrialists who greedily exploited the area's resources. Tarbell saw modernity's dark side: "the destruction of beauty, the breaking down of the standards of conduct, the love of money for money's sake, the grist of social problems facing the countryside from the inflow of foreigners and the instability of work." On one particularly scarring day, she watched as charred bodies were carted off from a smelting furnace that had just exploded. "Unforgettable horror," she mourned. She took in the truth about a ruthless economic order co-opting the land. "Like the charred bodies carried across the road," she rued, "it was an unforgettable thing."[67]

Stretched physically, emotionally, and financially, Tarbell returned home to Titusville in 1882 to reassess her future. A short time later, her mother invited Reverend Theodore Flood, editor of *The Chautauquan*, the main organ of its namesake institution (now a "movement"), over to dine. Flood listened as Ida told him about her training and teaching; here was someone who could help him convey complicated ideas to the magazine's 50,000 lay readers. The editor finally stopped the conversation to ask Tarbell to help him with the journal's production. She agreed and within months established herself as *The Chautauquan*'s go-to person for editorial advice and ultimately its most effective writer. Eventually she started using her pen to navigate the political terrains she had witnessed in Titusville and Poland: women's rights and religious reform, scientific progress, and the inequity of power. She wrote heavily researched, passionately argued pieces on behalf of eight-hour workdays and urban reform, embracing social Darwinism as a way for Christians to better understand current economic dislocations. Over time, her social criticism sharpened. "The eighties dripped with blood," she later noted, "and men struggled to get at causes, to find corrections, to humanize and socialize the country." With her prodding, *The Chautauquan* "interested itself in all of this turbulent and confused life."[68]

The turbulence was nowhere more apparent than in her hometown, Tarbell finally recognized. Throughout the late 1870s and early 1880s, while working beyond immediate view of Petrolia's developments, she had stayed informed by way of regular family visits and conversations with her father and brother. The message she received—and saw evidenced in her father's sallow face—was a disquieting one, reminding her of what she had witnessed in rural Ohio. For over a decade, despite the efforts of moral reformers, Petrolia had been descending into its own disarray, for reasons pertaining more to finances than malfeasance. Economic progressions in the petroleum sector had broken the backs of Titusville's men, and the town itself had grown divided, bitter, and defeated, all because of oil's failing dream. "Here was a product meant to be a blessing to men," Tarbell puzzled, yet "it was proving a curse to the very ones who had discovered it, and developed it." And so she began to contemplate a more forceful response, one informed by her evolving religious convictions, faith in a sisterhood more equipped than ever to revolt, and confidence that, despite man-made chaos, reason and reasonableness could prevail. "Cherish your contempts," writer Henry James once advised her as she struggled to accept her role as agitator. "Cherish your contempts . . . and strength to your elbow."[69]

In the mid-1880s, she determined to do just that. The close-up view of her father and the Oil War spurred her on. By then, the battle for Petrolia had essentially come to an end, with John D. Rockefeller claiming a decisive psychological as well financial victory. For the hundreds of independent oilmen who fought him and lost, existential crisis followed. Franklin Tarbell was among the broken. Growing up, Ida remembered her father as a loveable eccentric, known for his gentleness; in the wake of his refusal to "cast his lot with the Standard Oil trust," he was "grim faced" and plagued by worry. Having lost his distressed business partner to suicide and mortgaged his house to offset company debts and continuing to bleed money, he joined his son Will on a move to the Dakotas to try his hand at wheat farming. The experiment failed, and Franklin returned home, defeated yet again. Franklin's daughter kept filing away the evidences of an economic system gone wrong, making mental notes of the pain it was causing the men on whose shoulders that system once rested. Hers was not a simple fatalism, however. Looking at her father, she saw damage but also dignity; despite all the pressures, he refused to cave to someone else's authority. "Success," she wrote later, "lay in being your own master." "I am sure my father would rather have grubbed corn meal and bacon from a piece of stony land which was his own than have had all the luxuries of a salary." In her initial view of the circumstances surrounding Franklin's collapse, the absence of that kind of stick-to-itiveness among his peers angered her most. "I looked with more contempt on the man who had gone over to the Standard than on the one who had been in jail. I felt pity for the later man, but none for the deserters from the ranks of the fighting independents."[70]

Against this backdrop the writer started to firm up her moral critique of capitalism. Her target was not free enterprise itself but rather the manipulation of it by men with evil designs. "There was born in me a hatred of privilege . . . of any sort," she would recall of that awakening.

As the next steps of her career unfolded, her commitment to a truly egalitarian capitalism, one defined by the value of "production by individual laborers," would evolve, as would her commitment to an ever more flexible Christian faith. The searing effects of her father's struggles further loosened her trust in the God of her Methodist upbringing, as did her further embrace of scientific theories that pushed the boundaries of biblical convention. "But that which shook me hardest," she would remember, "was a continuous series of discoveries about human sufferings, inequalities, greed, ignorance, all so inconsistent with the notion of a merciful force active in the world." Tarbell retained her sense "that this force was at work," yet began to grapple intellectually with its agency in her life and the world. Where better to test it all than in Paris?[71]


WHILE SHE CROSSED the Atlantic for a sojourn in France, oilmen of her father's ilk were crossing the continent. Of the oil hunters' wanderlust Tarbell would later write, "Fortune was running fleet-footed across the country, and at her garment men clutched." Tarbell's sentimentalized words belied the fact that the oilers looking west were once proud, now displaced producers desperately in search of a second chance. As last-gasp attempts at solvency, their journeys were risky, for who could imagine sufficient oil in Texas and California and territories in between?[72]

Willing to challenge mainstream opinion that no oil flowed west of the Mississippi River, the wildcatters who left Pennsylvania for the Far West were also eager to upset the logics of faith and capitalism that John D. Rockefeller and his team had enforced back home. Rockefeller's conquest of Petrolia's oil culture lent proof to a theory that Max Weber would a short time later articulate as universal. With Standard's ascent came confirmation that a second stage of capitalist development had consumed the oil business, one geared to the prescriptions of a rational, Calvinistic Protestantism that privileged coordination and control over willful acceptance of risk, raising to power a class of men who were "calculating and daring at the same time, above all temperate and reliable, shrewd and completely devoted to their business, with strictly bourgeois opinions and principles." What Rockefeller could not predict—and Weber would overlook—was the way a wildcat ethic would relocate and flourish again in the speculative mode.[73]

As they straggled westward, the wildcatters left behind a social system stamped with their influence. However much Rockefeller and reformers tried to erase them, the cycles of oil's blessings and curses that beset the oil patch and the rolling bouts of pathos that descended on its citizens during oil's first season would long endure and be replicated elsewhere. And the new nation that early oilers helped define and awaken to the enchantments of crude would not forget its first encounter with the economic and religious power of the material coaxed out of the ground. But in the immediacy of their travels west, these legacies and their effects on a modernizing society were not their concern; mere survival was.

With his radical spirit in tow, a battered Lyman Stewart sought that kind of future for himself when, out of answers in Petrolia, he contemplated a move. Although the 1870s were a difficult decade, the western Pennsylvania native, Civil War veteran, and devout and determined Presbyterian oil hunter had stuck with his dreams. One priority he held to was to apprentice younger oil entrepreneurs and offer support whenever he could. In the early years of the decade, while enjoying his last moments of prosperity before accruing heavy debt, Stewart had supported a team of brothers from California who had traveled east to hunt for Pennsylvania's black gold. Lyman developed a close relationship with the most ambitious of them, Wallace Hardison, that resulted in a partnership. Despite Stewart's struggles, in 1877 the duo managed to acquire control of some land in the developing Bradford field. Hardison and Stewart were complete opposites in many regards. Hardison was a large, charismatic, impatient man with a penchant for diving in to the next oil project, whereas Stewart was defined by his uprightness. Of average build, with a pronounced Vandyke beard lending him an air of sophistication, the Presbyterian elder never traveled or worked on Sunday, never drank alcohol, and always did his best to help his workers understand why such moral observance would better their lives. An oilman with a fierce independent streak, he also believed that independence could only be exercised properly with a Christian moral compass. Despite their differences, the two men complemented each other and worked well together. Although their venture in the Bradford field failed because of Rockefeller's stranglehold, they were anxious to try again somewhere else.[74]

Hardison thought Kansas made sense, but Stewart set his sights "even further west." "There were reports," he explained, "that extensive oil lands could be had for practically nothing in California. The idea of the new open country, with the opportunity for unhampered effort, appealed to me very strongly." In the winter of 1882 Stewart and his eldest son boarded a train. "What I was to find in the west I knew not," he would write. "Except that it was opportunity and that was all I asked." In his possession was a small Bible that his wife had given him. "That Bible was to be my guide and protector, my inspiration during the hectic and discouraging times ahead."[75]

# CHAPTER TWO

# Worlds of Wonder

When Lyman Stewart and his son William arrived in Los Angeles in early 1883, the West felt a bit like home. Greeting them were former allies from Titusville, men who had fought the Oil War, then fled for new proving grounds along the Pacific coast. These welcoming friends helped Stewart make contacts with local powerbrokers in the business, including I. E. Blake of the Pacific Coast Oil Company. Blake arranged a deal with Stewart allowing the Pennsylvania transplant to lease land from Pacific Coast Oil. An excited Stewart then wired Wallace Hardison, requesting his help rounding up funds and workers. Hardison quickly returned to a state he knew well with enough capital to begin drilling and thirty-five roughnecks on hand.[1]

As Stewart soon discovered, the topography of the West was difficult. California's complex geological formations were challenging to the uninitiated; steep slopes, tilted rock walls, and the constant presence of water caused endless problems, resulting in lost or damaged equipment and one delay after another. Over time Stewart would hone his skills as an oil scout, all while relying again on his nose to identify subsurface pools. But initially, every one of his strategies met with failure. By mid-1884, after a year of futility, Stewart and Hardison were $183,000 in debt, with no further borrowing options. Making matters worse were

winter rains that had flooded their wells earlier that year. "I have suffered from the blues ever since," Lyman despondently told his brother
and investing partner Milton. "I have nobody to blame but myself." He
continued, "I had grown quite conservative after so many failures of
my plans and decided never to undertake anything again in the way of
a 'big thing,' but this was such a tempting opportunity that I not only
took hold of it for myself but got the friends whom I felt anxious to
help to join with me in the venture. This is what troubles me most."
Among his backers were his sisters and church (including its pastor)
back in Pennsylvania, who had supported Stewart's earlier ventures and
stuck with him as he moved west. In his time of desperation, Lyman as
always leaned on theology for some (if never total) comfort. "I sometimes think that perhaps the dear Lord loves us too much to give us the
success which for long seemed to be just within our reach," he confided.
"I know that it is all for the best ... but still I seem constantly to be
under a dark threatening cloud and many wasteful hours and much
suffering seems to be my present lot." Unfortunately, the cloud would
linger.[2]

During the next few years, Hardison and Stewart suffered repeated
defeats. Due to ongoing contractual disputes and their bitterness at
being assigned difficult territory, they became convinced that their
plight was largely the work of the men at Pacific Coast Oil's helm.
Once again Stewart bared his soul to Milton. "It seems as though the
Almighty has put the stamp of His disapproval upon our operation
and I believe it is just punishment for our entering into an arrangement with such a set of wicked monopolists." But in 1885 they received
better news. The "wicked monopolists" were willing to let them prospect anywhere, with promises of support in exchange for refining rights
(Pacific Coast Oil owned a refinery; Hardison and Stewart did not).
The two men pressed on with a quicker step. Finally, at the close of that
year, producing wells came in for them in the Puente Hills, southeast of
Los Angeles. The cloud was lifting.[3]

Meanwhile, the two oilmen aligned with a powerful accomplice,
Thomas Bard, a Pennsylvanian responsible for California's first gusher
in the 1860s. Bard was convinced that oil rested beneath his land in the
Ojai Rancho, north of Los Angeles. By 1890, the three men were hitting pay dirt, raising a tough question: whether to expand or maintain

operations. Bard and Hardison insisted on staying the course, Stewart on adopting new modes of integration. From his uneven dealings with Pacific Coast Oil he had learned that lasting success would only come in the region's undeveloped economy if a company operated in each sector: production, transportation, refining, and marketing. Despite the rift, for the moment, unity prevailed. The harmony owed not just to the partners' increased corporate stability but also to their shared belief that in turn-of-the-century Southern California, independent oilmen and their Christian capitalist values had the rare opportunity to root themselves in fruitful fields. Why jeopardize such promise?[4]

On these common principles the men officially forged a new corporate entity in late 1890, the Union Oil Company of California. Thomas Bard was named president, but Vice President Lyman Stewart, owning 53 percent of Union stock, truly ruled. In the coming years he would wield his authority with a gentlemanly but unbending tenacity out of desire to save a world he feared lost to monopolism and other secular sins.[5]

Stewart's renewal on the West Coast was a major chapter in independent oil's incremental rebirth on that same soil. Driven out of the East by the Standard Oil juggernaut, a diverse lot of small oil producers desperately worked to reestablish themselves on western frontiers, anxious about the difficult environmental and economic conditions that confronted them but relieved that, for a while longer at least, they could stick with their trade. The trails they walked toward the Pacific Ocean and Gulf of Mexico were charted by an equally keen band of oil scouts and saddlebag saints—spiritually attuned itinerants whose contact with the land made them the vanguard of US oil's westward march. For some, oil hunting assumed explicit priority as a professional duty, for others it was a hobby, and for a few it represented a chivalrous quest to create alternative communities in a time of unsettling societal change. For all, it seemed, the encounter with trans-Mississippi terrain and its hints of subsurface crude reawakened a wildcat spirit that had been squelched in Pennsylvania's Petrolia. Set apart from John D. Rockefeller's machinations, men of Stewart's class could envisage again their own divine destinies.

Yet, even as Stewart's horizons finally expanded, so too did those of his giant nemesis. While Stewart's cohort reimagined oil's fate in continental terms, Rockefeller's started speaking of it in global terms. Neither was alone in its lofty aspirations. In distant lands, European entrepreneurs and corporations, missionaries and church folk approached the twentieth century immersed in rapidly expanding circuits of petrocapitalism. Even though a transnational venture by the 1890s, oil remained dominated by the United States, whose unmatched access to and exploitation of the natural resource came to define its place in the world. At this critical juncture, petroleum reinvigorated Americans' habit of viewing their society as set apart, as uniquely equipped by God to usher all humanity forward into a modern epoch. For wildcatters like Stewart, this dawning reality brought on a heightened burden. They were now contributing to a kingdom-building project much bigger than their own. In its restless sprawl, oildom was remaking the world in its image, lending credence to an emerging truth in the business: neither petroleum nor those who pursued it could ever stay still.

WHEN LYMAN STEWART traveled to California, he followed paths blazed by contemporaries who had been far less patient with conditions in Pennsylvania. Already in the 1860s, as Pithole came and went, oil hunters of all kinds began infiltrating terrains to the south, west, and north, anxious to ride the next wave of discovery well before Pennsylvania's inevitable decline. Since they never achieved a momentous breakthrough of the kind witnessed in Titusville in 1859, no great attention was forthcoming. Yet their quiet labor laid the groundwork for future revelations.

The scale of this labor was not completely hidden from view. In an 1865 published report, Alexander Von Millern, a geologist at the Royal and Imperial Academy of Arts and Sciences in Vienna, offered a firsthand look at oil's emerging production sites. He covered Pennsylvania but also outlined oil hunting farther afield, in Ohio, Indiana, and Colorado. In some cases, oil had been identified; others evidenced only oil fever. "Our people are taking the infection," offered an Ohio newspaper that Von Millern quoted. "Politics, the war, drafts, conscriptions, high taxes, and even our lumber business, all are in danger of being forgotten in the rage for petroleum, but so far nary 'smell' of 'ile' has been struck." Of real interest to the professor were places where "ile" *had* been struck.

He rendered his impressions in scientific script laced with religious allusion. "I have just returned from . . . Ohio and West Virginia," he told his readers, and "now [submit] information as to the . . . minerals and lubricating and illuminating oils, which have been stored away for countless ages . . . destined by the Great Creator and Author of events to become serviceable, and now just beginning to be developed for the benefit, appliances and usefulness of the human race." Von Millern and his associates were fully aware of two other landscapes where oil development seemed bound to take root.[6]

Thanks to Benjamin Silliman Jr., Southern California emerged as a curiosity for trend watchers. In 1864, East Coast financier Thomas Scott, who was then also assistant secretary of war, hired the professor (and George Bissell's expert consultant) to investigate mineral investment opportunities in Nevada and California. Silliman mapped out areas where asphalt veins and outcrops, bituminous shale and fossils, and patterned ranges and "beltways" of hills seemed to promise reservoirs of subterranean liquid. He eagerly commented on the wonders he encountered. "The oil matter is beyond all comparison the most important game started by my year's work," he explained in a letter to his wife. "Providence" had played a crucial role in molding the natural forces that bore gifts of carbon. Now it was his turn, through "wanderings in search of all oil & asphaltum," to make the properties God ascribed to them serve the white man's civilizing enterprise. He was particularly spellbound by the hued oil slicks that glossed the sea near Santa Barbara. Long known to navigators, the gloss nevertheless left Silliman certain of oil's presence and in awe of geological time. "Think of the flow of oil from the upturned edges of these strata going on for an unknown time," he pondered to his spouse. "Is it not wonderful that with such a hint men have been so long in comprehending the plain meaning of nature's language. My friends now may amuse themselves in investing in colors equally gorgeous [as] the fortunes they will make of it!"[7]

Whatever Susan Silliman thought of her husband's exuberance, it soon rubbed off on the man who paid his way. Upon receipt of the report, Scott's Philadelphia & California Petroleum Company acquired control of 75,000 acres of territory along the Pacific coastline. During the late 1860s, it took the lead among the estimated sixty-five corporate compctitors in drilling wells in the Ojai region around Santa Barbara, the area Silliman had identified as particularly promising. Additional encouragement came from Pennsylvanians who had made their way west and become excited about prospecting there. Between 1865 and 1867, the company sank several wells, one of which, under the direction of Thomas Bard, Lyman Stewart's future partner, spudded California's first gusher. Bard's well would remain modest in output, compared to the highly productive ones he witnessed back home in Pennsylvania, but its reported "15 to 20 barrels of oil per day from a depth of 550 feet" made it the first "commercially productive" California oil well. By the late 1860s, though, the state's nascent petroleum sector had petered out. Unsatisfied with the quality of the oil, which had the uncompromising density of asphalt, and unable to compete with Pennsylvania's cheaper crude, which made its way by rail to San Francisco, California's first oilmen momentarily channeled their corporate energies elsewhere. Stewart's arrival in the Golden State in 1883 would coincide with the revitalization of its oil sector.[8]

At this point, California remained a curious but marginal player in the oil realm. More significant were finds back east and across the US-Canadian border in Ontario. There, industrialist James William Miller, who aspired to be the next Abraham Gesner, Canada's kerosene king, acquired the gummy bitumen beds located in the "Great Enniskillen Swamp" in Lambton County, just west of London. In 1858, Miller's team happened upon a substantial oil deposit. Whether Miller's find actually predated Edwin Drake's at Titusville is debatable; that Miller set a Canadian oil boom in motion is not. A London, England, report of 1862 pegged Ontario's rock oil as the British Empire's answer to Pennsylvania and a source of illumination it so desperately craved. Only imperial oversight was needed. "A flood of wealth is poured by nature into the lap of Canada," the report observed. "Our brethren . . . invite us to aid them, and to share with them the yet greater profits to arise from CANADIAN NATIVE OIL, its manufacture, transportation, refinement, and final sale." "It is for Englishmen to say whether they will ignorantly surrender to foreign hands so great a commercial advantage." The English would help, but over the coming years it would be the locals of Lambton who turned Miller's discovery into an oil outbreak with international reach.[9]

Many rank-and-file drillers did not need an official report to point them to opportunities farther afield. Men like R. Mortimer Buck, a Union veteran whose Civil War command of the Michigan Cavalry earned him fame in his hometown of Paw Paw, believed that their fortunes were tied to a mercurial liquid, not an unchangeable land. Life in oil entailed movement. Immediately following the war, Buck traveled back to Michigan, then east, across the Canadian border and into Ontario, where he started to drill. By 1866, his Ida Oil Well Company had struck pay dirt near Lambton County. In subsequent years the Methodist gentleman, respected for looking after his fellow soldiers during the war and his community in the years that followed, carved out a career that spanned decades and borders. Petroleum's impetuses drove him in many directions, and he dutifully tested each path.[10]

They drove countless others south as well. After the Union's victory, many Confederate veterans fanned out in search of liquid riches in their defeated region. Texas loomed large in their imagination. By October 1865, a team was boring land around Nacogdoches, where "tar springs" were known to exist; in 1866, four oil companies were formed to expedite the effort. One of them was headed by a former Texas general, whose well in Hardin County made him the first official corporate petroleum prospector in the state. Two Civil War veterans of another stripe, meanwhile, helped transmit excitement about oil to the Southwest through their work with parishioners and the pen. Benjamin Taylor Kavanaugh and William Fletcher Cummins were practitioners of natural theology whose ministerial work took them to remote places that happened to hold extractive promise. The itinerant mode compelled them, as Methodists, to circulate their faith. It also impelled them to test the inscrutabilities of God along the way, particularly those that seeped from the ground on which their horses trotted.[11]

More than anyone, Kavanaugh prompted the 1866 corporate burst in Texas's oil sector. Born in 1805 in Kentucky, the studious teen followed the pious example of his father, a Methodist cleric. In 1819, he dedicated his own life to Methodism while attending a revival. "This miracle of grace was so vivid and powerful," he testified, "that I can not better describe it than with Ezekiel to say, 'The heavens were opened, and I saw visions of God.'" Kavanaugh coupled his spiritual and intellectual visions by becoming a missionary with the American Sunday School Union and ascending into higher leadership and education. His vita during the 1840s and 1850s included administrative roles with the Indian Missions District of the Sioux and Chippewas and the American Colonization Society, as well as an MD from Indiana Asbury University (later DePauw University), a medical practice in St. Louis, and a professorship in obstetrics and gynecology at the University of Missouri. While in Missouri, he also pastored two Methodist congregations. He spent the Civil War as a Confederate chaplain and surgeon before resuming ministerial work in 1865, this time in Texas.[12]

Transferring south allowed Kavanaugh to take another step in his commitments to Christian service and scientific progress. While overseeing parishes in the Houston area and practicing medicine, he found time to scour Texas for mineral deposits, an interest he may have acquired while briefly ministering in a mining district of Wisconsin. Equipped with a divining rod that he called his "mineraloger," the unassuming renaissance man crisscrossed the state's southeast during the late 1860s, applying the rudimentary geological techniques he had acquired through the years. Kavanaugh scrupulously recorded every detail of his encounters with Texas's soil, mapped his journeys, and sketched his impressions, all to educate the public in the ways of the natural world. He summarized his findings in articles for newspapers throughout Texas. Later, his wife, Mary Margaret, compiled his reports in a manuscript titled "The Great Central Valley of North America Considered with Reference to Its Geography, Topography, Hydrology, and Mineralogy, and Other Prominent Features of the Valley." His publications and business ventures (he cofounded the San Augustine Petroleum Company in 1866) led one observer to declare him "largely responsible for the contemporary interest in potential oil in East Texas." While the payoff did not come immediately, Kavanaugh's preliminary stabs at the earth opened eyes. "Some day a great oil field will be developed in the valley of the Neches," the preacher predicted in one commentary, referencing the marshland around Beaumont.[13]

William Fletcher Cummins helped to sustain the interest in black gold sparked by Kavanaugh. For a time during the 1860s, their careers mirrored each other. In November 1859, just two months after Drake's Pennsylvania strike, Cummins left his home state of Missouri and headed for Texas. The decision to leave was borne out of a family squabble. His father, John, was a Methodist cleric in the Springfield district, a man revered by all, especially William. "I had [no] higher ambition than to be as good and great" as him, Cummins would say. Yet he eventually grew distant from his father. In 1857, when William was seventeen years old, a party of surveyors led by paleontologist S. C. Swallow came to Springfield to map its geological formations. They stayed at the Cummins residence, and William helped guide the team. On daily excursions he learned how to collect fossils, identify animal species, and map the puzzling terrain. "In that month's time," he stated, "I became thoroughly enthused with the idea of being a geologist." John allowed his son to continue this pursuit; at every chance, William scampered off to discover vestiges of the Silurian age, then consulted with Swallow, at work elsewhere, about his findings. But when another Methodist preacher started railing against Swallow's science, claiming "it was impossible to be a geologist and a Christian at the same time," the Cummins men faced a dilemma. Thrust into an awkward position, John asked William to cease his exploration and focus on being a minster. When William refused, John threw his son's fossils into a well with an ultimatum: abandon study or leave. Brokenhearted, the teenager left.[14]

As civil war consumed his new home of Texas, Cummins worked through his own upheaval. He decided to stick with his goal of becoming a preacher but could not forget the fascinations of his first geological hunts. In the early 1860s, Cummins glimpsed a future where he could privilege both callings. While riding his circuit, he continued to comb the terrain for fossils. On one occasion, he discovered ore, which Confederate operatives subsequently commandeered to smelt into weaponry. Then, in 1862, he stumbled upon another find. While conducting evangelistic services in East Texas along the Louisiana border, he was alerted to the area's asphalt sediments. It was customary, he later recalled, for locals to illuminate their religious meetings "by setting fire to slabs of the raw material dug from the asphalt beds and piled on scaffolds built for the purpose." Surrounded by oil-fueled flames of revival and overtaken by his alluvial obsessions, he pondered the significance of that bituminous soil. The curiosity lingered and intensified after his reappointment later that same year to the San Augustine circuit, the exact terrain that Kavanaugh would study in 1865. There, amid salt springs and oil slicks, Cummins witnessed war. Although not an enlistee, he defended the Confederacy by scouting out (and in one instance shooting at) small bands of Union soldiers that infiltrated the area, conveying wounded men to field hospitals, and assisting surgeons as they operated on the injured.[15]

After the war wound down, Cummins maintained a dizzying pace. Soon he was expending less energy on ecclesiastical matters and more on the scientific methods he had learned from S. C. Swallow. While he continued to accept temporary ministerial callings, from 1870 forward he devoted himself to working the land. For a time he plied his trade with the geological department of the Texas Pacific Railroad, scouting out new routes, testing mineral deposits, and digging wells for water that could be used to cool locomotives. The work excited him about what lay underneath Texas's topsoil, and as he continued to report his findings, state, federal, and corporate officials took notice. A culminating experience occurred in 1880. While camping in Northwest Texas, Cummins and his companion discovered a reptilian fossil, which they subsequently shared with paleontologist Dr. E. D. Cope of Philadelphia. According to Cummins's recollection, Cope "at once declared it to be the most important find that had been made in the state, as it belonged to the Permian formation, the existence of which in Texas had not at that time been admitted." Cummins continued to investigate what would become known as the Permian Basin. After three years of fieldwork, his findings made their way to the US Geological Society and into print in the Texas Geological Survey's *Second Annual Report* and, years later, the *Journal of Geology*. Cummins's knowledge of the state was now noticed. Scientists eager to learn more about geological time and entrepreneurs searching for spots to invest in carbon extraction—coal and oil, mainly—absorbed his findings, then pleaded for more. By the early 1880s, around the same time Lyman Stewart arrived in California ready to help reignite oil fantasies in that field, Cummins was directing his energies and rapidly expanding knowledge of the earth toward the same end in his adopted home state of Texas.[16]

DURING THE 1880S AND 1890S, oil hunters pursued their prize in California, Texas, and places in between with a drive equal to that witnessed in 1860s Pennsylvania. Their desire to escape Standard's grasp spawned a sense of last-chance urgency. Yet the West's resplendent landscape also stirred them and, coupled with oil's charms, made them prone to utopian dreams. Already an abstruse exercise in deciphering earth's enigmatic forms, oil hunting in the continent's farther reaches became an intensely spiritual act of becoming one with its natural wonders.

A major amplifier of oil's allure in the West was the religious orientation of spiritualism. This movement cohered around notions that spirits of the dead not only survived but sought to communicate with the living, that their realm—the spirit world—was more advanced than the human world, and, by extension, that through continued communion with the spirits, earth beings could acquire wisdom in moral and ethical issues. Since its emergence amid the religious ferment and scientific revolutions of the mid-nineteenth century, spiritualism had appealed to Americans by stressing individual free thought over churchly conventions, angelic revelation over rationalism, and, importantly for oil culture, personal interrogation of the natural world for transport to a higher spiritual plane. The West provided spiritualists with hospitable warmth. Its natural grandeur was ideal for the serenity and self-expression they deemed central to their being. California served as their crossroads, San Francisco their hub. The movement took root there in 1857 when its rituals attracted a small, learned class of citizens. That same year devotees started a newspaper called *Banner of Light*, which spread word of seances and lectures and invited easterners to "reap a rich harvest, materially and spiritually" on the Pacific coast. The recruitment worked. By the late 1860s, the movement was shaking the foundations of California's religious establishment. "Spiritualism is spreading rapidly in this coast," wrote one exuberant "Friend of the Cause." "I never saw anywhere such an eager desire to investigate the phenomenon." Mark Twain himself felt the quake. In an 1866 article titled "The New Wildcat Religion," the San Francisco satirist informed readers that spiritualism was mainstream. He asked that they be tolerant: "I can remember when Methodist camp meetings and Campbellite revivals used to stock the asylums with religious lunatics, and yet the public kept their temper and said never a word." While admitting his preference for the staid Presbyterianism of his household ("You never heard of a Presbyterian going crazy on religion"), Twain acknowledged that the wildcat religion of his day was the practice of "good and worthy persons." It was in America to stay.[17]

More incisively than Twain realized, his use of the word "wildcat" connected spiritualism to the ethos of the West's mineral extraction zones. It was no accident, for instance, that celebrity mystic Abraham James, who went on to strike oil in Pennsylvania, was first exposed to spiritualism while visiting his brother in California during the state's gold rush. In the years that followed Twain's pronouncement, spiritualism grew not only along the California coast but also within mining communities across the mountains to the west, if for slightly different reasons than those informing the San Francisco elite. For centuries mining and metallurgy together had forged a conviction in those who toiled under the earth that their efforts were sanctified, the tactile materials they handled modes of transubstantiation. Much like Emanuel Swedenborg, a founding father of spiritualism in Europe and himself an expert in metallurgy, colliers saw minerals not simply as the gods' reward but as a living linkage between the ancient and the eternal, the worldly and the heavenly. For Swedenborg, once designated the king of Sweden's assessor of mines, there was no fixed gulf between earthly life and the life that lay beyond death. In the physical essences of the earth, he identified the continuity between these perceived spheres. Meanwhile, in Britain's coal country—places like Yorkshire and Cornwall—and its colonies, spiritualist rituals thrived among commoners with ties to dissenting Protestant sects. In their worship and work, they willingly accepted the role that spirits played along with clerics and the Bible in setting terms for life. Countless numbers of them brought that experiential and mystical form of Christianity to the western United States when they were recruited to work in mountain rock pits.[18]

The spiritualist proclivities of the West's miners spilled over into oil culture by century's end. The extractive and spiritual journey of one Montana miner turned Texas oilman typified that easy transition. During the late nineteenth and early twentieth centuries, he ran his own copper and iron ore mining company. He also read intently in spiritualist periodicals, dialogued with seers, actively built Helena, Montana's spiritualist community, and in very personal ruminations grappled with the meaning of the cosmos. For answers to life and business, he turned to an astrologer in Titusville, Pennsylvania, as well as to a spiritualist thinker on the East Coast. The miner regularly bore his soul to the latter, asking for help with contacting his deceased wife in one instance, begging for truths about raw materials in the next. The sage assured him that his labor was priestly. In taking minerals out of the earth, he was releasing them to the ether, allowing them to transmute into higher forms, synthesize with human need and desire, and serve as further reminders that the universe leaned toward unity. Adding that "many of the writers of the Bible" ("particularly the author of the 'Revelations'") were alchemists, the mentor persuaded the mentee that this understanding of the universe as an organic orb stemmed from both Christian and classical thought. The miner embraced that encouragement as he turned to oil drilling in Aransas Pass, Texas. As much as he received from his spiritualist community he wanted to give back, and he was convinced that petroleum was—as the town's boosters advertised—"the Magic Wealth Producer." As he went about establishing his oil operation, he spoke unhesitatingly in grandiose terms about "doing something handsome for the cause." "I am determined to get my oil business started this year," he wrote family in Montana, "and when oil is struck here, this place will fill up with thousands of people, and then building will begin on all sides." For the rest of his career he would keep chasing that desire, never fully realizing it but never wavering from the doctrines that spiritualism had supplied him.[19]

The Montanan surely felt at home in Texas, for spiritualism was already prevalent there in the 1890s among its local residents, preachers, and politicians, as well as its oil hunters, including proud Methodists like Benjamin Kavanaugh and William Cummins. No wonder Kavanaugh encountered so many friendly audiences. At the same time that Kavanaugh combed East Texas for oil, he lectured widely on the "electric theory of astronomy," which propagated the notion that electric currents and magnetic fields were life-giving forces, evident in every form of animal and plant life and essential to the functioning of the earth's biosphere, atmosphere, and axial rotation. Boldly opposing Newtonian theory, which attributed earth's energy to gravitation, Kavanaugh leaned on inductive reasoning, his senses, and appreciation of ancient mysteries—hallmarks of a Methodism cast in spiritualist dye—to make his case.[20]

Cummins's thinking about minerals was just as audacious. During the late 1880s, as he delved further into geological research and searched for oil, he assumed a militant stand against ministers who seemed to reject the freedom of the individual mind, labeling them "jackasses" and "false prophets." Cummins began to question the literalness of scripture, seeking a more holistic view of the universe and the riddles of life all around him. For insight, he digested Henry Drummond's *Natural Law in the Spiritual World* and Dante's *Inferno*, the poetry of Walter Scott and the psychology of Thomas J. Hudson, and the treatises of Herbert Spencer and Charles Darwin. Cummins's freethinking faith made room for evolution, but even in this new respect, it held close to a belief that the human, natural, and supernatural were bundled together in a productive organic whole. "I believe that the whole substance of Christianity is a biology, the science of life," he declared. While Kavanaugh and Cummins did not overturn the reigning scientific paradigm, their dabbling in esoteric fancies reinforced their status in Texas as experts regarding the elusive energy source of oil.[21]

By the 1890s, truly paradigm-shifting finds were beginning to occur in spiritualism's heartland of California, permanently linking the movement to petroleum's fortunes. The most momentous discovery occurred in a colony called Summerland. The community, which bore the name of spiritualism's heaven, was the creation of Henry Lafayette Williams, a former Treasury agent, and his wife, Katie, both ardent freethinkers. In 1885, the Williamses purchased several acres of land east of Santa Barbara and started selling lots to fellow spiritualists in hopes of establishing a haven. Pinched between mountains and ocean, Summerland soon became a mecca of meditation and fellowship, a place of pilgrimage for California spiritualists. To guarantee his community's financial future, Williams started prospecting for oil. The Santa Barbara coast had remained a target for oil hunters ever since Benjamin Silliman and other surveyors piqued interest in the region's grease-slicked waters and shores. Throughout the entire second half of the nineteenth century, experts were convinced that the "bituminous effusions" on the south slope of the Santa Ynez Range, which angled into the ocean waters, contained viscous gold. Wrote one early explorer, "The asphaltum, or hardened bituminous matter, occurs in the greatest abundance on the shore at Hill's range, about 6 miles west of Santa Barbara, and lies along the beach for a distance of a mile, in large masses." Summerland occupied that very space, as Williams knew well.[22]

In 1887, Williams sank two wells at depths of five hundred feet. Oil began to percolate up, but he wanted more. He found it once he began drilling on the beach. The prospector and his Summerland neighbors noticed that the closer the well was to the ocean, the more it would produce, and in the adjoining tidal area, gas bubbled at the surface. Williams eased closer and closer to the shore, wondering how he could reach that water-covered reservoir beyond the ocean's break. In 1896, he came up with the answer. He and his team built three piers that stretched three hundred feet from the shoreline into waters thirty-five feet deep. They attached a cable tool rig at the tip of the piers and started to drill. By the following year, Williams was pumping crude from underneath the sea's floor. Within months twenty-two other companies were busy building a dozen more piers and four hundred more wells, rapidly expanding the innovation that Williams had conceived: offshore oil exploration. For Williams, who would die just two years later, the invention meant that the self-contained world he had created for his fellow saints could live on and, with it, the new age to which he had dedicated his life.[23]

From California to Colorado, Montana to Texas, enterprising individuals with chimerical visions were ensuring that the American West would be part of petroleum's unfolding prospect. As of 1890, though, Pennsylvania crude remained the coin of the realm, the foundation on which the entire industry could rely while other continental terrains were tested and opened to production. Thus, Standard Oil's grip on Pennsylvania guaranteed its role as the ultimate adjudicator of the US petroleum market. Yet, by the time Henry Williams started puncturing California's ocean bottom, Standard and the entire US oil sector were starting to realize that petroleum's progressions would also involve land and people well beyond US borders. The phantasms of a better world through oil that compelled Methodist geologists and spiritualist entrepreneurs to synchronize their faith and vocations and press on were part of a worldwide phenomenon.

Continental Europe was already under petroleum's spell. By 1890, amateur oil engineers had been actively hunting oil in Romania and

Galicia (a region overlaying present-day Poland, Hungary, and western Ukraine) for over a half century. There a key breakthrough came in 1853. Teamed with Ignacy Lukasiewicz, a University of Vienna–trained pharmacist based in Lvov, salt mine inspector Joseph Hecker distilled kerosene from crude and, more critically, created the first affordable kerosene lamp for application on a commercial scale. A year later Lukasiewicz opened the first oil mine in Bóbrka (in present-day Poland) and, in 1856, Europe's first refinery in neighboring Ulaszowice. By 1859, Galicia's kerosene business encompassed 150 villages and contributed the lion's share of the 36,000 barrels that European producers sent annually to the market. For decades, this part of the Austro-Hungarian Empire would remain among the five largest oil-producing lands in the world. One historian quips that as late as 1909, "Galicia sparkled like a gem on the tip of every oil driller's tongue, and its oil industry held the hopes for retirement in comfort of many a London waitress turned investor."[24]

During this same chronology, Russia-based entrepreneurs also scoured their continent for an alternative to the "Yankee invention," desiring to supply Europe with their brand of illumination. In the 1870s, chemist Robert Nobel, a Swede, traveled through the Caucasus to Baku, the financial center of Azerbaijan, then under Russian control. At that time Baku was experiencing an oil boom. "Oil is in the air one breathes, in one's nostrils, in one's eyes, in the water of the morning bath ... in one's starched linen—everywhere," one traveler marveled about Baku's industrial "Black Town" suburb, where two hundred refineries were active. Recognizing the potential, Robert and brothers Alfred and Ludwig purchased a refinery and rapidly expanded their corporate hold over the European kerosene market. Soon they could legitimately boast that they were driving "American kerosene ... out of the Russian market" and Europe as a whole.[25]

The Nobels had rivals. The Rothschilds, a prominent European banking family, established the fast-rising Caspian and Black Sea Petroleum Company in the 1880s. After Ludwig Nobel's sudden death in 1888, the Nobels ceded a good deal of European oil power to the Rothschilds, and with the aid of Marcus Samuel, a merchant based in London, began looking to the Far East, where, as one historian notes, "they saw hundreds of millions of potential customers for the 'new light.'" Like his father, who as a "shell merchant" once bought and sold knickknacks and seashells from sailors, Samuel could spot a niche. He noted the potential of the oil tanker, a creation fashioned in part by Ludwig Nobel, who saw the value of transporting oil in tanks in the hull of a ship. Aided by allies in the British government, Samuel gained access to the Suez Canal. By 1890, his ships were sailing the waterway, conveying kerosene to Asian markets.[26]

The Nobels and Rothschilds now stood alongside Rockefeller in a rapidly expanding global arena of petroleum products. They were soon joined by a Dutch rival. For generations, colonists had reported seepages of "earth oil" in the Dutch East Indies (later Indonesia). While surveying a crop in Sumatra in 1880, the manager of a tobacco company learned of sludge puddles from which locals drew oily material to light their torches. During the following decade, he gained rights to the land and started creating a viable enterprise. His death in 1890 prevented him from seeing the fruit of his labor: the freshly minted Royal Dutch company. Under the leadership of Jean Baptiste August Kessler, Royal Dutch made gains in the difficult, swampy terrains of the East Indies, and by the late 1890s the company was a major player. In the early 1900s Kessler sought a partnership with Samuel, whose Shell Transport and Trading Company was vying with Royal Dutch for control of the East Indian fields and the Asian market. Samuel had struck oil in Borneo in 1898. The Borneo product did not easily yield kerosene, yet Samuel perceived what he called "the tremendous role which petroleum can play in its most rational form, that of fuel." Samuel's instinct, slightly ahead of the time, spurred him on. Henri Deterding, the new chairman of Royal Dutch, and Samuel both soon realized that their competition made each company vulnerable to larger peers. In 1907, they merged to create the Royal Dutch Shell oil company. Deterding followed up on this triumph by purchasing the Rothschilds' Azerbaijan oil fields. Royal Dutch Shell—or simply Shell—was born.[27]

Oil was, of course, not the only commodity that propelled dizzying transcontinental trade at this stage of the Industrial Revolution. Cotton and rubber were also thrust into more expansive flows of capital and conquest that remade—in violent fashion—the world map. Yet oil was unique in important ways. Whereas cotton and rubber enterprises depended overwhelmingly on indigenous workforces, the hunt for crude necessitated significant importation of westerners, whose engineering faculties, no matter how rudimentary, were in demand. While oilers were clustered together in smaller work sites than those witnessed in cotton, they had greater levels of community contact with locals than the highly isolated South American rubber extraction zones. The new global oil zones of the 1890s thus reflected a peculiar arrangement of imperialist hierarchies. Western oilmen clearly dictated things but had to engage in considerable cultural give-and-take with native laborers for the sake of efficient progress. These exigencies in turn shaped a complex weave of corporate initiative and oversight. Though attached to the nation- and empire-building imperatives of the age, oil's merchants also moved in overlapping circles of collaboration and competition that cut across state boundaries. Theirs was a free-flowing endeavor by necessity, reflective in part of the still nascent structures of the broader industry.[28]

Oil also captured the spiritual imagination of world residents in a way that other commodities did not. To be sure, coal, cotton, and rubber had long evoked their own narratives of deific favor. Across ancient Asia and Africa, cotton pickers equated the material with supernatural power and the vagaries of fate, while in the nineteenth century English cotton kings deemed their business a "spectacle unparalleled in the annals of industry," proof of Christian Anglo-Saxon superiority. Their contemporaries pointed to rubber and especially coal as the reasons why the British enjoyed God-given dominion over the earth. Yet everywhere oil was found, people believed it could move them like no other mineral into a higher state of civilization. Oil's capacities to illuminate the darkness and lubricate modern machinery held enormous universal attraction in an era when monumental transformations beckoned.[29]

Like John D. Rockefeller and Lyman Stewart, many of the entrepreneurs who navigated the intercontinental networks of crude thus did so with the conviction that their labor was a religious undertaking. If not quite as outspoken as their American counterparts, Dutch oil hunters like Kessler approached their vocation with a similar ethic, shaped by their native country's Calvinist heritage, which saw hard work as one's covenant with God. Saddled with outsider status, Jewish oilmen carried an extra burden. In central Europe, they used their trade to uplift their communities. Joseph Hecker, for example, saw his oil work as a chance to raise the standing of Galician Jews, who occupied the bottom rung of their rural province, Europe's poorest. Hecker's colleague Ignacy Lukasiewicz joined him in advancing Galicia, but with Catholic convictions in mind. After his first success at refining crude and in the decades that followed, he supplied free oil to Galicia's Catholic monasteries, sponsored a Catholic parish, and used profits to fight Galicia's poverty and alcoholism. At his mine in Bóbrka, he established an insurance agency called Brotherly Funds to offset workers' emergencies. "Father Ignacy," as he became known, earned a reputation for saintliness that grew alongside his expanding enterprise.[30]

The industry's reliance on a global network of itinerant labor also helped to link oil to a sense of higher calling. While executives did their part to recruit workers from local pools, their operations could only succeed if educated Western engineers agreed to impart their knowledge to the uninitiated. By the 1890s, thousands of such itinerants were following multidirectional paths to Europe's and Asia's oil patches, offering their expertise to locals and melding the physical and metaphysical aspects of their work in one spirit of discovery. One Standard scout traveled extensively at this time, including to Japan, where he conjoined analysis of rock formations and drilling methods on the Asian island with careful unpacking of its cultural dynamics. While in letters home he reflected on spiritual insights derived from his travels, his communion with nature, and his observation of Japanese labor practices and family life, to colleagues he was even more deliberate in mixing theological and technical analysis. One striking moment occurred while he watched Japanese drillers, surrounded by solemn villagers absorbed in ritual, dig wells, a harrowing process that involved the dangling of a man by his feet, enabling him to draw out dirt, mud, and rock to deepen the hole. "Knowing the danger of his position before the digger is lowered, he says a prayer, bids good-bye to his associates, and goes down to his living grave! It requires some stoic virtue to go through this process every day." By the end of his journey, Standard's tactician had succeeded in conveying his own oil wisdom to locals and compiling an exhaustive report. Still, he did not want to stop—oil scouting had exposed him to fascinations he could never abandon. "There are so many things, connected with this country and its people, which came within my notice, since being here, worthy of comment and consideration, it seems I could write a book on them."[31]

Countless other engineers voiced this same awe when conducting their work. Included among them were drillers from Lambton County—the heart of Canada's first oil field. Following James Miller's discovery of oil there, local Ontarians devised a unique pole-tool rig system, which consisted of wood tubes (later, wrought-iron casing) screwed together, through which ran the string of tools, topped by the bit that would puncture the earth. In the US system of drilling, tools were openly suspended from a cable; by using poles, Ontarians held otherwise loose drilling equipment together, allowing drillers to plumb unknown terrains with greater efficiency and without jeopardizing their precious instruments. Over time, roughnecks who worked in Petrolia (the registered name of Lambton County's largest boomtown) mastered the drilling technique and accepted contracts to take their expertise abroad—to Galicia, Russia, Sumatra, and Borneo. Armed with technology and presumptions of racial superiority, they approached their fieldwork as crusaders, charged with summoning a source that could illumine "barbarous" societies out of the darkness. One Ontarian in Sumatra used his diary and missives to process the challenges of work among the "heathen." His words oozed with condescension when he expressed contempt for the 560 cleaver-bearing "Coolies" under his management who "struck for more money," and disgust with a native funeral procession that involved men "laughing and shouting" in tribute as they carried the corpse ("one of the most unhuman affairs I ever saw," he scribbled). Yet over the course of his days in Sumatra—not unlike the Standard scout's in Japan—his perspective gradually made way for more local inspiration. He learned to speak Malay by singing from a book of Malay hymns, then took his new language skills to the worksite, where his communications and relations with employees improved. Over time, his view of local religious rituals—funerals included—became less critical. When he finally left Asia, he echoed the sentiments of another Ontario driller who admitted that the global fields he had committed his life to had altered his Christian worldview. "Since I have crossed many seas, since a new hemisphere, a new earth, has been passing beneath my gaze, like a panoramic ribbon, I have added lessons, and mine eyes have seen His glory in other forms."[32]

Finally, the global marriage of religion and oil also occurred at the institutional level, where oversight of oil's multidirectional, multinational expansion relied on concrete ties between church and capital. The American Protestant minister Josiah Strong famously stated that such a partnership would be critical to the "civilizing" of the world. "Commerce follows the missionary," he declared in his 1885 treatise *Our Country*. Oil's expanding empire produced the fruits of that kind of collaboration. In the East Indies, Dutch and Western missionaries helped open up the region for oil hunters, supplying them with advance knowledge of terrain and cultures. In return, the oil tankers that began to transport crude also conveyed missionaries to ports that might otherwise have been unapproachable. Meanwhile, missionary churches provided basic needs and spiritual nourishment for petroleum's proletariat and in return counted on them to spread word back home of the evangelism being carried out by the church's workers.[33]

This mutual dependency was on striking display in the West Indies, whose small role in the globalization of crude was partly thanks to Louisa Harriet MacKinnon. Lady Dundonald, as she was known, was the daughter-in-law of former British admiral and radical politician Thomas Cochrane, the Tenth Earl of Dundonald, whose interest in asphalt collected from Pitch Lake, the natural tar pit on Trinidad, and association with kerosene inventor Abraham Gesner led to creation of a family-run business. The Cochrane clan saw in Trinidad a future for their Presbyterian faith, as well as petroleum, and built a mission. After MacKinnon's husband died in 1885, the family project he had inherited from his father passed to her. The responsibility of managing a small but viable extraction venture that shipped asphalt to the United States was heavy enough, not least because she resided in Scotland. But the venture also included a church, school, and convalescent home. For help she partnered with a missionary, who became the eyes and ears of the entire enterprise. Besides keeping his patron updated on church attendance, the cleric also charted the business's fiscal ebbs and flows. In 1897, he was spirited: "The pitch labour has increased to such an extent . . . that it has afforded labourers great joy," he wrote MacKinnon. One year later, he relayed discouraging news that a corporate competitor was encroaching on their domain and laborers were threatening to strike. As times turned rough, he stepped up his role as pastor to soothe workers and dampen their resistance. "You must remember," he told a woman, "the Saviour has not promised to take His people to heaven on flowery beds of ease, for

He has plainly told them in the Scriptures that they have a cross to bear and in the world they shall have tribulation ... [yet] if they abide in Him they will be able to overcome also." Thanks to the missionary's maneuvers in church, on the worksite, and with corporate rivals, the enterprise survived into the next century. MacKinnon's partner reveled in his position as cog in a cause that spanned an ocean. He signed letters with a pledge that said much about the bond he and his kind shared with oil and its kind: "Your Obedient Servant."[34]

EVEN WITH THE oil booms in Galicia and Baku and the quiet inroads along many other shores, the global footprint of oil remained largely American. By the 1890s, petroleum registered as a sign of the United States' shining imperial prospects. When Josiah Strong spoke of a burden to civilize the world through the dissemination of Christian, capitalist values, he assumed that Americans would shoulder the most weight. Because of their supremacy in crude, oil's apostles proclaimed, Americans could bask in that new season of authority.

Assuming the Puritan conceit of a special "errand to the world," contemporary pundits took pains to highlight how oil remained America's trump card. The US oil industry, they bragged with regularity in national print, was far better equipped than any other to expand its global reach. More than any other national group, they pointed out, Americans filled the payrolls of foreign drilling operations in the East Indies, financed the start-up oil companies of the West Indies, and spread knowledge of petroleum to the rest of the planet. Yes, Russia's corporate ambitions were a concern, but its oil industry paled next to the voluminous holdings of US companies, which allowed them to dictate production, pricing, and labor flows. The US oil industry also was unassailable because of its economic ingenuity and resilience. Staffed with the "best American skill," it boasted the most advanced engineering methods, transportation system, and workforce in the world. At the start of a new century, one booster underscored, the United States possessed wells over 5,000 feet deep, 20,000 oil tank rail cars, 100,000 miles of pipelines, 250,000 oil workers, and an annual production rate of "53,000,000 barrels of illuminating oil," to go along with 50 million barrels of oil for other purposes and a cumulative production total of

740 million barrels. American oil was encircling the earth, squeezing it into submission. "If we put the oil produced into barrels, and then placed those barrels end to end," the booster boasted, "we have enough to reach all around the world and some to spare." As a different commenter stressed, with disregard for the hardship many smaller oil companies faced at the time, while other sectors lost ground during the 1893 financial crisis, US petroleum grew: "Amid the general demoralization, when the nation seemed hastening to positive ruin, one splendid enterprise alone extended its business, multiplied its resources and was largely instrumental in restoring public confidence."[35]

Such success, it was believed, stemmed from another distinguishing feature: stout leadership. In one writer's estimation, the US petroleum sector embodied "American civilization" like none other. Stocked with rugged individualists, it was also led by men of Christian character—"blunt in business" but "trustworthy and deservedly esteemed for liberality and energy"—whose global aims aligned with the nation's founding principles of liberty for all. "The salutary, far-reaching effects of such management," he exclaimed, was that "by reviving faith and stimulating the flagging energies of the country," oil's executives "exerted an influence upon the common welfare words and figures cannot estimate. Petroleum preserved the thread of golden traffic with foreign nations." US oil, raved the exuberant writer John McLaurin, "has found its way to every part of Europe and the remotest parts of Asia. It has penetrated China and Japan . . . reached the wilds of Australia, and shed its radiance over many a dark African waste. It is the true cosmopolite, omnipresent and omnipotent in fulfilling its mission of illuminating the universe!" Oil, America's gift from God, was now America's gift to the world.[36]

The most important bearer of that gift was Standard Oil, which became synonymous with America's growing global status. John D. Rockefeller's position as US statesman par excellence rose swiftly during the 1890s, even as his standing in the domestic sphere slipped. In what would prove the first round of a protracted judicial struggle, the US Congress passed the Sherman Antitrust Act (1890), which "declare[d] unlawful trusts and combinations in restraint of trade." The sweeping, if also imprecise, antimonopoly proclamation was passed with Rockefeller in mind. The Ohio Supreme Court followed up by declaring

Standard Oil of Ohio a monopoly and forcing it to disband its trust. Other states joined in the assault. Aware of their lost footing, Standard executives skillfully reorganized. They utilized a loophole in New Jersey's state law that allowed them to dissolve the trust but then regather their interests in a "holding company." In an effort to attract revenue, the state permitted companies to incorporate there while holding stock in companies elsewhere. So in 1899, Standard Oil of New Jersey, or simply Jersey Standard, increased its capitalization from $10 million to $110 million, absorbing stock (and with it, financial influence) in the other Standard companies. "Terminology had been changed," a historian writes, "a holding company for trust—but the effect was the same. Standard was again secure behind its bulwarks." Regardless, public displeasure mounted with each next step Standard took on US soil. As Pennsylvania pools dried up, the Rockefeller conglomerate shifted focus to the Lima field, which straddled Ohio and Indiana. In 1893 alone, despite that year's financial panic, five hundred wells were drilled in the field, drawing 2.3 million barrels of crude. By the turn of the century, Standard Oil of Indiana (formed in 1889) would join Standard New York (Socony) and Jersey Standard as the prime movers of Rockefeller oil. All the while, public outcries intensified. Embattled workers, farmers, and populists who decried monopolies of any kind targeted the Rockefeller group as a sign of everything wrong with society. No cry was louder than Henry Demarest Lloyd's. In his 1894 diatribe *Wealth Against Commonwealth*, he wrote apoplectically of Rockefeller, "He is . . . a depredator . . . not a worshipper of liberty . . . a Czar of plutocracy, a worshipper of his own Money Power over mankind. . . . If our civilization is destroyed, it will not be by . . . barbarians from below. Our barbarians come from above."[37]

Rockefeller and company were able to weather this initial torrent of odium in part because of their imperial gaze. They readily flexed their own brand of "hard" and "soft" power to extend America's material and moral empire. On the first score, they challenged each competitor head-on through savvy marketing and agents in the field. In Asia, where the Russians, English, and Dutch were beginning to sell kerosene, Standard quickly spanned out. The most valuable market was China, where by the early 1890s the corporate giant was aggressively targeting its 400 million potential consumers. Standard's ambassadors did not enjoy free rein; for some time, a chronicler notes, they confronted "mandarins who insisted that the Chinese must burn peanut oil and . . . priests who excommunicated any peasant daring to use kerosene to light his hut." Similar resistance surfaced elsewhere. But Standard's men persisted and transformed China into their company's largest Asian market, its efforts there being the largest US financial venture in all East Asia. Other societies also opened their doors. US consulates reported Standard's progress in India, Borneo, Burma, Malaysia, and many African locales. By 1890, reports showed, "millions of gallons of oil" were being sent "to all parts of Latin America—coastal towns, plantations, ranches, and mining camps." Europe was more vexing; yet there too Standard triumphed. Initially, US diplomats in Germany and neighboring countries fretted at the inroads made by Russian kerosene, sometimes due to anti-American lobbying. Yet over time, Europeans soured on the Baku alternative, finding it did not burn as vibrantly as the American brand. While oil from Galicia and the Caucasus would continue to leave a mark, by 1900 Standard's dominance in Europe was well established. Soon, striking workers in Baku (a young revolutionary named Josef Stalin among them) would cement that standing by setting Black Town's refineries ablaze.[38]

Americans had a much more favorable view of Rockefeller's fortunes abroad than at home. Even Washington wanted to help Standard sell its products. The hyperbolic John McLaurin was a former independent oilman. Still, he gloated over Standard's international success. "Russian competition, the extent and danger of which most people do not begin to appreciate, was met and overcome by sheer tenacity and superior generalship," he wrote about his former opponent's muscular world conquest. "The advantages of capable, courageous, intelligent concentration of the varied branches of a great industry were never manifested more strongly."[39]

Rockefeller's increasing involvement in philanthropy accrued public favor too. The 1890s marked a shift in his priorities. Throughout the frenetic post–Civil War years, the deep-pocketed Baptist had remained committed to his church. Several medical setbacks, however, changed his perspective. Doctors' warnings encouraged him to pull away from business and contemplate avenues for quieter service. Apathy factored in as well. By 1895 he was missing board meetings and writing fewer memos; in general, as a confidant would explain, his profession had "ceased to amuse him, it lacked freshness and variety and had become merely irksome and he withdrew." The following year Rockefeller let John Archbold assume control of the business, formally resigning in 1897. His retirement was never announced, however, and he would continue to hold on to the titular presidency of Jersey Standard, along with his whopping 30 percent share of Standard stock. This ambiguous status meant he would remain the principal target of criticism when animosity toward Standard reescalated in the first decade of the twentieth century. On a day-to-day basis, though, Rockefeller was free to do other things.[40]

Charity especially. Rockefeller's giving ultimately pioneered modern practices of philanthropy but was fundamentally an extension of his first love: missions. Since his youth, he had tithed to the church in support of its evangelistic efforts, of which foreign missionary campaigns seemed most deserving. His wife, Cettie, had dreamed before marriage of being a missionary. She and her peers formed a women's auxiliary of the American Baptist Home Mission Society to address the needs of African American women and girls in the Jim Crow South. Foreign fields, especially China, remained her passion, though, and the same was true of her husband. He made his first financial contributions to the missionary effort in China at the same time that Standard started selling kerosene there. It was the beginning of a decades-long commitment to funneling aid across the Pacific and, soon, across other oceans as well.[41]

That same zeal for moral outreach inspired Rockefeller's first grand charitable experiment: the University of Chicago. With this venture, Frederick Gates became Rockefeller's philanthropic manager. Gates had been a successful pastor of a large Baptist church in Minneapolis. "Devoutly religious he unquestionably was," a historian would say of him, "but at heart he was a businessman, shrewd, alert, aggressive, and capable of driving hard bargains." An appointment as secretary of the American Baptist Education Society showed Gates how he could move people to action. He took up the agency's primary charge to reestablish the then defunct University of Chicago as a prominent Baptist institution that could fill a void in Western higher education. Local Baptists saw Rockefeller as a prospective benefactor. As Gates knew, though, a competing group of Baptists in New York, led by the prominent Reverend Augustus H. Strong, was lobbying Rockefeller to donate $20 million for the creation of a flagship university in their city. Strong and Rockefeller were friends as well as family (Strong's son married Rockefeller's daughter). Undeterred, Gates advanced a powerful proposal for a Chicago-based institution "with an endowment of several millions" that would boast an infrastructure "equal to any on the continent," while commanding the services of "the ablest specialists" in both humanistic and scientific studies. The institution would be "wholly under Baptist control as a chartered right, loyal to Christ and His church, employing none but Christians in any department of instruction, a school not only evangelical but evangelistic." Gates won over Rockefeller, who came to believe that the Midwest, his home region, and Chicago, its emerging flagship city, deserved his help. His impressions of the Chicago project grew stronger as he talked with other prominent Baptists, including Thomas W. Goodspeed, a well-known professor at Baptist Union Theological Seminary in Chicago. Another Baptist minister, the thirty-three-year-old dynamo William Rainey Harper, told the oil king he envisioned the new university as a world-class institution that would hire the best faculty at the highest wages, create a first-tier graduate school, and rival England's and Germany's best universities. Rockefeller preferred a cautious start before aspirations for global dominance were entertained.[42]

Nevertheless, the final results were not so out of tune with Harper's glowing ambition. In May 1889, after a walk with Gates on West 54th Street in Manhattan, Rockefeller pledged $600,000 to the start-up of the school, well over half the targeted $1 million. Gates and his peers were elated. At a meeting of the American Baptist Education Society held the next day, attendees broke out in "tumultuous cheering and applause" at word of the gift, then sang the doxology: "Praise God from whom all blessings flow." More checks from Rockefeller followed; after the second gift of $1 million, delivered in 1890, Harper agreed to become the University of Chicago's first president. His forwardness had paid off. In the fall of 1892, Harper looked on, worried but proud, as the school opened its doors in expectation of students. They came, as did the outstanding faculty he had predicted. Five years later, when Rockefeller finally agreed to visit his creation, he pronounced the university "the best investment I ever made in my life." Then he teased, "The good Lord gave me the money, and how could I hold it from Chicago?"[43]

In 1892, Gates went to work for Rockefeller full-time to help organize his charitable giving. "I am in trouble, Mr. Gates," the oil baron said. "The pressure of these appeals for gifts has become too great for endurance." Rockefeller was completely inundated with personal pleas for cash, many of them originating on the mission field. Gates quickly discovered that Rockefeller was virtually funding his own mission society. As Gates described it, "He was in daily appeals from individual Baptist missionaries in every region of Baptist missionary endeavor. . . . His office, his house, his table was beset with returned missionaries, each comparatively ignorant of all fields but his own." Gates tackled the task with customary doggedness. "We cut off every one of these private missionary appeals," he would recall. "We referred every applicant straight back to the missionary executives in Boston. . . . Mr. Rockefeller then gave not thousands as formerly, but hundreds of thousands, every dollar of which was expended by the experienced board." Meanwhile, Gates helped the benefactor channel even more funds into the University of Chicago—almost $35 million over the course of twenty-one years. Gates urged Rockefeller to approach his giving like the big-time oilman he was. Rather than continue as a wildcatter in the business of evangelism, Rockefeller needed to let his managerial grasp of capitalism and bureaucratic sensibilities translate to his charity. By 1900, Gates and his boss were ready to branch out and use Standard's profits for more dramatic service to society.[44]

WATCHING ALL THESE developments from afar, Lyman Stewart wrestled with the possibilities and limits of his own global reach. Following the incorporation of Union Oil in 1890 he entered a decade-long stretch of corporate fits and starts, which coincided with a period of theological reassessment. Unlike his fellow independent oilman John McLaurin, Stewart could not bring himself to revel in Rockefeller and Standard Oil's international exploits. Yet neither could he shake their specter. As he anticipated the turn of the century, Stewart harbored conflicting outlooks. While feeling enabled by good fortune to expand his business, intellectually—theologically—he could not help but see the world as frightfully lost, its future as one of steady decline until God intervened one final time. Stewart lacked the confidence of Rockefeller and Gates, along with the financial prowess and buoyant theology of social regeneration that nurtured it. So he swayed from one pole of the hope-despair spectrum to the other, his fatalism never far from the surface.

Stewart's company was likewise unsettled throughout the 1890s. In the months that followed incorporation, the young company faced one threat after another, some external, many self-made. In 1892, an English oil company made waves by arranging the shipping of oil from the new Peruvian field to the US West Coast. The move threatened to undercut Union's improving but still vulnerable position in the competitive California market. Fortunately for Union, political outcry against the British company led Congress to slap a draconian tariff on Peruvian crude. More challenges followed, however. It initially seemed good news when, late in 1892, a prospector by the name of Edward L. Doheny struck the first huge oil find in the state, just north of downtown Los Angeles. His lucky strike at shallow levels led to a boom that put the field on the map. But even as Doheny and countless others scrambled to erect derricks and draw oil from deeper realms, the financial crisis of 1893 made the strike bittersweet. Los Angeles crude flooded the market, and prices dropped, while many vulnerable oil companies struggled on the heels of Wall Street's punishing slump. "We have been going through a wild financial panic," Stewart admitted to a friend at the time. The next year, a strike against the Pullman railroad car company encouraged socialist leader Eugene Debs to organize a wider boycott across the US railroad system, stalling trains nationwide and leaving Union unable to move its product. Meanwhile, Union's attempt to convince railroads to switch fuel from coal to oil fell apart, as did talks among producers of the glutted Los Angeles field to organize for the sake of pricing stability. Unlike many of its competitors, Union retained enough cash to survive the onslaught, but Stewart grew weary about additional dark disturbances on the horizon.[45]

The picture was already gloomy within the company ranks. The frayed bonds between Union's founders belied the corporation's name. Bitter infighting erupted between Stewart and Thomas Bard, whose respective allies formed warring parties. The camp that circled around

Stewart demanded that Union continue to integrate while aggressively innovating and marketing new products, in particular fuel oil. Like Marcus Samuel and other forward-looking strivers in the business, Stewart operated in a manic mode, constantly testing new technologies to improve his company's exploratory and drilling returns and its capacity to move crude quickly—be it through longer pipelines or by bigger oceangoing vessels. And he sensed earlier than most of his peers that a new age was dawning in which petroleum's primary appeal to people would be as an energy source for their machines; within the guild he would soon come to be known as "the apostle of fuel oil." Bard and his allies held that Union should stick to one thing—drilling— and let others do the innovating in parallel spheres. The tussle between the two grew personal. Stewart self-righteously lambasted Bard for his poor leadership. Looking back on the tumultuous early 1890s, he was blunt with his partner: "The management was in your hands and was so largely characterized by lack of progress and loss of ground that it might be rightfully considered as the period of retrogression." Bard, meanwhile, railed against Stewart's impulsive ventures. One of the last straws for him involved Union's other partner, Wallace Hardison. Strapped for cash, Hardison started selling his shares to the two other partners. As of 1892 he was no longer a major shareholder. In 1894, he enlisted in a Peruvian oil venture, becoming the California front man for the company, charged with selling the oil in the face of increased tariffs. But in 1898, he was in a better position to approach Stewart with a new plan for stateside speculation, this time using Union's undeveloped lands in California. Stewart, always enamored of Hardison's drive, bought in. Bard made it known he was steadfastly against the venture. "I have more than once defeated similar attempts of Hardison to secure, through you, control of our company's property and 'God helping me, I will defeat this.'" When the California plan proceeded, Bard stewed.[46]

Looming over all these battles was the prospect of another struggle with Standard Oil. The discovery of the Los Angeles field, combined with increased production off the Santa Barbara coast and elsewhere in California, led Standard Oil to begin making surreptitious inroads in 1895 and 1896. "The Standard's agent here says his company is not going into the fuel oil trade here," Stewart told a colleague in the fall of 1895, "but I don't take any stock in the statement." Stewart was panicked about this very prospect, especially as he had used most of his Union shares as collateral for debts. With the added stress of fighting Bard, Stewart contemplated the unthinkable of conceding to Rockefeller and selling him a piece of his beloved company, if only just to survive. The option actually had surfaced before. Stewart's brother Milton, whose hatred of the Rockefellers knew no bounds, had nixed an earlier plan to sell Standard a minority interest. Should Standard "get a little more stock," Milton argued, "we would be at the mercy of the worst set of thieves and robbers the world ever saw." When Lyman nonetheless made overtures to Standard in 1895, he was rebuffed. Standard's men were in no rush to dole out heavy funds. Stewart tried yet again in 1896, when it was more apparent that Standard was about to enter California. The major company entertained this proposal, exchanged preliminary contracts, and sent agents to survey Union's holdings. "I have spent six days with a couple of representatives of the S.O. Company in going over our oil fields," Lyman wrote Milton. "They are evidently well satisfied and ask only till September 10th to give us an answer." The answer did not come by that date, and when it arrived days later, it was bad news. With slightly less gusto, Stewart made a final overture in 1898. He wished to maintain some property, but as Standard kingpin John Archbold himself replied, Standard wanted it all. As a last gasp, Stewart fielded one other offer, this one from European investors—likely the Rothschilds. Bard traveled to England to assess matters and found them unacceptable; the deal fell through. Crestfallen, Stewart begged Bard to find another European buyer, but to no avail.[47]

As the reality that a buyout was not forthcoming settled in, Bard and Stewart's combat intensified. Bard attempted a takeover by acquiring majority interest in a number of subsidiary companies, including the Torrey Canyon Oil Company. Stunned, Stewart sought allies on the Torrey board. He found one in R. W. Fenn, a Union engineer who got his start prospecting in Peru. A former missionary there, Fenn shared Stewart's passion for evangelism. That connection helped ensure Fenn's support for Stewart's interests and a vote against Bard's. In November 1898, Union's board of directors elected Stewart president in place of Bard; Fenn was elected secretary but returned to his missionary work a short time later. Bard, meanwhile, promised a lawsuit; in his words, he was determined to send "the company to the devil." After another year of maneuvers—with Bard attempting another takeover and Stewart secretly marshaling a defense—the men parted ways. In November 1899, Stewart's control of Union was once and for all reasserted; William Stewart, his son, was elected vice president. Bard sold his holdings and retired from the company. His next major step would be a political one as a California Republican member in the US Senate. Curiously, his entry into politics would with time heal his fraught but prosperous friendship with Stewart.[48]

As Stewart contemplated his life at the end of the century, mixed feelings lingered. Union was in better shape than ever, despite the internal fighting. Thanks largely to Stewart's aggressive leadership and obsession with integration and innovation, Union was well positioned to be Standard Oil's only major competition in California once the latter set down permanent roots there in the new century. Yet Stewart also continued to harbor doubts. He pledged to oversee his company's continued growth in the next decade; yet the pressures that came with that promise continued to wear him down. More importantly, in his mind, they continued to steal time and energy away from what he really wanted to be doing.[49]

And that, quite simply, was to save the world. Although he groused about Rockefeller's investment in America's moral empire, charging him with hypocrisy, Stewart also wished to be such a patron. Since his years as an apprentice tanner in western Pennsylvania, he had envisioned heading off to the mission field one day to proselytize his faith. Now, as an established oilman, he sought other outlets for that unfulfilled dream. Even the chaos of the past decade had not prevented him from starting to locate new avenues of influence. Upon his arrival in California he had confidently stated, "Los Angeles is to be the great city of the future, and if we occupy the ground now we may be able to lead . . . for years to come." On that count, Stewart busied himself in several church and community activities, especially interdenominational agencies like the YMCA and Union Rescue Mission. Still, Stewart was ever anxious to do more for his nation's spiritual health, more for his God.[50]

Then, in 1894, Stewart attended a religious summit that transformed his theology. It also set his vision of philanthropy fundamentally apart from Rockefeller's. At the Niagara Bible Conference, held in southern

Ontario, hundreds of conservative preachers and laypeople from across the Anglo-American Protestant world gathered to contemplate biblical prophecy. At the center of the proceedings was the doctrine of dispensational premillennialism, which—as one historian succinctly puts it—"offered a dark view of the present and an anxious-yet-anticipatory belief that Armageddon was impending." Premillennialism held that Christ would come back to earth before the millennium of peace promised in the Bible began and that the moment of his arrival would occur suddenly, soon, and amid the madness of a humanity in decline. By contrast, the majority view among Protestants at the time was that Christians could prepare the world to enter the millennium, after which Christ would return (hence the label "postmillennialism"). Theirs was a buoyant end-times belief that nurtured patience and confidence in God's people and a commitment to the betterment of society through the creation of Christian institutions with vast cultural power and the spread of knowledge and moral conduct, all in order to pave the way for their Lord's second reign. By contrast, the advocates of premillennialism did not believe that God's people could do anything in advance of these end times other than wait expectantly. Shunning man-made answers to the world's problems, their doctrine was attuned to a messianic notion of time that underscored the inescapably cold and discordant realities of the modern world, whose troubles only the Messiah could resolve in his final, rapturous return.[51]

Yet anxious waiting did not paralyze premillennialists; rather, it turned prophecy into a task of the highest order and an impetus for action. The Niagara attendees were heavily influenced by Anglo-Irish theologian John Nelson Darby, who added a supplemental theory to premillennialism known as dispensationalism. Darby divided history into distinct epochs, "dispensations," in which God dealt with humanity differently. Assuming they were living in the last of those dispensations, the devotees who joined Stewart in Ontario lapped up Darby's teachings and started scouring the planet for evidence of their Messiah's return. Two obvious clues to watch for, in their estimation, were the return of Jews to Israel (ensuring the biblical location for Christ's arrival) and the decline of civilization into a state of wickedness that God would address by sending his son a second time. They scoured scripture too. Rejecting emergent scholarly approaches that questioned the inerrancy and infallibility of God's word, dispensationalists built what they believed to be an airtight hermeneutics that got them closer to the Almighty and his absolute truths. Unlike their progressive counterparts, they insisted that the mysteries of the supernatural shadowed human activity across time and that, in the ultimate sense, these mysteries were impenetrable. Yet they also readily applied Darby's mechanics of exegesis to decipher as much about God's laws and sovereignty—and timeline—as humanly possible. Even as they hungrily devoured scripture, they also spurred each other on to share their true faith. While mingling at conferences and church, they strategized ways to "evangelize the world in this generation" and offer salvation to as many lost souls as possible before time ran out. Theirs was to be a tireless march through the present darkness toward heavenly bliss.[52]

Dispensational premillennialism made perfect sense to Lyman Stewart, independent oilman. It combined a speculative spirit with supreme trust in the supernatural, engineering sensibilities with alchemic obsessions, and it was premised on a view of the world that expected ebbs and flows in fortunes, human powerlessness in the face of giant forces, and a general slide toward cataclysm. Stewart's life, as well as the world around him, seemed to cry out for such theological insight. He returned from Niagara convinced that the next phase of his life must follow a drive to save people across the oceans—the Pacific especially—before God's judgment rained down upon them. Stalled by professional tumult in the late 1890s, he pledged never to allow his business to curb his higher calling again.

WESTERN OILMEN MAY not have abided by the finer points of Stewart's end-times doctrine, but they largely approached the new century with an air of expectation—as if one dispensation were ending and another beginning. After a winding stretch of development, the Golden State seemed poised to become synonymous with gold of the liquid variety. Activity was brewing in Texas as well. In the territory southeast of Dallas where William Cummins traversed during his pursuit of revival and oil, a driller hired by the city of Corsicana to locate water found oil instead. The 1894 discovery transformed Corsicana from a sheltered farming community into an industrial center. As these signals made their way to dominant petroleum players in the East, the hunch began to grow that the skeptical John Archbold may have to make good on his promise to drink every gallon of oil discovered west of the Mississippi River. Lyman Stewart and his fellow independents sensed that their own successes, however modest in comparison to those realized by large companies in the East and other parts of the globe, were about to bring the leviathan down upon them again. Stewart was not the only one of them to pause to consider ways to get out of the business before it was too late—even if that meant selling his livelihood to the enemy: Rockefeller. Yet the excitement of their finds and a rising global petroleum industry and market that they watched in wonder kept them anticipating rather than doubting the next progressions of the industry writ large. Having escaped the leviathan once before, they decided they could do it again. After all, in coming west, Standard was entering *their* territory, a space of extractive promise they had long imagined and possessed as their own. They were convinced that God had granted them the dreams and the rights to occupy it and the tenacity, intuition, and technological wherewithal to develop it, which no one could steal away.[53]

Even in their most optimistic mode, Stewart and his fellow oilers in the West could not possibly have imagined the fields of extractive promise about to be opened to them by a one-armed oil hunter who had walked among them. Patillo Higgins toiled in Southeast Texas as the inheritor of a well-formed, well-traveled wildcat faith. He had digested the independents' geological writings and scoured parts of the country for crude, internalized their obsession for the spectacular and utopian possibilities of oil, and pledged with them to fight evil monopolists and protect daring, risk-taking individuals' right to achieve profit and salvation on their own terms. In January 1901, the Spindletop discovery offered independents the opportunity to step into the twentieth century as equals of Standard and Rockefeller, not outliers. With his correct intuition that something big rested beneath Beaumont, Higgins also helped redraw the rules and boundaries of the entire global oil enterprise. If he did not immediately grasp the momentousness of the Spindletop discovery, his former partner George O'Brien did. As news of the Lucas 1 gusher spread, pandemonium set in. Rushing to the scene, at a fairer clip than Higgins, O'Brien was overcome by chaos. "Has the world gone mad?" he murmured to himself while dodging zigzagging buggies. "Never have I seen such a sight. It is only with God's help that we will be able to cope," he thought. "The whole world will soon be at our doorstep."[54]

# CHAPTER THREE

# Dawn of the Gusher Age

George O'Brien was right. In the days following Anthony Lucas's discovery at Spindletop on January 10, 1901, the world seemed to besiege Beaumont. Overnight, tourists and speculators arrived in the burgeoning town, which sat thirty miles inland from the Gulf of Mexico. Several came from Galveston, a coastal city still reeling from the hurricane that had destroyed much of it five months before. On January 20, a Sunday, five hundred excursionists dressed well enough for church took the train to Beaumont to gawk. Arriving at 1:00 p.m., they made their way to Spindletop, where guards caved to pressure as onlookers broke through fencing that ringed Lucas's well site. By 6 p.m., the crowd was heading home "hilariously happy." "It was a most exciting day," a newspaperman reported. "The weather was fine, and the Beaumont people were on the streets in thousands. All manner of carriages, buggies, and fashionable traps and automobiles were whizzing through the throngs, and the hum and noise of talk made the air so full of noises one could scarcely hear distinctly." It was "unlike a Sunday," he added, "and more resembled a great circus day or some big festival." The spectacle grew more dazzling as market-savvy rail lines offered expanded service to as many as 15,000 people a day and teased the nation with advertisements of oildom's wonders.[1]

Weaving through the bewildered onlookers were the impatient business types who wrestled for a piece of the action. Speculators drove up property values as they snatched up every parcel of land. At the Crosby House hotel, the heart of the wheeling and dealing, men standing on chairs fought to be heard as they auctioned off leases, some legitimate, others fraudulent. One particular acre was purchased for $8 then repeatedly resold in frantic trading that left the final purchaser owing $35,000. No wonder the traders who entered the Crosby carried suitcases with $100,000 in cash, and no wonder barbershops were equipped to make change for $1,000 bills. Even more heated was the building boom around Spindletop, where oil hunters scrambled to replicate the Lucas team's fortune. In no time, they hastily assembled two hundred derricks on a 2.5-acre tract, a forest of fresh-cut lumber piercing the clouds.[2]

Robert and J. Edgar Pew were among the business types who ventured to Beaumont on the heels of the Lucas gusher. They represented a family company with a refining center in Toledo, Ohio. Robert arrived first on January 16. Though overcome by the rush of people and put off by the suffocating air, he also saw possibilities for profit. The abundance and affordability of Spindletop crude, coupled with shipping access through the Gulf of Mexico, left him brimming with enthusiasm. After taking stock of the possibilities, he wrote to company executives, "We could put oil into *all* of the Atlantic coast cities for less than one fraction of the cost of transportation from Ohio." Unable to endure the hot, humid, and riotous southeastern Texas frontier, Robert soon departed the area, leaving his younger brother to bear the load. Edgar Pew was far less impatient with Beaumont; he seemed to like it, in fact. Even the outrageous cost of living—$1 for breakfast, $20 for a ride to the well site—did not deter him. Armed with a .41 revolver and wary of confidence men, he strove to find honest locals to help him hunt oil.[3]

Over the coming months, Edgar proved himself to his superiors back home. With patience and calculation, he mapped out where his company could start drilling for and storing oil, reporting each advance to his boss, uncle Joseph N. Pew. Gradually he forged an alliance with a local whose personality perplexed him. Was Patillo Higgins honest or a huckster? Pew concluded that he was "sort of a crank," plagued by a high opinion of himself but trustworthy. "It was he who made the original claims and organized the original company for Spindle Top [*sic*]," Pew explained to his head office. "He had some prestige, of course, from this and has been able to get other money to put into this." With cash in hand Higgins was exploring new terrain outside Beaumont and suggested that Pew come along. Intrigued with the wildcatter's intuitive grasp of the land, Pew could not resist taking a risk. "I have an arrangement with Higgins to go down there again the first of the week and will probably stay there a couple of days with him," he told his uncle. Crank or not, Higgins was a man with vision, and unlike many of his colleagues in the trade, J. Edgar Pew was willing to bet on it.[4]

As the Pew brothers instantly realized, Spindletop was a game changer for their industry. The titan of all oil strikes, it announced the onset of Texas's gusher age and, with it, a frantic rush of production that would alter the balance of global petroleum for generations. Spindletop also sent a signal to the nation as a whole. Its occurrence in the first month of 1901 gave notice that the new century of US power, influence, and affluence would be fueled by southwestern crude. No one was happier about that than the men who had been chasing it. After decades of scouring distant terrain with only intermittent success, the small producers and oil hunters who had long awaited a major breakthrough west of the Mississippi finally achieved it. More than survival, Spindletop gave them muscle in their protracted struggle with Standard Oil.

Yet Spindletop also rendered their immediate concerns more rudimentary and internally focused; not all was favorable under oil's limitless flow. Faced with a reckless abandon that made Titusville seem quaint by comparison, Beaumont's independent-minded oilmen struggled to bring their communities under control. The unparalleled unruliness of the Spindletop rush—the rampant corruption, religious radicalism, and extreme racial violence—would linger in the region's oil culture for years to come. In that initial moment, corporate-turned-civic leaders like the oil-rich Baptist George Carroll grew increasingly wary of the speculative fury nonconformists like his onetime partner Patillo Higgins promoted; they urged fellow independents to tame some of the unruliness that had given wildcatting a bad name. Meanwhile, in response to the proliferation of church-based oil ventures and the rise of apostolic and antinomian tendencies in local pews and drill sites that followed the

Spindletop discovery, Beaumont's self-identified better classes struggled to carve out more deliberate, rational steps for the advancement and stability of their businesses and community. Their efforts sparked the first round in a protracted battle for authority over the soul of wildcat Christianity.

Against this backdrop of booming oil and religiosity, opportunities arose for a few independent companies to grow into small majors. Although they would stay loyal to their roots as family-run businesses, the Stewarts' Union Oil Company and the Pews' Sun Oil Company jumped at the chance to compete with majors on firmer footing. Having suffered under Rockefeller power in Pennsylvania, the Pews especially looked to Texas as a promised land, with J. Edgar as their Moses. While hardly risk averse, Pew was a steadier hand than Lyman Stewart, reflecting new attempts to impose order in a boundless field. Yet the families mirrored each other in many ways, not least in their staunch Presbyterianism and fierce anti-Standard streak. Even as they started visualizing a loftier corporate status, both remained steadfastly determined to counter John D. Rockefeller with all their being.

SPINDLETOP WAS EVERY bit the seismic event Higgins prophesied it would be. There had been booms before, but nothing like this. In an era when any well that produced over 100 barrels per day was still considered a success, during its initial weeklong gush Lucas 1 produced an estimated flow of 100,000 barrels per day. A year later, the field's cumulative annual production total of 17.5 million barrels astounded experts. Such staggering statistics made the hyperbole of pundits seem credible, even commonsensical. A newspaperman boasted that the Texas oil rush would "eclipse in significance, extent, and human interest . . . the gold fields of '49, and even that pathetic melodrama of the Klondike." Spindletop was the El Dorado of its time. Yet the underside of history making was less gilded. For weeks after the Lucas find, Beaumont endured a frenzy that left everyone aghast at the debauchery. Many locals bemoaned the fact that "Spindletop" had become "Swindletop," a home for peddlers, prostitutes, and the ugliest drudges of the earth.[5]

All the usual challenges of an oil boomtown accumulated in Beaumont to exponential degrees. The oil contagion brought the expected "service" workers to town and, with them, an industry of pleasure that remapped the area into safe and unsafe zones. During the first two years of the Spindletop boom, Beaumont's saloons grew in number from twenty-five to eighty-one, with several clustered in a red-light district some called "Hell's Half Acre." Eighteen bars and four hundred prostitutes operated within its three-quarter-mile circumference. Call girls often worked hand in hand with saloonkeepers, receiving a 25 percent commission on the liquor they sold while sweet-talking the men. A majority housed themselves in brothels, which ranged from establishments lodging twenty occupants to the sketchier two-person "crib houses." Overseeing the enterprises were notorious madams like New Orleans transplant Ruby Belle Pearson, who operated Beaumont's biggest and most expensive house, and "Gold Toothed Sadie" and "Big Annie," African American managers of smaller, cheaper niche enterprises. Guns and card tables were ubiquitous too. Walking the streets of Hell's Half Acre became hazardous, as pistol-wielding gamblers shot craps and sometimes each other, and bloodying fights regularly spilled out into the streets. As one blunt local reckoned, the entire scene was "pretty raw."[6]

Searching for a toilet, a drink of water, or even a breath of fresh air was no less hazardous. Within thirty days Beaumont's population had exploded from 6,000 to 50,000, leaving washrooms and landfills in short supply. Desperate individuals who paid to wait in long outhouse lines weathered the sight and stench of surging raw sewage, while people learned to pinch their noses at the stink of fresh waste. The only beneficiaries of the situation were enterprising garbage hounds like a local female pig farmer labeled "Mrs. Slop," who collected the town's refuse for a price. Well emissions were another culprit behind Beaumont's foul air. Out in the fields, drillers encountered an unexpected beast, hydrogen sulfide gas, which was prevalent along the Gulf Coast. "All of those domes had that sulphuric [sic] gas," a driller remembered. "If you got two or three good whiffs of it it just knocked you out. I was knocked out with it." He also "was blind there for quite a while." At night, the region's dense air forced vapors low to the ground, where they became even more lethal. Beaumont's residents were hardly immune to the threat, as noxious fumes wafted into town, filling children's nostrils and stripping the paint off homes. Sulphur poisoned the local water source so badly in places that even boiling was inadequate to remove the impurities. In no time, barrels of fresh water were more expensive than barrels of oil.[7]

Fire, of course, was the most destabilizing agent of all. In March 1901, just two months after Lucas's team filled their makeshift reservoir to the brim, sparks from a passing train set the lake of oil ablaze. The "spectacle of unparalleled grandeur" created a sense of panic among the oilmen that all their handiwork would be destroyed. "When we found there was no possible hope of saving the oil," Lucas later explained, "we started a counter-fire about a mile below the oil lake" to "choke" the original conflagration. Townspeople realized their greatest fear when the second fire made contact with the initial flames. As the two fireballs exploded as one, the ground quaked, blasting scalding oil into the air. Killed by absence of oxygen generated by the explosion, the original inferno died, but across the charcoal-covered hill tiny fires continued to flare alone, giving off the impression that the purgatory was just briefly quieted.[8]

Beaumonters viewed the firestorm as a stark reminder of their vulnerability in the new petroleum age. Oil workers did not need such reminders. There were many ways to die on a rig, which is why the men who staffed them were required to sign "death warrants," legal forms stating their acceptance of all the dangers they would encounter. Yet fire affected workers in a unique way. Explosions on the derrick floor or in storage tanks announced the presence of death with a particularly dreaded cadence, and the poisonous smoke that accompanied them added to men's worries about how long the burn would last and what they would find once the darkness dissipated. "Finding" was the worst part, something one worker realized after watching a colleague ignited by gas. "He was burned—well, you couldn't even recognize him," he recalled. "We found him under a tree, where he had crawled with no feet. Didn't have any feet on him. I got out there, and he asked for a drink of water.... Just black flesh had fallen off awful.... He was gasping.... [H]e must have inhaled that flame down in his lungs. He died a terrible death." Laborers found their pain compounded by the lack of proper medical and postmortem care. Crews in isolated drill sites did not have the time or expertise to handle a dying man or a dead body, and in the early years of the Beaumont boom, few medical aides were there to assist. One of the area's only morticians was overwhelmed, orbiting the well sites as quickly as possible to pick up the deceased, whose crushed and charred corpses were sometimes simply left by the road like strewn garbage in need of disposal. "I pronounced a benediction over several of them," he explained when remembering the task of retrieving and burying bodies. "I done the best I could. Quoted a little Scripture rather than just drive off just like you was leaving a dog."[9]

Excessive oil production was also a problem. The rule of capture had always encouraged a pell-mell rush to sink wells, but not to the degree witnessed around Spindletop. On Spindletop itself, an initial forest of 200 derricks grew over the course of the first year into a jungle of 440. With so many gushing wells, one antiquarian later quipped, "it was a wonder the whole section didn't collapse into a huge oil-soaked crater with all the oil and gas being suddenly removed from their pockets." As wood-framed derricks went up in droves, the gas pressure responsible for driving the oil to the surface dropped precipitously. But the drilling went on; wells were drilled so closely together that men could jump between them without ever touching the ground—an unintended safety valve for those fleeing fire. Not until the summer of 1901 was some semblance of a safety code enforced, but those working the fields had little time for restraints of any kind. Their job was to produce in record numbers, which they did, leaving observers in a state of awe. By the end of Spindletop's first year, one technology journalist marveled, "Beaumont oil is burning in Germany, England, Cuba, Mexico, New York and Philadelphia. By its energy steamers are being propelled across the ocean, trains are hastening across the continent . . . and this, too, while half the world is either unaware or incredulous of the value of this fuel." The onlooker rightly pinpointed Spindletop's propitious timing at the dawn of petroleum's fuel age. Electricity was depressing the need for kerosene, but the automobile and other machines were beginning to require larger supplies of oil for propulsion. Absent from this paean was acknowledgment of the human toll of Spindletop's boundless reach.[10]

The oil boom imperiled the physical and fiscal health of Beaumonters, threating their community's long-term viability. Rampant fire, horrific sanitation, death, and rapid depletion had been the telltale signs of an oil boom since the days of Pithole in Pennsylvania, as was speculative fury. But in Beaumont, the wildcatting was especially wild. Spindletop generated hundreds of upstart oil companies, most incorporated on a whim by crafty individuals with lofty aims but limited means (later known as "poor boy" drillers), making the boom there a high-stakes poker game played by men with questionable hands.

Spindletop's relative isolation contributed to its chaotic brand of capitalism. As of 1900, Southeast Texas remained drowsy and undeveloped. On the eve of the Spindletop discovery, the "Queen of the Neches," as the small river town was called, had yet to experience any serious buzz of economic activity. Travel to Dallas, Houston, and New Orleans still required a daylong train ride. When the oil boom arrived, Beaumont thus lacked access to the economic expertise needed to build a viable financial infrastructure. When searching for assistance in their costly ventures, wildcatters like Anthony Lucas and Patillo Higgins could beg for help from investors in the distant Northeast, pester the handful of local men with modest means, or proceed on shoestring budgets. Even in the wake of the Lucas geyser, the stampede of poor boys without cash or credit created a "manic period of lease-swapping, claim-jumping, and land-grabbing" that quickly turned the rice town into what one pundit called "the capital of a nightmare."[11]

Several other factors contributed to the mania in Beaumont. First, the coarseness of the region's crude actually created instant demand for the otherwise subpar material. Heavy in asphaltic and sulfuric content, it made better fuel oil than kerosene. Never were oilmen so pleased with their second-rate find. Proximity to the Gulf of Mexico also proved a boon. Even the most limited producer could string together a pipeline to move crude to sea-faring tankers that sat at Port Neches or in Sabine Lake, just to the south, which connected the Neches River to the gulf. The political culture of Texas encouraged wildcatting as well. The state's hostilities toward Standard Oil, ensconced in antitrust legislation implemented in the 1890s, opened up room for oilmen of Higgins's ilk. Factored together, all these components created one giant crease of opportunity for the wildest prospectors to emerge. As J. Edgar Pew would later recall, Spindletop turned the business on edge by introducing "a new set of oil men." They had "pluck and energy" but limited wherewithal. While veteran oilmen from Pennsylvania took their time warming up to Spindletop's potentials, upstarts bombarded the region with cheap equipment, stock options and lease agreements—some of them crooked, most of them "made in honest belief"—and an appetite for risk. "Such promotions," Pew observed, "were mostly carried on by men of the South, with no previous oil experience, but who honestly believed that thousands of barrels of oil would continue to flow daily from their wells for ten years or more."[12]

Local religious culture also nurtured a rabid gambler's mentality. For generations, Texans had embraced a reality of tough choices with perilous ends. In their rush to farm land and raise families, in their circuit preaching, church planting, and dealings with banks and government, they calibrated their lives to chance and contingency, to a constant bet on what would come next. Oil amplified that attitude. In earlier oil patches, families, friends, and even congregations had rallied behind risky quests for crude as if taking such chances together was a natural extension of community values. Oilmen such as Lyman Stewart had long asked those they worshipped with to invest with them too. The same solicitations made their way through the gulf region as well, but on a Texas-sized scale. Compared to Stewart's insular circle of investors, speculation at Spindletop was a sprawling enterprise, involving extended family, not just close kin, and entire denominations, not just single parishes. When the daring individuals in charge of the operations failed, so did entire societies. Yet everyone, it seemed, was always ready to try again.

The San Jacinto Company, for instance, was one of nearly 150 companies that filed charters immediately after the Lucas discovery (these comprised less than a third of the 500 total companies formed during the boom). San Jacinto was the creation of a speculator with an abnormally large list of contacts. Reverend J. B. Cranfill was the owner and editor of the popular church newspaper the *Texas Baptist Standard* and financial secretary at Baylor University in Waco. (Earlier, in 1892, he also had been the Prohibition Party's candidate for vice president.) Cranfill was a Bible-wielding warrior, known for taking on schismatic clerics. That he was ill prepared for wildcatting did not stop him from trying. In 1901, after quitting his job at Baylor, he formed San Jacinto and started aggressively marketing it in Baptist newspapers and soliciting fellow denominationalists across the country. Thousands of dollars of stock commitments followed, mostly from clergymen and their wives with whom Cranfill had a rapport.[13]

By late 1902, San Jacinto was in trouble, with water flooding its wells and its prospects fading fast. In a September letter to stockholders, Cranfill relayed the difficult news that his company would not be able to honor its financial commitments. "As I often said in the advertisements which I sent out for this Company," he reminded his supporters, "no one can tell how long the oil will last." Then he reminded his friends of the liabilities they had assumed. "Everybody who bought the stock took the chances on this, and all of the stockholders know as much about it as those of us here on the ground." Some of Cranfill's investors, however, unsure of what he meant, wrote with requests for cash payouts. Others threatened to sue. The minister of First Baptist Church in Cincinnati, Ohio, said that he would not (at that moment, at least) join a lawsuit against Cranfill but wrote scathingly of the entire operation. Of a lawyer compiling the complaints, he queried, "From your words . . . am I to understand that the stock of the Refining Co. is valueless[?]. . . . I have too much invested to lose." He added, "[As] a 'far off' investor [I] appreciate your interest in us stockholders, and hope you win." The cleric paired his legal correspondence with his defunct stock certificate and mailed the entire package to Cranfill, undoubtedly to indicate that such exploitation of church resources and poor management was unacceptable, not to mention ungodly.[14]

Whether or not Cranfill took the message to heart, his company collapsed. While he returned to his church calling, his peers dealt with the fallout. Such was the drastic turn from anticipation to despair that accompanied so many of the long-shot ventures in early Beaumont oil, leaving investors large and small hanging by thin financial threads.[15]

BEAUMONT'S VIOLENT BOOM spawned another beast: a business entirely dependent on racial hierarchies. Propped up by the prevailing ideologies and theologies of the day, the patricians and proletariat of southwestern petroleum mapped out their oil patches on a grid of apartheid. As one scholar puts it, turn-of-the-century oil acquired a "specific look." Pale-faced oilers occupied the most hospitable of generally inhospitable jobs, housing, and natural environments, acquiring the bulk of financial returns with the least bodily harm.[16]

From its beginning, oil operated according to rules of white supremacy. To a degree, it mirrored other industries in the late nineteenth century, such as coal. The coal industry made allowances for miners of various ethnicities, particularly those with a white hue, but burdened African Americans—when they were even allowed to enlist—with heavy stigmas and the toughest jobs. Nineteenth-century petroleum provided even less opportunity for blacks. Before Spindletop, oil production centered on places with relatively low African American populations. And unlike coal, which required massive workforces, early oil production (and even refining) involved smaller, homogenous teams, usually consisting of men who already knew each other. These factors meant there was little chance whatsoever for the marginalized to penetrate the ranks. Ideology mattered too. In the post–Civil War years the mythology of oil cast petroleum as a material essence for American unity and US imperial might, furthering a brand of Yankee individualism that excluded African Americans and the "nonwhite" other. For all its claims to cherish liberty, wildcatting at home and abroad was to be a white man's game.[17]

Already regimented, US oil's racial proscriptions hardened considerably once transferred to Texas. The cotton-growing territory bounded by Houston and Dallas to the west, the Oklahoma and Louisiana borders to the north and east, and the Gulf Coast to the south was steadfastly aligned with the Jim Crow order and its underlying violence. During the decade that preceded oil's arrival, 110 black citizens were reportedly lynched to death in Texas, a total surpassed only in Mississippi and Georgia. East Texas, where most black Texans lived, recorded more lynchings between the 1890s and 1920s than any other section of the state. Horrifically representative was the experience of a black man charged with rape in 1892. Though he had been sentenced to hanging by the law, local citizens demanded he be given to them instead. Officials relented—provided that the lynching occur beyond the community's borders (so as not to upset children). At the agreed-upon spot, men bound the condemned to a stake and doused him with kerosene oil, soon to be abundant in proximate supply. The woman he was convicted of raping lit the first match, while upward of 6,000 people watched. Nearby, a disturbingly commonplace event occurred over a decade later. Gun-toting white vigilantes sought revenge for a black resident's perceived slighting of a white peer. They riddled twenty-two black bodies with gunshots and left them on roads and in brushes and weeds.[18]

This "reign of terror," as the *Galveston Daily News* called it, occurred just as the ideology of the "Lost Cause" grabbed hold of the old Confederacy. At the heart of this creed rested notions of white supremacy and a reimagined, romanticized history that stressed the noble virtues of the antebellum South and painted the Confederacy's Civil War as a heroic struggle to preserve them. Besides minimizing slavery as a root cause of the conflict, the ideology also suggested the South had been forced into secession, war, and Reconstruction by a radicalized few (abolitionists and freed blacks) but would rise again, to the benefit of the entire nation. William Cummins and other former Confederate warriors who had traded guns for geological equipment and started scouring Texas for crude supposed that oil might fuel the region's resurrection. After the war, the Methodist circuit rider Cummins had joined the Ku Klux Klan and, hooded and cloaked in white, terrorized local black residents. Along with scientific inquiries and theories of oil's abundance, he touted the constitutionality of states' rights and white superiority. For him, black gold and the Lost Cause went hand in hand.[19]

Religion was the glue that bound them. Cummins and his peers considered it their sacred duty to reestablish the racial order, viewing the reassertion of white Democratic Party power following Reconstruction as an act of "redemption." That sense of duty energized white Christian citizens, with tangible results. Clerics and lay leaders frequently stood at the front of the lynching gangs that punished East Texas's black residents.[20]

The white oilers who populated the Beaumont field enacted racial standards with a similar ferocity. Spindletop crude immediately registered with locals as a material of such import that only white males could handle it. Simply put, nonwhite men were not allowed anywhere near a derrick. At the time, a few other Texas industries, such as shipping and lumber, were beginning to carve out room for African American laborers. But in oil, apartheid was unassailable, extending even to the proverbial "death warrant"—the labor contracts all oil workers signed releasing their employers from responsibility for bodily harm and death. Only white males over the age of twenty-one were allowed to sign. A local preacher recalled that black men who broke this rule were immediately put in their place; on one occasion his own brother led the purge. "They rounded up a bunch of niggers working out there and scared them pretty bad and that's about all the trouble they ever had. They never come back no more." By edict and vigilantism alike, blacks were banned. At best, they could drive trucks, dig holding ditches, or do a job that white men refused: laying pipeline through the region's bug-infested swamps. They might also hope to do prep work for the latter task, hacking away trees to create a right of way and then lugging heavy pipe—each segment stretching twenty feet and weighing six hundred pounds—from rail depots. Indian and Mexican laborers had to abide by the same rules. On the few occasions when nonwhite workers found their way onto drill teams, they performed menial service. Despite his own history of harassing local African Americans, Patillo Higgins hired "several darkies"—though only to shovel out earthen reservoirs, not pull levers or sink pipe. As a Beaumonter remembered when asked about the involvement of blacks and "Red Bones" (his epithet for Indian African Americans from Louisiana) in the business, the message was matter-of-fact: "Of course [they] would do hard labor . . . building tanks . . . muleskinning, but outside of that—all the work's done by white people." African Americans would be reduced to that work profile for quite some time. As late as 1940, black oil workers accounted for 0.5 percent of all employees in US oil exploration and production and 3.0 percent of all refinery workers.[21]

Racial lines also bounded oil's living arrangements. While in the field laying pipe or digging ditches, black workers were quarantined in their own tents and, despite their drastically reduced pay, forced to fend for themselves where food was concerned. Hunting sustained them, with poor working stiffs trapping rabbit where they could. White workers, meanwhile, enjoyed a much higher quality of lodging and food, all supplied by the company. Housing in the oil town was no different. White male workers with families preferred quieter sections of Beaumont and Gladys City, the suburb named after Higgins's utopian venture (and favorite female pupil). Those who could not claim white privilege lived to the east of Spindletop in a hamlet called "South

Africa." Local Frank Dunn explained that it "was named that because there were so many [African Americans] that worked in earthen tanks and so forth like that, that they called it South Africa." According to Dunn, the quarantine of nonwhite workers appeased white elites and workers: "They decided that it would be better off to have [black men] away from the field. They felt like at that time that they were taking up jobs that some white man probably would be glad to have. And they decided that it would be best to have them removed." As Dunn's contemporaries saw it, blacks were best kept out of view in the neighborhood as well as on the work site for the good of everyone, white women and children especially.[22]

Even the boomtown's red-light district was off-limits to the inhabitants of South Africa. They had to look for fun elsewhere or take their chances in Hell's Half Acre, where they were at the mercy of their white hosts and the town's ragtag police force. Black versus white fisticuffs were common, as were scenes of policemen pulling African American men from saloons and transporting them to jail in a wagon dubbed the "Black Moriah." Facing an uphill battle, the few law enforcers operating at the time meted out selective justice. Locals approved: "The only people they would arrest would be a nigger shooting craps. And they'd catch those niggers, jerk them up and fine them, put them in jail and all that kind of stuff—beat them up. But the white people went on just like they wanted to." Relegated to the most menial jobs and forced to the margins even of Beaumont's shadow society, East Texas's "South Africans" revealed the severe limits of oil's promise for a better tomorrow.[23]

Those constrictions would continue to inform the oil industry for decades, despite the liberty-loving image it sold to the public. The speculative frenzy and racial othering that swept Spindletop in fact reinforced each other. They drew on and incited the same emotional flings of expectation, dispossession, and dashed dreams and together shored up a conviction that the white citizens of a reborn Confederacy possessed the sole right to lead American society into the next stage of petroleum's enlightenment.

ANOTHER CATALYST OF Beaumont's boom was Pentecostal Christianity. This Holy Ghost–filled gospel emerged at the very same time as the

Spindletop discovery and began transforming the rapturous spirituality seen in earlier oil patches into an institutional structure. In its teachings of health, wealth, and blessedness before God, Pentecostalism found a natural entry to the emerging order of petroleum, where broken bodies and longings for healing and happiness proliferated. Empowering for some, upsetting to others, this holiness movement electrified Beaumonters as they adapted to the harsh circumstances into which oil heaved them. That same spiritual energy produced a weariness of born-again euphoria among Beaumont's more modest oilers, which evolved in equally strong measure and sparked their own quest for order.

The same month that Lucas struck oil at Spindletop, a former Methodist preacher named Charles Parham made history by guiding Bible college students in Topeka, Kansas, through a practice of "glossolalia," or speaking in tongues. In the form of worshipful chants, they spoke a mysterious language vouchsafed by the Holy Spirit to the most devout. Parham also began preaching a "full gospel" message that included promises of physical restoration for ailing Christians who trusted in God. His beliefs gained attention throughout southwestern Missouri and southeastern Kansas, a zinc and lead mining district. He enjoyed a particularly strong connection with workers whose silica-dust-filled lungs and arthritic joints begged for the relief he promised and whose tolerance of taxing labor in places of unfathomable darkness preconditioned them for the hyper-supernatural truths of salvation and sanctification that he taught. "Their belief world—protean, eclectic, and dynamic," one scholar offers, was already tuned to "his message that believers could bring the forces of heaven to bear on the material world to effect miraculous change, most especially on and in their own bodies." Parham essentially rearmed the region's colliers with a highly experiential spirituality that for generations had animated mining cultures around the globe. Parham's nascent Pentecostalism bore a family resemblance to the Methodist spiritualism of the oiler-preacher William Cummins, whose own fascinations with terrestrial and extra-terrestrial truths had been sparked on the very same southwestern Missouri soil.[24]

Parham's teachings soon spread to Texas. By 1906, he was active in Houston, sharing his faith in the Holy Spirit with its white and black denizens. Among them was William J. Seymour, an African American

Christian who had fled north to escape the poverty and racial subjugation of Louisiana before returning south to Houston. Inspired by Parham, Seymour joined the movement; soon after that epiphany he accepted a pastorate in Los Angeles. In the spring of 1906, he oversaw an extended religious revival at an old African Methodist Episcopal church on Azusa Street. In its musty confines lively worshippers collectively sang and prayed, spoke in tongues, and got baptized in the Holy Spirit. The event would become known as the Azusa Street Revival and the formal start of modern Pentecostalism. Tantalizing for its emphases on the presence of biblical miracles in modern times, Seymour and Parham's Pentecostalism quickly spread throughout the West, including in Southeast Texas, where Parham and Seymour had first met.[25]

Spindletop's version of the Azusa Street Revival was less a novelty than an intensification of the region's spiritual fervor. By the time big oil arrived, Beaumont's pews were already overflowing (as one resident noted) with "apostolics" and "Holy Rollers" doing enough "shouting and hollering and jumping . . . to shake the whole house." As traveling preachers like Cummins came to realize, the pockets of black Christian congregational life and the small white churches amid the region's pine trees and swamps had always fostered the charismatic piety that would enliven Parham and Seymour's movement. After Spindletop, with oil's orgasms all around, the shouting and shaking redoubled. Inspired by the conditions they now faced, many of Beaumont's apostolics used revivalism to process the ecstasies and the excesses in spiritual terms— to celebrate oil's arrival and mourn its effects. On the Lucas oil discovery, they praised God for his blessings. Chants of gratitude quickly turned to laments when fire spread at the Lucas well. Closest to the action were a number of black holiness churches in "South Africa," whose frightened worshippers prayed for relief from the conflagration and pledged to leave the town altogether, never to return. Farther afield, black and white Christians sang songs of deliverance and heard sermons that painted oil as the devil's handiwork. "The earth is the Lord's and the fullness thereof," ministers pronounced as they declared the Lucas fire a dire warning that oil drilling was invading the Lord's domain and about to combust the entire region. Others promised catastrophe if the violations of God and nature continued: "vast underground fires . . . would burn until the country collapsed"; more gushers would "submerge the entire coast under a sea of oil which would ignite and destroy all living beings." Having triggered the highest expectations of prosperity, the Spindletop strike also evoked scripture's darkest parables.[26]

In the months that followed, the Beaumont area remained an epicenter of emotive Christianity. It was increasingly a destination for preachers associated with the Pentecostalism of Parham and Seymour. William Joseph Philp, a Methodist minister, watched the spreading wave of Pentecostalism with great interest and some respect. One tiny church caught his attention. "Why they was very Christian-like in their actions—those Apostolics," Philp insisted, his tone betraying his awareness that many of his peers viewed Pentecostalism skeptically. Its pastor, named "Gibson," "couldn't hardly read, and he'd pick up the Bible and he read and he'd get to a certain word and he'd say, 'I can't call that name and [so he would] call it 'Jim,' and go on, and then he'd get so happy he'd just grab that table and sometime maybe, jump plumb up on it." Gibson was mesmerizing, Philp admitted: "he'd get the people . . . emotionally worked up . . . some of them praying and some of them just a-hollering. . . . They're building churches now, I think, around over the State. Those, Assembly of God, they call them now." "Christianity is a wonderful power," Philp figured, "and when people know they are going to live again, why they try to prepare for that second life." The joy he witnessed in Gibson's audience stemmed from the assurance that "they was going to go to Heaven when they died," he added.[27]

Philp was just as taken with the large holiness revivals he witnessed, where preachers who did not identify as Pentecostals preached a similar message. Sometimes led by "scholars" (ordained ministers), at other times by grade-school dropouts like Gibson, the tent meetings that popped up on a regular basis could be counted on to convulse the town. One evangelist named "Threadgiver" was among the "scholars" who arrived. "He come down there and he began to preach," Philp remembered, "and he built the morals of the people up." At those meetings, people did not just listen—they swayed and spoke in tongues, they prayed out loud, they walked the "sawdust trail" forward to receive their blessing, and they sang. Among their staples were "Traveling Through This World of Woe" and "Shadow and the Cloud," whose familiar refrain about the Israelites fleeing Egypt spoke of the Holy Spirit's manifestation as "a fire by night and a cloud by day," images that spoke to the atmosphere that enveloped Texas oil country.[28]

Pentecostal-style awakenings were hardly the only revivals to shake Spindletop, though. Methodists, Baptists, Presbyterians, and even Catholics found reason to gather as communities anxious to beg for God's gifts. With a sense of partnership, they went about constructing congregations that could provide cradle-to-the-grave ministries. "We organized a little Sunday school and we just sent around and gathered up all the children and folks that we could get," one woman from an outlying oil community called Batson recalled. "We had a few Catholics there that came right into the services and worked in the church with us. We had all denominations in the church." When it came time to worship, she explained, the eclectic flock gravitated toward the familiar: "we used to sing the old-time hymns because everyone seemed to know them." Everyone seemed to know how to coordinate interdenominational revivals as well. Philp's Methodist church joined with a Baptist congregation to organize interchurch meetings attended by over 1,000 people. In their eyes, doctrinal differences mattered little when both groups were trying to save the community. Other collaborations involved barnstorming preachers, rollicking gospel music, and various enticements to draw the area's rowdies into communion with their Christ. Church folk often sold their message with a meal—picnics involving grilled meat, "a lot of cakes and bread," and makeshift swings, built near Spindletop's derricks to attract workers. "The drillers and the roughnecks would come down there and help eat our chicken and be delighted," one resident recalled. "One of the old gaugers [sic] there [would] come down there with his crew and we'd all have a time eating chicken and cake and swinging and drinking ice water and stay there until time to go home."[29]

Meant for enjoyment and instruction, mass meetings were also designed to foster social propriety. Since Titusville, the flip side of revivalism had always been reform, the urge among oil-patch believers to stabilize and better their booming society through public enforcement of Christian moral standards. Amid the unprecedented ruptures of their environment, including the disorienting proliferation of apostolic and Pentecostal piety, Beaumont's religious establishment felt that something more than preaching, singing, and swinging was required. Christians had to step up in the fight to restore order in their town.

In the days that followed the Lucas gusher, as laborers of all types poured into the area, Beaumont's Christians configured a plan for rolling back the migration's ill effects. Their initial steps resembled those taken by their predecessors in 1860s Pithole; temperance was their loudest rallying cry. While acting in smaller packs to infiltrate and expose the goings-on at local saloons, they also coordinated more systematic responses. Members of the local Women's Christian Temperance Union (WCTU) chapter organized drives to counter any encouragement of alcoholic consumption, even when it came from medical experts. Following a declaration by local doctors that it was safer to drink whiskey than the sulfur-saturated municipal water, WCTU activists started boiling and dispensing free water alongside their pleas for restraint. The same Beaumonters also cheered on militant Prohibitionist Carrie Nation, who purposefully visited Spindletop's most notorious bar. "She didn't have her hatchet with her," one female observer noted. "She just went in there and gave them a tongue-lashing." Beaumonters' justification for infiltrating pubs improved after they succeeded in voting in local Prohibition laws. They did so by convincing oil executives of the crusade's worthiness. "You can't work derricks and drink whiskey," they pleaded; several oil chiefs agreed and signed on. Activists, businessmen, and friendly politicians forced the matter to a vote, and the dry side won. Bootleggers promptly proceeded to flout the rules and frustrate the rule makers. Yet, symbolically at least, the oil patch's Prohibitionists had gained the upper hand, lending proof in their mind that a two-headed gospel of revival and reform could curb the oil patch's worst vices.[30]

If there was one individual who embodied that type of thinking, it was George Carroll, Patillo Higgins's elder at First Baptist Church and former partner in the Gladys City enterprise. Carroll was highly respected, which was why his opinions mattered. In the eyes of his fellow Beaumonters, he "was one of the finest characters that ever walked in shoe leather." By 1903, Carroll was convinced that oil's arrival marked a bad turn for his community. Though one of the richest men in Beaumont—enjoying fortunes in lumber as well as oil—he regretted the town's infusion of prosperity and profligacy. In response, he pledged to do all he could to muster his willpower, his wealth, and his church to tame the transgressions.[31]

Carroll assumed the role of his community's Reverend Darius Steadman, of Pithole fame. One local marveled at the toughness the Baptist elder displayed when raiding bars: in one instance, Carroll "shaved his [long] beard off, put on an old rough suit of clothes, and an old cap with the bill turned backwards ... walked in there and sat around a little while till he'd seen the roulette game going on, the dice gaming going on, the poker games going on. He said, 'Boys, I don't know if you know who I am, I'm George Carroll. You boys are under arrest.'" "Like rats leaving a burning vessel," the "boys" fled, handing the crusader a victory, along with some satisfaction. Other acts of resistance transpired via quieter means. The civic-minded man strove to provide an example of decency, even in the most mundane matters. For instance, Beaumonters fretted over the dust and mud whipped up by the wagons that transported oil, making their tight streets smog-producing thoroughfares. The Baptist had a solution. "George W. Carroll has set a good example by sprinkling the street in front of his residence with oil," exclaimed the town's broadsheet. "All streets should be thus sprinkled to keep mud off the paved streets."[32]

Carroll was equally adroit at using politics to extend his causes. In 1902 he vied for the governorship of Texas on the Prohibition ticket and two years later sought the vice presidency of the United States on the same platform. He had more success back home, where he was elected alderman from Beaumont's Third Ward. In the meantime, he founded the local YMCA chapter and poured his profits into Baptist causes, especially his own First Baptist Church and Baylor University, which in May 1901 readily accepted his initial gift (more would follow) of $75,000, stunning for that day. And in 1904, following once again in the shoes of church editor and wildcat oilman Reverend J. B. Cranfill, whose previous run for office on the Prohibition ticket likely inspired him, Carroll purchased the *Baptist Standard*. Cranfill, finally past the wreckage of his failed oil venture and now having sold his magazine, would go on to lead southwestern Baptists in other high-profile capacities. Carroll, meanwhile, would secure his place at the front of a rising tide of petroleum-incited moral zeal.[33]

Carroll focused his search for order simultaneously on spiritual and fiscal immoderations. He remained anxious not only about the brass tacks of his business but, relatedly, also about the charismatic outpourings of the local church, which seemed only to accentuate the chaos. During the heyday of the boom, he thus operated alongside other Christian executives interested in imposing a semblance of coordination on small producers before the chaos of Spindletop overwhelmed them. In the absence of Rockefeller and his heavy-handed quashing of the wildcat ethic (which relieved them), capitalists of Carroll's class were left to enforce at least a modicum of rationality among those who worked proudly under the broad canopy of independent oil. Calculating and temperate, they recognized that the rabid speculative spirit driving men to places like the Texas coast could be damaging, as could the lease swapping and land grabbing that followed. While the world of oil erupted around the spot that Higgins prophesied contained great wealth, garnering his profile as an undisciplined and unpredictable oilman some level of praise, in little time his peers again grew wary of his kind.[34]

The post-Spindletop careers of Carroll and Higgins brought these emerging discrepancies into full view. In his corporate dealings as much as in his moral crusading, Carroll accepted but did not court risky ventures. No doubt he was fully aware of the gambles several of his colleagues in the church took in hopes of winning instant riches. There was, of course, the clergyman easily roped in by his colleague, J. B. Cranfill. The publisher of another denomination's major paper, the *Texas Christian Advocate*, also boasted his own oil company. Yet another endeavor, presumably carried out by Bible believers, was simply dubbed the Christian Oil Company. A group of women based in Joplin, Missouri, Pentecostal, perhaps, created a corporate entity called the Young Ladies Oil Company. Texas was inundated with audacious amateurs who thought they could defy the odds and, with God guiding them, bore through to earth's riches.[35]

Carroll, then, preferred a slightly different way. During the 1900s he distanced himself from Higgins and built an empire known for probity. He hired cautious workers and paid them well, enforced modesty on his worksites, and did not overreach in his finances. Fiercely protective of the individual's relationship with God and right to glean truths from the Bible, in business he jealously guarded the independence of producers against monopolism. Yet he also held tight to the conviction that with personal liberty came a great deal of personal accountability—that God entrusted true freedom only to those who could manage it within a moral community. Unlike Higgins, Carroll allowed no room for apostolic or antinomian impulses, resisting the assumption that any man who accepted Christ's gift of grace could ultimately follow his own moral path. Carroll instead adhered to a contractual theology that blended Old Testament injunction with modern commercial code. Along with Lyman Stewart and other oilmen who held that success was contingent upon reciprocity with God, Carroll believed the onus was on him to honor his Father by observing biblical practices of tithing, Sabbatarianism, worship, temperance, and service. In business, those practices required evenhandedness over competitiveness in dealings with others (especially other Christians) and the nurturing of work atmospheres organized around principles of rectitude. Do this, they believed, and the returns on their contract would be exponential; fail, and the cost would be chastisement. God's promise was unbending: he would honor fidelity with profit but punish backsliding with loss.[36]

Whereas Carroll proceeded with prudence and foresight, Higgins bolted ahead without a blueprint. Both men remained wildcatters at heart, accepting the mysterious workings of suprahuman forces in their businesses and lives, along with all the personal hazards that arrangement seemed to offer. But Higgins did not merely accept the risks. He reveled in them, as if they validated his anointing. That tendency showed itself in the years after the Lucas gusher. Having secured a small payout from his original deal with Anthony Lucas (guaranteeing 10 percent returns) and maintained a few of his own leases in the area, Higgins immediately threw his financial wherewithal into acquiring more land and brokering deals between his Higgins Oil and Fuel Company and other companies. He boasted of being a "horse trader" whose wheeling and dealing had magical ends for a lot of people. "I didn't buy me a little steam yacht, and this and that and the other . . . and run with the devil and everything." Oil "was my only horse," he joked, and "I done good with it": "I helped people that needed something to eat and something to wear. I helped build that country up." In terms of his bottom line, Higgins seemed destined to weather major hits and a steady stream of painful misses. Yet failure and rejection of any sort only propelled him toward the next deal.[37]

Bombast and complaints aside, Higgins's gains were notable. While he was never able to join oil's establishment, he did manage to leverage his folk hero status for gain. According to two biographers, "Hundreds of letters poured in describing the character of the land that people had, noting comparisons with Higgins' descriptions of oil-bearing surface indications and inviting him to analyze their properties, often with partnerships or royalty interests." Higgins answered only a few, but the contacts were substantial enough to allow him to snatch up land in outlying sections of Southeast Texas like Sour Lake, Saratoga, and Batson, where oil production accelerated once Spindletop's pools began to dry up. His company soon generated interest from larger corporate bodies. A year after seeing his company strike it big at Spindletop, his Higgins Oil and Fuel Company was absorbed by the Houston Oil Company, leaving him to create anew. He immediately formed the Higgins Standard Oil Company with designs to wildcat again in the outlying fields. In tagging his company with the "Standard" label, Higgins once again revealed his supreme confidence that he was the one commissioned to lead America into its oil future. In 1903 he published an expansive seventy-two-page brochure selling his wares, boasting of his brilliance and exploits, and touting his pioneering role at Spindletop. It was *he* who was responsible for Beaumont's riches, the publication announced, not the "two-by-four-headed Beaumont skeptics whose brains . . . 'could not balance a feather on the scales of knowledge.'" The Prophet of Spindletop, he intimated, was about to make good on another round of prophecies.[38]

WHATEVER HIS PEERS thought about him, they found it nearly impossible to avoid the Higgins machine. Higgins held the keys to Southeast Texas development: a grip on locals' illusions, an intuitive sense of the land, and a wealth of experience navigating both. Even Carroll ultimately could not desist from doing business with him again (a brief, largely failed effort in 1911). For this reason another oilman came calling, hoping to glean something from Beaumont's ultimate charismatic. J. Edgar Pew saw Spindletop through the same eyes as Carroll—as a bedlam in need of cleaning up—yet he was willing to be flexible in his opinions for the sake of profits.[39]

Pew's arrival in Beaumont, just weeks after the Lucas gusher, occurred at a critical time for his family's petroleum firm. He was the nephew of Joseph Newton Pew, an oil pioneer from western Pennsylvania. Growing up during the 1850s, the elder Pew experienced the same social revolutions that his contemporary Lyman Stewart lived through just a few miles away. As Old School Presbyterians, the Pews gave time and money to their church and its conservative ministry, but not at the cost of their own principles. When their denomination came out in defense of slavery, the Pews joined other disgruntled congregants to found the Free Presbyterian Church. Prior to the Civil War, their farm served as a way station on the Underground Railroad. As family lore recounts, "It was not unusual for one or the other of the Pew children to be roused from bed to hitch up horses and drive a band of escaping slaves to their next refuge." Like their neighbors, the Pews harbored a staunch belief in personal liberty, whether framed theologically or politically. That same conviction shaped their commitment to free market capitalism, which Joseph fully absorbed. At the age of eleven, he grew fascinated with oil speculation in Titusville, just forty miles away, and at twenty he moved to the boomtown to start a business.[40]

For the next three decades, Joseph Pew and his company floundered in the dispiriting environment ruled by Standard Oil. By the 1870s he was overextended and struggling with paralyzing debt brought on by dicey decisions. Like Stewart, though, he earned last-chance relief by investing in the new oil field at Bradford. Pew recovered enough to start a natural gas company in 1876 with Edward Emerson. The two recognized sooner than most that gas was an emerging fuel for heating boilers and pumping oil wells. In the late 1880s they decided to move into oil, seeking to integrate operations "from wellhead to consumer," a strategy they saw Standard master. The opening of the Lima pool in Ohio spurred them on. But Sun Oil Company of Ohio, which they formalized in 1890, was no match for the Rockefeller conglomerate. Even as Sun partially integrated by building a refinery in Toledo, it struggled against Standard's cutthroat tactics. Sun's survival, as a company historian admits, came only through its ability to deal "in the leftovers bequeathed by Standard." Increasingly frustrated with Emerson's cautious business approach, Joseph sought an out and in 1899 finally forced the issue. Emerson, who was older than Pew and in failing health, sold his shares and sailed off on a retirement trip to Europe.[41]

Now firmly in charge of Sun Oil, Pew pointed the company toward Texas. A few years before Spindletop, Pennsylvania petroleum operator and Pew associate Joseph Cullinan had ventured to East Texas to prospect for crude, convinced it presaged oil's future. His hunch was rewarded with the Corsicana oil strike of 1894, which allowed him to plant roots in the state as head of the Joseph S. Cullinan Company. Pew had turned down Cullinan's invitation to invest in the Corsicana venture, so as soon as word of Spindletop spread, he was anxious not to miss out on another Texas boom. Within a few weeks of Lucas 1's geyser, his nephew, J. Edgar Pew, traveled south, his task straightforward but hardly easy: give Sun a chance to make it in the business. Edgar exceeded his superiors' expectations. Quickly he purchased forty-two acres of land at Port Neches, just outside Beaumont, on which reservoirs and tanks were immediately constructed. He recognized that the real challenge at infrastructure-starved Spindletop would be obtaining sufficient storage and transportation. With holding vessels in place, he oversaw the construction of a pipeline running from the Port Neches company base—"Sun Station"—to the Spindletop field. Pew was ready to start transporting crude back to the company's refinery.[42]

Sun's senior officials began reorganizing the company in anticipation of large next steps. In the spring of 1901, Joseph Pew with eldest son Arthur E. Pew incorporated Sun Company of New Jersey, eager to make it the shining light of the Sun network. The elder Pew also remained president of the Sun Oil Company (Ohio), but the Sun Company of New Jersey was ascendant. One of its first initiatives was to give Edgar near carte blanche "to buy and sell oil, oil leases, and lands and transact such other business for the company" as he saw fit. Sun then began building another major refinery on its new eighty-two-acre plot in Marcus Hook, southeast of Philadelphia, in the fall of 1901. Seven months later it was completed and ready to begin receiving shipments from Beaumont via the SS *Paraguay*, a Great Lakes ore-carrying ship that Joseph bought and repurposed for long-haul transport. Edgar's initial oil shipments headed north to Toledo via train, but by 1903 the *Paraguay* was responsible for carrying 400,000 barrels of Texas oil to

Marcus Hook—roughly 10 percent of all gulf oil shipments that year. Within a brief eighteen-month period, J. Edgar Pew had given Sun a foothold in the Southwest.[43]

His gumption was absolutely necessary. The Spindletop blitz created a new level of competition between independent oil firms that aspired to major status. Two in particular registered as key combatants with Sun. Spindletop driller Anthony Lucas was responsible for what became Gulf Oil. In his quest for funds, Lucas had partnered with Pennsylvania prospecting firm Guffey & Galey as well as the Mellon banking family of Pittsburgh. In the years following Spindletop, the Mellons—brothers Andrew and Richard and nephew William—proceeded to buy out (and in the case of James Guffey, oust) their partners until in 1907 they took full control of the rechristened Gulf Oil Company. The other peer to the Pews was the company founded by Joseph Cullinan, whose presence in nearby Corsicana allowed him to be among the first to stake huge claims in the enormous Spindletop field. On March 28, 1901, partnered with Arnold Schlaet and backed by a group of investors, Cullinan formed the Texas Fuel Company (aka the Texas Company and ultimately Texaco). The fact that Cullinan already had storage facilities in the area gave his company an advantage. Also critical was his ability to seize control of valuable leases from a syndicate headed by former Texas governor James Hogg, who had been instrumental in preventing John D. Rockefeller's oil giant from entering the state. Cullinan relocated Texaco's headquarters from Beaumont to Houston in 1905 and that same year oversaw the establishment of a European subsidiary. Mirroring Gulf, Texaco grew rapidly through integration, set on controlling as much down- and upstream capacity as possible.[44]

Going forward, then, the challenge for J. Edgar Pew and Sun was to continue expanding in an environment flush with rivals and unpredictability. Pew's efforts proved vexing. He complained regularly to his uncle and boss of the region's difficult landforms and people. Spindletop and the fields that subsequently emerged around it were hard to read; while in some instances "attempts to flow wells" would succeed, in others a well would "flow for a little bit . . . [then] quickly diminish and . . . become a gasser." Dangerous gas was always on his mind. He warned his colleagues repeatedly that the material he was extracting for them posed numerous hazards. "You will find it an entirely different grade of oil to handle and must be handled most carefully," he wrote. "Would suggest that you also take it up with the refinery and give them very careful warning." For good measure, Pew reported on the fatalities that the lethal gas had already created—eight dead of fire ("one little girl") in one instance, 120 derricks burned in another. No less taxing was navigating the region's mania. Pew hated the fact that Sun had to rush in headlong. Knowing that approach would deplete a field's longevity, he nevertheless resigned himself to it, fearing "there may not be any oil for us to get" if he hesitated. The commercial climate bothered him as well. Absent any oversight, he complained, Spindletop was bursting at the seams with inexperienced "natives" who did "careless and incompetent work." And then there was fear of the great enemy, Standard Oil. Although confident that Texas's aversion to Rockefeller would hold, Pew suspected secret agents at work, around every corner, scheming to ease Standard's entry into the area.[45]

Personnel matters were just as gnarled. While Pew maintained vigilant watch over external corporate circumstances, he struggled to smooth Sun's internal dynamics. On more than one occasion, he was forced to deal with worksite injuries, one of which resulted in a lawsuit. There was also constant racial strife. In the spring of 1902, a local Beaumont newspaper provided news of Sun's brand-new ship, the *Paraguay*, but also noted violence between two of its workers. "Deputy Sheriff George McGriff came in from Nederland bringing a white man named James K. World and a Negro named Will Jones," the daily reported. "The Negro had a flesh wound in his right arm caused by a bullet. Both were employed by Sun Oil Company and were at Sun Station." When detailing these human relations failings to Sun executives in Toledo and Marcus Hook, Pew wrote with an air of resignation. Despite his own abolitionist heritage, he seemed to believe that Sun's labor practices could not help but echo the region's racial apartheid.[46]

Pew pressed on. He felt he had little choice but to set caution aside and deal with one of the emblems of the region's abandon: Patillo Higgins. Shortly after arriving in Texas, Pew oversaw Sun's purchase of the Lone Star and Crescent Oil Company, whose Spindletop well sites bordered Higgins's. Over the course of the next few years, they became collaborators. Higgins himself was eccentric, and Pew knew it. Still, as the Spindletop boom receded slightly in 1902 and 1903, he started relying on Higgins's parochial knowledge to ramp up exploration of surrounding lands, especially near test zones in Sour Lake, Batson, and Barbers Hill. Pew figured that to stay afloat, let alone succeed, in Southeast Texas, he was going to have to hope that Beaumont's notorious fortune hunter—dismissed for his unpredictability by many of Pew's peers—did not do too much damage to his or Sun's reputation.[47]

When all was said and done, Higgins came through for Sun, though not without some hand-wringing on Pew's part. Flush with cash after the Spindletop strike, Higgins had spent hundreds of thousands of dollars buying land around emerging production sites. He knew that other companies would come calling to acquire parts of his domain. Pew thus found the negotiations difficult but rewarding, and over the course of three years he came to rely on Higgins's savvy to help Sun gain an advantage. Writing to headquarters in 1904, Pew spoke of yet another potential deal with the Prophet. "This is the place Mr. Higgins offered us to drill," Pew explained, "the best showing of anything I have seen anywhere. I have been trying to keep pretty close to him and have been advising him to keep everything quiet, and can no doubt get something out of him, at least." Though critical of Standard's surreptitiousness, Pew nevertheless practiced his own subterfuge when the stakes were high. Sun committed to the hush-hush plan for further development of the area in question (Barbers Hill, between Beaumont and Houston); yet in subsequent correspondence Pew admitted frustration. "Mr. Higgins has himself . . . been trying to put down wells there for a couple of years, but is thoroughly impractical and has not made a success of getting a well done yet." He voiced other annoyances, such as with Higgins's untrustworthy drilling equipment and constant stalls, overcommitments to investors, and inability "to get anything done." Pew and Sun's patience paid off—if not spectacularly at the modest-producing Barbers Hill, then certainly back at Spindletop. Even as other wells there began to falter by early 1904, the ones that Pew acquired from Higgins continued to flow. Whatever their hesitancies, Pew and Sun officials could not help but be grateful for their eccentric ally. By 1905, Sun was a well-established entity in and around Beaumont because of its almost exclusive relationship with the man who started it all.[48]

Pew also dealt with a handful of other enterprising capitalists in the area—"some of the best people in town," he explained—Beaumont's George Carroll types. While enamored of the independent streak that pierced the Spindletop phenomenon, the Presbyterian businessman ultimately gravitated toward entrepreneurs who shared his preference for good civic, church, and corporate governance. His membership in Beaumont's esteemed Central Presbyterian Church, to which he tithed thousands of dollars during the course of a decade, placed him in the heart of the town's illustrious class. Sitting next to him in the pews were several leading oil executives, including chief officers of the Guffey-Gulf and Texaco operations, all of whom gave just as generously to the church in hopes it would help anchor the community.[49]

Pew also preferred his peers' way of building strong companies through steady innovation of technology and careful streamlining of well-to-refinery operations. Early in Sun's Texas venture he transformed Sun Station into a model hub of oil containment and transportation. He also encouraged the use of new drill bits that promised to revolutionize the industry, one of which his foreman created to guide his drill through craggy soil and 134 feet of rock. The bit became the company's new weapon. News of it spread to Walter Sharp and Howard Hughes, who copied and refined the device, selling their "Sharp-Hughes roller bit" for hefty profits. (Hughes would go on to start his own oil tool company and build a fortune for his more infamous son to assume.) For Pew, such encounters confirmed his belief that the best way to build a Texas oil empire was to forge relationships with oilmen of like minds and temperaments, fostering creativity and a patience for development within company ranks.[50]

By 1905, Sun Oil had joined Texaco and Gulf as one of the rising stars of the independent sector, all thanks to Spindletop. To be sure, none of these burgeoning companies enjoyed free rein. They faced challenges from dozens of smaller start-ups and also watched warily as Shell and Standard shifted attention to the region. Still, Texaco and Gulf in particular expanded aggressively. They built refineries throughout the Southwest, extended distribution and marketing capacities nationally and internationally, and moved into Oklahoma when fields there erupted in the second half of the decade. Absent in Oklahoma and committed to Marcus Hook as its refining center, Sun experienced slower progress. Yet it too redefined the entire industry with its success. Soon the "independent" moniker would no longer apply merely to smaller companies that opposed Standard; rather it would be a descriptor of the degree to which they were (or were not) vertically integrated, of capacity rather than conviction. By that measure, Gulf and Texaco would soon evolve into "major" oil companies, Sun into a "mid-major." Yet, Sun and the Pews would continue to wield the "independent" label proudly, with conviction, as evidence of their close association with Texas and, more importantly, their staunch adherence to the core philosophy of independence at the company's and the family's core.[51]

WHATEVER LABEL THEY assumed, the oil companies that emerged out of the Spindletop bonanza did so armed with enough clout to collectively rival Rockefeller. Already by 1900, Standard's grip on domestic oil had weakened. Its hegemony in Pennsylvania meant less now that the region's production was in steep decline, and its relatively small footprints out west meant that any attempts to attain control there would face considerable odds. The survivors of Standard's early onslaught were evolving into powerbrokers, able to dictate the terms of their existence.

While Texas provided the greatest spark for independents' ascent, California was also critical to their long-term prospects, thanks in large part to Lyman Stewart and Union Oil. The always-charging Stewart followed up on corporate restructurings he orchestrated in 1899 by vaulting Union onto a new plane of operational expansion. He was aided by the 1900 discovery of oil in the Kern-McKittrick region of the Central Valley. The strike did not measure up to oil eruptions in Southeast Texas, but it was as momentous for Union as Spindletop was for Sun. Union's production rose dramatically, as did its involvement in refining and transportation. Signaling those gains was Union's construction of a tanker named the *Santa Paula*, which began shipping crude out of the region with profitable returns. Under Stewart's headship and the increasing involvement of his son William, Union became the integrated corporation he had once dreamed it would be. Union's enlarged capacities, like Sun's, now belied its reputation as a family-run, independent corporation. Yet, like the Pews, the Stewarts refused to see themselves in any other terms; in their eyes, they still stood alongside and for the small producer.[52]

Standard Oil's advances reinforced the sense of pride—and insecurity—that the "independent" label prescribed for those who bore it. In 1900, Standard officially planted its flag in the Golden State by purchasing the Pacific Coast Oil Company, eager to make up for lost time. In 1906, Standard renamed Pacific Coast Oil and merged it with Standard Oil of Iowa to create Standard Oil of California (Socal). Lyman Stewart once again grew anxious. His pugilistic brother and fellow Union Oil stakeholder Milton Stewart now seemed resigned too. "Am very sorry those fellows are arranging to get a foothold in California production," he wrote from Titusville, "for it means control of the business, just as in this country, I fear." A few months later, during Union's breakthrough in the Central Valley, Lyman expressed further exasperation. Standard agents, he surmised, had infiltrated Union's ranks with intentions to sabotage. "They [Standard Oil Company] have made the statement recently," he told Milton, "that they knew all about the details of our business as they had their agents in our employ." "In any event," he sulked, "we will" have a "nice plant to sell to the Standard when they absorb this coast." Lyman again attributed his woes to a failure to uphold his contract with God. For some time now, he noted, Union had let its morals slip by allowing men to work on Sunday and imbibe in its camps. Since arriving in California, he had done what he could to recruit preachers for his worksites, succeeding even at securing a full-time salary for a pastor at the company's Torrey Camp. Yet it was not enough, and he was wracked with guilt, which he expressed to a colleague. "Confidentially, I sometimes feel that the Lord is having a controversy with us because of our Sabbath work and also because of our employing intemperate men in such responsible positions as that of drilling and pumping wells in such territory as we have to work."[53]

Despite their doubts, Lyman and Milton concluded that they needed to forge ahead in faith and business. Earlier cycles of uncertainty had frequently thrust Lyman into a paralyzing fatalism. In the face of the new challenges, though, he grew bold and determined. Dispensational premillennialism, his theology of the end times, laid out human history as an elaborate pattern of epochs, distinct phases of development in which God dealt differently with his people. On another level, the early 1900s represented a new dispensation in his life and career.

That was certainly so on the business side of things. Anticipating Standard's encroachment, Stewart pushed Union to continue plumbing the Kern-McKittrick pool, acquire additional land, build a pipeline, and integrate more quickly. By 1905, Union could boast a brand-new refinery in Bakersfield, in the heart of the valley's oil fields. The timing was propitious because just a few years later Union would strike it big again, further necessitating the storage and transportation infrastructure that the company had committed to. In 1910, Stewart arranged control of an extant well site in the Lake View district of the Central Valley. His payout came on March 14, 1910, this time on a Spindletop scale. At the point that Union's team reached 2,200 feet, the earth shuddered, spewing oil and gas skyward. An oil chronicler would later write that the "blast was so terrible that the derrick disappeared into the crater it made. The column of oil, 20 feet in diameter, gushed higher." The crew chief could barely be heard yelling ecstatically, "My God, we've cut an artery down there."[54]

Meanwhile, Union pursued opportunities across the California state line. Like his father, William Stewart was a gambler who wanted to grow the family company aggressively, well beyond the bounds of its California compounds. "We wish to urge on you the pressing necessity for most thorough and vigorous efforts to secure the necessary funds to extend our business," he wrote Lyman matter-of-factly. At William and Lyman's urging, Union's chief foreign representative searched for wider production, transportation, and marketing potentials. While overseeing Union's move into the country's Pacific Northwest, he also struck a deal with the American-Hawaiian Steamship Company by which Union would supply it with 500,000 barrels of fuel oil per year. The arrangement built on earlier agreements, brokered by Lyman Stewart, to supply oil to the Oahu Railway and Land Company and a few Hawaiian sugar refineries.[55]

The territories the Stewarts most coveted, though, were in Asia and South America. Union's lead representative was charged with forging connections in those locales, even as he pressed for Union to expand eastward toward Europe as well. One of his biggest coups came through a nifty manipulation of White House policy. Union's agent managed to convince President Theodore Roosevelt that a pipeline running along the Panama Canal, which Roosevelt was scrambling to complete, would be good for the American oil business. Union—not Standard—won the right to lay that pipeline, thereby securing the right to stretch its influence beyond California to terrains under Standard control. Much as the Lake View strike served notice that Union was California oil's true powerhouse, the Panama Canal deal proved that its international prospects were gleaming too. Thanks to all these victories, Union approached the 1910s as the "dominant producer" in the West. It was, as one historian notes, the only oil corporation outside Standard Oil "to have maintained a continuous independent existence since 1890 as a major integrated oil company."[56]

As Lyman Stewart's corporate achievements mounted, his spiritual life grew in ways that further suggested he had crossed a threshold. Convinced that disrespect for his Lord had tainted the moral fabric of his business, he set out to undo the damage. In a 1901 letter to one of his managers, he demanded a halt to all Sunday work. Labor on the Sabbath was "unfair" to Union stockholders who uphold the Lord's Day, he explained, before adding, "It is also unfair and unjust to yourself because there can be no true success in business without the Lord's blessing." To a superintendent he laid down the law on alcohol: "Many corporations have found it necessary to adopt a rule not to employ men who drink or who even frequent drinking places. This will be the rule in the future for the Union Oil Company's employees." In the name of good business and good behavior, Stewart was no longer going to allow hedonism to creep into his ranks. Fresh reports from men on the ground appeared on his desk to assure him that the level of drinking among his workers was dropping precipitously. If heaven seemed to be shining on him again, he felt it was due to his determination to shore up his relationship with God.[57]

All the while, the oilman's devotion to church and charity intensified. With his son taking on heavier burdens of company leadership, Stewart channeled more of his energies toward philanthropic causes.

Throughout the 1900s he remained committed to supporting religious agencies like the YMCA and the Union Rescue Mission, as well as missionaries affiliated with his church. Much like Rockefeller, Stewart was inundated with financial requests from individuals (an estimated 10,000 during his lifetime). Many of them tugged at his heart strings with pleas for help in evangelizing the world. Stewart also grew eager to apply the teachings of premillennialism to a close reading of current events. He regularly attended prophetic conferences and rigorously read *The Truth*, the movement's leading journal. "This magazine had providentially fallen into my hands," he would tell his children, "and I found it exceedingly instructive, and particularly helpful because of its sounding continually a note of warning to . . . apostasy." A relatively late convert to the millenarian movement, the spiritually hungry oilman felt that he needed to make up for lost time before time ran out.[58]

Wanting to toil for Christ in advance of the world's end, Stewart tested ways of making his charity count. One of his first experiments involved Occidental College, the local Presbyterian institution of higher learning. Stewart was angered by the liberalization of American higher education, something he saw epitomized by Rockefeller's University of Chicago ("the greatest school of infidelity in America," he charged). He also believed that a Bible-based school like Occidental was essential to establishing Los Angeles as the beating heart of the emerging American (and global) economy. To its president, John W. Baer, he stated his belief "that a great commercial-industrial empire is to be built on this coast." Of utmost importance to its success would be the "strong spiritual foundations . . . laid substantially by having our young people thoroughly instructed in the Scripture." When, in 1906, Baer asked Stewart to contribute to the school, the oilman pledged $3,000 per year. But as the school started teaching a curriculum Stewart considered secular, the donor contemplated taking his money elsewhere. By 1911, his relationship with Baer was frayed, and in 1914 Stewart canceled his pledge, writing his brother in explanation that "it seems to be a sin for a Christian to contribute to the support of Occidental." Utterly convinced that apostasy was seeping through society, he ratcheted up his charitable giving but now sought greater design and control of its use. A 1911 letter to a pastor friend signaled his intentions: "it certainly is possible to give some Scripture portion to every person in the world during the next ten years, if the Lord's people awake to their opportunity, and I believe that if the work is not accomplished in the next ten or twenty years that it will never be done during this Dispensation." In seeking to revolutionize his philanthropy, Stewart would, in a way, follow in the footsteps of his archfoe, John D. Rockefeller.[59]

A DECADE AFTER Spindletop, Stewart and his cohort of independent oilmen found themselves harnessing a freedom and power that had eluded them for forty years. From oil's awakening in Pennsylvania to the end of the nineteenth century, the hegemony of the Rockefellers in the corporate and churchly realms had seemed unassailable. Now, the Rockefellers and their company were on the defensive. With the dawn of the gusher age and the succession of oil booms in Texas and California, emergent companies such as Gulf, Texaco, Sun, and Union started to close the gap in production, refining, and marketing. Whereas at the close of the 1800s Standard controlled 90 percent of all refining capacity in the United States, by 1910 it could claim only 63 percent and independent companies 37 percent. While still unmatched in its integration of production, refining, and distribution, Standard approached the 1910s on a downward slide relative to the upstart companies of Texas and California. "Though certainly through no choice of its own," one oil chronicler recounts, Standard "was now forced to accustom itself to the distasteful reality of significant and lasting domestic competition." Union and Sun, virtual twins in their corporate profiles, lagged behind Texaco and Gulf as competition to Standard. Yet they all had reason to be excited about their roles in challenging big oil.[60]

And buoyed independents suddenly found politicians, the courts, and the public more willing to listen to their pleas for assistance in the fight against the Standard behemoth. But the Pews, Stewarts, and their allies in the empowered independent oil sector wanted more than to be heard. They sought revenge. By 1910, and with increasing breadth in the decade that followed, Standard became the hunted, and oilmen of J. Edgar Pew and Lyman Stewart's stock, the hunters. The struggle would play out in the realms of politics as well as business, and more quietly in the realms of philanthropy and Protestant missions, at home and across the Pacific Ocean. It would involve some familiar voices of dissent, none more important than Ida Tarbell's. New voices would be heard too, including that of J. Howard Pew, the incoming president of Sun Oil, who along with his cousin J. Edgar would help usher the company into a new era.[61]

One veteran of Texas crude who would not be heard was Patillo Higgins, the wildcatter who started it all. In the years that followed the excitement of Spindletop and his work with J. Edgar Pew, Higgins carved out a life that strayed little from the one he had enjoyed before 1901. He continued to dream big about oil's redemptive potentials. Setting his sights on San Antonio, where he would later settle, he imagined finding oil under the city and linking it to a deep-water port next to Aransas Pass. The port would be its own city, a planned community he would call Higginstown. He also continued to write. In 1917 he published *Oil Shark Net Building*, a book excoriating big oil refining companies for "get[ting] rid of the small independent oil refineries" and taking advantage of the consuming public. He lambasted major oil corporations for "running over our fields, gutting them of the best oils," and using it all "to supply foreign countries." The diatribe was in keeping with the antimonopoly politics of the day, but no one took Higgins seriously enough to listen. And he continued to prospect for oil, always his primary obsession. As the Spindletop field began to deplete and decline in the mid-1900s, Higgins explored far and wide throughout Southeast Texas, hitting modest returns in some locations, missing out on opportunities in others, and most of the time carrying heavy debt. He started and folded several new companies—including a failed project with George Carroll and the short-lived Wonder Oil Company—but mostly kept plodding along on his own. In the late 1920s he struck oil at Barbers Hill, which, as one of his biographers asserts, "finally freed [him] from the financial shackles under which he had labored most of his life." Even still, the riches he garnered were never substantial, just enough for his family to worry less.[62]

Higgins did find other fulfillments in his fifty years of life after Spindletop. Family was one of them. On the heels of Spindletop Higgins and his mother used some of their oil earnings to support people in need and adopted several children, a majority being young girls. Even though he was their legal guardian, Higgins—as he was wont to do—developed a fondness for one of them. When Annie John turned eighteen, the forty-five-year-old Higgins announced his love for her. In the fall of 1907 he proposed, and a few months later the two were married. Having gone to the Baptist church as Patillo's daughter, Annie left as his wife. Soon thereafter the Higginses had their first child, a girl. Patillo called her Gladys.[63]

*part two*

---

# CARBON GOSPELS

Oil derricks and tanks surround a church in 1930s Kilgore, East Texas.

PHOTOGRAPHED BY RUSSELL LEE, LIBRARY OF CONGRESS PRINTS AND PHOTOGRAPHS DIVISION.

# CHAPTER FOUR

# Trust Busting

W hile the Pews and Stewarts were building their empires, Ida Tarbell was tearing down another. In the early 1900s, the muckraker from Titusville burst onto the national stage with a raw passion she shared with oilmen who struggled in the titan's shadow. That shadow was her precise concern when she secretly traveled with a sketch artist to Cleveland's Euclid Baptist Church in the fall of 1903. It was the first time she would measure up close the countenances of a person whose actions had caused her father's downfall. What she witnessed surprised her. The Machiavellian prince she had supposed him turned out to be, in her estimation, a pathetic imp.

For two hours she watched as John D. Rockefeller served in his public role as deacon and Sunday School teacher, and she marveled at the authority he wielded in those capacities. Listening to him, she heeded a "pleased and satisfied" devotee. "His talks . . . are uttered in a natural and rather agreeable voice, and with evident sincerity of feeling," she noted. The oilman's oratory quickened as he turned to parables about the price and benefit of serving God and giving on his behalf. "You must put something in if you would take something out," he told his audience, drawing on financial lessons of his life. Listening to the layman wax eloquent, Tarbell wondered how he so easily glanced over memories of those he trampled while making his money. She pondered, too, the inadequacy of his philanthropy as repayment for such loss. "May not Mr. Rockefeller come to see finally that the injustice and wrong it takes to build such a fortune as his are only equaled by the weakened manhood and the stimulated greed engendered in its spending?" Condemnation came next. "And he calls his great organization a benefaction, and points to his church-going and charities as proof of his righteousness. To the man of straight-forward nature the two will not tally. This is supreme wrong-doing cloaked by religion."[1]

But make no mistake, she added, pointing to his profile: Rockefeller *was* paying for his sins. "It may even be that it is because Mr. Rockefeller has begun to see vaguely that he will never, never be able to give away enough to drown the wrong he has done that his face has taken on its terrible pathos." Several features struck her as proof of a failed individual: expressionless eyes that "see everything and reveal nothing"; lips like a "slit" slanting to "a melancholy angle"; a bald head with "stripped away . . . eyelashes and eyebrows"; in total, an amphibious looking face, "dead, like a devil-fish." Then there was his demeanor. When ensconced in the audience, Rockefeller occupied the church's last row, anxious to protect his back. His head swiveled like a lizard's, nodding at the preacher's word, then wrenching to see who was beside or behind him. "It is pitiful, so pitiful," Tarbell pondered, "that one cannot watch John Rockefeller sit through a church service and ever cease to feel that he is one of the saddest objects in the world." Artist George Varian hurriedly captured that sadness in black and white. Overall, Tarbell concluded, Rockefeller was a ghastly figure out of keeping with his reputation for conquering aggression. "This is the oldest man in the world, a living mummy."[2]

After digesting the scene, Tarbell and Varian quietly exited the church. Moved by the experience, she retreated to record her thoughts, torn by a question of fairness: Should she expose the repulsiveness of this man or tread lightly? She decided to take the harder line.[3]

Tarbell published her thoughts about Rockefeller in a 1905 issue of *McClure's Magazine*, the journal with which she was closely associated. The release of her character sketch, accompanied by Varian's artwork, caused a stir; known for authoring essays that blended opinion with data, Tarbell here offered only opinion—biting and layered with attacks. Moreover, her article took the oil titan to task in a different way, not just for his business practices but also for his churchgoing and charity, features of his life that seemed less odious. In justification, publisher Samuel McClure insisted, "The works of a man's life . . . cannot be separated. It is the intimate and intricate relation of the Rockefeller Business Code with the Rockefeller Religious Code that makes it imperative the public study the man and his influence." For her part, Tarbell showed no compunction. Perhaps it was the fact that her father passed away just as she was finishing the piece. This was her chance to vent. But it was also an extension of her transformed theological convictions. Rockefeller was not only guilty of greed but was also emblematic of a hypocrisy that had crept into the Christianity of her youth. In no small way, she saw her stabs at him as an opportunity to level charges against the religious system he helped prop up.[4]

Tarbell's exposé came at a key phase of a public war on Rockefeller and Standard Oil, one that she fought alongside independent oilmen, who she believed still stood for her father's values. By then, Tarbell was the queen of muckraking journalists, morally charged scribes who turned their fervor against the Rockefeller machine as an affront to everything decent about American Christian democracy. Aiding Tarbell were wildcatters like the Pews and Stewarts, who saw her as their voice, their weapon, their way to shift public opinion and influence the establishment. Even as they labored to compete with Standard on a more level corporate field, they also cheered as Tarbell brought the oil baron to his knees through a succession of printed words. Rockefeller hardly stood a chance. Tarbell and her allies would herald the Supreme Court's 1911 antitrust ruling to dismantle Standard as a political triumph and vindication of their worldview. Rockefeller and Standard would see it as simply another beginning.

And in a way it would be exactly that. In the decade that followed the takedown of the Standard Trust, major and independent oil began to compete in the realm of charity; henceforth the politics of allocating wealth would rival the politics of acquiring it as the pivotal rupture between the two sides. Eager to extend the giving impulses of John D. Rockefeller Sr., yet frustrated with conventional strategies of corporate and Christian evangelization, the Rockefellers decided to build a modern philanthropy geared to global humanitarianism. Swiftly, the individualistic, salvific emphases of Senior's faith gave way to the ecumenical, internationalist ideas of his son. Working with friendly clerics, John Rockefeller Jr. made the Rockefeller Foundation and his own charitable initiatives an unassailable force for progressive ideals. Animated by a theology that encouraged adjustment of biblical understanding and application to modern intellectual developments and by an expressed confidence in the human ability to transform the world through scientific methods and an optimistic faith, Junior came to epitomize the modernist wing of his church. By embracing those principles, he helped set the stage for a modernist-fundamentalist clash that would erupt in China before ricocheting back to America.

The flare-up, though, was largely due to Lyman Stewart and his fundamentalist allies, who began to construct a web of alternative religious institutions aimed at offsetting the Rockefellers' expansive philanthropic ambitions. Inspired by *The Fundamentals*, statements of doctrinal orthodoxy that Stewart's Union Oil fortune sponsored, these traditionalists were determined to uphold the primacy of an active, all-powerful God, the authority of an infallible Bible, and a scriptural injunction to evangelize lost souls. Stewart did not speak for all his peers in independent oil when he declared himself a fundamentalist. The doctrinal strains of his brand of Protestantism would remain a subset, albeit an increasingly important one, of the broader cult of wildcat religiosity to which he belonged. Yet, even in his sectarianism, he reflected wider confluences of thought within his sector and its culture, notions that underscored the right of individuals to manage the inevitable mysteries and volatilities of their chaotic world as free agents, accountable only to God. The collateral damage of Stewart and his brethren's oil-fueled animosity against the Rockefeller worldview would be a permanently fractured Protestant Church.

TARBELL'S SEARING PROFILE of Rockefeller in 1905 came on the heels of an intense few years during which her indignation toward the man grew exponentially. Her ire was infectious and soon filtered through the ranks of a reform-minded citizenry bent on curtailing big business and challenging the injustices of the period.

On a basic level, Tarbell's personal assault on the churchgoing Rockefeller grew out of her wrestling with God and the ghosts of her youth, which came to a head during her stay in turn-of-the-century Paris. There, amid the flourishing of Paris's bohemian lifestyle, Tarbell discovered a world of infinite complexity and opportunity to pursue the career in composition that had budded with her early work at *The Chautauquan*. Freelance writing was her primary means of putting food on the table, and eking out an existence was difficult, but over time she enjoyed successes, with several of her articles gracing the pages of popular American dailies. While writing, the perennially curious *femme travailleuse* also attended lectures at the Sorbonne. She delighted in lessons on historical investigation and narrative writing and applied them to her immediate goal of crafting a book about Madame Roland, the French revolutionary who lost her life to the guillotine. For all the enticements of Paris, Tarbell also probed her own comprehension of humanity and the divine. Far removed from the confining Pennsylvania valley of her youth, she pressed the intellectual limits of her faith. Ironically, a Methodist sense of duty spurred some of the reevaluation. Writing home, she assured her parents that despite all the signs of her enjoyment in France—jaunts to quaint chateau towns, meanders through museums and galleries—she was staying true to their values. "You mustn't think I am getting Frenchy in my morals because I do things here which I don't at home. I only do these things to see what the French life is really like." On that count she taught Sunday School and played the organ at the nondenominational American Chapel of Paris. But those very commitments actually pushed her further beyond the theological comforts of Titusville. After attending a service at the chapel, she expressed frustration to her brother with orthodox Christianity: "I am just home from church where I heard a senseless sermon on heaven. . . . If people who preached would only try to give a little more incentive to stay on earth and behave themselves for the sake of behaving themselves, instead of holding up heaven as a reward of merit, I'd have more hope for the church."[5]

Tarbell's admissions hinted at a metamorphosis in her theological sensibilities, which positioned her further on the edge of mainstream Christianity but never in complete opposition to it, an ambiguity she welcomed. In her personal encounter with Christianity she now traded Methodism's emphases on outward displays of a transformed heart for the inner focus of Quakerism. Staying silently in touch with the divine and "let[ting] it work its way with me" became her modus vivendi. The highly devotional Tarbell's evolving theology also demanded disciplined yet flexible thought. "Pure religion forces no man's spirit," she emphasized, for "its very essence requires that the spirit be free . . . for learning what the divine has to teach it." The creeds and ceremonies forced upon devotees had become counterproductive to that essential task, she asserted, and she lamented the concomitant substitution of honest grappling with blind devotion. Particularly galling to her was the theological infighting she witnessed between modernist and fundamentalist Protestants. Those debates "affect me as having nothing to do with my religion," she announced; "they belong to that effort, always so strong among men, to formulate their thoughts and feelings into a creed, which those who do not know it or deny it are to be forced or persuaded to accept." Tarbell saw sincere, godly pursuit of intellectual truth as an exercise in humility, in coming to terms with human fallibility, something schismatic ideologues ignored. "Of course this leaves me a tiny atom in the universe," she explained scientifically; yet "as a matter of fact, that is what I am, my only business being to be a sound atom, one that works with and not against the beneficent spirit in things—there lies my immortality."[6]

Tarbell's fresh gospel also promoted action, not passivity. Monastic in its espousal of quiet contemplation, her faith nevertheless rested on the presupposition that its strength could only be evidenced in application for public good and in altering social systems of wrong. On this score, Tarbell maintained respect for institutional Christianity, even as she nudged Christians toward all-embracing awareness. "According to the Christian system as it is laid out in the Bible," she asserted, "society should be a brotherhood . . . of men of all colors. Moreover, it takes men as they are, pagan, Christian, idolator [sic], scoffer, Catholic and Jew, and it lays down the set of principles which are essential for their living together in a just and peaceful society." To Tarbell, the essential precepts of Christianity could be distilled down to the beatitudes—the construction of a "brotherhood of man" through commitment to core virtues: "hungering and thirsting after righteousness; merciful, pure in heart, meek in spirit, a peace-maker, willing even to be persecuted and reviled for righteousness' sake." As much as it sounded like salvation through rote, Tarbell's blueprint in fact held that redemption could only be realized through citizens' own sincerest yearnings for spiritual wholeness. "This conception of men in their relations to one another," she concluded, "is not the fruit of doctrinal struggle, church organization, of theologies however sound and essential, but rather of the travail of the spirit." By that she meant it would only come from the accumulated spiritual capital of each individual's "striving in solitude and silence to enter into a fuller understanding of the divine."[7]

It still had years of maturing ahead of it, but Tarbell's theology was formed enough by the early 1890s to lend her Paris work an ethical edge. While other freelance journalists of the day tended to write tales of the rich and famous in hopes of gaining inroads with editors, Tarbell gravitated toward accounts of the working class—the dignity she saw represented among rank-and-file city dwellers and the injustices that they and their counterparts faced throughout the Western world. Be it in western Pennsylvania or in Paris, she wanted to be the voice of the poor. Armed with new methods of research and writing, she gave sharper accounts of that class and drew more revealing insights, and as she continued to wrestle with theological issues that had long racked her with uncertainty, guilt, and excitement, the prose assumed a moralistic bent.[8]

It was that very combination that made her attractive to an entrepreneurial publisher with his own moral bent named Samuel (S. S.) McClure, who watched with interest as Tarbell's dispatches made their way across the Atlantic Ocean to American press outlets. In 1892, McClure set up a meeting with Tarbell in Paris, wanting to see if she would contribute to the publication he was starting: *McClure's Magazine.* The publisher was conceptualizing a new form of journalism that combined sensational reporting of society's most terrible blights with technical innovation (the accompaniment of photography, for instance), stirring narrative, and passion for universal improvement through the provision of information. McClure sought to agitate the public into action by raking up its immoral muck. He was impressed with Tarbell's inquisitiveness as well as the education in writing she had undertaken in Paris and thought she might be perfect for that task. For her part,

Tarbell was equally enthralled with her interlocutor's traits. "His utter simplicity, forthrightness, his enthusiasm and confidence captivated me," she said. Thus was born a relationship that would soon redefine American journalism and industry.[9]

That relationship budded in the following years. In 1894, Tarbell formally accepted McClure's offer and returned to the United States to set up shop in New York City, home to the magazine. By the end of the 1890s, Tarbell had completed a number of important essays, including a biography of Abraham Lincoln, which was serialized over several months and then released as a two-volume book in 1900. Her next assignment was the defining one of her career. At first she began mapping out a study of Standard Oil's global influence, in particular its ability to earn huge profits through exportation of its product without incurring much of the risk involved in the transportation and distribution of the material. Upon her return to the United States, she visited Titusville briefly, at which time she gleaned more insight from family into the unequal workings of the oil industry. She also took time to reacquaint herself with the devastation wrought by oil on places like Pithole, now abandoned. She decided to dig into her own past and come to terms with the specter that had always hung over her life. A more expansive history of Standard Oil was in order, she decided.[10]

Tarbell's timing was impeccable. In 1901 American society was fully immersed in the Progressive era, a period during which citizens coalesced in a multitude of reform movements and interest groups in an effort to solve the social and economic plights of a rapidly modernizing society. McClure's journalists—men like Upton Sinclair and Lincoln Steffens, who joined Tarbell on the circuit—added to the urgency of the period by revealing the darkest aspects of a nation undergoing rapid and overwhelming change. No threat seemed more daunting to US citizens than that of big business and the seemingly unlimited freedom large corporations enjoyed to unleash their interests on the mass public. In 1890, US Congress had passed the Sherman Antitrust Act, which forbade companies from conspiring to restrain trade, secure monopolies, and commandeer excessive power in their respective industries. Though it would take time for the federal government to act on this law, the 1890s saw several states use antitrust legislation to file lawsuits against large corporations. Standard was often on the receiving end of that litigation, including in Texas, where in 1894 Governor James Hogg and his attorney general invoked the state's antitrust law (passed in 1889) to sue the large oil company. The investigation into Standard's practices of price fixing and rebates resulted in several indictments (Rockefeller escaped unscathed). As the new century dawned, concerned citizens were clamoring for more of that type of action. Tarbell's investigation of Standard Oil would have a ready-made audience—provided she could craft a compelling story.

For two years, Tarbell tore into the files—newspaper clippings, corporate summaries, courtroom records, and her own interviews—to construct an unassailable case against the Rockefeller monopoly. Her model was Henry Demarest Lloyd's 1894 book *Wealth Against Commonwealth*, an exposé of Standard Oil that helped initiate an era of anti-Rockefeller journalism. Like Lloyd, Tarbell was determined to reveal all the schemes and contrivances that greased Rockefeller's conquest. Yet, where Lloyd wrote out of an almost irrational determination to punish, Tarbell approached her task with greater balance, in hopes of convincing those who needed it rather than simply preaching to the converted. And with a daring that Lloyd lacked, she reached out to Standard's own men. In nothing short of a coup (assisted by mutual acquaintance Mark Twain), she convinced Henry Rogers, one of Standard's powerful executives, to supply her with a firsthand account of Standard's business practices. Over the course of 1902, she met regularly with the oilman. The fact that Rogers was a former independent oilman who had lived in Rouseville, Pennsylvania, at the same time as Tarbell (and knew her father) helped ease the conversation, as did their shared circumspection. Their concerns about Christianity and the church—Rogers's impatience with his family's Presbyterian pastor, Tarbell's with mainline religion as a whole—helped forge their union and keep them talking about matters beyond the boardroom. "We parted on very good terms after this discussion of our mutual religious view," Tarbell penned on one occasion, "and he gave me a cordial invitation to come back." From her dealings with Rogers, she gained knowledge of Standard's manipulation of the railroads, surveillance strategies, price-fixing measures, and range of tactics utilized to suppress competition and secure its monopoly. By the fall of 1902, she was ready to start sharing that expansive insight with her reading public.[11]

The first installment of Tarbell's exposé appeared in *McClure's* in November 1902. For the next two years the magazine published a total of nineteen chapters, subsequently combined in a mammoth two-volume book called *The History of the Standard Oil Company*, released in 1904. Readers applauded its fearlessness. No one had ever laid bare the calculations and corruption of a major American corporation with such shrewdness, such incisive yet entertaining prose. And to do so as a pioneering woman in a profession of men made the accomplishment all the more impressive. Tarbell was famous. "Her pen has made the name of Miss Ida M. Tarbell a familiar household word throughout the land," offered one enthused reviewer. Samuel McClure marveled too, with a playful gibe: "You are today the most generally famous woman in America. People universally speak of you with such a reverence that I am getting sort of afraid of you."[12]

It was her words themselves that thrust Tarbell into the limelight. Hers was a powerful case for why Rockefeller symbolized "all that was wrong in national life." There was no denying her contempt for the man; she wore it openly in her running, biting commentary with Rogers about Rockefeller's hypocrisy ("Now, Miss Tarbell, that isn't a Christian remark," he would chuckle) and in her prose, which came peppered with scorn. Her short two-part character sketch of Rockefeller, researched in 1903 but not released until 1905, allowed her the chance to voice that indignation in full. In truth, Tarbell had been hesitant to visit Rockefeller's church. "It seemed unwise, like spying," she later recalled. But it was too difficult to resist. And in the end her visit to Cleveland's leading Baptist tabernacle proved cathartic in a way, a last purge of her Rockefeller preoccupation. Later, when looking back on the days surrounding her Standard Oil publications and drafting an outline for her autobiography, Tarbell admitted she almost let the entire affair get the better of her. "I must have something on muckraking," she jotted down in her notes. "Here confession will be good for the soul. The last thing that I was through the Standard Oil Company [affair] was a muck-raker. Having that formula there was a period when I was in danger of becoming one. My inability to let go of the Standard Oil; the obsession that I had." Conflicted or not, when Tarbell released her written assessments of Rockefeller and his company to an awaiting audience, she hit the mark; as far as a vast majority of Americans were concerned, she had unveiled the oil emperor, putting all his warts and neuroses in clear view, and sent a warning signal to the nation that his type must no longer rule.[13]

But she offered another message as well. Tarbell's treatment of Rockefeller came couched in a romanticized view of her protagonists—independent oilmen like her father, who scraped and clawed for a living and, in her mind, upheld America's founding principles. In that spirit, she did not condemn petrocapitalism as much as she petitioned to clean it up. "Life ran swift and ruddy and joyous in these men," she wrote glowingly of her oil-chasing heroes. "There was nothing they did not hope and dare." In contrast to Rockefeller, small-producing oilmen struck Tarbell as the last hope to recreate the "whole" and "perfect man in the Bible sense." This Bible-based viewpoint matched her conviction that oil-fueled capitalism had to remain egalitarian if it were to thrive. She theologized oil's land and labor too. Shaped by her eclectic readings in Methodist and Quaker theology and Christian socialism, she painted the struggle with Standard as one to protect the productive value of the producing being. "It is the partnership of the two—land and labor—which produces wealth," she declared. Because of big oil, she lamented, "labor had been made dependent on capital by capital's theft of the land which God gave to all." Tarbell wished for an ethic of possessive individualism that would endure among men and women like her parents, and on the soil they turned over, for generations to come.[14]

TARBELL'S EPIC ACCOUNT of the nation's capitalist kingpin helped inspire a chorus of Christian leaders and cultural critics who opened the new century with intensifying critiques of the Standard conglomerate. If in the 1890s Rockefeller was spared slightly from the heaviest of blows, by the early 1900s, fewer people were willing to hold back. That he was helping expand US interests abroad or constructing a university with global aspirations mattered little. The man and his kingdom, many believed now, were rotten to the core.

The moral critiques started to fly from all points on the political spectrum, but none were more damning than those lobbed by social-justice-minded clergymen and scholars. Among the former was Washington Gladden, a staunch advocate of the social gospel; for Gladden and his peers (clerics like Walter Rauschenbusch, lay activists like Jane Addams), true Christianity fostered an organic view of humanity, in which the spiritual and physical conditions of any one citizen were linked through union with an immanent God to the spiritual and physical condition of all citizens. Rauschenbusch wrote, "The ideal society is an organism, and the Christianizing of the social order must work toward an harmonious cooperation of all individuals for common social ends." In Rockefeller, Gladden saw a disregard for the collective good that undermined the New Testament. His strongest venting of anger toward the man came in 1905, just a few months after Tarbell's character sketch. Gladden publicly denounced his church's acceptance of "tainted money" from the oil king. His judgment referred to Rockefeller's $100,000 donation to the Congregational Board of Foreign Missions. The fact that the board itself solicited the donation and that Rockefeller wanted to honor his Congregational-raised wife with it did not register with Gladden. "The organization which he represents has been and now is a gigantic oppressor of the people," he trumpeted; his "great fortune has been built up ... by methods which are at war with the first principles of morality." As soon as Gladden's remarks hit the newsstand, they stuck: Rockefeller was dark as sin, the Congregational Church guilty by association.[15]

Among the scholars who leveled their charges against Rockefeller, meanwhile, were members of the University of Chicago's first-class faculty—the one that William Harper was so proud of recruiting. In 1899, renowned economist and sociologist Thorstein Veblen published his pathbreaking *The Theory of the Leisure Class*, which exposed the brutalities of the Gilded Age capitalist system and the comfortable numbness it created through promotion of "conspicuous consumption." In the age of Rockefeller, he posited, men and women derived meaning and identity by way of their purchasing power and their ability to escape menial labor. Veblen's was a clear attack on Rockefeller's luxury-obsessed class; yet he did not discomfort Rockefeller or university brass in quite the same way that Edward Bemis, another faculty member, managed to. Perhaps that was because Bemis's charges bridged two realms: Veblen's academic and Gladden's ecclesiastical. A young political scientist, Bemis entered tenuous turf when he wrote in favor of municipal gas ownership and railroad unions. That he offered his comments at a prominent city church, full of Christian donors, especially galled university brass. "Your speech at the First Presbyterian Church has caused me a great deal of annoyance," President Harper wrote his underling. Bemis was eventually fired.[16]

Independent oilmen joined the chorus of mounting anti-Rockefeller opinion. Considering his long-standing antipathies toward Standard, it was no surprise that Lyman Stewart was one of the most outspoken. Even as his Union Oil Company began to grow dynamically during the early 1900s, he did not shy away from opportunities to assume a public stand against Rockefeller and his conglomerate. Unlike social gospelers' critiques, however, Stewart's emerged from the orthodox side of the spectrum. Already in the 1890s, Rockefeller's close associates in the Baptist Church—men like Augustus Strong and William Harper—were coming under scrutiny from the staunchest of conservative Protestant clergy for their openness to modernist readings of scripture, which subjected it to historical and scientific scrutiny. The fact that Rockefeller aligned himself with representatives of an evolving liberal wing of the church did not sit well with Stewart. But he was just as agitated by the way Rockefeller seemed to flaunt his money in Christian guises. The fact that the University of Chicago was fast becoming "the greatest school of infidelity," as he liked to repeat to colleagues, came as no surprise to him, because the man behind it was himself an infidel, whose machinations in the corporate realm revealed his true shadiness. The "millions that Rockefeller is giving," Lyman told his brother, were an attempt to gloss over that. They also reflected the false notion that "the more we give the greater will be our dividends in salvation." The oil giant was trying to buy his way into heaven. While Stewart joined Gladden and Veblen in his critique of Rockefeller's materialism, then, he took a different tack by stressing the personal dimension of that failing: the oilman's heresy was not that he shunned society's collective good but that he flouted the essential truth of salvation through grace alone and that, by way of his extravagant giving, he told others that shallow works mattered more than what was in a person's heart. Stewart's concurrent attempts to shore up his company's moral standards by encouraging personal religiosity (through temperance, oil field preaching, and Sabbatarianism) marked yet another attempt to rebuke the Rockefeller way.[17]

Yet how else to fight the infidel? By 1906, when Standard Oil of California was officially formed, the Stewarts—Lyman, Milton, and William—jumped into another sphere of stinging critique and contestation: politics. They had never shied away from that realm. Throughout the 1890s, Lyman and his former partner, the politically connected Thomas Bard, had consistently lobbied the state legislature to protect the interests of independent producers against incursions by foreign oil (Peruvian, for instance) and regulations that threatened to diminish their returns and autonomy. Even after their final break played out in 1899, Stewart and Bard remained cordial. Stewart endorsed Bard's failed bid for reelection to the US Senate in 1904; Bard, in return, supported charities Stewart gravitated toward. Their political inclinations grew sharper in the early 1900s as the struggle with Standard reached a climax. Wanting allies in the fight, Union worked hard to woo small producers into a united front. Stewart ensured that they received copies of Henry Demarest Lloyd's *Wealth Against Commonwealth*, along with a personal note outlining Standard's evil acts. The producers chose to form their own alliance, absent Union, but the effort was only the beginning of Union's political activism. What had already occurred in Texas during the 1890s—legislative and legal pushback against Standard's monopoly—was about to escalate in California, and Stewart watched with keen interest as the drama began to unfold. But he did not simply watch; he stoked prevalent antimonopoly feelings among independents and the public with hopes of generating a formal political resolution.[18]

He also assisted the federal antitrust suit that began to target the Standard empire. By 1906, Washington was committed to a thorough investigation of the oil industry and Standard's dominance therein. Along with a supportive Congress, President Theodore Roosevelt sought to put some teeth into the federal antitrust law and enhance his own reputation as a trustbuster. James R. Garfield, the commissioner of corporations, was placed in charge, and his cross-country inquiry eventually brought him to California. The California inquest took nine months to complete and involved testimony from vital members of the Golden State's oil establishment. The testimonies painted a picture of collusion between Standard and the railroads and in general of Standard's predatory style. Stewart happily bore witness to those questionable strategies.

He also helped in an unintended way. Over the course of the previous decade he and his brother Milton had been courted and rejected by Standard Oil on a number of occasions, raising the level of angst he had about Union Oil's future: the question of whether to sell and give into the leviathan or press on was a constant worry in his life. Stewart now had the chance to glean some satisfaction from his troubled dealings with the big oil company. He submitted preliminary contracts to government lawyers that outlined Union's previous failed negotiations with Standard, who used them to argue that Standard had pursued business agreements with leading California oil producers that were designed to destroy competition. Stewart shied away, however, when asked for more documentation. Standard was already more than displeased with his submissions, and he feared reprisals. Stewart told the commission he would not hand over other records unless subpoenaed, which never occurred. But both his deliberate and his inadvertent support of the government's case helped draw Garfield's council closer to a decision that he and his fellow independents would cheer: Standard was in violation of trust laws.[19]

Behind the scenes, Lyman corresponded with Ida Tarbell, likely supplying the muckraker with firsthand facts to strengthen her case. Tarbell's *History of the Standard Oil Company* greatly pleased Stewart. "I have read Miss Tarbell's first chapter in the history of the Standard Oil Company," he wrote Milton, "and I see that she has laid a good foundation for establishing the fact that the Standard Oil Company did not build up the oil business but were simply parasites feeding upon an industry already established." To what level Stewart's words to Tarbell proved critical for her efforts to take down the trust is unclear, but considering his profile as one of the "ruddy and joyous" independent oilmen she romanticized in her treatise, they likely provided her sufficient encouragement to stay the course.[20]

That course led to Standard's political downfall on a national, not simply state, level. By the middle of 1907, Washington had seven suits pending against the conglomerate and its subsidiaries, which added to the list of states carrying out similar actions. Roosevelt, wielding his metaphorical "big stick" to beat down overbearing corporations, infused the onslaught with added emotion and drove the legal initiative to charge Standard under the Sherman Antitrust Act with trade violations that bolstered its monopoly at the cost of market competition. "Every measure for honesty in business that has been passed in the last six years, has been opposed by these men," he bellowed. Adding fire to the populist takedown was Democratic mainstay William Jennings Bryan, who asserted that Rockefeller needed to be put in jail. But it was government lawyer Frank B. Kellogg who shouldered the heavy lifting by presenting the government's main antitrust case to the federal court. Kellogg was a champion of independent oilmen, who in his eyes reflected a purer capitalism. He brought those sympathies with him into the two-year-long case that involved 444 witnesses (including, dramatically, Rockefeller himself), 1,371 exhibitions, and a final 14,495-page, twenty-one-volume report. In 1909, the federal court ruled Standard guilty and demanded mandatory dissolution. Off on a hunting trip in Africa (and no longer president), Roosevelt hailed the ruling with typical glee: this was "one of the most signal triumphs for decency which has been won in our country."[21]

Standard's legal team immediately filed an appeal with the US Supreme Court. When that failed on May 15, 1911, the sprawling company finally faced its fate. Much like Roosevelt, Bryan hailed the 1911 verdict, but he also used the occasion to scold the nation—Christians especially—for being slow to fight against Rockefeller-level greed, forcing government to do the dirty work. For her part, Tarbell wanted little to do with the drawn-out legal takedowns of the big company. She was moving on. As she would later admit, "I could have made a good killing out of that long investigation, for more than one editor asked me to analyze the testimony as it came along or give my impressions of the gentlemen who appeared on the witness stand. . . . But I had no stomach for it."[22]

Watching the winding process unfold, the Stewarts, Pews, and their peers *did* have a stomach for it and cheered. They wrote Kellogg with their appreciation. One producer made clear to him that the verdict was historic: "There is no doubt but that the independent interests have been aided and bettered by what the Government has done. The rigor of monopolistic control and abuses has been broken by the proceedings of the Government through all its departments, but especially through the dissolution suit." Standard appeared slain.[23]

THAT WAS HARDLY SO. "The business of the Standard Oil Company will go on as usual," Standard's lawyers casually noted after the Court's final verdict in 1911, "although changes will be made in order to comply with the statute law and the decisions affecting it." The most dramatic of those changes was the conglomerate's immediate dissolution into thirty-four different companies. The largest of them would be Standard Oil of New Jersey (Jersey Standard), preserving nearly 50 percent of Standard's total value; then Standard Oil of New York (Socony), with 9 percent; and in roughly descending order, Standard Oil of California (Socal), Standard Oil of Ohio (Sohio), and Standard Oil of Indiana (Indiana Standard, eventually renamed Amoco). Dismembered, the Standard monopoly may have appeared weak, but in fact the carnage represented a fresh start. Although they would remain linked to the networks forged earlier, Standard affiliates gained their liberation from headquarters in New York and a sense of rejuvenation. "We felt the change all along the line at once," a future executive at Indiana Standard admitted. "The young fellows were given the chance for which they had been chafing."[24]

And who would benefit most? Rockefeller. Even though he was encouraged to dump shares in Standard prior to dissolution in order to prevent inevitable losses, Rockefeller refused—he would stay loyal to the end. Following dissolution, stock shares in succeeding companies were distributed "pro rata" to Jersey Standard shareholders. Within a year of the 1911 Court ruling, stock for the various Standard spinoffs had doubled, and in one case (Indiana Standard), tripled. No one benefited more than the baron, who owned a quarter of all shares. His personal wealth rose by $200 million, making him the nation's first billionaire. Theodore Roosevelt would return to presidential politics in 1912. Once again he ran on an antitrust ticket, an easy proposition in the face of the Standard companies' new success. His blaring populist refrain sounded familiar: "The price of stock has gone up over one hundred percent, so that Mr. Rockefeller and his associates have actually seen their fortunes doubled. No wonder that Wall Street's prayer now is: 'Oh Merciful Providence, give us another dissolution.'"[25]

The year 1911 and the months that followed marked a fresh start for the Rockefeller family as well. For its patriarch, it was time to turn the corporate reins over to other men. John D. Rockefeller formally resigned in 1911, leaving John Archbold in charge of Jersey Standard. The decision came on the heels of a painful time; bad publicity weighed on him. At each stage of the antitrust controversy he had stayed engaged. Out front he did his best to offset the scathing image portrayed by Ida Tarbell, whom he derided with the moniker "Ida Tarbarrel" and called "that misguided woman." He presented himself in a softer light in his own autobiography, published in 1909 at the height of the federal court case, and hoped some friendly journalists would do the same. In that vein he sought to carefully explain to the American people that Standard's business model was right for the new century. They needed to face that fact. "The day of individual competition in large affairs is past and gone," he declared. "It is too late to argue about advantages [and abuse] of industrial combinations." "They are a necessity." Behind the scenes, meanwhile, he acted as a general, rallying the Standard legal team and ensuring it did not get "caught napping." On all battlegrounds, his was a tiring march toward the final verdict of 1911. Once it was delivered, his burden lightened considerably.[26]

That, in turn, allowed him to systematize the family's charitable causes, a quest in which he partnered with longtime advisor Frederick Gates. The Rockefellers would certainly maintain considerable influence over Standard's splintered corporate realm and continue to shape its boardroom culture. The next generation of Standard leaders—men like Archbold—would take the lessons and allegiances forged during Rockefeller's headship into the executive offices of the Standard offshoots they now ran and remain loyal to the founding family. Thanks to their extensive shares in the Standard network and widespread ties in business and government, the Rockefellers would, in short, remain heavily invested in its next steps. Going forward, however, they would focus on the delivery, not the accumulation, of Standard wealth.[27]

Following the founding of the University of Chicago in 1892, Rockefeller's charity had entered a dynamic phase. Gates provided the spark. "Your fortune is rolling up, rolling up like an avalanche," he thundered to his advisee. "You must keep up with it! You must distribute it faster than it grows! If you do not, it will crush you and your children and your children's children!" Gates was a fierce defender of Rockefeller and took on all detractors who lambasted his privilege to make *and give* money with impunity. "The fact is that nobody is so well able to administer the wealth of the country for the good of the country as the man who makes it," Gates retorted. But behind closed doors, Gates implored Rockefeller in his own frank tone. A letter he sent his boss in 1905 laid everything on the line: "I have lived with this great fortune of yours daily for fifteen years. It has been impossible for me to ignore the great question of what is to be the end of all this wealth." Gates envisioned two paths: a first in which Rockefeller's riches were channeled methodically through established institutions into the hands of the people and a second in which carelessness resulted in God-given profits passing into the "sinister" "unknown."[28]

Besides advocating for the first path, Gates also provided a blueprint for giving, one that laid out a key shift in priorities: from emphasis on the individual to focus on the social, from short-term campaigns for revival to the construction of long-lasting institutions, and from the explicitly to the implicitly religious. On the latter score, he insisted that missionary support continue in the scheme, provided it be allocated with well-defined and broader goals. The Rockefellers had always supported evangelistic and missionary endeavors. Throughout the late nineteenth century Rockefeller gave to Dwight L. Moody, the most famous revivalist of his day, and doled out hundreds of thousands of dollars to the multitude of preachers and missionaries who asked for his help. That was precisely the problem—Rockefeller's first love of Christian proselytization had almost broken him, with a steady stream of requests for money from missionaries and preachers proving overwhelming. Gates was a cleric who shared the ultimate goal of converting individuals to Christ, but by 1905 he was determined to make those efforts calculating, not simply heartfelt. That year, during which he wrote Rockefeller his ultimatum, Gates drafted a letter asking him to give $100,000 to the American Board of Commissioners for Foreign Missions, one of the most important interdenominational missionary organizations of the day. In it he carefully laid out reasons why and how the donation would result in lasting impact. It would help save souls, of course, but Gates saw even wider impact—a civilizing one as well that illustrated the bigger picture of dominion he had in mind. "Missionary enterprise" was also "good business policy," he noted, and when combined with the application of technological know-how, it was a formula for revitalizing the globe. Gates wanted an imperial campaign with no limits: "I think the subject of foreign missions should command the interest of patriots and philanthropists . . . of men of commerce, of manufacture, of finance, of the bankers, importers and exporters of our country, and of all who have the wellbeing of their own country or of mankind at heart." His aim was nothing less than the "peaceful conquest of the world" through the enabling of religious, moral, commercial, scientific, and philosophical progress.[29]

In that sense, Gates spoke for a rising segment of Protestant leaders who were beginning to envision a form of Christian global outreach that championed a wider humanitarianism. Drawing on social gospel notions of an immanent and indwelling divine, which underscored God's presence in the world *and* in worldly matters, and postmillennialism, which emphasized humanity's duty to construct a golden age of peace and righteousness, this cohort imagined international engagement as an organic whole, folding spiritual and material aims into one initiative. They also exuded the confidence in technology and scientific methods of modernization that intellectuals in the progressive movement at the time conveyed through their writings and instruction. According to some, the engineer was to be exalted, as much as the evangelist, as an apostle leading humanity into its gilded epoch of completeness. A Methodist theologian encapsulated the belief: "There must be an adequate physical organization of the world before there can ever be fully developed soul-life in it, and the engineer is making that physical organization of the world." "Hail, Engineer, coagent of the millennium." Such thinking shaded Gates's conceptualization of Rockefeller's philanthropy and his prods to shift emphases.[30]

Several local and international undertakings illustrated the effect of Gates's new outlook on Rockefeller support of traditional missions and evangelism. In 1905, John D. Rockefeller fielded a request for funds from the Evangelistic Committee of New York, which wanted to organize a revival "in the poorer parts of the city." Gates and his associate, Starr Murphy, were skeptical. "I have no more confidence in the permanent value of these spasmodic evangelistic movements than Mr. Murphy has," Gates wrote the patron; "perhaps it might be wise to make a contribution of a thousand dollars toward the thirty thousand which they want. But if this is done, it should be with the mental reservation that if they come back next year, we will make them give satisfactory reasons, drawn from actual experience." Rockefeller appreciated the advice but was conflicted, his Baptist guilt bubbling up: "Should we not make it at least two or three?" he replied. Because of the luminaries involved in the project, esteemed civic leaders like Cleveland Dodge, Gates, Murphy, and their boss agreed to donate, but only at the $1,000 mark. The following year, and annually until 1919, when the Rockefellers finally ceased giving to the initiative, members of the Evangelistic Committee solemnly (no doubt anxiously) wrote Rockefeller with another petition, replete with the multiple-page report that Gates demanded, outlining the tangible outcomes of the previous year's revival and reasons why support should continue. The number of converts was but one minor statistic of interest. Other accomplishments now dominated the page: evidence of "business methods" adopted to streamline the ministry, total receipts and detailed expenditures to indicate how many local associations had been recruited as allies, and statements of purpose that underscored the goal—mirroring Gates's—to transform civil society as well as wounded souls. Surely it was a draining process for the petitioners and probably never satisfactory where the monetary return was concerned—Gates and Murphy remained skeptical and urged Rockefeller to give modestly. Nevertheless, they were always sure to sign their requests with a cheerful refrain: "I simply want to lay this before you, Mr. Rockefeller, grateful for what you have done for us." "We covet your prayers more than we do your money."[31]

Gates's influence reshaped Rockefeller's giving to foreign missionary enterprises as well. A couple of campaigns caught their eye for the degree to which they demanded new thinking. One of them involved a trusted leader in worldwide missions: John R. Mott, the prominent Methodist layman who served as chairman of the World Missionary Conference held in Edinburgh, Scotland, in 1910. Following the conference, Mott devised a scheme, which he presented to Rockefeller, to construct an institutional apparatus of missiology—the Missionary Research Library—that could facilitate informed outreach to the unreached peoples of the world. Gates needed guarantees that the money would generate results of "permanent importance"; he was not interested in funding "spasmodic" evangelism. For the next few years Mott labored to convince him; in the process, Mott himself became more convinced by the idea. Writing to Rockefeller, he admitted, "The more I have reflected upon the setting apart of the money necessary for both funding and building the more I have been impressed by the advantages of the plan." Mott now envisioned an ideal of global Christian cooperation that could mirror "the Peace Palace at the Hague," which had "incarnated the idea of a peacable [sic] settlement of disputes between nations." Gates grew pleased: expanding Christendom was no longer Mott's sole goal; reaching "all mankind" through an expansive ministry of societal regeneration according to Christian principles was. Once hints of sectarianism were sifted out of Mott's proposal, Rockefeller money was forthcoming.[32]

Rockefeller money made its way into another agency that increasingly widened its purview as well. During the mid-1890s and again with greater urgency between 1909 and 1922, word spread of the Ottoman Empire's persecution of Christian Armenians, a genocide that would result in well over 1 million deaths. Western missionaries in the area began to gather ground-level information and convey it to religious and political leaders in the United States. Protestant periodicals such as the *Christian Herald* alerted readers to the crisis and coordinated a response. Money for traditional ministry in the region was no longer enough, they declared. American Christians needed to donate to disaster relief for the embattled region's refugees. The response became more formal in 1915, linking religious charity to government sanction. At the urging of Henry Morgenthau, US ambassador in Turkey, and with the endorsement of President Woodrow Wilson, leading philanthropists Charles Crane and Cleveland Dodge, whose family was tied to missionary work in the Near East, formed the American Committee for Armenian and Syrian Relief, which over the next few years raised $20 million. In 1919 it was rechristened Near East Relief and charged with coordinating an even wider campaign to feed and house Armenians and to supply the region with medical and technical support, as well, eventually, as industrial and agricultural education needed for its rebuilding. What began as an exercise in charity morphed into a full-fledged doctrine of humanitarianism, an expansive initiative that the Rockefellers—under Gates's guidance—readily stepped forward to fund.[33]

Near East Relief's appeal to "inter-denominational, international, and inter-racial idealism" and application of "practical philanthropy" was precisely the type of approach that Gates encouraged the Rockefellers to adopt. Already in the early 1900s, Gates was helping channel Rockefeller funds into scientific and medical outlets designed to improve the inhumane conditions in which many American citizens lived. These included the Rockefeller Institute for Medical Research; the General Education Board, which sought to improve education for southern blacks; and the Rockefeller Sanitary Commission, which tackled hookworm in the South. Gates and Rockefeller soon decided to test their vision for structural reform on an even larger scale. In 1909 Rockefeller signed a deed that allocated 72,569 shares of Jersey Standard, with a value of $50 million, to three joint trustees: his son John D. Rockefeller Jr., his son-in-law Harold McCormick, and Frederick Gates. That first donation of oil was to create a trust known as the Rockefeller Foundation, whose stated purpose reflected the evolution of Rockefeller and Gates's thinking over the previous few years. The deed announced that the foundation's main aim was "to advance the civilization of peoples of the United States and its territories and possessions and of foreign lands in the acquisition and dissemination of knowledge, in the prevention and relief of suffering, and in the promotion of any and all of the elements of human progress." Of note was its intended global reach, for which Gates lobbied. "Is there not something within us," he asked rhetorically, "an instinct which is the harbinger of better things, an instinct of humanity which cannot be fenced in by the boundaries of a merely national patriotism, a sympathy which transcends national boundaries and finds complete expression only when it identifies us with all humanity?"[34]

In 1911, at virtually the same moment that the Supreme Court was pondering its final decision on the antitrust case, Congress considered a bill to incorporate the Rockefeller Foundation. According to one sympathetic biographer, the senior Rockefeller had "nothing but the public welfare in view in [his] conception of a great agency, controlled by the best trustees obtainable, to which he would assign the bulk of his fortune for philanthropic objects. Its purpose was not to perpetuate wealth, but to distribute it." Skeptics in Washington saw things differently: to them this was yet another "indefinite scheme for perpetuating vast wealth . . . inconsistent with the public interest." It was a Trojan horse whose threat to democracy was as menacing as Standard Oil's.

After three years of negotiations, a more moderate tone toward Rockefeller's philanthropy began to prevail, though not in Washington. After introducing concessions to the bill, the Rockefeller team made a final petition to Congress in early 1913, but the Senate failed to consider the measure prior to adjournment. Rockefeller's advisors adopted plan B and immediately petitioned the New York State Legislature for a charter, which it received that same year. The Rockefeller Foundation was formed, the lofty mantra "To promote the wellbeing of mankind throughout the world" emblazoned on its deed.[35]

While somewhat anticlimactic, the formal creation of the foundation marked a critical juncture, not just for Rockefeller philanthropy but for American philanthropy as a whole. In the years that immediately followed, the Rockefeller Foundation would grow quickly in size and vision. Like the corporate giant whose money filled its coffers, it would construct a mammoth institutional apparatus consisting of a board of trustees and sprawling staff of managers, advisors, and office personnel, layers of oversight and reporting, government partnerships, and a propensity to shape public policy as well as transform minds, souls, and bodies. And with similar proficiency, it would start penetrating foreign fields in South America, Africa, and especially Asia, where the Rockefeller captivation with China would once again loom large.[36]

THERE TO HELP guide the new endeavor was John D. Rockefeller Jr. In the years following the family's pivotal 1911, he assumed greater influence in its dealings. While his stamp of leadership in Standard's corporate actions would never be explicit, through his continued investments and business ties he sought to shift the company toward an ethical and cosmopolitan outlook. Just as the father had been the face of Standard's fiscal might, the son wanted to be its moral compass. But of utmost importance to him was the philanthropic agency Gates had helped create. In that capacity, Junior became not just the moral guardian of a rapidly expanding nonprofit operation but also the target of opposition from men like Lyman Stewart, "fundamentalists" in their determination to defend their orthodoxies of church, the corporate realm, and now charity.

Junior had been there all along, playing a crucial role in the emergence of Rockefeller philanthropy during the early 1900s. Like Gates, he accepted that role as a result of deep conviction. As a child, reared by extremely devout parents, Junior could not help but be consumed with church life. Of its effect on him, a contemporary would write, "What he did, where he went, with whom he went—all such decisions were inextricably bound up with this central purpose [to be a good Christian] which sprang from a deeply ingrained religious faith." More so than his father, who wore his faith easily and freely traversed the boundaries of churchly and worldly affairs, Junior was prone to prudishness. His personality, shaded by a constant pattern of guilt and introspection, certainly contributed to his embrace of a more somber piety, as did the insecurity he shouldered of being the son of a rich man who cast a long shadow. While he attended Brown University, his religiosity continued to evolve in ways that lent it even greater seriousness. Rockefeller flourished there, especially under the tutelage of its clerical president and professor of political economy Elisha Benjamin Andrews. Andrews was a social gospeler with a scientific mind who believed that business needed to operate in the best interests of the public, that government had an important role to play in the economy, and, most strongly, that all citizens had to labor together, with the latest tools at their disposal, for the betterment of society. "The world painfully needs two more classes of missionaries still," he preached to his pupils: "social missionaries to the rich and political missionaries." Swayed, the Baptist scion determined to fill the void and commit to a vocation of Christian civil service.[37]

That calling would take some time to take root. Rockefeller started work at his father's oil company in the fall of 1897. He was to apprentice in the firm with designs for promotion, and toward that end he was assigned to the office that oversaw Senior's business and philanthropic affairs. There, his boss, Frederick Gates, patiently, painstakingly tutored him in the essentials of the Rockefeller empire. "No father could have been more kindly or helpful to his own son than was Mr. Gates to me," Junior would later write. Gates, meanwhile, was impressed with his underling's energy and "large capacity for work." By 1901, Gates later reflected, Rockefeller "may fairly be said to have completed a postgraduate course in business and benevolence." Soon, however, the young man was thinking less warmly about the first facet of this job description. Even though he had begun climbing company ranks—he was made vice president in 1901—Junior's appetite for the corporate side waned. His exposure to boardroom (and backroom) politics as well as media scrutiny of his father factored in. But mostly, it was his ripening passion for philanthropy that caused him to rethink his future.[38]

He pondered and stewed throughout the first decade of the new century, during which his work with Gates expanded. The two made a formidable team, with Gates supplying much of the lofty vision and Rockefeller a good deal of the real-world muscle. "Gates was the brilliant dreamer and creator," Junior recalled. "I was the salesman—the go-between with Father at the opportune moment." In actuality, Rockefeller provided a lot of the ideas too. He was eager to apply the concepts and methods he learned at Brown and make his office a lively lab for solving society's problems. Like his college mentor, he harbored a confidence that the challenges humanity now faced could be addressed through the collaboration of experts in effectively managed organizations. Rockefeller was particularly fixated on issues related to poverty, disease, and education, and those very concerns helped inspire Rockefeller charity's first ventures. With the aid of the experts he ably recruited—yet another emerging talent—Rockefeller joined Gates in establishing the Rockefeller Institute for Medical Research, the Rockefeller Sanitary Commission, and the Bureau of Social Hygiene, for which he was directly responsible. Satisfied with these accomplishments, he was far less so with business. His father had succeeded at multitasking, simultaneously governing Standard, his own investments, and his charity; Junior did not have the will to do the same. By 1910, realizing he "could never be happy in this business atmosphere," he began resigning several (not all) directorships in Standard- and Rockefeller-affiliated companies and turning to the thing that stirred him most.[39]

His mission expanded considerably after the creation of the Rockefeller Foundation in 1913. In the decade that followed, Junior became proficient in multitasking within the philanthropic orb. There was the foundation itself and its mushrooming apparatus of medical and scientific initiatives that could, in Rockefeller's words, "cure evils at their source." One of the first notable successes was the establishment in 1913 of the International Health Commission (later Board), which built on the work of the Sanitary Commission and extended it world-wide. Under the headship of Dr. Wickliffe Rose, the International Health Commission undertook a campaign to eradicate hookworm around the globe, which eventually reached into fifty-two countries on six continents. More controversial was the foundation's Department of Industrial Relations, started in 1914, with a mandate to heal ties between labor and management. The department was immediately scrutinized as an initiative too closely tethered to Rockefeller business interests. All these ventures kept Rockefeller busy. He hired managers, recruited experts, raised funds, helped facilitate negotiations with government officials at home and abroad, and as president of the board of trustees shepherded the foundation's leaders as they assessed possibilities for outreach. In the latter capacity he set the tone at the foundation's first meeting, at which trustees wrestled with the fundamental objective: just what, exactly, constitutes "the well-being of the world?" Gates and Rockefeller made their opinions known. The foundation was to "confine itself to projects of an important character, too large to be undertaken, or otherwise unlikely to be undertaken, by other agencies." Funding applications that proposed programs of local charity or relief were excluded; those attacking "the root of individual or social ill-being and misery . . . [and] more far-reaching in their effects" were to be considered. When Gates and Rockefeller said the well-being of the world, they meant exactly that.[40]

Rockefeller's commitment to the foundation did not preclude him from personally delving into charitable causes related to the church. Like his father, he remained committed to funding missionaries, evangelists, and church ministry—perhaps more so. Unlike his father, whose financial giving transpired in an epoch of relative calm within American Protestantism, Junior was thrust into contestation. The battle lines between liberal and conservative Protestants began to be drawn in the late nineteenth century over the rise of the social gospel, new academic scholarship that measured the accuracy of scriptural stories and claims through a scientific and historical lens, and related intellectual trends such as evolutionism. In the eyes of conservatives, these progressions undermined the authenticity and authority of the

Bible, its teachings about Christ, and the core commission for believers to evangelize the lost. Whereas liberals in different degrees sought
to modify traditional beliefs for modern societal needs, fundamentalists dug in to resist and roll back any challenges to orthodoxy. The
battle itself reached a feverish pitch in the first two decades of the
twentieth century.

In that milieu Junior was forced to become a culture warrior. There
was little question as to which side he would join. The Rockefeller name
was already attached to one of the most visible intellectual centers in
the country, at which teachings of liberal Protestantism were being
generated. University of Chicago Divinity School professor Shailer
Mathews, an advocate of social-justice Christianity and scientific scrutiny of the Bible, was one of the leading lights in the movement. Junior's
own intellectual outlook planted him firmly alongside Mathews on the
Protestant spectrum, and as the modernist-fundamentalist controversy
began to tear denominations apart, he became all the more animated
in his effort to advance liberal ecumenical causes. On one occasion in
1917, while speaking to the Baptist Social Union, he delivered a clarion
call for Baptists—and all Protestants—to unite. What should the future
of Christianity look like, Rockefeller asked in his sermon, subsequently
published in the *Saturday Evening Post*. "It would pronounce ordinance,
ritual, creed, all non-essential for admission into the Kingdom of God,
or His Church. A life, not a creed, would be its test; what a man does,
not what he professes; what he is, not what he has." Speaking as a social
gospeler, he added, "Its object would be to promote applied religion, not
theoretical religion. This would involve its sympathetic interest in all
the great problems of human life; in social and moral problems, those of
industry and business, the civic and educational problems. . . . It would
be a church of all people." His ecclesiology was simply an extension of
his worldview and of his overriding dedication to forging a practical
Christianity that everyone—not just churchmen—could embrace as
relevant for the times and that served as a major cog in the crusade for
sweeping social reform.[41]

Rockefeller did not simply talk of practical Christianity—he used
his personal pocketbook to grease its institutional development. One
of his first significant steps came in 1908, when he promised to underwrite at least 5 percent of the first year's operating budget of the newly

formed Federal Council of Churches (FCC), an ecumenical agency that could oversee cooperative ministries among Protestants of various denominational affiliations. Rockefeller's giving to the FCC continued to rise in the 1910s, even as he took on other ecumenical projects, such as the Committee on Cooperation in Latin America, overseen by John Mott and Robert Speer, two FCC stalwarts, and the Interchurch World Movement, which received upward of 100 million Rockefeller dollars. In 1911, Gates wrote to Junior, "Sectarianism is the curse of religion at home and abroad; a blight upon religion, whether viewed from an economic, intellectual or spiritual standpoint. The union of evangelistic denominations would solve more problems of human progress than any other single reform." Rockefeller wholeheartedly agreed, which is why he endorsed all of Gates's efforts to "present a unified program of Christian service and to unite the Protestant churches of North America in the performance of their common task." Junior did not abandon revivalistic religion altogether. Throughout the 1910s and 1920s he pledged generously to several evangelistic crusades, which, however much they may have frustrated Gates for their lack of systematic focus on large-scale social returns, appealed to the Rockefellers' Baptist roots. He gave especially freely to high-profile campaigns orchestrated by Billy Sunday, the Dwight Moody of his day, who communicated regularly with Junior and Senior as "dear friends." Yet, by and large, Junior preferred the steadier progressions of ecumenical partnership to the frolicking, Bible-thumping revival of Sunday's muscular variety.[42]

And in that regard, the type of preacher who interested him most was the sage, not the showman. Just as his career as champion (and bankroller) of liberal Christianity was taking flight, Rockefeller grew close to a pastor who would become his trusted ally in the cause. Rockefeller was introduced to Harry Emerson Fosdick through Gates's mediation in the early 1910s. Thereafter a relationship budded. From a long line of clergymen, Fosdick and his brother, Raymond, were staunch proponents of the social gospel and quickly found a viable outlet for their interests in the Rockefeller Foundation (of which Raymond would assume the presidency in 1936). Harry, though, would work most closely with Rockefeller in the church realm. During the 1910s, Fosdick quietly carved out a career as a professor at Union Theological Seminary and pastor of New York's prominent First Presbyterian Church in Lower Manhattan. Gradually his theological writings and sermons earned him attention among not only progressives such as Rockefeller but also conservatives, whose abhorrence of his teachings rivaled only their hatred for Shailer Mathews in Chicago. For Fosdick, true Christianity had immortal answers for every facet of human existence and was "intelligible for modern living." "Religion can be an utterly conventional and meaningless affair, or it can be a vital force in life," he would observe. "Man's spiritual life is a good deal like a twig in a bonfire: if it falls out, toss it back on the fire, and it adds to the fire." Positive in his rendering of a personally empowering and socially transformative theology, Fosdick was also unbending in his defense of it against sectarian ideologues and willing to draw a line in the sand. "You cannot fit the Lord Christ into that Fundamentalist mold," he growled when excoriating his opponents' rigid theology. Rockefeller lauded Fosdick's willingness to take on the militants of the church and began to look for ways to channel that drive toward his own aims.[43]

By the early 1920s, that process was already well underway. Personally, the two men were building an abiding friendship based on profound mutual trust as well as shared political outlook. Soon Rockefeller would gush to Fosdick about "my great affection for you, my full appreciation of what you are doing for the world . . . and of all you mean to the Christian world." The partnership was budding professionally as well. Rockefeller began to woo Fosdick to pastor his home church. That venture would take time to bear fruit. In the meantime, he managed to convince the minister to partner with him in a difficult assignment unfolding across the Pacific.[44]

THE ASSIGNMENT THRUST Fosdick into the trenches of a bitter contest between the two sectors of oil politics that had animated the previous decade's anti-Rockefeller animus. It also placed him in the crosshairs of one of the Rockefellers' most determined critics: Lyman Stewart.

By 1911, Stewart had also shifted his career goals and achieved a fresh start. Already frustrated with how the corporate world sapped the strength he wanted to deploy in his burgeoning philanthropic work, his love of oil waned further as he waded into the antitrust case against Standard. Disgusted with big business and disillusioned with bureaucrats, he became convinced that petroleum was corrupt to the core. While he cheered Ida Tarbell and the Supreme Court in their takedown of Standard Oil, his cynicism would not abate. On top of that, he was growing increasingly agitated as Protestantism's traditional institutions turned liberal and, in his mind, away from the Bible. By 1911 he was ready to reconnect fully with the original vocational desires of his youth and devote his life almost exclusively to evangelistic causes. He would finally be that missionary he always wanted to be, though a missionary in an executive's pinstripes. With the help of his brother, Lyman began erecting a philanthropic apparatus that he hoped would offset the Rockefellers'. It included the Milton Stewart Evangelistic Fund and his own financial initiatives, which he mobilized in several different capacities.[45]

In one of their first major undertakings, the Stewarts commissioned a series of articles defending their Protestant dogma. Besides providing the vision and money for the project, Lyman, the project's true architect, also played the part of manager. As Gates and Rockefeller were also known to do, he surrounded himself with experts. He established a separate organization, Testimony Publishing Company, based in Chicago, with an executive committee comprised of conservative Protestantism's leading lights, many of whom were affiliated with the city's Moody Bible Institute. The team enlisted dozens of authors to write twelve volumes of tracts containing ninety essays. The thought pieces tackled every subject that conservative Protestants considered threatening to orthodoxy, including doctrinal flashpoints like the virgin birth and the deity of Christ, the Bible and modern criticism, and a host of "isms": socialism, Mormonism, evolutionism, Catholicism, and atheism. Released intermittently between 1910 and 1915, *The Fundamentals*, as they were titled, found a way into homes, seminaries, churches, and missionary bases where the battle between fundamentalism and modernism was intensifying. Three million volumes were issued before the end of World War I.[46]

*The Fundamentals*'s statistical success paled next to its symbolic impact. With words as their weapon, Stewart's men established the theological parameters of a movement that would upend American Protestantism. For the next generation fundamentalists would hold fast to the principles laid out in this treatise as they attacked liberalism on every front.

The documents and the process through which they were created also reaffirmed Stewart's fierce sense of independence. Cloaked in the guise of ecclesiastical politics, this was in fact another exercise in antitrust agitation. As he looked out on the Protestant world before him and the role of the Rockefellers in shaping it, Stewart grew all the more distraught with the overbearing and misguiding influences of large, distant institutions. In the case of the gospel, oversized and questionably run denominations and Christian associations were letting liberalism creep into American Protestantism and undermine true Christianity from within. One organization that Stewart scrutinized was the American Bible Society, which for copyright protection prohibited the missionaries he funded in China from using its translated scripture in full. "Bible societies are apparently disposed to make a trust of their business," he vented to Milton, underscoring a wider trend. What was a good Christian to do when faced with monopolism in the pews?[47]

As witnessed in *The Fundamentals*, the answer involved free market solutions. Mirroring his own predilections, those who Lyman put in charge of the enterprise were nondenominational in spirit and eager to produce a commodity that could be marketed to and placed in the hands of consumers directly, without middlemen or a giant apparatus getting in the way. Faced with a competing product—"modernism"—they hustled to assemble a more appealing package. Skirting denominational leaders with an enticing pitch to the masses, local laity, and religious workers, as well as "thousands of good honest men today preaching error because they don't know the truth," Stewart promised to deliver straight to the people a "living gospel truth." With this attempt to win their market share and encourage others to separate themselves from the apostasy of their competitor, *The Fundamentals's* executives hoped to form a new autonomous body of believers, coalesced around shared conviction in the power of individuals to grasp God and his wisdom of their own volition.[48]

That same motive drove Stewart's other philanthropic investments. Besides bankrolling *The Fundamentals*, Lyman also constructed a cathedral—the nondenominational Church of the Open Door in Los Angeles—and a school, his counter to the University of Chicago's Divinity School, named the Bible Institute of Los Angeles, or BIOLA. Whereas the former became the West Coast's epicenter of revivalism and prophecy, the latter served as a training site for thousands of young men and women eager to evangelize the remotest parts of the globe. That included South America, where by 1920 Stewart was funneling financial support in staggering proportions. He was particularly supportive of the Central American Mission (CAM), a nondenominational "faith-based" mission solely dependent on private rather than large-scale institutional gifts, founded in 1890. His support of South American missions in general grew out of his personal determination to "give the WORD OF GOD to Spanish-speaking and other Roman Catholic peoples." The fact that the continent was a key frontier for Union Oil and that petroleum exploration and marketing south of the Mexican-American border would only happen after the opinions of foreign capitalists softened there certainly influenced his decision to support agencies like CAM. "Many of our missions have a commercial aspect to their work," he told his brother point-blank. Stewart recognized the benefit of having missionaries on the ground selling the capitalist creed. Though never voiced in such explicit terms, his efforts to turn foreign hearts toward God were also intended to prepare them for the coming of black gold.[49]

As much as South America touched a nerve, Stewart's obsession was Asia. For several reasons, beginning with his eschatology, his concern with missionary work there assumed special urgency. Through his immersion in a widening network of premillennialism, he came to view evangelism as the last gasp of an ever-darkening world. Unlike John D. Rockefeller Jr., whose embrace of a postmillennial, progressive gospel and concomitant humanitarianism reflected his comfortable standing in the world and a confidence in man's ability to transform it, Stewart shouldered the insecurities of a volatile social and economic system and the conviction that Christians had neither the time, need, nor ability to restructure the world. He agreed with Rockefeller and Gates and their liberal cousins that the "engineer" should be exalted as an agent of technological wonder and modernization; he liked to count himself a member of the engineering guild and visualize his labor in these very same terms. Yet he rejected the comprehensive social engineering Rockefeller and Gates expected of these modern apostles, as well as the fantasy (in his mind) that these forerunners could guide humanity to a perfected world order. Engineers were to build better machines that made life more tolerable—and profitable—in the here and now; otherwise, the best any Christian could do was save as many souls before the impending apocalypse. That charitable impulse was buttressed by his grasp of capitalism's service to the church. In his mind, money was to be made and spent in the present in order to convert souls and minister to the saints here and now, before the world collapsed. Always the speculator, willing to assume risks for a higher calling, he had no patience for elaborate, scientifically coordinated and science-focused foundations that seemed to diminish the sacred and the spiritual; in fact, he believed good Christians had to fly in the face of them. Stewart's financial plan, one historian notes, simply "demanded expenditure for the kingdom, not stockpiling for the world." Because of this open-pocket policy, he "was always hard up for cash," but he never let this constant stress stop him from giving freely.[50]

In Asia Stewart identified a particularly ripe field for his brand of Christian witness. Even as he believed he was watching the demise of American Christianity, he took solace in the fact that Christian converts in Korea seemed to be amassing in proportions far greater than anything seen in the United States. Could it be that Koreans would one day bear responsibility for Christianizing the globe? And he drew sustenance from the positive reports that flowed into his office from Southeast Asia and across China, where conservative missionaries seemed to be making a marked difference, building Bible institutes and holding large meetings. One aggressive agency in the region was the Bible Union of China. Through cash and Union Oil stock, Stewart ensured that it received his monetary support as well as his help with monitoring other missionary agencies affiliated with the FCC and ensuring that the fundamentals of the faith were being preached. Of course, once again, Stewart's special concern for Asia also had much to do with business. As Union continued to expand its presence in the Pacific Rim, China's oil-producing possibilities and burgeoning market potentials proved especially attractive. Under the leadership of foreign field managers such as John Baker, whose own résumés revealed dual labor as missionaries and oilmen, Union was determined to break open the Asian frontier both for God and black gold.[51]

The problem for the Stewarts was that the Rockefellers and Standard Oil affiliates had their sights set on these lands as well. China had always been special to the Rockefellers. Senior had begun his own private charity work by giving to Baptist missionaries there, and "oil for the lamps of China" was one of Standard's first marketing ploys, signifying the company's appreciation of the untapped consumer demand for kerosene that existed in the Asian country. By the 1920s Socony was trumpeting that refrain in an effort to stretch its consumer base from the Great Wall in the country's north to Hainan Island in its south. Thanks to Frederick Gates, Standard profits also made their way into China in the form of an ambitious philanthropic blitz. He spent the early years of the century exploring ways to construct a university there, an Asian version of the University of Chicago. A 1909 report commissioned by the Rockefeller-financed Oriental Education Commission emphasized the challenges of such a venture; besides revealing the difficulties of selling the idea to Chinese officials, the report also documented widespread opposition from missionaries. "The missionary bodies," Gates later recalled, "were distinctly and openly, even threateningly hostile to it as tending to infidelity." He put the plan on hold, but once the Rockefeller Foundation was up and running and the successes of Dr. Wickliffe Rose's hookworm campaign began piling up, Gates revisited it, this time with a focus on the "gradual and orderly development of a comprehensive and efficient system of medicine in China." The plan quickly came to fruition. In 1914, the Rockefeller Foundation created the China Medical Board, which began distributing grants to improve medicine in the country and, most importantly, conceptualize the Peking Union Medical College. Instead of a University of Chicago, Rockefeller proffered to China its Johns Hopkins University. It opened in 1921.[52]

China was transformative for Rockefeller philanthropy. In the face of opposition from several missionary boards, Gates's turn to medicine reconfirmed the foundation's desire for a nonsectarian, nonreligious thrust. "The work of missionaries . . . has seemed to me to offer little promise," he reported to the China Medical Board. "China needs modern science but the missionary schools avoid science as leading to skepticism. China needs modern medicine but the hospitals and missionaries are merely proselytizing agencies. The spirit of pure compassion . . . that animated the Good Samaritan in his ministrations, our missions seem not to have caught." Despite his pessimism, Gates did not endorse abandoning missionaries altogether. He preferred, rather, to fold the training of missionary doctors into medical education advanced at all levels, in all sections of the country. In the years leading up to the opening of the Peking Union Medical College, a few willing missionary agencies agreed to assist that strategy, but conservative opposition continued to sour him on such partnerships. Meanwhile, John D. Rockefeller Jr.'s personal encounter with China reconfirmed Gates's philanthropic model. Junior was never the same after his visit to China during the year of the medical college's official opening. "Father was persuaded that while American philanthropy had an important role to play in the modernization of China, traditional American missionary work had become outmoded and irrelevant to the needs of the country," his son David would recall. "The lessons drawn by each of my parents had not only an enduring impact on them by also on the lives of my brothers and me." Junior was convinced: the way to transform China into a beacon of modern progress was to help light its way with fuel, with education, and with medical experts who could heal.[53]

The competing approaches of Stewart and Rockefeller helped bring the fundamentalist-modernist battle to a crucial pivot in Kuling, China, a favorite conference site for missionaries. The clash began in 1920 with the arrival of William H. G. Thomas and Charles G. Trumbull. Thomas was an Oxford-trained seminarian who preached premillennialism and biblical inerrancy; Trumbull was editor of the *Sunday School Times*, a centerpiece in the crusade against liberal thinking. Both men believed that mainline Protestants had abdicated their authority in Christendom by embracing secular intellectual trends. Afraid that Christian witness was eroding in China, they determined to set things right. In Kuling they led meetings and implored listeners to fight for the fundamentals. Sponsored by the Bible Union of China, with backing from the Stewarts, the convention drew large audiences from China's biggest Protestant agencies. Once back in North America the two men used the pulpit and print media to awaken conservatives to liberalism's global threat. Thomas made the biggest splash. In January 1921, he warned the Presbyterian Social Union in Philadelphia about the inroads of modernism abroad. His comments subsequently framed an article, "Modernism in China," that rocked the Protestant status quo through its wide distribution in the *Princeton Theological Review* and *Sunday School Times*.

China's missionaries were "divided into two camps," he wrote, those who undermined and those who upheld the "truth." However much he claimed simply to be the messenger, his conclusion came wrapped in advocacy: Asia was slipping further away from Christ.[54]

Confronted with charges of apostasy, liberal Protestants recruited Harry Emerson Fosdick to travel to China and fend off the onslaught. Prior to his departure, Rockefeller wrote letters of introduction to Socony and Jersey Standard managers in China and supplied travel funds so as to guarantee that missionaries aligned with the FCC could hear Fosdick's case for a culturally sensitive, internationalist church. "I believe you can render most important service just at this time," Junior told his ambassador, "and I count it a privilege to be a partner with you in the enterprise." The animosities Fosdick faced during his China travels in 1921 were indeed intense, catching the wider public's attention. One Socony employee, a Catholic, wrote home during the extended period of Protestant infighting with detailed reports of what he saw happening. The portrait he offered highlighted his annoyance. "I do not suppose there are a greater lot of fakers in existence than missionaries," he proclaimed, "or that anybody knows less about the Far East than they do." With a frankness that must have made his devout mother nervous, he concluded, "Christianity is a nauseous mixture out here after you see it in the process of administration to our Chinese 'brothers,' and in common with all foreigners, I should prefer to see the Asiatics retain their old pagan worship, as they are 1000 times better off."[55]

It is no wonder, then, that Fosdick's commission in China was so daunting. After visiting a few major cities and speaking to friendly crowds, he went to Kuling. There, twice daily for an entire week, he addressed 1,000 agitated missionaries. Fosdick would recall this as one of the most "strained and difficult" circumstances he had ever encountered. "It was like walking a tightrope," and the "tension was terrific." Poised, he championed a culturally inclusive faith that made room for change and closed his final sermon by invoking unity: "The task to which we are called is enormously difficult. God help us so to fulfill it and to preach the Master to the life of our generation in the terms of our generation, as he ought to be preached—Lord of our life and God of our salvation." Fosdick wanted to win his liberal Protestant friends "peace with honor," and he did, for the time being. Still, after witnessing troubles on his Asian tour, Fosdick returned to the United States disillusioned, then preached a sermon that shook the Protestant world.[56]

The damning homily, delivered from his pulpit at New York's First Presbyterian in May 1922 and subsequently published for a wider readership, was titled "Shall the Fundamentalists Win?" An appeasing diplomat abroad, Fosdick became a zealous field general once he returned to American soil. He used his sermon to draw a line between the "intellectually hospitable, open-minded, liberty-loving, tolerant" people who followed his creed and the intolerant fundamentalists who traded in "tiddledywinks and peccadilloes of religion." His was a plea and a warning: "We must be able to think our modern life clear through in Christian terms, and to do that we also must be able to think our Christian faith through in modern times. Now, the people in this generation who are trying to do this are the liberals, and the Fundamentalists are on a campaign to shut against them the doors of the Christian fellowship." "The present world situation smells to heaven!" he doubled down, and "now, in the presence of colossal problems, which must be solved in Christ's name and for Christ's sake, the Fundamentalists propose to drive out from the Christian churches all the consecrated souls who do not agree with their theory of inspiration. What immeasurable folly!" Biting in his appraisal, Fosdick nevertheless insisted that right thinking and a generous spirit promised to prevail. Meant to inspire tolerance, Fosdick's homily instead exacerbated hostilities and helped make the rift between liberals and conservatives a permanent divide. "If ever a sermon failed to achieve its object," he would later admit, "mine did." "It was a plea for good will, but what came of it was an explosion of ill will . . . making headline news of a controversy that went the limit of truculence."[57]

The fallout from the sermon augured the fracturing of American Protestantism yet to come. Fosdick immediately faced a conservative faction that demanded his removal from the pulpit of First Presbyterian. One critical Presbyterian pastor fueled the campaign with his own damning homily titled "Shall Unbelief Win?" With pressure growing, the General Assembly of the Presbyterian Church in the United States of America opened an investigation into Fosdick's conduct in 1923. Leading his defense was Presbyterian lay leader (and future US secretary of state) John Foster Dulles. Although he escaped formal censure, the writing was on the wall, and in 1924 Fosdick resigned. Having urged him for years to accept a pastorate at his Baptist church, John D. Rockefeller Jr. finally won his confidant over, though not without further hesitation. Fosdick had always expressed concern about leading a church flush with Rockefeller money and rich congregants, and he maintained that stand. Although an ordained Baptist, Fosdick was by then theologically opposed to the practice of requiring baptism by full immersion for membership. But Rockefeller persisted, addressing each concern. Worried about adult baptism and rich congregants? We will build a bigger, more independent church to service the wider metropolitan area, he said. In response to Fosdick's concern with being a "private chaplain" to the richest man in the world, Junior jested, "I like your frankness, but do you think more people will criticize you because of my wealth than will criticize me on account of your theology?" Fosdick softened and agreed to the pastorate at Park Avenue Baptist Church. Then, when its doors opened in 1930, Riverside Church welcomed Fosdick to preside over what its patron hoped would be a grand experiment in ecumenism and the epicenter of a bolder liberal Protestantism. From a sparkling and stately edifice in Morningside Heights, funded by Rockefeller cash and Socony stock, Fosdick set out to answer his rhetorical question in the definitive: Shall the fundamentalists win? No.[58]

FUNDAMENTALISTS, OF COURSE, were intent on answering that query differently. Lyman Stewart, however, would no longer be there to guide them. At the time that Fosdick delivered his infamous sermon, Stewart was eighty years old, cognizant that his time was short. He could feel good about where his business stood at that juncture. By then Union Oil possessed 800,000 acres of land, produced more than 18 million barrels of oil per year, and oversaw a vast grid of wells, pipelines, refineries, and service stations. Thanks to that success, Stewart could give to his chosen ministries at an even more dizzying rate.[59]

That is not to say he was done trust busting, however. The everstretched Union Oil was susceptible to takeover by stockholders. Percy Rockefeller (Junior's cousin) and his Wall Street associates were among those who tried. Percy and his conglomerate's attempt failed, but in 1921 the English-Dutch Shell Oil came close to achieving that end.

After acquiring a one-fourth interest in Union Oil of California, Shell brokers announced that Union Oil's new affiliate in Delaware would ratify a plan to merge with their conglomerate. This news set off a political firestorm, prompting the US Senate to call for federal investigation of "the attempt of foreign interests to take over a big American oil company." Loyal Union stockholders rallied to stave off the "Shell grab." With the aid of the press Stewart begged Californians to fight "the forces of [the] Royal Dutch Shell combination"—that "motley aggregation recruited from many races . . . manned by a regiment of Rothschilds and equipped by a plentiful supply of ammunition from the British treasury"—and "get aboard the Union Oil Associates' bandwagon." After eighteen months of wrangling, Union Oil Associates (longtime California stockholders) gained the necessary shares to offset Shell's maneuvers, and on March 20, 1922, the *Los Angeles Examiner* declared victory: "Union Oil Saved from Foreign Control."[60]

Having left the comforts of retirement to fight this last battle, Stewart retreated again to the quiet of home and church. One year later, at the age of eighty-three, he died of complications from pneumonia exacerbated by his contest with Shell. Seven weeks later Milton Stewart passed away. As company boilerplate offered in response to the two brothers' sudden passing, "Thus the mild-mannered, evangelical, picturesque brothers, who had helped launch the Oil Age on its way sixty years before . . . passed from the scene." An editor of *Petroleum World* offered an equally glowing appraisal of Lyman Stewart, calling him the "dean of western oil men," whose "name was known wherever oil was spoken of and his three-score years of square dealing in business and kind personal interest in all around him had earned the friendship and respect of thousands." A proud wildcatter to the end, Stewart, colleagues proclaimed, had embodied the strength of the self-made man, the fortitude of the true servant of Christ, and the founding virtues of the business that had allowed him to give so much.[61]

Colleagues did not state so explicitly that by the time of his death, Stewart had stoked flames of discord within his church and drawn the oil business's internal combustions into another public sphere of influence. Stewart's theology (a call to save souls before Christ's sudden return), sense of capital (a mandate to make and spend cash quickly), corporate strategy (an incessant drive for new pools), and politics (a need to protect access to crude and take down the trusts) were dictated by his attachment to the high-risk realities and sacred diktats of his vocation. During the last decades of his life, his fight to defend those commands had spilled over into the realm of philanthropy. In the years ahead, in no small part because of his legacy, some of the fiercest contests between major and independent oil would transpire in that very same realm.

Both sides would wage that war willingly. In the wake of the fundamentalist-modernist flare-up, Rockefeller and his allies in business and the church would firm up their civil religion of crude and advance a melded system of theological and corporate ecumenism. Rockefeller's theology (a call to restructure society in advance of Christ's millennial rule), sense of capital (a mandate to manage profits carefully and deploy them for long-term causes), corporate strategy (a cautious pursuit of industrial order), and politics (a need to wed corporate, churchly, and government ambitions in the name of international accord) were dictated by his privileged standing in his sector, his proximity to power, and the social-service convictions he brought to his vocation. In the coming years he and his partners in major oil would act on those convictions in ways that secured their hegemony in the business and the nation's hegemony in petroleum's emerging global realm. It would be left to subsequent generations of independent oilmen, led by Sun Oil's Pew family, to carry out subsequent strikes against that dawning world order and forge a popular front to counter the next perceived threats of a Rockefeller-inspired monopoly.

But as much as they remained animated in that internecine struggle, independent and major oilmen were also cognizant of shared existential threats that they needed to oppose with arms locked in one purpose. Even as the fundamentalist-modernist controversy thrust the nation's Protestant establishment into crisis, a broader culture war played out, forcing men of Stewart's and Rockefeller's stock into alliance in defense of their business against a new generation of muckraking journalists, an emerging class of agitated oil workers, and a society that began to scrutinize the oil industry's role in American life.

# CHAPTER FIVE

# American Plans

C ombatants in the churchly realm, petroleum's patricians spent the period between World Wars I and II confronting a common foe: oil's proletariat. The Rockefellers and Pews learned firsthand that the struggle would be a bloody one, for they had helped create it.

The lessons for both families started during World War I. Now the face of his family and its vast corporate holdings, John D. Rockefeller Jr. had weathered an especially brutal year in 1914 when the coal mining company he still directed hired gunmen to suppress a miners' strike in Ludlow, Colorado. They opened fire, murdering thirty-three people. It would take years for Junior to process the massacre. Guilt ridden, he reached out to experts for help with reconceptualizing capitalism's approach to labor management. One of them advised him to focus not just on correcting "economic questions" but on healing the "personal antagonisms . . . arising out of prejudice and bitterness and individual antipathies" festering in his business. Over the coming months, Junior would apply that counsel, but he had insufficient time to adjust fully before another killing season unfolded at Standard refineries in Bayonne, New Jersey, between 1915 and 1916. In a series of violent clashes, thousands of strikers dueled with Standard's armed guards and policemen in demand of better pay and safer conditions. By the time order was restored, the only details that captured attention were that sixteen laborers had been shot dead and Rockefeller was once again associated with pulverized bodies.[1]

J. Edgar Pew, meanwhile, both dealt and suffered the terror that plagued oil politics. In the fall of 1917, activists from the Industrial Workers of the World (IWW), a radical union, wanted to organize Oklahoma's oil workers. "Come to Tulsa," they trumpeted; "we want to get the heads of all these big concerns and want a representative in each company!" Pew instantly became a target. Though still connected to his family's Sun Oil Company, he was also president of Carter Oil Company, which was in a standoff with unionists. As the local newspaper reported, Carter Oil "discharged a number of IWW men in its employ, determining that it would give sustenance in no way to such an outlaw band." His family was targeted too. Late in the evening of October 29, 1917, a bomb rocked the Pews' Tulsa home. "So great was the explosion," reports stated, "that window panes were shaken out of the building next to it on each side and in the windows of some of the houses across the street." Remarkably, the sleeping husband, wife, and son escaped unharmed. The house itself was destroyed, with floors splintered and walls caved in, plastering ripped from each room and the supporting beams left ready to fall. "That Mr. Pew and every member of his family were not killed in their beds," a repulsed reporter surmised, "was a miracle."[2]

Before daybreak, police charged an IWW oil worker with the crime, but there was no resolution. He did not confess. More troublesome for the public, the politics this unrepentant roughneck represented were not going away. There were serious questions in need of answers, one commentator underscored: "What can be done toward closing this festering sore of sedition situated right in the heart of this city?" No one seemed to have long-term solutions to the labor war, but in the short term, revenge seemed easiest. A few days after the explosion, Tulsa police raided the local IWW headquarters, arresting seventeen men. While on the way to jail the accused were abducted by fifty black-robed and hooded men who called themselves the Knights of Liberty. The armed assailants drove the IWW prisoners to a remote ravine, then performed a ghastly ritual in ceremonial silence. One by one the captives were stripped down, bound to trees for flogging with a cat-o'-nine-tails, doused in hot tar and feathered, then released into the woods with the parting promise of death were they ever to return to Tulsa. This was no random act by an average mob. Investigators hired by the IWW and the American Civil Liberties Union found that the rite of torture was well orchestrated, with police consent, by some of the oil town's leading citizens, including a former assistant police chief, a prominent pastor, and members of the chamber of commerce.[3]

J. Edgar Pew was purportedly there too, robed and hooded and ready to inflict pain on those he believed responsible for attempting to hurt his family, his business, and his country. At that moment, his goal was not to heal "bitterness and antipathies" but to punish.[4]

Such vindictiveness animated the entire oil industry in the late 1910s and 1920s. At first, oil's blue-collar activists took advantage of wartime conditions to rally for better labor conditions and a living wage. Their inspiration came packaged in a radical Christianity that said Jesus was on their side, not Rockefeller's or Pew's. Yet their hopes were dashed repeatedly, and although labor's assault on corporate oil was furious, it was also short-lived. The brevity of their attempt to change the industry was due in part to the unique religious and work practices of the oil patch. However much the IWW tried to convince its constituents that only collective action would secure their livelihoods, especially in southwestern towns like Tulsa, roughnecks and roustabouts harbored fantasies, conveyed to them in their pews, that they too could still make it big on their own. Top-down strategies would also quicken labor's demise. During the 1920s, the Pews, the Rockefellers, and their peers stifled unions and advanced an "American Plan" that offered a gentler, church-supported "welfare capitalism" as the answer to bad industrial relations. Fair, well-managed oil companies, they promised, were their workers' best launch into the abundant life that all of America in the Roaring Twenties so desired.

Oil's corporate leaders also hoped to win the public relations war. Rocked by unprecedented scandal and industry missteps, they battled a second wave of muckraking journalism, which deemed the oil business completely immoral. Their task was to portray their business differently—as a godsend to a modern nation on the move. That, in turn, required another "American Plan" of sorts: cleaning up their corporate sector and winning the hearts and minds of Middle America. The Pews and Sun Oil were among the trendsetters on both fronts. Through their leadership in oil's largest guild, they helped consolidate petroleum through implementation of industry and ethical standards and a public relations campaign that celebrated oil's throwback values of industriousness and stewardship. By the end of the decade, oil would once again shine in the nation's imagination as quintessentially American.

THE OCTOBER 1917 bombing of J. Edgar Pew's house marked a climax in a workers' rebellion that consumed the oil industry during the late 1910s. There had been several outbursts of violence before, much of it precipitated by anarchists and IWW radicals, whose tactics left the nation's largest cities racked with fear. Oil executives were among the targeted. In November 1915, shortly after an assassination attempt on John D. Rockefeller Sr. was thwarted, Jersey Standard president John D. Archbold escaped death when the gardener at his Tarrytown, New York, estate found dynamite in a crease of the residence's driveway, just fifty feet from the front door. Had Archbold been out for a drive instead of sailing on his yacht, his automobile likely would have triggered the device and its lethal blast.[5]

Anarchists threw bombs to terrorize the corporate elite and public into accepting labor's demands for better wages and working conditions and additional rights, but the workers' revolt of the late 1910s had a different side as well, one with religious resonance and a subtler militancy. For what turned out to be a fleeting moment, America's industrial workers entertained socialist answers to the trying economics and politics of the war years, melding class solidarity and religious zeal. One historian notes that in the shadows of World War I, "the IWW was reviving, in syndicalist, class-struggle terms, the revolutionary, system-rattling energy of prophecy; the anti-capitalist fervor of a religion of the dispossessed." The militants who stormed the refineries of Bayonne and oil territories of Texas, Oklahoma, and California may have adhered to a Marxist formula of disruption and change, but for many of them, Jesus was the true inspiration.[6]

Granted, the concept of a humble, heroic "carpenter of Nazareth" guiding workers to their rightful place atop the economic order was neither new in the 1910s nor unique to the petroleum sector. America's industrial underclass had long owned a fiery spirituality that sought revolutionary change. Animated by New Testament teachings of justice, union-friendly Christianity at the turn of the twentieth century synthesized material and spiritual concerns and took root in mines and factories, on shop floors and docks across the nation. There, in their own vernaculars, toilers affirmed their trust in the Son of God, who stormed the elites of his day, and in a living principle that said their sweat was not in vain. They echoed the words of a striker-sage who wrote of his beloved Christ, "Despised as we are despised; hunted as we are hunted— he seems like one of our kind, with whom we may clap fraternal hands across the centuries . . . since his ideal of universal brotherhood based upon toil is not forgotten—and is about to be realized." Christ was a "proletaire," wrote another sage, "whose words made systems, states and empires turn to dust." Even skeptics within the labor movement, whose Marxist convictions were drained of overt religiosity, endorsed a manifesto of class warfare that came laced with spiritual metaphor. Should workers need a God, a dubious labor impresario sighed in 1910, may it be a God "of the working class, by the working class, for the working class," one whose deific fists would smash the capitalist machine, whose sword would slay the enemies of true democracy.[7]

As widespread as that belief was among workers prior to World War I, it was most forcefully perpetuated in the shadows of World War I, especially by the IWW. At its founding in 1905, IWW spokesmen William D. Haywood and Catholic priest-turned-activist Thomas Hagerty stated that their guild would "confederate the workers of this country" and "have for its purpose the emancipation of the working class." Membership was granted to all wageworkers, regardless of creed, color, gender, or race, who shared the conviction that "no commonality of interest existed between employer and employee" and that the struggle between them was inevitable and necessary. By 1914, with membership beginning to climb to its estimated peak of 150,000 (realized in 1917), the IWW's message was penetrating numerous work settings. Yet the IWW considered the recruitment of oil workers a key project, organization of coastal oil refineries and mid-continent oil fields the most cherished victory. Vital to the emerging economy, petroleum was considered a prime site for strike action; vulnerable to the toughest features of that economy, petroleum's workers were ripe for mobilization.

The IWW was not the only labor union to mobilize, but its leaders wanted to ensure it stood at the head of the pack.[8]

The actions of one of the Bayonne strike's instigators showed that they were able to do so with great effect. Socialist idealist Frank Tannenbaum had made a name for himself in 1914 when he marched protestors—his "Army of the Unemployed"—into New York's finest churches to disrupt services with calls for poverty relief. "Tonight we eat and sleep indoors at the expense of the rich," he declared. After getting jailed for stampeding St. Alphonsus, a Catholic cathedral, he said his agitation on behalf of industrial unionism stemmed from moral impulses. "It is my belief that a real religion lies not in the sleek, fat priest who raises his eyes to the heaven, forgetting the poor who live in a hell on earth, but in the man who throws himself, heart and soul, in an endeavor to help make out of this hell a place to live in." Tannenbaum understood that the IWW's campaign needed to center on religion—as target *and* inspiration. He knew that the men and women he and his fellow unionists sought to enlist were often devout, entrenched in ethnic congregations, usually Catholic or Jewish, and well versed in religious idiom. Whether or not members of his Army of the Unemployed continued to wear their faiths firmly or loosely, or not at all, Tannenbaum recognized the power that those faiths could continue to have over their lives. Why not marshal it for class revolution?[9]

He took that game plan to Bayonne where, in July 1915, he roused strikers with his pleas for justice. On July 22, he spoke to a crowd of 2,000 workers, whose day of protest had included the death of one of their own. Besides encouraging them to press on, Tannenbaum also organized a public funeral for the fallen striker, intending once again to blend sacred ritual and agitation. As much as he recognized the strong grip of traditional creeds, he also believed that the workers' movement could itself function as a "religion." "The labor movement has a profound spiritual influence upon the workers who join its ranks," he would reflect a short time later. "It takes the isolated man of limited experience, of narrow view, of little power . . . to a world outside and beyond his control and gives him a means of escape." After his initial appearance in Bayonne, officials told Tannenbaum not to return. But Tannenbaum dared them. When he reappeared on July 26 to speak to the protestors, the local sheriff beat and arrested him. Bayonne's corporate leaders and law enforcement eventually managed to ban the IWW from its refineries, but not before Tannenbaum's spirit of rebellion had spread. In the fall of 1916, the workers—10,000 altogether—won concessions from Standard, including a raise in pay.[10]

By then, the spirit had spread to the oil lands of California and the Southwest, where the fight escalated. The prevailing sense among activists was that they were entering the high-stakes chapter of their campaign. They were right to think so, because organizing the region's oil sector had always proved difficult, and the future was dim. There had been success in the past, but it was spotty. The first serious effort to unionize the region's oil workers occurred after the Spindletop discovery in 1901. Within a year of the Lucas gusher, Samuel Gompers, head of the American Federation of Labor (AFL), sent organizers to Beaumont to drum up support. Over the course of the next decade, as oil companies in the area rapidly expanded their drilling and refining operations—and simultaneously sought to curtail their workers' power and pay—the AFL managed to establish local chapters and, in flashpoints of heated crisis, win important demands, all but the most important: formal union recognition by the corporate heads. Yet, once crises were averted, area workers did not make a fuss about the absence of that guarantee. Most found it too costly and inconvenient to maintain a union anyway. Under duress it made sense, but not when crude was flowing, oil pricing was right, and bosses were paying. As a result, by the end of the decade the union movement had foundered. According to one of Texas's first labor chroniclers, it not only foundered but "vanished," leaving laborers without protection.[11]

That condition changed rapidly between the summer of 1916 and the fall of 1917. Workers revolted out of confidence as much as a sense of crisis. Although they faced rising living costs and oil's fluctuating wartime pricing, the roughnecks and refinery workers of Texas, California, and Oklahoma also knew that with wartime Washington desperate for their services, they held a bargaining chip.[12]

The oil sector as a whole grew in importance during World War I, as its prime product became a staple for Western economies and militaries. Winston Churchill's crucial decision as first lord of the Admiralty to switch his warships' fuel from coal to oil, in hopes of upping their speed and efficiency and thus gaining an advantage against Germany, was but one clear indicator of that rapid transition. Almost overnight, Britain's naval supremacy became wedded to its access to the world's new energy source and all that entailed geopolitically. "Mastery itself," Churchill chimed, "was the price of the venture." British—and American—quests for mastery of oil now extended to Mexico as well, a second indicator of the sector's rapid rise. In the wake of Spindletop, oil scouts had moved southward to explore salt domes along Mexico's gulf coast. Former circuit preacher William Cummins, in fact, finished his career there. Between 1901 and 1915 he spudded wells for the East Coast Oil Company in virgin territory near Topila ("So I can claim to be the first developer of oil fields in that part of the Republic!" he would later boast). But no one, let alone Cummins, was as successful as Everette DeGolyer. In 1909, the professionally trained geologist began work with Edward Doheny's Mexican Eagle Petroleum Company. His innovative analytics culminated in the eruption of the Potrero del Llano No. 4 well in June 1910, which set Mexico's boom in motion, drawing British and US companies to its eastern shores. By 1917, Mexico was second only to the United States in petroleum output and, for a time, the leading oil exporter in the world. That same year the Mexican government's new constitution granted it full control of the country's subsoil resources. The act inaugurated a twenty-one-year battle with foreign oil companies, whose substantial interests in the region now seemed threatened. In the shadows of world war, then, oil was vaulted to a loftier, unprecedented, and more vulnerable economic status. The West's political and corporate leaders were fully aware of that fact.[13]

So were workers in the US oil patch. Their first maneuver transpired at Goose Creek, due west of Beaumont, Texas. Dissatisfied with the bonuses operators offered to assuage them, Goose Creek oilers formed an AFL local. Several other chapters soon dotted the region. California union organizer Walter J. Yarrow helped them coalesce and coordinate a conference in Houston with corporate leaders. But that meeting in mid-October 1917 merely heightened tensions. Ross Sterling, president of Humble Oil and Refining Company, site of the fiercest labor action, said it was fine for unions to exist and men to enlist. But, he added, "this company will continue to exercise the right to select its own employees and to deal with them directly and not through the medium of a 'labor union' or other organization." Join a union, and you would stand free but alone, outside Humble's doors. Those were fighting words that reverberated far and wide. In reply, on November 1, 1917, 10,000 oil workers, representing seventeen Texas and Louisiana gulf fields, declared a strike. "What a sight it was at Goose Creek," one striker mused, "a big field with 800 wells and 75 to 80 drilling rigs running one day and down the next, with not a walking beam moving and not a rotary turning." The fight spread. In Yarrow's California, AFL oil workers expressed solidarity with their south-western brethren, even as they targeted their own concerns: unfavorable wages and a twelve-hour day. Thanks to the guidance of Yarrow, friendly allies in Sacramento, and jitters among California companies, which feared losing lucrative government naval contracts, the oil workers got their way. A government settlement dated November 24, 1917, granted them an eight-hour workday and a wage increase to a guaranteed $4 per day.[14]

Even as strikers elsewhere continued fighting to be heard, their counterparts in Oklahoma were just beginning to trigger an insurgency. There the mantle of leadership rested with the IWW. The IWW had assumed an active presence in California and the gulf area, but due to coordinated efforts by corporate and government (and to a degree AFL) leaders to paint the "Wobblies" (IWW members) as a "vicious class" and an "arch enemy of our Nation," the radical union found those regions to be tougher terrains. But Oklahoma was ready for flaming movement politics. Present there since 1906, when Oklahoma's oil industry was born, the IWW began growing exponentially in 1914 as the state's oil boom and crisis in agricultural labor made calls for worker' rights appealing. Buoyed by its Agricultural Workers Organization, whose membership rose quickly, the IWW accelerated its recruitment of oil workers in hopes of constructing a united front for rural-industrial class warfare. To its target audience it sold an ideology of syndicalism, which envisioned the trade union as the heart of a cooperative society that would arise in the aftermath of a general strike. "A hodgepodge of ideas, emotions, and militancy," one IWW historian explains, "American syndicalism was characterized by both a distrust of anything not emanating from the working class . . . and a contempt for established law and political action." As a blueprint for sea change, quite simply it wanted to "build a new society within the shell of the old."[15]

As the IWW's campaign hit a crescendo in 1917, that "hodgepodge" of militant sympathies and blueprint for sea change were infused with radical Christianity. In their soapbox proclamations and through their expansive print media, Wobblies spread the gospel that Frank Tannenbaum encouraged. They did so in Texas and California as well and in the latter received a level of support from clergy. Though far from willing to enlist in the IWW crusade, some California clerics defended it as an all-American enterprise, not some foreign threat. One pastor told parishioners to support IWW's persecuted members as "the example of Christ" and align with the "Prince of Light" against the "powers of darkness" represented by corporate greed. But Oklahoma was particularly well conditioned for the sacralization of IWW politics. An earlier wave of socialist protest had already melded local religion with anticorporate agitation. When describing the early days of mobilizing his neighbors, an Oklahoma socialist later reminisced, "They were looking for delivery from the eastern monster whose lair they saw in Wall Street. They took to their socialism like a new religion. And they fought and sacrificed for the spreading of the new faith like the martyrs of other faiths." That new religion gained further traction in Oklahoma during the war years. "May the great God of heaven help us to secure our liberty and freedom," activists declared in 1915. "Give us Socialism and the religion of our Lord and Savior Jesus Christ."[16]

Such sentiments, though engendered by unique socioeconomic circumstances in agrarian strongholds of the state, filtered through the syndicalism that Wobblies proselytized to mid-continent oil workers in 1917. Aided by expansive print media (the IWW produced sixty-six different serial publications between 1905 and 1919), the movement's philosophy pervaded the ranks of Oklahoma oil workers. In union literature, laborers in the booming Cushing Field and Glen Pool, refining hubs of Tulsa, and pipeline lanes across the state encountered the same radical Jesus that their counterparts in the East and Far West entertained. Even as they learned of the materialist and class-oriented dogmas of their movement, always the IWW's priority, they could read texts that seemed theological: texts that condoned an Old Testament–style prophetic faith that called on downtrodden people of God to transform all aspects of their society and texts that underscored a New Testament–style millennialism that said revolution was coming, so too the end of time and, with it, judgment for capitalist oppressors and false teachers of the church—and for Christ's toilers, "a world shorn of all its present deficiencies."[17]

While they read of this future, they also sang about it. Nothing moved Wobblies like their rallies, held in halls and tents—revivals, really— and the singing of "hymns" that raised them in one voice. Raiding hymnbooks used by evangelists like Dwight Moody and Billy Sunday (false teachers, in their eyes, whose business-friendly Christianity they despised), IWW activists twisted church songs into union canticles. Among the most popular was "There Is Power in a Union" (a play on "There Is Power in the Blood"). Even more so than the printed word, Wobblies' litany of choruses distilled revolutionary ideas down to their basic application and united them in an emotive mode. "It was their vision that made them powerful," James Jones later wrote in his novel *From Here to Eternity.* "And sing! you never heard anyone sing the way these guys sung! Nobody sings like they did unless it's for a religion."[18]

Despite their evangelistic passion—indeed, because of it—IWW activists in Oklahoma and throughout the West faced mounting obstacles. If 1917 represented a banner year for them, it also served as their denouement. By October of that year, corporate and community leaders had resolved to roll back the IWW. With Bolsheviks securing power in Russia and American fears of communism reaching a feverish pitch, the IWW faced an increasingly impatient public as well. Those oppositional forces coalesced in the vigilantism that followed the October 29, 1917, bombing of J. Edgar Pew's house, dubbed by IWW sympathizers the "Tulsa Outrage." Hours after the near-lynchings, IWW sympathizers received another message. As Tulsa's major daily reported with some glee, "Later in the night, large printed signs appeared on the front door of the I.W.W. headquarters, in railroad stations, on telephone poles, and elsewhere. They bore these words: 'Notice to IWW's Don't Let the Sun Set on You in Tulsa.'" The warning was signed "Vigilance Committee." In the following weeks, the warning was backed by more force. Throughout Oklahoma, Texas, and California, hundreds of Wobblies were killed, deported, or imprisoned under the Espionage and Sedition Acts of 1917 and 1918, marking the beginning of a corporate and government campaign to suppress the IWW that would last a few years.[19]

Amid the suffering, Wobblies looked for comfort to another side of the radical Jesus whose persecution reminded them that as much as revolution could change the world, martyrdom could too. By 1918, their day of dreaming of revolution was done. As one chronicler admits, "The heart had gone out of the IWW."[20]

DURING THE FOLLOWING decade, organized labor as a whole would be stripped of its soul. The days of rallying workers of the oil patch were essentially over. Mobilizing oil's proletariat had always proved daunting. Amid the dizzying economic transformations of the 1920s and the era's pro-business politics, it became virtually impossible.

Self-inflicted lesions contributed to labor's woes. Following the collapse of the IWW, leadership in oil's unionization passed to the AFL. In the summer of 1918, oil workers from California, Louisiana, Texas, and Oklahoma successfully petitioned AFL president Samuel Gompers for a union, chartered as the International Association of Oil Field, Gas Well & Refinery Workers. A few months later the international held its inaugural convention at the Labor Temple of El Paso, Texas, where it ironed out a constitution whose concluding line reflected the evangelistic elements of the event: "Cherish the union, for it teaches you how to live; have faith in the union and it will comfort you in need; have zeal for the union for in its growth you will find happiness for yourselves and your fellow men." The creed went unheeded. Smoldering differences soon broke at the surface of internal politics. The union's state-level initiatives won some gains. By 1919, the international could hail the founding of its monthly magazine, *International Oil Worker*, and a total of 101 local charters with a membership exceeding 20,000. But unity was fleeting. That was apparent at the international's 1920 convention in Fort Worth, where hotly contested elections created two factions, one consisting of 10,000 members from California, the other comprising slightly fewer members from the remaining forty-seven states. California locals muscled for their slate of executive candidates, inciting bitterness from other state representatives and spelling an end to the abbreviated era of good feelings. Factionalized, by 1922 the international was a shadow of its original self. It reached its peak membership of 24,800 in 1921, but by 1922 that number had dropped to

6,100. From there it would decline swiftly to 300 in 1933. A new generation of leaders would have to remobilize the flock, but for oil's labor leaders in 1922, that reboot was too far in the future and too unrealistic to even imagine.[21]

What else caused the swift decline? That was the question oil's first unionists were left grappling with. Despite the zeal that fired up IWW and international workers, their spirit of insurrection was no match for a business and culture of oil that injected its own zeal into the oil patch's work zones in 1920s America. That energy flowed both ways, downward from the corporate level but also upward from the rank and file.

Asked what caused the demise of his movement, one international executive offered a succinct answer that stressed top-down oppression: big business's "American Plan" and its blatant assault on unionism. Beginning in 1920, US industry leaders carried out advertising and labor relations campaigns that portrayed unionists as communist and un-American. Powerful corporate heads swore they would not negotiate with unions and insisted their employees sign contracts rejecting any collective action. Already demoralized by the splintering of their movement, members of the international faced added pressures from oil's corporate bosses, who took advantage of the union's fragility. One company in the gulf region forced each of its employees to sign "yellow dog contracts" that stated they would pledge "not to join the union," that "employment was on a day-to-day basis," and that the company "reserved the right to hire and fire without cause." With no alternative, workers signed, handing what little control of their labor they had acquired in the previous few years back to their superiors.[22]

Yet the top-down imposition of corporate prerogatives was subtler than such yellow dog contracts implied. Accompanying business's iron-fisted attempts to restrict workers were velvet-glove endeavors to mollify them through provision of pension plans, cash benefits, stock ownership, recreational outlets and health services, and membership in company-run unions. This softer strategy of welfare capitalism placed employers in paternal rather than adversarial relationships with employees. Anchoring welfare capitalism was the presumption that any solution to the daunting "labor question" would come via environmental improvement and human uplift. "One of the reasons there are so many labor troubles is that we have forgotten the human element," one oil king admitted. "Labor is being looked upon as a commodity . . . that may be bought and sold," he continued. "We sometimes forget that we're dealing with human beings. . . . The big thing we've got to do is inject the spirit of brotherhood into the labor question. There is no other way." That sentiment quickly permeated America's oil patches.[23]

The oil king who uttered that admission was John D. Rockefeller Jr., welfare capitalism's architect. His embrace of the new labor management philosophy was ensconced in his "Rockefeller Plan," which he instituted at the Colorado Fuel and Iron Company (CFI) after the Ludlow massacre of 1914. One of the few corporate directorships he decided to maintain after his turn to philanthropy kept him in charge of the CFI; it was a decision he would regret. Remorseful, he set out to reform industrial relations in his corporate domain. "Rather than fight independent trade unions with guns or injunctions," one historian quips, "[Rockefeller] chose to fight them with kindness." His course of action hinged on the establishment of an advisory board comprised of employers and employees. The plan's constitution required employees to "elect from among their number representatives to act on their behalf with respect to matters pertaining to their employment, working and living conditions, the adjustment of differences, and such other matters of mutual concern and interest as relations within the industry may determine." Together, it was believed, managers and laborers could carve out optimum conditions for collaboration. Part penance, Rockefeller's concession also marked an attempt to recover his reputation and prevent the United Mine Workers of America, heavily critical of Rockefeller, from organizing his company's workforce. But most of all, it was an attempt to enact his theology of humanitarian service. "In no field of human relationships is the spirit of brotherhood on which the church was founded more profoundly needed than in industrial relations," he declared.[24]

The unveiling of the Rockefeller Plan in 1915 in fact marked a revitalization, not the creation, of that theology. The Rockefellers had already begun to grasp for clearer Christian answers to the plagues of industrialism in the early 1900s. At that time Frederick Gates drafted several statements defending the paternal strictures of welfare capitalism. "The spirit of unionism seems to be wholly selfish," he pronounced in a piece titled "Capital and Labor." Unions, he charged, operated out of a "spirit to rob, to confiscate, to absorb remorselessly, cruelly, voraciously, if they can, the whole wealth of society." Yet Gates also acknowledged the deplorable conditions that created the demand for such guilds. Environment, not biology, he underscored, was the determining difference between the laborer and the capitalist, rich and poor. "The blood that courses in their veins is just as pure . . . and probably better than that of most of the aristocracy," he charged; it was only "because they have been living from childhood and working from childhood in the mines" that the poor laborer despaired and sought radical redress. His parting words demanded action. "It is for us who have means, not to resist the claims of these people" but to "cut down their hours of labor. Improve their living conditions. Give them opportunities for music, for pictures, for whatever can cultivate them in mind, whatever can beautify and adorn them in body." Gates's solution to the labor problem was a heavy dose of Christian largesse and a small degree of sacrifice. "Let us ourselves share to some extent the manual labor of the world, and . . . let us undertake [to] build up society in all [its] parts as a whole to a higher level."[25]

Whereas Gates stressed the paternalistic—and patronizing—aspect of early welfare capitalism, Rockefeller's moves in the wake of Ludlow leaned farther toward partnership. Indeed, his drift from Gates was notable. When Gates reacted to the labor protest of the 1910s, he strongly condemned the "labor monopoly" and its "organized and deliberate war on society." Rockefeller, by contrast, embraced a liberal doctrine that proposed representatives of labor and capital work with hands clasped in unity. His courage to do so grew out of his relationships with two younger confidants, men who more fully than Gates recognized the predicaments of modern industry and more anxiously recalibrated their spirituality in an effort to ameliorate them.[26]

William Lyon Mackenzie King provided the initial spark. A graduate of the University of Chicago and Harvard University, where he earned a doctorate in economics, King was both learned and earnest in his intellectual life, wanting to put it to service in his native Canada. Politics provided him with an outlet. During the first decade of the twentieth century he was elected to the Canadian parliament as a Liberal and instrumental in drafting the country's Industrial Disputes Investigation Act and establishing a government office for labor affairs. After his party's ouster in the 1911 election, King returned to the private sector and agreed to Rockefeller's request for help restructuring his company's labor management. He headed the Rockefeller Foundation's Department of Industrial Relations between 1914 and 1918. The two grew close. Based on their shared commitment to the social gospel (King was Presbyterian but fluent in ecumenism and a practicing spiritualist), they constantly exchanged ideas about how to translate, in King's words, "God's love for humanity as expressed in Christ's life and death" to the factory floor. Early in their relationship King scrawled in his diary, "I feel a perfect sympathy in all things as we talk together and have felt it since we first met. . . . Clearly, there is a spiritual or psychic power that has attracted and that attracts and holds." To a friend abroad he professed, "I have found in Mr. John D. Rockefeller, Jr. one of the best of men and . . . almost without exception the truest followers of Christ." Rockefeller was just as enthralled. "I feel I have found in you the brother I have never had and have always wished to have," he told King.[27]

They were an imposing duo when it came to reconceptualizing modern industrial relations. In King's mind, their duty was nothing less than to change the "scene of industrial strife into a valley of contentment & happiness." With the social-justice passion he wore as a politician and churchman, he set out to educate Rockefeller on the finer points of organized labor and to recode any of his remaining antiunion DNA. King wanted his friend to recognize that unions were vital in political economy and not the evil beasts Gates believed them to be. He introduced Rockefeller to labor leaders in hopes of framing a lively dialogue. He also coached him through government investigations that followed the Ludlow affair and convinced him to visit his Colorado operation. In the fall of 1915, King and Rockefeller traveled west, where they spent two weeks touring eighteen different CFI coal mines. They capped off the trip on October 2, 1915. After Rockefeller delivered a lighthearted lecture on company economics, King spoke about the Industrial Representation Plan (the "Rockefeller Plan") that he had spent months crafting, with designs to guide workers into their valley of contentment. He then distributed the document, printed in thirteen languages, to CFI workers, who voted overwhelmingly in its favor. It was the highlight of King and Rockefeller's collaboration. In 1918, King returned to politics, observing that his work with Rockefeller had "opened new horizons, refreshed and restored him, and enabled him to return to his first love better equipped than before."[28]

Rockefeller watched proudly as King subsequently ascended to Canada's prime ministership in 1921; yet he was still disappointed at losing a trusted advisor. Into the vacuum stepped Raymond Fosdick. Much like his preacher brother, Fosdick was a progressive Protestant to the core and determined to apply his faith to real-world problems. After graduating from Princeton University in 1905 and New York Law School in 1908, he was appointed New York's commissioner of investigations, charged with probing fraud and misconduct. While performing his duties and researching "white slave trafficking," he met Rockefeller, who at that moment was overseeing a grand jury investigation of the same issue. After comparing notes and exchanging wisdom on that tangled matter, Rockefeller eventually hired Fosdick to assist with the Rockefeller Foundation's Bureau of Social Hygiene, then in 1920 assigned him a more prominent headship in other initiatives, including the Rockefeller Institute for Medical Research and the General Education Board. Fosdick's service would culminate with his appointment to the presidency of the foundation in 1936. It was through his advising of Rockefeller on labor issues in the 1920s, though, that he became so invaluable. Fosdick became Junior's confidant, King's clear replacement as counselor if not entirely as brotherly friend.[29]

With the same verve as King, Fosdick urged Rockefeller to move farther to the left of the corporate-labor continuum. Fosdick in fact consulted regularly with King in order to present a united front that could prevent Rockefeller from sliding back toward the right. "His instincts are all in the liberal direction," Fosdick wrote King in 1919, but "I am fearful he may be misled by . . . others about 'open shop,' etc." "Collective bargaining is now an established fact," Fosdick continued, and "Mr. Rockefeller should . . . fight for it not only because it is the right end to be achieved, but because it is only through such a spirit of liberalism that revolution can be avoided—if indeed it can be avoided." Fosdick's insistencies stuck. Over the course of the next decade, he and Rockefeller carved out a far-flung educational campaign to inculcate workers, corporate leaders, and citizens with the knowledge that (in Fosdick's words) a "middle way existed between the extremes of militant unionism and business paternalism." Together they wanted to build corporate commonwealths, "communities of interest" where those who toiled and those who administered embodied reciprocity. Their message was delivered in schools, churches, and public settings across the land. "I believe that labor and capital are partners, not enemies," Rockefeller told one audience, "and that neither can attain the fullest measure of prosperity at the expense of the other, but only in association with the other." Meanwhile, he attacked executives who maintained harsh anti-labor tactics. In one instance he supported a study of the steel industry produced by the Interchurch World Movement, which called for an eight-hour workday (instead of twelve). When he learned that United States Steel rejected the proposal, he protested by selling his company stock. In another instance, he took on Indiana Standard for adhering to a twelve-hour-day, seven-day-week policy. As he possessed 15 per-cent of all company stock, Rockefeller's voice carried weight when he publicly railed against a labor policy that was "unnecessary, uneconomic and unjustifiable."[30]

By 1926, it was obvious that Rockefeller had no inclination to slide back toward the right in his labor politics. That fact was made manifest in the incorporation of the Industrial Relations Counselors (IRC), the culmination of Fosdick and Rockefeller's education campaign. With leading executives on its board, including one from Jersey Standard, $1.4 million of Rockefeller's money, and Fosdick's guidance, the IRC quickly became a leading consulting firm in labor relations. Its goal was to create an entire academic discipline, replete with fellowships, research centers, and libraries, in the nation's leading universities. By the end of the decade the IRC would prove successful in penetrating the nation's top schools and boardrooms with its philosophy. At that junc-ture, over three hundred major corporations were deploying employee representation plans of the kind that the IRC had engendered and that Rockefeller, King, and Fosdick had begun preaching in the midst of bloodshed during the 1910s.[31]

To THE CHAGRIN of union activists, Rockefeller and his team of social gospelers and brand of soft diplomacy were successful at sequester-ing organized labor in a political wasteland. Yet they were not solely responsible for the plight of the guild. In oil especially, the Rockefeller Plan succeeded because there already existed a desire for it at the local level and a sense among a rank and file battered by the violent swings of their profession that moderation was the best path forward. In the 1920s, the construction of an organic unity of shared interest and spiritual brotherhood was also an ambition acted upon from the ground up.

At regional firms like Carter Oil Company, an affiliate of Jersey Standard, the abstractions of welfare capitalism became concrete in several ways, starting with the worker's handbook, which served as a bible for each member of the community. "In a Company as large as this," the leather-bound, pocket-sized booklet began, "an employee often thinks he is a very small part of a large machine, and that what he does will hardly be noticed. We want you to know, however, that each employee has an opportunity to become an important part of the Company.... We hope that it will be a pleasure, not a task, to give the best that is in you." Thirty subsequent pages detailed the benefits that employees could look forward to as citizens of the Carter domain. Patterned after the plan that Rockefeller and King introduced in Colorado, Carter's policy stressed the freedom employees enjoyed to mold the company according to their prerogatives. Fair wages, reasonable hours, representation, pensions and vacation days, health and disability benefits, stock options, and regular promotions: these and other perks awaited the responsible and engaged Carter employee, whose feedback Carter managers promised was as cherished as their sweat. But these provisions were more than perks. Employers conveyed them to the employee as threads of commitment that wove the entire corporate body together.[32]

And in that respect, nothing bonded corporate bodies more tightly than the company town, another critical feature of oil's welfare plan, which literally mapped capital wishes onto physical grids. Already popular in other industrial sectors such as steel and coal, this strategy was of vital necessity to the oil sector as it dealt with spasms of development and dissent across the Southwest. One of the first to implement it in the region was the Benedum-Trees oil firm, which built "Trees City" next to its base in northwestern Louisiana. Unveiled in 1909, the bucolic-sounding village was not quite paradise, but it was impressive in its tidy composition of fifty brick homes and a playground, pool, hotel, medical facility, and movie house, all ideal amenities for raising children and providing escape from the causticities of oil. Benedum-Trees chose to face petroleum's human and environmental profligacy head-on by domesticating its workforce. Its philosophy spread in the post–World War I years. Oil companies constructed modest camps comprised of a few bunkhouses in some cases, virtual cities in others. The largest was Phillips Petroleum Company's encampment near Borger, Texas, in the panhandle, which boomed in the 1920s. At its peak it contained a thicket of buildings and a few thousand people (the town would eventually be called Phillips). One of the most celebrated company towns rested due south in the Permian Basin, where oil was just becoming a going concern. West Texas newspapers praised Big Lake Oil Company's "Texon" as the archetypal model town, a pristine oasis of Americana surrounded by foreboding dusty plains, opposite in every way from the usual boomtown. And as one endorsement of Humble Oil's company town in Cushing, Oklahoma, blared, that was exactly the point: "No rough-and-tumble boom town can compete with this neat cottage city, which has utilities and even home delivery of milk."[33]

Oil's proletariat did not need to be prodded. When companies built their towns, workers came and, with employee handbooks and guarantees of well-being in hand, pledged citizenship. Several factors specific to petroleum encouraged them to do so and, in the process, shun the potentials of unionization. With the exception of refining, where larger numbers of men clustered in one industrial complex, most oil work transpired in isolation, typically in remote locations, with small teams toiling to pinpoint drill sites, extract crude from the ground, or link pipe. Such toil demanded movement, a constant gathering of equipment and migration to another distant spot. As a way of life, in other words, early-twentieth-century oil functioned in a work regime defined by isolation and independence, a system very different, for instance, from coal mining, where, as one scholar notes, the concentration and permanence of a large labor force "provided the means for assembling effective democratic claims" through mass action. As witnessed on the Gulf Coast and in Tulsa, oil refineries offered greater opportunity for such united protest, but there too it was difficult to sustain. That is because most of the men who staffed those centers were not conditioned to think in such terms. Labor organizers in the region regularly complained that the men whom they had to woo were products of farm life, ill informed when it came to union tactics and goals and soaked in mythologies of self-sufficiency that shrouded their labor.[34]

The very dynamics that made southwestern oil workers increasingly hesitant to join unions in the 1920s lured them to the corporate compounds that firms like Benedum-Trees and Big Lake calibrated to the conventions of welfare capitalism. Constantly on the move, workers longed for the stability, however brief, that the oil camp or company town could offer; used to the tight-knit communities and community values of their youths, they embraced day-to-day existence in sheltered hamlets, even if it was fleeting.

The childhood of Estha Briscoe speaks to the allure of those places. Between 1921 and 1928, her family moved a dozen times so her father could work as a connection gang pusher—head crewman on a six-member team that installed pipe linking wells to storage tanks. "We learned early in life to deal with an endless procession of trying circumstances," she recalled, "attempting daily to adjust to changing situations as we accompanied our parents along the crude oil trail." In some instances, the Briscoes were forced to inhabit the barely habitable: tents "drawn tight to keep the cold wind from finding the cracks," old bunkhouses plunked down in the desert, ramshackle huts on the outskirts of town. It was a tough life filled with tragedy. "This is one hell of a way to make a living," Estha's father mumbled after a boiler explosion killed a crewman, whose body he helped pick up in pieces. "If I didn't have to do it, I'd never work another day in a damned oil field."[35]

Yet he also cherished the solidarity he shared with his men and the sense of freedom and adventure his job offered, which is why he and his family continued their endless sojourn. For Estha, the hardest part was the lack of stable friendships, and that is why she was always overjoyed when her family got to live in a company town. Her fondest memories were of life in Texon, where families would "share meals often, go on short trips together, keep each other's children, care for illnesses and share each other's joys or misfortunes." Her Texon network of schoolmates was especially large and active, and she relished the chance to play in near-ideal conditions. "Skates were a must," she later wrote. "The perfect sidewalks around each block were finished with a smooth surface, not too good for walking in the rain. But then it scarcely ever rained in West Texas, and the kids skated every day." The Christmas celebrated there in 1925 was the "brightest of my childhood," she remembered, for "we . . . were more prosperous than we had ever been"—comfortable and secure as well.[36]

Designed with those basic needs in mind, company towns were also meant to satisfy sacred longings and turn corporate bodies into godly commonwealths, puritan as well as pristine villages shielded from the foreboding blackness of the world. In places like Trees City and Texon, sponsoring companies ensured that steeples defined the skyline, providing direction. In Texon, the Briscoes attended First Baptist, where Estha's father unexpectedly assumed a leadership role. Seeing himself as an "old gang pusher," John Briscoe hardly felt cut out to be a deacon; yet at First Baptist he was called upon as "brother" to help facilitate worship and prayer. "I had never heard my father pray publicly before," Estha admitted, "but when he gave thanks for 'all the great blessings we have so recently received,' I wanted to shout 'Amen!'" While surprised by her father's public displays of spirituality, Estha viewed it all as a rather normal extension of the contentedness she and her family felt in their miniature utopia and the confidence that bred in her otherwise reticent dad.[37]

Briscoe's was a common experience. Church life in the company town seemed to assume a unique immediacy, especially where young families and their children were involved. A captive audience surrounded by manufactured niceties, compound kids nevertheless had to be won over with a truth that could change their hearts; at least, that is what the preachers who came calling believed. In company towns, revival was a regular occurrence, reports of conversion a celebrated break from otherwise predictable routines. Young Charley Spikes was one such heralded statistic. When he was thirteen, Spikes accepted the invitation of a traveling Baptist minister to walk the sawdust trail toward conversion. He recorded the event in his Bible:

CHARLES WINFRED SPIKES DOB 9-16-19
CONVERTED JUNE—1932 (SECOND BIRTH)
Revival Meeting—Rev E.Λ. Ingram
(30 Baptisms)

Trees Baptist Church
Trees, LA
Baptisted [*sic*] in Jeems Bayou

For the rest of his life, Spikes could flip back through his worn Bible and find a reminder of the day he and twenty-nine other members of his community accepted Christ.[38]

Granted, it was not always so easy to bring residents of company towns to that reckoning, as one itinerant preacher learned while ministering to clustered oil workers in Montana. On this remote oil patch, isolation and independence were all the more pronounced—as was the preference for fishing instead of worshipping on the Sabbath. To win residents over, he turned unconventional: he signed on with the subsidiary of Indiana Standard to work as a roustabout. Labor was tough, the men standoffish, but gradually the man they called "Mister Preacher" won their trust. During the week "Mister Preacher" talked theology while he dug ditches, triggering debates with crewmembers; then on Sunday he delivered a gospel attuned to the community. Rather than slam people with a fire-and-brimstone message, he solicited them with one of belonging. He designed his sermons to dovetail with his parishioners' lives and serve as parables of how biblical principles could apply in the here and now. His other ministerial strategies reflected that same goal. "Where people work six-and-a-half and seven days a week in a raw hole in the ground," he reported, "a preacher has to do other things than merely preach in order to justify his existence." And so he started organizing social and recreational outings, a community sing-along, and vaudevillian performances. The breakthrough followed. "The work on the ditch had sent the tide flowing in my direction," he recounted, "and much of the remaining opposition was broken up ... when I performed as a black-face comedian in a minstrel show given by the Catholics in the Basin to raise money toward the erection of a little chapel for their monthly masses. After that the West opened its arms to the preacher, together with many of the problems in its heart."[39]

Innovation, persistence, and perseverance: these attributes were required of those who sought to instill religious values in the corporate community. But above all else, coordination determined success. In the late 1910s and 1920s, southwestern oil patches in particular were witness to a scale of religious mobilization that transcended the focused activities of any one congregation or firm. Shocked by the ability of the IWW to co-opt traditional religious conveyances for the purpose of revolutionizing workers, large nondenominational organizations such as the YMCA stepped up their own campaigns to repackage a fresh and inviting "old-fashioned" gospel, one with which oil workers were more accustomed. No individual was more instrumental in jump-starting that campaign than J. Edgar Pew.

Pew's efforts to turn his company camps into godly commonwealths grew out of his violent clash with the Wobblies. After guiding his family's company through the chaotic Spindletop years, he had resigned as Sun's Texas agent in 1913. He was now a true son of the Southwest and eager to pursue new Texas and Oklahoma terrains that Sun could not open to him. Recognizing his talent, Jersey Standard hired him to oversee its subsidiary, Carter Oil. Graced with $34 million of Standard cash, Pew quickly turned Carter into a force on Oklahoma's erupting fields—Cushing the largest—which for a stretch of time in the 1910s made the state the nation's largest producer. But in 1918, on the heels of his year of terror in Tulsa, Pew returned to Sun. Although respected by Standard, the Texas-style wildcatter was too self-driven for the cautious major and moved at a hurried clip that worried Jersey executives. So along with his brother, John G., he formally rejoined Sun as vice president and a key member of the board of directors.[40]

Among his first duties was to tidy up Sun's southwestern operations in hopes of inducing peace and increasing its bottom line. Emerging from the "Tulsa Outrage," he was anxious to mitigate tensions and literally "clean up the mess." To his manager in the Caddo Camp, located just outside Ranger, Texas, site of perhaps the most raucous oil boomtowns, Pew offered practical solutions: "get them all imbued with the idea that the condition of the camp . . . is dependent upon them each individually," he insisted. "We have a large property out there, and are possibly capable of producing a lot of oil. Let us also see if we cannot make it a model property in every respect." In 1920 Pew and Sun officials also approved alterations to Caddo's social environment by upgrading its athletic facilities and housing, and in 1925 they instituted a stock-sharing plan, which allowed employees to "purchase Sun common stock with payroll deductions up to ten percent of their earnings." The company then matched every dollar they committed with a fifty-cent contribution. Sun followed up with other incentives such as a group life pension plan and eventually a company-run union called the Sun Oil Employee and Management Counsel. But Pew and his brethren were not just following the Rockefeller lead. They also stood out front in the crusade to reorient their workers' and industry's moral and political compasses.[41]

One of the clearest demonstrations of that involved the YMCA, which the Pews, like Lyman and Milton Stewart, had always generously supported. Also like the Stewarts, the Pews took old-fashioned evangelism seriously. Following the example of Sun's founder, who transported his workers to Billy Sunday revivals, Edgar and his cousin, Sun's new president J. Howard Pew, donated considerable sums to make sure the same preaching touched the ranks of their working class. Still, in partnering with the YMCA, the Pews wanted more than proselytization. The YMCA pledged to offer a program geared to the formation of a "healthy spirit, mind, and body," and when surveying their camps and the degree to which the entire labor system was broken, the Pews considered this capacious agenda a must.[42]

In 1919, Edgar assumed the regional chairmanship of the Committee on Welfare Work of the American Petroleum Institute (API), a body tasked with harmonizing "the whole situation" with labor. With the tenacity he demonstrated in oil exploration, he hounded his equals at sixteen oil companies, including Texaco, Humble, and Gulf, with solicitations to contribute to an annual fund. Between 1919 and 1920, he raised nearly $30,000, then partnered with the YMCA, which used every cent to busy oil workers with a full repertoire of entertainment, education, athletics, and worship. According to a ledger for the month of March 1920, at Caddo a total of 3,085 men took advantage of a range of activities that included community socials (260 men), "athletics" (130), and "baths" (871). Caddo workers were also encouraged to enroll in night school to learn "Business-English," arithmetic, and Spanish. "This is the young man's opportunity to fit himself for promotion in his chosen vocation by improving his education," advertisements read. "Get ready for the great openings in Mexico, Central and South America by acquiring a start in the knowledge of Spanish." While YMCA officials took pride in the breadth of their offerings, they also noted the gains made in what remained the most important measurement: numbers of souls touched. At one of their camps 430 workers attended religious meetings, more than participated in any other activity. After the first year of operation J. Edgar Pew was pleased. "On the whole," he told his friends, "I think this work has come up to expectations, and believe that it has shown its worth. The men located in these fields . . . have but little opportunity at best . . . for improvement of their minds or for amusement, all of which go so much toward contentment."[43]

Pew's was clearly a pragmatism blended with Protestant conviction that fueled so many of the welfare programs his class of executives introduced across the Southwest; yet still other displays of this philosophy made it so pervasive. Echoing the transcendent desires of an earlier generation of oilmen, some petroleum bosses sought to bind communities on even stronger foundations of shared aspirations and equality, where residues of hierarchical power still evidenced in the Rockefeller and Pew plans were eradicated altogether.

No one was more daring in that aim than Edgar Byram Davis. In the first decades of the twentieth century, he made millions of dollars through investments in foreign rubber plantations (he was the largest individual shareholder of the United States Rubber Company), then gave most of the profits to friends before joining his brother Oscar's oil venture near Luling, in south-central Texas. Edgar had come to believe God's hand was upon him during his time in the jungles of Sumatra, where he oversaw US Rubber's efforts to plant 5 million trees. "This was poisonous snake country," he recalled, "but to show God's Guiding Hand, I was given the faith to go through all those years in the East without wearing leggings or puttees." Davis was certain he was anointed with a special destiny and that fortunes and faith would align in Luling. It took time, however, for providence to kick in. Before he died in 1920, Oscar Davis had invested $75,000 in wells, all of which came up dry, something skeptical geologists had predicted. Already facing doubters, Edgar dove into the project and incorporated the United North and South Oil Company, a gesture toward national unity, then kept drilling. Even after the sixth attempt failed, he set down another well, debt be damned. On August 9, 1922, the seventh derrick erupted. For the next four years Davis rapidly expanded his empire in ways that he had promised his neighbors. Upon his arrival in Luling, he had become convinced God wanted him to deliver it from the area's oppressive one-crop (cotton) economy. Now, as riches poured in, he channeled them toward agricultural development and an expansive educational program designed to teach local citizens, trapped in the crop lien system, "husbandry techniques and methods for diversifying crops." Black gold was to be Luling's escape from white gold. That plan grew in scale when Davis sold his interests in the Luling Oil Field to Magnolia Petroleum in 1926. The $12 million that Magnolia paid Davis was the most lucrative oil deal ever recorded.[44]

The wildcatter immediately doled it out. He gifted funds to Luling for parks, churches, and community centers. More importantly, he established the Luling Foundation, an act its officials would later paint as a "thanks offering to God . . . for the Divine Guidance which he knew had led him to discovery of the rich Luling oil field." The foundation was charged with dispersing a major portion of Davis's payoff into his agricultural program and its training in "terracing; proper fertilization; crop rotation; improvement of beef and dairy herds, hogs, sheep, and poultry; [and] intensive tillage." While he backed the foundation in hopes of addressing the nation's rural challenges, upon the sale of control to Magnolia Davis he also announced he was handing one-quarter of his windfall to his employees in profit shares. The announcement was delivered at a thank-you barbeque that he hosted on June 5, 1926. No one had ever seen anything like it before. One report stated that between 15,000 and 35,000 denizens of area counties "were treated to 6 tons of beef, 5,180 pounds of mutton, 2,000 frying chickens, 28,000 bottles of soft drinks, 6,000 bottles of near-beer, 8,700 bricks of ice cream, 7,000 cakes, and vats of beans, potato salad, and coffee." When the sun set, Davis "handed out 100,000 cigarettes and 7,500 cigars and told his weary guests of his ambitious plans for the region." "I may go broke again," he conceded, "but it looks as though I would have the fun of giving away several millions of dollars before I do." For years people would marvel at the antics of a "share-the-wealth messiah who actually practiced what he preach[ed]."[45]

Davis may have represented a radical edge of welfare capitalism, but even in its moderate doses the program proved effective in turning workers back toward the familiar cultural setting in which they had been raised—a setting in which steeples, plain preaching about God's grace, and hymns like "There Is Power in the Blood"—not "There Is Power in a Union"—registered as normal. If anecdotes from Sun Oil's operations are indicative, by 1930 it seemed evident that oil companies had managed to repossess the hearts of their employees. When rumblings of strike action appeared on an Oklahoma field, Sun's manager promised that the Pews could count on "100 percent" loyalty. "I assured the boys that we would take care of them as we had always done in the past and that I did not think it would be wise for them to join any organization." The manager's pledge was solid, and Sun workers stayed true to their company's plan. A story circulating at the time suggests they did so out of heart-felt concern. When an on-site preacher prayed for God to bless the "pure and humble" in area oil fields (referencing Pure Oil and Humble Oil companies), a roughneck interjected, "Don't forget about Sun."[46]

FOR SUN AND its competitors, reclaiming the loyalties of the working class was one tough challenge; winning the allegiance of America's consuming class was another. In the booming 1920s, as new middle-class dreams of mobility heightened petroleum's importance, journalists scrutinized oil companies as a nasty blot on the American conscience. As much as they decried organized labor as un-American, oil barons, engulfed in scandal, themselves now bore the same stigma.

Such charges emerged from several different directions for several different reasons, but all of them hovered around the basic fact that with the dawn of the automotive age, America craved oil like never before. In 1916, Shell Oil chief Henri Deterding wrote to an associate, "This is a century of travel, and the restlessness which has been created by the war will make the desire for travel still greater." He meant travel by all means, but in the United States the automobile reigned supreme. In the year of Deterding's missive, there were 3.4 million registered cars in the country. Over the next decade, with Ford and General Motors racing to produce more product, that number would rise in staggering proportions. By the end of the 1920s, 3.4 million had turned into 23.1 million registered vehicles, and each year those vehicles were being driven farther, from an average per car of 4,500 miles in 1919 to 7,500 miles in 1925. That stunning transformation was global, yet also undeniably American. As of 1929, 78 percent of the world's total automobiles were in the United States. In order to drive those cars, motorists needed gasoline—a lot of gasoline. Fuel now surpassed light as oil's fundamental contribution to American life.[47]

So the question for oilmen was straightforward: how to keep America's pistons stroking and wheels turning. With a renewed determination they accelerated their search for domestic sources and better processes of tapping and distributing their liquid goods. As a result of their efforts, crude production increased by two and a half times during the decade, from 1.03 million barrels per day in 1919 to 2.58 per day in 1929. Yet, at each step of the way, they faced a litany of self-inflicted pressures and scathing press coverage from a new print media anxious to protect the interests of average Americans. Precisely because of their dependence on oil, Americans readily digested the era's muckraking journalism, which said it was time for them to demand more from oil's bosses. Caught in a conundrum, with the imperative to produce resulting in a pell-mell rush for new oil pools and more profits, those bosses of oil struggled under the weight of moral censure.[48]

As newspapers portrayed the situation, American consumers had every right to condemn the petroleum business for its deadly sins. The first of these was gluttony. Coming out of World War I, a time when they had enjoyed leverage in Washington, US oil companies were supremely confident they possessed the license to value their product and absorb their profits as they saw fit. But as consumers' stake in the gas pump increased, so did their criticisms of oil's pricing. Major newspapers kept readers informed of the latest price climbs and political pushbacks. Jersey Standard and Socony—and, with them, the Rockefellers, who were singled out as primary stockholders—once again found themselves targeted. At a meeting of the Senate oil investigating committee in 1922, Standard representatives were grilled about a price hike at the pumps. Wisconsin senator Robert La Follette asked how it was that the pricing of gasoline by "five leading buying companies" had "risen and fallen almost simultaneously during 1921 and 1922," a hint at collusion. La Follette also used the occasion to send a warning to the American people, predicting they would soon be paying $1 a gallon for gasoline (a prediction that would soon prove imprudent as gasoline prices plummeted to thirteen cents per gallon). For their part, Standard officials rejected La Follette's innuendo. "The crux of the gasoline situation is this," they argued: "the price is not fixed by the Standard Oil Company (New Jersey) nor by any other large company, nor by any association or group of companies. It is fixed by the consumer and expressed by demand." But few people, including La Follette, believed them.[49]

As La Follette indicated, it was not simply customers who felt gouged; government felt the same. In the waning days of World War I, US Secretary of the Navy Josephus Daniels jotted in his diary what so many Americans would come to believe: "President of Standard Oil Co & Mr. Doheny urged [me] to accept high price proposed. Standard gets unholy profits though Rockefeller may think they are holy." A North Carolinian with strict Methodist morals and populist antipathies toward big business, Daniels not only hated the fact that he had to cave to pressures and pricing wielded by large oil corporations; he also despised the work he had to perform as the navy's headman to protect those same corporations' interests abroad, particularly in Mexico. Big oil's constant push into that unstable region for more crude placed Washington in a precarious spot, and Daniels would come to decry the unevenness of that arrangement.[50]

The court of public opinion also leveled charges of greed against oilmen. Never content with what they already possessed, oilmen seemed perfectly willing to steal others' possessions. That narrative developed in parallel with the price-fixing storyline and revolved around the tragic case of Osage Indians in northern Oklahoma. Oil was discovered on Osage lands in the late nineteenth century. For the next twenty years it continued to flow at astronomical rates, spectacularly enriching the tribe's 2,200 members. According to the US Interior Department, Osage tribesmen were "the wealthiest people, per capita" with "property aggregating one and one-half billions of dollars." Due to perceived incongruences of race and open envy of their limousines and fine dress, white Americans turned the Osage into targets of derision. The "Red Men" were uncouth, journalists editorialized, and suffered from "a childlike lack of discretion in the management of their affairs." "Spending their money is a passion," jingoists added. "They will buy almost anything that strikes their fancy, from a case of chewing gum to a coffin."[51]

Racial bigotries notwithstanding, the Osage became another parable of oil's utter disregard for others. In accordance with a 1921 law passed by the US Congress, which deemed Osage people unable to manage their wealth, all Indians of the oil region were appointed with guardians, primarily white lawyers and businessmen placed in charge of royalties. By 1924, it was clear the system was rife with malfeasance. That year a report by the Office of the Indian Rights Association revealed "an orgy of graft and exploitation" in Oklahoma, where oil-hungry whites were using guardianship to seize the land. Journalists confirmed that oilmen were grabbing up every available holding, while besieged Indians looked on helplessly. The scathing Indian rights report forced Congress to research the claims. It found that at least six hundred guardians had swindled $8 million from Osage oil funds. Worse than the fiscal exploitation, Indian rights advocates charged, was that guardians were turning a blind eye as "girls [were] robbed of their virtue and their property." Rape was accompanied by murder. Early in 1922 the bullet-pierced body of Anna Brown, an oil-rich Osage, was discovered in a canyon. A few weeks later, assassins killed other members of her clan. "First it was one family," observers noted, "then another, but always death struck the wealthiest families of Indians, and always a member who controlled a large share of the fortune." By 1925, at least sixty Osage people had been killed, their land deeded to guardians. Agents with the Federal Bureau of Investigation uncovered troubling schemes; in some cases, white men were inducing rich Indians (often through marriage) to sign life insurance policies. When the rich Indians died, conveniently, the white men, who ensured they were designated beneficiaries, claimed the wealth. Two men who deployed such tactics were eventually charged with murder of one Osage family and, in 1929, sentenced to life in prison. Yet everyone knew that the conspiracy extended beyond these convicts, just how far no one could tell. Americans did seem to know that the "reign of terror" in Osage county was further proof that the oil curse was itself a cause for horror.[52]

Another sin was pride, to which the oil business seemed most prone in the 1920s. At least that was the takeaway from the decade's biggest oil scandal. It began in 1912 when President William Taft established three naval petroleum reserves at Elk Hills in Central California. Taft put these potentially (likely) oil-rich plots of land aside in order to ensure that the US Navy possessed future oil supplies. Oilmen agitated for a reversal and, throughout the presidency of Woodrow Wilson, pressured Washington to lease out the land. Secretary of the Navy Daniels denounced them, swearing he would "order marines to the oil fields" if they attempted to drill. Wilson's White House resisted leasing the land to oil companies, but Warren G. Harding's did not. New Mexico's Albert Fall, the new Republican secretary of the interior, lobbied for Washington to start transferring the reserves to firms owned by his friends. Harding agreed, and the transfers began. Fall dealt most closely with Los Angeles tycoon Edward Doheny and Harry Sinclair, head of Sinclair Oil. Why two wealthy oilers would take such a risk remained a mystery, but one commentator asserted a short time later that it boiled down to their "obsessive lust" and "ravening appetite for oil" "wherever it might be found." Fall's intentions were clearer. In exchange for giving Doheny and Sinclair access to one of the Elk Hills reserves and an additional one in Wyoming, called Teapot Dome, he was promised they would help fund a storage facility for the fleet at Pearl Harbor. Behind closed doors Fall was also gifted $100,000.[53]

Upon receipt of his reward, Fall retired to ranch life in New Mexico, but it took little time for word of the trade-off to spread. Snippets of Fall's deal filtered from the press in April 1922. The US Senate opened a full-fledged investigation. Over the next several months, the Senate committee uncovered one titillating secret after another, including Doheny's admission that his son had carried the $100,000 right to Fall's office in a "little black bag." The press pounced. By late 1924, one writer noted, Washington was "wading shoulder-deep in oil. . . . The newspaper correspondents write of nothing else. Congress has abandoned all other business." Seeking distance from the tumult in an election year, in which he sought to run on his own merits, Vice President Calvin Coolidge fired the deceased Harding's associates and appointed a bipartisan duo of prosecutors. The strategy got him elected in 1924, but the scandal continued until 1931, when Fall was finally convicted. Before entering jail Fall attended a final board meeting at Sinclair Oil, where he received a "vote of confidence" from the company's directors. Sinclair himself received a light six-month jail sentence, while Doheny was judged innocent. "You can't convict a million dollars," one senator chortled.[54]

Such blatant disregard for any higher authority or purpose magnified the public's disdain for Doheny's clique. As the Teapot Dome scandal unfolded, critics ratcheted up their moral critiques of the business and its political stooges. One exposé in particular encapsulated oil and society's slide. Upton Sinclair was a household name by then. Emerging alongside Ida Tarbell in muckraking journalism, he left his initial mark with publication of *The Jungle* in 1906, a novel that unmasked Chicago's meatpacking industry and led Theodore Roosevelt to pass the Pure Food and Drug Act and the Meat Inspection Act. Unlike Tarbell, Sinclair wrote with a heavy socialist hand to show readers the biting realities of capitalism. That political bent intensified after he witnessed the labor struggles of the mid-1910s (he himself traveled to Ludlow and marched with protestors on Rockefeller's New York headquarters), then moved to California. Once settled in Pasadena, Sinclair immersed himself in IWW politics as the organization tried one last time to mobilize longshoremen and demand the release of imprisoned Wobblies. But by 1924, he was enamored of oil discoveries near Signal Hill in Long Beach, one of two new fields in the reawakened Los Angeles Basin, the other being Huntington Beach, where derricks towered over sunbathers. After several trips to the hotspot, notebook in hand, he told his wife, Mary Craig, it was time for another novel. "Don't you see what we've got here? Human nature laid bare! Competition in excelsis! The oil industry—free, gratis, and for nothing! How could I pass it up?" Anxious to capture that mad dash for crude, Sinclair and Craig moved closer to Signal Hill, near oil plots that Craig managed to purchase. There they took in the full picture, a process aided by Craig's involvement in neighborhood meetings with property owners who sought to organize before larger firms bought up a few adjoining lots and drained their oil.[55]

Opening with a meeting of property owners on "Prospect Hill" and the panicked fits of oil leasing that consumed them, *Oil!* was published in 1927. Told through the eyes of Bunny Ross, son of oil magnate J. Arnold Ross, it is a coming-of-age tale on multiple levels. For Bunny, it is a journey into maturity and recognition that the petroleum world is a cruel, vexing place. He watches his father struggle to succeed as a wildcatter, yet embraces the adventure it requires; he helps his father discover a promising drill site, called Paradise, yet constantly urges him to embrace caution. "Listen, Dad," he pleads, "couldn't you stop your new developments, and put everything on a cash basis, and go slow? You know, that might be better, in a way; you're trying to do too much." "Son, but oil ain't cash; it has got to be sold," Ross answers, defending his manic pace. Through his presence at Paradise, Bunny develops a relationship with two sons of a local farmer, one of them named Paul Watkins. On account of the left-wing influence of Paul and his own college education, Bunny commits to a thoughtful, activist strand of socialism, intending to solve the capitalist injustices that oil helped create.[56]

Sinclair captures other evolutions and other illustrations of petroleum's heavy burdens as well. There is Bunny's father, who weathers the wins and losses of his business with a willingness to endure its pain. That system certainly does its damage. Early on Ross rides petroleum's World War I boondoggle to success and becomes a proud independent oilman eager to take on the majors—the "dirty crowd . . . [that] didn't think the little fellows had any business on earth." But as his career unfolds, he gets wrapped up in a syndicate that brokers a secret deal for government reserves. Under physical duress, Ross flees the country; nearing death, he gives his son a final hug and a large check, his inheritance. "Take your time," he warns Bunny, "and . . . don't let your self be plucked by grafters." On his deathbed Ross acknowledges the wisdom of his son: slow down and steer away from the false assurances of crude.

Then there is Eli Watkins, Paul's brother. Sinclair paints Eli as a charlatan who uses his family's proximity to oil to build a Pentecostal empire. Eli prays over the Paradise well, pleading for God's reward. When oil erupts, so does Eli's career. Soon he is everywhere, holding revivals at which church folk "break into ejaculations at every pause in the prophet's words." Eli wants to reach oil laborers too. At Paradise, with backing from oil executives, he softens workers' will with "bright lights . . . and the heavenly raptures, all free—and with a gambler's chance of heaven thrown in!" "The 'wobblies' also were trying to stir the revival spirit in their members, and use the power of song," Sinclair writes, but "feeble indeed was the singing in the 'jungles,' compared with the mighty blast of Eli's silver trumpets, and the hosannas of his hosts." In Eli's coming of age, oil and religion fuse structures of oppression together, tricking petroleum's underclass into believing that the ecstasies of the black stuff are theirs to enjoy too, in heaven if not on earth.[57]

Sinclair's novel garnered instant notice. While one critical reviewer thought it burdened with "a dreadful amount of radical sentimentality," most hailed it as one of Sinclair's finest literary creations and, in the lineage of Ida Tarbell, another stinging indictment of petroleum. Yet Sinclair's indictment stung more than Tarbell's. In Tarbell's rendering, oil was not as much to blame as the monopolists who ran it and destroyed honest entrepreneurs like her father. In Sinclair's, oil represented the worst of a capitalist system that destroyed humanity completely, a system that quashed otherwise hardworking, well-meaning men like Ross, encouraged the otherworldly fanaticisms of manipulative hypocrites like Eli Watkins, weighed heavily on young men like Paul Watkins as they tragically searched for a better way, and left innocents such as Bunny adrift in the modern world. Sinclair's, in other words, was a complete condemnation, which, socialist propagandizing aside, resonated with a public completely beleaguered by oil.[58]

Sinclair made that moral takeaway fully apparent on his last page. After Paul dies for his radical beliefs, his sister Ruth, one of Bunny's favorites, walks the derrick-dotted fields of Paradise in grief, only to fall into an open oil pit and die. Bunny's—Sinclair's—parting words leave little doubt as to what they wish for society: "Some day all those unlovely derricks will be gone, and so will . . . the graves. There will be other girls with bare brown legs running over those hills, and they may grow up to be happier women, if men can find some way to chain the black and cruel demon which killed Ruth Watkins and her brother—yes, and Dad also: an evil Power which roams the earth, crippling the bodies of men and women, and luring the nations to destruction by visions of unearned wealth, and the opportunity to enslave and exploit labor."[59]

WITH WORDS SUCH as those filtering through print, oilmen felt they were facing a political threat more nebulous than organized labor. A sick irony was not lost on them: at the very moment they should have been seizing control of a roaring economy, they were stuck on their heels, embroiled in scandal due to their missteps and saddled with tarnished reputations. But they did not stay stuck for long. Even as scandals began to break, they started refashioning their industry as the standard-bearer of pure all-American values, a boon for the nation, not its foulest blight.

Their attempts at an industry makeover began internally with a season of self-reflection. How could US petroleum act with greater modesty in both conducting business and connecting with the consumer? Some members of oil's highest echelon called for corporate leaders' honest grappling with systemic failures that muckrakers exposed. No one was more vociferous than John D. Rockefeller Jr. Once again, Indiana Standard angered him the most. He had challenged the company before, when it refused to budge from a twelve-hour-day, seven-day-week work policy. In the mid-1920s, he demanded the resignation of company boss Colonel Robert Stewart. Stewart was tied to a bogus trading company involved in the Teapot Dome scandal, through which government kickbacks were channeled to oil executives, but he refused to cooperate with any investigation or heed Rockefeller's call to resign. Driven by an indignation that he now shared with Ida Tarbell, with whom he had begun dialoguing in the early 1920s, Junior lashed out. Appearing before a Senate committee in 1928, he stated that "in the affair of Colonel Stewart, nothing less than the 'basic integrity' of the company and indeed of the whole industry was at stake." Something drastic had to be done. Junior engaged in a proxy war to win stockholders' support to oust the chairman; Stewart showered extra dividends on them in hopes of stemming the tide. In early 1929, the moral crusader got his wish. Armed with 60 percent of the stockholders' votes, Junior forced Stewart's resignation. One small cleanup was done.[60]

But as industry insiders such as Sun Oil executive J. Edgar Pew knew, the cleanup had to involve much more than sporadic public clashes and maybe even a visible hand of top-down oversight. In his mind, the key agent of change had to be the American Petroleum Institute. It was founded in 1919 as a way for oilmen of "every branch of the Industry" to "continue the co-operation and good fellowship" they had achieved during World War I. The API was more than a fraternity, however; it was a clearinghouse for industry concerns, a command post for application of industry-wide standards, and a lobby through which oil representatives could impress their wishes upon Washington and the public. The Pews were key to the organization from its very beginning. Both Howard and Edgar assumed significant posts in its national leadership apparatus and served on a number of its councils, one being the Committee on Welfare Work. In 1924, Edgar ascended to the top. At its annual meeting, the API found itself wracked with division over how to respond to federal regulatory initiatives and petroleum's ill standing in the public eye. Respected for his roots in both the northeastern and the southwestern oil fields and for his ability to bridge gaps—ideological and personal—Pew was voted the API's second president.[61]

He was not a pushover, however. In the coming years he guided the API through several heated debates. One concerned how and how much the industry should impose self-regulations. Unitization and standardization were the hot-button issues. Thanks to Pew, the latter gained substantial support. Prior to his presidency, most oil equipment varied wildly in size, making collective ventures beyond company lines nearly impossible. During and after his presidency, the API encouraged an overhaul and systematization of all equipment in order to promote uniformity. In Pew's eyes, standardization was "the greatest example" of how oil companies could fashion "joint operations" for a greater good. For his efforts, he was proclaimed the "father of standardization." Unitization, which sought to apportion production in any one field to rates of extraction voluntarily agreed upon by its producers, proved more difficult. Some insiders saw it as a way to offset charges of excess leveled against the industry by the Senate on pricing and to tame, if slightly, the rule of capture. Under Pew's watch the API considered the proposal, but opposition was fierce, including from within Sun's own camp. Edgar's cousin J. Howard Pew denounced any mandated regulations as wrong in principle because they undermined oil's founding laws and because they favored major oil companies, which could afford the patience and caution demanded by the plan. Edgar was more open-minded and supported voluntary unitization, but for the time being the entire proposal was shelved.[62]

A second debate was more daunting. In the wake of the Teapot Dome affair, President Calvin Coolidge formed an oversight body, the Federal Oil Conservation Board (FOCB), whose calls for regulation rang API alarm bells. Under Pew's direction, the API assembled a report for the FOCB that documented the oil resources still at America's disposal and denied the industry's wastefulness. Pew and the API were also determined to offset growing fears, backed by some statistics, that despite notable gains the United States still faced the prospect of oil depletion. For the first time (not the last), prevailing opinion suggested US domestic reserves had peaked. The Pews rejected the negative outlook. Howard accused majors and government of fearmongering their way toward regulatory power. "My father was one of the pioneers in the oil industry," he told oilman-opponent Mark Requa. "Periodically ever since I was a small boy, there has been an agitation predicting an oil shortage, and always in succeeding years the production has been greater than ever before." Regardless, notable oil leaders such as Requa and Jersey Standard's Walter Teagle rejected the API and called for government-industry partnership. Requa laid out the controversy in stark terms: "The roads diverge. One leads to cooperation, the other to obstruction of all cooperative effort. The industry must elect which one it will follow." Howard responded with his own stridence. As far as he was concerned, Teagle's friendliness with government was "bunk ... conducted for the sole purpose of creating good-will" for his firm. And Requa was undermining "those who have spent their lives in the development of the most efficient and effective industry in the world." For Howard, the only response to flaws in the system was no response. "I must confess," he wrote Edgar, "deep in my heart I have a conviction that the proper solution of this problem can only result from the ultimate working out of the economic law of supply and demand." Edgar entertained regulation at the state level only. But no answer sufficed, and the tangled issues of external regulation were left unsolved.[63]

In the meantime, Edgar achieved clearer victories in another realm he deemed essential to the recovery of oil's reputation: public relations. As far as he and his cousin were concerned, it was the most important responsibility assigned to the API. Among Edgar's first acts was to demand the resignations of four high-profile members of the API board who were linked to the Teapot Dome scandal, including Harry Sinclair and Edward Doheny. The Pews had long criticized Sinclair for his involvement in several questionable deals and, as Edgar quipped in a letter to his cousin, for carrying on as "a horse race man and gambler." Edgar believed the firings marked a first step toward earning "a sympathetic ear in Washington" and with the public. That symbolic purge was only the beginning of Edgar's much wider publicity campaign to regain the nation's trust. Howard was pleased. "I have personally been urging such a campaign for several years," he told his cousin. While Howard believed a few paid advertisements in prominent magazines would suffice, Edgar envisioned a complete program of proselytization through the dissemination of information. The public has to "know the truth about the difficulties of the oil business," he explained, "and the industry is entitled to have the protection which justly belongs to it, as a result of the truth being made known." In late May 1924 he set plans in motion for the creation of a "publicity committee" comprised of corporate heads and editors of trade publications and managed by a general chairman—"a thoroughly experienced oil man who would devote his entire time to this work." Pew wanted that chairman to demonstrate to all Americans that the oil industry was "not out of control," that its profits were "not unreasonable," and that the entirety of its operations aligned with market principles.[64]

But he also wanted to provide a fuller pedagogy that linked oil to Christian American values. In positive—not simply defensive—terms, Pew and the API set out to portray their business as pure. That meant shoring up the integrities of the industry itself. In consultation with the Pews, the API drafted a "code of ethics," which upon its unveiling in 1928 marked the industry's first substantive articulation of trade practices. More conspicuously, the API enhanced its educational drive, which included college lecture circuits, by mass-distributing a three-hundred-page volume titled *Petroleum Facts and Figures*. "In addition to having been sent to the 3700 members of the Institute," overseer Leonard Fanning relayed in a 1929 report, "a thousand copies were sent to editors of selected newspapers, to college libraries, to public libraries, to government officials, and to banking and other financial houses." Fanning was thrilled with the feedback. By all accounts, he stated, the volume "is informing the industry and the public as to the extent of the services rendered by the petroleum industry," as well as the "contributions of the industry to the labors of research, to the public welfare, and to national, state and municipal taxation . . . [and] the innumerable ways in which petroleum products enter into the daily life of the people." Morally upright, plugged into the public's best interests, and paying its dues—this was the oil industry that Pew and his allies wanted people to recognize, not the shameful one of Harry Sinclair's vein.[65]

Pew and the API took their publicity crusade yet one step further. It was not enough to inundate the public with voluminous data points; they had to "catch the eyes of the public and hold their attention" with glitz. With increased proficiency as the decade wore on, the API funneled articles, replete with illustrations, to US newspapers—at one point over 1,500 newspapers total, located "in all parts of the country." Petroleum, these feel-good write-ups proclaimed, was purely American; at the dawn of the automobile age, it was the "lifeblood of the nation." That sentiment was conveyed through API's folksy history lessons. In one piece, readers of the nation's dailies learned how George Washington was among the first to discover oil during his travels through Pennsylvania. "Washington many times declared petroleum would be a highly important industry," the API essayist underscored, fusing the legacies of petroleum and the country's iconic president. In another piece, readers were whisked away to the Panama Canal, the brainchild of the iconic Theodore Roosevelt, to see how the transportation of oil from west to east was raising their quality of life. Geopolitical gains were to be noted too, the article said, as the transfer of crude was placing the Panama Canal ahead of the Suez Canal as the most important transfer point in the world. Thanks to their adept exploitation of Roosevelt's creation, American oil companies were providing the "light of civilization" across two oceans and to the far reaches of the globe and making America rich in the process. Whether looking backward or forward, at home or abroad, API propagandists intimated, oil was America's—and by extension the world's—salvation.[66]

Of course it was not just the Pews and API transmitting that message in the 1920s. Across the industry as a whole, executives were learning from advertisers how to spice up their offerings. The most famous ad man of the decade was certainly on their side. Having grown up in a devout family, with a famed Congregational minister as his father, Bruce Barton knew the powerful hold visions of the holy could have over people. After becoming a journalist and publicist, he recognized just how supple those visions could be and how far they could stretch from pulpits into boardrooms. In 1925 he published his breakout book,

*The Man Nobody Knows*, which recast Jesus as a "man's man" who navigated his landscape and times with daring and resolve and mentored his disciples and followers with a conquering spirit. In Barton's parable, Jesus was the "world's greatest business executive" and had much to teach the corporate leaders of 1920s America. On the heels of that success, Barton toured to deliver the New Testament's sales pitch for corporate America in person, and oil's leaders were receptive to what he had to say. In 1928 he spoke to a group of petroleum executives and implored them to change their ways. For too long, he exclaimed, they had handled their product poorly, with no attempt to lift it "out of the category of a hated expense." As a result, gasoline—their black gold— was not cherished, as it should be, as a sign of "health," "comfort," and "success" but derided as a "bad smelling liquid," something "for father to grumble about in the family budget . . . [and] mother to economize on." "There is a magnificent place for imagination in your business," Barton declared, "but you must get it on the other side of the pump." He encouraged oil executives to "stand for an hour" at their filling stations, talk to real people, and learn "what magic a dollar's worth of gasoline a week has worked in their lives." Only then would they realize they were proprietors of liquid lure, the "juice of the fountain of eternal youth," the source of miracles, all of which they needed to shout from the mountaintop.[67]

To what extent Barton triggered their rethinking is unclear, but by the late 1920s oil executives seemed to have mastered his communications strategies. Evidence of that showed at the pump, Barton's hallowed ground. By then, the gas service station was oil companies' access point to the heart of America. They adopted flashy logos that helped customers not only identify their product but identify it with the nation's core virtues. There was Texaco's resplendent star and Sun's gleaming diamond, emblems of authentic value and success; Union's "76" and Phillips's "66," signaling America's founding and pioneering spirit; and Jersey Standard's red, white, and blue—all indicators of radiant patriotism. Sinclair's brontosaurus went one step beyond, linking business and Americana with the ancientness—and superior quality—of its brand. All these symbols "became the icons of a secular religion," one historian remarks, "providing drivers with a feeling of familiarity, confidence, and security—and belonging—as they rolled along ever-lengthening ribbons of roads that crossed and crisscrossed America." Functioning under these gleaming symbols were primed and polished stations, whose managers attended to every minutia. Rest rooms were to be pristine, products neatly arranged in eye-catching cases, decor fresh and in keeping with corporate aesthetics. There were to be maps on display—a lot of them, charting every state of the union, all intricately created and neatly packaged by the oil companies themselves. The oil company map was indeed the new staple of the era and a venerated commodity for the family with wanderlust. Then there were the attendants. Decked out in crisp uniforms, they were commanded to pump gas, provide air and water, offer directions, and sell company products with an inviting smile. As one Shell manual emphasized, salesmen were to be gracious and free of "personal opinions and prejudices," as well as articulate, always speaking the king's English to all classes of consumers, and always ready to serve.[68]

Whereas the service station was corporate oil's contact with the customer, the in-house company magazine became the customer's conduit to oil's wider world. Initially, the magazines were created to keep company workers informed and wedded to the corporate commonwealth. Whether it be Jersey Standard's *The Lamp* or Sun Oil's *Our Sun*, Indiana Standard's *The Torch and Oval* or Gulf's *The Orange Disc*, the template was the same. Inside the bright, full-color cover of a typical issue readers encountered articles and statistics documenting their company's progress and snapshot profiles of particular facets of the corporate family, be it oil truckers on America's roads or tanker crews on mighty oceans. No issue was complete without lighthearted witticisms and the honoring of employees. Gulf workers likely winced at the "Gulf-Grams" of wisdom their organ offered: "Every employee should have a lot of 'GULF PRIDE'—both in his engine and in his soul"; "The employees of the Drilling Department are the only ones who start at the top and work down—the balance of us have to work up." *The Orange Disc* also recorded employee accomplishments and letters, all of which it claimed testified "that a breathing, loyal Gulf Family really exists." In parting words, the magazines also implored their readers not only to embrace their belonging to their corporate families but to share in the enlightening of the world through support of oil's higher calling of service. Indiana Standard's *Torch and Oval* explicitly embraced the metaphor, calling on its readers and employees to be "Torch Bearers," messengers of hope in dark, tumultuous times. Just like the men who manned the company pumps, they too shared in a patriotic calling that could not be suppressed and the magic and miracles of laissez-faire capitalism that had to be spread.[69]

Over time, these corporate rags expanded their purview. Content-wise, they began embedding business matters in tales of humanitarian-ism and modernization. Combatting malaria in Asia, studying peoples of the Far North, bettering the lives of midwestern farmers—such broad themes, accompanied with Norman Rockwell-esque art, were *The Lamp's* way of announcing that those who flipped its pages would enter charmed dimensions and hidden corners of life in Standard's past and present world. The surfeit of reverie worked. Thanks to these pop-ular offerings, *The Lamp* outgrew its aim of connecting employees to become a monthly magazine with mass appeal. Demand for the publi-cation grew so dramatically that the company started selling subscrip-tions for $1 per year. What started as an inward glance had, by decade's end, grown into a wide-reading public's rose-tinted window onto the universe, with petroleum sparkling out front as a symbol of all that was righteous, prosperous, and good in society.[70]

HELPED ALONG BY J. Edgar Pew and the API's persistence and driven by top-down and bottom-up interests, dreams of stability for workers, and enticements of motion for a consuming public, the US petroleum business exited the 1920s in a better frame of mind, with a clearer sense of itself and its hold on the American imagination. In the dawning hydrocarbon age, with society clamoring for their goods and ultimately choosing Bruce Barton's Jesus over the IWW's, oilmen could feel that they had escaped their purgatory. Perhaps they *were* the high priests Bruce Barton declared them to be, handlers of the people's ultimate longings and harbingers of a golden epoch.

However blinded they may have been by their own embellishments and by the shiny symbols and stories they used to prop up their indus-try, oilmen as idealistic as Luling, Texas's beloved Edgar Davis and as pragmatic as J. Howard Pew were more than savvy salesmen. To varying degrees they also wrestled in the open with the economic, political, and cultural conundrums that unsettled their society and managed to force the nation to shine a light on itself. Their American plans, in other words, were not simply base marketing ploys but also honest attempts, spurred by Baptist and Presbyterian urges, to harness their industry to clearer standards of probity and virtue and the nation to an agenda of technological progress and mass consumption, with human values still factored in and the uplift of the world in full view. Of course, in their attempts to do so, they also bolstered economic interests that suppressed dissent through the extension of antiunion imperatives and quieted naysayers by propagandizing a commodity-hungry populace.

Not that their attempts to reassert influence went unanswered. Many others besides Upton Sinclair lifted their pen to articulate discontent with the caprices of petrocapitalism. One of those voices was Robert Lynd, the itinerant preacher who ministered to Indiana Standard oil workers in Montana. By the end of his stay in Wolf Basin, "Mister Preacher" had been transformed, something he revealed in an article he published in *Harper's Monthly*. Upon his arrival in Wolf Basin, Lynd wrote, he believed that "religion could be 'sold' to people just like anything else worthwhile." After his "baptism of fire" and his initial struggle to connect with his neighbors, he thought differently. During his days in the oil town, the earnest preacher came to learn that authentic community—authentic Americanism—demanded a different kind of spiritual nourishment, one that traded catchy Barton-esque promises of instant salvation and abundance for social consciousness and moral solidarity. "There was something portentous in the capacity of the people of the Basin to become interested in the more enduring aspects of life," he noted; their godly commonwealth was built not on foundations of petrowealth and the business ethic but on ground-level values of collective equality and belonging.[71]

After leaving Montana, Lynd earned a bachelor of divinity degree at Union Theological Seminary and a PhD in sociology at Columbia University. All the while he grew more steadfast in his critique of modern capitalism and the unjust practices he witnessed in Indiana Standard's company town. His exposé, "Done in Oil," which he published in another journal at the same time as his *Harper's* piece, was hard-hitting enough to catch the attention of John D. Rockefeller Jr. himself. Always wary of Indiana Standard's practices, Rockefeller appeared extra eager to hear what Lynd had to say about the company's labor practices, even if it was scathing; financial support followed. Robert and his wife, Helen, were eventually awarded a major grant from Rockefeller's Institute of Social and Religious Research. The finances supported their study of Muncie, Indiana, which would subsequently be published as *Middletown: A Study in Contemporary American Culture*. As a pathbreaking anthropological study, the Lynds' book challenged scholarly conventions in its focus on modernization and industrialization's adverse effects on the values, personalities, and class relations of an "average" midwestern town. As commentary, it built on Lynd's experience with oil and his conclusion that "business ideology" tore at the fabric of American life.[72]

Yet, however much Lynd and fellow critics portrayed oil's ideology as a caustic force in modern American life, the fact remained that it won the day. By the end of the 1920s, US petroleum's fresh fusion with American yearnings and identity was complete and on open display both at home and increasingly abroad. Its hegemony was never impenetrable or absolute; as the 1930s dawned, oil's luminaries faced more gathering clouds. Still, its leading lights could rest secure in the leverage they enjoyed over their society and in their power to lay claim to its soul.

# CHAPTER SIX

# Fightin' Oil

At the moment the stock market tumbled in 1929, steering the US economy onto a disastrous course, there was reason to believe that the fantasies of health and wealth Bruce Barton and the oil sector had sold the American public in preceding years would falter too. But thanks to a humble woman and a hard-luck entrepreneur, they only intensified.

At seventy years old, his wiry body hunched from rheumatism, Columbus "Dad" Joiner looked the least likely to court success. His ugly rig, assembled from spare machinery parts, and ratty team, comprised of "Doc" Lloyd, a trendologist with throwback spiritualist techniques, and untrained white and black roughnecks, merely added to the effect. A quintessential "poor boy" (an underfinanced operator who could only afford to drill in shallow pools), Joiner was a silver-tongued wildcatter whose aura seemed hard to resist. Blessed with strangely youthful, silky skin, which he attributed to eating carrots, the veteran also boasted total command of scripture. As a farm boy in Alabama, Joiner received all his education from his parents, who used strictly the Bible to teach him to read and write. He developed his penmanship by repeatedly copying out the book of Genesis, his vocabulary by digesting the entire

King James. As far as East Texans were concerned, he was the Patillo Higgins of his generation, and they loved him for it.[1]

Joiner was also a tenacious operator who ignored the naysayers and in 1927 set his sights on the agriculturally depressed area around Henderson to start drilling for oil. His promise to browbeaten Texans came laced with sacerdotal certainty that underneath their barren soil lay a "treasure trove all the kings of earth might covet." Armed with "certificates" and "royalty rights" guaranteeing future payouts, the salesman wooed locals with enticements to invest. He was especially keen on wooing widows. "Every woman has a certain place on her neck," he once explained, likely with a wry grin, "and when I touch it they automatically start writing me a check." Having scraped together enough cash to proceed, Joiner and his team attacked a drill spot resting on the property of Mrs. Daisy Bradford, a woman who agreed to Joiner's advances out of good business sense. Raised on the 1,000-acre farm purchased in 1840 by her esteemed grandfather, General Andrew Miller, then run by her father, the town's resident doctor, Bradford was considered an upstanding member of the community. After her husband died, she moved back onto the Miller acreage. As a local paper would describe it, from that point forward the widow's vocation was "wholly" about administering the soil "that responded to the first spade and pick thrust in the hands of her forebears. She found no monotony in this existence." At the age of sixty, though, Bradford grew restless with routine. Convinced that she could draw more from her farm, she struck a deal with Joiner that allowed his team to puncture the sod.[2]

Between 1927 and 1930, Joiner struggled to make his guarantees of crude come true; yet Bradford's commitment held. Even as he paused to acquire new funds, she coaxed his team along with her high spirits. Sometimes she did more than that. On one occasion, a frustrated Joiner, who was away raising money, told his foreman to abandon one dry well and drill another wherever "Mrs. Daisy" instructed. Perched on a hilltop with clear view of the site, Bradford guided the team until she yelled, "Stop, boys. Drill right there." On that very site Joiner finally hit pay dirt. In September 1930, his head driller began to see signs of oil in sludge drawn up by Daisy Bradford No. 3. By then the operation had attracted plenty of attention, especially on Sundays, when church folks dressed in their best made their way to the Bradford farm to partake in oil-viewing picnics. Once rumors of an impending gusher spread, 10,000 locals packed lunches and parasols and rushed to the scene. As one observer recounted, this was a "gala day," with cars lining the dusty road for miles, venders selling hotdogs and cold soda for outrageous sums, and optimism all around. When no gusher was forthcoming, they turned the festival into a vigil. Spectators constructed a makeshift shantytown, christened Joinerville, to stay close to the action. For the next month, they waited, expectancy undiminished. A few doubters emerged from the crowd. Scouts for major oil companies had considered Joiner's East Texas venture pure folly. Now they ridiculed the man for taking such a high-profile risk. "I'll eat your hat if that's an oil well," one of them chortled. "I'll drink every barrel of oil you get out of that hole," another added. It was the type of taunting Higgins had suffered.[3]

Like Higgins, Joiner had the last laugh. On October 5, after a long night of bailing and swabbing, audible gurgling could be heard in the casing. Then came the rush that electrified the crowd. One witness described the scene as "hilarious." "'Oil!' they cried. 'Oil!'" "Some jumped up and down with joy, tossing straw hats high into the air." One crewman pulled out his pistol and dangerously shot at the black spray in the sky (he was quickly wrestled to the ground). Joiner, meanwhile, turned pale at the sight of his creation and "leaned against the derrick for support." Scouts raced to the nearest phone. Having seen oil pour over Joiner's derrick and soak pine trees hundreds of yards downwind, one young surveyor for Shell sped to town to call his superior, who reacted with disbelief. "Son, are you sure you know what you're talking about?"[4]

In the hours after Daisy Bradford No. 3 came through, a mass of people deluged the Henderson area. As the onslaught began, locals honored Bradford and Joiner in sacrosanct terms. Joiner was a "second Moses" leading his people to the "milk and honey" of the "Promised Land." A woman of "indomitable faith and courage," Bradford had brought "liquid gold from the earth [and] industrial glory to the commonwealth." Immortalized, Bradford and Joiner now watched as the Bible-sized epic they had created unfolded on other people's terms.

Epic indeed. Between 1930 and 1941, East Texas experienced the largest oil boom in history, one that would conclude Texas's gusher age in spectacular fashion. Enshrouded by piney woods, ragtag drillers punctured woodbine sand and discovered an unfathomable truth: a lake of oil forty-three miles long, ten miles wide, and flush with 5.5 billion barrels. It was the largest pool ever discovered, with a capacity equaling a third of the total oil produced in the United States up to that time. Amid the towering derricks and exultant cries of discovery, locals caught up in the fury followed a familiar pattern by invoking their prophets and citing their own miraculous turnarounds to explain God's illustrious work. Nothing, though, came easy for this up-and-coming lot. If sheltered from the worst of a depressed economy, East Texans would suffer human devastation of unimaginable scale, industry infighting and bloodshed, and worry that their day in the sun would be short-lived. Rather than dampen their enthusiasm, these trying conditions encouraged them to embrace radical emphases that had always been present within wildcat religion but now surfaced with an irrepressible and irreversible vengeance. In 1930s East Texas, "pentecostal" impulses that had surfaced at Spindletop once and for all overtook "presbyterian" ones as the heart of a movement that now dreamed of greater glory for oil's average people.[5]

The politics of the reawakened oil patch soon bore the marks of this theology. Consumed with the black stuff and its democratic potencies, oilers in the southwestern United States started forming a more elaborate system of political association and lobbying with increasingly national reach. In the face of growing federal power embodied by the New Deal's "Oil Czar," Harold Ickes, they ramped up a populist juggernaut whose clout Americans had not seen evidenced since the 1890s. Responding to federal regulations and imposition of a New Deal in petroleum, they demanded a "square deal" in which they maintained control of the land—their rule of capture. As always, the people of the oil patch delivered those demands with end-times urgency, conscious that the rush to obtain oil always worked according to earth's (and God's) unknowable clock, with depletion (and Armageddon) an inevitability lingering on the horizon. Yet in East Texas they did so with more theological fervency and political awareness. If time was running out, what was any God-fearing person to do but drill, drill, drill? If plain folk could tap riches that improved their lives, why should the government stop them? With the Pew family's help, this sentiment fueled a more coordinated revolt against Roosevelt and the Rockefellers. Even as agents of major oil crafted partnerships with Washington and with increased resolve began to pursue global gains—efforts Texans identified as devilishly coercive—those who flocked to East Texas found fresh value in the wildcat ethic. On domestic soil, at least, oil's elites confronted a potent foe in a class of oilers who were utterly convinced that with a little luck, a lot of faith, and much dogged persistence they could determine their own fates.

DENIZENS OF THE West had ridden waves of oil fever before, but not on the same scale. Besides its sheer statistical precedence, the East Texas boom's unusual context mattered too. Struck at the very onset of the Depression, it operated at arresting odds with the prevailing mood of the day, making it particularly entrancing. More jobs, well-endowed citizens, bustling banks, prospering heartland towns, and a sense of better tomorrows: these were the peculiar circumstances that made East Texas an island of delirium during America's Great Depression.

Signs that the East Texas boom would rewrite southwesterners' futures first appeared on the lands they abandoned. Migration, of course, was a way of life at this time, the desertion of farms for factories in Los Angeles and Detroit standard practice among Depression-era plain folk who sought escape from their dustbowl conditions. Yet the cataclysmic nature of this resettlement also set it apart from more common relocation patterns. It is impossible to say just how many journeyed to this budding oil patch, but if the look of their vacated homesteads was any indication, the sojourn enlisted a multitude of people whose impulse to move was baldly unhesitant. That was folk musician Woody Guthrie's impression during an impromptu visit home around the time of Joiner's gusher. While riding a boxcar through eastern Oklahoma, feet hanging out the door, he grew curious. "Somethin has happened down there," he mused as abandoned houses rolled by. Guthrie asked a fellow traveler where the people had gone. "Chasin' th' boom," his mate offered, "a chasin' a boom."[6]

"Chasin'," Guthrie learned, had taken his former neighbors to East Texas, where drama like that he lived through as a child on the Oklahoma oil patch began to play out in exponential degrees. Shining like a lodestar for people begging for a decent wage in a difficult time,

East Texas lured more jobseekers than any boomtown had ever done before. As one resident offered, "The whole world was broke and everyone came . . . looking for work." The mass of people descending on this region immediately redrew its physical features. From Panola County in the southeast to Upshur in the northwest, between Cherokee County in the southwest and Harrison in the northeast—four corners of territory spanning a few hundred square miles—news spread daily of momentous hits, resulting in a ballooning almost overnight of local populations and pocketbooks. Longview, Gregg County's main center and the center of the action, was one of the largest towns in the area in 1930, with 5,000 residents; by 1940 it would be a small city of 15,000. Its financial outlook would change too: while in 1930 it registered as a place of modest folk whose annual wages and property values were far below Texan and American averages, by 1940 it would be home to predominantly middle-class people with an above-average standard of living. In the region as a whole, the booming 1930s would see population growth of 50 percent and a stark upsurge in revenue and property values, a demographic picture strikingly different from that of a tattered and stagnant nation.[7]

As witnessed in previous oilscapes like Spindletop, petroleum's mythologies of instant abundance and personal and societal progress once again pulsated through the community. As they settled over a materially transformed East Texas, though, they morphed into get-rich schema and sanctions for wealth that were institutionalized and singularly strong. Amid pumps, derricks, and church steeples, the prosperity gospel, which had always buttressed wildcat religion and sanctified risk and reward as a test of faith and a way to draw closer to God, acquired a red-hot verve that would permanently alter American economic, religious, and political life.

Of course those chimeras also masked tough realities that many East Texans could never escape, realities that worsened in the regime of oil. East Texans themselves recognized some of the negative trade-offs. First, the perpetual signs of industrial brawn marred their lives and made them yearn for tranquilities of yesteryear. Lazy rows of cotton and motionless pines had given way to ugly holding tanks and derricks, now constructed out of steel. In production centers such as Kilgore, citizens lived under a thicket of metal towers, arranged forty per block. One farmer spoke for many of his contemporaries when he denounced the machinery and men that had invaded his turf. Sure, he was making "a little money out of it," with two rigs pumping his land, but he still wished "they'd go away and leave us alone." Many of the workingmen who poured into the farmer's home region came to harbor similar negative sentiments. As the boom unfolded, rank and filers found themselves stratified in new ways, not according to class as much as to chance. There was a disquieting randomness to the entire affair. Experienced workers from California and inexperienced wannabes off farms in Arkansas, skilled drillers and burly roughnecks stood by the thousands in the same job lines, hoping to be among the hundreds hired to work on area oil sites. Together, the rejected tramped off to the soup kitchen once their names were not called. One field hand learned firsthand that the difference between spectacular success and mere survival was slim. For over a year he remained trapped in a cycle of temporary positions, often working only two days a week for thirty-five cents an hour and desperately trying to feed his family. Finally he landed the job he so desired. His experience was not atypical—months of apprehension followed by good fortune—but neither was it the norm. Countless journeymen never achieved that final victory and left for home, downcast, having learned the pitfalls of a labor-saturated market.[8]

In East Texas's tenuous new pecking order, African Americans by far had it the worst. Since well before the Spindletop strike due south, East Texas had been a turbulent borderland on which white farmers functioned as a privileged minority next to the majority of white and black sharecroppers, whose oppression typified the Deep South's cotton belt. Craving what little power they could muster, white East Texans of both standings leveraged their whiteness to claim racial superiority. This is why, in the first decades of the century, the natural red soil between Longview and Lufkin witnessed unmatched displays of lynching and Ku Klux Klanism. Little changed in the post-1930 regime of oil. Regardless of race, since most area farmers were tenants, even in the case of a discovery on their land, no windfall was forthcoming. Those who did happen to own their land often saw their proceeds from oil funneled straight to the bank, as repayment for debts owed because of previous cotton crop failures. Black farmers faced these and other insurmountable challenges. More vulnerable to the crop lien system than white farmers, the few among them who struck oil were certain to owe significant sums to local bankers and to have to deal with white financiers hungry for their piece of the petroleum pie. They also dealt with nefariousness similar to what Osage Indians had faced. Knowing black landowners were virtually unprotected in the legal system, white hustlers threatened them with violence if they did not sign over oil leases. One white lease hound recalled losing his crack at a deal with a black farmer because another white speculator had upped the ante with the threat of death. Rumor had it that the winning bidder "had killed quite a few negroes in Gregg County."[9]

For many white and especially black East Texans, then, thoughts of oil's beneficence were fleeting, soon to be replaced by preexisting torments and painful recalculations about self-worth. Yet oil's myths were hard to shake, especially when so many average folk did seem to benefit from streaming crude. Abusive to some, the phantoms of petroleum appeared kind to so many others, including the downtrodden. There were just too many cases of cunning and lucky strivers vaulting into an upper echelon of magnificent wealth for average folk to look away and not internalize or credit Texas oil's rags-to-riches fables.

Numerous small, independent oil producers who achieved substantive gains in this last shimmer of Texas's gusher age validated the fables. East Texas provided them with several unique advantages, beginning with complete liberty to attack the soil with their self-derived techniques. For months after Joiner's strike on the Bradford farm, major oil companies remained convinced that it was a lucky hit on a small pocket. Their surveyors were adamant in this. After two subsequent strikes, though, including one on December 28 by Ed Bateman, another poor boy who struck it rich near Kilgore, they scurried to catch up. Immediately their geologists, most aligned with the United States Geological Survey, were on their way, traveling the dusty, overwhelmed roads to Joiner country. Yet the nature of the East Texas fields perplexed them, and their initial doubts about a substantial pool coupled with their outsider status only reinforced the perception among locals that science was not the key to locating crude. Common sense and charismatic feel were. Assuming the same manner as Joiner's head driller, most East Texas oil hunters ignored or downplayed geology and stuck to gut instinct.

Oliver Winfield Killam was one of the many industrious hunters who preferred to use the eclectic techniques of an earlier era. "I haven't used any very scientific method," he would recount. "It's kind of a little geology and a little doodlebugology and a little common sense." Killam's seemingly haphazard approach was in fact driven by deep belief, confirmed regularly, that oil could be found best when a man was willing to sense, not just study, the earth. "We just think that oil gives off a ray of some kind that affects certain chemicals and indicates the presence of hydrocarbons in the ground. I think everything is susceptible of being detected if you know just what to do."[10]

Killam's words, echoing those of earlier hunters, reflected the privilege oil's lay practitioners still ascribed to kinesthesia in 1930s Texas. In the same guise as their predecessors, they continued to rely on psychic powers to locate oil. Amid the rush to find the black stuff, full-fledged, self-identified spiritualists once again garnered special favor. This was the case for Annie Buchanan, whose healing of individuals through application of olive oil *and* ability to detect crude remained legendary, somewhat to her chagrin. "I try my best to done quit but jus' can't do it," she admitted. "When God give you anythin' you jus' got to keep on." Then there was the handful of mystics who claimed that they had X-ray eyes, enabling them to see deep into the earth. One preacher, antiquarians recounted, was known to point "to the heavenly bodies, and with closed eyes . . . majestically prance around—suddenly stop, shudder as though he had palsy, and in a stentorian voice . . . declare that he was on the edge of an oil creek." Ridiculed by some, teased by others, the preacher nevertheless functioned comfortably in East Texas oil culture as someone who simply made apparent what many inferred: oil defied logic.[11]

Empowered by local acceptance of the commoner's authority, small producers were able to proceed with pure abandon. By August 1931, nine months after the Joiner strike, East Texas was home to 3,372 wells producing 1 million barrels total per day, most run by independents. As late as 1935, even after major companies had feverishly acquired any available plots, independent producers would still manage more than half of the 22,500 operational wells in the region. The surprise of Joiner's strike had given independents a head start that they would never relinquish. Once the "Big Boys" arrived, rank and filers maintained their upper hand by demanding astronomical payouts for the lucrative mineral rights they possessed. Upon acquiring capital for one portion of their land, they used it to develop another. East Texas's plebeians thus approached their futures fully aware of their ability to drive laissez-faire capitalism to ends even Adam Smith could not have dreamed possible.[12]

Adding legitimacy to their prosperity gospel was the fact that several of these plebeians quickly ascended the pecking order to the rank of the elite. Among East Texas's instant millionaires was Ed Bateman, the man responsible for jolting majors into action and an example of the status to which his kind could aspire. After discovering oil, he decided to take an easier way and sell his well to Humble Oil, pocketing $1.5 million in cash and $600,000 in future payments, an unbelievable sum for a once penniless man. Then there were those whose game was building empires and turning Protestant modesties on their head. With cigars and down-home charm on display, East Texas's new "Big Rich" rode extravagant volatilities and profits to power. Within no time, charismatic capitalists such as Sid Richardson, Clint Murchison, and Hugh Roy (H. R.) Cullen were an ascendant force with which the nation would long reckon. None among them, however, captured attention like Haroldson Lafayette (H. L.) Hunt, a prospector from Arkansas who sensed before anyone else that history was being made in East Texas. Seven weeks after Dad Joiner started making this history, he met with Hunt in Dallas. After a series of negotiations, Joiner, still struggling to pay off debts, agreed to Hunt's proposal of $30,000 up front and $1.305 million once production began. With one flit of savvy, Hunt gained control of the epicenter of the East Texas field, leaving pundits stunned by the "most astounding business deal the state had ever seen." Even when subsequent strikes proved the enormity of his field, Joiner remained content, happy to escape arrears and looking forward to prosperity in his old age. In his dealings with Hunt, he internalized a truth universal among his fellow warriors: within the capriciousness of the times, any wealth was a godsend and an undeserved thing, any dollar an exponential increase over what they'd had before.[13]

East Texans pondered the metaphysics of that condition in the context of spectacular church growth as well. The prosperity gospel took root most concretely in the pews of the region's bootstrap parishes. In several cases, the very aesthetics of extraction, at the heart of which stood houses of worship, made obvious the linkage between booming oil and blessedness. Not unlike in Pennsylvania's Petrolia half a century before, derricks littered the church properties in the area. Their presence there made sense. Church lots were larger and more open for development than the typical residential or business strip of land; they were also managed by people who would do anything to keep their poor congregations alive. A steady stream of discoveries in the area convinced them that this was their answer. The Spring Hill Church lot in Longview yielded early success. In late February 1931, Spring Hill's pastor and one of his parishioners spudded a well on the church's fifty-acre tract. To mark the event, congregants gathered for a service, at which the preacher preached and his parishioners sang. Having consecrated the dig, they waited for good fortune. They did not wait long. In March, at 3,598 feet, Spring Hill hit liquid gold, which in the first hour gauged two hundred barrels. The breakthrough was significant for many reasons, not the least being that it proved the East Texas pool extended one mile further to the north than experts first estimated. Of course, it also meant that the tiny temple could look forward to years of well-funded ministry.[14]

So anomalous in America's Depression era, well-financed ministry nevertheless became the expectation for East Texas congregations, Spring Hill Church a benchmark. No one knows for sure how many congregations crossed this same threshold of success, but those who did tended to celebrate oil finds in conspicuous fashion by erecting extravagant edifices. One Churches of Christ congregation located near the Spring Hill drill site consecrated its own boon by replacing the modest box-shaped clapboard hut it inhabited with an English Gothic style cathedral. The cost of construction, $18,000, signaled that mere survival was no longer a worry for this prospering body of believers. This congregation's encounter with abundance was repeated across the area, among Protestants and Catholics alike, making English Gothic a fad.[15]

The influx of cash trickled up the chain of ecclesiastical command as well. During the 1930s all the major white denominations in the area boasted huge income and membership gains that countered statewide trends. The Southern Baptist Convention (SBC) experienced the sharpest surges. From 1929 to 1940, the combined membership of the area's two district associations rose from 6,359 to 22,680, while total property values of churches reporting to both more than doubled, a contrast to outcomes posted by Texas's other SBC associations, which showed dramatic declines on all fronts. East Texas oil's institutional impact, moreover, emanated to farther points in the Southwest's Baptist sphere. Baptist educational institutions like Baylor University looked to black gold to sustain them. Baylor's Waco campus had been built on the fortunes of Texas's first oil boom, with millions of dollars donated by Spindletop veteran George Carroll. Now, in this difficult time, it petitioned petroleum's aid again. Wives of Texas oil's first wildcatters, women who had taken over their husbands' empires in the 1920s, often took the lead in supporting causes that met their theological priorities. For Mrs. W. J. McKie and Mrs. Verna McLean, heads of two different oil fortunes, that cause was Baylor. School president Pat Neff and his associates struggled during the Depression to generate the endowment necessary to stay afloat. The gift of crude thus became a particularly wonderful thing, worthy of gushing praise. Baylor would not just survive its tribulation, Neff stated confidently in public recognition of the McLean donation; it would become "bigger and better" and a "great modern university."[16]

No church folk boasted more gains from Depression-era oil than Baptists; yet none did more rejoicing than Pentecostals. On the socioeconomic ladder of East Texas, Pentecostals typically occupied the lowest rung. Baptists and Methodists suffered too during the 1930s, but they were the establishment to which the countless apostolic Christians of the area aspired. Musicologist Bill C. Malone would remember this longing well. While growing up in a family of tenant farmers in Texas's eastern section, he learned the social practices of his lowly class. "Tenants and other poor farmers paid deference to their 'betters' with respectful words and a tip of the hat." "People always knew who ranked above and below them." Malone's mother was fluent in this unspoken discourse, but she also grasped how to find empowerment in the dialects of her church. At the Tin Top Pentecostal Church, where she worshipped weekly, she internalized the message that salvation and divine blessing were her rights as well. After Daisy Bradford No. 3, such desires assumed a sensible feel. With liquid riches pouring into offering plates, even (especially!) the most marginalized folk could ascend to the higher order.[17]

Being able to escape (if temporarily) the harshest burdens of Jim Crow racism merely accentuated petroleum's redemptive properties and further justified white *and* black East Texans' illusions of earthly—and heavenly—treasure. In the same manner as their white counterparts, black parishioners drilled for oil on their church properties in order to generate funds for ministry. Black evangelists targeted East Texas during the 1930s for ministerial outreach and growth, cognizant of its emerging economic sway, hence importance to the advancement of black Christianity. African American laymen and laywomen who found crude underneath their private property, meanwhile, gave money to their churches in the same ratios as white Baptist benefactors.[18]

Mary Jackson's biography, sensationalized by the *Dallas Morning News,* served as inspiration. The daughter of an ex-slave from a Georgia plantation, Jackson lived on a "negro settlement" in East Texas. Unlike most of her neighbors, she owned her land (her father had barely succeeded in paying for it) and managed to hang on to it, even when (as she explained it) "times was ha'd and taxes high." Such perseverance paid off when oil was found on her acreage. With pomp and ceremony, she received $5,000 in cash, a check for $20,000, and guarantees for "8 per cent of the value of the oil flowing from the fields." "I'se rich," she told a reporter, tears in her eyes. Late into the night, she and fellow congregants "of the little church at the end of the street" prayed, wept, sang, and sawed strains of their favorite spirituals on their fiddles. Even as realization of her wealth—their wealth—sank in, "Mammy Mary" and the congregants looked west onto their horizon of glowing derricks and the "throb of engines."[19]

Of course, white newspapers like the *Dallas Morning News* liked to identify churchgoing African Americans' riches as signs of their society's health and thereby glance over its vilest bigotries. "Luck was with the Negroes" too, one newspaperman was quick to note. Take the example of Dad Joiner's black crewman, he offered. Even when no money seemed forthcoming, the loyal helper kept fueling the wildcatter's rig with fresh lumber. The humble worker was rewarded once Joiner made his million. And take the example of a poor "negress" whose parents had been slaves. Freed by their master, they received a plot of land on which to farm. One of their daughters took responsibility for the soil after her parents passed away, and even when saddled with heavy taxes, she stayed, never willing to abandon their legacy of perseverance and strong belief in the good graces of the Almighty. Thanks to the discovery of oil on her land, the newspaperman concluded, that woman was now drawing $25,000 from leases: "the struggle is over for her." His message was clear: wherever oil was in play, godly, capitalistic strivers could dream boldly, regardless of race.[20]

Though white pundits used stories like "Mammy Mary's" to justify a social and economic system that in the main kept black citizens mired in racist violence, these tales nevertheless resonated with East Texas's black residents in paradigm-shifting ways. Caught up in oil fever and the bootstrap mentality that it engendered, African American wildcatters and their brethren saw their hunt for crude as the endeavor that would finally break them free.

No one adhered to this hope like Jake Simmons Jr., a black entrepreneur who first hit it big in oil in 1920s Oklahoma. It was in the 1930s, though, that Booker T. Washington's protégé really began applying his capitalist verve. Trained at Tuskegee Institute, Simmons was one of the first African American oil hunters to travel to East Texas after the Joiner find. He initially planned to buy leases from black farmers, but within the first month of his stay he added another agenda. Hearing his clients' stories of lynching and disenfranchisement, he offered them refuge in Oklahoma. Over the next few years, in a process that would expand exponentially during the 1930s, Simmons simultaneously brokered oil leases in East Texas and sold land in East Oklahoma to nouveau riche black Texans who wanted a better quality of life. His was an easy sell. Edythe Fields grew up near Longview and remembers when her father, a farmer and Baptist pastor, was won over. Having made considerable money from oil on his land, her father wondered what to do next. "Mr. Simmons," Fields recalls, "came in and just talked him into moving." Joining the Fields family on the move was the Ryan family, who at Simmons's urging sold off their oil royalties and relocated to the Sooner State. Mrs. E. C. Ryan explained Simmons's approach in matter-of-fact terms: "He was a good salesman and influenced us. He said Muskogee County was a good place to live, that it has nice schools and nice people. We bought 240 acres. We decided to move out here and raised cotton and corn and had lots of cattle."[21]

Simmons was more than a shrewd trader, however. Always careful to maintain contact with those he brought to Oklahoma, he also sought better conditions for the Texans he could not lure north. On that score he worked with a prominent white businessman in Longview to buy up leases from black landowners and secure his constituents' fair dealings with banks and the law. Simmons's association with the Longview leader only partially shielded him from local white supremacists who hated the fact that the sharply dressed black businessman was making swift gains in their home territory. Their racist rage and rumblings of violent pushback increased as Simmons hired a white lawyer to defend the title claims of his African American clients. But Simmons did not flinch. A staunch Methodist, he also supported the National Association for the Advancement of Colored People. In both capacities he used his oil wealth to broker deals of another kind—legal ones that guaranteed civil liberties. In 1938 he filed the first court case against segregated schools (*Simmons v. Muskogee Board of Education*), which traveled all the way to the US Supreme Court before being dismissed. By the late 1930s Simmons's reach was indeed expansive. Linking two regions and two racial communities through the prospects of crude, he managed to fasten the prerogatives of oil hunting to societal uplift and human rights. He would press these prerogatives further in the post–World War II years.[22]

Already during his first forays into East Texas's oil fields, though, Simmons embodied the combination of human energy and higher purpose that was engulfing the area. By the mid-1930s, just as Simmons's business and the work of countless booming white and black churches began to flourish, East Texans were not simply translating oil's abundance into unprecedented institutional advancement. They were also wrestling with its theological designs.

BUOYED BY SUCCESSES and looking to future gains, East Texas church folk knew intuitively that oil time was transitory, that during booms they lived on borrowed time. Writing in 1933, one local captured this sentiment when he titled his reflections on home "Where Oil Flows Joy and Woe Curiously Mingle." Showers of riches today meant floods of misfortune tomorrow, he lamented. This was a fact of life in any Petrolia, where the ephemerality of everything weighed heavily on the soul. For many East Texans, the transaction was more fundamental than that. Blessed by God with oil, they assumed a sense of responsibility to use it for Kingdom-building objectives, before their dispensation suddenly ended. Theirs became an acute expectancy that assigned end-times significance to petrocapital and paid homage to an all-powerful being who "giveth and taketh" suddenly but is always there. Conceived in extraction zones at an earlier time, their way of thinking about health, time, and wealth now reached full bloom.[23]

Oil's temporality registered most tangibly with East Texans through their scarred bodies. Mirroring human experience in Titusville and Spindletop, residents of the East Texas fields weathered the sight and stench of death. From the outset of the boom to its end, they regularly awoke to news of oil-related tragedy in their morning papers. Yet, due to the breadth and sustained haste of East Texas drilling, misfortune came to command their space in unrivaled degrees. Fire was so commonplace that it hardly warranted press coverage. The 1934 blast that killed two workers and injured ten others at a Kilgore refinery was big news only because of the people involved. The company's vice president lost his nephew in the explosion, and the other casualty was an insulator from Dallas with roots in West Texas. Among those who suffered injury was the eight-year-old son of a refinery worker and six local firemen. Conflagrations always reminded oil-patch citizens that they lived amid constant danger, but this one seemed particularly searing. No respecter of class or geography, it was truly democratic in its devastation, affecting families across the state and social spectrum. It also showed that as much as the drive for East Texas crude was remapping the Southwest, its attending tragedy was too.[24]

As commonplace as death and battered bodies were in 1930s East Texas, they did not go unanswered. In response to the broken and dying, local church people once again turned to patterns of apostolic spirituality that had appeared in the wake of the Spindletop discovery. While living under the shadow of dangerous steel barbicans, East Texans not only embraced but also formalized the type of "full gospel" religiosity—attuned to body, mind, and soul and the miraculous signs and wonders of the cosmos—that had always been present in extraction zones. The widening popularity and institutionalization of faith healing manifested that continuity. During the 1930s, healing services proliferated as the answer to oil's heavy physical tolls. Besides generating advance press as large, exciting meetings to which all East Texans (afflicted or not) were encouraged to flock, they also managed to generate an outpouring of testimonials, often published in local papers or church news, of individuals transformed.

The testimony of John Abernathy was typical. Before becoming a wildcatter in the late 1920s, Abernathy had served as a US deputy marshal in Oklahoma Territory, during which time he carved out a reputation for courage (which even Theodore Roosevelt lauded) for his ability to kill wolves barehanded. Ranchers paid him handsomely to perform this task. "Catch 'Em Alive Jack" was a legend. In the late 1930 he was chasing another kind of prey. While drilling for crude, however, Abernathy quickly found out that his muscles were no match for a machine. As he began to apply power to lift his swab and its loaded fluid to the top of his rig, his cable snapped. At the same time the equipment plummeted fifty feet to the floor, "like a wild coiling snake," the freed wire encircling the man's waist and jerking him into the drum. Abernathy's colleague quickly killed the power. "Had he not been right on the job," Abernathy would testify, "my body would have been torn to pieces or cut in two. From the time I heard the crash and felt the fearful coil of that cable around my body I felt I was a goner." Fellow workers, his wife, and a doctor thought Abernathy was gone too and called the morgue.[25]

Eventually Abernathy awoke, suffering from crushed ribs, a damaged back, and blindness, from which doctors believed he would never recover. Over the next few months the frail man improved, but never fully. Eyes badly crossed and plagued with pain, he looked for an alternative and found it in the "doctrine of divine healing" preached by a Pentecostal minister, Reverend H. B. Taylor. For an entire week Abernathy attended Taylor's services, gleaning as much truth as he could until finally, at week's end, he was healed. He would later convey in a testimony published by the YMCA in 1936 that Taylor "prayed with me and for me, and I prayed most fervently for myself. Soon my eyes became straightened so I could see with them as well as ever; the injuries in my back began to heal; and I returned to my family, feeling that I was on the road to recovery. Whatever the reader may think, I believe that my prayers were answered." The wolf catcher turned wildcatter ended with an insistence that his story was fact, not fantasy, testifying to "a marvelous change in my thought and life."[26]

Whereas the mysteries of the body and its pain nudged East Texans further toward the full gospel tenets of Pentecostalism, the jarring nature of the quest for crude intensified their apocalyptic purview. In this climate of chaos, when languid lifestyles gave way suddenly to industrial fury, old methods of interpreting the present in light of the past and future also gave way. If once informed by gradualist understandings of God's unfolding designs for his people and his Kingdom on earth that more closely aligned with the postmillennial beliefs of mainstream Protestantism (that which the Rockefellers adhered to), amid the ruptures of the oil boom East Texans traded millennialism for a messianic eschatology that accepted the convulsions and uncertainties of the modern moment both as natural by-products of a fallen humanity and sinful world and as mysterious workings of God, who was preparing to send his Son to regather the saints. Through this endtimes awareness, the saints could rest assured that the spasms consuming their society were signs of—indeed, steps toward—the Messiah's return and the radiance that awaited them in the afterlife.[27]

Concrete shifts in doctrine accompanied East Texans' reimagining of their place in present and future time. During this decade of upheaval, area Protestants began to jettison the softer optimism of postmillennial theology, which held that Christians could perfect humanity and usher it into the millennium, for a hard-core premillennialist theology once harbored by fundamentalists associated with the Moody Bible Institute in the North and its institutional twin, the Bible Institute of Los Angeles (BIOLA). Thanks to BIOLA benefactor Lyman Stewart's philanthropic efforts, the strictest form of premillennialism—dispensational premillennialism, which leaned on literal readings of biblical prophecy to decipher God's intentions for humanity in the present and future soon to come—became increasingly popular within conservative circles during the interwar years, conspicuously in North American oil patches. Just as Stewart had done as head of an oil company and global charity, residents of these locales rigorously decoded signs of societal strain as evidence that Christ's return was nigh. Their duty? To marshal their labor for the rapid spread of the gospel and prepare society for the end of time by alerting it to its vulnerability and need for salvation.

Few oil patches could match 1930s Texas for the heatedness of end-times thought. At this juncture the ministerial careers of J. Frank Norris and John R. Rice took off. They became arguably the two most prominent fundamentalists in mid-century America. While Norris began using his oil-funded Fort Worth pulpit and radio station to educate southwesterners in the canons of dispensationalism, from his pre-millennialist church in Dallas Rice printed and distributed his organ of apocalyptic thought, *The Sword of the Lord*. The pastors they trained took their teachings to East Texas's grass roots and refashioned the area into a hothouse of prophetic belief. Norris protégés Frank M. Mullins and Jesse Wood encountered a ready-made audience of disciples who, caught up in sharp undulations of wealth and despair and the intuition that one day it would all come to an end, needed no stretching to think in their terms. That Christ's return could happen anytime, without warning, made complete sense in a place where miracles happened at any time, without warning. So did the call to action that followed. If the world (like their boom) was about to end, what was left to do but capture souls and subsurface pools and extract expeditiously before their allowance expired? In this cosmology East Texans absorbed a larger truth that they represented a last glimmer of hope, that they alone had the courage to stare down end-times darkness with uncompromising drive. During the region's struggles with violence and tragedy, residents of America's new Petrolia thus trusted heavily in the Bible's prophetic teachings about the end of the world to get them through the shadows. Listening to their preachers wax poetic about the trials of this life as preparation for the next, then reading about oil's latest wreckage, they could not help but nod in agreement.[28]

One cataclysm in particular drew these abstract and existential threads together in a totalizing view of the world that forever altered East Texans' time consciousness. It transpired in New London, just a few miles from Joinerville, the makeshift shantytown locals had erected when monitoring Dad Joiner's discovery well. On March 18, 1937, at a brand-new school built for the sons and daughters of oil workers, seven hundred total, students gathered for their last class of the day. Paid for with tax revenues from the town's oil business, the million-dollar structure was the envy of administrators across the country. As if to give credit where it was due, in one classroom pupils faced a chalkboard on which was scrawled "Oil and natural gas are East Texas's greatest mineral blessings. Without them this school would not be here and none of us would be here learning our lessons." In another classroom, a shop teacher switched on a sanding machine. The simple act ignited a pocket of gas fed by underground pipelines crisscrossing the town. The explosion occurred underneath the first floor, which was subsequently blown upward toward a collapsing roof, hurling pupils into the air. As her classroom disintegrated, a young girl heard her teacher cry, "Jesus, help us; Jesus help us." Others in out-of-body states watched as the walls around them rose into the air, sat suspended, then crashed to the ground.[29]

The aftereffects of the New London explosion were profound. On the technical end, government investigation of the tragedy led to mandatory implementation of malodorants to detect escaped gas. But it was the human toll that mattered. Hearing the explosion, roughnecks and townspeople from miles away rushed to the scene to see if the children were okay. The Texas Rangers, Red Cross, and media followed. Upon arrival they found bodies that had been propelled out of windows and still-living victims suffocating under mounds of rubble. People started clawing with bare hands to get at the wounded. They dug for eighteen hours, aided by heavy equipment transported from area drill sites. In the end, three hundred students died, one-third of the town's underage population. Most had been burned beyond recognition or blown to pieces, making identification by and psychological healing for their parents nearly impossible. Finding himself on one of his first assignments, a young Dallas reporter named Walter Cronkite was as traumatized by the scene as his subjects. "I did nothing in my studies nor my life to prepare me for a story of the magnitude of that New London tragedy," he would later admit. "Nor has any story since that awful day equaled it."[30]

Citizens of East Texas dealt with this collateral damage by seeking spiritual cover. For weeks after the explosion, letters poured into Texas governor James Allred's office from all points of the globe. Schools in France, foreign ministries in Mexico and Japan, even Adolf Hitler's office in Germany contributed to the barrage. All the letter writers expressed sympathy rooted in shared human pain. The explaining was left up to local ministers. No one blamed the catastrophe on divine judgment for egregious sin or dwelled too long on the goodness of a caring God. Rather, East Texas pastors, white and black, Baptist and Pentecostal, rearticulated the sacred paradox that operated at the heart of their society. On earth, any abundance in life was a mere interval along a continuum of pain. On the oil patch especially, hellacious reversals of fortune, rather than an easy progression to a fanciful end, were the norm. This was because "when you strike oil," as one local admitted, "you let loose Hades." New London's disaster confirmed this very point. As another local lamented in despair, "All the billions . . . of the great East Texas oil field will not repay the stilled laughter of a child—one boyish grin, the toss of a vivacious curly head is worth all the oil gushers in the land." "Today," he continued, "New London is the most poverty stricken community in the world—its towering steel derricks no longer monuments to the commercial success of man, but sentinels of a fate that . . . brewed its bitters in Hell's own bowl." Yet rather than dwell on their despair, East Texas's pastors charged, citizens needed to renew their faith in an active Christ who expected them to use whatever prosperity they had in their passing moment to prepare for his return. One Baptist pastor implored everyone to internalize this sense of expectation: "Surely God is beginning a revival here at New London that is destined to sweep America and the world, 'Even so, come, Lord Jesus.' These dear oil field people can set the world an example for consecration and they will." Another spiritual leader echoed the charge. New London residents, in his estimation, had "already turned . . . toward the rising sun of tomorrow, letting the shadows fall behind . . . saying in their hearts, 'God, we drank the bitter cup to its dregs, and can still say, Thy will be done.'"[31]

East Texans knew that the shadows would never leave, that cruel death was part of them. Their dreamtime demanded that they be realists. But this historic consciousness also demanded that they not sit still or fail to attack social—and political—evils that beset them quickly, in the here and now.

LOCAL RESIDENTS ATTUNED to crude's boom-bust cycles and end-times thought embraced politics as a way to deal with their period's violent swings. Following patterns seen on earlier oil patches, local small producers once again channeled their anger with the major oil companies into a heated political assault, this time administered by an emerging network of regional guilds. Their revolt mutated in another way as well. With eyes trained on Washington, they believed they were witnessing the union of two leviathans: "big oil" and "big government," Rockefeller and Roosevelt. In 1930s East Texas, wildcatters began looking for ways to evoke change in Washington. At the heart of their struggle stewed another age-old question: Who held the right to control the land and its lucrative subsurface materials?

At the moment of its arrival, East Texas crude set off ferocious competition for the region's submerged liquid gold. With nearly 3,500 wells up and running by August 1931 and dozens more coming online daily, things quickly became dire. Rampant Texas crude production drove US oil prices down precipitously. Major companies feared "competitive suicide" in the Southwest and collapse of the entire industry; Jersey Standard's chief executives were not the only ones to express dismay at the prospects. Even those in Texas who did not see the world through Standard's eyes recognized the precariousness of the situation. Not only were prices falling because of overproduction, but East Texas's underground oil pressure was too, and with it hopes of long-term yields. Against its inclination for a hands-off approach, the Texas Railroad Commission (TRC), the state's primary regulatory agency for oil and gas, decided to step in. In April 1931 the TRC issued its first proration order for the field—an attempt to limit the allowance of crude that wells could draw out of the ground—and called for voluntary shutdowns and compliance by all producers as a way to prevent the dangerous glut of petroleum from doing permanent damage to the market. Between July and August of that same year, Governor Ross Sterling, a former oilman, took more drastic measures. After declaring East Texas in a "state of insurrection" and overrun with renegade drillers and criminal elements, he instituted martial law. Thousands of National Guardsmen and Texas Rangers trudged into Henderson to set up a base of operations that the TRC's commissioner dubbed "Proration Hill."[32]

It was appropriate lingo, because for the first half of the decade East Texas became embroiled in civil war. Even as the TRC and state government saw some of their concerns allayed by increased adherence to conservation ideals and concomitantly rising oil prices, the quest to regulate East Texas was almost futile. With each step that authorities took to impose proration, locals filed suit. At one point a judge insisted that "petitioners . . . pool their complaints" in order to reduce the heavy burden created by so many separate dockets. But there were heavier consequences with which to deal. As the militia imposed its will on local producers, producers fought back. One man resisted the TRC by encasing his well controls in a concrete blockhouse, making its yield impregnable and impossible to measure. Other subversives padlocked wells, planted lookouts who could shut down valves when authorities approached, or operated strictly at night. They armed themselves too. The Henderson resident who fired on three TRC agents investigating his oil lease was hardly exceptional. Nor was the anonymous bomber whose dynamiting of a Gladewater well achieved its twofold purpose: to blast devices preventing the free flow of his crude and inform authorities that he would do anything to foil their efforts, even if it meant destroying his own drill site.[33]

Backlash against authorities was only one face of anarchy. Another was the rampant criminal activity that victimized average East Texans as much as it did state authorities. Most producers spent far less time battling authorities than they did finding ways to acquire, transport, and sell "extralegal" "hot oil" (produced beyond stated quotas). Through the first half of the 1930s, renegades did whatever they could to get their hands on surpluses: a few robbed company depots and some stole from church drill sites to get to this sought-after reward, though most simply overproduced. They then secretly constructed pipelines and marshaled trucks to move their product and hired spies with guns to protect it. Oil's bootleggers were relentless. After joining authorities on a midnight raid of hot oilers, newspaperman Carl Estes was thunderstruck. "Al Capone at the height of his reign as gang lord of Chicago's underworld never got away with anything any more high-handed than [what] the writer witnessed with his own eyes," he told readers. What Estes saw with his own eyes, East Texans saw with theirs: the ruinous effects of the rabid drilling and full-blown fracas that had beset them at the moment Joiner set them on their different course. Still, even as they came to that realization, they preferred forms of redress that involved the voluntary enlistment of regular citizens who had the greatest stake in the game and grasp of local circumstances.[34]

As natural centers of collective life, local churches fashioned themselves into one key facet of social and political response. Besides offering basic sustenance to those caught in the violence of oil production (by housing workers in their sanctuaries, for instance), they also devised ministries to change minds and hearts. One congregation used large trucks to transport workers from oil camps to its meeting hall, while another formed a sister church right in the heart of a drilling zone and recruited members off the derricks. Yet another parish enticed oilers with sermons about how to do right amid crude's vicious cycles, the titles of which—"The Oil That Failed," "Man's Greatest Discovery"—were splashed across the news. Lay religious organizations such as the Women's Missionary Union and the YMCA, meanwhile, carried efforts of amelioration further by championing faith-based answers to prostitution and poor living conditions, health hazards and hot oil that included wider structural reform of the social system. Upon the backs of East Texans themselves, these institutions argued, rested the responsibility to draw abundance out of the earth, distribute it fairly to the most people, ease the pains of its disruption, and put it to work for Christ's glory.[35]

Over time, this churchly mission folded into a political one that both reinforced and recalibrated the wildcat imperative. True, Depression-era East Texans harbored a variety of political opinions that did not easily amalgamate. Following the lead of outspoken pastors like J. Frank Norris, some of them stood guard against anything that smelled of socialism. Others appreciated the populism of old, James H. "Cyclone" Davis's variety, which regenerated itself during the boom. Already in his late seventies, the former East Texas populist politician and Democratic member of the 64th US Congress (1915–1917) stepped back into the limelight in 1932 to lambast those who sat idle while injustice prevailed. "The extortioners have got the common herd in this country and have had hold of them fifty years," he blustered. "Hence, we have millionaires and mendicants, bread lines and busted banks, purse proud plutocrats and poverty-stricken farmers, all because our statesmen will not regulate commerce so as to establish justice and domestic tranquility." East Texans typically claimed space in between Norris's and Davis's ideologies, with a slight preference for Cyclone's side. They championed a politics of economic redistribution, community values, and local, democratic protections against the forces of collectivism, monopolism, and centralization. Above all else, they championed a politics that guaranteed their right to handle the resources on and under their land.[36]

Just what exactly this entailed became clear only in stages. In the immediate wake of Joiner's discovery through to the end of the decade, one dimension of East Texas petropolitics remained constant: a driving anticorporatism that identified major oil and its desire to impose strict stabilizing measures as the ultimate threat. Tensions between the majors and the independents had eased in the 1920s but never abated completely; lingering animosities resurfaced with a vengeance in the 1930s. Having missed their first crack at the East Texas pool, Gulf, Texaco, and Jersey Standard were determined to make up for lost time once they entered the game. Their aggression precipitated what one contemporary called the "greatest conflict ever waged between the major oil companies and the independents." Able to operate on a level playing field, at least for the first while, small producers waged this war with fresh confidence. Yet major companies had extra political tools at their disposal. Repeating cycles of the previous era, they lobbied for expensive conservation controls such as proration and strict unitization (imposed rates of allowable extraction), which, due to their economies of scale, boosted their leverage in the field. And with increasing determination, they sought to enlist Washington in the campaign. Although sympathetic to the majors' read on the crisis, wanting a good price for their oil, and willing to contribute to conservation—but only to the degree it helped, not hindered, their tenuous bottom lines—independents believed that Standard and its partners were ultimately after something else: absolute control.[37]

The independents' revolt manifested in various ways. One was a ratcheting up of populist rhetoric that connected the will of the people to broader "share the wealth" political campaigns. Louisiana governor-turned-senator Huey Long, whose sustained politicking against Standard in the late 1920s and early 1930s put him in good stead with the Southwest's homegrown oilmen, had mastered that type of campaign. Inspired, East Texans wrote and read political commentary that borrowed Long's language. "The Standard Oil Company of New Jersey and its subsidiaries [are] the worst enemies this country has had since the carpet-baggers were run out . . . shortly after the civil war," columnist Carl Estes crowed, in that vein. While other companies pay "the horny handed and honorable sons of toil in the ranks of Texas's great army of farmer royalty owners," he continued, Standard looks after only itself. Its other crimes? Cavorting with Washington to compel Texans to "keep the oil in the ground for the sake of conservation." "Stand up and fight this band of Judas Iscariots," Estes implored in biblical (and Huey Long) idiom, for they "are demanding thirty pieces of silver for the birthright of the people of Texas." Fluent in this vernacular, oil-fixated East Texans remained ready throughout the 1930s to crusade behind their region's loudest politicians, be they Long or their very own governors Miriam "Ma" Ferguson and W. Lee "Pappy" O'Daniel.[38]

Adding to this legion of populists were anti-Standard evangelists whose experience with Standard elsewhere reinforced their credentials. One of the most important (if also curious) for the way he connected petroleum-fueled populism across borders was Cameron Townsend, a missionary in Latin America. Townsend's barnstorming came naturally. His two ministries—Wycliffe Bible Translators and its affiliate, Summer Institute of Linguistics (SIL)—received their earliest backing from Los Angeles's Church of the Open Door, his (and Lyman Stewart's) home congregation. In the 1930s Townsend made his way into Mexico where, with the assistance of liaisons like Columbia University anthropologist (and former anti-Standard IWW radical-turned-intellectual) Frank Tannenbaum, he was introduced to President Lázaro Cárdenas. Reciprocity followed. While Cárdenas granted Townsend access to Mexico's hinterland, allowing him to bring in translators and proselytizers, Townsend offered Cárdenas an educational infrastructure through which rural Mexicans could be integrated, unified, and "modernized." Townsend's political advocacy grew out of this tight relationship. In early 1938 Cárdenas told Townsend how difficult it was to handle US and British major oil companies, which refused to negotiate fairly with Mexican labor unions. Less than a month later, Cárdenas nationalized the companies, reigniting a political storm that had been swirling since the 1910s. Deeply sympathetic to Cárdenas's position, which he framed as the people's defense against "big oil," Townsend promised to help. He penned articles praising Cárdenas and undermining the narrative of Mexican aggression that Jersey Standard's *The Lamp* actively conveyed to its readership. "Teach the Greasers 'Thou Shalt Not Steal,'" *The Lamp* railed against the Cárdenas regime. US Ambassador to Mexico (and former naval secretary) Josephus Daniels agreed with Townsend that Standard's propaganda was reprehensible because it painted the Mexican people as "uncivilized and degraded" and "of a lesser breed." The deluge of misinformation, he declared, had to stop.[39]

Armed with funds from Cárdenas and a letter of endorsement from Daniels, Townsend set aside his pen and embarked on a tour of the United States, speaking to church congregations, college audiences, and anyone else who would listen. Unable to meet with President Franklin D. Roosevelt, something he hoped Daniels's letter would facilitate, he nevertheless gained an audience with Wall Street leaders, including a Standard executive. But his message truly resonated in the oil-saturated Southwest, the new home base of his ministry. There he told Americans that they needed to extend "Christlike friendship" to their Mexican brethren to help them escape the clutches of exploitative oil companies ("selfish trusts"). Blended into his homilies was a critique of Washington. "The truth of the matter," he asserted, "is that [Cárdenas] gave Mexico New Deal developments without New Deal borrowing or New Deal taxation." In Cárdenas Townsend saw the Western Hemisphere's next William Jennings Bryan, the famed American populist of yesteryear. Fiscally responsible, sensitive to the will of the people, and desiring citizens' control of their natural resources: this was the type of leader that both Mexicans and Americans needed. Cárdenas failed to survive the storm and eventually resigned following his failed reelection bid in 1940, but the sentiments Townsend conveyed to the US oil patch reinforced its imperative to stare down the corporate establishment. They would also help its believers make fresh sense of their wildcat faith on a rapidly expanding global stage.[40]

East Texans ate up such religiously infused anti-Standard bluster, but they also knew that preachers, traveling evangelists, and politicians could not always deliver on-the-ground results. Inspiration was one thing, political implementation another. So they looked for other avenues through which they could act out, rather than just voice, their populist agitations. That desire engendered a constellation of political bodies that began channeling ground-level discontent and economic interests into a state- and nationwide reformist movement.

These associations arose to guarantee protections for small producers in a way that the Texas Railroad Commission would and could not. As the TRC and its backers in major oil started pressing for court injunctions to restrict production by small producers, independents battled back by petitioning judges to stop what they saw as an assault on their livelihoods. That legal wrangling, combined with TRC's pseudo-military actions against suspected hot oilers, convinced independents to organize. In 1933, they founded the Independent Petroleum Association of Texas, later reconstituted as the Texas Independent Producers and Royalty Owners Association (TIPRO). Founding executive Jack Porter knew that his peers' only recourse was united action. With the help of high-profile producer Glenn McCarthy, he began consolidating local chapters and mounting a legislative challenge to the majors. He recognized that much work had to be done, not the least being to educate his constituency in political trends, but he was confident that with some heavy lifting in the short term, long-term prospects would brighten. Porter spoke bluntly about the chance of upending big oilers: "There are more of us than of them, and if we work together we can get the job done."[41]

Besides boasting numbers, TIPRO could also claim the diversity of its constituency as politically advantageous. It truly spoke for all types of independent producers: swashbucklers and serious types, rising stars in the industry as well as a middle-of-the-pack majority. Of the swashbucklers, Sid Richardson stood out as representative. Like Porter and McCarthy, Richardson prided himself on being a "good-ol'-boy oilman" with deep Texas roots. This was a man, some have noted, who "with equal ease ... negotiated for leases while drinking buttermilk with Baptist ranchers and traded properties with fellow oilmen while downing more potent beverages." Those who occupied the middle-of-the-pack majority, however, were every bit as dynamic in their blending of talents and interests. The world of 1930s independent oil welcomed people of various backgrounds and social standings as productive contributors to the community. Farmers who wanted to drill their own crude, roughnecks who dreamed of becoming self-sufficient oilmen, amateur geologists and charismatic oil hunters, Masons and Methodists, longtime East Texans and newcomers to the area: independent oil's guild flourished because of its inclusivity. Uniting them in oil's drama were two essentials: the readiness to gamble on a drill bit and the ability and desire to cut a lucrative deal.[42]

Another essential, which evolved as the decade wore on, was a willingness to fight the federal state. As concerns with Texas oil crises percolated up to Franklin D. Roosevelt's administration, triggering calls in Congress and the White House for greater government oversight, the fervent religion and politics of East Texas began to coalesce in a distinctive brand of antiliberal, anti–New Deal dissent. Texans were like most southerners in the early 1930s in that they voted for Roosevelt's Democratic Party—overwhelmingly. East Texas's oil region was the bluest of them all, voting over 90 percent for the Democratic candidate in 1932. Little would change by 1936 when Roosevelt garnered 87 percent of the Texas vote. Beneath the veneer of one-party voting trends, however, was a fomenting dissatisfaction with Washington Democrats and particular unease with Roosevelt and his handling of their beloved commodity.[43]

The emblem of their disdain for the Democratic establishment and target of their wrath was Harold Ickes. Any propensity East Texans exhibited to embrace Roosevelt's measures and government aid to farmers and the poor was offset by their hatred of the man who denoted the New Deal. From the moment he became secretary of the interior and petroleum administrator, the curmudgeonly Ickes saw it as his special calling to clean up East Texas, which he claimed threatened "disastrous results to the oil industry and to the country." Convinced that US oil depletion was a real concern that could eventually expose American weaknesses, he readily assumed the mantle of the nation's supreme conservationist. "Oil is a harvest which is reaped only if the seeds are planted long in advance," he announced in defense of a steadier management of the material. Educated in the trust-busting progressivism of the early twentieth century and puritanical in temperament, Ickes, in short, believed in the efficacy of strong government regulation as the answer to oil's problems. Though wary of big business, he was even leerier of small producers and consumers, whom he deemed unknowledgeable and unpredictable. His handling of oil through the Depression into World War II would be predicated on the certainty that he could handle the lesser of two evils—major oil—and, through rigorous application of his skills and negotiating abilities, ultimately forge a prosperous relationship between Washington and the world of Standard, Texaco, and Gulf.[44]

Independents sensed from the beginning that Ickes had more in mind than reining in oil's excesses—that he wanted to share power with the majors and, where needed, squeeze small producers out altogether. When the National Industrial Recovery Act (NIRA) of 1933 established the Oil Code, which gave Ickes additional power over Texas production, independents howled. They agreed that some controls were needed, but bestowing that responsibility solely on one man in Washington struck them as wrongheaded. Again, with passage of the Connally Hot Oil Act of 1935, which increased governmental powers to "curtail contraband oil" and handed Ickes greater leverage, independents vented their discontent. Even after Ickes lost a bit of clout with the Supreme Court's voiding of the NIRA in 1935, his authority in the business could not be reversed. By 1937 Ickes was truly oil's "czar," if unofficially, and could boldly claim, along with his supporters in the nation's largest oil companies, that the "Federal Government and the Oil producing states in . . . common effort" had restored sanity to Texas's Petrolia and saved its beleaguered soil.[45]

East Texas wildcatters saw things differently, though; in their estimation, stated in newspapers and sermons, Ickes was a "dictator" and a sign of what awaited Americans in the last days: a twin-headed beast of Washington and Wall Street, ready to do Satan's handiwork. With ever-heightening angst and fervor, they rallied their church organizations and oil associations against the interior secretary's agenda. Ready to lead them to concrete results was an oil family they considered one of their own: the Pews.[46]

As HEAD OF Sun Oil, with ties to East Texas, deep roots on the East Coast, and a growing presence in Washington, the Pews emerged in the 1930s as the spokesmen for disgruntled wildcatters whose fused passions they now helped shape into an assault on the New Deal. Through the strength of their politicking and the expanse of their political connections, they began to funnel grassroots dissent toward viable political outcomes in a way that would presage a political phenomenon of the post-Depression years.

The Pews had earned their right to speak for East Texans through thirty-plus years of steady operation in the Lone Star State. Depression-era economics did not slow them down; quite the opposite. Due to its conservative financial practices in the 1920s, Sun emerged unscathed from the Wall Street crash and banking crisis that followed. Unburdened by debt and flush with cash, the company expanded its production, refining, and transportation capacities through the 1930s. As J. Howard Pew would later write, "The depression was in many ways the best period we ever had." The company's foothold in Texas anchored its success. By the mid-1930s it owned 7 percent of the total acreage in the East Texas field, from which it drew crude that was piped south, then loaded onto one of fifteen possible tankers for transport to Marcus Hook in Delaware. But Sun did not rest; it continued to invest heavily in new production and transportation systems that allowed it to maximize the Texas-Philadelphia connection, which made it competitive against even the largest, fully integrated companies, including archnemesis Jersey Standard. Innovations in pipeline construction were especially important in this regard. During the 1930s Sun completed 150 miles of gathering lines in the East Texas field, as well as a major north-south link to the company's gulf refinery and shipping depot. As it entered the 1940s, it was about to become a major stakeholder in the Big Inch pipeline, designed to run from Longview, Texas, to Philadelphia. All these efforts, combined with its inventive refining and marketing, demonstrated Sun's quest to compete with the giants of its industry.[47]

Sun's ongoing labor and public relations initiatives helped strengthen ties with East Texans as well. The relative absence of organized labor, of course, helped it forge such strong bonds. Despite measurable gains in some areas (Southern California and the mid-continent region of Oklahoma), oil's major union, the International Association of Oil Field, Gas Well & Refinery Workers, continued to struggle with recruitment. Some shifting momentum was evident in the late 1930s, after the international, now renamed the Oil Workers International Union (OWIU), affiliated with the Congress of Industrial Organizations (CIO) and started implementing industrial unionism in the major gulf refineries of Port Arthur, Beaumont, and Houston. But it was not enough to reverse patterns in East Texas. OWIU locals experienced increased membership in Longview and Kilgore, and the language of CIO activists, which condemned major companies for "dominating" their workers, did resonate with some roughnecks to an extent. Yet, by and large, East Texas laborers remained too independent minded, unwilling and unable to unite, divided by strict racial proscriptions, and too scattered to muster any attack on corporate oil or support a labor-friendly New Deal. Texas locals, one observer noted, remained "storm-wracked islands of unionism in a sea of open shop oil."[48]

Sun happily and effectively navigated (and guarded) that open sea. One of the last truly family-run oil businesses, a fact it trumpeted proudly in this time of duress, it continued its "family approach" to labor in the 1930s by fine-tuning company welfare programs it had instituted in the 1920s. Counter to an industrial pattern of layoffs and wage cuts, it maintained a steady rate of employment. Even during the heaviest pressures of the Depression, it kept all its employees on the payroll; two-thirds of Sun employees were working five days a week, the other one-third, six. Their labor was rewarded with an average weekly wage of $25.48, in keeping with industry standards. J. Howard Pew maintained his belief that the inability of "purchasing power to maintain itself" had caused the Depression. As he explained in 1932, "Even before the depression it was plain that continued prosperity demanded the main-tenance of a broad-based buying power such as could be assured only by . . . liberal wages and salaries." Pew's philosophy drove him to keep employees operating at a fair wage, but it also animated his politics. In response to the New Deal's pro-labor provisions, particularly the 1935 Wagner Act, which extended the power of workers and labor unions to bargain collectively with their corporate employers, he buttressed his defense of the employer's right to raise or reduce employee wages at his discretion, reiterating his justification of a conservative paternalism.[49]

That paternalism and the Pew presence in East Texas worked to shore up Sun's image as the people's petrocompany. By now Sun was, in truth, a full-blown mid-major, but it did not choose to sell itself as such. Since its breakout at Spindletop, it had carefully guarded its aura as a Texas independent that refused to give up on the values that had made it flourish. During the industry-government infighting of the 1930s, Sun thus became the media darling, the corporate entity that exemplified what to do right. Described as "square dealers" by newspaperman Carl

Estes, Sun's executives were the antithesis of Standard's men because they abided by rules of "real conservation" with focused concern on local environments and economic health (rather than on their own bottom line), took care of their workers, and stayed true to the needs of "the little man and royalty owner[s]" with which they collaborated.[50]

The Pews assumed another role as oil's anti–New Deal generals. Edgar and Howard earned the label honestly but wore it with increasingly different degrees of conviction. In the early stages of the oil crisis, Edgar continued to serve the aims of the American Petroleum Institute (API) and educate producers about the need for voluntary regulations and standardization. His efforts came to a head—as well as a pivot—in late 1931. At a meeting of the Texas Oil and Gas Conservation Association, attended by the likes of H. L. Hunt, he urged independents to police themselves with greater coordination and resolve. Then, while addressing the API Division of Production in Dallas, he resurrected a proposal for the unitization of oil field development raised a decade before and, more strikingly, spoke out against the rule of capture. "It is no longer of any use to inveigh against government interference with business, or to denounce as revolutionists any who disagree with us," he charged. "The country, the world, looks upon us as trustees for a vital resource. Our administration of that trust has not been satisfactory." Having witnessed the brutalities of the East Texas fields, J. Edgar Pew could no longer ignore the necessity of business-government cooperation. The adopted son of the Southwest admitted that it was incumbent upon his peers to concede the value of such a partnership, at least temporarily. He continued advocating that middle path even after he relocated to Philadelphia in the mid-1930s.[51]

As the decade unfolded, then, it was Howard who became Sun's most vociferous spokesperson for the wishes of the wildcatter. He had always been the most outspoken Pew, but now his words carried special weight. As he watched the economic depression play out and subsequently the Roosevelt administration's attempts to correct it through the extension of federal largesse and economic restructuring, he grew increasingly agitated: the staunch laissez-faire principles that his father and church had instilled in him seemed under attack.

He did not act alone, but the seriousness of his intent thrust him into the lead of a legion of silk-stockinged dissenters. Various facets of the sprawling New Deal program, not the least the racial and social upheaval it seemed to provoke, upset businessmen of his stock. As Roosevelt recruited black and Jewish citizens to his coalition and raised some prospect of civil rights advancements, the staunchest of white corporate conservatives railed against him. Funded by a number of Texas oilmen and northern industrialists, the Christian American Association, headed by reactionary Vance Muse, was hardly fringe in its pronouncements against the president. "That crazy man in the White House will Sovietize America," Muse seethed, "with the federal handouts of the Bum Deal. . . . Or is it Jew Deal?" Muse raged against New Deal support for labor unions as well, fretting that they would force white laborers to join "organizations with black African apes whom they will have to call 'brother' or lose their jobs." In the foul atmosphere of 1930s politics, there was plenty of room for Muse's caustic attempt to roll back Roosevelt and all the "isms" (communism, socialism, atheism) registering as alien to his "traditional" Americanism. By virtue of his earnestness to kill the New Deal, Pew breathed in some of this air; yet he and his family were adamant that their ideology made no room for Muse's brand of anti-Roosevelt vitriol. When the Pews once were publicly accused of anti-Semitism, Howard and his politician brother Joseph N. Pew Jr. demanded an immediate retraction; anti-Semitism and racism, Joseph retorted, were "despicable and un-American and deserve[d] universal condemnation." Moreover, others pointed out, they were out of keeping with a family that once aided and abetted those fleeing slavery.[52]

What invigorated J. Howard Pew most—and allowed him to work alongside xenophobes who shared his opposition to the New Deal—was rigorous, philosophical defense of liberty in all its measures. In his many lectures, church and company talks, and opinion pieces, which he produced prolifically, Pew made it known that his was an unshakeable faith in "freedom of the conscience . . . freedom of religion . . . freedom to dream, to think, to experiment, to invent, to match wits in friendly competition—freedom to be an individual." "That is America's Christian heritage," he professed. "That is America's strength." Pew was a Christian libertarian to the core. His resoluteness on that score placed him at the heart of a labyrinth of organizations that spanned denominational and class divides and brushed over ideological nuances separating small and big business interests, low- and high-church proclivities. While his family, along with the Catholic, Delaware-based gunpowder- and dynamite-producing DuPont family, assumed a founding role in the American Liberty League, the highbrow lobby for ultrarich conservatives, through his ardent Protestantism and leadership in the Presbyterian Church he rubbed shoulders with members of the Church League of America, National Laymen's Council, and Christian Business Men's Committee, which espoused the interests of the middling evangelical type. The common denominator was his determination to derail what he considered a dangerous Roosevelt ruse to seize authority for the presidency over the people. Everyone who knew him knew he was dead serious in this quest. Of Pew a perturbed US senator once remarked that the "stiff-necked, bushy-browed, six-footer" had the constitution of "an affidavit."[53]

That was most clearly evident in the realm of petroleum politics, the spring from which his fretting about diminishing freedom flowed. Unlike Edgar, Howard grew more, not less, determined to resist the New Deal's encroachment on his sector as the decade wore on. On that count, a revealing division with his cousin surfaced before the US Congress's Cole Committee, which held hearings in Washington in 1934 to assess federal involvement in the stabilization of oil production. Rejecting claims that uncontrolled supply from East Texas was injurious to pricing and the consumer, Howard also starkly opposed any federal conservation initiative. In his most quotable statement, he adamantly rejected the fears of scarcity that were redoubled in the 1930s by government's and major oil's predictions. Oil was not depleting, he declared; nor was the loss of resources a real worry. Focus needed to be on facilitating discovery, not holding tightly, desperately to the discovered. "Regarding future supplies of oil," he stated unapologetically, "frankly I may say I feel but small concern. Nature has been bountiful in the supply of this resource, and we have barely scratched the surface. I am not in favor of preserving supplies of petroleum for the use of generations yet unborn." Howard did voice support for state-level "police protection" of producing fields, as well as an interstate compact to prevent theft and transportation of hot oil, but Washington altogether needed to stay out of his boardroom and refineries and off his derrick floors. With another flourish of bravado, he announced that he did not want a "nurse" for his or anyone else's business. In contrast, Edgar, testifying at the same hearings, repeated his concession that for the time being at least, Washington had to restore a semblance of order to protect the short-term viability of small producers and the long-term well-being of consumers. Sometimes a nurse is needed, he intimated.[54]

J. Howard Pew's muscular defense of the wildcat ethic reached well beyond the halls of Congress and the single issue of conservation. Under Ickes's command, the Roosevelt administration endorsed other strategies to regulate the petroleum sector, including gasoline taxes, price-fixing measures, and labor codes, and at each step of the way Howard was there with a response, garnering losses in some cases, victories in others (the defeat of price-fixing measures and the National Recovery Administration were particularly satisfying for Pew). Meanwhile, he lectured widely to corporate lobbies in hopes of convincing them of the righteousness of his vision of the oil sector. One of his most popular political sermons was his unabashedly titled "The Oil Industry: A Living Monument to the American System of Free Enterprise," which he delivered in several settings, including at the API annual meeting in 1938. The speech was celebratory in its praise of the petroleum sector's heritage and hard-hitting in its determination to paint oilmen's wars with New Dealers as an epic clash, with American nationhood itself resting in the balance. "The persistent effort to bring industry, business, commerce, and enterprise, under government domination is a flat denial of all the lessons of the century and a half of the industrial age," he inveighed. And to attack industry in such a way, he continued, was to destroy the guidepost to which the "discipline, character . . . and morale of the people" was calibrated. It was up to oilmen to save their society. "With so many political witch doctors abroad in the land teaching communism, fascism, planned and dictated economies, government paternalism . . . I urge you to guard well that heritage and to turn a deaf ear to all their sophistries." Each oilman before him, Pew petitioned, had a "part to play in the great drama of life" and a role to assume in the takedown of tyranny.[55]

The object of Pew's greatest scorn was well aware of his barnstorming. After one meeting with Pew and his fellow independents, Harold Ickes admitted he faced a formidable bunch: "They were a sober lot of men." The soberest of them all, Howard was relentless and creative in his politicking. In a way, he had to be, as national party politics did not yet provide clear space for oilmen like the Pews. To be sure, Joseph Pew, Howard's brother, boasted deep connections inside the GOP. Angered by New Deal petroleum measures in the early 1930s, he became active inside the party and served as a delegate to the Republican National Convention. From 1934 to 1940 he gave over $2 million to the party, representing one portion of more substantial Pew donations to the GOP. Despite their generosity, the Pews could coax little return from national Republicans. Wanting a conservative like Ohio senator Robert Taft to take the reins of the party, they were stuck with the likes of Wendell Willkie, the Democrat-turned-Republican political centrist from Indiana who expressed his disdain for them. "I don't know Joe Pew," Willkie insisted, "but I am 100% against his policy of turning the Republican Party back to the days of Harding and Coolidge." The GOP's 1940 presidential candidate went so far as to ridicule Pew's type: "The good Lord put all this oil in the ground, then someone comes long who hasn't been a success at doing anything else, and takes it out of the ground. The minute he does that, he considers himself an expert on everything from politics to petticoats." Willkie mocked their power, and independents determined never again to let a politician get away with that sin. Hamstrung at the national level, for the moment the Pews focused on state-level and movement politics. They bought up popular media outlets such as the *Farmer's Wife*, the *Farmer's Journal*, and the *Three Star Extra* radio program on the NBC network, extended their leadership in Christian business associations, and through those channels transmitted their anti-Roosevelt doctrine into the homes of average Americans. Even if they could not yet gain a satisfying hearing with Washington politicians, the public was starting to listen to them.[56]

And some degree of clearer-cut political success did soon follow, hinting at challenges yet to come once the pall of the Depression had fully lifted. By the time Willkie suffered defeat in 1940 at the hands of Roosevelt, who earned a third term, the Pews were wary of another rising New Deal threat to their standing: what Howard deemed a "super cartel" of Washington and major oil interests combining for global influence. Once again the matter arose because of Ickes's maneuvers. With the latest geological surveys in hand, Ickes sounded the alarm bells: despite East Texas's boom, peak oil was a real and impending threat.

After he was named petroleum coordinator for national defense in May 1941, seven months before the United States' entry into World War II, that sense of dire urgency grew. As he reflected in his brief primer for the public, *Fightin' Oil* (1943), his commission was extraordinarily demanding, requiring a special touch: "There is no denying ... I have wondered if our production and transportation of petroleum could possibly keep pace with the growing military and essential civilian needs. If it does, let me say right here ... that we will have been a witness to a miracle worthy of the saints." Convinced that victory in war and sustainability beyond would require broader partnerships and oversight, Ickes conceived of the Anglo-American Petroleum Agreement. Through this arrangement, formally proposed in 1944, he wanted Britain and the United States to establish an alliance with each other and the Western world's largest oil companies in order to manage international petroleum supplies, demands, and drilling. An International Petroleum Commission was to oversee the entire operation, with Ickes implanted in a key role. Of immediate concern to all parties was the Middle East, where a series of oil discoveries in the late 1930s was hinting at its future importance in the petroleum world. How would the two nations and their agents in oil manage its emerging fields?[57]

However much Ickes promoted the initiative as a pragmatic step forward for the international community, the agreement faced stiff opposition from the beginning. The Pews and their legion of independents loudly sounded the alarms that centralization and monopolization of oil governance were in full swing and that Ickes's scheme was a surreptitious ploy by government and major oil companies to wipe them out. Once again they identified Roosevelt's right-hand man as the most "toxic of the New Dealers." Their opposition was more substantial than name calling, however, with the Pews out front. Through Joseph Pew's newly acquired magazine, *The Pathfinder*, Sun's public relations people spread word of the Anglo-American Petroleum Agreement's nefarious intents. In one damning story, *Pathfinder* warned its readers of rising dangers in Middle East politics and Zionist-Arab tensions, all to emphasize the misguidedness of Washington's interests there. It also charged that "government concessions to big oil companies [were] a kick in the teeth for independent oil operators back home." J. Edgar Pew, meanwhile, generated press by demanding that Washington ease exaggerated fears of depletion by returning "oil control by the federal government to private enterprise under state law" and empower, not inhibit, wildcat operators in the mid-continent. Edgar had returned to his family's antistatist fold. Howard took the strongest action by directing open letters of protest to the Senate Foreign Relations Committee, in which he painted the agreement as license for an "evil cartel system," and by speaking out against it at government hearings, including one at which Ickes was present. Ickes's plan, Pew barked, was "a deliberate attempt to place the American petroleum industry under the bureaucratic control of the federal government" and expose it to foreign interests.[58]

Ickes was flummoxed and left in a tough spot, with his detractors gathering steam. "Some of the industry are seeing ghosts where there are no ghosts," he complained to Roosevelt. Roosevelt agreed but, in the name of expedience, withdrew the agreement from Senate consideration in 1945 and let it sit. Ickes would not recover. In early 1946, he faced off against Roosevelt's successor, Harry Truman, over the president's proposed hiring of western oilman Edwin Pauley as undersecretary of the navy. Used to having his say in the White House, Ickes submitted a letter of resignation in order to force Truman's hand. To his surprise, Truman accepted it. "It was the kind of letter sent by a man who is sure that he can have his way if he threatens to quit," Truman later mused. Stunned, Ickes slinked off into a new career—journalism—leaving his enemies delighted. With Ickes out of the picture, the Anglo-American Petroleum Agreement faltered again, this time without recovery. Opposition now mounted in the State Department, where officials listed reasons first cited by the Pews for killing Ickes's deal: it was anticapitalist in spirit, placed Washington at the center of a cartel of multinational companies, made US interests vulnerable to foreign powers, and represented government meddling at its worst. Grassroots antagonism grew too, especially in the Southwest, where local residents openly declared Ickes's deal a sellout of US interests and destructive of their livelihoods. Truman heard the criticisms and let the agreement die a quiet death.[59]

THE FUROR STIRRED up by Ickes's international agreement, leading to his eventual demise, obscured other wartime developments that were beginning to leave a more profound impact on the future of faith, politics, and oil in postwar America. Wildcatters welcomed some of them and rued others but across the board recognized that they and their battle were crossing another threshold.

Despite the Pews' and independent oilmen's complaints with the New Deal's encroachment on their pools, profits, and church pews, wartime Washington would in fact be good to them. Thanks to the US military's largesse, Sun's fortunes emblemized the wildcatter's silent ascent. From war's beginning to end, the Pews' assaults on Harold Ickes captured headlines; yet when the interior secretary visited their Marcus Hook refinery in 1943, they softened their tone, knowing that some collaboration with Roosevelt's "Oil Czar" was best for business. Sun's ledger bore proof of this auspicious bond. Sun Shipbuilding and Drydock Company quickly emerged as the nation's most prolific producer of oil tankers. Between the Japanese attack on Pearl Harbor in December 1941 and Japan's surrender in August 1945, Sun built hundreds of freighters and destroyers and, with one stroke of the pen by Navy Secretary Frank Knox, won a government contract for tankers worth $350 million. Sun's refining was just as lucrative. With its innovative Houdry catalytic cracking units working full blast, efficiently converting crude petroleum into high-quality gasoline, it produced the finest and largest quantity of aviation fuel in the land. By 1945 J. Howard Pew could boast to Ickes that Sun had blended its billionth gallon of aviation fuel for the armed forces, outpacing any competitor, including its main competitor, Jersey Standard. All the while, Sun kept pressing for gains in extraction and distribution, privileged access to the Big Inch pipeline out of Texas, and political clout that came via the Pews' new proximity to Washington. Sun's annual operating income rose accordingly, from $131.5 million in 1939 to $600.8 million in 1944, leaving its executives primed for peacetime and a burst of expansion.[60]

With their coffers full of federal dollars, the Pews and their fellow independents, particularly those with close ties to Texas, would proceed to expand their churchly influence and infrastructures as well, processes that would accelerate in the months that followed Japan's surrender. As the Lone Star State's gusher age came to an end, wildcat religion broached another beginning. Having debated among themselves for two generations about the proper limits of their enthusiasm for God and black gold, wildcat Christians came to embrace, not resist, their fury and all the outcomes it invited. No longer would the Presbyterian inhibitions of the staid independent suppress the propensity of charismatic and Pentecostal prophets to chase crude with all vigor and senses trained on the prize, impatience exposed to the world, as if the end of the world were nigh. Even the bushy-eyebrowed, silk-stockinged, affidavit-looking Presbyterian J. Howard Pew would agree that in the postwar years, at the height of US power—yet with the survival of capitalism, democracy, and the heart of the nation resting in the balance—only an all-out, uninhibited imperative to drill new soil and save lost souls would suffice.

At the same time that independents and their wildcat religion approached peacetime feeling emboldened, they also felt besieged. "Besieged" was a familiar emotion for them, consistent with what they had felt in the 1930s; yet it gained new traction in the waning hours of war. Even as Allied victory became certain, providing reason for hope, they watched with ascending horror as the dawning internationalist vision of Roosevelt, Ickes, and the Rockefellers—liberal Protestantism and major oil—was entrenched in the United Nations Charter of 1945 and then championed by the Federal Council of Churches (FCC), the nation's largest and most imposing Protestant ecumenical organization. Much to the chagrin of Cameron Townsend's populist conservative friends, the FCC seemed more powerful than ever and, thanks to expanding corporate and government aid, poised to reach new heights in the postwar years.

As if Pew, Townsend, and their peers in wildcat Christianity needed any further confirmation of this, an important meeting took place in the Middle East in February 1945, shortly after the first failure of Ickes's Anglo-American Petroleum Agreement. It transpired on a US warship and involved President Roosevelt, on his way home from the Yalta Conference, and the warrior king of the Arabian Peninsula. While sipping dark coffee under a blazing sun, the two set in motion the shift of US petroleum interests to foreign fields.

*part three*

---

# PETRO WARS

Ibn Saud and Franklin D. Roosevelt meet aboard the USS *Quincy* in the Suez Canal's Great Bitter Lake, 1945. A kneeling William Eddy serves as interpreter and liaison.

# CHAPTER SEVEN

# Holy Grounds

On February 12, 1945, Saudi Arabia's King Abdulaziz ibn Saud and his large entourage boarded the USS *Murphy* to sail to meet Franklin Roosevelt on the Suez Canal's Great Bitter Lake. Ibn Saud, as the king was commonly known, immediately transformed the destroyer into a vessel befitting his bedouin sensibilities. A canvas tent was erected, seven sheep were penned for future consumption, and rugs were laid out on which he could consult with his advisors and, facing Mecca, lead prayer. The voyage north was taxing but exhilarating. US envoy William Eddy was pleased with how the USS *Murphy*'s shipmen and Ibn Saud's retinue "fraternized without words." So too was Ibn Saud, who gifted each US sailor a gold dagger or money.[1]

The formal rendezvous proved just as rewarding for everyone. At 10 a.m. on February 14, the Arabian king, his advisors, and Eddy crossed the gangplank to Roosevelt's cruiser, the USS *Quincy*. The visuals of sheep grazing in a makeshift corral near the *Murphy*'s fantail (where the slaughtering took place) and other signs of the "ancient past" invading a "modern man-of-war" mesmerized Roosevelt's crew. During the next five hours, over lunch and the coffee that Ibn Saud personally served Roosevelt, the two men struck an accord. Ibn Saud believed they were twins, close in age and burdened with similar responsibilities and infirmities (with the president paralyzed from the waist down by polio and the king hampered by war wounds). Their frailties bound them. Upon hearing of his confidant's ailments, Roosevelt gave him a wheelchair that matched his own. "This chair is my most precious possession," Ibn Saud would later boast, "the gift of my great and good friend, President Roosevelt, on whom Allah has had mercy."[2]

Politics fed that rapport. Over the course of their conversation, with Eddy translating, the host guided while the guest dutifully followed. At one point, Roosevelt noted that with advanced irrigation, Saudi Arabia could develop its agricultural sector, so it would become more than adequate to feed a growing population. Ibn Saud thanked him for the advice but replied with a jab: What good was the "development of his country's agriculture and public works, he asked, if this prosperity would be inherited by the Jews?" The king was alluding to the pressing topic of the day, the postwar fate of Palestine. Roosevelt asked how the king would resolve the plight of Europe's persecuted Jews, who yearned for their own homeland. "Give them and their descendants the choicest lands and homes of the Germans who had oppressed them," the monarch replied. Why should they impinge on Arab domains? "What injury have Arabs done to the Jews of Europe?" Sensing his friend's irritation, Roosevelt assured him that "he personally, as president, would never do anything which might prove hostile to the Arabs" and that "the U.S. Government would make no change in its basic policy in Palestine without full and prior consultation with both Jews and Arabs." Ibn Saud expressed his gratitude and allegiance. By mid-afternoon the historic meeting was complete. Upon his return to Washington, Roosevelt penned letters to Eddy thanking him for his service and to Ibn Saud reaffirming the pledge he had made under Egyptian skies. In March, shortly before his death, he told Congress about his afternoon with the king: "I learned more [about Palestine and the Near East] by talking with Ibn Saud for five minutes than I could have learned in exchange of two or three dozen letters."[3]

Much would soon change, of course. Later that year, President Harry Truman started pursuing another direction in the Middle East. "I'm sorry, gentlemen," he told state officials, "but I have to answer to hundreds of thousands who are anxious for the success of Zionism; I do not have hundreds of thousands of Arabs among my constituents." Ibn

Saud thought he had secured a covenant with Washington, not just a handshake between honorable men, and now fretted over the imminent founding of Israel. Still, he preferred to deal with Americans instead of other Western powers like the British, who had always questioned his authority. The earnestness he witnessed among Americans while sailing the Suez convinced him they had purer interests in—and a better grasp of—Arabia's future. Why sacrifice that deep investment in his people's economic future on the altar of Palestinian politics?[4]

Ibn Saud would stick with the United States in no small part because Eddy and his American cohort of Arab advocates—"Arabists," as they would be called—stuck with him. On the heels of the historic agreement he helped broker, Eddy, the son of a Presbyterian missionary, became the adjudicator of two nations' postwar dreams of economic progress. At the moment they met, neither Roosevelt nor Ibn Saud comprehended the degree to which Arabian oil would alter the trajectories of their two societies. Hints of that future reciprocity had emerged over the course of the previous two decades, though, as major oil companies accelerated their global advancement. With rising fears of depletion in domestic fields, they turned toward South America and especially the Middle East. Several vanguards aided their advance, as did the sense that a shared monotheism would play a role in global oildom's dawning modern order. Carrying out the heaviest labor were petroleum geologists and engineers, whose explorations demonstrated new scientific techniques for reading foreign topographies. In order to locate subsurface minerals in distant quarters, they also had to learn about the spiritual auras that enshrouded them. In ancient lands that circled the Persian Gulf, God—the West's Jehovah, the Arabs' Allah—was omnipresent in their negotiations. There to help them navigate was a vast network of missionaries among whom Eddy had grown up. From these veterans of Muslim encounter, oil's forerunners learned how to read the soil as Ibn Saud approached his: as holy ground.

In the years following the Roosevelt–Ibn Saud rendezvous, as Arabian crude began to flow, the reality of a new epoch in international oil production settled in. For operatives tied to major oil and to Washington and the Rockefeller vision of liberal democracy and international cooperation, expectations prevailed that this new stage in global development would lead to universal prosperity and peace. While many

of major oil's apostles shared the ecumenical worldview of the Rockefellers, not all of them expressed it in explicitly sacred terms. Some
willingly dropped doctrinal particularities altogether for the sake of
universal brotherhood and international service. At a time when the
tinderbox of religious sectarianism in the Middle East seemed ready
to explode, their cosmopolitan and "secular" proclivities made sense.
However expressed, their enthusiasm helped transform the oil venture in Saudi Arabia itself into a model of postsectarian exchange for
the world's postwar era. Such hopes, which Eddy and his allies articulated in upbeat parlance, glossed over the social fissures plaguing their
expanding oil empire. They were also jarred by the creation of Israel
and the push by Jewish oilmen to place their fledgling state on equal
footing with its oil-rich Muslim neighbors. In the face of such challenges, Eddy proceeded with deepening resolve to impel Washington
to forge a "moral alliance" between the United States and Saudi Arabia.
By 1953, which brought the installation of a new US president and the
death of Ibn Saud, Washington would begin to entertain his call.

Eddy's efforts as a cultural broker were in keeping with the work
his missionary parents had performed. For generations, missionaries
had trekked the crescent curling eastward between points in Syria and
Yemen. The specific aims of their journeys varied; yet the American and
British subjects who tarried in the deserts and oases of this territory
all considered their service critical to the realization of its modern age.
Some perceived that they were also paving the way for oil.

Missionary work was foundational to every venture that Westerners
undertook in advance of petroleum. Beginning in the early nineteenth
century, missionaries affiliated with the nondenominational American
Board of Commissioners for Foreign Missions (ABCFM) set their
sights on the Levant, the Holy Land, which they viewed as a place of
"ancient promise" and "hardened" spiritual soil. Since Christ's day, they
believed, false religions had dimmed the sparkle of that place. Bearing Ivy League degrees and surnames like Bliss, Eddy, and Dodge, the
paladins of ABCFM flocked to the Middle East determined to clear
away the "debris and rubbish of ages" that had obscured Christ's truth
and replant a "living" faith. The hardened soil was difficult to penetrate,

however. Try as they might to convert non-Protestant peoples in the region—Muslims in particular—ABCFM crusaders suffered frustration and demoralization. By 1857, the ABCFM could count in all of Syria, its most promising field, only 317 Arab congregants. In response, its agents changed course and focused less on building churches than on constructing schools and hospitals. One of their impressive achievements was the founding in 1866 of the Syrian Protestant College, designed to instill discipline and democratic values in Syrian students, as well as equip them for careers in engineering and medicine. Situated on a bluff in the Muslim district of Beirut, with a panoramic view of the Mediterranean, the college was presided over by its first president, Daniel Bliss, and Reverend David Stuart Dodge, president of the board of trustees. Its prominence atop a hill literally made it the gleaming beacon of revamped Protestant missions in the Middle East. By 1900 evidence of that work abounded in the valleys below as well. Ninety-five American-run schools were operating in Syria by then, with a total enrollment of 5,300, and countless Syrian Protestant College–trained doctors and pharmacists had been deployed in the countryside to serve rural villages.[5]

The Dutch Reformed Church contributed significantly to the revamped missionary activity. Visionary-scholar Samuel Zwemer had established its first base of operations on the Arabian Peninsula in 1889. His record of winning Muslims to Christianity was never great, but his ability to recruit missionaries to the Middle East left its mark. Dozens of young, smart individuals digested his published treatises, which called upon Western Christians to meet Muslims on their intellectual as well as physical turf in order to usher them through "an open door into Christianity." The Arabian Mission grew accordingly. By 1929, it encompassed five outposts (Basra, Bahrain, Oman, Kuwait, Amarah) and a staff of forty-five. Such growth occurred on account of the mission's adaptation. Its staff still maintained the type of evangelistic strategies that Zwemer had employed early in his career. In 1921, the Basra base purchased an old war launch to proselytize tribes in the marshland between the Tigris and Euphrates Rivers. The boat was paid for by the Milton Stewart Evangelistic Fund and promptly rechristened the *Milton Stewart*. Yet, notably, the Arabian Mission also increased its service through education and medicine, the latter of which it considered crucial. Zwemer believed that due to the physician's "honor in Muslim society . . . medicine was the battering ram of Christian mission." Zwemer's was an overly optimistic charge. Besides the continued difficulties missionaries encountered when trying to translate physical care into spiritual care, among the most indispensable of the mission's trained medical staff were Muslims who never felt the need to convert to Christianity. So it was that a pharmacist in Zwemer's camp was remembered upon his sudden death as a believer in spirit if not creed: "he was loved and trusted by all & though he never saw his way to confess Christianity, he lived a life that showed he was more a Christian than he was willing to admit." But Zwemer was also right: if not a battering ram, medicine could be a feather of peace that promoted fellowship. That is why the mission built seven missionary hospitals in the early twentieth century, able to treat 100,000 patients a year.[6]

As witnessed at the Arabian Mission, these wider missionary endeavors intensified under the shadows of World War I. The collapsing Ottoman Empire instilled their work with certitude; the Armenian genocide gave it urgency. Since the 1890s missionaries in Anatolia and Syria had warned Washington of the atrocities Turkish leaders were committing against their Armenian Christian population. Cries for intervention intensified during World War I as killings escalated. Amid the carnage, a Congregational fieldworker wrote President Woodrow Wilson, "One could wish that such a power as the United States should become so strong on land and sea that such a government as Turkey would never dare to commit such a horrible crime." The missionary recommended an American policy "that brandished 'a great gun' in 'one hand' and 'the Gospel in the other.'" Wilson took notice, as did American Christians who, through agencies such as the American Committee for Armenian and Syrian Relief (as of 1919, Near East Relief), followed the lead of Charles Crane, Cleveland Dodge, and the Rockefellers in lobbying for Armenian aid. As the Ottoman Empire failed, affiliates of ABCFM and Syrian Protestant College sensed time was on their side. With more workers in the field and support from back home, they believed, the oppressive style of Islam they associated with the Turks would give way to an enlightened brand that supported democratic values—and one day, they hoped, a new Christian order.[7]

At this precise juncture of political ferment, drill bits joined Bibles as a co-agent of change. Oil had long been known to exist in the Middle East; since ancient times, its seepages had been spotted throughout Mesopotamia. A few oilmen cited that history as reason to start surveying the plains and ridges of Mesopotamia and Persia. The cleverest was a Turkish-born, British-trained engineer by the name of Calouste Gulbenkian, whose familiarity with oil in Baku (where his Armenian father locked up several oil leases) convinced him that the Turks were sitting atop liquid gold. He supplied the Turkish hierarchy with a survey that predicted huge finds in its eastern provinces, a territory that encompassed much of today's Middle East, including Syria and Mesopotamia (Iraq). The predictions excited Sultan Abdul-Hamid, but the Armenian massacres of the mid-1890s forced Gulbenkian to flee to Britain. The plan was resurrected in 1912 with the founding of the London-coordinated Turkish Petroleum Company (TPC), in which the enterprising Armenian, now a powerbroker with connections to Royal Dutch Shell, held significant shares. Under Gulbenkian's guidance, the TPC comprised a consortium of Europe's largest oil companies, with the aim of procuring exclusive exploratory rights in Iraq. World War I complicated its advances, yet also provided extra impetus. Although the entanglements of wartime geopolitics curtailed easy movement, Winston Churchill's mandate for the British to find and control petroleum for its war machine inspired action. In the wake of World War I, Gulbenkian and TPC would be anxious to help with that task.[8]

That eagerness placed them in competition with another British subject, William D'Arcy. Made rich by foreign mining interests, D'Arcy became obsessed with oil exploration in Persia (present day Iran), which rested outside the Ottoman Empire. A devout Catholic, he stewed over the mysteries of ancient holy lands. Why did the lamps of Persian temples burn with such brilliant white flames? With what material did Zoroastrians, "the fire worshippers," feed "the eternal fires of . . . the Temple of Solomon" whose ruins rested near Masjid-I-Sulaiman, in the Persian Empire's southwest corner? Petroleum? Intrigued, in 1901 D'Arcy negotiated a concession with the Persian government for sixty years of exclusive access to Persian territory, excluding its five northern provinces. He immediately sent a crew to drill near Chiah Surkh on the border of Persia and Iraq, but years of difficult drilling produced little. By 1908 D'Arcy's finances were failing. That year he received help in the form of a partnership with the Scottish-based Burmah Oil Company, subsequently formalized with the 1909 creation of the Anglo-Persian Oil Company (APOC, eventually British Petroleum). George Reynolds, D'Arcy's field manager, then shifted the company's focus to a second spot, near Masjid-I-Sulaiman. On May 26, 1908, Reynolds brought in the Middle East's first commercial well. D'Arcy was saved. "When the first black fountain spouted to heaven," one sentimental journalist reported, D'Arcy "fell on his knees, crucifix in hand, and offered historical prayers of thanks. His life's work and his faith in God were justified. Here was wealth—vast wealth waiting to be put to the service of the Church." D'Arcy did indeed start pouring his riches into the Catholic Church. Meanwhile, APOC quickly built a thirteen-mile pipeline to the Arabian Gulf and constructed a refinery at the gulf's head in Abadan, consolidating tasks aided by the British government's investment (ultimately a controlling share) in the company. In 1913, APOC contracted with Churchill to provide his navy with oil. After the war, the company rushed to resecure its hold on Persian fields and became the major player in the quest for "mastery" of the Middle East's great prize.[9]

That APOC's advances were swift was in no small part due to tie-ins with missionary outposts proximate to its discoveries. At the start of World War I, when British forces seized the southern Iraqi town of Basra from the Ottomans, making it their bridgehead in Mesopotamia, APOC gained control of the valuable triangle of production, refining, and transportation that would center its operations going forward. Basra and the nearby towns of Abadan and Ahvaz served as hubs. APOC's sway in turn guaranteed its access to those towns' extant Christian missions and hospitals, the latter being especially coveted. APOC's crews always battled the worst health trials imaginable, including the plague. Medical missionaries were essential to their survival. Even after APOC constructed its own hospital system in the 1920s, church-based health services remained essential collaborators when smallpox and cholera epidemics spread, as they did repeatedly. Inoculation of entire communities (one round totaled 25,834) was required. The Arabian Gulf's missionaries gave APOC another critical advantage: soft diplomacy. The British needed friendly accomplices on the ground to help them maintain the regional control they had gained during World War I. Missionaries offered exactly that. "I am a firm believer in the mission," one official scribbled on a pad in 1924, recording his conversation with the Arabian Mission's overseer, John Van Ess. In the official's mind, it stood as a "tribute" to Christianity's indispensable role in imperial progress. Van Ess had already begun offering that assistance years earlier. As he would later remember, in 1908 "an Englishman, named Reynolds, came to my house in Basrah and asked me to hire forty mules for him. He said he was going across the border into Persia to prospect for oil." Those mules ferried Reynolds to the place of APOC's first discovery. Van Ess's support of APOC increased with time. In the 1920s he befriended Sir Arnold Wilson, APOC's director of the Mesopotamia region, and in 1924 supplied him with an erudite theological study of Islam.[10]

Van Ess also offered a summary of Christian influence in the Persian Gulf, with hopes of instructing Wilson on the opportunities and challenges that awaited APOC. Through its multifaceted work in serving the physical and spiritual needs of the region, "missionary enterprise in the Persian Gulf has been an unqualified success," he declared. Going forward, missionaries could be vital to the modernization of the region by supplying "the people with a distaste for the old and the reactionary and an ambition for the new and forward looking." "Missionaries are distinctly an asset to government in its task of controlling alien and backward races," Van Ess bluntly surmised. In a subtler tone he insisted that they could serve as vital liaisons, "interpret the West to the East," and "equally . . . enable the West to appreciate the aspirations and difficulties of the East." Devout emissaries of his kind had long lived among Arabs, "eating their food, sharing their hardships and their problems, along the whole coast of Arabia, throughout Oman, the whole range of Ibn Saud's territory and Mesopotamia," he explained. "What this daily contact on the common level of human joy and sorrow and need means by way of mutual interpretation and sympathy, who can estimate!" Van Ess was ready to enlist his platoon of Christians in Arnold Wilson's civilization-building campaign.[11]

By all accounts, Wilson took that message to heart. Speaking before the Royal Geographical Society in early 1927, he repeated almost verbatim Van Ess's 1924 report. "There is no greater influence for good in the [Persian] Gulf," Wilson declared, "than the Christian missions; no Europeans are so universally respected as are the missionaries, such as Zwemer, Van Ess, Harrison." Enabled by the calmed circumstances Van Ess and his peers helped ensure, Wilson's APOC expanded its hold on the area. While APOC's explorations spanned out from Masjid-I-Sulaiman, improvements in drill technology allowed it to plumb greater depths. The wells that came in outperformed comparable wells around the world in terms of yield, and unlike elsewhere, it was soon found, they did not dwindle over time but increased in productivity as oil was released from the porous, fissured limestone. Meanwhile, at Abadan, APOC's refinery grew rapidly. Whereas in 1919 3,379 Persian, Indian, European, and "other" workers staffed it, in 1927 its payroll numbered 14,033. Thanks to the dredging of an estuary connecting Basra to Abadan and the Persian Gulf, those workers saw their refined product ship out to ports around the world in huge tankers.[12]

The Turkish Petroleum Company made inroads as well. In 1927 it hit a gusher at Baba Gurger, near Kirkuk, in Iraq's northern quadrant, exposing an immense field that would enrich the company. The strike precipitated negotiations between the world's largest oil conglomerates: TPC, APOC, Royal Dutch Shell, Compagnie Française des Pétroles, and the Near East Development Corporation, a consortium of five US oil companies headed by Jersey Standard, Socony, and Gulf. Sensing the dawning significance of Middle Eastern oil and anxious to protect their hegemony, they agreed to the Red Line Agreement whereby each company promised not to seek individual concessions in the former Ottoman Empire without securing prior agreement from the others. The pledge was mutually beneficial. It encouraged a deliberate pace, which the TPC—renamed the Iraq Petroleum Company (IPC) in 1929—adhered to especially well. Following its breakout with Baba Gurger, IPC restricted its production levels in Iraq in order to maintain output and pricing in an increasingly saturated global market. Meanwhile, the pledge allowed APOC and US companies to step up their exploration inside the red line without causing panic among their competitors.

The Red Line Agreement also benefitted Calouste Gulbenkian, who on account of spearheading the negotiations was awarded 5 percent of the total shares in the shareholding agreement. "Five Percent"

Gulbenkian, as he was nicknamed, proceeded to distribute his wealth to the arts, schools, hospitals, and churches. Two churches received generous support: St. Sarkis Armenian Church in Kensington, England, and St. James Cathedral of Jerusalem, home to the Armenian Patriarchate. With oil money he wanted to provide a spiritual gathering place for displaced Armenians whose lives, like his, had been disrupted by genocide and geopolitics. As much as his quest for mastery of Middle Eastern crude helped guarantee fuel for war machines, his greatest hope was that it would ensure peace for his own broken people.[13]

By the time of the Red Line Agreement, which formalized Western oil's dominance in the Middle East, American oil executives were increasingly confident that big developments there were on the horizon. A new class of scientifically trained geologists offered them that certainty. Although they continued to face skeptics in the US oil patch, whose commitments to the doodlebugs of yesteryear remained strong, these trained vanguards of the business gradually carved out positions of authority in the 1920s and 1930s as prospecting assumed wider range. Those years would be especially dizzying ones for them in Saudi Arabia. Under a blazing sun with endless sand on the horizon, they drew upon cutting-edge strategies and religious sensitivities to facilitate the extension of American influences in the region, just as William Eddy's parents had hoped would happen and just as Eddy himself was making possible.

American entry into the Middle Eastern blitz of Bibles and drill bits had a lot to do with the outsized agency of two men. Harry St. John "Jack" Philby, petroleum's Lawrence of Arabia, was a restless journeyman with lusts for travel and power. A graduate of Cambridge University, he was originally assigned to the Punjab as a colonial agent, before transferring to Basra during World War I. There he attended Arabic worship services at the church pastored by his new friend, John Van Ess. After the war, British authorities ordered Philby to the Arabian Peninsula to monitor Ibn Saud, whose challenge to the British-backed sharif of Mecca for kingship over the Arabs was cause for worry. Philby, as he was prone to do, carved out his own path: he came to believe Ibn Saud should rule. As Ibn Saud proceeded to conquer the peninsula,

Philby's star rose in the eyes of the bedouin king, even as his ties to Britain grew strained and, by 1929, were severed altogether. The following year he converted to Islam. "Allah has opened my heart [and] guided me to accept this religion in the rooted belief and full conviction of my conscience," he stated publicly. Philby could now officially serve in Ibn Saud's court. His first task was to tackle a fiscal crisis, tied to the global economic depression. Muslims were pilgrimaging to Mecca in decreasing numbers, from 100,000 per year in the 1920s to 40,000 in 1931 (and 20,000 in 1933). Ibn Saud needed another revenue stream. Philby's answer: subsurface minerals. Privately, he told the king that he "and his people were like folk sleeping over a vast buried treasure, but without the will or energy to search under their beds." He offered a Koranic verse as inspiration: "God changeth not that which is in people unless they change what is in themselves." Philby said it was time to break convention and invite foreigners to find that buried treasure; he knew someone who could help.[14]

That man was Charles Crane. Since the early twentieth century, the rich American Presbyterian philanthropist had generously assisted Arab societies. As cohead of the American Committee for Armenian and Syrian Relief and the King-Crane Commission (the post–World War I American-headed council charged with assessing prospects of national formation among peoples formerly ruled by the collapsed Ottoman Empire), he had inserted himself into the snarled politics of the Middle East. Over subsequent years he financed several schools and missions to help cultivate Arab culture and foster understanding between Muslims and Christians. In 1929, he visited the Arabian Mission in Basra to learn of ongoing developments in Ibn Saud's kingdom to the south. One of the mission's leaders agreed to guide him to neighboring Kuwait to call on Ibn Saud. Ikhwan marksmen from the Wahhabi sect of Islam (nomadic militiamen loyal to Ibn Saud) ambushed the caravan. Ibn Saud was distraught that members of his own constituency had carried out the raid, killing Crane's missionary guide. He wrote Crane with regret and invited him to Riyadh. The memorable meeting occurred two years later. To what degree Philby orchestrated it (as he claimed) is uncertain; whatever the case, in March 1931 Ibn Saud feted the philanthropist and in a quieter moment awed him with his cantor's "chanting of that passage in the Koran which relates to the birth of

Christ." Crane radiated admiration, noting he "had followed the King's career with close interest for some years, and [that] his interest was all the keener as he knew that His Majesty was all the time working . . . for the welfare of Islam." He was just as glowing in reports he relayed to his confidant, Franklin D. Roosevelt. "Ibn Saud is the most important man who has appeared in Arabia since the time of Mohammed," Crane wrote. "He is severely orthodox, manages his affairs, his life and his government as nearly as possible as Mohammed would have done." On the last day, king and confidant talked about the kingdom's lack of water for agriculture. Could Crane help? The entrepreneur offered to enlist some of the geologists and engineers with whom he was familiar. On March 3, 1931, with more ceremony, Crane boarded his ship, leaving Arabia behind.[15]

One year later, the first surveyor, Karl Twitchell, arrived ready to serve the king's interests. Crane had recommended him to jump-start exploration for water—and oil. The engineer set out into the desert and, after crafting a promising survey, convinced the king to pursue commercial investment in oil exploration. Twitchell himself began contacting potential backers. He nearly wooed the Near East Development Corporation, the US oil conglomerate in Persia, but its lawyers concluded that the Red Line Agreement prohibited it from entering Saudi Arabia. Unbridled by that compact, Standard California (Socal) soon emerged as a potential corporate partner with Twitchell and the Saudis. Socal's recent success in Bahrain, an island twelve miles off the Arabian coast, precipitated its interest. Bahrain's amir, whose favorable dealings with American missionary Paul Harrison warmed him to American interests, had granted Socal a concession in 1929. On June 1, 1932, its well came alive, signaling that oil existed on the Arabian side of the Persian Gulf and suggesting the same arc of deposits extended into Arabia. Against that backdrop and with Philby lobbying on its behalf, Socal finalized a contract with Ibn Saud. It was framed as a sacred covenant, with two key clauses, one economic and the other civil. First, Socal maintained exclusive right to "explore, prospect, drill for, extract, treat, manufacture, transport, deal with, carry away and export petroleum . . . and other hydrocarbons" for sixty years. Second, "the Company or anyone connected with it shall have no right to interfere with the administrative, political, or religious affairs within

Arabia." The corporate title under which Socal would operate was the California Arabian Standard Oil Company (CASOC).[16]

Bolstered by visions of Bahrain's success and the backing of a monarch, CASOC oil hunters set out into Arabia to find the next big thing. They did so as advanced technicians—and amateur theologians. By then, corporate leaders were clamoring for college-trained experts who could advance new interpretations of oil accumulation and revolutionize technologies in prospecting now so essential to the business's next steps. On tougher, global terrains, relying on sight and senses to find crude no longer seemed viable. Science answered the call. At institutions of higher learning such as the University of Oklahoma, students began to learn the latest mapping techniques, involving topographical charts, three-dimensional models, and coded renderings of anticlines. They studied how to measure surface-level stratigraphic layers of outcroppings that signaled traps of oil and gas. In fieldwork with the United States Geological Survey, meanwhile, they handled telescopic alidades and plane tables and tested new technologies like seismic reflection. Armed with these advanced tools—but also anthropological awareness—they went out into the world better equipped to locate liquid gold. Like their predecessors, they peered at new environments through a fish-eye lens, digesting and disseminating all the information they could about foreign faiths.[17]

The mentors to whom they looked for inspiration demanded that inclusive vision. At the University of Oklahoma—where the premier oil geologist of the day, Everette DeGolyer, discoverer of Mexican oil, was trained—Professor Charles Gould taught cutting-edge techniques while holding firm to the belief that his faith and science should coexist. Tension between those two realms arose in the 1920s when some scholars starting questioning biblical orthodoxies pertaining to the origin and age of earth, and fundamentalists in the church responded by intensifying their defense of creationist beliefs. But at a time when contemporary geology did not yet possess the tools to determine accurately the age of fossils or fossil-bearing rocks (seismology and carbon dating were still in its future), Gould could hold firm to the natural theology of yesteryear. On one hand, that meant he ignored abstract debates about earth's origins and focused instead on teaching an applied science, whose goal was to equip geologists to analyze material that was already there, stuff they could dig up with their hands and feel with their fingers. On the other, that meant he could meld his service to science with service to the church. In that regard, he loved to speak to congregations about the global advances of petroleum geology and show them how to read the book of God and the "book of nature" as one. In talks to church youth he referenced nature as a text "never complete at one place"; mysteries abounded, with "line(s) omitted, Page(s) torn across, Chapter(s) missing." Geologists were to "reconstruct the record" but also realize that theirs would be an "eternal search for truth." Only God knew the fullness of his creation, but should not the geologist pursue it with all his mind and soul? On this plane, then, and considering the unresolved voids in his guild's epistemology, Gould could legitimately argue for a unity of knowledge that said God and geology should coexist. Other leaders in the oil patch eagerly argued that same point. At Baylor College, President Pat Neff promised that traditional theology and applied science would continue to work hand in hand. "The professor who teaches geology" will not only know "something about the age of rocks," he declared in a speech, but "also . . . something about the 'Rock of Ages.'"[18]

That same seamless sensitivity toward geological and spiritual matters translated to the field. One of DeGolyer's contemporaries outlined the need for such traits. His must-have list included knowledge of the "entrapment of hydrocarbons" but also "an open mind that is imaginative and unfettered by prejudice, be it technical or otherwise." The author titled his report "A Gift from the Gods." In his intimations, the oil hunter's unprejudiced mind also had to leave room for a full accounting of the sympathies that shaped the territories under investigation. To understand foreign grounds, one also had to grasp their gods. Even in this age of rapid scientific professionalization, faith remained one of the oil hunter's guides. Another of DeGolyer's peers—a PhD-holding Jersey Standard scout in northeastern Peru—acted on that promise by donning, simultaneously, the hats of rock hound, botanist, zoologist, ethnographer, and theologian. His expeditions through Amazonia involved several months of inching along by boat and foot, striving to map miles of terrain, up to five hundred in a single circuit. By 1926, he had coded the oil seepages and anticlines in the area. But the expert was not done. He toiled for another six years, searching for oil but also meticulously gathering thousands of rocks, fossils, animal specimens, and amphibians, while compiling a database of jungle flora and fauna. "Never mind the snakes, send us more anticlines," his frustrated boss rued. Meanwhile, he recorded impressions of river villages and their religion. He was struck by the animism that pervaded his hosts' worship and connected them to natural organisms around them. Perhaps that was because his hosts' holistic spirituality resonated with his own evolving spirituality. In letters home, he parsed his discoveries about local geography and gods as an unquenchable polymath, a man on a never-ending search for deeper truths. In reply, he received sermons from his home church. While opening these missives under the jungle canopy, he once again acted as intercessor, making sense of foreign grounds and gods while entertaining fresh takes on his own.[19]

While the Standard man never found the big pool, his work in the Amazon affirmed the new standards of his profession, which oil executives celebrated. In the midst of the guild's revolution, J. Edgar Pew spoke to the American Association of Petroleum Geologists (AAPG). "We are all seekers after knowledge," he opened. Yet the geologist's searching transpired in the most difficult of terrains—the "Fifth Dimension," a realm animated by "something 'what ain't'—'yet is,'" where hard science and the art of patient observation meet. For encouragement Pew turned to the Old Testament story of Elijah, whom he thought—in partial jest—the AAPG should adopt as its patron saint. Banished to the desert by King Ahab, Elijah wandered until Jehovah guided him to a widow, who only possessed a bit of meal and a cruse of oil with which to make a cake. Elijah blessed the scant supplies, Pew recounted, "and behold! Thereafter there was always ample ... meal in the barrel and oil in the cruse. ... And the barrel of meal wasted not, neither did the cruse of oil fail." Pew told his listeners to keep wandering the deserts and listening to Jehovah: the fate of the world rested on their ability to perform such miracles.[20]

As the 1920s unfolded, petroleum's "Elijahs" helped US oil companies begin to locate—not simply envision—large finds. South America received initial attention. Standard geologists' exploration of Peru was meant to build on momentum that got underway due north in Venezuela, whose oil industry boomed after a 1922 blowout of a well along Maracaibo Lake. Virtually overnight, oil companies—including

Sun—poured into the region and turned Venezuela into the largest exporter in the world. The process of making Venezuela's economy oil dependent had profoundly disruptive effects on its society. It was initially disruptive for oil corporations too: even as they hurried to develop the field, the costs of building an infrastructure of transportation, communications, and housing became crippling. Sun was one of the entities that failed. By 1925 it controlled 800,000 hectares of land; yet within months, after a stretch of failed wildcat wells, it had to withdraw. Cash-strapped, it terminated its operations, clearing its payroll of two hundred employees. The company's first stab at internationalization had failed, and for the next three decades its concentration would again be domestic. Its deeper-pocketed competitors—Gulf, Jersey Standard, and Socal—meanwhile came to control 98 percent of Venezuela's reserves. Despite the challenges of their South American fields, oil's corporate magazines—including Sun's—heralded the work their petroleum hunters were conducting in the continent's dense jungles. In this age of celebrity explorers, oil's Elijahs entered center stage. On front covers and in accompanying texts, oil rags such as Jersey Standard's *The Lamp* profiled the lives and careers of geologists who were tussling with unforgiving vines along the Amazon's shores in hopes of finding obscured clues to oil's whereabouts and, along the way, meeting (and documenting) strange others—plants, people, and beliefs beyond conventional register.[21]

It was in the Middle East, though, that the exigencies of oil exploration caught up to the romance. By the early 1930s, oil magazines were replacing silhouettes of South American jungles with outlines of Arabian sand dunes. In part that was because Arabia tapped different longings than Amazonia in the Anglo-Christian mind. The lands circling the Persian Gulf contained holy sites with lifespans longer than that of Christianity. And whereas geologists in the Amazon labored under jungle canopies in obscurity, in the Middle East they worked "out in the blue" (as one traveler recounted metaphorically), eyes wide open to all that awaited them. That was the expectation of otherworldly importance that rested on CASOC oil hunters as they started surveying their company's concession zone along the eastern edge of Saudi Arabia. Gradually, with the aid of a camera-bearing, high-winged monoplane, the inspectors' purview sharpened. Gadgets were not enough, however.

They also relied on area tribesmen for help. Early on CASOC hired an English-speaking bedouin named Khamis as its guide. Besides helping them traverse unknown topographies, he taught the Americans manners. "Do not ask the Bedouin a direct question when you first meet him," he advised, because "you are a stranger." The proper method involved supplication. "If you seek directions, greet the Bedouin as a friend, saying 'Peace be on you.' To this he will reply, 'And to you, God's peace.'" As CASOC's surveyors quickly learned, much of their success would rest on their ability to connect with the residents of a fastidiously devout society. CASOC's forerunners faced the challenge head-on: they digested Islamic theology and history, applied Koranic teachings to camp life, and adopted the *ghutra*, the native Middle Eastern headdress, protective against the desert's harsh elements and complementary to the biblical beards they all grew. They tried to blend in, both physically and intellectually. When North Dakotan—and quintessential CASOC forerunner—Thomas "Tom" Barger arrived in Saudi Arabia, he immediately began devouring all the information he could about the place, beginning with a study of John Van Ess's *Spoken Arabic of Mesopotamia*. "After three months I already know more of the language than most of the people at Casoc," he bragged to his wife, "but I can't get two swelled up about it because it is always this way. The geologists have to learn quickly in order to talk to anyone but their partner."[22]

As a Catholic, Barger came to appreciate how faith gripped his hosts. Nighttime confabs were the most enlightening. "The diplomacy around the campfire is wonderful," he told his spouse. While seated around the warm flames, listening to his Arabian peers recite poetry and tales of Muslim martyrdom, he felt he had direct access to the soul of the place. Inspired, he replied with quiet testimonies of his own. "Remember the Bible I bought in New York before sailing?" he asked his wife rhetorically. "It is very readable, and the proximity of the scenes of action makes it more interesting. These people have many of the Old Testament stories in their Koran." Khamis, he added, liked to repeat "whole sections" of scripture, "which he must have learned from rote." For Barger, the "perfect naturalness" of the stories his Muslim brethren told, some of which jumped out of the crisp pages of his Bible, grounded his faith in unexpected ways.[23]

That reciprocity served CASOC well. By early 1934, its geologists were convinced that their target was the limestone humps along the coast, dubbed "Dammam Dome." In 1935, CASOC drillers began probing the dome. By the end of April, the first rig was up, ready to be staffed. Headed by experienced Texans, the drill shifts also relied on Arab workers, making communication a challenge. As one CASOC chronicler remembers, makeshift signals were the best everyone could do. "The crews developed a Texas pidgin English with which to communicate, along with gestures, grunts, and shouts." No matter, the work proceeded. After the first well showed potential, five more wells were drilled in succession, and company heads in San Francisco consented to develop a camp for workers and staff on a 70,000-acre plot. Drilled over a period of several months, those five wells failed to produce the imagined outcome; but then Dammam No. 7 responded. On March 3, 1938, the well, now at a staggering depth of 4,727 feet, erupted with an initial flow rate of 1,585 barrels per day. By the end of March, it was flowing at over twice that amount. It had taken fifteen months for No. 7 to reply, but it was now obvious to everyone in the petroleum business that Saudi Arabia was about to become a major player. The Persian Gulf as a whole seemed alive with that promise. Just a few days earlier, on February 23, 1938, the Kuwait Oil Company, a collaborative venture between Gulf Oil and APOC, had hit pay dirt.[24]

With Kuwait, Bahrain, and Saudi Arabia online, all at once in the late 1930s it seemed the fused goals of drill bits and Bibles were coming to fruition on a scale that earlier missionaries to the Middle East could not have imagined. For some of their offspring, that marriage stirred worry that they had ceded influence to oil's voracious marketplace imperatives. Ultimately, a chronicler of the Arabian Mission would lament, "The high moral character the American missionaries enjoyed was compromised." But in the immediate wake of oil's discovery, the dominant sentiment in the mission was one of pride that petroleum might finally set the stage for a new era of Arab enlightenment, perhaps even Christianization.[25]

American oilers and Arabists kept at that project, despite the constraints of strictly Muslim Saudi Arabia. CASOC's oil operations continued to expand in the wake of the 1938 strike; the entirety of

Arabia's eastern portion, it seemed, was ripe for exploration. In need of finances to pursue wider gains, Socal agreed to equal partnership with Texas Oil Company (Texaco). As CASOC's maneuvering broadened, so did its attempts to construct a community on its 70,000-acre plot. By late 1939, CASOC's camp on the Dammam Dome, named Dhahran, consisted of several portable structures: offices, bunkhouses, bungalows, and a hospital. In accordance with the covenant signed with Ibn Saud, there was no church; yet a sense that oil work served higher aims penetrated the camp just the same. On occasion, that sense of mission crept into the open, in celebration of the ecumenism that had animated geologists' campfires. Such ardor was on display in 1939 when Ibn Saud made his first visit to CASOC's operations to open the valve through which oil would fill tankers at Ras Tanura. It was a royal affair, punctuated with rituals, including the presentation of each of CASOC's resident children to the king in homage. Pleased with the progress made and eager to extend his nation's covenant with the US oil company, Ibn Saud paused long enough from the testimonials of shared manifest destinies to sanction CASOC's broader control of lands beyond the original concession area. The space granted equaled that of Texas and California combined.[26]

Farther afield, other missionary agents of ecumenism were beginning to propagate the notion of shared manifest destinies with equal effect. The Arabian Mission's outposts around the Persian Gulf planned larger hospitals, while medical work under Paul Harrison's headship was extended into Oman, and schools in Bahrain grew. Meanwhile in Beirut, a new generation of Arabists was emerging. As symbolized by the ascent of thirty-four-year-old Bayard Dodge to the presidency of the Syrian Protestant College and, simultaneously, the renaming of the college as the American University of Beirut (AUB), that transition had already started in the early 1920s. Dodge was the great-nephew of the first president of the school's board of trustees and the husband of Mary Bliss, daughter of Howard Bliss (who preceded Dodge in the presidency). Seasoned by Beirut politics and the violence of the Armenian genocide in a dying Ottoman Empire, Dodge knew instinctively how to navigate difficult circumstances. His savvies vaulted AUB to an apex of influence by the late 1930s. Bolstered by grants from the Rockefeller Foundation and Dodge's decision to throw open the doors of its faculty to Arab as well as American professors, AUB earned a reputation among Middle Eastern elites as a place that nurtured strong minds, nationalist sympathies, and a healthy internationalist tone. Among the Levant's rising class of professionals and future leaders, AUB was simply "the great Oriental queen."[27]

One of those emerging leaders was William Eddy, a product of the missionary Brahmins of Beirut. His grandparents and parents had been among those who sought to Christianize the Middle East through the ABCFM. After growing up in Syria, he attended Princeton University, then served in the US Marine Corps during World War I, at which time he was awarded a Purple Heart for bravery. Following World War I, he earned a PhD in English literature at Princeton in 1922, then accepted a faculty position at the American University in Cairo (AUC), an institution patterned after AUB. For the next six years Eddy reacquainted himself with Arabic and Islam. His mastery of both soon became legendary. "In Egypt he used to stand on the street corners with holy men and they'd chant forever," his daughter recalled. "People would gather around and listen and say, 'Here's this American who knows the Koran.'" "He knew pages and pages of the Koran by heart." Eddy's Arab peers wondered why he would not convert to Islam. "Our Prophet was the greatest and the last of all the prophets, of whom Jesus is one," his colleague submitted. Eddy respected the verve with which his friend proselytized his faith but said he was content with his own. Such tact would later make him an effective diplomat.[28]

The professor's steps toward that diplomatic service accelerated in the 1930s. Struggling to raise a family in Cairo, he resigned from AUC and returned to the United States to teach at Dartmouth College. Immediately he adopted a breakneck pace of outreach that fed his desire to teach the humanities and religion and share his passion for the Middle East. Those commitments increased in significance when he accepted the presidency of Hobart and William Smith Colleges in 1936 (the former all male, the latter all female), an Episcopalian school in upstate New York. Eddy reinvigorated the colleges' mission. In a 1937 chapel sermon he beseeched students to resist the clamor of modernity, "shed the foolish disguises and distinctions of our day," and, as "children of eternity" and citizens of the world, pursue a unity of knowledge and experience, across denominational and national lines, that could quietly raise up all humankind.[29]

As specters of war collected over Europe, he widened his campaign to sell that message of global ecumenism. It was a two-pronged crusade. Behind closed doors, he agreed to assemble with Francis Sayre, US assistant secretary of state, and other Washington insiders to "discuss frankly with each other," in Sayre's words, "whether any plan seems feasible and practicable to make our Christianity more virile and dominant in the world today." Like Sayre and other fellow ecumenical warriors—such as John D. Rockefeller Jr., who joined him—Eddy wanted to guide the troubled world toward international cooperation based on premises of religious brotherhood. Eddy's goal was to ensure that Muslim societies were cared for in that formula. At the same time, in the fall of 1940 Eddy traveled cross-continent speaking on behalf of his school and its Christian vision. Titled "The Power of God and the Secular World," his prepared talk warned that in the face of the hulking fascism of Adolf Hitler, a truer demonstration of might would only occur if God-fearing citizens wielded compassion for the overwhelmed peoples of the globe. "You and I who believe in Christendom are not doomed to weakness. We serve the only totalitarian King!" he declared. "We who follow Christ need only to cover ourselves from head to foot with tolerance, reverence, and charity, and then wherever we walk, we shall find ourselves standing on holy ground." Eddy's was a plea for residents of the world to engage their tumultuous times and, especially in lands under fire, such as his beloved Middle East, to throw every ounce of their being behind a program of utter human transformation.[30]

Much like the geologists who roamed the earth during his lifetime, in other words, Eddy wanted Americans to see the world as an undifferentiated organic whole, with soil, souls, and nations in need of mutual atonement and restoration. In the shadows and wake of war, he would become more convinced that petroleum and the attending civil religion of crude that he shared with Rockefeller was the channel through which to achieve that collective well-being.

EDDY'S ROLE AS cultural broker evolved dramatically during World War II. A pivot point in his own career, this period of rapid change also marked the true dawn of an oil-fueled American Century. Even while under clouds of global cataclysm, Eddy and his co-champions of a civil religion of crude began imagining a postwar international system shaped by American prerogatives. This quest to inaugurate an epoch of US predominance derived much of its purpose and vim from the humanitarian and political ambitions of petroleum's first family.

If there was a symbolic beginning to this epoch, it was Henry Luce's *Life* magazine article of 1941. With a somber pen, Luce outlined what was at stake for humanity. "No other century has been so big with promise for human progress and happiness," he wrote. "And in no one century have so many men and women and children suffered such pain and anguish and bitter death." Because of their isolationism after World War I, Americans, Luce asserted, were partly to blame. He begged them now to wield (softly) their imperial might, embrace their nation's super-power status, and create the American Century. Much like Eddy, Luce wanted to steer his fellow citizens into a new interventionist mode that would acknowledge the interdependence of nation-states and the need for the United States to guide them. National security was at stake. Defeating totalitarian threats required the steady, outward stare of a concerned US electorate, he insisted. It also required US investment in global development. As he indicated on the page, as well as in person a month earlier at the American Petroleum Institute conference in Tulsa, Luce believed the loyalty of foreign societies would be won through economic and technological uplift, not merely ideological inculcation. He paid tribute to oilmen for their "skills and techniques" and "world-wide" vision. Armed with those useful traits, oilers—and Americans as a whole, he asserted—had to take the reins and usher the citizens of earth into shared prosperity.[31]

Couched in Luce's proclamation was an unspoken assumption of the role religion and religionists had to play in the construction of a new world order. That emphasis came naturally to him. Like Eddy, Luce was born on the mission field, and that heritage would always press upon his politics. So too would the influence of the Rockefellers. John D. Rockefeller Jr.'s missionary support during the first three decades of the twentieth century had been profound in China, where Luce's parents were active. "Mr. Junior," as he was fondly known in the Luce house-hold, would leave deep impressions on Luce and shape the faith-based internationalist project Luce began envisioning during the 1940s, even as the Rockefeller commitment to global fields shifted.[32]

The evolution of Rockefeller philanthropy had a lot to do with internal family dynamics. By the late 1930s Junior, now in his sixties, was convinced that headship of the Rockefeller Foundation and family wealth should pass to his heirs. Federal legislation forced that decision. New Deal taxation reforms, which raised estate taxes precipitously, encouraged him to distribute his riches to several "irrevocable trusts" for his wife and six children. Of special interest to him were the financial fates of his five sons, John D. Rockefeller III, Nelson, Laurance, Winthrop, and David. In 1940, the five Rockefeller sons, with Junior's blessing, agreed to incorporate a fund of their own, combining their individual charitable assets and finances. "It is to be known as the Rockefeller Brothers Fund," John recorded upon its official incorporation, "and is to serve as a convenience for all of us in connection with our personal contributions."[33]

These maneuvers freed Junior to return to his love of charity—though, there too, not without change. He was now a thoroughgoing ecumenist. During the late Depression and war years, he remained plugged into the work of the Rockefeller Foundation but also expressed renewed passion for his churchly ventures, provided they were widely inclusive. At one point, Junior submitted a paradigm-shifting letter to the Northern Baptist Convention, his home denomination, in which he stated that his giving would come with even stricter stipulations. Henceforth his money would only support ministries "interdenominational or non-denominational in character, which interpret the Christian task in the light of present day needs and which are based not so much on denominational affiliation as on broad, forward-looking principles of cooperation." Always disdainful of sectarianism, Junior crossed another threshold to declare a higher loyalty, transcending his Baptist membership, to "the oneness of Christian purpose." Critics accused him of shunning his parents' Baptist faith, but others—including his own aging father—endorsed his stand. Soon Junior was earmarking his Jersey Standard stock for the Federal Council of Churches and the World Council of Churches, gifts which by 1946 totaled $1 million. He also continued to back Riverside Church and Harry Emerson Fosdick, whose leadership in the war years leaned further toward the progressive pole. Fosdick opposed war and racism and championed "a world federation . . . that will transform the world into a community." Junior acted on those cues, right through to the minister's retirement in 1947, and endorsed that "world federation" Fosdick touted, the United Nations, seeing it in the same light as did its first general secretary, Dag Hammarskjöld: as a "secular church" in which the era's knottiest problems could be handled with "firm moral purpose" and collective pursuit of higher truths. Junior's endorsement of this humanist agency was punctuated by his 1946 gift of the Manhattan land upon which its new headquarters would be built. Always a social gospeler at heart and evermore global and ecumenical in his purview, Junior embodied the sense of US responsibility to the world that Luce called for in the decade's first days.[34]

His sons extended that rationale a step further by shifting from a social to a technocratic gospel of global development. The third generation of Rockefellers bore the imprint of their family's faith differently from one another. This was especially true of John and Nelson, who assumed the mantle of family leadership. John, who inherited his father's brooding Baptist self-reflection, wore it as a heavier burden. Throughout his career in philanthropy, he undertook initiatives for "civic betterment" with a punctiliousness that both Junior and Senior would have recognized. Nelson was less overtly pious but just as serious about extending family expectations of Christian civil service. His charm, affability, and attraction to politics (and the love of the accolades that came with it) positioned him outside his father's norm, as did his notorious infidelities. Yet his subsequent fights against poverty and environmental degradation, disease and communism were Rockefeller to the core, as was his belief that private-public partnerships and a reliance on expertise could solve the world's structural problems. "The Brotherhood of Man and the Fatherhood of God was not a cliché for Nelson," a eulogizer would generously offer upon his death; "it was a call to action, the motive force of his life."[35]

Personal idiosyncrasies aside, Nelson, John, and the other Rockefeller brothers collectively reoriented the family philanthropic thrust. As John assumed greater authority in the Rockefeller Foundation during the 1940s, he attempted to shift it from research to application of knowledge. He wanted to give greater concreteness to its abstract founding pledge to hasten "the well-being of mankind." John also encouraged tie-ins between the scientific work of the foundation and the fight of democracy against totalitarianism and communism. In that regard, he urged it to turn toward development work. "What I proposed," he explained, Western biases in full view, "was that we should select a number of carefully selected backward areas and be prepared to render them assistance in health, agriculture, nutrition, and public education, not to mention population programs." Nelson endorsed that plan. His heavy investment in the Rockefeller Brothers Fund's developmentalist agenda was an extension of personal undertakings he had assumed in the late 1930s and early 1940s. Following his graduation from Dartmouth College (where he wrote a senior thesis on the Standard Oil Company), Nelson and his young wife, Mary Todhunter, embarked on a yearlong tour of the world. He used the opportunity to visit with diplomats, missionaries, and businessmen to see how they associated with the indigenous populations with whom they worked. Nelson "expressed his approval of the activities of missionaries who came in close contact with foreign nationals," one historian writes, but criticized "the aloof attitudes of diplomats" and businessmen, the latter of whom seemed hamstrung by "narrowness caused by their career." The lessons of that trip stayed with him as he grew into his post as director of the Creole Petroleum Company, a subsidiary of Jersey Standard in Venezuela. Upon joining the Creole board in 1937, he traveled through Latin America to observe company operations. He was struck by the way that Creole kept its Venezuelan workers segregated in compounds and ignored the abysmal living conditions of bordering towns. Such tactics, Nelson believed, were bad both morally and politically, particularly in a time of worldwide unrest.[36]

His subsequent visit to Mexico drilled that point home. In 1939, at the behest of his father and Jersey Standard, Nelson traveled to the villa of President Lázaro Cárdenas, who was at the height of his efforts to expropriate US oil companies. Cárdenas explained why his people were so upset with Standard. US hegemony had deep psychological effects, he said. The symbolic nature of US corporate relations in Mexico "is often more important to our people than is their own physical or economic well-being." By the end of the discourse Nelson had glimpsed foreign oil operations from the other's point of view; if not quite as sympathetic to Cárdenas as outspoken evangelist and Cárdenas defender Cameron Townsend, Standard's missionary capitalist sensed what was wrong with the entire picture. No longer should US oil companies run roughshod over the environs they tapped for profit.[37]

Nelson backed up that insight with policy. In the late 1930s he and Venezuelan president General José Eleazar López Contreras remapped relations between Creole and the government. While the two men differed as to who deserved majority interest in the country's oil ventures, they agreed that a more equal partnership, close to if not entirely based on a fifty-fifty ratio, was required. Nelson also agreed that Creole needed to build a refinery in Venezuela, help enhance the nation's agricultural infrastructure, and invest in resource development programs that would ease the society's entry into the modern economy. He outlined these goals in a hard-hitting speech to Jersey Standard executives. It was time, he said, for Standard men to "speak the language and develop an understanding of the customs, habits, and psychology of the people" with whom they worked. Moreover, they needed to commit to the socioeconomic needs of their host countries. There would be a price to pay if they did not. Borrowing from Cárdenas's lexicon, he continued, "When the people become convinced—rightly or wrongly—that the owners have disregarded the responsibilities of their stewardship, they can withdraw through legislative action or otherwise these privileges of private ownership." Test the patience of the people, in other words, and suffer dire consequences. Rockefeller closed by emphasizing the goodwill that could come from a corporation's honoring local values; such ethics would be "good business from the dollars and cents point of view." If Jersey Standard and its counterparts were willing to meet their hosts halfway (or at least close to it), the future of capitalism, democracy, and the American way would still shine bright amid darkening shadows of totalitarianism.[38]

Even as a young man, then, Nelson had developed a keen sense of what was required for the United States and its oil enterprises to stay viable in a war-torn era. Washington noticed. During World War II, in conjunction with his Good Neighbor Policy toward Latin America, President Roosevelt named Rockefeller head of inter-American affairs in the Office of the Coordinator of Inter-American Affairs (OCIAA). Funded by Washington with help from the corporate sector, the OCIAA was to "provide for the development of commercial and cultural relations between the American Republics ... thereby increasing the solidarity of this hemisphere and furthering the spirit of cooperation between the Americas in the interest of hemisphere defense." Rockefeller was to ensure that Allied-friendly film, radio, and advertising saturated Latin America before Nazi propaganda did. Other assignments followed, including his appointment as assistant secretary of state for American Republic affairs, a platform he used to coordinate the Inter-American Conference on Problems of War and Peace in 1945. That same year, he joined the US delegation at the founding of the United Nations in San Francisco.[39]

As Nelson's evolving career as oilman–philanthropist–political operative demonstrated, the stakes of a petroleum-fueled American Century increased as World War II unfolded. The US global hegemony that Henry Luce spoke of in 1941 was far from secure during the heated months that followed his pronouncement. Oil itself served as a fulcrum of war. Most immediately, both sides needed it to feed their military machines as they advanced on the enemy or fended off invaders. In the longer term, Britain and Germany and their allies considered oil the key to securing viable futures for their modernizing societies. If oil was "the prize" of World War I, by World War II it was an elemental staple, essential for survival.

Even amid Rockefeller's wartime work in South America, the Middle East began to assume paramount geopolitical significance for the world's powers. Eminent geologist Everette DeGolyer reaffirmed that future trajectory. After traveling through the region in early 1944, he drafted a survey of the crescent's prospects. He estimated that, at minimum, the "proven and probable reserves of the region" (encompassing Iran, Iraq, Saudi Arabia, Kuwait, Bahrain, and Qatar) equaled 25 billion barrels. "The center of gravity of world oil production is shifting from the Gulf-Caribbean area to the Middle East," he announced. His words were a eulogy for US oil: its heyday of exportation was at an end. But they were also a wake-up call, a prediction about an immediate reorientation in the industry that would dictate world politics long after World War II ended. It was clear that the heart of that shift would be Saudi Arabia. While DeGolyer formally placed Saudi Arabia's reserves at 20 percent of the Middle Eastern total, amounting to 5 billion barrels, informally he guessed a larger figure of 100 billion barrels. There was no doubt that Ibn Saud's kingdom would hold the seat of power in the Middle Eastern empire of crude. US officials now warmed to that prospect, and their enthusiasm for CASOC's fledgling fields grew.[40]

DeGolyer's predictions—and Luce's vision—made the work of William Eddy all the more vital as his own war years played out. As with Luce, Eddy's fluency in the Rockefeller-styled civil religion of crude had grown out of a life spent on the threshold between his family's American roots and his attachments to a foreign society. As war erupted, he remained certain that the United States could achieve great things in the Middle East—but only if the region's traditions were fully respected. He brought that mind-set to his wartime military service. In 1940, when the United States was unofficially mobilizing for war, he resigned his college presidency and returned to the US Marine Corps as a lieutenant colonel. He received an assignment with Naval Intelligence and the Office of Strategic Services (OSS), precursor of the Central Intelligence Agency, with a post in Tangier, Morocco: his mission was to shore up defense of North Africa against the Germans. The assignment proved crucial to Allied maneuvers in a zone deemed sensitive because of its potential oil reserves. Upon his arrival in January 1942, Eddy instantly observed that Tangier was a shadowy place teeming with double agents, criminals, and state operatives from every part of Europe and Africa. The dexterous spy finessed his way through these circles. Navigating a Spanish-hosted dinner with German and Italian envoys in one instance, he conferred with hidden Arab and American sentries in another, all to gather the information his superiors asked of him. Meanwhile, he maintained a routine that included Sunday worship and devotional observance during the week. Due to his expert maneuvering, Allied forces were able to carry out Operation Torch, the invasion of Vichy North Africa, in November 1942. Eddy was now a known asset in Washington. With that notoriety came more opportunity. A deal was struck whereby he would remain a marine corps officer but serve on loan to the OSS, tying him to the State Department.[41]

What followed was the most far-reaching assignment of his illustrious career. "In view of the increasing importance of our relations with Saudi Arabia arising from our interest in its petroleum resources," a memorandum for the president dated May 31, 1944, read, "you may wish to consider the appointment as Envoy Extraordinary and Minister Plenipotentiary to Saudi Arabia of Colonel William A. Eddy, United States Marine Corps, former college president, and Arabic scholar." Eddy, the memo underscored, was perfect for this vital post; Franklin Roosevelt agreed. Eddy readily accepted the assignment, the full description of which included an open-ended duty to acquaint himself with "personalities, problems, currents of thought, wants, needs, and aspirations, both political and nonpolitical, with particular reference to American interests, friendly and helpful relations between the United States and the local governments and peoples, and the attitude of their governments and their respective nationals regarding these matters." One month after his arrival in Jeddah, he headed to Riyadh, the kingdom's capital, to meet with Ibn Saud. The king was pleased he had an American ambassador who spoke his language and seemed to care for his people's well-being. He urged Eddy to do more. While traveling from Riyadh to Dhahran on the coast, Eddy was stunned by the hardship he witnessed everywhere, some of it exacerbated by a recent drought. The experience turned him into the lobbyist Ibn Saud wanted him to be. Over the next few months the king and the American legate forged a friendship that would last until the ruler's death in 1953. That relationship helped grease negotiations between Saudi royalty and the US military as they ironed out the terms of an airbase on the peninsula and of Roosevelt's visit to the region in early 1945, Eddy's first key accomplishment. By the time Eddy joined Ibn Saud and Roosevelt aboard the president's cruiser for that historic rendezvous, he operated in full confidence that both men counted him as the vital and trusted link between the two nations.[42]

By the end of World War II and the dawn of the Cold War, the American Century ideal had moved from nationalist posturing to government policy. The result was a blend of humanitarian idealism and political realism, expressed in economic development projects of sweeping effect. Oilmen remained at the vanguard of all such endeavors.

If there was a symbolic bookend to Henry Luce's 1941 clarion call for US leadership, it was the 1949 inauguration of Harry Truman's Point Four Program. Now entrenched in a standoff with an ideology of materialism, Washington sought to combat communism by empowering state and nonstate actors to advance a diplomacy of reconstruction. "We must embark on a bold new program for making the benefits of our scientific advances and industrial progress available for the improvement and growth of underdeveloped areas," Truman proclaimed. "All countries, including our own," he added, "will greatly benefit from a constructive program for the better use of the world's human and natural resources." Critiqued by some as gentle colonialism, heralded by others as a sign of US beneficence and smart politics, Truman's blueprint bled principle and pragmatism into an unmitigated drive for Pax Americana.[43]

The Point Four Program did not concentrate on the Middle East alone. Early on, government and corporate leaders focused on modernizing rural societies in Asia and South America to prevent their alignment with communism. Nelson Rockefeller had much to do with such efforts in the Western Hemisphere. Despite being relieved of his duties with the OCIAA when Truman came to power, he continued to expand his Latin American initiative under the auspices of the American International Association for Economic and Social Development (AIA) and the International Basic Economy Corporation (IBEC); the former was slated as a philanthropic foundation, the latter as a clearinghouse for business enterprises in the region. Besides putting out $1 million of his own money and asking his brothers to do the same, Rockefeller made strong-armed pleas to oil executives, underscoring their weakening position in places like Venezuela as reason to "support the kind of activity that I'm proposing." The executives opened their company coffers—to the tune of over $14.5 million for AIA over the next twenty years and $12 million for IBEC. With that support Nelson initiated a plethora of projects that made US technical expertise available to developing nations. Meanwhile, Rockefeller's earlier efforts to transform Creole Oil into a petri dish for developmental strategy bore fruit too. By 1950, Creole oversaw several company towns in which its native workers were encouraged to "deruralize" (in the words of company promotional literature), reorient their notions of labor and family life, and, through immersion in company-sponsored churches, transform their communities into bastions of democratic, capitalist, and Christian vitality.[44]

The type of developmental strategy Rockefeller spearheaded in the spirit of Point Four soon made its way to the Middle East, where—to an even greater extent than in South America—business assumed the reins. When Harold Ickes failed to finalize the Anglo-American Petroleum Agreement and assert Washington's control in the region's oil patch, he essentially conceded authority over development schemes to the private sector. Buoyed by optimistic reads of Middle Eastern crude, corporate officials eagerly assumed it. Jersey Standard director John R. Suman parroted Point Four policy experts when he spoke of corporate oil's capacity to pave the way. The Middle East is "one of the most depressed areas of the globe," he told a group of oilmen. Yet by "pouring hundreds of millions of dollars into the drilling of wells, the building of docks and refineries, the laying of pipe lines and the construction of whole communities, this area can be transformed into one of promise and its society into one of hope." Socal and Texaco executives in Saudi Arabia internalized that language and drew up a blueprint to facilitate the kingdom's societal restructuring. They did so, first of all, with an eye to necessary changes within the American-Saudi corporate arrangement. With the momentousness of its work on the Arabian Peninsula sinking in, CASOC changed its name to evince the two nations' joint commitment to postwar-era expansion of their oil interests. It relabeled itself the Arabian American Oil Company: Aramco. More changes followed. Jersey Standard purchased 30 percent of Aramco, Socony, 10 percent, with Socal and Texaco retaining 30 percent each. By decade's end, Aramco stood as a sprawling, multilateral venture, with the corporate heirs of John D. Rockefeller calling the shots. Yet one other factor contributed to the remaking of Aramco into a singular agent of development. Ibn Saud barred nongovernmental organizations in his kingdom, and although he held missionaries in high esteem, his theocracy required that Islam rule unequivocally. Left without help from the nonprofit sector, a vital engine for American developmental schemes elsewhere around the globe, Aramco was left entirely on its own to carry out the monarch's quest for modernization—without offending his god. Eddy stepped forward to help the company pilot through tempestuous waters.[45]

Eddy was better positioned than anyone else to merge the ecumenical and economic intentions in Saudi oil fields. His role as adjudicator changed in the immediate postwar years. A family crisis in late 1945 had forced him to return to the United States, where he was named special assistant to the secretary of state for research and intelligence, an assignment that saw him provide critical assistance to passage of the National Security Act of 1947 and formation of the Central Intelligence Agency, successor to the OSS. But the Middle East continued to beckon. In October 1947, he resigned from the State Department. "I decided on my own initiative to return to private life to have more time for my own interests and to look after my personal affairs," he wrote his superior. Eddy was not entirely forthcoming; frustration with the White House's growing support of a Jewish state had much to do with his decision. But the chance to reconnect with Ibn Saud's kingdom was the ultimate lure. "My personal and professional interest for some time has centered on Saudi Arabia and the Arab countries in general," he detailed in his resignation letter. "I have found a happy combination in the offer of a position with the Arabian American Oil Company as adviser on political relations in the Near East." Eddy was thrilled to be connected again to the oil works of the desert, all the more since his new role gave him flexibility to advise from afar.[46]

The son of Beirut immediately went to work. At the time Aramco hired Eddy, its principle aim was huge: to carry out a massive, $500 million expansion of its operations. At this juncture it employed roughly 20,000 workers, 4,000 of whom were American—drillers, engineers, and managers who helped oversee 13,000 Saudi laborers and an additional 3,000 employees from India and other corners of the Middle East. Needing ambassadors like Eddy to bind this increasingly sprawling empire together with a shared sense of mission, Aramco assembled a legion of visionaries ready to accomplish that task. Through their proliferation of corporate boosterism as well as practical instruction on how to live and labor in a land saturated with God and black gold, Eddy and his peers were charged not only with wrapping Aramco in a myth of enlightened capitalism but also animating ground-level operations with a tenor of intercultural and ecumenical exchange.[47]

The institution that Eddy and his men created within Aramco to carry out these tasks would soon become enormous, the likes of which global oil had never before witnessed. Aramco called it the Government Relations Organization. Designed as a multitiered agency, with a central base in the Saudi Arabian oil patch and channels of communication reaching all the way to Washington, the organization immediately turned into a haven for impassioned experts on Arab culture who saw the oil company as the best outlet for their aspirations. Their profiles matched that of David Dodge, who joined Aramco in 1949. Dodge was a son of the Middle East (his father was AUB president Bayard Dodge) and a scholar of it too, with graduate training in Princeton University's Oriental studies program under his belt. When Eddy introduced him to corporate brass as a potential hire, he stressed Dodge's "unusual drive within himself to study and increase his knowledge" of the Middle East as one of his qualifying attributes. Fluent in Arabic and regional customs, committed to a spirit of internationalism that stemmed from their own faith, and eager to trade a career in Washington for a less certain (but more lucrative) assignment, Eddy, Dodge, and those who joined them in the Government Relations Organization saw Aramco as the vehicle through which they could transform their adopted homeland. In short order, they filled all the critical posts that the organization devised for its separate divisions in research and translation, as well as government and local affairs.[48]

Three of David Dodge's colleagues bore the heaviest burden of bridge building. The most influential of them was Tom Barger, who headed the Local Affairs Division. While prospecting for oil in the 1930s, the geologist had proved a skilled mediator between Western and bedouin interests. At Aramco, Barger was thrust into ongoing negotiations between the company and local leaders. He responded to requests for water tanks, truck axles, talcum powder, and material supplies of every kind with the aplomb that would make him so effective. He initiated engineering programs to improve area canals and water supplies, while also educating locals in new forms of agriculture and husbandry. By the end of the 1940s, Barger was well respected for his determination to make Aramco's presence in the area tangible and welcome. "Tom was ever the didact," one of his colleagues later surmised. "He was always teaching. He was always trying to explain to the Bedouin how the world was round."[49]

Two of Barger's associates demonstrated similar ardor. After spending the war years working for the US Office of War Information in Cairo, Egypt, George Rentz moved to Dhahran in the summer of 1946 to assume command of what became known as the Arabian Affairs Division. Aramco envisioned it as a think tank that could generate research and provide guidance and translation services both to other divisions of the Government Relations Organization and to other branches of the company. An accomplished historian with a doctorate in hand, Rentz was as serious about his scholarship on the Arab world as he was about Aramco's public works, and that combination would make him a formidable influence within the corporate regime for the next twenty years. Joining him in the quest to forge philosophical as well as political ties between Aramco and Arabs was William Mulligan, whom Rentz hired shortly after arriving in Saudi Arabia. Mulligan had spent the war serving with a US Army Air Force communications squadron in Yemen, so he knew the area well. Prior training in classical Arabic and Islamic studies at Hartford Seminary in Connecticut had prepared him for his wartime work, and at Aramco he immediately resumed the status of savant. For the next thirty years he studied, wrote about, and taught Arab history and culture to Aramco's minions, as well as to those in classrooms and boardrooms around the world who shared his passion.[50]

From the very outset of their work in the 1940s, the ever-expanding Arabian Affairs Division registered with residents of Aramco's domain as an imposing lot. "These 'Arabists,'" one construction worker from the United States lightheartedly recalled, "showed an alarming incidence of Ivy League degrees, transfers from the Foreign Service and PhDs in esoteric subjects." By the 1950s, the portables that first housed them had been replaced by stately offices in the administrative complex in the center of Aramco's unofficial capital of Dhahran. Once a dusty camp built to hold workers at CASOC's first successful well, Dhahran now housed 10,000 Aramco workers and family members. According to some of its American expats, the company town looked like Bakersfield, California. This "outpost of American civilization" also served as the hub of a wider orb that included two other company compounds, Abqaiq and Ras Tanura, production and refining sites consisting of 5,000 residents each. From their vantage point in Dhahran, Aramco's cultural specialists looked out on an expanding petroleum kingdom, which they were anxious to sell to the world as a parable of progress, a story of how a culturally sensitive, religiously attuned Western corporation partnered with a revered monarch to modernize a slumbering society.[51]

The proficiencies of their academic training beyond engineering informed Aramco's government relations men as they built their organization into the company's own virtual state department. Between the desks of Rentz, Mulligan, and Barger alone flowed a steady stream of information that made its way into policy and propaganda. Ever the fact finder of the cohort, Rentz scoured the peninsula to harvest knowledge of Arab society, then organized it in a research library that Middle Eastern studies programs around the world came to envy. Rentz's data points inevitably found their way to Barger, who would use them to determine new strategies for deploying corporate resources to assist development—whether through the use of oil equipment to drill water wells or the application of novel engineering techniques for irrigation and agricultural projects. The data came alive once it reached Mulligan's eyes and ears. Talented with the pen, Mulligan twisted the driest details into lively prose. Stories of corporate-community partnerships made their way into Aramco's print media network. Looking back on his Aramco career, Mulligan acknowledged, "Many of the Americans had a bit of missionary zeal, and by that I don't mean Christian missionary but, you know, spreading American doctrines, technical expertise and all of this. We were very proud of what we could do and very glad to show people how to do things."[52]

Even if they did not concede it, Mulligan, Rentz, and Barger were missionaries in function as much as form. On a personal level, all three came to their work from abiding faith traditions. While Rentz was a mainline Protestant, Mulligan and Barger were Catholics who seemed to grow more devout as their days in Saudi Arabia played out. Already core to their personal lives, religion became their professional preoccupation in Dhahran as they took up the task of binding together Islam and Christianity, the Muslim peoples of the Middle East with the "civilizing" mission of the Western oil company. As they proceeded to forge a viable intelligence agency, one that could supply Aramco with all the necessary facts but also sow and spin valuable insights for a wider Arabist public, they found themselves nudged deeper into the realm of theology.[53]

The duties attached to their theological endeavors were manifold. At the highest level of corporate exposure, they sought to cloak Aramco's entire operation in mutual respect for the holy. They worked tirelessly as academic specialists in Islamic studies, publishing and presenting original scholarship and building curricula vitae that would be attractive to major universities around the world—all in an effort to augment Aramco's reputation as a site of intellectual and theological exchange. Meanwhile, as Aramco ramped up its print media, which included a newsletter (eventually magazine) titled *Aramco World*, Mulligan especially helped ensure that the pages were full of educational stories about the cross-cultural unions forged in Aramco's domain. In some cases, colorful tales were told to highlight the religious authenticities of Arabia and the divine authority that the Saudi king enjoyed over it and its people. In others, Mulligan and Aramco's press corps drew out examples from the grass roots—a Saudi girl and her American classmate with hands on a globe, an Anglo-American engineer and his Arab roustabout with hands on a drill bit—to illuminate "the cooperative spirit that Saudis and Americans brought to . . . the Aramco venture." The portrait of Aramco as a soulful place for the gentle shepherding of different cultures toward modern bliss was highly skewed. But it enhanced the reputation of Middle East oiling.[54]

Aramco's image also benefitted from the Arabists' missionary work on two other planes. Of the highest importance was their service as deacons of goodwill to the Saudi king. Their most urgent task was to moderate the pressures placed on Aramco by a Muslim theocracy whose moral imperatives for daily life—enforced by a "religious police"—were unbending. It was up to the government relations Arabists to ensure that Aramco's employees did their utmost to honor the codes passed down from the sovereign and in general abide by sharia law. While some freedom for Western behavior (imbibing homebrews, for instance) was allowed within Aramco's compounds, in general Aramco's expats had little choice but to behave as their Muslim peers behaved. Why not do so with a respectful—even inviting—mind-set? That was the message Mulligan and Rentz passed on by way of the educational materials they helped produce, to which Aramco employees were exposed prior to departure for the Middle East. At Aramco's training facility in Long Island, New York—later Sidon, Lebanon—prospective employees took a six-week seminar in basic Arabic and Islamic thought and history. The content came via documents such as Mulligan's lecture on "Muhammad," which he delivered at seminaries in the United States.

Aramco made sure that Saudi Arabs did the teaching and that recruits learned to socialize with their mentors. One Aramco employee later remembered the experience as edifying. "There were many things we learned at the Aramco school that fall of 1948," he would write, "but none was more important to me than the realization that an understanding of Islam was vital to an understanding of the Arab world. Islam was fundamental to the life of the Saudi Arab." "But was this really so different from our own way of life in America?" he pondered. "I was to learn ... that Christians and Moslems could be good friends. Only an open mind was necessary, for open-mindedness was the beginning of understanding."[55]

The work of Aramco's deacons was deeply political as well. Besides bombarding newly arrived workers with manuals, memos, and prompts to respect Islamic law, they did all they could to prop up the king's political standing. Ibn Saud faced pushback from fundamentalists in his midst who questioned his allowances for a Western company and its infidel workers. To help him fend off that criticism, Aramco's ambassadors used their pens to herald him as an anointed leader who could vault his society into wealth and well-being without sacrificing tradition or faith. Their lobbying ultimately affected corporate policy. By 1950 it was becoming clear that Aramco would need to adjust its financial arrangement with the Saudi government in order to keep it friendly to the cause. In Venezuela, government reformers now demanded fifty-fifty profit sharing with Jersey Standard and other US companies. "The total purification of the Venezuelan oil industry, its ritual cleansing, will remain impossible until the companies have paid adequate financial compensation to our country," Juan Pablo Perez Alfonzo bellowed on behalf of reformers. With this model now in place, Saudi Arabia began to desire more from its US allies. Thanks in part to the advocacy of Aramco's Arabists, in 1950 officials on both sides would strike a fifty-fifty profit-sharing deal.[56]

Far less conspicuous but no less important to Aramco's dreams of development was the second role the Arabists played as unofficial diocesans of the company town. Not unlike Rockefeller's Creole Oil Company, Aramco recognized the value of religious activity in its communities. Aramco enlistees did too. Upon arriving in Dhahran in 1948, one fresh recruit found an oil society explicitly Muslim on the surface, yet dynamically catholic underneath. At a party in Ras Tanura during Christmas of his first year, he entered into theological conversation with the other guests. From a Saudi Arabian official, Indian nurse, Lebanese diplomat, Egyptian businessman, and Iraqi oil worker, he learned about the essence of the Muslim faith—its emphasis on peace and goodness, its totalizing hold. "Islam is my life," the Iraqi explained. "It can only be accepted as a vital part of one's being." After considerable exchange between the Muslims, Christians, and nonbelievers in the group, the American host "took out the Bible and read aloud, from the Gospel of Matthew, the story of the first Christmas. All the guests, even the [secular] Egyptian, listened with rapt attention. As we separated later I felt that we all experienced a deepened sense of brotherhood, one with another." That project of understanding extended to rigs as well. When Muslim roughnecks in Ras Tanura protested that they were not getting enough time to pray, an American manager with whom the enlistee associated took the advice of a sheikh and not only provided them with extra time but joined them in devotion. "Each day when the Arabs take time to pray," he offered, "I take time to read a verse or two from the Bible." Such was the practical side of a corporate citizenry bonded by belief "in the book."[57]

Yet how to promote that ideal without offending the king's Islamic theocracy? That question pestered Aramco's middlemen. They were fully aware of the theological and ecumenical exchanges taking place around them, as well as of American workers' desires to worship in established institutional settings; yet they were wary of testing their hosts' doctrinal inflexibility. The Arabists thus devised a clandestine ecclesiastical system. As Mulligan would tell an editor at *Muslim World* in Hartford (in confidence and code), theirs was a "very real progress . . . made in the dark of the moon." With their associate Floyd Ohliger in command, Barger, Mulligan, and their colleagues made the key steps toward that progress between 1948 and 1950. First, they firmed up the terms under which Protestant and Catholic groups in the Aramco compounds could operate; active for over a decade, these practicing Christians wanted clarification of their freedoms. Ohliger approached the king's advisors to gain formal acceptance of Aramco's church life. He was told to "carry on Christian religious services . . . quietly and without fanfare." On this sensitive matter Ohliger thus earned a handshake agreement with the Saudis: proceed but as phantoms. Aramco came to see the surreptitious nature of that agreement as necessary for everyone's protection. Under sharia law, no foreign faith could operate inside the king's domain, and anyone who broke that law faced severe punishment. Moreover, in accordance with the oil company's founding concession agreement, Aramco had "no right to interfere with the administrative, political or religious affairs within Saudi Arabia." So any formal breach of the sovereign's Islamic rule was obviously out of the question. The handshake approach, which continued into the early 1950s, protected the king as well; conservative critics would pounce were he to make any public allowance for Christianity. Officially, a company memo put it, "activities by non-Muslim religious personnel are completely forbidden in Saudi Arabia, and missionary activity is doubly taboo."[58]

Granted tacit approval for collective worship from the monarch, the Arabists worked with his advisors to map out company-wide rules for a Christian underground. Conspicuous Christian rituals such as weddings and burials were banned; baptisms and first communions were allowed. Rules for worship got more complicated. A 1950 meeting attempted to spell them out clearly: "(1) No church structures, as such; (2) Services to be restricted to persons who are already Christians—in other words, there is to be no proselytizing or missionary work among the Arabs; (3) Clergymen are not to wear any particular vestments of their office when not conducting services; (4) Clergymen to travel on certificates identifying them as 'teachers.'" Enacting these rules was a jumbled process, however. It was agreed that congregations, not the company, would pay for visiting clergymen—"teachers"—so as to minimize formal association. Catholic and Protestant devotees were free to meet in their homes and company clubhouses, but never beyond the Aramco compound, never with advance advertising or anything "in writing," and never with Muslims (or non-Christian Palestinians) present. In those rooms where they chose to practice their faith, Catholics and Protestants alike were to ensure that their interiors did "not take on the appearance of a church, such as permanent altar, pews, et cetera." Henceforth, Aramco's good Christians were to gather as "morale groups" that worshipped in respectful anonymity.[59]

Constraints aside, those morale groups rapidly proliferated. Between 1950 and 1954, Aramco's diocesans monitored a steady growth of cell groups, categorized as "R.C." (Catholic), "Canterbury" (Episcopalian), and "P.F." (Protestant Fellowship). In 1950, Barger informed prelates in Rome that there were already 2,200 Catholics in the Aramco compounds. By the mid-1950s there were over 3,000 active Catholics, while the "P.F." encompassed several Sunday schools, women's service groups, Bible classes, and youth fellowships. Other progressions were notable as well, such as allowances in 1954 for permanent clergymen to settle in Aramco's camps and "the importation of Bibles for non-Muslims [for] private use." Challenges cropped up along the way, none more vexing than those created by evangelical Protestants who wanted to proselytize with the public fire they felt their faith demanded. Yet, by the time Ohliger retired in the mid-1950s, the underground was alive and well. A contemporary memorandum marked "Employee-Directed Morale Groups—Confidential" praised the advances and dismissed those (evangelicals) who still demanded more religious freedom in the Saudi desert. "More thoughtful persons," it read, "appreciate the fact that the present arrangement providing religious services in relative convenience is only slightly short of miraculous in the circumstances."[60]

Less quantifiable was the spirit of ecumenism that enveloped the Aramco religious underground. In the definitive meeting of 1950, Ohliger, Barger, and the Religious Services Committee laid down one other commandment, which reverberated with Rockefeller sentiment: sectarianism of any kind was not allowed. "It is important," Ohliger underscored to Aramco's religious cells, "that the Christians present a unified front. There must be no friction as to Catholics versus Protestants, Methodists versus Presbyterians, et cetera. We must make sure that the actions of one group do not upset the applecart for the others." He added another caution. "We should work for a unified group. As a matter of fact, we will fail if we try to do otherwise." His fellow Aramco citizens internalized his encouragement. By the mid-1950s, Aramco's morale groups would exude the ecumenical confidences that the men who staffed Aramco's Government Relations Organization had long been preaching. Think together, and think big, beyond borders—that was the theological as well as economic imperative now operating at the heart of global oil's juggernaut.[61]

ARAMCO'S GOVERNMENT RELATIONS men proved highly adept at promoting the worldview that William Eddy sold to powerbrokers in Washington and places farther afield. The stories that these consuls of big oil crafted were compelling—but also distorted. Not only did they obscure the exploitative dimensions of Aramco's invasion of Saudi society, but they also brushed over cracks in the system that began to surface in company operations at this very same time. These underlying frictions, coupled with Ibn Saud's primary worry—the status of Israel—tested Eddy and his associates' exuberance for Aramco's constructive role in the Middle East.[62]

If you listened to Eddy speak on his lecture circuits, the doubts that Aramco's Arabists harbored were difficult to discern. On a consistent basis—with rising determination, perhaps, as threats set in—Aramco's lead diplomat sold his employer to leaders in the Middle East as a model of social responsibility and to Washington as a showpiece of US capitalism. His chock-full itinerary kept him on the road and in the air for a good part of the late 1940s and early 1950s, a burden eased only slightly by his and his wife's permanent relocation to Beirut in 1951. A talk titled "The Impact of an American Private Company on a Middle East Community" typified his relentless corporate evangelism. In it Eddy underscored the momentousness of his employer's role in building a modern state. Aramco "furnishes 90% of all the revenues of the Saudi government," he noted, before listing the by-products of that fiscal stream: the construction of roads, harbors, sewage systems, and schools and the provision of water wells, dug with Aramco equipment, making agriculture possible. Eddy was even prouder of the human relations his company had nurtured. It had already provided jobs for over 20,000 "non-Americans, mostly Arabs." "Many Arabs who had never received such wages as those they now receive from ARAMCO have learned the ideas of thrift, saving, planning for the future and continuous employment," he emphasized. Aramco was also fostering an Arab professional class by providing promising young men education in the trades or in engineering at AUB. And Eddy was pleased with the intercultural contact that Aramco was providing its employees. "Arabs and Americans are working on the job, on machines, together," he exclaimed. "The result has been an unusual fraternization, unusual because difference in religion, language and background would seem to prevent it; but such fraternization has been the result of men working together."[63]

The actual contours of Aramco's world did not entirely measure up to Eddy's sunny presentation, however. Aramco's labor system itself was riddled with flaws. On different occasions in the late 1940s and early 1950s, its Saudi worksites erupted in protest. The first strike occurred in June 1945 when hundreds of laborers at the Ras Tanura refinery stopped work to decry their limited food rations. One month later, 137 Arab drillers in Dhahran struck to protest their unequal pay and benefits; their financial compensation was lower than that of American and other foreign laborers, and they wanted swift redress. By July 16, 700 workers had joined the drillers. More resistance followed, as 1,700 Italians who were helping build the Ras Tanura refinery abandoned their tools and said they were "fed up" with being treated "just like the Arabs." They demanded better living conditions. Then, on August 4, all 9,000 Arab workers stationed in Dhahran and Ras Tanura coordinated a strike that lasted for three days and finally forced Ibn Saud and Aramco officials to respond. Shortly after it ended, Eddy had a private meeting with an agitated Ibn Saud. Company and palace ironed out a resolution in which Aramco promised to build a hospital and new housing for Arab employees, treat "workers with similar skills and responsibilities the same," and give them a pay raise. For their part, Aramco's government relations men remained sympathetic to the workers but also perplexed: just how to deal with a labor force with "practically no industrial skills" or discipline, "high illiteracy," and "time problems." "All adds up to a huge training need," one of their briefs concluded.[64]

Other systemic flaws exacerbated matters. In response to the 1945 strikes, Aramco created its human-relations-focused Arabian Affairs Division, soon home to George Rentz. Rentz signed on with Aramco on the condition that he and his wife and young daughter be allowed to live inside the company's American camp at Dhahran. His spouse was a Coptic Christian, Arabic-speaking Egyptian from Cairo with dark-hued skin. In making that request, Rentz was—as William Mulligan would later note—essentially undermining the "Texas *herrenvolk* atmosphere that pervaded the town." Well into the 1950s, Aramco's living quarters—20,000 persons strong by the middle of the decade—adhered to strictures of race familiar to the residents of South Texas and South Africa alike. In the American Camp at Dhahran, white workers inhabited ranch-style homes with picket fences, waved to their children as they boarded buses for school on weekdays, then on weekends played with them in the compound's swimming pool. At "intermediate camps," based in Aramco's three main towns, Italians, Indians, and other non-American workers settled in barracks with more limited amenities. Saudi workers lived in the General Camp, which had the barest infrastructure and little access to recreation and leisure. Arranged by this grid, Aramco was, one scholar puts it succinctly, a "Jim Crow enclave" lifted from the American oil patch and reconstructed on Saudi Arabia's eastern shore.[65]

Word of Aramco's social tensions eventually reached the public. The Rockefellers themselves heard about the situation. In the late 1940s, advisors to the family's financial portfolio, which still included major shares in Jersey Standard, toured Aramco's facilities. They wanted to see how a company in which they wanted to invest (to the tune of 30 percent of the Socal-Texaco joint operation) handled itself. Shocked by the inequities of the place, they not only filled their reports with dismay but tried to remove some of the most racist managers in Dhahran. The contrast with Creole Oil's communities in Venezuela was arresting. One official with the US State Department wrote in a report on Aramco's troubles that Socal and Texaco were "a disgrace to the American enterprise." His reaction was tied to reports in the Pakistani press in which fifty Aramco Pakistani laborers spoke about the horrible treatment they received in Saudi Arabia. There, the Pakistani public learned, they encountered "American officers drunk with racial arrogance . . . all too primed to subject young Muslims to an unscrupulous 'lynch-the-nigger' treatment." The press coverage upset US officials, who told an Aramco chief that further promotion of the company in the region needed to be tamped down. "Particularly dangerous," they explained, are such "phrases as 'a spectacular example of American enterprise abroad' and 'a prototype of the kind of thing President Truman had in mind in his 'bold new program' of American guidance for 'undeveloped areas.'" Aramco was now a plague to the Point Four initiative Truman had unveiled in 1949.[66]

Such criticism pricked the consciences of Aramco's Arabists. Eddy assisted a US State Department investigation. The report he helped draft admitted Aramco's substandard amenities, pledged improvement, and noted the difficulties of dealing with labor demands while assuaging a stridently antiunion Saudi royalty. It also pinned protests by workers and whistle-blowers on communist influences facilitated by secret cell groups in Aramco installations. Exaggerated or not, these latter claims indicated the escalating pressure in the Middle East stemming from communist and nationalist movements that now attacked foreign oil corporations as symbols of capitalism's evil. Aramco would incur more of this wrath from radicals who (as one subsequent protest announced) wanted to "overthrow . . . first, ARAMCO, second the Saudi Government, and third, Islam," and also the "Christian dogs." "There will be no easy short-cut to the solution," Eddy concluded.[67]

Eddy reacted with even greater dissatisfaction to a concurrent political development, the birth of a Jewish state in Palestine. As far as he was concerned, there was no more menacing threat to the Aramco model of cosmopolitanism than Israel. By 1947, the once hesitant President Truman had warmed to the partitioning of British-controlled Palestine into two independent states, one Jewish and the other Arab. UN endorsement of this plan prompted his shift, as did the barrage of encouragement from Zionists and American evangelical Protestants, who underscored the significance of Israel to Christ's second coming. They were not outliers; polls conducted in 1947 revealed that twice as many Americans supported a Jewish independent state as did not. At the same time, Truman heard from resisters. Ibn Saud publicized the agreement he had ironed out with Franklin Roosevelt, leading to public awkwardness. And Arabists such as Eddy sent memos to the State Department warning that a Jewish state would be a threat to neighboring Arab nations and Arab-American relations, as well as a drain on US national defense.[68]

On May 14, 1948, the British army retired its flag in Jerusalem, and a short time later, David Ben-Gurion, head of the Jewish Agency, declared Israel's independence. "We extend our hand in peace and neighborliness to all the neighboring states," he offered in a gesture of cooperation. "The State of Israel is prepared to make its contribution to the progress of the Middle East." Two hours later, Truman recognized the new state. Even before the politicians finished expressing themselves, a street-level clash between Jewish and Arab stakeholders in Palestine flared. The violence would last for a year. It did little to dampen the ardor of American Zionists who had long dreamed of this moment. For others, the bloodshed confirmed the logic, introduced by Charles Crane, that establishment of a Jewish homeland in the region would trigger generations of conflict.[69]

Aramco's corporate missionaries guided their firm and their king through the difficult days. In the lead-up to 1948, Eddy counseled Ibn Saud, who queried why "freedom-loving Americans [who] supported Lebanon and Syria against French oppression and defended Greece and Turkey against intimidation by neighbors to the north" did not see Palestinian liberty in the same light. The massaging worked; Ibn Saud told Aramco and its allies in Washington that the partnership would continue, as there was too much at stake for his people to kill the enterprise. Eddy assured him that company policy would remain different from US government policy. Aramco agreed to reroute the Trans-Arabian Pipeline it was building between Saudi Arabia and the Mediterranean through Syria and Lebanon instead of Palestine. It also honored another of the king's requests: to ban all Jews—not just Israelis—from working at or traveling to Aramco's base. Not even Jewish US government personnel were allowed. In 1950, Aramco designated religion a "bona fide occupational qualification" for its operations. Despite some opposition, the US State Department approved, arguing that "American-Saudi relations required equilibrium between American ideals and Saudi demands." US courts agreed, ruling that Aramco's ban on Jews was necessary and legal, if not ideal.[70]

Once past this political fury, Eddy redoubled his boosterism. Lecturing on the virtues of Aramco would remain one key aspect of his elocution, speaking out against Israel's privilege another. In his eyes, the two overlapped. As he watched Washington, US corporations, nongovernmental organizations, the United Nations, and Israel begin to apply strategies of development to the Jewish state, Eddy's ire increased. Whatever energy Truman's Point Four Program guaranteed the Arab Middle East appeared to be headed toward the Jewish and Christian

Holy Land. Eddy's frustrations boiled over at a meeting in January 1951. Dubbed the "Conference on President's Point IV Proposals for the Near East," it was held at Nelson Rockefeller's New York City home and included elite statesmen whose familiarity with UN humanitarian and development missions inspired them to think in ambitious terms. Eddy was asked to speak about "regional plans for the Near East." He began by affirming the symposium's aim to expand initiatives related to "conservation of water resources, irrigation, control of malaria and other diseases, and technical aid in the field of finance and banking." Such efforts "are already underway," he confirmed. The major agenda item followed. As he later relayed to colleagues, the attendees' chief concern was to "define a large, bold, and imaginative project for the area which would result in cooperation and integration of the resources of the Near East." They asked Eddy if he thought a Jordan Valley Authority, "with simultaneous development of dams and hydro-electric power in the Litany River in Lebanon," might be the answer. Rockefeller's group essentially wanted to bring the Tennessee Valley Authority to Israel, to create massive economic transformation but also "peace between Israel and at least two of its neighbors." Eddy's response was "a flat 'No.'"[71]

Eddy denounced the idea of using a mammoth project to merge Arabs and Israelis, Muslims and Jews, into one worldview. Any such proposal, he predicted, would only further alienate Arab leaders, who would see it as a "thinly disguised stratagem" for US-backed Israel to establish economic control of the rivers and their resources. The idea reeked of American grand thinking at the cost of ground-level awareness. Instead, Eddy countered, the Point Four Program had to guarantee direct US support of Arab societies alone, with their prerogatives always in mind. Eddy also insisted that before any such program was implemented, the United States had to ensure that Palestinian refugees driven off their land by the Israelis were relocated onto viable farms in northern Syria and Iraq. Though taken aback by Eddy's blanket dismissal of their overall plan, his listeners agreed that US funds had to be directed toward the refugees and close attention paid to the construction of viable agriculture, transportation, and small industry based on local resources. The Rockefeller group believed funding for these projects could be channeled through a corporate body like IBEC. On that note, Eddy warned that Israel was sure to oppose "any large-scale aid to Arabs which does not flow through Israel and does not help to entrench Israel as the leading nation of the Near East." His counterparts admitted "fund-raising activities of the Zionist organizations in this country are still following openly the doctrine that Israel should be the workshop and the banker to exploit the Near East." That is exactly what Eddy feared.[72]

Eddy had reason to be concerned that Arab nations would be swamped by a surging Jewish state. Already by 1951, Zionist enthusiasm combined with American money and Israeli government initiative was inciting a mad dash of economic growth. A good deal of this momentum, Eddy surely knew, was driven by Jewish oilmen, such as Rudolf Sonneborn, whose ambitions now clashed economically as well as politically with Aramco's. Sonneborn, of Baltimore, had a decades-long devotion to Zionism and friendship with David Ben-Gurion, Israel's first prime minister. During the 1940s, Sonneborn was instrumental in financing transport for Jews fleeing Europe to Palestine—a process that linked him to the famous vessel *Exodus*. By 1951, he was head of several campaigns charged with raising millions of dollars for Israel and tirelessly exhorting his American Jewish brethren to empty their pockets on behalf of their holy land. He also served as president of the American Financial and Development Corporation for Israel, which oversaw the economic structuring of the nation during its infancy. Sonneborn's close associate in this enterprise was fellow Baltimorean Jacob Blaustein. In the early twentieth century, Blaustein cofounded with his father the American Oil Company, a major portion of which was purchased by Indiana Standard in the 1920s. Blaustein continued to manage American until the early 1950s, when the company became a full subsidiary of Indiana Standard—now known as Amoco. While Blaustein remained on the Amoco board, he shifted focus to philanthropy on behalf of Israel. Intensely pro-Israel—if not an outright Zionist—and onetime president of the American Jewish Committee, Blaustein was every bit as dedicated as Sonneborn to the Jewish state's success. Behind the scenes he worked channels with the White House to ensure that the funneling of financial loans, technology, and arms to Israel went smoothly. He also personally reminded President Truman that "Israel can be counted on 100% as our U.S.

ally" in the fight with global communism and that it "is the best friend American[s] ever had in the Near East."[73]

But oil was at the top of Blaustein's docket. By 1951, after the Israeli Knesset passed favorable oil legislation offering generous royalties to oil companies willing to explore Israeli terrain, Blaustein's recruitment of them was full-blown. A geological survey released that year added momentum. The two American geologists who conducted it were optimistic: "Each of the eight geological provinces has all [oil] possibilities," they reported, with the most promising being "Negev, foothills of Judea, co[a]stal plain, Dead Sea Valley." "Test drilling should start at once," they declared. Blaustein and the Israeli press noted that this was a "race against time." The state's oil consumption had doubled between 1949 and 1951, making the resource the "largest single import item" for the fledgling society. The price of foreign oil, mostly Venezuelan crude with exorbitant transportation costs, was quickly becoming prohibitive. Oil had become Israel's greatest commodity and most urgent need. "Since Israel no longer flows with milk and honey," a journalist quipped, "Israelis feel it would be only fair to have it flow now with a bit of oil." In the following years, Blaustein would dig into his job as Israel's supreme oil booster, anxious to coordinate plans for foreign firms to make their way to his homeland's promising tracks. He knew oil was critical to Israel's prospects in the modern Middle East. A US State Department official agreed with his sense of proportion: "A big strike might do for Israel in the Mid-East what industrial revolution did for England in the 18th century."[74]

Eddy wanted the same—but for Muslims, not Jews. At the very least, he wanted US support for Israel not to unravel the progress he saw in Saudi Arabia. In the coming years, with Israel's oilmen busily combing the Bible land's earth for oil and Aramco's mass workforce doing the same on Islam's sacred soil, he would grow convinced that the legacy of Truman's decision of 1948 would be a dark one where Muslims and the Middle East were concerned.

By 1953, THE geopolitics of the Middle East hung in the balance. At the start of that year, Dwight Eisenhower assumed the US presidency, promising a freshening of US policy in the region. In November, Ibn Saud's death marked the end of an era of oil discoveries and political diplomacy that Eddy helped oversee. Eddy took advantage of the transitional time to remind American leaders of what was at stake. In a speech at the Naval War College in Rhode Island, Aramco's emissary reiterated his fears of a permanent divorce between American and Muslim peoples. He saw the real possibility of an uprising of religious resistance taking hold of Palestine, led by the Ikhwan al Muslimin (or Muslim Brotherhood), an organization with political tentacles spreading across the Middle East that Eddy had helped the CIA profile. A last gasp of potential remained, he said, for "three hundred million Muslims, not yet militarized, [to] offer to the U.S.A. a potent friend or a dangerous enemy. The choice is still ours.... If we choose wrong, then may God have mercy on our souls."[75]

Otherwise, Eddy stressed the good that could come out of continued commitment to Muslim Arabs and the type of ecumenism practiced at Aramco. The Aramco kingdom was a microcosm, he suggested, for how the United States and Saudi Arabia, and by extension the entire Middle East, could bond by way of a shared commitment to monotheistic religion. Equally impressive, in his mind, was the earnestness with which Aramco's partner—Ibn Saud—had set out to transform his society without aborting its soul, to modernize it without cutting it loose from ancient creeds. Eddy intimated there were lessons in that persistence that all citizens of the world could learn. On that bedrock of belief in the enduring power of faith amid changing times, Americans and their brothers in the Middle East could draw close. In a speech to the Middle East Institute in Washington, he called on Americans to "recognize a moral alliance of Christianity and Islam." "It's always seemed to me that not enough was made of the common ground between these great religions," he mused. "We have not only the belief in one God ... we also share with Islam many of our prophets and much of our Scripture. We share the beliefs in reverence, humility, charity, the brotherhood of mankind, and the family as the sacred unit in society." Eddy's call for Christian Americans to embrace their Muslim cousins stemmed from his own theology of grace, as well as his own family's rootedness in the Muslim holy land; but it also contained a pragmatic edge. "It wouldn't take very much for us to mobilize all of that historic religious sentiment in the fight against Russian communism," he implored. All that was required was for the United States to extend a hand of friendship and say, "Your worship of your God and our worship of the same God; your veneration of our prophets and our admiration of your Prophet make us brothers in arms in the moral crusade to keep religion free and alive throughout the world." Such evocation of shared piety and devotion would "be not only a fine thing for us to do as Christians," he offered, "but also it would be a fine thing for us to do as Americans."[76]

Eddy and his colleagues were about to gain some reward for their steadfast commitment. Soon after ascending to the White House, Dwight Eisenhower would seek to construct a political consensus based on shared Judeo-Christian values. His would be a call for all American Protestants, Catholics, and Jews to create "one nation under God"—a republic populated by "people of the book" (the Bible, the Torah, and the Quran) and buttressed by monotheism that could spread religious freedom and democratic values worldwide and roll back the encroaching influences of atheistic communism. With Arabists like Eddy and Aramco's government relations men urging him on, the president would attempt a bolder progression—to turn his tri-faith America into a quadrilateral. Alongside Protestants, Catholics, and Jews, Eisenhower hoped Muslims at home and abroad would join in a coalition of the faithful to fight the Red Menace and transform the globe.

# CHAPTER EIGHT

# Wildcat Redemption

At the same time that William Eddy and Jacob Blaustein were consolidating oil's hold on the Middle East, a revivalist by the name of Charles Fuller was trying to carve out a less conspicuous influence. Fuller's life prior to 1947 had been a whirlwind of success. After jump-starting several gainful business enterprises and pastoral ministries during the first decades of the century, he had risen to fame as a radio evangelist. By 1939, Fuller's *Old Fashioned Revival Hour*, broadcast weekly from Long Beach, California, over the Mutual System, enjoyed an audience of 20 million. By 1942 the program played on 456 stations, making it one of the most popular prime-time shows in America. Fuller had reason to believe that his radio ministry would continue to flourish after the war and worked hard toward that end. Yet, in the wake of world conflict, he began shifting his attention away from edifying his flock with sermon and song to educating it through study of scripture. He decided to build a divinity school.[1]

Fuller's plan to construct a seminary entered its critical phase in the spring of 1947. He was adamant that his school open in September—despite the fact he still had to enlist faculty and students and locate a campus. Fuller's impatience worried his partner in the venture, pastor Harold Ockenga, who monitored operations from his esteemed Park

Street Church in Boston. While skeptical of Fuller's breakneck timetable, he did not let reasoning get in the way of enthusiasm for making
Fuller Seminary a West Coast version of what his beloved alma mater
once had been. The faculty Ockenga wooed, the wages he offered them,
and the promises of grandeur that came with the pledges all stemmed
from his firsthand knowledge of Princeton Seminary, which he singled
out as the "best-equipped" divinity school in America, if also, in light of
its recent liberal turns, a tragic illustration of "departure from the faith."[2]

Sustained by Ockenga's letters of encouragement, Fuller pressed
hard to organize a board of trustees, buy real estate in Pasadena,
and market his new seminary. Small triumphs followed, including
recruitment of well-known Christian businessman R. G. LeTourneau
for his board, an all-star faculty of evangelical sages, and thirty-nine
enrollees, including graduates of Ivy League universities. Despite
the stress of a six-month blitz, Fuller and Ockenga had managed
to make their Princeton happen. It was an impressive effort worthy
in some respects of the aggrandizing speech that Ockenga delivered at the school's inaugural convocation. With Christian culture in
the West as his theme, he signaled that Fuller Seminary's founding
was part of God's plan to redeem Western civilization. Those seated
before him, he charged, were "heirs" to the Reformation, burdened
with the task of fighting Satan's proxies: communism, atheism, and
secularism. Yet in the next breath he declared it time for brethren to
practice an "ecclesiastically positive" agenda, not just a defensive one.
On this note he stressed another meaning of "the West," for it was
in territory nearer the Pacific, where East Coast liberalism had less
pull, that evangelicalism could achieve its breakthrough. Ockenga
intended his creation to be a momentous renewal of Christendom
and reversal of secularism in American life.[3]

After opening his seminary, Fuller started tackling its daily challenges,
still convinced that it could be the flagship of a smarter evangelical
Christianity. In 1949 he thanked Ockenga for making intellectualism
a priority. "The whole effort could sort of die on the stem without you,"
Fuller admitted. "But with your wise guidance under God, I believe
it can take the place of conservative leadership and save the day for
fundamentalism." Lofty intellectual achievement, however, obscured
financial struggle. The school depended on its founder's portfolio,

which was fine at first, considering the health of his radio ministry. But with each new strain on his purse, accentuated by the costly purchase of property in an explosive California economy, Fuller lost his where-withal. Ockenga worried with Fuller about the lack of solidity. "I too hope that we will so be able to broaden the base of income through numerous givers to the Seminary [and] that there will be utterly no need to pare down the evangelistic and Bible ministry." Two years after the school's opening, things seemed dire. "Financial conditions tight-ening down rapidly," Fuller telegrammed Ockenga. "Have had one cut in dividends of endowment fund; others may follow; believe it is time for utmost scrutiny of expenditures." Fuller decided on a quick fix. He would form a petroleum company; surely the black stuff could cure his ills. He couched his corporate strategy in the guise of deific appoint-ment: he called it Providential Oil.[4]

Charles Fuller and Harold Ockenga dreamed big because they believed strongly in the movement they represented: the "new evangel-icalism" of the early postwar years, led by a new generation of conserva-tive Protestants who wanted to strip away the rigid fundamentalism of their predecessors and build a broader coalition of Bible believers that could impose itself on the nation. If ridiculed just a short time before for their backwardness and decried by famed liberal minister Harry Emerson Fosdick as a blight on the church, Fuller and Ockenga's allies approached the 1950s confident that their message was gaining traction from California to South Carolina, West Texas to Washington and that they were the emergent mainstream. Independent oilmen had a lot to do with their confidence and with their freshly packaged fire and brim-stone. In their attempt at revitalization, new evangelicals underscored the moral imperatives that had shaped the wildcat ethic over previous generations. What was required in America's darkest hour of the Cold War was for individuals to reclaim a personal relationship with Christ and all the liberties and market freedoms it promised, then prompt fel-low citizens to be born again lest they succumb to socialism, secular-ism, and the looming state. Backed by new monies that the Texas boom and wartime buildup had stuffed into their coffers, independents bank-rolled the construction of a culture industry of philanthropy, education, and media, one that stretched beyond Protestant boundaries but was particularly efficient in propagating the new evangelical message.

Their front had a political dimension as well, which gained footing amid heightening tensions with the Soviet Union and major oil's Middle Eastern blitz. In reaction to the first threat, independents fought for policies that could shore up the United States' homegrown energy sources. Their defining struggle, framed as a defense of faith and family values, pertained to offshore oil and resulted in their gravitation toward a Republican Party that now welcomed them with open arms. Regarding big oil, they raised existential questions: Why should anyone place trust in conglomerates like Aramco that compromised with foreign regimes, especially Arab-Muslim ones that rejected democratic ideals and sought destruction of the United States' most important new ally in the Middle East: Israel? Was Washington's collusion with petroleum's majors not antidemocratic as well and a step toward Soviet thinking? Though assisted by these external Cold War pressures, which lent credence to their harangues about America's vulnerability, wildcatters' ability to seize this moment was largely self-created. Melding eschatological expectation with wonder for technology, corporate know-how with dirt-under-the-fingernails resolve, they sold themselves and their Christian Americanism to the US citizenry as the way forward. At the end of their surge in the 1950s they would still speak in dour terms about a nation that was lost, but theirs would be a jeremiad delivered from a position of authority, not—as it had long been—one of desperation.[5]

OBSCURED BY EARTH-SHAKING geopolitics in the Middle East, proponents of independent oil and wildcat religion experienced their own quakes during the late 1940s and early 1950s. Much of the drama had to do with rapidly shifting—and directly related—institutional structures within the corporate and churchly realms. J. Howard Pew was at the center of it.

The season of pivotal change began in 1947 inside Sun Oil's Philadelphia headquarters. After thirty-five years of bullish leadership, during which his company grew forty times over, Pew resigned as Sun's president. He was only sixty-five years old and still unrelentingly driven, but in his mind the time had come for Sun to change. His brother Joseph, Sun's vice president, felt likewise and tendered his resignation on the same day. Both had long anticipated this moment. For sixty years Sun had operated as a family business, and by World War II executives and employees alike noted this with pride. Many outsiders praised the arrangement too. In contrast to the muscle flexing of multinationals, Sun reminded them of simpler times when any man and his kin could extract crude and a livelihood on their terms. But by 1947 the complex corporate realities of the hydrocarbon age had caught up with them, and the Pews knew it.[6]

Rather than fight these realities, they decided to nudge Sun into its new era. Under their watch Sun's shareholders elected a board of directors, which included thirty-seven-year-old Robert G. Dunlop Jr., who replaced Howard as president. Dunlop's climb through the company ranks had been swift. After graduating from the University of Pennsylvania's Wharton School of Business, he was hired at an accounting firm that serviced the nation's major banks. In the wake of the banking crisis of 1933 and the New Deal's drastic measures to curtail it, Dunlop found himself out of work and out of sympathy with Franklin Roosevelt's government. Naturally he jumped at the Pews' offer to work for Sun. One of Dunlop's first assignments was to certify that Sun honored the National Recovery Administration's strict codes of industry and labor "fair practices," imposed by Roosevelt's New Deal, and his deft handling of the difficult task put him in good stead with his boss. Dunlop grew closer to Howard during the war as the two teamed up to defend Sun's laissez-faire principles at industry proceedings in New York and negotiate aviation gasoline contracts with Washington. By war's end Dunlop was company comptroller and Howard's mentee in every way. The two men even looked alike, with perfectly pressed suits and silk ties anchoring their daily dress. Dunlop lacked Pew's intimidating brow but not his starchy mien.[7]

Considering their affinity for each other, it is little wonder that Dunlop stayed true to Pew's precedents. Dunlop did his best to ensure that Sun's philosophy stayed the same. Under his watchful eye the fiftieth anniversary of Sun's Marcus Hook refinery in 1951 opened with prayer. "Almighty God, we ask thy Divine blessing," it began. "Incline the hearts of employers and those whom they employ to mutual forbearance, fairness, and good will. May we remember the service and sacrifice of those who helped build our industry. May Thy guiding spirit continue to be with the officers and employees of our Company that their mutual understanding may be for the betterment of us all." Also under his guidance Sun adopted an official creed, the first line of which read, "We believe in America as a land able under God to enrich its people both materially and spiritually, even more abundantly in the future than it has in the past." And at his urging, Sun's promotional literature sparkled with praise for the Pews' gospel of free markets. "Sun grew by pulling on its own boot-straps," he trumpeted, and by maximizing its assets (low-cost raw materials, advanced technology, tested fiscal principles) and wise leadership. In "J. Howard Pew and Joseph N. Pew Jr., we have more than the advantage of a blazed trail; they are sources of immediate guidance, counsel and inspiration."[8]

Pew basked in the veneration, welcomed his adjusted standing in Sun's structure, and rededicated himself to his family's Christian canons. Continuity was his aim as well, and he used his authority as Sun's new director of the board to champion Dunlop's vision—his vision—at every turn. Rare would be the occasion in subsequent years when Sun executives, gathered in the walnut-paneled boardroom of the company's head office, did not absorb Howard's strong opinions and cigar smoke. And rarer still would be the occasion when Sun's strategies did not play out exactly as he intended. Company officials knew that for as long as their chief was alive, some things would never change. Yet, at the moment of his resignation, their chief was also cognizant that his more flexible status meant he could brandish power beyond office doors, and this excited him. Pew had always harbored strong religious and civic commitments but acted on them as supplementary to his business's bottom line. In this next stage of life, he was determined to reverse the order. The engineer-executive became the philanthropist.[9]

This metamorphosis culminated in 1948 with the founding of the Pew trusts. Fifty years earlier Lyman and Milton Stewart had taken it upon themselves to fund a conservative counterweight to Rockefeller charity. Now it was J. Howard Pew's turn. In 1948 he and his three siblings incorporated the Pew Memorial Trust to "help meet human needs" through support of "education, social services, religion, health care and medical research." Fear of the US Treasury certainly informed their decision. By funneling their Sun stock into a foundation, they could avoid steep inheritance taxes. Politics was a motivation as well.

As a unit, the Pew children were determined to use their fortunes to support conservatism, and the Pew Memorial gave them the mechanism to do so.[10]

So did the smaller trusts (six total) established by the Pew siblings at this time for their personal purposes. The most important of these was the J. Howard Pew Freedom Trust. Second only to the Pew Memorial in assets, Howard's trust outshined all the others when it came to proficiency. His goal, articulated in his trust's pithy constitution, was transparent: "to acquaint the American people with the evils of bureaucracy"; "to expose the insidious influences which have infiltrated channels of publicity"; "to acquaint the American people with the values of an open market, the dangers of inflation, the paralyzing effects of government controls on the lives and activities of people"; "to promote the recognition of the interdependence of Christianity and freedom." Pulling no punches where politics was concerned, Pew also held nothing back when bankrolling allies for his cause. He was as aggressive about giving his money away as he had been about making it. For the remaining years of his life, he would devote his whole energy to financing a vast network of schools, churches, social agencies, and media outlets that could help him roll back the legacy of Franklin D. Roosevelt and the Rockefellers.[11]

Already in the early 1950s, the breadth of Pew's funding was staggering. Howard had plugged himself into overlapping circuits of anti-liberal crusading in the 1930s, and as he shifted his vocational focus at the dawn of the 1950s, those circuits remained of top concern to his checkbook. He was particularly drawn to agencies that reflected his preoccupation with free enterprise capitalism and Christian libertarianism, values he saw entrenched in his family's roots, undermined by the Roosevelt administration, and now in desperate need of protection against what he perceived as America's continued slide toward socialism. On that score, he sought out organizations run by clerics and corporate types whose expressed purposes were to defend his brand of the American way. Among his favorites were Spiritual Mobilization, a Los Angeles–based libertarian lobby run by free market, self-help Congregational guru James W. Fifield Jr., and the Christian Freedom Foundation (CFF), based in New York and run by businessman-preacher-author Howard Kershner, whose editorship of the CFF's

*Christian Economics* magazine and intent to transform political thought through every media form made him a vital link between the "Old Right" of the 1930s and the postwar "New Right." Loving Kershner's ambition because it matched his own, Pew quickly became the CFF's primary donor.[12]

Pew's willingness to transcend denominational lines in order to build a viable Right connected him to Catholics as well, including William F. Buckley Jr., then a young Yale University graduate. On account of his 1951 publication of *God and Man at Yale*, an upbraiding of his alma mater for sacrificing individualism and belief at the altar of secular collectivism, Buckley was well on his way to becoming what one historian calls "the preeminent voice of American conservatism and its first great ecumenical figure." Buckley's conservatism was shaped by his father's wildcat worldview, which mirrored Pew's. By the time the son had entered Yale, the father—William F. Buckley Sr.—was a heralded independent oilman whose career had been built on discoveries in Mexico in the 1910s and Venezuela in the 1920s. A devout Catholic, fully committed to the traditions of his church, he was also a fiercely independent thinker who even as a young man refused to accept any notions from on high without carefully processing them. And in oil, few matched his daring. "At the root was a tenacious philosophy of independence," his family would write affectionately; "W.F.B. was often called (by himself and by others) a gambler, but the strong conviction was basic. He was primarily resolved to prove and practice his philosophy, which he wore like a panache, and then to make money." "Will Buckley," they added, "cannot be pictured, at twenty, working for someone else; at three score and ten he was still, above all, an independent oilman in a world of oil Titans, whom he held in no awe." When asked to fund a series of lectures at Yale Law School titled "Conservative Principles in American Life," a response of sorts to Buckley's *God and Man*, Pew welcomed the chance. And when, in 1955, Buckley released the inaugural issue of his new magazine, *National Review*, its back cover carried endorsements by corporate and political leaders. None was more glowing than that supplied by J. Howard Pew.[13]

Pew's philanthropy and politics naturally overlapped with those of another prominent Catholic steeped in oil. Born in 1885, just three years after Pew and the senior Buckley, Ignatius O'Shaughnessy was similarly imbued with the restlessness of oil's second generation. After graduating from St. Thomas University in St. Paul, he made his way to Texas to work in the insurance business. But oil caught his attention. During World War I O'Shaughnessy established the Globe Oil & Refining Company, based in Oklahoma, and shortly thereafter formed other companies geared to production, Lario Oil & Gas Company being the most successful. By the mid-1930s, he was a force in the industry. His contacts extended widely, and at times he partnered with others in the business to further his reach. One such relationship was with independent oilman Fred Koch. For a time in the late 1930s and early 1940s, the two men oversaw the Wood River Oil & Refining Company in Illinois, but that partnership—marked by testiness on both sides—ended poorly. Perhaps that is why O'Shaughnessy preferred to work alone and run his own base of operations in the mid-continent region, where he was deemed "King of the Wildcatters." Always generous with his charity, he created a mechanism for giving in the I. A. O'Shaughnessy Foundation, established in 1941. Prompted by the estate taxes legislated during the Roosevelt years and following the lead of Frank Phillips of Phillips 66 Oil Company, who was among the first oilmen to realize the financial benefit of such a move, the Minnesotan transferred the first $190,000 of his assets to his foundation, an amount that would quickly balloon. Like Pew, O'Shaughnessy prioritized a variety of causes, including the arts, youth and antipoverty programs, and medical aid. He also contributed to an array of religious organizations, including the National Conference of Christians and Jews. But from the beginning he was most eager to channel his wealth toward two institutions: St. Thomas and the University of Notre Dame. His first significant gift to Notre Dame came in 1942 in the form of a $100,000 check to support its liberal arts program. More would soon follow.[14]

O'Shaughnessy and Pew's shared outlook meant they swam in the same philanthropic and political waters. One exception to that rule was O'Shaughnessy's partisan preferences during the 1930s and 1940s. Like most Catholics of his generation, he associated with the Democratic Party; an invitation to a Roosevelt White House dinner in 1937, personal notes from the Truman White House, and even President Harry Truman's consideration of him in 1946 for an ambassadorship in Australia were fruits of his ties to party brass. Yet O'Shaughnessy's relationship with the party began to diminish, especially as the 1940s gave way to the 1950s and frustrations among conservative business-men and churchmen with the New Deal legacy intensified. O'Shaugh-nessy aligned with Pew in that regard. While serving together on the executive committee of Harold Ickes's Petroleum Industry Council for National Defense, they stood among the independents as checks on Ickes's central power. And by the early 1950s they were speaking the same language of dissent against the liberalization of the Democratic establishment.[15]

They found themselves sending checks to the same places as well. O'Shaughnessy considered higher education vital to American soci-ety in the era of nuclear bombs and communist threats, and in Notre Dame he was impressed by the potential to pair humanistic study with Catholic tradition. With that in mind, in 1952 he donated $2.5 million to Notre Dame for construction of a new liberal arts building, subse-quently named the O'Shaughnessy Hall of Liberal and Fine Arts. The oilman explained his generosity at the laying of the building's corner-stone in May 1952. "To many persons today the whole notion of liberal arts denotes the idea of long-haired men sitting under a tree compos-ing what they may even call poesy. To these people I should like to say as emphatically as I can that the liberal arts represent the most prac-tical, useful, indeed indispensable field of learning in the world." How so, he asked rhetorically? Besides arguing the virtues of liberal arts as a bond between faith and learning—education "in the light of eterni-ty"—O'Shaughnessy stressed their political benefits. "By definition," he said, "the business of liberal arts is to liberate": to liberate oneself from socialistic thinking (which he saw creeping into Washington), group conformity (of the kind that fueled Nazism), an overbearing state, and the soul-killing dazzle of modern technology. O'Shaugh-nessy was convinced that only the private college could deliver the "intellectual weapons with which to resist invasion by totalitarian ide-ologies." "It is only logical that the truly liberal, that is, free-making disciples be taught in schools that themselves are free." Two years later Notre Dame's Hall of Liberal and Fine Arts opened its doors, ready to produce the thinkers O'Shaughnessy wanted for the world. The fol-lowing year J. Howard Pew wrote a more modest check of $35,000 to assist Notre Dame's economics program. A masterful fund-raiser, Notre Dame president Theodore Hesburgh thanked Pew and urged him to visit the campus and stay in the inn built with the money of Ernest Morris, Pew's friend. "I trust that God ... will grant you ample blessings for the wonderful effort you have put forth in the interest of Christian education for young men," he closed.[16]

Ecumenical in his bankrolling, Pew nevertheless channeled most of his energy and funds to evangelical causes. While serving as chair of the National Lay Committee in the National Council of Churches (NCC), recent successor to the Federal Council of Churches (FCC), Pew grew agitated with the liberal drift of his own Presbyterian denomination and of America's Protestant mainline as a whole, which he attributed to the proliferation of progressive ideas espoused by John D. Rockefeller Jr. By 1955, when the committee was disbanded, Pew was disgusted with the direction of his church and eager to find other ways to push back against left-wingers in the pulpits and pews as well as in the political apparatus of the nation. He found it in the loosely coordinated movement that conservatives called the "new evangelicalism," which would come to be the beating heart of post–World War II wildcat Christianity. An outgrowth of dissatisfied conservative Protestants who wanted to distance themselves from the bitterly dogmatic fundamentalism of the 1920s and 1930s, the new evangelicalism of Harold Ockenga and Charles Fuller's ilk avowed an irenic, cooperative, and engaged orthodoxy, whose eagerness to connect with rather than isolate from society matched the general optimism of wartime and postwar America. Several individuals and institutions would emerge as representatives of this new wave, none more illustrious than evangelist Billy Graham and his numerous ministerial outlets. Among them was the Pew-funded magazine *Christianity Today*, which new evangelicals hoped would offer a strong defense of conservative theological values in a culturally appealing manner.[17]

As a gathering force and symbol of united purpose, however, no other organization could match the National Association of Evangelicals (NAE), founded in 1943 as a clearinghouse for evangelism and conservative theological causes and as a mechanism to offset the FCC/NCC. But it was also a political federation binding together disgruntled anti–New Deal churchmen. One of the driving personalities behind the NAE was Ockenga, whose charge that evangelicals had "suffered ... defeats for decades" because of the "terrible octopus of liberalism" encapsulated his constituency's feelings. Ockenga initiated the NAE with a vision of crisis, saying it was "the only hopeful sign on the horizon of Christian history today." Meanwhile, the NAE's mouthpiece, *United Evangelical Action*, offered members advice on current events, monitored government policy, and disseminated complaints about Congress's acquiescence to liberal interests. The NAE's field office in Washington filed grievances against bills seeming to challenge conservative principles and behind the scenes knitted together what it deemed an evangelical "Secret Service" of "trusted, loyal, evangelical people in every city and region of America who [were] in a place of any importance or influence, in public life or education or business circles." J. Howard Pew provided substantial funds for NAE campaigns. NAE officials thanked him by ensconcing him in the organization's furtive "inner circle" of reengaged Christian generals.[18]

That others within the NAE and orb of new evangelicalism were grateful for Pew's support became evident in the career of Charles Fuller. When the evangelist formed Providential Oil, he believed he had found the key to his seminary's success. He was hardly the only one at that time to bank everything on gushing crude. Unprecedented demand had made oil a hot and expensive commodity in the five years since the war, and with rising prices came rising expectations that it could make any venture capitalist rich. In the early 1950s oil hunters poured into developing fields in West Texas's Permian Basin. The boom attracted new breeds of oilmen, including Ivy League graduates such as George H. W. Bush, who brought their eastern capital and sensibilities with them to Midland and Odessa. It also wooed risk-taking "outsiders" from Los Angeles who, upon settlement in West Texas, became the "insiders" in the business. They chased after that authority in creative ways, marshaling their ties to Tinsel Town glitz, locking in investments from Bob Hope, Bing Crosby, and other celebrities. One wildcatter made special note of the Los Angeles investors who used Hollywood beauties to promote West Texas crude. "They had a whole bunch of models come out to the rig, every one of 'em nude. They had them working the tongs and the brake and all that, every one of 'em nude. I suppose they sold a lot of interests in [the well]." Fuller surely disapproved of these tactics, but his scheming was no less earnest.[19]

Fuller proceeded cautiously at first while prospecting for land. Steel shortages and labor strikes held him back further, but by the summer of 1952 he was firmly entrenched in the Southwest, with a base at Ada, Oklahoma. In his first report to Ockenga, he guardedly described his undertaking as "very favorable." "I am fortunate to have the . . . help of Mr. Currin, executive vice president of the bank in Shawnee. He is a fine Christian man who has been interested in our Hour [radio ministry] for years, a pillar in the Southern Baptist Church . . . who is interested in our Seminary. He knows a lot about oil out there and is advising us." By late 1952, Fuller was exuberant. Providential was reporting thirteen productive wells, each drawing 2,000 barrels daily. Fuller informed Ockenga that a major company was trying to buy up his leases but that through "prayerful planning" he was going to find a way to keep putting down wells. How could it not go in his favor? "I want you to know, Harold, that God is working a miracle out there. It really frightens me—actually I do not want to say too much—but I am confident that the next six months will see great strides ahead." "If you had been with me this past week I think you would have been speechless. I can't write it." With his rigs pumping, Fuller could once again dream big for his school and movement.[20]

But after a promising start, Providential Oil began to fail, leaving the evangelist despondent. Fuller's wife wrote to Ockenga pleading for help for her frazzled husband. By early 1954, the problems were manifold. In Oklahoma, Fuller's trusted manager turned out to be a "hotheaded Texan" who woefully mishandled production. There were no more booms to imagine near Ada, just mangled remnants—corroding steel towers, demoralized roughnecks—of promise. In his California fields Fuller faced circumstances that were even more trying because they were acts of God. Terrible weather patterns had left his rigs' pipes frozen and his wells full of sand. Echoing Job (but lacking the prophet's perseverance) he wrote his friend bemoaning the callousness of their Maker. "Why the dear Lord has permitted adverse results . . . I do not know." He did know that wildcatting was for the headstrong, and it was time to get out. "I just cannot go on with more oil investments," he told Ockenga. "The strain has been terrible."[21]

Foiled by oil, Fuller and Ockenga chalked the evangelist's experience up to unfortunate circumstances, then looked to petroleum again by soliciting favor with new evangelicalism's patron. Around the time Fuller's operation was collapsing, J. Howard Pew invited Ockenga to speak at a meeting of forty petroleum executives. Ockenga sermonized on three themes: the need to train ministers in "sound theology with sound economics, politics, and diplomacy," the need for "sound Americanism by a grass-roots movement of evangelism," and "the spiritual nature of the recent oil threat" (presumably the rise of foreign oil exports and federal regulation of domestic offshore oil). His initial encounter with Pew grew into a pattern of engagement and an itinerary of lecturing to businessmen around the country. Ockenga's subsequent visit to Houston marked a high point since it involved a luncheon with one of the Lone Star State's richest oilmen, Hugh Roy Cullen. Pew, meanwhile, offered to assist Fuller Seminary, essentially guaranteeing its survival, which thrilled Fuller: "Harold, I do not know how to express to you my appreciation for your getting the Pew Foundation interested in the Seminary." Fuller's friend offered all the encouragement he could in return, as well as insistence that going forward the answer to their troubles would be twofold: Pew and the "bigwigs" in Texas.[22]

OCKENGA'S ADVICE TO Fuller merely confirmed what evangelical leaders already knew—that oil barons were critical to their movement's prospects. For their part, the "bigwigs" of Texas crude recognized that their own interests were well served by alliance with new evangelical powerbrokers of Ockenga and Fuller's variety. At the same time that Fuller was drilling to keep his school alive, independent oilmen were immersed in their own struggle to regain a hold in a political economy that had shifted further in favor of major companies. The cachet that wildcat preachers like Fuller and Billy Graham enjoyed promised them a much-needed advantage in the court of public opinion. These clerics could also lend a critical hand in the political arena, which heated up during the late 1940s and early 1950s over issues of oil exploration and regulation, political clashes sparked by a few surprising discoveries of crude.

The political backlash against "big oil" and "big government" stirred up by independent oilers at this time was animated by their vulnerability. Their apprehensions stemmed from what major oil was accomplishing in the Middle East. However much they wanted to supply Americans with American oil and earn a healthy living out of it, independents sensed their dream was dying as US oil exploration and extraction shifted abroad. On one hand, the expanding demands of an automobile-reliant suburban society were pushing domestic reserves to the limit; on the other, foreign fields were producing abundant supplies at a fraction of the cost. Whereas the cost of producing a barrel of US oil averaged seventy cents in 1948, a barrel of Saudi Arabian oil cost only twenty cents. Moreover, processing crude overseas was far less cumbersome, as operators abroad did not have to abide by quotas set by the US government or spend money to regulate gas emissions. Foreign oil made better business sense. But that was only half the problem for US independents, the less troubling half. Much more disquieting was Washington's seeming determination to handcuff them in their quest to supply fellow citizens with the fuel they so craved and, worse yet, their fellow citizens' obliviousness to their plight.[23]

The trials came in various forms. Most obvious was the growing presence of imported crude, which between 1945 and 1950 reached historic proportions. Speaking before the Subcommittee of the Senate Labor Committee in May 1950, Oklahoman H. B. Fell of the Independent Petroleum Association of America (IPAA) described the trying conditions his brotherhood faced. "Since 1948," he explained, "there has been a deterioration and curtailment of activities within the domestic petroleum industry. It is our opinion that the principal factor causing this recession . . . has been excessive imports of petroleum and its products into this country in continued increasing amounts." Meticulous and measured, Fell's talk nevertheless reached an emotional crescendo when statistics were introduced. In 1946, 377,000 barrels of crude were imported daily into the country, 419,000 exported, a fair quotient for his brethren, Fell admitted. Yet, in the first quarter of 1950 alone, 820,000 were imported and 265,000 exported. What did this reversal mean on the ground level? How was the foreign oil breaking the backs of average Americans? By stealing jobs: some 15,000 between August 1948 and February 1950 alone, Fell declared. In the second place, foreign oil prohibited small producers from playing the new game on a level field. "There are 2525 oil producers in Oklahoma," he offered; "between 98 and 99% of these producers are strictly independents." These were the men who generated local economies by opening up productive fields. Yet these were the men now under attack.[24]

But Fell believed the situation was worse than this. Who was aiding importation? The world's seven major oil companies—the "Seven Sisters," as a pundit designated them—who, with sanction from the American and British federal governments, now looked to commandeer and convey foreign oil sources and dominate markets with a renewed sense of possibility and diminishing care for the US oil patch's rank and file. What was at stake for the American people? Not simply loss of their autonomy and agency to the monopolistic ways of the multinationals but defenselessness against warring hegemons. "If an emergency came and foreign oil was shut off," Fell insisted, "we would have an inadequate supply for national security." "We must build up within the borders of the United States ample excess productive capacity for war needs," he added. Weakened American labor, national economy, and national security: these were the hazards of the current situation, which Congress needed to address with "immediate action."[25]

Fell's allies faced yet another challenge as well: a suspicious consuming public that lacked sympathy. At the same time that they petitioned Congress for stricter import quotas, independents fretted over a reawakened moral critique of "big oil," which lumped them in with the majors as the same greedy lot. Circling congressional hearings on exports were fiercer calls for regulatory oversight of the gas industry and the dismantling of the oil industry's sacred cow—the depletion allowance, the tax law that allowed oilmen to deduct a high percentage from the gross income they earned from producing wells and write off financial losses they incurred from failed exploratory wells. Led by staunch New Deal senators Paul Douglas and Hubert Humphrey, oil's opponents demanded that it start playing by rules that benefited all of society, not just its special interests. For independents, however, the challenge cut deeply, because it undermined the only mechanism they had to compete with their outsized peers. Without concessions from Washington—a tax write-off for their costly and tenuous exploration of North American pools—their fight against exporting majors would become moot. Why keep demanding an open market when you have nothing to sell?[26]

Cognizant of the challenges, wildcatters responded in two ways, first by ramping up their exploration overseas. Prohibitive costs made this a difficult proposition, but several of them pressed forward. By the mid-1950s, 233 US operators were active in fifty-one countries. In some cases, small producers compensated for their limited funds by collaborating; the American Independent Oil Company was formed as a combination of corporate entities to explore the Middle East. Other well-heeled oilmen, like H. L. Hunt, surveyed international possibilities on their own. For mid-majors like Sun, the move to the global arena was a bit more manageable. Under Robert Dunlop's leadership, Sun broadened its range of production, refining, and transportation to assume—once again—an international dimension. It opened up a subsidiary in Canada, contracted to purchase crude from the Middle East, and established a Foreign Operations Department to explore South America, the Caribbean, and Pakistan. The efforts would soon produce major gains across the board, especially in Venezuela, which it returned to in the 1950s, three decades after abandoning its first operation there. Sun also expanded its transportation system to service its global aims. Already a stakeholder in Texas's Big Inch pipeline (with interests second only to those of Jersey Standard), it jumped at a chance in 1951 to become one of five partners in the construction of the Gulf Line, designed to move petroleum out of the Permian Basin to the Gulf Coast. Waiting on Texas's south coast were Sun's newest tankers, ready to convey this crude to the Delaware plant in record time.[27]

Of particular interest to the most daring wildcatters was Israel. With the exception of Shell and Socony, major companies avoided investing in the Jewish state because of both its political instability and their abiding ties to Arab nations. However, favorable laws introduced in the early 1950s, which allowed companies to harvest all the oil and profits they could with a minimal 12.5 percent royalty owed the Israeli government, enticed the independents to take the risks needed to reap the large reward. One of the most active operations in the Dead Sea area, four miles from Sodom, was Kerr-McGee Oil Industries, half-owned by Oklahoma governor-turned-senator Robert Kerr. The Kerr-McGee crew, reporters in Israel relayed, comprised twenty "seasoned American field men," roughly one hundred Israeli workers who provided the manual labor, and a few "selected Israelis" who were being trained to manage equipment and teams on their own. A few other Canadian, American, and Israeli firms, including Catawba Oil, the elder William F. Buckley's company, joined Kerr-McGee in hunting for Israel's black gold. In all cases Jacob Blaustein and the Israeli government spurred them on, and in many cases the prophetic importance of this Bible land added incentive for wildcatters. Assuming some of the strategies of earlier oil explorers in the region, they plumbed scripture for clues to oil's whereabouts with a heightened expectation that came from toiling in the very territory where they believed Jesus would soon return. Blaustein welcomed their enthusiasm, so much so that he readily engaged in informal exegesis with wildcatters like Russell Brown, a board member of the IPAA who sent the Jewish oilman Bible verses proving oil's past and future importance to Israel and all God's people.[28]

Such was the enlivening side of wildcatters' world turn. Their second response was self-protective, to shore up domestic production, and for this they leaned on political action. Knowing that they could never match the majors' advances abroad, independents spent the early Cold War years expanding their network of associations that could lobby Washington for import and tariff restrictions and, above all, guard their depletion allowance. Of their enemies and the task before them, Texan Jack Porter spoke bluntly: "There are more of us than of them, and if we work together we can get the job done." At his urging, independents ramped up support for the IPAA and the Texas Independent Producers and Royalty Owners Association (TIPRO) as a way to head the grassroots charge. Porter saw that much work had to be done—not the least of which was educating his constituency in national political trends—but he was confident that with some heavy lifting, the long-term prospects of the wildcatter would brighten considerably.[29]

Before long his call to action was embraced by church folk and rewarded with top-down support. Through their extensive interpersonal and institutional ties, powerbrokers associated with the new evangelicalism and independent oil associations together imposed their concerns on politicians, several of whom claimed personal ties both to church and to oil.

Oklahoma statesman Robert Kerr was one of these types. His stature as wildcat oilman extraordinaire, which he leveraged for access to Israel, had a lot to do with his company's breakthrough in 1947, one of two key continental discoveries of that year. Kerr-McGee accomplished what no other petroleum company had in the industry's history: hunt oil in the deep sea. In the fifty years after Henry L. Williams's offshore find near Santa Barbara, drillers had explored shallow waters along coastlines but never beyond sight of land. Kerr-McGee abolished this convention. Determined to prove that more was possible, that the Gulf of Mexico was ripe for such experimentation, and that risk-taking independents should lead the charge, the small company ventured ten miles off the Louisiana coast and started patching together a flotilla of old World War II barges. From this "platform" Kerr-McGee fished for and found its prize. The strike sent shockwaves through the industry. While oil rags heralded the "spectacular Gulf of Mexico discovery" as "revolutionary," Kerr-McGee's competitors immediately began mustering their finances and technologies and setting out to sea.[30]

Reveling in his offshore find, which added to his personal wealth and reputation among fellow independents, Kerr basked in another glow in 1948 when he won a seat in the US Senate. As Oklahoma's governor the Democrat had already labored to meet independent oil's needs, and now as a senator he promised to meet them on a much larger stage, all to the satisfaction of Porter, the IPAA, and their mutual friends. Upon arrival in Washington, Kerr assumed responsibility for independent oil's most critical initiatives, including organization of a special hearing before the Senate Labor Committee, at which advocates like H. B. Fell could speak.

Fell's speech in May 1950 in fact followed one of Kerr's most ambitious projects, passage of the Kerr Gas Bill, which sought to limit the Federal Power Commission's regulation of natural gas sales by independent producers, who controlled 80 percent of the market. Kerr and fellow Democrat Lyndon Johnson of Texas championed the bill as insurance against overbearing cost formulas that would stymie gas production and result in higher consumer expenditures. The Senate watched Kerr and Johnson face off against fellow Democrats Paul Douglas and Hubert Humphrey, who argued for the commission's right to rigorous oversight. At the end of the monthlong tussle, the

Senate voted overwhelmingly for passage of Kerr's bill, but after the House passed it by a slim margin, the decision was left to the president. On April 17, 1950, Harry Truman vetoed the bill, setting off a storm of protest across the Southwest and a cascade of congratulations from the Douglas-Humphrey camp. "God bless the president of the United States," Douglas trumpeted. "He has once again shown he is the true defender of the common people."[31]

Kerr thought differently, of course: Truman had erred, Douglas was too liberal, and it was he who truly defended the commoner. Even after this defeat—more so, in fact—Kerr proudly and tirelessly crusaded for the dispossessed, working all his connections in Washington to give small producers the protections they deserved. And though he clearly served the needs of a wealthy few—independent oil's conspicuous successes, of which he was one—there was no denying the force of his grassroots appeal. Amid the domestic oil supply crisis of the late 1940s and early 1950s, constituents' letters poured into his office charting devastating personal effects. Many, like one Oklahoma City pumper's unpolished plea, came from oil's struggling masses. "We oil field employees would feel more secuer on our jobs . . . if this foreign oil was stoped from flooding our markets," he wrote. "It is a shame for our Pipe Lines to lay idle and our People out of work, And let the American Markets be flooded with Foreign Oils. So I'm pleading You My Senator to give us you'r Support in stopping this thing which is hurting every Oil Co and Employee in Our grand State of Oklahoma. And you'r best is all we can ask of you." A healthy portion of missives came from local royalty owners, particularly women, who in the tradition of yesteryear managed their families' petrofinances while their husbands farmed the land. "As I am a royalty owner in Texas County," one Oklahoma farmer's wife wrote tersely, "I am writing in regard to the reduction on the Percentage Depletion of the gross income from oil and gas. I DO NOT want it lower than 27 ½ %. Sincerely Yours."[32]

But Kerr did more than answer the people's letters. He went and spoke to them, on oil and his faith, in a manner that politicized wildcat Christianity in a disarming way. In plenary after plenary—dozens between 1947 and 1952—he addressed oilmen in the IPAA and American Petroleum Institute (API) and called on them to work as one unit for the sake of the threatened small producer; his pleas always assumed moral urgency and grand context. At the national gathering of the API in November 1949, Kerr beseeched his brethren to assume their rightful duty as head of America's two-hundred-year-long quest for self-rule and righteousness. "The golden age of this people, who, under God and in a land of freedom have travelled farther along the pathway to the stars than any other" was in neither the past nor the present, he declared. "The golden age of America is in the future, in the development of her limitless resources, in the boundless courage of her people, in the hearts and souls of her sons and daughters." Lest they get too taken with liberty, Kerr cautioned that theirs was a heavy responsibility, as well, to guarantee America's international security (by supplying its primary energy source) and protect the natural resource that made their independence possible. On this latter score he opined that conservation was essential to good business and good citizenship. "The story of the 'Grapes of Wrath' was not born of hard hearted landlords," he averred, but rather "the product of neglected lands." Having lived John Steinbeck's story, he knew firsthand the pains of land mismanagement, and as an oilman he spoke to his audience with a special knowledge of earth's vagaries. What should be their response? An ecology that enhanced the oilman's standing as protector of the soil and its subsurface wealth, an ethic of stewardship that linked the wildcatter's providence to judicious use of the minerals and made him essential to every aspect of the nation's well-being.[33]

Even as he spoke to business lobbies on the virtues of independent oil and conservation, the statesman paused frequently to preach to his fellow churchgoers. By virtue of his unmatched successes in oil and profile in Washington, Kerr became one of the Southern Baptist Convention's (SBC) star laymen. He implored SBC groups to embrace a special role in the economic, political, and spiritual advances of their country, and his homiletics mesmerized. On one occasion he delivered a speech at the SBC's national meeting in 1949 titled "Always Bearing Our Witness as Christian Citizens." Kerr drew from his politics and corporate experience to craft an allegory that could spur his audience on for Christ. For working folks such as himself, he offered, it was important not to feel "overwhelmed by the realization of . . . insignificance" or "dismayed by the vastness of . . . the unexplored present, and the uncharted future." Kerr admitted feeling this inadequacy until a quiet moment in the Gulf of Mexico sparked something inside. Seeing a light on a distant shore he was comforted by thoughts of the dedicated lighthouse keeper who kept wandering men (offshore oilers included) on course. What stirred him was not the lighthouse keeper but a sense of the keeper's job, one that all Christian laity shared: the burden of spreading spiritual light to the world. "If we would bear witness for the Master, we must follow His footsteps as He goes to the crossroads where men and women live and work." With a final flourish he warned that the crossroads were many, the waiting world dark and expansive. But no worries—God's commission was also the Christian's joy and comfort: to march "with upturned faces into the rising sun."[34]

ROBERT KERR'S FIND off Louisiana was revolutionary, but no more so than what happened in Alberta during that same year, 1947. In the dead of a Canadian winter, patient oilmen found crude in the Leduc field, south of Edmonton. Since its first strikes during World War I, the Canadian province had enjoyed few petroleum breakthroughs. The Imperial Oil Company had poured millions of dollars into exploration throughout the region, all to no avail. But under the guidance of Vern "Dry Hole" Hunter (colleagues mocked his failures) an Imperial team took one last chance on an unassuming patch of farmland. There they triggered a small geyser. Anticipating a huge strike, Imperial asked Hunter to set a date to bring in the well, which caught him by surprise: "The crew and I were experts at abandoning wells but we didn't know much about completing them. I named February 13 and started praying." On the designated day, before five hundred freezing witnesses, Hunter commanded his roughnecks to open the valves and flare the well. With the ground rumbling and a concoction of crude and gas spewing from the pipe, flames shot into the air and could be seen in Edmonton, where Imperial executives partied in black ties. Within days other companies were pouring into the western province. Alberta was now a player in international petroleum.[35]

Much as Kerr's gulf discovery vaulted him into a loftier standing in the oil patch, the Alberta strike lifted an otherwise obscure politician from the Canadian West into a high-profile role as someone who could link the independents' empire across national divides. Alberta premier Ernest Manning enjoyed no formal standing among Democratic and Republican elites, of course; yet this was his very strength. Buoyed by his province's entry into international petroleum, yet removed from the direct heat of US politics, Manning could speak frankly about US petroleum's internal fracas without getting dragged into it. In the 1950s he used this leverage to solidify north-south ties between Alberta and the American Southwest and make his dominion a wildcatter's paradise, welcoming of producers who shared his faith. Buckley and Catawba Oil Company, O'Shaughnessy and Lario Oil & Gas Company, and J. Howard Pew and Sun all made their way to Manning's terrain.[36]

Manning's worldview had been cultivated through years of tireless work in Alberta's Social Credit Party, the most successful North American populist movement of the twentieth century. While still an aspiring politician, Manning came under the tutelage of Social Credit's two leading lights. The first was Clifford Hugh (C. H.) Douglas, a British engineer turned political philosopher who believed that the Great Depression was caused by an inefficient, monopoly-controlled capitalist system that in failing to provide average people with purchasing power had "immobilized consumption" and essentially frozen the economy. The science of wealth redistribution he championed included a price-adjustment mechanism to ensure a "just price" for consumers and state provision of "social credit"—money—to citizens so they could purchase local goods and services and energize the economy. William "Bible Bill" Aberhart, the preacher-politician whose teachings won him the premiership of Alberta in 1935, provided the theology of Social Credit—the soul to Douglas's science. A warring fundamentalist in the heated 1920s, Aberhart did all he could to shore up orthodoxy by founding the Calgary Prophetic Bible Institute, speaking in churches, and preaching on his radio program, *Back to the Bible Hour*. Aberhart pursued politics with the same zest through Social Credit's platform of anti–big business, community values, and economic redistribution. His agenda, which included a promise to give each citizen $25 per month, earned him Alberta's head office, where he served for eight years. Having been educated by Aberhart at his Bible Institute, Ernest Manning slid easily into leadership in the premier's camp. Even prior to Aberhart's election, Manning could be seen traveling the countryside with the barnstorming politician, junkets that the press referenced when labeling them a father-son team.[37]

In 1943, following Aberhart's sudden death, Manning ascended to his mentor's political post of premier and simultaneously became Alberta's minister of mines and minerals. Whereas Aberhart was a fundamentalist who waged war for his beliefs, Manning was an irenic evangelical who bore witness to them in a tactful tone. This combination made him an instant ally of the new evangelicalism's clerical and lay leaders in the United States. Between 1943 and 1947, Manning in fact made it his mission to enlist in several of the movement's undertakings. He organized branches of the International Christian Business Men's Committee, spoke on behalf of Billy Graham and the Gideons, an association of Christian businessmen, sat on ministerial boards, and saw to it that America's leading revivalists made their way north to Alberta. His pause from work to host Charles Fuller on a three-day provincial speaking tour in 1947 typified his resolve to prioritize his faith initiatives over political ones.[38]

In truth, however, he never considered the political secondary. Manning believed that if linked to evangelism, politics could serve as an essential rejoinder to society's problems. "We cannot purify polluted water in a well merely by painting the outside of the pump," he would say; purification needed to happen first through a personal relationship with God and second through a willingness to act vigorously for social reform. His message that statecraft and faith should mix and that Christian citizens needed to take ownership of their communities stirred the masses at home and abroad. "As I travel," he offered in 1950, "I frequently meet those who think it strange that a man in public life should be interested in the Bible. . . . I wonder why." "If you are a realist you cannot deny the fact that beneath and behind all of our human and material problems there lies the one basic problem of man's broken relationship to his God." Under Manning, Social Credit continued to rally for plain people who sought escape from the clutches of eastern banks and corporate elites. Manning did not follow C. H. Douglas's doctrines to the fullest by constructing alternative credit-creating agencies and scrip. In his politics as in his religion, he was more centrist than hard-core. But he did make government responsible for leveling capitalism's playing field and sustaining a "share-the-wealth" spirit.[39]

Manning's administration of oil reflected this pragmatism. As minister of minerals he was anxious to develop Alberta's oil supplies: this, he believed, was the easier ticket to collective wealth. His schema received a momentous boost with the Leduc discovery. Proximate and overseen by a politician who shared their values, Alberta's oil breakthrough struck embattled independent oilers as a spectacular opportunity for their business, their politics, and, for many of them, their faith: here was a new, exciting plain on which they could reap profits and sell the virtues of local crude to a North American citizenry pressed by Cold War anxieties and paranoid about controlling foreign influences, be they Saudi or Soviet. Recognizing this, Manning spent the years after the Leduc strike making his dominion their destination of choice.[40]

His speaking itinerary grew accordingly during the late 1940s and early 1950s. Even as he continued to traverse the continent preaching on the radio and in pulpits about the essence of conservative Christianity, he assumed a more pressing schedule of business engagements, especially with executives, engineers, and politicians in the Southwest's oil sector. Preaching in the region's churches on Sunday, he sermonized in its oil associations Monday through Saturday. He completed the latter task with equal enthusiasm because in his mind Alberta had a God-given gift to offer all North Americans: a cheaper, safer supply of oil, mined in accordance with Christian principles. His was a totalizing conviction that the purest faith and fuel values were those that allowed individuals to draw freely the fortunes of God's word and God's earth. As Manning's reputation grew, so too did the volume of his daily mail, which became inundated with requests from US citizens for his autograph, photo, or latest speech.

American oilmen were among those sending the requests. A few different aspects of Manning's outlook appealed to them, the first pertaining to policy. As his province's oil business grew, Manning framed a petroleum plan that maintained Social Credit's share-the-wealth imperatives. His mineral policy was simple but tough: to "ensure that the natural resources of the Province [were] developed in the interests of the people as a whole, under the most equitable conditions and with the greatest measure of freedom from regimentation." What did this mean? Though welcoming of corporate investment in Alberta's fields, Manning set firm limits. Oil companies could lease no more than 200,000 acres of Crown land for exploration and had to pay hefty deposits in advance of their work, which was reviewed yearly. Once oil was discovered, companies could continue leasing half the allotted land, but they had to set aside the other half as a Crown reserve, territory owned and managed by the provincial government. "By this procedure," Manning proclaimed, "the Government precludes all possibility of any monopoly getting control of the natural resources of the province." There was another way that the producer's loss became the purchaser's gain. Once a company developed a field it had to pay royalties (up to 15 percent) back to the people of Alberta. In this manner, Manning added, citizens were guaranteed that private enterprise would be "properly directed" toward the public good. And it guaranteed that citizens would get their piece of petroleum's lucrative pie. Some US oilmen, independents included, found Manning's policies heavy-handed, and their wishes for less government handling would eventually force him to soften his stand. But even in their caution, independents openly celebrated his stand against big oil. In this Canadian outpost they saw a politician who was leveling the playing field for corporations of any size and staring down the "tyranny of monopoly."[41]

If Manning was a free enterpriser with a plain-folk edge, he was also a prime mover who privileged the engineer over eastern intellectuals and bureaucrats. This trait too—one grafted from Douglas—struck a chord with American allies. In his handling of oil, Manning relied on technological experts to draft reports and policies, design the mechanisms to extract and protect the province's resources, converse and compare notes with tacticians in other parts of the world, and generally manage everything. There was nothing surprising about this approach, since the superstructure of post–World War II petroleum demanded special knowledge. Still, Manning's reliance on technical thinkers was also testament to the Social Credit experience, which privileged those who thought in utilitarian terms and sought to make society better through the application (not abstraction) of truth. In this sense, Manning agreed with Imperial Oil's president, who told an audience of engineers at a national gathering in Calgary in 1954 that their status in the West was singular, for they had imagined their region and its resource-rich civilization into being. As Manning would add in one of his own addresses to engineers, theirs was the great privilege and responsibility to mold physical material into a shape that God had intended for it. The importance Manning placed on engineers allowed him a special hearing with the petroleum guilds that he frequented throughout North America. Able to speak to them as someone who shared their deep distrust of knowledge-makers on Wall Street and in the Ivory Tower—those operating far from the dirt, grease, and splendor of their immediate environments—Manning struck a chord that rang deeper than politics. It was existential.[42]

Yet another aspect of Manning's oil ideology resonated widely: its connection to cosmic purpose. Manning, like Aberhart before him, held to a dispensational premillennialist view, which encouraged him to decode signs of societal strain as evidence that Christ's return was nigh. His eschatology grafted onto contemporary theories of petroleum geology. At that moment M. King Hubbert, a founder of the social movement known as Technocracy, which underscored the importance of engineers in the management of society and had ties to Social Credit, crafted his theory of "peak oil," holding that US domestic production would crest by 1971, then steadily decline. This prediction confirmed Manning's belief that the world was entering its last phase. Not only did time seem to be running out for America—God's City on a Hill—but it was now favoring non-Christians located in the very place to which Christ would return: the Middle East. His response was twofold: first, to train Western Christians' eyes on the Middle East, where rising oil production and politics seemed to portend Christ's return, and second, to extract expeditiously whatever oil was left under their soil before their dispensation expired. In Manning's scheme, wildcatters offered North Americans a last glimmer of hope: they alone had the courage to find new reserves and inspire patriots with pure capitalist drive.[43]

With remarkable ease Manning thus filtered eschatology and economics into a political creed that could unite oil-patch citizens in the United States and Canada. In his speeches, writings, and legislation, he shaped the way millions of Christians in both countries thought about energy and their place in the world and synchronized theologies of salvation and stewardship with the politics of entrepreneurialism and access to nature's resources. His networking on behalf of this dogma was invaluable to the construction of independent oil's political apparatus. Even as he spent the early 1950s traveling on a north-south axis to the United States, networking with like-minded evangelicals, he also approached oil producers as partners in Alberta's cause.

At a summer meeting of the Interstate Oil Compact Commission, held in Banff, British Columbia, in 1952, Manning thanked his guests for taking their conference north of the border: "May I pay tribute to the good judgment of those responsible for arranging to hold this year's meeting in the province now recognized as the Texas of Canada." A short time later he paid tribute to Texas in person by speaking at the Mid-Continent Oil & Gas Association in San Antonio. Texas's oilmen publicized his plain-folk qualities in advance of his arrival. "One of the most important 'oil executives' in North America is a tall, slim fellow who lives on a small farm, helps with farm chores from cattle feeding to riding a tractor, conducts a weekly religious broadcast and is paid about $15,000 a year by his Provincial Government." Manning used these opportunities to encourage his brethren to take a forceful stand for Christian democracy. "The world situation today is precarious," he proclaimed at the Banff gathering, striking a conspiratorial tone. "If we are content to sit back and leave to a handful of men in the world councils of today the responsibility of trying to work out some master plan to superimpose on the human race, from the top down, in the hope of solving this tremendous problem confronting all mankind . . . we are not being realists." Manning demanded grassroots action: "we have to recognize that as individual citizens, we have an inescapable responsibility to do our part to that end, and I am convinced that it is only when we as individual citizens assume that responsibility that we will see progress made." Oilmen from both sides of the forty-ninth parallel flooded Manning's office with requests for written copies of this speech so that they could spread the word. Revival was coming.[44]

MANNING'S TRAVELS THROUGH North America's oil patches, along with his heavy investment in the emergent new evangelicalism, helped increase possibilities for wide-scale collaboration within the independent oil fraternity during the Cold War's first decade. But preachers and oilmen knew that in order to survive the erupting international climate and seize upon their breakthroughs, they had to do more than drill holes and pray for redemption. With something bigger in mind—societal transformation—they set out to market a mythology that spoke to everyone, not just those who lived and breathed petroleum. In parallel with their fights in Washington, they began to construct a culture industry to prove their worth as true patriots uniquely positioned to transmit the truths of Christianity and capitalism to a nation besieged by dangerous foreign influences.

New evangelicals and their allies in oil pursued that power through deft use of mass media, at which evangelist Billy Graham was particularly adept. Graham's ties to clerics and businessmen in western oil patches thickened organically during the early years of his ministry. In 1950, following a series of evangelistic services in Dallas, he made the city's First Baptist Church, the hub of Texas oil's "big rich," his official home congregation. Already acquainted with J. Howard Pew, Graham secured close association with other prominent oilmen by joining First Baptist, including Sid Richardson, Clint Murchison, and H. L. Hunt. As his ministry continued to mature into the ultimate indicator of new evangelicalism's vitality, the evangelist paid tribute to these swashbuckling men. In 1951 his new movie company, World Wide Pictures, released its first film, *Mr. Texas*, which told the story of a rancher turned oilman who learned how to abide in Christ. After premiering it in the Hollywood Bowl, Graham took *Mr. Texas* on the road, showing it at stadium revivals across North America. The warmest reception came in Fort Worth, where Richardson watched as a rags-to-riches, sinner-to-saint life story that echoed his own played out on screen. The Western world, Graham intimated, had much to learn from the regenerated wildcatter.[45]

That notion was strikingly at odds with Hollywood's, whose portrayals of Texas crude at this very juncture reinforced negative perceptions of the state's oilmen. During the early Cold War period, movie producers readily translated tales about the Lone Star State and its swashbucklers onto the silver screen. Most famously, they released *Giant*, the movie version of Edna Ferber's 1952 novel. With its star-studded cast and stunning on-location scenery, *Giant* paints a vivid world in which the quest for oil is essentially impure because it serves no other end but greed and causes even well-meaning people to succumb to the lure of money and, in the process, jettison all happiness and basic values. In order to address this dark image, southwestern oilmen had to locate an alternative, one that portrayed them as the last pure capitalists who did not trade morals for an edge in the marketplace but stayed true to oil's—America's—founding vision. And in order to accomplish this, they had to demonstrate their own fallibility and an eagerness to recalibrate their careers according to godly precepts of yesteryear.[46]

It was natural for Graham's movie company to take the lead in this venture. Following the 1951 release of *Mr. Texas*, World Wide Pictures' team of moviemakers, headed by Dick Ross, knew that a grander sequel was in order. Unlike their first undertaking, which filmed amateur actors in modest locations (such as Abilene, Texas), the second, they promised, would boast a bevy of first-tier actors and be shot "against the background of the world's most fabulous city ... Houston!" By hitting these spectacular notes, Graham's moviemakers hoped to exceed the number of converts (100,000) created by their first film and generate a level of excitement that could enhance Graham's revivalist imperative on a global stage. Despite their huge ambitions, Ross and his associates settled on a simple title for their film that conveyed the importance of righteous living in the local setting: *Oiltown, U.S.A.*[47]

Ross carefully wrapped his narrative around the life of fictional oilman Lance Manning. Like *Giant*'s money-grubbing Jett Rink, portrayed by James Dean, Ross's Manning represents everything wrong with 1950s society. A relentlessly hard-driving oiler obsessed with the quick buck, he is also a hard-living lost soul unable to do anything with his wealth other than drink and gamble it away. Manning's foibles are not entirely his own fault. A widower who cannot escape the sadness of losing his life partner or the shadow of her presence (her oversized portrait hangs on his mansion's dining room wall), he lives with a recklessness stirred by profound grief and an inability to move on. Still, most of Manning's struggles are self-made. Caught up in the booming petroleum business of Houston, he exhibits a callousness and lack of charity cast by proximity to his rugged place and indulgence in its worst excesses. As a wildcatter who chases affluence with abandon, Manning is, by all measures, the American dream gone wildly bad.

But he also personifies its redemptive potential. At the very moment Manning hits rock bottom in his life (marked by an alcohol-induced outburst against his daughter, Chris), he also sees a ray of hope. Sorry for his outbreak and begging for forgiveness, he starts reading his Bible again, something his deceased wife did. But it is a crisis followed by complete submission to the gospel that transforms him. While working in his posh office one day, Manning hears about an explosion in a town on the coast, south of Houston. Knowing that Chris is in the area boating with friends, he rushes to the scene. Panicked, he finds her bandaging the wounded and directing local residents to safety, away from the inferno. The visual of his daughter's sacrifice softens him for what comes next. On a memorable day in a Houston football stadium, Manning listens intently to Graham preaching salvation. At sermon's end, he walks the "sawdust trail" and prays the sinner's prayer, then commits his wealth to spreading God's word.[48]

Ross's script covered all the basics of evangelicalism's salvation message and managed to fold them into real-life features of Texas crude. He worked hard on this count, capturing real anecdotes and images from area oil operations (including searing ones spliced from the Texas City disaster of 1947) and recruiting Houston's oil elite for help. Local oilman and Billy Graham friend Earl Hankamer was Ross's closest confidant. Hankamer was a fixture in Texas Christian circles, hence the ideal contact. He chaired the board of deacons at Second Baptist Church in Houston as well as the board of trustees at Baylor University. To the latter he gave millions of dollars in hopes of facilitating the type of education—Bible based, market friendly—that he believed essential to the training of the next generation of oil-patch citizens. But the Christian lay leader also served out front for many of Billy Graham's key initiatives. Besides acting as chairman of Graham's 1952 Houston Evangelistic Crusade, an undertaking that involved thousands of volunteers, and dealing directly with city officials, Hankamer also functioned as a liaison between the Billy Graham Evangelistic Association and area sponsors. In addition to being one of the city's most "prominent oilmen," Houston papers proclaimed, Hankamer was one of its most prominent Baptist churchmen.[49]

Through Hankamer's connections, Ross won the right to film in the Houston Petroleum Club, at key city landmarks, and in a real-life oil baron's mansion. With its southern colonial style, graced with white pillars and a grand driveway, and its elegant interior, Hankamer's own abode was perfect as Manning's home. The real Houston oilman enjoyed hosting the make-believe one and savored each opportunity to help Ross's team. In Hankamer's opinion, *Oiltown* was destined to be "far-reaching in its influence and effect," and he wanted to be part of the momentous effort. Ross shared Hankamer's faith in the film and at the same time marveled at the sway a Christ-honoring wildcatter could have on his church. At the end of filming, he thanked the Christian oilman with words of highest praise: "Eternity alone will reveal the grateful appreciation which all of us feel so inadequate to express for your generousity [*sic*] and your consecration. . . . May God richly bless and prosper you for all you did as unto Him."[50]

In anticipation of *Oiltown*'s release in the spring of 1953, Hankamer did his best to disseminate its message in hopes of redeeming his peers. Lance Manning was *one of them*, Hankamer intimated to his friends, and it was time they refasten the wildcatter's ambition to a personal faith in God. Hankamer secured the Sam Houston Coliseum for the film's premier, held over a three-day stretch in March, and did all he could to publicize it. In large print on oversized posters, he and Ross spread word about the movie's timely and timeless truth: "Welcome to Oil Town, U.S.A.!," it boomed. Why a story about Houston, it asked, and not about Pittsburgh, Chicago, or Boston? "Well," the placard explained, "the story of Houston is the story of the free enterprise of America . . . the story of the development and use of God-Given natural resources by men who have built a great new empire, and with it, a fabulous central city: Oil Town." Houston exemplified America in all its extreme possibilities, the poster added; imagine what God could do with it were it to accept "Jesus Christ as Saviour and Lord"![51]

The positive responses to *Oiltown, U.S.A.* thrilled Hankamer and his friends. During its first run in Houston, 36,000 local citizens packed the Sam Houston Coliseum to see their city's redemptive narrative flashed on the screen. After each evening's showing Billy Graham offered viewers a chance to follow Lance Manning's example and pray the sinner's prayer. Two-hundred-and-fifty people accepted the invitation on the first night alone. This was just the beginning of *Oiltown*'s global journey. Those gathered in Houston not only lent Graham's movie their rapt attention but also supplied funds to show it around the world. Graham's plans for revival in Great Britain were just taking shape, and with the illustrative aid of *Oiltown*, he intended to tell Europeans that they too had something to learn from America's encounters with God and black gold. Graham had yet another target in mind: the Korean War front and Korean Peninsula as a whole. During a recent visit there he had been pleased to see the "most religious army we have ever had." *Oiltown* was at its heart a tale about a local community; yet Graham saw in its saga of personal empowerment plenty of inspiration for soldiers—and South Korean citizens—to take into the battle with communist imperialism.[52]

GRAHAM AND HIS movie's message cut to the heart of the Southwest's sense of regional and religious independence, as well as the new evangelicalism's emerging priorities. But they also added color and conviction to wildcat politicking, which, even as *Oiltown, U.S.A.*'s production unfolded, was reaching a feverish pitch. This politicking played out because of developments in the oil frontier that Robert Kerr was instrumental in uncovering in 1947: the Gulf of Mexico. Thanks to the cultural front forged by independent oilmen and their allies in evangelical pulpits, it resulted in one of the first major, successful displays of the oil patch's determination to fight the federal government, portending what was to come in partisan politics.

Even as southwestern independents celebrated the monumental Kerr-McGee strike that shifted exploration to the Gulf of Mexico, they grew wary of a foe that had its own aspirations for offshore oil. That foe had begun signaling its intentions years before. In 1945 President Harry Truman issued an executive proclamation that placed the federal government in charge of oil deposits off the Gulf Coast. At the time—even though Robert Kerr had not yet shown how to access it in deeper waters—experts believed that this seabed held millions of barrels of crude, thus a potential windfall. By then, numerous oil companies, ranging from the imposing Shell and Texaco to the smaller Sun and Kerr-McGee, were acquiring state leases that let them explore thousands of acres of the gulf's "continental shelf." The prospect of losing the funds generated by this practice incensed Texans especially. For a century they had believed that their state held sole ownership of waters stretching three leagues (10.35 miles) into the gulf. This arrangement had been passed on to them from the Republic of Texas, which had gained its authority upon independence from Mexico. For Texans,

Truman's initiative was an insult to their heritage. But it meant more than this. In 1939 the Texas Legislature had earmarked all revenues from exploration in the tidelands for public education. By the mid-1940s parents saw offshore leasing as a way to guarantee their children's access to higher learning. Other Truman critics—including a dethroned Harold Ickes—would soon rally around that same notion. "The off-shore oil belongs to all the people," the former secretary of the interior would bark in his new career as a journalist; "save the tidelands for the schools." In challenging the status quo Truman thus did more than trigger a storm in the Lone Star State's legislature; he set one off in its local communities as well.[53]

Developments during the late 1940s accentuated the tension. In 1947, the Supreme Court rendered a decision in favor of federal jurisdiction over California's tidelands, another key battle zone. Justice Hugo Black explained the ruling succinctly: "California is not the owner of the three mile marginal belt along its coast, and the federal government ... has paramount rights in and power over the belt [and] dominion over the resources of the soil under that water including oil." Although the ruling applied only to California, state officials and an informed public knew that it had direct consequences for Texas as well. Washington would soon be on their doorstep. Even prior to the ruling, Texas attorney general Price Daniel advised Governor Beauford Jester that the California decision would trigger a fight on their turf. After the ruling, Jester and Daniel responded harshly. While the former called the decision a "further invasion of states rights," the latter condemned it as the greatest "blow struck against property rights of a state since the Civil War." "There is no protection against the greed of the totalitarian-minded bureaucrats," Daniel would later add. Texas legislators reacted in their own stern manner by passing legislation that extended their state's jurisdiction to twenty-seven miles into the gulf (Louisiana officials did the same). Truman answered back, charging that the federal government regarded "the natural resources of the subsoil and sea bed of the continental shelf ... subject to its jurisdiction and control." Behind all the legalese rested an obvious fact: Texas was at war with Washington.[54]

The struggle intensified in the months surrounding the 1948 presidential election. Vocal opposition to Truman's Democrats spread quickly. Texas Democrats were divided, and many considered alternatives. State

Republicans, perpetual runners-up, were gleeful and convinced that they could break the Democratic lock. One official asserted that nothing would make the "Republican Party stronger in California, Texas . . . and the other coastal states . . . than a strong leadership in favor of state ownership." Developments in the national party offered this official added encouragement. At their national convention, Republicans drafted a platform that included a pledge to restore "to the states . . . their historic rights to the tides of submerged lands, tributary waters, lakes and streams." Meanwhile, they nominated New York governor Thomas Dewey for president and California governor Earl Warren for vice president. Warren was relentless when campaigning and eager to frame the tidelands controversy as a family-values issue. During one of his more impassioned whistle-stop speeches in Fort Worth, just before the election, he thanked his audience for joining his state in the fight against federal greed. Citing Texas and California's shared pioneering values and dominion over their resources, he implored listeners to continue "stemming the tide" under the fresh counsel of the GOP. Much more than pride and dollars were at stake: "the heritage of every child in Texas" hung in the balance.[55]

For those southwesterners who appreciated Warren's words but not yet his party, there was another vehicle for voicing dissent: Strom Thurmond's States' Rights Democratic Party. Thurmond was a longtime Democrat from South Carolina with staunch segregationist convictions, whose ambition for a third party certainly grew out of concern with Truman's progressive stand on civil rights and a desire to protect the South's racial order, but the tidelands debate drove him as well. In his stumping across the South he promised to keep Washington's hands off the Southwest's petroleum. The Southwest's oilmen, headed by Hugh Roy Cullen, heard him and, in varying and secretive degrees, bankrolled him. Louisiana oilman and "political boss of the Delta" Leander Perez spent the most backing Thurmond's Dixiecrat charge. Cullen, Perez, and their associates helped the South Carolina politician steal victories in four states, even as Truman pulled off a stunning win over favored Republican Dewey. The significance of the campaign extended beyond the outcome at the polls, however. As one historian notes, the "tittle-tattle about the tidelands represented the most significant opportunity to date for conservative economic forces in the region to consolidate an anti–New Deal constituency." Truman's surprising electoral win killed this opportunity but not the anger that had generated it.[56]

The tidelands struggle drew to its climax in the early 1950s, and that is when the combined energies of independent oil and the new evangelicalism produced a major political turn. After another Supreme Court ruling in 1950 reaffirmed federal control over tidelands off the California, Texas, and Louisiana coasts, Cullen's allies once again looked to the Republican ticket in 1952 as a way to reverse the order. To be sure, they looked to old allies as well. Cullen pleaded with Robert Kerr, in a letter dated February 1952, to abandon the Truman Democrats who had stymied the Kerr Gas Bill, designed to protect independents' free rein in the gas market, and disappointed their constituents in so many ways. It was time for Democratic senator Kerr to reassess. "You are now considering a matter so important that it overshadows national politics, the budget, our international commitments—even the tragedy of Korea. This matter is the tidelands controversy." "It is all-important," Cullen averred, "because if the tidelands are confiscated by the Federal government under the dangerous theory of 'paramount rights,' everything will go. If this theory is allowed to stand, there will be no United States as we know it." Kerr did think deeply about the matter but stayed true to his partisan home and for the first time found himself on the wrong side of prevailing sentiments among his peers. By now it was obvious to Kerr's fellow wildcatters that federal tidelands rulings were negatively affecting offshore leasing and state revenues. They determined to address the problem once and for all, through rigorous grassroots action and machinations within the GOP.[57]

As witnessed in the lobbying of Walter Hallanan, their labor on those fronts easily melded political, economic, and regional passions into one Puritan-sounding jeremiad. Hallanan was an oilman from West Virginia who ran his Texas-based firm (named Plymouth Oil Company out of reverence for the nation's roots) from a distance. He was also chairman of the 1952 Republican National Convention. Wearing all those hats he used advertisements in industry newspapers and hard-hitting sermons to excoriate Truman's handling of oil and nudge citizens of the oil patch toward a new alternative. During a speech in Sinton, Texas, Plymouth's operational headquarters, he painted the oil industry as the "outstanding symbol of free, competitive enterprise" and the force that had lifted "America out of the darkness, lethargy and drudgery . . . into the light." He also made clear that rank-and-file oil-patch families were custodians of this remarkable resource, morally equipped to handle the burden, yet in need of awareness about the threat of socialism, which had skulked its way into Washington. Hallanan reminded his listeners that the "crisis" they faced was spiritual, demanding a response from the heart. "As we face the morning sun of tomorrow," he motioned, "let us all re-dedicate and re-consecrate ourselves to the proposition that Socialism and Americanism will not mix any more than oil and water. Let us squarely face the fact that we are to have one or the other. Let us restore together that our Republic, founded in faith, conscience, compassion and law, shall continue in freedom, in dignity and in peace." Like Texas's firebrand preachers, Hallanan beseeched true, red-blooded Americans to take a stand for those values before Washington snuffed them out.[58]

Other independents bellowed as well. During the early 1950s, at the height of the tidelands debate, high-profile independents like H. R. Cullen, Sid Richardson, H. L. Hunt, and J. Howard Pew bombarded religious organizations with the message that Washington had overstepped its bounds. Pew and Hunt's deep connections to Christian anticommunist networks were especially valuable. Hunt's Dallas-based Facts Forum gained national attention in 1952 as a sounding board for McCarthyism and its strident attacks on anyone and anything that seemed friendly to socialist thought. Though able to reach a wider public in southwestern conservative circles, Facts Forum programming penetrated the ranks of oil-patch evangelicalism with special effect and directed this constituency's angst toward all things Washington related, including the tidelands "oil grab." Pew preferred a quieter path to mobilization. Through his charitable trust he delivered steady donations to Christian anticommunist and women's groups that monitored federal policy in oil. One of the most important was the Washington-based Women Investors Research Institute, headed by Catherine Curtis, which gave Pew the evidence needed to warn evangelicals of a federal assault on their rights to land and resources.[59]

Hunt and Pew's information gathering, coupled with the activism of high-profile preachers, including Charles Fuller's partner Harold

Ockenga, helped wildcatters generate support for their case within the GOP and with its rising leader and Texas son, Dwight Eisenhower. One of the most important clerics to help the recruitment of Eisenhower and public support for a Republican reversal of the tidelands charter was Billy Graham, whose proximity to Texas crude now placed him in an important political position. Although close with Pew, Graham seemed most willing in this instance to work with Sid Richardson. Having met Graham at his Fort Worth crusade in 1951, Richardson came to consider him a spiritual confidant and ally. Between the fall of 1951 and spring of 1952, he and Graham worked together to pressure Eisenhower to run for the presidency. Ensconced in Paris at the time, serving as supreme commander of the North Atlantic Treaty Organization, Eisenhower was on the receiving end of several petitions from both Democrats and Republicans begging him to run on their presidential ticket. But the oilman and preacher were among the most insistent suitors. When Richardson traveled to Paris in early spring of 1952 to woo the general in person and implore him to guide the GOP, he carried two letters of support, one from Clint Murchison and the other from Billy Graham. Eisenhower's decision to lead the GOP was ample evidence that these pleas from the oil patch were answered.[60]

More evidence of an answered call came when, via an open letter sent from Paris to his Texas campaign manager, wildcatter Jack Porter, the presidential candidate voiced his opposition to a proposed congressional bill designed to allocate offshore oil revenues for federal education. His letter of late March 1952 came with a campaign pledge that Porter, Richardson, and Graham heartily endorsed: to end all talk about federal profits from the tidelands and simply restore control of them to the states that once held jurisdiction—California, Texas, and Louisiana in particular. "Once again," Eisenhower declared, "I agree with the principle that federal ownership in this case, as in others, is one that is calculated to bring about steady progress toward centralized ownership and control, a trend which I have bitterly opposed." Wanting to steal thunder from GOP contender Robert Taft, the political darling of conservatives, yet not lean too far away from his centrist base, Eisenhower added a caveat with hopes of bridging intraparty divides: "Of course, I agree with all other patriotic citizens who believe that the U.S. with an eye to its own national security should always take effective steps to prevent unjustified and unfair exploitation of natural resources. (Witness our once abundant timberlands.)" "But," he concluded, "this can be done without Federal ownership."[61]

Graham, Richardson, and their allies worked well together during the campaign as well. Richardson poured his funds (approximated at $1 million) into the Eisenhower campaign and convinced his friends to do the same. Graham, meanwhile, worked evangelical circles to enlist oilmen of modest standing, such as Earl Hankamer. Although unable to match the wealth of a Richardson, Hankamer equaled his fellow wildcatters' commitment to the cause. Thanks to the ardent activism of men like him, Texas preachers and oilmen won their victory. In the days leading up to the election, pastors across the state called on followers to kill the liberal goliath that Roosevelt and Truman had been growing in Washington for years. Though broad in scope, with Cold War anxieties about communism front and center, their proclamations resounded with the demands of the wildcatter, which held that the nation's survival would only be guaranteed when its most daring entrepreneurs had the chance to extract material from the earth and put it to use for the furtherance of a Christian America. Richardson and Texas's "big rich" joined the chorus and celebrated each Eisenhower vote.[62]

So did lesser lights like Hankamer, who shared his joy with Graham when all the politicking was done. The first of Hankamer's thrills had come when Graham secured tickets for him and "the boys" (Graham's term of endearment for oil associates) to the 1952 Republican National Convention. The second of Hankamer's thrills came on election night. Basking in Eisenhower's triumph, he and Graham penned jubilant notes about their nation's brighter future. "We must be deeply grateful that the election went the way it did," Graham offered. "If it had gone the other way, it could have meant disaster." The Texan expressed similar thoughts in his reply. "I thoroughly agree. . . . I made the statement yesterday that I thought he would go down in history as one of the greatest of all presidents. If you have not already done so, I think it would be most effective for you to write General Eisenhower a personal letter, assuring him that you and a large group of your friends are remembering him daily in prayer."[63]

By the mid-1950s, corporate and church associates had constructed an interlocking movement for independent oil and the new evangelicalism, the breadth of which few—including Harold Ockenga—could have imagined a decade before. Their survival stories and successes—Fuller Seminary, Pew Trust, Eisenhower, *Oiltown, U.S.A.*, drill sites in Alberta and the gulf—were significant on their own. Together they signified a rising cultural and political force that now promised to cause further rumblings within the Republican Party and beyond.

Billy Graham's meteoric rise after his first flirtation with Texas crude in the early 1950s would be yet another symbol of that gathering wind. In April 1957, the *Ladies Home Journal* profiled the ten richest men in America, which included seven oilmen: Sid Richardson, H. L. Hunt, Clint Murchison, Joseph N. Pew Jr., John D. Rockefeller III, Paul Mellon, and Howard Hughes. Graham was friend to at least five, including John D. Rockefeller III. The first few on that list, though, stood out for their proximity to the preacher. In no small part that was because they worked and worshipped in Texas, a place the evangelist saw as his second home. Later in life Graham would joke with some seriousness that while his roots remained in North Carolina and the Presbyterian pew, he was at heart "a Baptist and a half-Texan." But the bonds of friendship that linked Graham to his allies in oil were, by this juncture, also philosophical. Temperamentally, Graham and the Pews leaned toward a certain puritan refinement, while their counterparts in southwestern crude—products of the wild 1930s boom—embraced the eccentric and to mixed degrees the immodest. One journalist's depiction of Richardson as a "wildcatter with the body of a barrel cactus and a predilection for poker and bourbon and yellow terminology" could be applied to a whole swath of his kind. Yet by the 1950s, with Texas oil shining as a life source of the new evangelicalism, such differences hardly mattered. What mattered was that the moral and market imperatives that had shaped the Richardson and Pew ethic over previous generations were fully formed, fully fused, and being propagated with unprecedented force. What was required in their dark hour, they believed, was for individuals to turn inwardly and reclaim a personal relationship with Christ and all the personal—and economic—liberties it promised, then outwardly to prompt fellow citizens to be born again lest they succumb to socialism, secularism, and the state. Graham and his allies now owned a national stage from which to deliver that antidote to all the world's ills. In 1959, Graham spoke at Richardson's funeral and, in tribute to the reclusive oiler, essentially praised his entire breed of "big rich" and their bare tenacity, which had made that national stage possible. "He was willing to go to any end to see that our American way of life was maintained," the preacher puffed.[64]

Directed toward his wildcat friend and his kind in Texas crude, Graham's eulogy also spoke to broader dynamics in the realms of petroleum and Cold War politics that now engulfed America. Even as political battles in the 1950s over tidelands exploration, continental oil production, and the importation of foreign oil divided US oilmen and churchmen—pitting Washington and the majors against the independents of the Southwest—the specter of international communism loomed large. The "American way of life" to which Graham referred when extolling Sid Richardson's liberty-loving virtues was one that oilers of every stripe embraced. As the Cold War heated up and fears of a Red Menace marching across the globe intensified, that way of life seemed increasingly vulnerable. In response, wildcatters, major oilmen, and the preachers and religious activists in their respective corners curbed their animosities toward each other and, for the sake of national survival, joined together to fight a common foe.

# CHAPTER NINE

# The Great Game

O ne month after the *Ladies Home Journal* profiled America's megarich, Billy Graham sent further notice to the world that his ministry was ascendant. His New York City revival, begun in mid-May 1957, sent that signal. On one level, this triumph occurred because of his appeals to a growing evangelical base. Yet it also had much to do with the ecumenical backing and message that Graham enjoyed and delivered. The Rockefeller family's support (John and David's in particular) was of immense importance, both financially and politically—this was very much their town. In return, Graham worked hard, in a way he might not otherwise have done in Dallas or Houston, to stress interfaith unity as a godly virtue. In his appeals to monotheism as the anchor of society, Graham would speak the political lingua franca of the day, which called on a Protestant-Catholic-Jewish citizenry to rise up as one nation under God.[1]

Yet Graham's pleas for a Judeo-Christian consensus were not simply designed to rally citizens around a tempered theology of belonging; he also wished to remind them of their singular purpose to serve as a light of truth to the spiritually lost. The evangelist set that tone on his opening night, May 15, 1957. The sermon he delivered in Madison Square Garden was laced with stark proclamations. In staccato, but with an inviting southern drawl, he listed off worries about the world that required a strong spiritual—by insinuation, political—response: urban blight and the loss of law and order; racism, secularism, and declining morality; teenage delinquency, communism, and the nuclear threat; and "Middle Eastern problems." America was living in a "night of total crisis," he thundered. The answer? Christ's empowerment of the individual and the revitalization of a government, culture, and marketplace that honored that solution. The evangelist wove that theme through his closing invocation as well. He asked people to exit their seats, walk toward his stage, and petition God for salvation. "I want you . . . to present your life and your heart to Christ as Saviour. You'll have a new power to live in Christ. That's what it means to be born again. You become a partaker of God's light." He poked the devout too. "I'm going to ask every Christian here to concentrate in prayer that there may be a . . . sense that God is here." Only through focused supplication, he insisted, would the lives of the lost be changed and hope brought to this world of sin.[2]

The weeks that followed saw the preacher take the city by storm. Large crowds forced his team to extend its inaugural New York City Crusade, initially scheduled for a few weeks in May 1957, until September 1. Graham poured himself into each meeting, pleading with sinners to repent. According to the crusade organizers, who cited a cumulative attendance of 2.4 million and 61,000 spiritual decisions, they did repent, in staggering proportions. Graham's ministry would never be the same, in large part because of his savvy. As he preached to New Yorkers, he clearly did so with the booming voice of a Texas wildcatter, but also with arms stretched out in inclusive fashion, in a manner that affirmed the values of religious liberty that defined the "American way" and set America apart from other secular and socialist societies. Striking a chord with conservative Christian Americans, he also managed to please more progressive ones and in general hit the right note with all Americans. Amid the anxieties of the Cold War, Graham's was a rallying cry for people from all walks of life to stare down their godless enemies as one.[3]

That was Dwight Eisenhower's cry as well, which both factions of US oil embraced. From the very outset, his administration was intent on governing behind a phalanx of centrist politics and an all-embracing religiosity that could demonstrate the superiority of American democracy to the world and contain the communist threat. Domestically, the construction of that united front involved a rigorous and sweeping attempt by both business and labor to sell democracy's core principle—free market capitalism—as God's master plan for modern society. The petroleum industry had honed its marketing prowess in the 1920s, at which time it appealed to the American people as the quintessence of God-sanctioned free enterprise. It reveled in its role during the 1950s as harbinger of the Eisenhower agenda, eagerly supporting the White House's attempts to sell it at home and abroad. For Arabists in major oil, men such as William Eddy, that initiative extended even further; the time was now, they declared, for the United States to shore up relations with Saudi Arabia and Arabs in the Middle East. Eisenhower heard them and, in a series of historic exchanges, fortified a moral alliance of these oil-dependent societies. He did so by reframing the American way as quadrilateral, not just trilateral, involving Islam as well as Judaism, Protestantism, and the Catholic faith. With petroleum as a critical backdrop, the canopy of Cold War America's consensus widened considerably, if momentarily.

That same momentum played out on global oil patches, as Eddy and the Rockefellers' civil religion of crude and the wildcat Christianity of the Pews together achieved a highpoint of impact that would stretch into the early 1960s. The expansive doctrine of major oil's proponents inspired them to expand their role in the "great game" of securing souls and oil sources for Christian democracy, not only in the Middle East but around the entire globe, all amid the death struggle with the Soviets. Backed by Rockefeller money and ideology, oil hunters-turned-Cold Warriors spanned into Africa and deeper into South America to test the earth and their concepts of development. To an unprecedented degree, independent oilmen joined this global outreach, as if it were their ultimate duty. They used their petrocapital to fund missionaries who could penetrate the jungles of South America with the Bible, then infiltrated the same terrains with their drill bits in tow in pursuit of economic conquest and a desire to construct model communities of Christian democracy in an attempt to make Pax Americana a local reality. Henry Luce's American Century, it appeared, was in full bloom.

DURING THE EARLY Cold War years, corporate oil attempted to unite behind a shared political agenda. Internal divisions, derived from background battles over domestic oil reserves and the expanding role of Washington and major oil companies in the Middle East, always worked against the full fusion of interests. But when larger threats arose, oil's constituents found room for collaboration, just as they had managed to do in the 1920s. Their looming danger of the 1950s was global communism. In an attempt to contain the Red Menace, major and independent oilers, along with their workers, labored together to cloak their nation in capitalist consensus.

Oil's attempts to coalesce in such manner began before Eisenhower was there to urge them on. One flashpoint in this advent of industry moral fervor occurred in New York City. On April 23, 1950, 4,000 men and women belonging to the Catholic Petroleum Guild celebrated "corporate communion" at St. Alphonsus Cathedral. The 1950 service marked the tenth year such a meeting was held, but it transcended any that had come before. An oil trucker had come up with the idea in 1941: Why not implore fellow workers of the Catholic faith to attend Mass together each year? By the late 1940s, thousands of oilmen and women observed the special Sunday in New York, Newark, and Boston. The Catholic Petroleum Guild provided the extra impetus. It was consolidated in 1948 with a fourfold purpose: "to pray for every member of the petroleum industry, both living and dead"; "to promote success of the petroleum industry and prevent any major disaster"; "to seek divine guidance in all dealings of management and labor"; and "to stimulate the observance of Petroleum Sunday among all creeds in the industry by encouraging them to attend their churches in groups at least once a year." Fifteen oil companies endorsed the 1950 gathering. As evidenced by a list that included Jacob Blaustein's Amoco, William Eddy's Aramco, the Pews' Sun Oil, and the Rockefellers' Jersey Standard and Socony, every denomination of petroleum and faith seemed eager to sponsor the event.[4]

That the largest of the 1950 "Petroleum Sunday" celebrations occurred in St. Alphonsus said a lot about a newly welcomed ally in the postwar petroleum apparatus: organized labor. Thirty years earlier that exact parish had served as ground zero for Frank Tannenbaum's "Army of the Unemployed" as he tried to corral oil's proletariat into the

Industrial Workers of the World and trigger class insurrection. That revolt had failed, leaving organized labor badly weakened. But as the postwar age of abundance arrived, trade unions were no longer outliers or the persecuted.

Global war had changed the status of the union movement. As with all heavy industry during World War II, the oil sector saw renewed activism by emboldened labor leaders fully aware of the nation's need for crude on the front lines and in America's factories—hence, for a happy workforce to supply it. The most powerful union at the time was the Oil Workers International Union (OWIU). In 1937, two years after the International Association of Oil Field, Gas Well & Refinery Workers changed its name to the OWIU, the newly minted union aligned with the Congress of Industrial Organizations (CIO). As an army of different units, with the OWIU's platoon of roughly 65,000 members leading the way and smaller independent oil unions such as the Industrial Workers Association following suit, oil's unionists entered the 1940s able to demand more of their employers and the government. One of their earliest campaigns took place on the Gulf Coast, which accounted for roughly 30 percent of the national refining capacity. Over the course of 1942, Texas oil workers coordinated a mammoth campaign enveloping refineries at Baytown, Port Arthur, and other satellite worksites. Their tactics ranged from membership drives and strike actions to colorful processions. In Texas City, south of Houston, OWIU activists led an "Oil for Victory" parade and rally during which workers and community organizations (a high school band, the fire department, pastors, even the mayor) walked together from the refinery to the city hall. Those on the front line held a "sixty-foot banner advocating 'Boil Hitler in Texas Oil—CIO.'" Union activity continued to expand in the postwar years amid scaled-back wages in a demilitarized economy. The mobilization culminated in a national strike of 43,000 oil workers in 1945, which proved how far and fast OWIU and its partners had climbed out of irrelevancy.[5]

By the time the Catholic Petroleum Guild organized in 1948, oil unionization was on a very different footing, ready to influence the industry in a way Tannenbaum would not have imagined possible. It was also a much more moderate force, compared with the IWW renegades of yesteryear. Due to both external pressures and internal ideological shifts, petroleum's burgeoning guilds entered the 1950s with a desire for societal rapport rather than revolution.

The external pressures were heavy and involved high politics. Worried by the postwar flurry of industrial strike action in which oil workers were one key part, a Republican-led faction in the US Congress steered passage of the Taft-Hartley Act in 1947, which outlawed many of the tactics unions had used to recruit members and shut down plants. It also imposed loyalty oaths (pledges of anticommunist commitment) on all union officers, essentially purging labor of radicals and radicalism. The act encouraged the OWIU to plant itself in the political center (although it had never leaned as stridently left as other CIO affiliates). By the time OWIU members merged in 1955 with employees in growing petrochemical plants to form the new, dominant union of the industry—the Oil, Chemical, and Atomic Workers Union (OCAW)—oil's primary labor organization functioned as a facilitator and protector of workers' interests in the capitalist order rather than as a conduit for protest against that very system. This was a common scenario for organized labor in the 1950s—massive membership, moderated political tone, and acquiescence to corporate capitalism—but it was an exaggerated one in the arena of oil.[6]

Organized labor also faced pressure from oil corporations, which responded to strike action with physical and psychological warfare. A glaring illustration of this transpired in California when, in September 1948, OWIU organizers told their union's 17,000 members to stop work at refineries and oil fields owned by several companies, including Texaco, Shell, and Union. With its current contract expired, the OWIU wanted to garner a twenty-one-cent-per-hour pay raise for its members; the oil companies offered a twelve-cent raise instead, prompting the OWIU to strike. The subsequent fight at Lyman Stewart's old company was particularly acrimonious. In mid-October, Union officials attempted to evict workers and their families from their company-owned dormitories, this after it compiled a "blacklist" of 972 employees and promised never to rehire workers who participated in strikes. Legal authorities stepped in to prevent Union from carrying out the eviction, but the political damage was done. Union employees reacted bitterly and took to the streets outside their compounds to protest, in one case holding signs that read, "America Ends Here; Beyond This Point 'The Iron

Curtain'—Union Oil Co. Controls the Public Roads, Free Speech, Free Assembly." Despite months of picketing, Union and California's other oil firms won the day. While some of the workers' basic concerns with on-site living conditions were addressed, the major item—a substantial pay raise—was not. The OWIU accepted the companies' offer of a twelve-cent bump. When all was said and done, even top officers of the CIO admitted defeat and apologized for "letting down its workers."[7]

Whereas corporate oil's victories came through force in some instances, most of them came during the late 1940s and early 1950s by way of propaganda. Even as they won victories in Congress, oil leaders were determined to maintain an upper hand by pouring finances into an incipient red-baiting media, which tarred organized labor with the damning communist label. One of its prominent voices was University of Notre Dame law professor Clarence Manion, whose writings and (as of 1954) *Manion Forum* radio commentaries were popular with school ally J. Howard Pew. As one labor newspaper reported, it was oilmen who were the "top fund contributors to Manion's anti-union lobby," with insiders such as Hugh Cullen and Walter Hallanan setting the pace. The latter distributed rallying cries to fellow oilmen on Plymouth Oil letterhead, "warning against . . . 'the plan of a merged one big union to take over the federal government and set up a dictatorship of the proletariat.'" The *National Petroleum News* echoed this sentiment and instructed oilmen to "battle socialistic control" in all branches of industry and government and "go to work *selling* our American way of doing things." A long to-do list of lobbying followed. "We must realize that an attack on the freedom of one industry or one profession is an attack on all. The battle of the doctors against socialized medicine and the power companies against government duplication of power facilities is our battle too."[8]

With the savvy and flare that Bruce Barton had imparted to them in their difficult 1920s, American oilmen also sold a gentler pro-business, antilabor doctrine designed to nudge rather than bludgeon workers into submission. They blitzed their rig and refinery floors with instructional pamphlets that taught marketplace principles. One popular booklet, titled *American Capitalism*, laid out the development of Western capitalism and refuted its Marxist critics in accessible terms. Over a dozen oil companies bought tens of thousands of copies ( Jersey

Standard purchased 20,000) to distribute to their employees. Petroleum firms, meanwhile, peppered popular magazines with "educational" ads that laid out the virtues of capitalism for the benefit of the underclass. Even as it battled employees in the trenches in 1948, Union Oil used full pages of national newsprints such as *U.S. News* to show how average laborers could invest in it and earn the types of dividends that were vaulting its roustabouts and mechanics into the middle class. The "largest individual Union Oil stockholder owns only 1% of the total stock," one announcement explained, so "profits of Union Oil . . . don't go to a few millionaires. They are split up among thousands of average American *capitalists* . . . whose combined savings have made Union Oil . . . possible." On some occasions, Union used elaborate pie charts to document the money that blue-collar folks were pocketing because of their faith in the company. Trust petrocapital, Union purred, and watch your mundane concerns melt away—and with them the need to picket.[9]

At the center of oil's marketing blitz was the purest symbol of postwar bliss: the family. Amoco (Indiana Standard) was a trendsetter in this regard. After a 1947 survey revealed how to better pique its customers' curiosity, the company began a multiyear blitz to sell itself to the public. Its tactics veered slightly away from Union's pie charts. "The key to a successful institutional ad," a spokesperson explained, is to offer "the story of free enterprise without employing the hackneyed phrases and platitudes usually associated with an argument." Show rather than tell, in other words. A favorite ploy was to profile newlyweds in brief narratives—accompanied by a picture of a smiling couple. In one such ad, titled "How to Stay Happy After Your Wedding Day," an omnipotent Standard voice predicted success for the young male breadwinner—a Standard employee—and his bride, "for they both know from experience that one of the best ways to stay happy is to be able to earn a good living at worthwhile work that is enjoyable." Without bombarding the reader with statistics, as Union was prone to do, Amoco still got the message across that its generous payroll, propped up by a free enterprise climate, was the key to the average working couple's long-term happiness. Key to their children's too. While some corporations delivered Norman Rockwell-esque photos of sleeping cherubs with accompanying messages of fear ("Will they inherit socialism?" one oil ad read), others, such as Socal, bragged of scholarships it had designed to offset college costs for those seeking "to promote American leadership in democracy." Socal wanted everyone to know it was a great "citizen of the west"; it estimated that 138 million people would stumble across that message in their newspapers over the coming year. It hoped the encounters would leave them ready to frequent its gas stations and feeling good about its efforts to inculcate America's youngest with time-honored lessons of patriotism, democracy, and civic duty.[10]

Oil marketers courted female consumers with special determination. Women were beginning to trickle into the working ranks of the petroleum and petrochemical industries at this time, and the American Petroleum Institute (API) wanted to make that fact known. Yet, in the overwhelmingly male (and masculine) domain of oil business, it was the female consumer who captured the full attention of the petroleum salesperson. Besides gracing many an ad for gasoline and plastics, white housewives were also lifted up by petroleum marketers as metaphors for all the goodness crude had wrought in society. The API helped sell that message by supplying newspapers with talking points. "Every American woman struck oil the day Col. Edwin Drake brought in the country's first petroleum well back in 1859," one duly informed pundit declared. "That's the claim of the American Petroleum Institute's Oil Industry Information Committee, which declares that discovery meant perhaps as much to women's emancipation as the 19th amendment which gave them suffrage." The liberation petroleum now effected for womanhood was spectacular, he continued. "Oil has helped give them freedom from drudgery" and "made it possible for them to be better homemakers and better citizens." From vitamin pills to floor polishes, wax paper to washing machines, sewing machines to baby strollers, oil's products were easing wives' way into modern living. And thanks to oil's moisturizing properties, it was beautifying them, too, and altering the way women gossiped about one other. "Oil has been a big factor in changing the whispered saying of grandmother's time, 'She looks old at 30,'" he joked, "to the admiring comment nowadays, 'she looks young at 40.'" Through the 1950s housewife, executives sold oil—as a component of other products, like plastic or petroleum jelly—to the masses as an indispensable commodity that could guarantee them the look of the smart consumer and make them the envy of everyone on the block.[11]

With that kind of coaxing, it is little wonder that oil laborers started to temper their politics. Never entirely, mind you. Throughout the 1950s the OWIU would continue to encourage protest action at opportune times, most notably in 1952 when it joined a coalition of oil unions to lead a nationwide refinery strike. Labor leaders chalked up a key victory that included a fifteen-cent-per-hour wage increase. In his "State of the Union" address at the twenty-second OWIU convention later that same year, OWIU's president delighted "that our Union dug deep into the profit pocketbook of the oil industry." By 1956, he would boast of doubling income among workers of the OCAW and foresee more increases to come—an annual "paid vacation of four to six weeks," "medical and hospital insurance so complete that you will never have to write a check to a doctor," and "payment of all costs for four years of college for your sons and daughters." The perks he promised were hypothetical, but his point was to underscore the benefits that both industry and labor could now expect to achieve together. API officials agreed and highlighted swift growth in industry wages and profits. Between 1946 and 1953, API statistics showed, the industry's workforce increased by 440,000 workers. Over the same stretch, despite rising living costs, wage raises had increased oil employees' buying power by 20 percent, placing them near the very top of all industry standards. By the mid-1950s, common opinion held that working in the prospering oil business was a safer, happier, more lucrative venture than ever before. Correspondingly, common—though not absolute—opinion within the labor ranks was that it was better to ride than resist oil's wave of spectacular growth. Looking back on the oil industry's labor-management arrangement, a study produced in the 1960s would conclude that due to oil companies' conscious choice "to maintain the highly acceptable economic position of its employees," no union could "be expected to gain the prominence and power enjoyed by several of the national unions in other major industries." To some, Marxists' worries that the proletariat would trade class leverage for cars and cul-de-sacs seemed to be coming true.[12]

Signs of a blue-collar desire to commune with America's rapidly expanding middle class radiated from within oil's proletariat. While the OWIU tamped down radicalism within its ranks, it also propped up the type of values that oil rags sold to workers and a wider public as essential to life in the Cold War era. The OWIU's Ladies Auxiliary worked hard on this score, rallying women behind union causes and educating them as leaders in America's emerging suburban society. "The local auxiliary is a friend of clean union halls," OWIU women pledged, as well as "of 'family night' meetings which bring union members, their wives and children together [and] makes the Oil Workers known as supporters of every wholesome civic authority." Domesticated in their community consciousness, white OWIU members also eased back into a confined racial order. Despite a burst of interracial activism within the OWIU during the 1940s, in the post-Taft-Hartley years white oil workers realigned with Jim Crow. The trade-off they made—comfort at the cost of racial equality—did not sit well with all OWIU laborers. One labor editorialist titled an article "White Union Members Must Ask Fair Deal for Negroes" and bemoaned the racial persecution black workers contended with at OWIU's plants. "The Negroes pay their dues as we pay ours, but can't enjoy the same protection, pay or benefits," he charged. But the editor could do little: as they reached their zenith of membership and influence in the 1950s, petroleum unions remained conspicuously white. Whereas black workers comprised 3 percent of the total national workforce in oil refining in 1940, by 1960 they would represent 3.1 percent, a minuscule gain. And of all oil sectors, refining was by far the most welcoming of African American labor.[13]

Resting on a platform of shared race and acquiescence to the postwar economic order, petroleum's collective sense of citizenship was also forged out of common—and outspoken—commitment to Judeo-Christianity. As they had already started doing through the Catholic Petroleum Guild, workers and labor leaders often drove the enterprise. Besides coordinating special gatherings to consecrate the oil business with prayer, they did their best to ensure that local churches, pastors, and parishioners helped make the petroleum profession the clearest symbol of faith-based Americanism. Catholic workers in New Jersey and Baptist and Pentecostal laborers in South Texas recruited their contemporaries in the pews with a zeal that blended their faith in God and oil with an undying sense of patriotic responsibility. That same outlook framed their collaboration on a global scale as well. In 1952, the OWIU for the first time participated in the Conference of the Petroleum Committee of the International Labor Organization (ILO) in The Hague. "The basic purpose of the organization," OWIU's ambassadors explained, was "to serve the cause of peace ... social justice" and guarantee "living conditions, working conditions, and wages of workers (including petroleum workers) throughout the world." The OWIU's commitment to this global body essentially tied it to an ecumenical mission of transnational, trans-sector democratic action. That spirit of solidarity intensified as Cold War tensions mounted. By 1956, the OWIU's representative to the international body was hailing it as a conduit for Christian democratic values. "Together the workers and industry can build the mold of peace," he declared to his brethren. Workers and management now owned a rare and urgent opportunity, he believed, to disseminate freedom and human rights around the world out of shared "moral obligation." Labor, too, he intimated, was eager to spread the civil religion of crude.[14]

Still, US oil's powerbrokers sold such moral imperatives to fellow Americans with the most explicit resolve. Throughout the early 1950s, oil companies proselytized faith as the bedrock of American civilization. Confronted with countervailing forces of atheism and socialism and Cold War nuclear and geopolitical tensions, Americans, they charged, needed to cling tightly to spiritual truths. Amoco drove that point home with an advertisement that drew on all of petroleum's popular tropes—family values and free market patriotism—with a child's tug at the heart. "Where are we going, Daddy?" read the words below a photo of a little boy in a tweed suit. "Where are we going this time? Could it be ... To church?" "That's the shortest *long* trip in the world," Amoco emphasized, "Perhaps only a block or two. But it can lead all the way to Peace of Mind." Peace of mind for parents who worried about their "*little fellow* ... starting to grow up without formal religious teaching ... without training in knowledge of God." And peace of mind for a society under attack. "What would the world be without God? What will our children be, without training in knowledge of God? If we let this happen, and something goes wrong, how can we ever face them in their hour of need?" Amoco's petition was simple—for mother, father, and child, hands held, to head to church. "Your greatest gift to your children is faith in God," the ad concluded. The petroleum industry, with labor and management's arms now locked in relative unity, pledged to follow the same path.[15]

ALREADY BY THE start of the Eisenhower era, the oil industry had cloaked itself in a political mainstream reinforced by demographic uniformity and consensus-building religiosity. The Eisenhower administration not only welcomed oil's intercessions along this line but also built on them as it sought to reify America's Judeo-Christian values and forge a moral alliance of monotheistic societies against the advancing threats of global rebellion.

Petroleum was hardly the only business or public voice to work overtime in the 1950s to promote an "American way" of free enterprise, class harmony, religious devotion, and civility as the path forward for the nation. "The conversation on consensus," one historian writes, "was carried on in many different registers and by many different voices" over an extended period before it reached a crescendo during the presidency of Dwight Eisenhower. Yet, once it reached that crescendo, it is fair to say that corporate and religious leaders assumed the crucial roles in this campaign. Oilers were among the most eager (and deep-pocketed) to lead the charge.[16]

Eisenhower himself placed tremendous emphasis on the aspect of faith. Famously the president-elect delivered a blazing sermon to a New York audience just before Christmas in 1952. He told a well-heeled crowd in the Waldorf-Astoria ballroom that "the great struggle of our times is one of spirit" and that "if we are to be strong we must be strong first in our spiritual convictions." Americans "have to go back to the very fundamentals of all things, and one of them is that we are a religious people." "Even those who are, in my opinion, so silly as to doubt the existence of an Almighty, are still members of a religious civilization," he added, "because the Founding Fathers said it was a religious concept that they were trying to translate into the political world." In the most memorable line of the speech, Eisenhower told his listeners, "Our form of government has no sense unless it is founded in a deeply-felt religious faith, and I don't care what it is." From the out-set of his presidency, Eisenhower would use civil religion to bind the nation together and inspire it in the battle with what he called "godless communism." His determination to consolidate Protestants, Catholics, and Jews—Judeo-Christians, as the by then popular expression went—made sense in light of demographic changes overtaking the country. During the 1950s, as many Americans bruised by war looked for quiet suburbs in which to retreat and raise families, the percentage of citizens claiming church membership surged, from 49 percent in 1940 and 57 percent in 1950 to 69 percent by decade's end.[17]

But the "tri-faith" ideal was not simply an organic extension of social change; Catholic, Protestant, and Jewish business leaders deliberately manufactured it. The fact that Eisenhower delivered his Christmas sermon of 1952 at an annual gathering of the pro-business Freedoms Foundation was no accident. In the wake of that speech, executives of several large companies, with personal networking flow-ing through Christian libertarian organizations like Reverend James Fifield's Spiritual Mobilization, urged the new US president to extend his campaign. Landmark decisions followed. In 1954, while speaking on the business-sponsored American Legion's *Back to God* radio pro-gram, Eisenhower reminded the "millions" of Americans who "speak prayers" and "sing hymns" in different theological tongues that their spirit was united—that "In God is Our Trust." A year later, he was even more upfront in reclaiming the nation's religious roots: "With-out God, there could be no American form of Government, nor an American way of life. Recognition of the Supreme Being is the first—the most basic—expression of Americanism." One year after that, the US Congress passed a joint resolution declaring "In God We Trust" the national motto of the United States. The same day (July 30, 1956) that Eisenhower signed the resolution into law, he signed another law requiring that the motto be printed on all US currency and coins. Meanwhile, Eisenhower's allies in the corporate realm encouraged him to sanction related initiatives that included creation of the annual National Prayer Breakfast, the introduction of prayer at White House cabinet meetings, and the reaffirmation of his predecessor Harry Truman's decision to designate Independence Day a national day of prayer.[18]

Oil's bosses moved through these circles of influence with ease, praying alongside the president and breaking bread with statesmen and CEOs. Yet the sheer economic and cultural power of their industry also distinguished their role in the tri-faith project. It was impossible for Eisenhower to ignore their presence. Between 1948 and 1958, American business as a whole soared, with gigantic corporations such as General Motors and US Steel recording huge profits and dividends. Of the top twenty-five companies during this time, eight were based in petroleum, and seven of those were clustered in the top sixteen (Jersey Standard, Gulf, Texaco, Socal, Socony, Amoco, and Shell). Eisenhower maintained close relationships with many of the petrocompanies' leading lights. Some, like Sid Richardson (simply "Sid" to Eisenhower), freely exchanged letters of advice with the president on church, state, and corporate matters. While Nelson Rockefeller occupied several positions in the Eisenhower administration (including that of the president's special assistant for psychological warfare), the Rockefellers as a whole had the president's car, reflecting the special power they and their corporate offspring continued to hold. And through participation in private enterprise lobbies such as the Freedoms Foundation—on whose board of directors sat Helen Pew, Howard's wife—the president's hobnobbing with America's oil giants grew all the more intentional and intense.[19]

The advertising prowess that oil companies had long demonstrated served the president's agenda too. In a 1955 piece for the *New Republic*, political scientist Robert Engler relayed a statistic harvested from the API that claimed oil companies spent $50 million a year on "nonmarketing public-relations expenditures." This was on top of other "local relations" campaigns oil firms carried out, which encouraged managers to infiltrate "youth groups, fund-raising drives, church activities, boards of education, boards of regents, library boards [and] social clubs." The statistic also did not count the millions of dollars they funneled indirectly into friendly causes. "Gulf, Standard (Indiana), Socony-Vacuum, Texas, Sun and others," Engler noted, "have contributed to such 'free enterprise' propaganda vehicles as the American Enterprise Association and the Foundation for Economic Education, with the Sun Oil Company probably the most willing to be so identified publicly." That power of persuasion now worked in Eisenhower's favor. Whether through propagation of pie chart advertisements or emotive portraits of cherubs and churchgoing parents, petroleum's ability to appeal to the core concerns of the American people was a boon for the president's goal of answering the looming enemy with marshaled faith.[20]

Other avenues of communication served this tri-faith ideal. As illustrated by the triumvirate of Jacob Blaustein, Ignatius O'Shaughnessy, and Robert Kerr, oil's religious statesmen delivered the message directly to the people. They held tightly to their theology, but in their minds the cataclysms of the Cold War required a level of cross-faith engagement. As president of the American Jewish Committee (AJC), Blaustein lectured widely on the virtues of religious freedom and belonging in the age of pluralism and menacing communist threats. "We have faith in the philosophy of American integration which, in effect, is 'unity in diversity' and calls for the attainment of a balance between becoming part and parcel of America and at the same time retaining group identity," he avowed to one assemblage. "But much as we believe in our own ideas, we do not conceive that the mantle of Moses has been placed on our shoulders—or on anyone else's." Blaustein's was the religious tenor of mutual nation building Eisenhower tapped for political gain. O'Shaughnessy spoke and acted with that same intonation. Even as he focused most of his charitable giving on Catholic causes, the petroleum magnate's desire to see people of the book united in defense of freedom culminated in several ventures in the early 1960s. One was the formation of the National Conference of Christian Employers and Managers (and its subset, the National Conference of Catholic Employers and Managers), a "continuing education institution" designed to inculcate in citizens theological, moral, and corporate principles and to complement organizations such as the AJC. Another was his pledge to University of Notre Dame president Theodore Hesburgh and Pope Paul VI to fund construction of Tantur, a Catholic-sponsored interfaith institute and research center in Jerusalem, which would come to fruition later in the decade. For this significant gesture toward the tri-faith ideal, O'Shaughnessy would eventually receive a national brotherhood award from the National Conference of Christians and Jews, to which the Catholic oilman had long donated money.[21]

As outspoken as they were, the Catholic oilman and his Jewish counterpart could not match Kerr when it came to promoting Cold

War consensus. Throughout the 1950s and early 1960s, the Baptist executive-statesman crisscrossed the United States and Canada, rallying members of oil and church communities behind the Eisenhower ideal. It did not matter whether he was speaking to Catholic, Protestant, or Jewish clerics, to members of his industry, or to fellow Democrats or Republicans—disseminating a doctrine of sacred unity remained his only priority. In one setting, the Tulsa Council of Churches, he voiced concepts seemingly lifted right out of Eisenhower's repertoire: "The United States of America with its 165 million people . . . are resolved that under God and with his divine guidance our way of life shall not be destroyed. Our freedom and liberty shall not be lost." In another setting, the API, he was unabashedly redundant in his speechmaking. "Under God, we of this generation . . . must unite as we have never united before . . . [and] bring about the full mobilization of our abundant spiritual, mental, and physical resources." "Under God," he finished with a flurry, "we must develop and maintain an undying resolve that we will prove worthy of our free way of life by sustained all-out effort and by continuing our all-out effort to do this job, no matter what it may cost." Heartfelt, Kerr's pleas to his brethren in oil and in Catholic, Protestant, and Jewish parishes were fixated on containing communism, which in his estimation represented the ultimate handiwork of Satan himself.[22]

Thanks in part to oil luminaries' heavy political lifting, the religious tripod of Eisenhower's American way seemed strong and steady by the time he began his second presidential term. Yet, all the while, he had remained concerned with a fourth leg of American political life: Islam. That apprehension had much to do with global circumstances.

Throughout his first term Eisenhower had fretted over communism's possible encroachment in the Middle East, not an unlikely scenario considering the upheaval there following the establishment of Israel, the homegrown challenge to Western economic interests, and the rise of Arab nationalist sympathies and charismatic leaders such as Egypt's General Gamal Abdel Nasser. Anxious to contain the threat, and by extension keep Arabs (especially Saudis) and their oil reserves in the fold, Eisenhower and Secretary of State John Foster Dulles started implementing several actions. The boldest transpired in Iran in 1953 and targeted popular secular nationalist Mohammad Mosaddegh.

Appointed prime minister of Iran in 1951 by Shah Mohammad Reza Pahlavi, who recognized—warily—the majority bloc that the skilled politician had built in Iran's parliament, Mosaddegh maneuvered for greater power and by early 1953 had gained it. That allowed him to press forward with his plan to nationalize the Anglo-Iranian Oil Company (APOC)—formerly Anglo-Persian and soon to be British Petroleum—and expel foreign oil personnel. By then, corporate leaders with APOC had grown exasperated in their dealings with the Persian government; since the mid-1930s they had been on the defensive, lobbying to maintain the sixty-year oil concession that William D'Arcy had secured in 1901 and doing everything in their power (they claimed) to staff APOC with Persian nationals, improve labor and living standards within the company community, and supply social services "on a colossal scale." But all for naught, it seemed. Now, challenged by Mosaddegh's government and desperate to maintain their holdings in the region, which included the sprawling refinery and company compound at Abadan—the largest in the world—British authorities called for a boycott of Iranian oil. When that did not fully succeed, they looked for a swifter end to the matter by recruiting an equally concerned Eisenhower administration and supplying the Central Intelligence Agency (CIA) with information it needed to carry out a coup. During a week in August 1953, under the direction of Allen Dulles—John's brother—the CIA orchestrated the overthrow of Mosaddegh and by extension shored up Shah Pahlavi's monarchical hold over the country.[23]

The Iranian coup would represent the Eisenhower presidency's most forceful—and politically fraught—intervention in the Middle East, but it was far from the last move. Increasingly wary of pro-nationalist leaders and movements in the region, whose anti-Western declarations only grew louder after the 1953 coup, convinced that they were proxies for communism or at the very least vulnerable to communist interests, Eisenhower and the Dulles brothers launched other initiatives to win the hearts and minds—and shadowy wars—of the Middle East. One of these included CIA-sponsored efforts to spread "black" propaganda and secure the secret trust of local leaders in a way that delegitimized revolutionary aims, a method with which war-worn William Eddy was familiar. Yet it was one of Eddy's other predilections, religious diplomacy, that caught Eisenhower and Dulles's eye. The moral alliance between

Islam and the Christian West that the Aramco booster preached to anyone who would listen now became the blueprint for American engagement with the Middle East.[24]

The course of action that Eisenhower and Dulles subsequently adopted would come naturally to the two politicians. A serious-minded Presbyterian, Dulles saw at the heart of the Cold War struggle a spiritual warfare between the godly and the godless, religion and irreligion. In his mind, individuals and institutions of faith had to take the lead in the fight. Eisenhower's convictions were tied to his membership at Washington's National Presbyterian Church, pastored by Dr. Edward L. R. Elson. Elson was Arabist to the core. Outside his primary ministry he traveled and worked extensively on behalf of the American Friends of the Middle East (AFME), which he founded, and the Foundation for Religious Action in the Social and Civil Order. Elson, like Eddy, was determined to swim upstream against the Zionist tide and ensure that Muslims were heard in proximate halls of power. Dulles and Eisenhower built on these initiatives and looked to the US government's Psychological Strategy Board (PSB) and the United States Information Agency (USIA) for help. Following Eddy's line of thinking, the PSB created a master plan for earning the United States favored status in the Middle East, one that underscored cross-cultural exchange through educational and interfaith programs. When the USIA assumed control of Voice of America (VOA), a global radio system, it immediately began broadcasting religiously themed programs into the Arab region. VOA's director ensured that they foregrounded America's "great spiritual heritage" and made "our audiences realize—that the strongest bond between freedom-loving peoples on both sides of the Iron Curtain is their *shared* faith in spiritual values."[25]

The Eisenhower White House did not stop there, however. During the middle years of the decade, as political upheaval overtook parts of the Middle East and Gamal Nasser agitated the British into a showdown over the Suez Canal, Washington accelerated its information gathering and dissemination. The USIA oversaw an aggressive campaign to publish pamphlets and booklets that portrayed communism as hostile to Islam. Titles such as "Why a Moslem Must Reject Communism" wished to elicit the right response. The USIA also set up libraries in Arab cities such as Damascus and Cairo, hoping Muslim religious leaders would study pro-American and anticommunist texts, then carry their lessons to their people. In short order, the libraries became popular destinations for imams, teachers, and students alike, with each library averaging over 250 visitors a day. Just as successful were the colloquia that brought Muslim intellectuals to the United States, where they visited the White House before convening at Princeton University. There, former American University of Beirut president Bayard Dodge guided Princeton's seminar participants into deep dialogue about faith and governance in the Cold War era.[26]

Eisenhower and Dulles believed much more still had to be done to solidify their moral alliance with Muslims, particularly at the highest levels of government. In Gamal Nasser they saw a formidable foe. Eisenhower, long fascinated with Nasser, had at one point seen him as the answer to stronger American-Arab relations in the region. But the general's radical leanings and dealings with the Soviets squelched that potential. The United States needed an alternative go-between who brandished religion as a political strength. Eisenhower and his advisors settled on Saudi Arabia's ascendant King Saud (Saud bin Abdulaziz Al Saud). While not as dynamic or beloved as either Nasser or his own father, Saud fit the bill. Wanda Jablonski, a rising force in petroleum journalism, helped nurture this belief with a series of articles in *Petroleum Week* derived from her own travels through the Middle East, in which she raved that Saud was "deeply religious—with no sham about it," displayed an "anticommunist record . . . better than even America's," and was surely ready to "prove to be the key link between the West and the highly strategic Arab world of the Middle East." For these reasons, Eisenhower told his team, "If we could build [Saud] up as the individual to capture the imagination of the Arab world, Nasser would not last long." Eisenhower and his counselors had high expectations—they wanted Saud to be the Muslim "pope," a spiritual leader who could show his followers the light of a new political age.[27]

The president and the "pope" nourished this relationship through correspondence and a sequence of diplomatic gestures. In letters written in 1956, Eisenhower voiced his optimism to Saud that the bonds between godly nations would be strong, as well as further encouragement for the Muslim leader to "exert your great influence to the end that the atheistic creed of Communism will not become entrenched at a key position in the [Muslim] world." The budding alliance received its greatest boost in 1957, when the White House and US congressional representatives welcomed the Arabian king to Washington for an official visit. The press found the nine-day spectacle impossible to ignore; Saud's coterie was, as insiders recalled, "excessively large ... with some Saudis sleeping in tents across from the White House," and the open-car caravans in which the president sat next to the king and the king's young son offered juicy photo ops. On more substantive levels, the special guests were honored at a banquet sponsored by the United Nations, at which UN General-Secretary Dag Hammarskjöld welcomed Saud as "the King who is ever-striving for peace." Saud was gracious in his remarks to the gathering and anxious to praise the United Nations for priorities of peace that it shared with his Muslim faith. "We believe in human, spiritual and moral values," Saud announced, as well as "in the right of everyone to a free and safe life, and a fruitful co-operation among mankind in their common interest." The most substantial outcome of the entire affair was the joint statement that Eisenhower and Saud released at the conclusion of the trip. Beginning with a nod to the "spiritual, geographical, and economic" importance of Saudi Arabia, it included several key points of agreement, including promises to uphold the UN Charter, the right of Middle Eastern peoples to "maintain their full independence, live in peace, and enjoy economic freedom and prosperity," and a military partnership with continued allowances for a US presence at the Dhahran Airfield in exchange for US weapons and assistance in the training of Saudi Arabian armed forces. Aramco and Eddy's vision, it seemed, had finally taken root.[28]

That vision received further sustenance in the year that followed. A few months after Saud and his entourage departed Washington, Eisenhower helped honor the city's new Islamic Center and Mosque. In stockinged feet, he and his wife, Mamie, shuffled into the mosque's prayer room, which faced Mecca, to pay respect. Then, with Arab League ambassadors looking on, he assured his Muslim allies that "America would fight with her whole strength for your right to have here your own church and worship according to your own conscience." When Western media spread reports of the president's overtures at the Islamic Center, the White House received the praise from Muslims in the Middle East that it had wished for. One imam singled out "America's deep belief in religion" as a basis for its great strength as a nation. Seeking to take advantage of that opening, Eisenhower's pastor, Edward Elson, traveled to the Middle East, officially on behalf of the AFME, unofficially as the president's conciliator. At John Foster Dulles's urging, the cleric was to carry a letter of presidential endorsement to King Saud, with whom Elson was to meet. "Aware of the common bond of faith in God which has always been important to the relationship between Saudi Arabia and the United States," it read, "we were certain Your Majesty would find it of interest to receive one so closely associated with the spiritual life of our nation." Elson's stated purpose was to discuss "the important role of religion in the life of our nation and the deep respect in the United States for those who walk parallel paths to God." Letter in hand, Elson became the first American clergyman to step foot—officially—in Saudi Arabia. His talks with Saud went well, just as they did with Jordan's King Hussein and Egypt's President Gamal Nasser. Elson was unsettled by Nasser's admission of his Soviet ties, as well as by the Egyptian secret police, which censored the sermon he was to deliver at a local church. But as the Presbyterian made his way through Lebanon, Syria, Iraq, and Iran, lands that enthralled him because of his fascination with the missionaries who had settled there a century before, he grew cautiously optimistic that America was gaining traction. He was also pleased to find that President Eisenhower was "exceedingly popular" among his hosts, "particularly for his spiritual qualities and for his statesmanship."[29]

Elson returned to Washington and delivered his report to the White House and the assistant secretary of state for Near Eastern affairs. Although he noted that underlying tensions in the region remained palpable, he voiced his pleasure that Eisenhower's doctrine was winning allegiances. Abroad as well as at home, it seemed, the Protestant-Catholic-Jewish-Muslim quadrilateral was proving a potent sword and shield against the communist beast.[30]

WHILE ELSON TRAVELED the Middle East, oil's attachés were extending their reach in new continental fields, particularly Africa. Amid the rapid wave of decolonization there, they accelerated their quest to gain soil and souls for Pax Americana before the Reds arrived. In this race against the Cold War clock, which sped up as Eisenhower's presidency gave way to John F. Kennedy's, sector divides in oil faded into shared purpose. Much like the majors and the Rockefellers—indeed, alongside them—independent oilmen assumed their own projects of global exploration and evangelism with intent to quell the Red Menace.

The Rockefellers remained at the center of the action, though their own vocational trajectories assumed new directions, with critical implications for global oil going forward. Fittingly, 1959—the centennial of the American oil enterprise—inaugurated a new era of change for oil's flagship dynasty. Much as Billy Graham had touted his New York City revival two years prior as a one-hundred-year commemoration of the Businessmen's Revival of the 1850s, petroleum insiders heralded their industry's centennial with books, memorabilia, and celebrations that once again singled out crude's role in constructing modern America— this, even as they acknowledged shifts of petroleum power to places abroad. The calendar also marked time passages of a personal sort for the Rockefeller clan. In 1959, Nelson became governor of New York State, having achieved a dominant electoral win in 1958. The move to Albany marked the culmination of his two-decade wanderings through political echelons. And within the family, it solidified his status as kingfish, one he cherished. He was the "self-acclaimed . . . leader of our generation," his brother David would gibe. John Rockefeller certainly continued to exercise influence on the Rockefeller Brothers Fund and family philanthropy, witnessed especially in the promotion of new agricultural initiatives (hybrid seed production, for instance) that would help spark the Green Revolution in Asia and Latin America. Meanwhile, David Rockefeller was working his way up the ladder at Chase National Bank, an institution long associated with the Rockefeller oil interests. He assumed its presidency in 1961, launching him into a lofty role as ambassador of global capitalism. As they contemplated their next steps in the 1960s, Nelson and his less imperious brothers focused on new horizons of personal, philanthropic, and political impact.[31]

Their contemplations assumed greater symbolic significance when, on May 11, 1960, their father passed away. He had been frail with cancer for quite some time and thus shielded by his second wife, Martha Baird (Junior's first wife, Abby, had passed away in 1948), in their Tucson, Arizona, home, where he eventually succumbed to pneumonia.

Before burying his cremated remains next to Abby's in the family cemetery, a modest-sized group of family members gathered in Riverside Church—Junior's beloved cathedral—for a memorial service. After quiet reflections, the five Rockefeller brothers exited the sanctuary and at the request of the press reassembled for a photograph. Tellingly, his biographer writes, "Nelson reflexively stepped forward to arrange the shot and to reserve the most prominent place in the lineup for himself." With Nelson in the front, the third Rockefeller generation was now fully in charge of carving out new tracks for the business and faith of the forefathers.[32]

In the coming years, that would involve a stepped-up campaign to further the domestic and global initiatives the brothers had introduced two decades earlier. They reiterated those goals in the RBF Special Studies Project, initiated in 1956 and published in 1961. Over the course of several months, the project convened business leaders, scholars, journalists, military and labor officials, and scientific experts to develop core concepts for foreign and domestic policy. On the domestic front, three panels were tasked with investigating the socioeconomic challenges to American society, educational reform, and "the power of the democratic idea" in American life. Their high-altitude takeaways meshed the Rockefellers' liberal idealism and practical outlook, a blend passed down from Frederick Gates. Community values were the touchstone: "Within . . . community there need not and should not be uniformity," the report read. "Diversity of religion, culture, philosophy, social organization, expression, and ideals is to be expected." To govern a dynamically pluralistic organism of this sort, Americans needed a reinvigorated democracy, one built on "belief that the purpose of a society is to emancipate the intelligence and protect the integrity of the individual men and women who compose it," all for the public good. The foreign policy panels offered similarly grand statements of singular purpose in a fractured world. "The American creed," they stated in support of a vigorous internationalism, "can be fulfilled only under conditions of peace and in a world so organized as to make possible free exchange, free communication, and free movement of people and goods. No one nation and no one geographic area alone is capable of preserving the basic right of man." "Freedom is part of the world," they emphasized, "or it does not have a valid existence anywhere." Soft toned in its delivery of these principles, the report was sharper edged in its support for the containment of communist ideology. While "committed to the basic idea of the consent of the governed" and willing to allow nonthreatening communist societies to function on their own accord, the report drew a clear line in the sand where Soviet communism was concerned: by nature it was imperialistic, and as such US foreign policy by nature had to head it off with equal aggression.[33]

Determined to propagate this American creed, the Rockefellers wore the Cold Warrior label proudly in the early 1960s and with their financial clout carried the fight for capitalism into new global zones. David's work became particularly crucial in this regard. The Chase CEO wanted his bank to continue its "strong tradition of civic involvement," "broaden and deepen" its involvement in the global community, and be "perceived as a modern, progressive, and open institution." With that as his primary, stated goal, he started traveling extensively to cobble beneficial relationships with economic and government officials in developing countries. One new field that held fresh interest for him and the Rockefeller strategy was Africa, a region on the cusp of becoming one of oil's next great global producers.[34]

There he found willing but vexing partners. Based on previous experience in South America, where he had been involved with his brother's International Basic Economy Corporation (IBEC), he had overseen the creation of the Chase International Investment Corporation (CIIC). Much like IBEC, CIIC looked for viable enterprises in which it could invest, with emphasis—as David put it—on projects that came with a "'know-how' partner who understood the business and the local economy." By the early 1960s, CIIC's gaze stretched to far-flung regions, including Iran, where it established a development bank. Nigeria was next. One of CIIC's initial investments was a textile mill in Lagos, purportedly the first American-based industrial project in the country. Chase's operations in Africa would encounter difficulties. Due to extant ties to colonial banking systems and, concomitantly, rising nationalist policies that worked against outsiders, the newly independent African nations were hesitant to do business with the US bank. Over time, those inhibitions softened, providing Rockefeller access to the continent's major markets, including South Africa. His experience was not uncommon for Western business interests. When he began to invest in economic development plans for African locales, he was joining a battalion of American state and corporate entities looking to plant their presence in postcolonial terrains that were now open for business but also susceptible to communist influences. Among the forerunners of capitalist warriors were oilmen in whose circles David Rockefeller felt especially free.[35]

US oil companies, government officials, and labor leaders were at this very same time beginning to cultivate Africa for economic yields. The hunt for commercial quantities of petroleum had been ongoing in Africa since the early twentieth century, but it did not start to reap favorable outcomes until the 1950s. By 1957, drilling was underway in Egypt, Gabon, Nigeria, Angola, and Saharan Algeria, with promising— if not yet impressive—returns. The activity on the continent was the talk of the industry, garnering special attention at the World Petroleum Congress held in New York in 1959, where oilmen such as J. Howard Pew learned of inviting prospects. Leaders of the International Labor Organization's petroleum branch were equally excited. In emerging African states, the ILO sensed an opportunity to inculcate in workers the "democratic way of life" that American unionists were advancing at home in partnership with their corporate peers. The organization also saw in Africa's emerging economies grounds on which to combat a common foe. "Our motives are simple enough," ILO representatives declared: first, "we are impelled by the spirit of brotherhood to assist the people of other lands to attain that way of life"; second, "[we are] keenly aware of the deadly nature of the communist threat. . . . We know the fight against totalitarian slavery is a fight to the finish. Therefore we know the security of our country is linked with the success of democracy everywhere. To that extent, it might be said that brotherhood and enlightened self-interest go hand in hand." By 1963, all key proponents of the American way were hoping to draw Africa into their fold.[36]

The surge grew thanks not just to the global banking community that Rockefeller was revving up but also to the US government and oilmen, one in particular. In 1961, President John F. Kennedy appointed Harvard professor Roy Gootenberg to expand the US Department of Commerce's international trade mission program. Gootenberg proceeded to recruit high-profile US businessmen who could promote American enterprise and products in developing nations around the world. Africa caught Gootenberg's attention in 1963. The mission there would be of key importance diplomatically because the host nations—Uganda, Kenya, Tanganyika, and Zanzibar—had just achieved independence. While assessing candidates Gootenberg was overjoyed when he read the credentials of one—a black oilman. Due to their lack of leadership in industry and the types of large-scale business ventures the United States wanted to sell to global partners, African Americans did not usually join the trade missions, Gootenberg later explained. For their part, "the Africans," he added, "wanted to see businessmen of some influence in the United States," regardless of race; yet the presence of nonwhite American delegates always greased the wheels of economic negotiation. "So Jake was a find; he'd been successful in an area where white business dominated and white business was not having anything to do with black businessmen."[37]

"Jake" was Jake Simmons Jr., the black wildcatter from Oklahoma who was one of the first on the scene at the East Texas discovery in 1930. Now a powerbroker with a national reputation, Simmons had a golden biography as far as Gootenberg was concerned. For his part, Simmons saw more opportunity. "I am going to Africa to get me an oil concession," he told his wife. His motivations were more complex than that, however. His continuing commitment to the philosophy of racial uplift through entrepreneurialism that he had inherited from his mentor, Booker T. Washington, made him sensitive to the needs of emerging societies in Africa. Washington had acted on that same commitment. In the early twentieth century, at the request of German colonial officials, he had helped transfer strategies of industrial and agricultural education from the American South to Togo. Sixty years later, his understudy looked to repeat that experiment, though with greater accent on the democratic virtues of free markets and free subjects. Simmons openly wore his wildcat faith on his sleeve. Cognizant of the momentous challenge that communism and the Cold War posed, he was willing to concede that large corporations, national governments, and the David Rockefellers of business needed to be involved in the capitalist formation of fledgling economies. Still, Simmons never let anyone forget that he was an independent at heart. When offering a brief background on US oil history to his African contacts, he would finish with a rhetorical flourish: "You know every major oilfield in America wasn't found by majors but by independents like me. Let's make a deal."[38]

Simmons also acted from an intense Christian faith. "You need God in your life to get anywhere," he liked to say, before reciting a Bible verse for backup. By the time he journeyed to East Africa in 1963, his was a familiar name to anyone who belonged to the African Methodist Episcopal Church. From the 1930s to the 1960s, he occupied the esteemed position of president of the trustee board of the historic Ward Chapel Church in Muskogee, Oklahoma, was a major contributor to the denomination's seminary, and joined other lay committee members in selecting the church's bishops. His avid faith was on regular display in his local congregation. He loved to preach. "When you looked and saw him coming up and sitting on the front seat," a fellow parishioner commented, "you knew that Jake's going to talk this morning. That Jake—he could talk. And he'd do it often." "He was very enlightened on the Bible," congregants recalled. For Simmons and his family, church life was all-consuming, requiring participation in church meetings multiple times a week and a devotional life during the remaining moments. The fervent Christian brought that same sense of commitment with him to Africa, hoping that in addition to signing on to large-scale economic plans, his hosts would recognize the blessings of personal, spiritual transformation.[39]

The Commerce Department mission benefited tremendously from Simmons's fervency. The team of seven arrived in East Africa on October 27, 1963, carrying 445 business proposals from US companies for everything from industrial and agricultural equipment to pharmaceuticals. By the end of the trip in November, 240 of the proposals would be under serious consideration. Unquantifiable, though, were the positive feelings of exchange that emerged, due largely to Simmons's presence. The heads of state with whom the Americans met were most eager to hear from him. In Dar es Salaam, capital of Tanganyika, government officials asked Simmons to address a special assembly on the status of blacks in American society. For the moment, Simmons suspended his own criticisms of US race relations to offer a glowing account of the "opportunities capitalist America offered its citizens, both black and white." It was a speech right out of Booker T. Washington's repertoire, and it garnered instant praise. The Voice of America featured it in a broadcast to the entire continent. The broadcast led with a biographical tease: "An American Negro businessman has told an African audience that Americans of African descent have had conspicuous success in American economic life." Consider the man in the spotlight: "Mr. Simmons's business is mostly with white American customers, and he cited this to show that Negroes are in business in America not only to serve their own people ... but to compete for business in all sectors of American life." Gootenberg was thrilled: Simmons's role in the tour, he observed, guaranteed "real public-relations impact."[40]

Simmons was not done doing business, however. When the assassination of President Kennedy cut the East Africa mission short, he decided to stay on the continent to see if he could harvest his own economic gains. In the 1950s, while operating his own firm, Simmons had developed a reputation for chasing oil leads into uncultivated territories, then brokering deals with major oil companies, whose financial wherewithal he lacked. One such deal involved Liberia and Phillips Petroleum, the rising Oklahoma major. Due to Robert Kerr's unwillingness to endorse Simmons's plan to explore the West African country (Phillips insisted that Kerr-McGee oversee drilling), the deal fell through. In 1963, Simmons tried again, this time in Nigeria, to which he journeyed after wrapping up the US trade mission. Through persuasion, he secured a meeting with Nigeria's minister of mines and power. The minister immediately took to the oil hunter. "I didn't know an African-American was in the petroleum business," the official confided. "You are most welcome to my country, my brother." Simmons proceeded to ask about oil concessions, claiming (falsely) he had Phillips's guaranteed backing. Roy Gootenberg later remarked that the bluff, typical of his associate, was brilliant. "Here was a swashbuckling independent black oil operator who writ large by becoming a member of an official U.S. mission, then going to Nigeria with his credentials and getting in on the ground floor of an exploration franchise [by] representing an oil company that had not had him on their rolls at all."[41]

Simmons's maneuver worked. Nigeria was coming alive with oil exploration at the time, much of it generated by non-American companies such as British Petroleum, Shell, and Italy's Azienda Generale

Italiana Petroli. But the lack of production frustrated Nigerian officials. It was at that precise time that Simmons made his pitch to the country's mineral minister and won a provisional oil concession, which he offered as bait to Phillips. Seeing Nigeria as the place where it could become a full-fledged global operator, the Oklahoma company jumped at the chance. With Phillips now behind him, Simmons returned to Nigeria in 1964, then again in 1965, and secured a license that awarded Phillips access to 1.3 million acres of drillable land. He also negotiated for other concessions, including an 897,000-acre plot on the Niger Delta. From there he moved into Ghana to gain more ground. "Most of these new African states were secretly hoping that they would have oil struck on their territory," Simmons's colleagues noted, "but they were holding back because they felt the big oil magnates of the world would just use up their oil and they wouldn't get very much out of it. Simmons gave them a bit of relaxation, knowing he was a black fellow who knew something about oil. They listened to him." Much as he had done in Texas decades earlier, Simmons sympathized with the outsiders, whom he considered his people, and worked hard to ensure better ends for them—and himself. By 1965, with oil booming in Nigeria, he was richer than ever. "Jake made more money than anybody who ever went on a trade mission," a Washington insider would later quip.[42]

Thanks in part to Simmons, Africa as a whole was now on the petroleum grid, adding further evidence that its future rested beyond US shores. That truth dawned with blunt force as fields well north of Nigeria, in Libya, began to erupt. Evidence of significant oil surfaced there in 1959, but the country would become known as the "jackpot" of African oil in the early 1960s, with the independent Occidental Petroleum Company and its impresario, Armand Hammer, leading the way. By 1965, Occidental would stand as the world's sixth-largest petroleum exporter, producing 10 percent of all oil exports. By decade's end it would, for a time, outpace Saudi Arabia. If Libya and Nigeria reinforced the ways in which oil's map was changing, they also indicated the new role that risk-taking independents like Hammer and Simmons were assuming in the petro-order. Faced with exceedingly challenging—indeed, dangerous—political conditions in untested lands, the petroleum industry's risk-averse major companies needed their cousins to accept the burden. Independents gladly picked up that gauntlet and, as one industry rag proudly announced, began to "encompass the globe." Who better to serve as the tip of capitalism's spear and fight communism along the way than its warrior class?[43]

THOSE WARRIORS JOINED big oil's generals to fight in South America, petroleum's most vulnerable production zone. That continent had already yielded two generations of exploration and production. Yet, as the Cold War heated up in the late Eisenhower and Kennedy presidencies, its significance grew exponentially, to oilers for what its vast hinterlands might still reveal and to proponents of Pax Americana as a sensitive region of democratic-communist competition. While the Rockefellers continued their labor in ways familiar to them, small oil producers pressed to make the oil patches of Venezuela, Ecuador, and Peru their test cases for free market democracy.

David Rockefeller and his brothers continued their instrumental role in shaping these Latin American landscapes. Nelson's corporate and political work in Venezuela and Brazil had started years before, laying the groundwork for the family's increased influence in Latin America during the height of the Cold War, much of it wielded quietly, even secretively, in boardrooms and government offices. David's own exposure to South America had come in the early 1950s, when he was placed in charge of Chase's Latin American activities. His first trip through the region was, in his words, "a watershed event in my life. I saw that banking could be a truly creative enterprise . . . and that Latin America was a place where economic development might take hold with spectacular results." Along with Nelson, David readily bore the unofficial label of missionary capitalist to the Americas' Southern Hemisphere. Under his watch, Chase built its portfolio in Brazil through Inter-American Finance and Investments, an entity it created. By 1962 the bank's leverage in the country was enhanced by way of US government sanction. At President Kennedy's command, David created the Business Group for Latin America, charged with propping up capitalist interests and countering the rise of left-wing politicians, an accented fear in the wake of the Cuban Revolution of 1959. The Business Group eventually morphed into the Council for Latin America (CLA), which would uphold the original commission to disseminate free enterprise discourse throughout Latin America. David also signed on to Kennedy's Alliance for Progress, an initiative that echoed Nelson Rockefeller's mid-century "Good Neighbor Policy" in its explicitly stated attempt to "enlist the full energies of the peoples and governments of the American republics in a great cooperative effort to accelerate the economic and social development of the participating countries." While David disagreed with Kennedy's emphasis on "state-directed economic development" programs, preferring the effort be directed through "private enterprise and investment," he was fully committed to the larger goal of nurturing markets as a strategy for hemispheric growth and security. When Kennedy died in late 1963, so did the alliance, but Rockefeller's Business Group, then the CLA, continued to advance its very same aims.[44]

Through banking and boosterism, the Rockefeller reach stretched ever deeper into South America's emerging cities and resource-rich hinterlands. By 1965, Chase was financially—and politically—active elsewhere, including in Honduras, Argentina, Colombia, and Peru. As historians have scrutinized at length, Nelson and David's heavy involvement with Latin American businessmen and statesmen placed them in the middle of covert operations that the United States carried out to undermine left-wing political candidates in nations where—as in the case of Brazil—strong nationalist and anticapitalist sympathies were brewing. On a number of occasions in Brazil, the strategy produced results. CIA operatives and Rockefeller partners in Brazil's business echelon played a surreptitious role in defeating left-wing candidates in Brazil's 1962 congressional elections, then had a direct hand in the military-led coup of 1964 that ousted the country's nationalist president, João Goulart. In the messy realm of anticommunist crusading, US government officials and their corporate allies, including the Rockefellers, felt that no means was too heavy-handed when trying to ensure the future of democratic capitalism.[45]

Rockefeller oil interests also acted on that philosophy in the South American interior. Even as Jersey Standard lost ground in Venezuela and Brazil to emerging nationalist oil corporations, the flag bearer of Rockefeller influence pressed forward in exploration, production, and marketing in less-well-trodden terrains. In a 1964 issue of Jersey Standard's *The Lamp* readers learned of its progress in Paraguay via a story that melded faith and petrofueled development in the type of parable readers had come to expect from the company rag. The photo-laden piece transported the reader into the boundary land of Chaco, Paraguay, close to the Bolivian border, where Mennonites—who arrived from Canada in the 1920s—lived in isolation. They in fact cherished their autonomy on religious grounds, but life on the boundaries was growing increasingly difficult for their farming economy and the education of their young. For the good of the colony (comprising 117 little villages) and the development of the country's economy, readers learned, the Paraguay government, backed by loans from the United States and Jersey Standard, built the Trans-Chaco Highway. When it opened in 1962, the region was transformed. A visitor observed that the road was "making economic life better, it has brought optimism to the colonies." "It must be optimism that now motivates increasing numbers of Mennonite youngsters to seek higher education in Asuncion," *The Lamp* surmised, and "that this year led the Mennonites to send representatives to Europe to seek new markets. Isolation in the Chaco is ended. . . . New businesses are starting—there is now an Esso [Jersey Standard] station there." Such was the scenario that David and Nelson Rockefeller dreamed of for an entire continent.[46]

The Rockefellers' wildcat counterparts had similar dreams. By the late 1950s and early 1960s, the culture industry that evangelicals and independent oilmen co-created was making its presence felt on foreign fields, including some of the remotest, where Standard geologists had trudged in the 1920s. Considered to be beyond their reach prior to World War II, the jungles, river basins, and plateaus of Amazonia now opened up to them, in no small part because missionaries inspired by Billy Graham were doing the groundwork. With a singular purpose to produce yields quickly, oilers and evangelizers worked in tandem to make their labor count in cosmic terms. Although they detested the Rockefellers' religion and politics back home, in these highly coveted and contested foreign terrains the enemy became the ally.

At one level, the Cold War partnerships between missionaries and oilmen marked a continuation of patterns witnessed earlier in the century when the two groups exchanged invaluable support in places as far-flung as Persia and Bahrain. That type of reciprocity mattered all the more in Cold War South America, where oil companies such as Sun were restarting their operations, yet still faced stiff odds because of difficult topographies. Although initial surveys of Amazonia had not produced a windfall for Jersey Standard, by the mid-twentieth century large companies such as Shell and Gulf had penetrated the area and achieved some success. Other firms like Sun followed, eager to examine the soil under the forested canopies of Venezuela, Ecuador, and Peru. Besides facing the thickest, most inhospitable jungles, their oil hunters had to confront the fearless tribes that inhabited them. As journalist Wanda Jablonski recounted in 1958, in Venezuela Shell oil crews were forced to "dodge arrows" while they drilled and deal with death at the end of a spear. Craving any knowledge of the country's remotest parts, for their very safety as much as their financial gain, Shell's men begged for insight into how to manage the unfamiliar. They often received it from missionaries already in the area. Among the most "hostile Indians in the world," Jablonski offered as an example when surveying the South American landscape, were the "Aucas" (officially the Waorani tribe) located to the southwest of Venezuela and in Amazonian Ecuador, whose only contact came through missionaries. Shell oilmen solicited and welcomed the proselytizers' ground-level intelligence. In return, the petrofirm offered them supplies and even shelter, illustrating the quid pro quo value of such exchange.[47]

Several US missionaries working with conservative agencies like Cameron Townsend's Wycliffe Bible Translators, its two affiliates—the Summer Institute of Linguistics (SIL) and the newer Jungle Aviation and Radio Service (JAARS)—and small organizations like the Missionary Aviation Fellowship (MAF) gladly welcomed corporate oil's help in their effort to evangelize the Amazon Basin. Townsend, the unquestioned leader of this entire endeavor, was absolutely determined to blanket every corner of South America with his salvation message.

As he had already demonstrated while helping President Lázaro Cárdenas battle major US oil companies in the 1930s, Townsend took an eccentric approach to his work, at least from an American evangelical standpoint. While he pleased conservative supporters with his emphasis on biblical teaching, he also embraced aspects of the Rockefellers' developmentalist gospel. Townsend was inspired by the anthropological work of several Rockefeller-funded scholars. The spectrum of agencies that supported his own work—Jersey Standard, the Pew Family and Charitable Trust, and the US Agency for International Development—further demonstrated his openness to a blend of idealism and pragmatism not dissimilar from the Rockefellers'. Some naysayers questioned his willingness to allow JAARS's airplanes to convey Catholic nuns and priests to their own bases in central South America. Others criticized his willingness to align SIL with the United Nations Educational, Scientific, and Cultural Organization (UNESCO) in cooperative literacy programs. To the first accusation, Townsend responded, "After working for thirty-five years in Latin America I've never known of a priest or nun being converted through a 'chip-on-the-shoulder' attitude toward them. I've known several who have been won through kindness." Besides, he added, even if the Catholic hierarchy hated his work, at the grassroots level he and his Catholic brethren were essentially working toward the same goal of winning indigenous people over to spiritual freedom. To the second he responded, "We would never get ourselves in a position with anybody that would weaken our testimony. However, this doesn't mean we should not accept opportunities to reach indigenous peoples with the Word just because it's an agency of UNESCO that opens the door." That same pragmatism placed Townsend in other in-between stands—generated, for instance, by his pilots' transportation of nonreligious emissaries to outposts of importance, his missionaries' collaboration with state and corporate interests, and his willingness to mediate between US and South American governments. In that milieu of murky associations, Townsend's labor once again connected him with oil.[48]

On one hand, Townsend's organization provided inspiration and the means for missionaries to connect their labor—wittingly or not—with the advance of petroleum. By Wycliffe's twenty-fifth anniversary in 1959, Townsend's enterprise was mammoth. He had a lot of support to offer. In 1960, he reported that 200 new recruits would be joining the Wycliffe organization that year, before underscoring his goal of 6,000 total members within twenty years. He also highlighted a growing JAARS fleet that now included twenty-six planes, responsible for flying up to 2 million people a year into the heart of South America, as well as to the Philippines and Papua New Guinea. Joining his ranks and those of affiliated missionary agencies such as MAF were young men and women who eagerly followed Townsend into South America's remote areas. Graduates of evangelical schools such as Wheaton College and Prairie Bible Institute in Alberta, they wanted to win the Cold War with communism and unbelief. So they made their way into the unknown center of the continent to witness their faith. One of the first leaders in their ranks was Jim Elliot, who set off for Ecuador to evangelize the Waorani with one simple purpose in mind. "Our orders are: The Gospel to every creature." Elliot, a Wheaton graduate, along with his wife, Elisabeth, fresh out of Prairie, were joined by four other couples equally committed to that charge. In their efforts to carry out "Operation Auca," they relied on the airstrips and flight plans that Shell workers had carved out during their exploration a few years prior. They also drew on Shell's surveys documenting previous contact zones and, most importantly, used Shell's old camps as bases from which they could reach tribal villages. The murder in 1956 of Elliot and his four male colleagues by Waorani warriors stunned Americans and made the "Auca Five" instant martyrs. It also reaffirmed evangelicals' resolve, shared with their allies in oil, to draw the world's "lost" peoples and their hidden riches into God's master plan.[49]

The most illustrative example of Townsend's aid in melding the interests of faith and oil involved his provision of petrodiplomacy for inquiring states. In answer to the government of Peru's inquiries, he recruited a man who could help open up the country's interior, someone whose ties to petroleum came through its service sector. R. G. LeTourneau already seemed to know everyone in oil and evangelicalism. He had achieved his success in the 1930s while turning his heavy machinery manufacturing company, R. G. LeTourneau, Inc., into one of the nation's largest. His expansive philanthropic work benefited a host of prominent evangelicals, Billy Graham, Charles Fuller, and Ernest Manning included. Meanwhile, he joined J. Howard Pew in speaking on behalf of the National Association of Manufacturers and free enterprise (and against the New Deal). Via the Christian Business Men's Committee International he championed bootstrap initiative in the boardroom as well as the church pew. Inside his factory, he trained workers in a mechanical gospel. There, through lectures, chaplain services, and company publications, they learned how scripture was technologically sound—how the laws of traction and torque applied to evangelism and how grades of steel illustrated stages of Christian growth. Like Pew, LeTourneau gained economic clout in the 1940s. During World War II his factories in Illinois, Georgia, and Mississippi buzzed with activity, with a focus on earthmoving machinery. LeTourneau products carried men ashore at Normandy and carved roads out of jungles in the South Pacific and deserts in North Africa. At war's end 70 percent of all such equipment used by the Allies had been built in his plants. Already producing land-moving machines for resource extraction, in the late 1940s he expanded his influence by building offshore platforms that could offer any oil company access to the sea. His first platform, the industry's first mobile unit of its kind, was commissioned for George H. W. Bush's Zapata Off-Shore Company. LeTourneau unveiled the 4,000-ton apparatus in 1954. A few months later, at a ribbon-cutting ceremony attended by Bush and a young George W. Bush, he handed over control of it for service in the Gulf of Mexico.[50]

LeTourneau's second launch to influence in oildom came when he relocated his operation to Longview, Texas. Coaxed by local anti-Standard journalist and wildcat booster Carl Estes to come to East Texas, LeTourneau soon found that his new plant allowed him proximity to the area's flourishing oil companies and to the expanding international market they sought to capture. Workers in his 88,000-square-foot mill produced twenty-five tons of molten steel every three hours and then transported it to the factory, where behemoth machines were built for use in the world's mines and oil fields. For LeTourneau the massive enterprise promised a massive religious payoff as well as a financial one. As he told an audience at a world trade conference, the machines he exported promised a new order. "God gave us the raw materials to work with for nothing, and there is plenty to be had if we go to work and produce the things we want." In building machines that could exploit nature's reserves, LeTourneau believed he was acting out God's will for humans to harvest the earth. Conversant with Ernest Manning in end-times belief, he was certain that the harvesting needed to be expeditious because Christ would surely return soon.[51]

In South America he displayed the same willingness as his brethren to fuse a crusade for lost souls with a campaign for minerals. His key venture transpired in northeastern Peru. Cameron Townsend brokered it. The two men knew each other well. In addition to running a massive business, LeTourneau also founded a technical institute in Longview, which trained Christian students to be pilots and engineers; many of them ended up working in Townsend's sprawling missionary operation. But Townsend had become especially enamored of a side project that LeTourneau had been carrying out in Liberia, which involved the construction of a self-sustained colony of missionaries and native Liberians, meant to demonstrate the vibrancy of modern capitalism. While LeTourneau's equipment carved out living and farming space for the community, it also lent help to a Liberian government that wanted to build roads and infrastructure. Townsend believed this same type of "third-world" development project could assist the cause of Christian democratic freedom in Peru. "We still have to carry Christ to the jungle Indians, but we have another job too," he wrote LeTourneau. "The eastern foothills of the Andes Mountains are being colonized by several hundred Peruvians," he continued, "but they need help. They need your machines and your program. Mr. LeTourneau, it will take them 50 years with hoes and axes to do what you can do for them in a year." Townsend in essence wanted LeTourneau to do in eastern Peru what government and business were doing for Mennonites in western Paraguay. And once again, oil was at the center of it all.[52]

In the late 1950s, Townsend helped finalize a deal between LeTourneau, Peruvian president Manuel Odria, and Peruvian oilmen, whereby the American engineer would complete thirty-one miles of the Trans-Andean Highway, linking the Amazon's hinterland with the Pacific and opening lines of commercial transportation. For Odria, the plan promised to prepare the hinterland for Mobil (formerly Socony) and Gulf's Peruvian subsidiaries, guaranteeing—he hoped—a new line of assets for the nation. The major oil executives believed they would find the liquid resource that could offer Peru—and their companies—that kind of profit. LeTourneau, meanwhile, earned his own significant prize: a million acres of uncultivated land on the Pachitea River, near the town of Pucallpa. Land secured, the engineer-evangelist began transporting his heavy equipment from the United States, a tedious process requiring a 4,500-mile trip from Mississippi through the Gulf of Mexico and up the Amazon River. Once there, the Christian engineer's machines leveled dense foliage and flattened land for farming and a community, which he named Tournavista. As with his Liberian enterprise, but on a grander scale, he determined to build a community of natives and missionaries that could implement his plan for a Christian economy that could serve as a blueprint for "third-world" societies and a buttress against encroaching communism. It was time for "technical missionaries" to excel, LeTourneau proclaimed. "Machinery in the hands of Christ-loving, twice-born men can help [Peruvians] to listen to the story of Jesus and His love." He promised that profound transformation would follow. "We can't feed the world, but our machinery in the hands of consecrated Christians can open the door to let us in and open . . . the hearts to let the Lord come in, and then the initiative which they lack will come, and that, plus the teaching in the use of machinery will enable them to feed themselves."[53]

By the time Chaco's commune of Mennonites welcomed completion of its road in 1962, Tournavista's residents—now numbering roughly 15 North American families and 125 Peruvian families—were already benefitting from theirs, which transported their treasures to and from the thriving compound but gave petroleum vehicles the right of way.[54]

IN ITS TRIANGULATION of religious, economic, and political interests, Tournavista accentuated in one small space the breadth of Cold War America's fight with communism in the world's toughest trenches. For US petroleum's allies in Washington and on Wall Street, that fight necessitated an all-out assault on even the slightest hint of collectivist, anticapitalist ideology, be it in the isolated interiors of South America or the Niger Delta, American suburbia or the refineries and union shops of California and the Southwest. Under the canopy of the Eisenhower consensus, church- and corporate-sponsored attempts to shore up the American way created a unity of belonging and purpose, casting a gloss over the nation's drive to capture the globe.

As Eisenhower's presidency ended and Kennedy's came to a tragic demise, the gloss quickly wore off. Petrofueled consensus gave way to petrofueled contentiousness, not an uncommon pattern in American life but a pronounced one nevertheless as the nation entered the tumult of the mid-1960s. The power shifts that began to play out would indeed be jarring and permanent, particularly for the Rockefellers' civil religion of crude. On foreign terrains, that gospel was about to be hit hard by the realities of ancient religious divisions. As Edward Elson continued to return to the Middle East to monitor its politics and its opinions of the United States, his optimism about a moral alliance between the United States and Arab societies began to fade. Perhaps, he worried, shared monotheism and modern aspirations were no match for eons-old sectarianism and deep-seated attitudes of difference. Growing more disillusioned as he aged, William Eddy shared that doubt. With oil assuming even greater import in the geopolitics of the region, he watched as Arab and Israeli, Jew and Muslim engaged in a bitter phase of warfare, bringing to a close the short-lived fantasy that Eisenhower had crafted with Jewish and Muslim leaders.

The consensus of a Judeo-Christian-Muslim nation was also suscep-tible to political violence in the domestic sphere. Eisenhower himself recognized that fact, though not necessarily with sufficient foresight. Whereas in public he welcomed wildcatters into his political fold, behind closed doors he increasingly railed against what he considered their extremist political and religious views. Throughout his presidency his centrism showed itself in an insistence that the welfare state and New Deal order be propped up to a modest degree. "Should any polit-ical party attempt to abolish social security, unemployment insurance, and eliminate labor laws and farm programs," he told his brother, "you would not hear of that party again in our political history." "There is a tiny splinter group," he continued, "that believes you can do these things. Among them are H.L. Hunt . . . a few other Texas oil million-aires, and an occasional politician or business man from other areas. Their number is negligible and they are stupid." Feeling betrayed by Eisenhower Republicans, the "stupid" wildcatters from the Southwest would once again mount an aggressive response, this time with intent to take over the GOP. Nelson Rockefeller and his ecumenical politics and faith would feel the first—but by no means last—serious blow.[55]

The wildcatters' response to the Rockefellers and global disruptions in petroleum would transpire in the economics of oil as well. In the 1950s, a Canadian geologist declared it time to develop another car-bon source: the 54,000 acres of oleaginous muskeg that circled Fort McMurray, north of Edmonton. Wanting to extend Alberta's profile on an international stage as the alternative to Saudi crude, yet wary of spending the exorbitant funds needed to extract oil from the Athabasca tar sands, Premier Ernest Manning solicited the corporate sphere. No company accepted his invitation, until Sun Oil appeared. Pew had always been fascinated with the Athabasca region. He kept a thick file marked "Athabasca Tar Sands" in his Philadelphia office and showed it to anyone who would oblige him. At Manning's invitation, he took the biggest gamble in company history and, in 1952, committed $250 million to the creation of Great Canadian Oil Sands, Inc. It was the largest single private investment ever made in Canada. By the early 1960s, Pew and Manning were nursing this investment together, contemplating the enterprise's next steps, and dreaming of how, as business partners and brothers in Christ, they could, through their operation, redefine their church and corporate domains. Soon R. G. LeTourneau's earth-moving machinery, having already leveled South American jungles, would be working Alberta's bog and tarry soil in search of its hidden wealth.[56]

*part four*

# CRUDE RECKONINGS

An abandoned gas station serves as a religious billboard, 1974.

# CHAPTER TEN

# Power Shifts

O n an eventful day in western Canada, in 1964, fifty finely dressed city types, belying the primordial muskeg and boreal forest encircling them, inaugurated an ultramodern enterprise. The spot rested on land butting up against the once sleepy fur-trapping town of Fort McMurray, Alberta, three hundred miles north of Edmonton. The buzz began in the morning, as the touring group of politicians, executives, pastors, and media arrived. Exiting an airplane, Alberta premier Ernest Manning and Sun Oil senior vice president Clarence H. Thayer caught the eye of photographers, as did fedora-wearing J. Howard Pew. Official proceedings opened with a luncheon at which the esteemed guests spoke. Pew, Thayer, and Stephen Bechtel, lead engineer, grandly predicted what was about to arise out of the bog. Bechtel announced that the project "rank[ed] high among the great industrial breakthroughs of the century."

Following lunch, the guests surveyed the small industrial compound, still in its earliest stage of development. Pew took stock of the towering conveyor belts, then paced the ground floor, where synthetic oil would be created out of sand. Followed by television network crews, the parade through the plant paused long enough for a playful—and meaningful—stunt. In front of cameras, a Sun Oil official poured a "pilot sample" of the plant's crude into an outfitted Land Rover. Alberta mines minister A. Russell Patrick then made history "by driving the first vehicle ever fueled by Sunoco gasoline refined from the Athabasca sands."

The opening ceremony itself assumed an air of religiosity. One of two Fort McMurray pastors present (the other also served as president of the chamber of commerce) led the assemblage in prayer, urging the luminaries to appreciate the weight of their handiwork, then bestowed "God's blessing" on the project. At the culminating moment of the entire event, Ernest Manning stepped to the fore and "praised the project as the finest example of free enterprise from which Alberta and the entire Dominion would profit." Then he drove a commemorative stake into the ground, soldered to which was a plaque declaring July 2, 1964, the official start of the "Athabasca Oil Sands Processing Plant of Great Canadian Oil Sands, Ltd."[1]

With his hammer and plaque, Manning signaled to the oil industry that Alberta was committed to innovating continental petroleum sources as a way to offset major oil's dependencies on foreign fields, guaranteeing security for North Americans in an untidy world. The presence of Manning, a devout evangelical living in expectancy of Christ's return, in Fort McMurray reaffirmed his dedication to the transnational network of believers that he had begun cultivating in the 1940s. The Great Canadian Oil Sands (GCOS) project would come to fruition through the soft diplomacy of "new evangelical" movers and shakers, including J. Howard Pew and Billy Graham.

Manning's posture on northern Alberta's peaty soil marked a power shift in the political, as well as the fiscal, ambitions of the wildcat faith. One month after the Alberta venture kicked off, Manning's American peers monitored the Republican National Convention in San Francisco. There, on successive evenings, a battle that had been brewing inside the GOP erupted on the stage and floor of the arena. When Barry Goldwater vanquished Nelson Rockefeller for leadership of the party in 1964, the wildcat wing served notice that its brand of religiosity and politics was ascendant. For independent producer J. Howard Pew, the coordinated attack on Rockefeller's "silk-stocking" wing of the GOP was animated not only by long-standing ideological differences within petroleum but also a basic desire: to get back at a family that had almost destroyed his father, Joseph Newton Pew, whose nineteenth-century oil and gas company foundered in the face of the Standard monopoly. Pew's allies did not earn the full victory they desired, as Goldwater's electoral defeat that November left right-wing Republicans demoralized and Rockefeller liberals convinced that their ecumenical vision would still carry the day. The subsequent guber- natorial rise of Ronald Reagan, whose "kitchen cabinet" came stocked with western oilmen, coupled with the comeback of Richard Nixon, tore that liberal poise apart.

Damaged by domestic politics, the Rockefeller wing was to suffer other setbacks on an international scale, particularly in the Middle East, where, unlike in Latin America and Africa, ideological boundaries were far more blurred. By the late 1960s, with US–Middle Eastern rapport in tatters, gone would be faith among William Eddy's allies that with Washington's support the Arab cause would trump Israel's. Israelis, meanwhile, would continue to consider oil the coin of the realm, an elusive national lifeblood with limited traces in the Holy Land, whose acquisition might require war. When war came in the late 1960s, it was intense and scarring and drew to a decisive end the fragile Protestant- Catholic-Jewish-Muslim consensus. It also pushed the Rockefellers' civil religion of crude to the brink of collapse.

THE 1964 GROUND-BREAKING ceremony in Fort McMurray occurred amid a decade-long period of negotiations that drew Ernest Manning and J. Howard Pew together in the construction of an engineering mar- vel. The Kerr-McGee firm had broken technological barriers in 1947 with the implementation of offshore drilling in the Gulf of Mexico. Now, proponents of Alberta's oil industry, which had come alive with the Leduc discovery that same year, sought innovation with similar impact. Their quest for the cutting edge would likewise be aided by the old-time faith.

Fascination with the muskeg that encircled Fort McMurray was hardly new. Indigenous peoples and fur trappers passing through the Athabasca region had always seen its bituminous sands as use- ful—for waterproofing canoes as well as for religious ceremony. Karl Clark, a metallurgist at the University of Alberta, had taken the lead in researching the sands for their commercial viability. In the 1920s he invented a separation process that boiled oil out of the soil and prepared the resulting tar for wider use as fuel. Eventually Clark, with help from the Research Council of Alberta, found an American investor. The alliance led to the construction in 1935 of a plant, under control of the newly formed Abasand Oils, Ltd., on the Horse River near Fort McMurray.[2]

Despite strong support from federal and provincial officials, the next ten years spawned one challenge after another. During the early 1940s, Clarence Howe, Canadian minister of munitions and supply, was anxious to mobilize the nation for war. On that front, he oversaw the creation of almost thirty state-owned enterprises, known as Crown corporations, in the manufacturing sectors. Oil, though, remained a vexing need. After its initial burst of activity in Ontario during the late nineteenth century, the Canadian oil industry had barely progressed, with occasional discoveries in the West spurring short-lived hope. And as of 1941, Abasand was falling far short of producing the fuel Howe wanted. Despite continued government subsidization, it could not process the abrasive deposits fast enough. Then, in November 1941, its plant burned to the ground, adding further woe. Ottawa assumed control of the replacement structure, but frustration mounted. Howe faced criticism from Alberta's members of Parliament, who demanded he commit more finances. One asked damningly, "If one Adolf Hitler had control of the Athabaska [sic] tar sands, does anyone believe for a split second that he would be worrying about the cost?" Howe's defense of the stalled Abasand project grew halfhearted.

For the impatient Manning, the oil sands represented more than a solution to a short-term wartime need—they were a means for his province to transition out of agrarian life. Once the war was over, political dynamics changed in his favor. Unsatisfied with its incursion into the business, the federal government stepped back and let the oil sector proceed without heavy oversight. Ottawa's hands-off approach allowed Manning to recruit oil companies to kick-start his province's conventional oil exploration, which resulted in Jersey Standard subsidiary Imperial Oil's discovery of the Leduc field. Yet, even as conventional oil came online, Manning remained eager to redevelop the oil sands; the potential windfall was too great to ignore. He was not alone in stating that desire. After further perfecting his technology, in the early 1950s

Karl Clark announced that the time had come for the province to move. Minister of Mines Nathan Tanner echoed his words, waxing eloquent at the province's first oil sands conference in 1951 about how the oil sands would offer North Americans continental security and ensure a "Christian way of life." "Communism and dictatorship have been able to take over in countries only to the extent that people refused to accept and apply the teachings of God in their lives ... and failed to take an active interest in public welfare," he explained. "We must realize that the service we give is the rent we pay for the privilege of living in this old world, and the higher rent we pay, the better place we shall have to live in." Tanner's was a twofold pledge that the Alberta government would do all it could to bring this godly endeavor to fruition and would carry out the task in a morally responsible manner, something the federal government had failed to do.[3]

Manning initially struggled to attract an investor in the risky Athabasca enterprise, but one entity finally answered the call. Unsurprisingly, as the province was already a haven for independent producers, J. Howard Pew appeared, checkbook in hand. Under the guidance of Sun vice president and future GCOS president Clarence Thayer, Pew's company had already begun sending geologists into the Athabasca area. Besides demonstrating a command of oil frontiers, Thayer had helped commercialize the Houdry catalytic cracking process, which placed Sun at the forefront of oil refining in the 1930s, so his high opinion of Alberta prospects was respected. Impelled by Thayer and his own obsession with the oil sands, in 1952 Pew committed a quarter of a billion dollars to the creation of Great Canadian Oil Sands. As a Sun insider noted, this "was a daring venture" that "jolted Wall Street's appraisal of Sun Oil as a conservative company." Pew and Manning would manage this investment together over the coming years, as business partners and fellow believers.[4]

Several factors forced GCOS into a spell of stagnation, however. For one thing, Alberta's conventional oil producers were dead-set against it, convinced it would reduce their profits. Politicians harbored doubts as well. What was the benefit of introducing another oil source into a saturated market? With the exception of a few months in 1956, when the Suez Canal crisis reduced the flow of world oil and created new demand for Alberta crude, the product lacked sufficient outlets. And despite Clark's efforts to lower the overhead, the cost of processing oil sands remained prohibitive. As the decade drew to a close, GCOS finally received a few positive jolts. In 1958, a geologist with California-based Richfield Oil Corporation submitted a proposal for "Project Cauldron." "The major production problem," he wrote with regard to GCOS, "is the natural viscosity of the oil which is hundreds of times greater than that of most other oils." So why not use the "heat and shock energy released by an underground nuclear explosion," he asked, to raise temperatures and reduce viscosity, then use "conventional oil-field methods" to capture the liquefied source? The scientist thought a nine-kiloton nuclear warhead would do the trick. The technology—under testing in Nevada—garnered approval from Manning's advisors, but public concerns with nuclear energy forced them to shelve it. Still, the level of excitement that the prospectus stirred up led some to believe that science was catching up to GCOS's costly challenge.

A less dramatic intervention helped ramp up interest in Alberta's oil industry as a whole. In early 1959, President Dwight Eisenhower, caving to pressure from Senators Robert Kerr and Lyndon Johnson as well as independent oil, instituted a mandatory quota on oil imports into the United States. Imported oil could no longer exceed 9 percent of the nation's total consumption. The quotas would last in some form for the next fourteen years, flustering executives of major companies invested abroad. One Socal CEO held little back in a lengthy, critical letter to the president. "The last thing your Administration desires," he summarized, "is to inhibit American venturesomeness abroad, or to have the oil imports control program used as the basis of an ideo-logical redistribution of income. Yet those are the very ends which the program . . . is on the way to accomplishing." A bane for major US oil companies, Eisenhower's act was a boon for the Canadian oil indus-try, which received an exemption (for continental security concerns). With even greater intent, US companies began moving north. Even as the Middle East captured ever-increasing attention, US imports from Canadian oil sources rose dramatically, from 4.9 percent of total US oil imports in 1958 to 11.7 percent in 1962. By 1967, imported Canadian crude would represent 18.7 percent of the US market, compared to 8.3 percent from the Middle East. Amid this intracontinental transaction, Alberta's oil sands finally seemed viable.[5]

In 1961, as it celebrated its seventy-fifth anniversary, Sun recognized it was time to move ahead. Its technological capabilities and diplomatic horizons had expanded in the years since it first committed to GCOS. By then, it was refining in Canada (Ontario) and Venezuela, carrying a payroll of 20,000 persons worldwide, and operating in every facet of the industry, making it one of the most successful mid-majors. During the diamond anniversary year, Sun president Robert Dunlop traveled 40,000 miles to speak at sixty dinners in each of the company's centers. "Pioneering petroleum progress" was his overlying theme in a speech that reminded employees of the company's lasting faith in God, country, and capitalism. "Sun grew by pulling on its own boot-straps," he preached, and thanks to the Pews, "we have more than the advantage of a blazed trail; they are sources of immediate guidance, counsel and inspiration." Because of them, Dunlop emphasized, Sun was also a company with "great moral values" geared to protecting human and national freedom. The CEO's message struck chords of familiarity in places like East Texas, where locals paid tribute to the "good citizen" that Sun had been, but it also drew in the Canadian workers who attended his dinner in Calgary in early fall. The timing was perfect. While East Texas represented a heralded past, Alberta, Dunlop intimated, was a new frontier on which Sun's "pioneering" progress could take another leap forward.[6]

J. Howard Pew's political and personal interests informed the decision to jump-start GCOS as well. Since the 1930s, he had vociferously defended domestic oil production as essential to national security. GCOS gave him the opportunity once again to drive that point home. "No nation can long be secure in this atomic age unless it be amply supplied with petroleum," he charged; "oil from the Athabascan area must of necessity play a role." In such innovation he also identified the source of strong companies and ultimately nations. "Unless projects of this kind were periodically challenged and solved," he reasoned when talking about the risk of the GCOS, "our organization would become soft and eventually useless."[7]

Pew's ties to Billy Graham–style evangelicalism also factored in. By 1960 Ernest Manning was one of its leading lights, and Pew noticed. In 1962, Manning published an essay in Graham's *Decision* magazine that blended prophecy with a nod to the good work that politicians and petroleum leaders could do. "In recent years, Alberta has become known internationally as the great oil-producing province of Canada," he began his homily: "Yet every time I look at an oil well and see the pump going up and down ... I say to myself, 'Some day that well will be pumped dry, but there is a cruse of oil which will never run dry— one that will flow on forever and ever.'" Manning's reiteration of his own bootstrap theology followed. "We should be anxious for people to know about the oil which in the lamp of God's Word produces a light that shines across the darkness of this world in order that men may find their way to Jesus Christ, the one who alone can save and who can solve their problems, whatever they may be."[8]

Pew, Manning, Sun, and the Alberta government moved ahead, although challenges loomed. Other companies such as Shell now expressed interest in Athabasca, but Sun was in the driver's seat, provided it could earn formal approval for its development plan from the Alberta Gas and Oil Conservation Board. The first cycle of petitions transpired between 1960 and 1962. Board members wanted several guarantees, among them that GCOS would not damage the province's conventional oil industry. After a few rejections and revised proposals, Sun finally won approval in fall 1962 and immediately began selling shares to raise the necessary capital. In 1963, Pew and Sun officials visited Fort McMurray to forge a plan whereby GCOS could become fully operational. The official ground-breaking ceremony in July 1964 gave the public a chance to glean the anticipation that had been building in boardrooms for a decade.[9]

Yet, even in the lead-up to that event, questions about the project persisted. Was GCOS's untested technology sufficient? And how should the province handle other oil sands proposals, such as Shell's? The uncertainties increased in the fall of 1963. In order to protect the province's conventional oil producers, Manning wanted to maintain the oil sands production quota at 5 percent of Alberta's total production. This was the exact output granted GCOS, leaving Shell in the cold. To some, Manning had essentially created a monopoly. Then, after fresh study of the operation, Bechtel engineers concluded that in order to be profitable, GCOS's plant capacity and production quota would have to be enlarged. Sun pledged to stick with the venture, provided Alberta's conservation board allowed it to expand the size of the project by 14,500 barrels per day—representing 7.5 percent of the province's crude production. Sun executives won approval for their new plan, in part because of new terms of purchasing, which would ease the other pressures Alberta's government was facing: while Sun would purchase 75 percent of the oil sands' production, Shell Canada Limited would now purchase the remainder. Sun moved into a final round of negotiations with the premier's office in early 1964. Though enthusiastic, Manning insisted that Sun make some concessions for rank-and-file Albertans: a commitment to build a pipeline that suited Alberta's economic and environmental interests, a pledge to hire "local labor," and an agreement that provincial residents "be accorded an opportunity to purchase up to 15% of the initial equity stock of the Company at the same price and on the same terms as those applying to the purchase of such stock by the Sun Oil Company." Albertans, Manning asserted, were not going to give American business a free pass. Although a realist who knew that some degree of cooperation with larger corporations was inevitable, Manning could not abandon his Social Credit antipathies toward Wall Street even at this critical juncture.[10]

Sun hedged. Besides imposing the extra burden of public investors, which added additional risk to an already risky enterprise, the Manning plan also seemed to reduce "Sun's ownership position" and compromise free enterprise ideals. In his dismissal of Manning's demands, one Sun official enunciated the broader complaint: "Government is . . . involving themselves in affairs of private enterprise to a peculiar degree in suggesting rearrangement of issued equity that a corporation might consider fits its corporate circumstances." Did the new provision mean GCOS directors would need to check with the government "on future issues of shares"? The commentator hoped his allies could still "impress the free enterprise atmosphere . . . as the project proceeds," but in his eyes the Pews' way clashed with the Province's way. Although appreciative of Manning's lobbying on behalf of the people, the Pews were not willing to let such appreciation override their company's bottom line. Sun and Alberta officials continued to negotiate through 1964 and early 1965, even as the project progressed.[11]

While Manning and Pew had become good friends by this point, conflicting interests still required ironing out. Enter Billy Graham. With their mutual ally serving as mediator, Pew and Manning began exchanging letters at a fairer clip. Soon the correspondence assumed a comity strengthened by talk about the Bible. Pew told of upcoming church conferences, forwarded favorite books (*Calvin*, by Francois Wendel; *The Man God Mastered*, by Jean Cadier), and asked if he could cite Manning's sermons in public talks. Manning implored the oilman to keep fighting for the fundamentals: "The need for aroused Christian laymen to take an uncompromising stand for the faith once delivered was never greater than at the present time, particularly in view of the fact that so many pulpits have become mouth-pieces for liberalism and even the outright denial of the divine authorship of Scripture." When Pew and Manning shook hands at GCOS's ceremonial unfurling in 1964, they were linked, as local lore offered, by "common commitment to Jesus Christ." When they met again a short time later, in Jasper, Alberta, a resort town nestled in the Rocky Mountains, they were joined by Graham. Between golf rounds, Manning and Graham schemed a near future when the evangelist would hold revivals in each Canadian city. By all accounts, the talks between Manning and Pew also went well. As their connections deepened, it became apparent to Pew that Manning's populist emphases served as protective cover for what was at its core an ideology of individualism and private enterprise, an ideology, in other words, that they shared. The premier, meanwhile, seemed willing to soften some of the populist defensiveness he had inherited from his Social Credit mentors and champion more forcefully a form of free market economy that Pew and his corporate cousins vigorously upheld. As Manning and Pew's relationship warmed, their wives grew close as well; unsurprisingly, so did GCOS's dealings with Alberta's government.[12]

By the summer of 1965, it was all systems go for the oil sands initiative. Sun and Alberta officials and the multitude of workers already congregated in the province's northern reaches once again looked optimistically to a future of full-on operation. R. G. LeTourneau's equipment began making the trip from Texas to Alberta, ready to help carve out the muskeg and scrub timber lining GCOS's unfinished plant site and—as he saw it—pave the way for civilization.[13]

AT THE SAME time that GCOS was redefining Sun and the oil industry, Pew was also helping champions of wildcat religion spark a permanent shift in America's partisan alignments. Even with a Republican in the White House during most of the 1950s, he and his corporate and churchly allies had grown dissatisfied with the political status quo. Despite their initial approval of Dwight Eisenhower as their heroic counterweight against Washington "landgrabs" in the West, independent producers found the president less likeable as his terms in office unfolded.

His legislation (or lack thereof) continued to shape their opinions of him. In 1956, Eisenhower vetoed a bill meant to exempt independent natural gas producers from utility rate controls the federal government sought for consumer protection. The producers insisted the regulation would kill their ability to assume costly risks, thereby stymying development of new reserves. Eisenhower agreed to an extent but grew agitated with "a very small segment" that seemed to be furthering "their own interests by highly questionable activities." "These include efforts that I deem to be so arrogant and so much in defiance of acceptable standards of propriety," he told Congress, "as to risk creating doubt among the American people concerning the integrity of governmental processes." The reversal angered oilmen such as Sid Richardson, who in response cast a protest vote for the Democratic ticket in 1956. Eisenhower's critics got louder the longer he resisted mandatory quotas on foreign oil. For a decade, small producers had been hounding Congress for protection. One such producer from Dallas begged his senator, Lyndon Johnson, to do something about that "foreign oil"; "no sense in bankrupting every independent oil man in Texas, for a few Arabian princes and because . . . Standard Oil of New Jersey claims they need the money." For his part, Eisenhower wanted to encourage free international trade, not protectionism. When he finally conceded to Congress in 1959 and instituted the quota that oil majors decried, small producers applauded, but only faintly. By then, Eisenhower had lost their trust.[14]

Eisenhower's consensus with wildcatters also waned for reasons other than oil. Over time, Eisenhower's credentials as warring defender of the Christian faith sagged. His invitation of Muslims into the fold did not sit well with those who—due to theology, corporate interests, or bald disdain for "Arabian princes"—saw Israel as the only US ally in the Middle East. Meanwhile, his doubters worried that while the Soviet Union was getting stronger, Washington was full of appeasers who did not want to take the battle right to the communists on foreign *and* domestic soil. For men such as William F. Buckley and J. Howard Pew, equally troubling was a moral drift in society they believed had accelerated on Eisenhower's watch. While they looked on anxiously as high courts outlawed religious practices such as prayer and Bible instruction in public schools, they deplored the rise of a beatnik culture of personal gratification that shattered Christian mores. For Pew, Buckley, and their peers, the president's loosely defined civil religion now registered as vapid and evidence of creeping secularism. Overall, the president's centrism left them feeling that the GOP—which, they generally agreed, was the party of their future—was still a work in progress. "We are suffering today from a one-party system," Pew articulated privately in the late 1950s. "If you can find any difference between the Democratic Platform and the Republican Platform, you have a more discerning eye than I have." The Republican candidate in 1960 did not convince them that things had improved; he was a carryover of Eisenhower, although with more anticommunist moxie.[15]

Their doubt about Richard Nixon also hinged on an issue that had long been their political bugaboo: eradication of the depletion allowance. In 1926, following Texas senator Tom Connally's lead, Congress had approved a provision enabling oilmen to deduct 27.5 percent from the gross income they earned from producing wells, along with all the losses from dry holes. Almost immediately, critics cried foul. In 1937, US Treasury Secretary Henry Morgenthau called the clause "the most glaring loophole" in the tax code. Harry Truman repeated that same accusation, calling it "inequitable" and "excessive" and a means of making the rich richer at the expense of public welfare. He asked Congress to kill the provision, but to no avail; few others would even broach the subject. "All efforts to close this loophole have been treated as an almost sacrilegious invasion of the oil industry's prerogatives," a pundit rued in 1955.[16]

That was again true in the 1960 election, when Nixon failed to win over all the independent oilmen, even though he came out in favor of the depletion allowance, while his opponent, John F. Kennedy, said he would revisit it. That latter announcement once again scared wildcatters into action. In their eyes, the depletion allowance was the mechanism that kept their careers alive. Whereas the huge majors could absorb losses, the very survival of their companies, they said, rested on their ability to write off losses as compensation for risk. Kennedy's pledge convinced many independents that the Nixon ticket was their only option. For some, though, Lyndon Johnson's presence on the Democratic ballot alleviated fears. Johnson had been one of their most ardent defenders in Washington. And as the 1960 campaign wore on, his oil-friendly politics seemed to rub off on his presidential running mate, who by October said he appreciated the value of the depletion allowance. Johnson did face backlash from Texas hard-liners, who at Texas congressman Bruce Alger's urging greeted him during a Dallas campaign stop with signs that read "LBJ, Traitor," "Judas Johnson," and "LBJ Sold Out to Yankee Socialists." But H. L. Hunt, Dallas's most extreme wildcatter, did not second the words. Despite attending First Baptist Church, where he heard barnstorming Reverend W. A. Criswell rail against the "papist" Democratic candidate—and despite allowing his own media enterprise, now called Life Line, to spread pamphlets and broadcast messages that did the same thing—Hunt voted for the Kennedy-Johnson ticket. He did so as a gesture of loyalty to Johnson, who had repeatedly offered such gestures of his own.[17]

Any lingering political uncertainties and mixed loyalties among wildcatters dissipated in the wake of Kennedy's victory. By 1962 the president was proposing tax reforms that would include a bill to reduce the depletion allowance to 17.5 percent. The measures were still in the works when he was killed in Dallas in November 1963, prompting conspiracists to accuse oilmen of masterminding the assassination. Eastern pundits frequently cited Hunt as the culprit. They unfairly "profiled Hunt as a bumptious superpatriot and cast aspersions on Life Line's finances and religious character," one sympathetic journalist would later write. Falsely or not, the accused did trade in Far Right reactionary politics; even Criswell, his liberal-hating pastor, worried that the oilman's Life Line programs had become too incendiary in their demands for "extreme patriotism" and a crusade to roll back communist influences in Washington. Yet, in their obsessions with the wildest of wildcatters in "Nut Country" (as Kennedy called Dallas), and in their focus on the surreptitious activism that converged in strident antiliberal, pro-conservative grassroots advocacy groups like the John Birch Society, journalists also missed the broader picture of political change. Alongside the Hunts of the wildcat realm were countless other fervent independent oilmen whose corporate and religious interests were encouraging them to seek—quietly, more responsibly—political leaders who would no longer fail them. For most, this increasingly meant supporting Republicans.[18]

Wildcatters such as Ignatius O'Shaughnessy fit this bill. The Catholic oilman approached his political giving during the late 1950s and early 1960s with the same type of deliberateness he exuded in his charity. Although he had once been invited to dine at Franklin Roosevelt's White House, O'Shaughnessy's partisanship shifted toward the Republican Right in the postwar years. He did not completely shut off the spigot of giving for Democrats, particularly at the state level. His was a realism that tried to account for every contingency and protection of his enterprise. "His basic theory was that they were all crooks but you had to work with them," O'Shaughnessy's grandson later recalled. But over time, O'Shaughnessy's giving also demonstrated greater ideological commitment. He donated money to Nixon in 1960, preferring him over fellow Catholic Kennedy, and also sent two substantial checks to the National Republican Committee and the National Television Committee GOP to underwrite promotional ads. In the wake of the Kennedy tragedy, O'Shaughnessy once again took out his checkbook and, without the fanfare of an H. L. Hunt, directed his funds to the one man he and his friends truly believed in: Barry Goldwater.[19]

The US senator from Arizona excited Hunt, O'Shaughnessy, and their corporate friends like no other political candidate in recent memory. Their commitment to him began in 1952, when the western libertarian took on Ernest McFarland, a two-term Democratic senator from the state and the Senate's Democratic majority leader. Goldwater offered a muscular message of anticommunism and anti–big government that caught the eye of conservatives around the country. "Now is the time to discharge those who have coddled communists," he railed. "Now is the time to put men into political office who will give their first allegiance to the principles of American freedom. Now is the time to throw out the intellectual radicals and the parlor pinks and the confused and the bumbling." Sid Richardson, H. L. Hunt, and Joseph Pew, Howard's brother, funneled funds Goldwater's way, which helped him pull off the upset win. By 1960, his message well honed, the Arizona senator was even more alluring to the emerging Republican Right. Already the citizen's group Americans for Goldwater had formed chapters in thirty-one states. That grassroots zeal intensified with the 1960 publication of Goldwater's *The Conscience of a Conservative*, a concise primer of conservative ideology. The idea for the book was borrowed. "Incensed at the liberal policies of the Eisenhower Administration," Buckley explained, former Notre Dame law professor turned conservative pundit Clarence Manion thought "a slim book" could "give fresh syntactical life to conservative doctrine, to stand in opposition to the prevailing political winds." Upon its release, *The Conscience of a Conservative* turned the Goldwater movement into a phenomenon.[20]

As 1964 approached and prospects of a run at GOP leadership heated up, the phenomenon spread, with housewife activists joining pastors, teachers, and businessmen in disseminating the Goldwater gospel. The John Birch Society, on whose executive board Manion sat, generated energy for the senator-candidate. Although he initially appreciated the controversial organization's help ("[Birchers] are the finest people in my community," he asserted), Goldwater's campaign advisors would work hard to sever any ties, real and perceived, between him and his extreme devotees. More important to the campaign were the rank-and-file Protestant and Catholic "suburban warriors" of the Sunbelt West, who harbored anticommunist sympathies but were also attracted to other fundamentals of the Arizonan's platform. They loved his tough talk about national defense, property rights, states' rights, personal freedoms, and the need to restrain Washington; they appreciated the primacy he placed on the traditional "3R's" of education (by way of ensuring that public schools did not become "laboratories for . . . the predilections of the professional educators"); and they cherished what he had to say about religion. His was a calculated as well as heartfelt approach, in this regard; at his advisors' prompting, he took strong stands against Supreme Court rulings outlawing school prayer and in support of Israel as it sought control of the Jordan River watershed. And he said he would ensure that Washington would protect all facets of religious freedom and moral truths rooted in God's natural law. "If we are true to our civilized heritage and to ourselves, we stand for order and freedom and justice, founded upon religious understanding," he told students at the University of Notre

Dame in 1962. Two years later, that message was gaining traction among a wider crowd.[21]

Listening to and reading those words, wildcatters could not help but dive into Goldwater's 1964 run for the presidency. While O'Shaughnessy—no doubt inspired by the senator's speech at Notre Dame—gave money, others in the oil club did that and more. J. Howard Pew, like his brother Joseph, was an early enlistee in the Goldwater movement and throughout the 1960s proved "overly generous" (as Goldwater associate Dean Burch once wrote) in his funding of the senator's career. Pew, who admired Clarence Manion but angrily rebuffed charges of belonging to the John Birch Society, gave Goldwater access to one of his sought-after constituencies. Through his deep association with a vast array of colleges, think tanks, and clerics, Pew ably channeled Goldwater's philosophy into the heart of evangelicalism. Oilmen of various economic statures joined Pew in the Goldwater blitz. H. L. Hunt, while still anxious not to hurt his relationship with Lyndon Johnson, discreetly used his media network to market Goldwater's ideas. As the national election drew nigh, Hunt openly stated his support for the Republican. Johnson's Democratic administration, in his estimation, had made too many "terrible mistakes" (such as appointing Chief Justice Earl Warren to head the investigation of President Kennedy's assassination). Closer to Goldwater's inner circle, meanwhile, were men steeped in the oil patch who assumed key advisory positions with the candidate's team. They included Henry Salvatori, the California-based head of Western Geophysical Corporation who worked as chairman of the candidate's California campaign, and Joe Shell, the Presbyterian petroleum producer from Bakersfield, California, whose political experience (he battled Richard Nixon for the California GOP leadership in 1962) added luster to his financial profile. Both Californians were critical to Goldwater's success in their home state, which would determine his fortunes. With petrocapital filling his coffers, Goldwater's fortunes seemed bright as the Republican National Convention approached.[22]

The fact that Nelson Rockefeller was also maneuvering for GOP headship only galvanized the Goldwater candidacy all the more. Rockefeller was anathema to the wildcat Goldwaterites, and they were anathema to him. As early as 1961 the New Yorker sensed that the Republican

Party was up for grabs, and he was anxious to do all he could to expose the reactionary sentiments of the opposing Goldwater wing. "For Rockefeller Republicans," one historian writes, Goldwater's rising Sunbelt movement represented "bad morals and worse politics." Aiming for an Eisenhower consensus he thought still governed American hearts, Rockefeller carved out a platform that stressed social and economic justice, government social welfare programs, and internationalist views of the world. To Pew, Rockefeller's candidacy was the most obvious sign that liberals were clawing to maintain a hold of party and country. Besides conjuring up bad memories of one family's near destruction of another's sustenance, the governor also registered with him as the face of a coercive system of centralization and compromise that had long threatened to emasculate his profession and the country's hallowed institutions and beliefs. When Pew looked at the Rockefeller campaign, he saw further proof of a society collapsing upon itself—like Rome or Carthage—because of power-hungry elites' weak thinking.[23]

Pew was hardly alone, which became clearer as the leadership race heated up. Despite weathering a number of early primaries with mixed results, Rockefeller headed into the California primary scheduled for early June as a solid favorite. There he met the full fury of his opponent's base. A year earlier Nelson had divorced his first wife and married Margaretta "Happy" Murphy, a divorcee with four children; the new-lyweds quickly conceived another child. Condemnations of Rockefeller's infidelities and infelicities came from all corners of the GOP, but nowhere were they more viciously delivered than in California. In the lead-up to the primary, Los Angeles cardinal James Francis McIntyre abruptly canceled Rockefeller's scheduled talk at Loyola Marymount University because he did not want to show even tacit support for an unrepentant divorced and remarried sinner. Sixteen evangelical pastors followed McIntyre's censure by releasing a joint statement that claimed Rockefeller had "struck a serious blow against the Christian concept of marriage." But that was tame. On May 30, three days before the California polls opened, Happy Rockefeller gave birth to Nelson Jr. The Goldwater camp seized the day, running ads that used family values as leverage. "Why are women for Goldwater?" asked one ad. "Because he is a responsible family man." "Mother . . . why are we for

Barry Goldwater?" another asked through the innocence of a child. "Because," mother replied, "children need the inspiration of example." Rockefeller's camp was equally vicious. Determined to expose Goldwater as an extremist who would destroy the world with one squeeze of the nuclear button, it painted him as a fascist dictator waiting in the wings. "We had to destroy Barry Goldwater as a member of the human race," Rockefeller's public relations expert conceded.[24]

When the polls in California closed, Goldwater had won, vaulting him to victory in the Republican race, which came to its conclusion at the party's national convention in San Francisco's old livestock pavilion. Between July 13 and 16, the Cow Palace was witness to a political earthquake. The seismic event was animated by the contempt Rockefeller and Goldwater and their respective sides held for each other. Rockefeller was the first to deliver his rhetorical blow. On July 14, he fought off jeers from Goldwaterites to decry their bigotries. While respecting dissent, he told delegates, he repudiated "the efforts of irresponsible, extremist groups [the John Birch Society especially] to discredit our Party by their efforts to infiltrate positions of responsibility . . . or to attach themselves to its candidates." They feed on "fear, hate and terror," he complained, boos now loudening, and have no program to solve society's chronic social and economic problems or guarantee peace for the world. "On the contrary," he charged, they "engender suspicion. They encourage disunity. And they operate from the dark shadow of secrecy. . . . There is no place in this Republican party for such hawkers of hate, such purveyors of prejudice, such fabricators of fear." As a common courtesy, Rockefeller followed up his speech by calling to congratulate Goldwater. "Hell," the victor fumed, "I don't want to talk to that son of a bitch." Goldwater got the last word. On the convention's closing night, he accepted leadership of the party with a speech that drew a clear line in the sand. The days of a Republicanism "made fuzzy and futile by unthinking and stupid labels" were done, he announced, before finishing with the turn of phrase that would both enshrine him in conservatives' memories and seal his fate in the general election: "I would remind you that extremism in the defense of liberty is no vice. And let me remind you also, that moderation in the pursuit of justice is not virtue!"[25]

Goldwater's edgy acceptance speech hampered his challenge of Lyndon Johnson later that year. Johnson won the presidency by a landslide that November. In the wake of Kennedy's assassination and amid the political reforms he had initiated, voters preferred stability and continuity, not ideological hard-lining. Rockefeller Republicans believed they had fended off a onetime threat—that the Right was dead, liberalism alive and well. Wildcatters, though, had other ideas. Goldwater could not have articulated their worldview in his Cow Palace speech any better, and now it was time to find others who would regroup a movement. Even in the bitter aftermath of 1964, Pew's allies in the parish and the petroleum guild worked to raise up candidates who could transform a short-lived phenomenon into permanent gain. They began at the local level, cheering on the likes of William F. Buckley Jr., who ran (unsuccessfully) for mayor of New York in 1965. And in 1966 they turned to other rising stars. One of their own, George H. W. Bush, an oilman from West Texas, would win a seat in the US House. Another, Ronald Reagan, spoke the wildcatter's language with an inviting lilt. With the help of his "kitchen cabinet" of advisors, staffed by oil-patch kingmakers such as Henry Salvatori and A. C. "Cy" Rubel, head of Union Oil, Reagan translated Goldwater's imputations into slicker supplications for citizens to reclaim conservatism as the answer to society's tumult. His gubernatorial victory in California in 1966 signaled that it was Rockefeller's ideology that was living on borrowed time.[26]

THE ROCKEFELLER WAY was living on borrowed time abroad as well. To be sure, the Pews and Rockefellers were united in subsidizing and amassing a phalanx of missionary capitalism against the communist left. Latin America and Africa were two critical zones in which that union prospered. The Middle East was another, in which it failed. There, clear lines of geopolitical and georeligious struggle that the Rockefellers and Pews navigated together elsewhere did not exist. Israel and its Arab neighbors and the heated politics of faith and petroleum that Jewish, Muslim, and secular states engendered polarized independents and majors, leaving little common ground. Independents would strengthen their accord with Israel, while majors would stay true to Arab societies in which they were already heavily invested.[27]

David Rockefeller himself saw the stark difference between the fantasy and reality of Eisenhower's ecumenical intentions for the Middle

East, particularly as they affected Israel, one of his new bases of business activity. Upon taking over Chase Bank he zeroed in on the area for his developmental schemes. His plans were not entirely new. Chase chairman Winthrop Aldrich had recognized the profitability of doing business there in the 1930s and created a petroleum department with a branch in Beirut. Rockefeller revitalized that approach. "I made the Middle East an integral part of my plans for international expansion," he noted. "I called on political leaders and banking officials in Lebanon, Kuwait, Saudi Arabia, Bahrain, and Iran during the course of a round-the-world trip in February and March 1962." On that occasion, the banker saw "signs of change everywhere," all due to the increased flow of oil wealth: highways, housing, airports, and desalinization plants were all being built, and "governments throughout the region were signing contracts with American and European companies to do the work." Considering their record of lucrative oil production, Rockefeller's negotiation with Arab states made sense.[28]

But considering the difficulty of bridging Muslim and Jewish interests, his willingness to court Israel raised eyebrows. The relationship began in 1951, when the Israeli government chose Chase as the US agent for Israeli bonds, whose sale was crucial to the country's economic emergence. Through those dealings Rockefeller forged reciprocating ties with American Jewish organizations and capitalists such as Jacob Blaustein. David, Laurance, and Nelson Rockefeller all knew Blaustein and exchanged honors with him on several occasions. Whether Blaustein, a registered Democrat, helped Nelson gain a surprise majority of New York's Jewish votes in 1958 remained unknown, but he toasted him at a banquet hosted by the Joint Defense Appeal (the fund-raising arm of the American Jewish Committee) in September 1959. After reminiscing about deep bonds by way of Standard Oil, Blaustein presented Nelson with the agency's Human Rights Award. Nelson's acceptance speech echoed Blaustein's aspirations, melding faith in God, humanity, and the market. "We in this country have a rich heritage in terms of our beliefs in the worth and dignity of the individual," he began. "It is a heritage that is importantly rooted in Judaism." "Our purpose to translate economic growth into individual well-being," he added, "is the touchstone of our dedication to the ideal of human dignity." Then he finished with a cue to international commitments:

"Millions of oppressed people, throughout the world, are, for the first time in history, resting their eyes on the distant hills of hope. They have caught from us and our Judeo-Christian heritage the concept and meaning of the freedom of the individual to develop himself to his full stature as a spiritual being." David's move into Israel to advance these same ideals thus placed him on shared ideological footing with his brother and with Blaustein.[29]

Yet it placed his corporate entity and the Rockefeller project as a whole in a tenuous spot. By the early 1960s his dealings with Israel and Arab governments, along with major oil companies, had grown significantly, as had the threat of reprisals and financial disaster. "We attempted to walk a tightrope of commercial neutrality in the region," he later recalled in an overly sanguine tone, but "we would hear complaints from the Arab world that we were contributing to the well-being of the Zionist state and should refrain from doing so." Anyone interested in Middle Eastern oil during the early and mid-1960s had to deal gingerly with the loyalties Rockefeller was trying to straddle. It was becoming increasingly obvious to world leaders and Western capitalists that neutrality was an impossibility and that united action among oil-rich people of the book was a pipe dream.[30]

If unintentionally, Blaustein's own labors in Israel contributed to that unsolvable tension. Although not as fiercely Zionist as fellow American Jewish oilman and Israel booster Rudolf Sonneborn, Blaustein was nevertheless passionately committed to advancing the fiscal and political interests of the Jewish state, in no small part through pursuit of domestic oil reserves. The emphasis he and his allies placed on crude as an essential life source for the Jewish people in turn raised the level of anxiety, which would reach new heights by the mid-1960s. The anxiety was internal as well as external, an existential as much as geopolitical problem for the young state and its citizens.

Within Israel, the matter of oil continued to be philosophically (and psychologically) vexing. In a contemporary article titled "Can Oil and Israel Mix?," journalist Ernest Aschner identified the intellectual conundrums that petroleum represented for Jews as they now sought to fortify their nation-state. On one hand, they had always regarded large, Western oil companies' schemes in the Middle East as "illegitimate and sinister" and "stigmatized [them] *a priori* as 'oil imperialism.'" Exuding degrees of anticapitalist and anti-Arab animus, early Zionists—many of whom harbored Marxist sympathies—decried the tentacles of influence major oil corporations were stretching across Muslim lands in the region. As a result, Israel was paralyzed by an aversion to crude that deemed it a curse—a base material on which only undignified societies depended. At the same time, Israelis desperately needed oil and could benefit mightily, Aschner asserted, were they to become "active partners and productive factors . . . in a business that has brought progress and prosperity to other countries." Crude, he insisted, could also be the nation's charm—not just a way of "obtaining capital so vitally needed for the upbuilding of the country" but a basis on which to construct vibrant communities and participate in a regional nexus of cooperation. Aschner's essay highlighted an innate tension that would cause Jews to view petroleum through a dark looking glass as something that could as easily break as advance their tentative future. Every oil-producing society faced such difficult paradoxes and distrusts. But because of prior hesitancies among many of its citizens, as well as its isolation in a region powered by Arab crude, Israel's courting of corporate oil and desperate hunts for the black stuff inside its borders would come laced with an extra dose of angst.[31]

As Blaustein, Sonneborn, and the Israeli government made substantive progress toward petroleum production in the early 1950s, that abiding sense of insecurity intensified. Shouts of exclamation and discernible sighs of relief were issued at each sign of a potential oil strike. After a stretch in the early 1950s when, with the Knesset's encouragement, independent US companies and emerging Israeli firms started drilling in select spots, Israelis finally had something to celebrate in 1955 when Lapidoth Israel Oil Prospectors Corporation spudded the nation's first commercially viable well near Heletz in the south. "The excitement was over-whelming and euphoria pervasive," oilman Zvi Alexander, in the United States at the time, recounted. "I remember hearing the radio commentator in New York saying, 'The Land of Milk and Honey is now flowing with oil, the riches of Arabia have come to tiny Israel.'" Six more drilling rigs were immediately installed; yet their motors soon stopped, the small pool quickly drained. Further disappointment followed. By the end of 1956, with the Suez crisis contributing to an already downward trend in its petroleum sector, Israel was reporting a dramatic drop-off in foreign capital investment in oil exploration and the potential need for further government funds.[32]

The dry period continued until 1962, leaving Israel reliant on unpredictable foreign oil supplies. Alexander was partly responsible for a wave of excitement that returned to Israel that year. After completing a UN seminar on oil exploration, he traveled to Oklahoma and Texas to observe the latest exploratory methods firsthand. Upon his return to Israel he applied his acquired knowledge on behalf of Lapidoth, his employer, in the northern section of the Heletz field. There, for a moment, Lapidoth's men thought they were going to be Israel's saviors. Alexander's team was drilling "one hundred feet below the producing horizon" when suddenly, he recalled, "the drill bit dropped six to eight feet. We figured that we had encountered a cavern full of oil." The crew was ecstatic, more so when an American engineer estimated that Lapidoth was sitting on a mammoth oil field. "For a whole week," Alexander explained, "we walked as if on a cloud. We considered ourselves great heroes, solving the second most important problem (the first was obviously defense) of the state, energy self-sufficiency." The oilers were soon disappointed. "When we perforated the well and started producing it," Lapidoth's lead driller lamented, "water replaced the oil after several days. The cavern was full of water with a thin film of oil on top. Our bad luck!"[33]

That string of bad luck and dashed dreams continued through the decade's middle years, during which Alexander transitioned into the public sector as supervisor of government investment in the oil industry. By 1965, when he accepted the job, he was dreading the proverbial question from Israeli officials—"We discovered oil in Heletz ten years ago, where are we now?"—to which he could respond with little substantive or good news. He could report one positive development: that at this juncture, with some level of calm restored in the region, US independent oilmen were once again flocking to Israel, pouring more fortunes and hard effort into exploration. As Blaustein had done earlier, Alexander nurtured relationships with them, including those whose strong evangelical beliefs caught him off guard but to whom he always responded with respect. After all, they were helping Israel find treasure it so desperately needed.[34]

Wesley Hancock was one such man. Hancock was a "Californian fundamentalist," Alexander remembered, whose Asher Oil Company received licenses to drill near Mount Carmel, in the coastal mountain range that butted up against Haifa in the country's northern section. The tribe of Asher, one of the twelve tribes of Israel, had settled in that area, and Hancock was convinced that it held oil deposits. There, the Bible says, Asher dipped his foot in oil, and the Old Testament sage Elijah disputed prophets of Baal over who could make water burn. Hancock believed both referred to petroleum (only oil-slicked water would burn, he thought). He had lofty plans for his drill operation—to help Israel but also the Jewish Diaspora. Hancock explained that he would use all his oil profits to fulfill Jeremiah's prophecy: "I will bring my people from the north country." Hancock was sure "people" meant Jews, the "north country," Russia. His plan was to buy Russian Jews from Nikita Khrushchev and bring them back to Israel. Alexander assured Hancock that he and Israel appreciated his "noble intentions." Unfortunately for Hancock and for Israel, the wildcatter's interpretations of scripture—and his fiancée's patience—failed him. After pouring over $1 million into two dry holes and beginning to drill a third, his spouse-to-be issued an ultimatum: "Either you marry and stay in California or continue fulfilling prophecy." Hancock returned home.[35]

Even if Hancock's circumstances were not the norm, dry holes and abandoned rigs in 1960s Israel were. By the mid-1960s hundreds of wells drilled throughout the country had turned up little. Some commercially viable statistics surfaced here and there, as well as hints of an offshore field, but nothing of the sort needed to resolve Israel's "second most important problem." With each round of failed drilling came further doubts that the embattled state would survive. Alexander kept selling Israel's oil prospects to American independents, Jewish ones included, but the routine was continually falling short. "Obtain[ing] financing for a speculative investment such as oil exploration, in Israel, was almost a mission impossible," he conceded. "Israel had not found oil in the previous ten years, in spite of active exploration activity and a very substantial outlay of capital." Making matters worse, of course, was the external squeeze that the oil-rich Arab nations, Saudi Arabia in particular, applied on Israel. Without energy self-sufficiency, how could Israelis weather the onslaught of hostile states? Since no oil was forthcoming, all that seemed to await them were the heavy blows, which, during the late 1950s and 1960s, were consistent. In addition to boycotting US corporations that traded in Israel—be it Coca-Cola or Xerox—the Arab League of nations sought to squelch the in- and out-flow of oil products with particular relentlessness. Oil was their domain, and they were determined to apply every ounce of the political wallop that afforded them.[36]

The forced departure of Socony—the only US major company to function inside Israel's borders—illustrated their determination. Socony had maintained a refining and marketing infrastructure in Palestine since before World War II, but in 1955 it agreed to honor a pact it had made with Saudi Arabia. The Saudis determined that no US company with which it was associated should contribute to the Israeli economy. Socony was then a 10 percent owner of Aramco, and in the interests of peace, Aramco's other US partners asked that Socony abide. Socony and Israel were thrust into uncomfortable spots and Jacob Blaustein into a mediating role. Socony voiced concern for the economic health of its workers and the Israeli economy, as well as for its reputation in the United States, were it to leave. The bottom-line fear, as conveyed to Blaustein, was that, "aroused by . . . an anti-Israel act by an American concern, and an unfair interference with the business of American companies by the Arabs," "both Jewish and non-Jewish" Americans would boycott Socony products. The implications for Israel were far more severe. Besides depriving the struggling nation of one of the two major oil firms that delivered oil products to it (the other being Shell), Socony's withdrawal might encourage other Western-based companies, including Shell, to do the same. Blaustein's diplomatic contacts also worried about the vacuum in Cold War relations such a move would create. One official warned Blaustein that conceding to Saudi Arabia in this case would cast "grave doubts on the reliability of international oil companies as responsible oil suppliers to long established clients." It would also "invite many a country to ask if it should not seek other arrangements (including trade with Russia) which may ensure it supplies, regardless of the possible whims of a Saudi tyrant in a virtual medieval country." Despite Washington's request that Socony not bow to Saudi pressure, it did. Blaustein, Socony, and their Jewish associates scrambled to find a compromise. Eventually, the company quietly transferred its refinery to Rudolf Sonneborn, who for the sake of Israeli survival and Socony's pride would continue the operation under the cloak of business as usual.[37]

More boycotts of oil companies connected to Israel would follow, but thanks to the well-connected Jacob Blaustein, the early 1960s would not be entirely bleak for Israelis. During the Kennedy and Johnson presidencies, the lobbyist maintained ties to the White House. His job—as he informed the two men—was to continue serving in a role begun under previous presidents "as a catalyst between Israel and the United States and the United Nations." By that he meant functioning as a liaison, an arms dealer, and a diplomat. He also nurtured ties with key officials like Secretary of State Dean Rusk, whom he feted at a 1964 annual dinner of the American Jewish Committee for his leadership in the Rockefeller Foundation and the State Department. In his meetings with Kennedy and Johnson, Blaustein never held back. He constantly begged that something be done about the Arab boycott and Saudi Arabia's vetting of religious affiliations of US corporate executives with whom it did business (in order to expose Jews), suggested channels for military support for Israel, and demanded that Washington "lead from strength" to contain Arab nationalism. He let both presidents know that on account of his family's substantial financial support of Israel, he had "large influence" there—and needed to be respected and heard.[38]

To what degree his lobbying factored into their thinking is unknown, but Blaustein saw plenty of wishes granted. Wanting to diversify its connections in the region, Kennedy's administration not only extended its good graces to secular Arab nationalist countries (accentuated by brief rapprochement with Egypt) but also reached out to Israel with a more generous hand, much to the distaste of Saudi royalty. Granted, it was not unconditionally generous—Kennedy also suggested that Israel allow Palestinian refugees, indigenous Arabs who had been expelled or displaced from their homes after the 1948 partitioning and founding of Israel, to resettle in the arid Jordan Valley and tap the Jordan River for irrigation. Israeli prime minister David Ben-Gurion was reluctant to accept the plan, which would allow Palestinians into a sensitive zone where Israelis, Jordanians, and Syrians were already vying for control of the river's vital resources, and he was adamant that Israel's main water source not be drained further. Arab leaders rejected it outright—no dealings with Israel were allowed. Unable to make peace, Kennedy settled for a stalemate and prevention of further bloodshed. Still, Kennedy's more pronounced support of Israel was notable. Johnson continued that trend with fiercer resolve. "You have lost a very great friend," he told an Israeli emissary upon Kennedy's death. "But you have found a better one." Johnson's support for Israel was almost surreal, testing to a degree even his heavily pro-Israel State Department's outlook, which nevertheless preferred a realistic approach that did not alienate Arabs. Besides standing on Israel's side as a sign of solidarity with his American Jewish Democratic voters, Johnson also remembered the warnings of his Baptist relatives: "If Israel is destroyed, the world will end." And he also saw in Israel the type of courageous last stand with which he, as a Texan, was so comfortable. "Israel, for him," a scholar offers, "was a latter-day Alamo, surrounded on all sides by compassionless enemies, and Nasser was the reincarnated Santa Ana, the Mexican general who laid siege to that fort."[39]

Diplomatic gains notwithstanding, Blaustein and his Jewish allies remained stuck in an uphill climb for Israeli energy independence. Contending with boycotts and the absence of oil reserves, the Israeli government had to work extra hard (and pay all the more) to secure available crude, as well as to convince the average Israeli citizen to conserve in this urgent time of need. David Rockefeller's enterprise now felt the squeeze too. In May 1964, the governor of the Saudi Arabian Monetary Agency (SAMA) sent Chase an official letter with blunt regards: "The Commissioner General of the Israeli Boycott Office of the Arab League has received information . . . that your bank is the headquarters for promoting the sale of Israeli bonds in all the states of the world." Chase was "supporting the Israeli economy," and that had to stop. "I am to express the sincere hope," he concluded, "that the Chase Manhattan Bank . . . will extend its maximum cooperation in avoiding any action which may be construed as jeopardizing its existing happy relationship with our group of countries." Next, the Arab League voted to ban dealings with Chase as of January 1965. Rockefeller knew this would be devastating—it would force closure of the Beirut office and result in the loss of $250 million in deposits (most from the SAMA). Adding to Rockefeller's conundrum was a follow-up from Aramco, which said that absent a favorable solution to the matter, it would halt its transactions with Chase. Tens of millions of dollars now rested in the balance. The aid of the US government, together with Chase's convincing plea that it was an "apolitical international bank" and that major Arab nations such as Saudi Arabia and Egypt would suffer along with Israel were the money flow stopped, eventually made the problem go away.[40]

Just the same, for Chase's CEO the experience drove home the point that the waters in which he was stepping were treacherous, the political balancing act he was trying to perform a nearly impossible proposition.[41]

WILLIAM EDDY AND Aramco's Arabists had been swimming in those waters for two decades and knew full well just how violently they could churn. Yet they too were caught off guard by the sharp political turns that came in the late 1950s and early 1960s. While they had applauded Eisenhower's efforts to frame a consensus American way that incorporated Muslims, as the new decade dawned they viewed that consensus with all the more angst. Muslims, not Jews, were in need of special treatment, they believed; yet Kennedy and Johnson's Washington did not grasp that. Realists with feet planted on Middle Eastern soil, they also sensed that the mix of Zionism, Arabism, Islamic traditionalism, and petroleum was toxic and bound to combust.

Eddy's colleagues did not take long to sour on Washington's dealings with their Arab neighbors. They had cheered King Saud's 1957 visit to Washington. "We all feel that the King's visit has been a highly successful and very useful affair," George Rentz wrote William Mulligan from the capital. But by early the next year, Rentz was voicing frustration with happenings in the Middle East. The continued rise of Arab nationalism and the anticolonial, anti-Western animus demonstrated by Gamal Nasser worried him. He lay the blame at Washington's feet, convinced it could have done more to commune with all Arab countries, not just Saudi Arabia. "Had the policy of our governments . . . been more intelligent and farsighted," he vented to a colleague, "Arab nationalism today would likely have fewer unattractive aspects in our view. So, in the last analysis, we have got to shoulder a share of the credit or blame for the character that Gamal proves to be." Nasser's alliance with a pro-Arab nationalist government in Syria in 1958, formalized in the short-lived United Arab Republic (UAR), drove that point home for Rentz, as did the Lebanon crisis later that same year. When pro-Arab/pro-Nasser Lebanese Muslims lobbied forcefully for Lebanon's pro-Western and Christian president Camille Chamoun to join the UAR, Chamoun, sensing his regime's vulnerability, asked for US military aid. Fourteen thousand US soldiers occupied the airport and port in Beirut for three months until Chamoun finished his term in office. Although Washington deemed its intervention a success for the way it demonstrated military strength and prevented revolution, in truth the affair enhanced Nasser's influence. Chamoun's successor would be a pro-Nasser, left-wing Muslim. One cynical pundit at the time summed up what many felt when he said in assessing the outcome, "It was as though the Marines had been brought in to achieve Nasser's objectives for him."[42]

Tension-filled US-Saudi relations did not help matters for Aramco's public intellectuals. While Nasser was turning the region's political reality inside out, striking fear in the hearts of conservative Muslim nations such as Saudi Arabia, King Saud's kingdom itself was immersed in internal crisis. In the years after his Washington visit, King Saud's reputation for lavish spending and weak governance raised discontent among his family and closest allies. While his reputation floundered, his brother, Faisal bin Abdulaziz Al Saud—Prince Faisal—earned Saudis' favor as a reform-minded leader with a clearer view of how to forge a nexus of Muslim nations to foil Nasser's agenda. Nasser's nationalist aims enjoyed popularity with certain sectors of Saudi Arabia, including a few individuals close to the royal family. Prince Talal, Faisal's brother, publicly criticized his family's regime and called for a freer, progressive government and ties to Cairo. In a moment of unity in 1962, Faisal and Saud ensured that neither Talal nor his ideology would feel welcome in their kingdom. Talal was banished to Egypt for the foreseeable future.[43]

Faisal became equally distrustful of a second insider, whose sympathies for pan-Arabic causes informed his political work. When King Saud appointed Abdullah Tariki the nation's first oil minister, Tariki relished his task. Left to his own devices by the vacuum of leadership created by the Saud-Faisal power struggle, the dashing gamesman looked for ways to increase Saudi petroleum revenues—and Saudi control of them. He even entertained the idea of nationalizing Aramco, a chilling proposition for US majors. Some of his determination was personal—as a former employee of the American-run oil company, Tariki became convinced that it had hoodwinked the Saudi government "into giving concession right to an enormous area for a song, because the Company was sophisticated and the Government negotiators were simple 'barefoot boys' who did not realize what they were doing." Tariki was also convinced that Aramco was hauling in excessive profits while refusing to honor the pledge it gave years earlier to raise its Arab workers' quality of life substantially. Although he would back away from his bold intentions, before his ouster by Faisal in 1962 the Saudi oil czar created an avenue for principally non-Western Arab oil-producing and -exporting countries to assert power over their product. Most notably he collaborated with Juan Pablo Perez Alfonzo, Venezuela's minister of mines and hydrocarbons, who was among the first to demand the fifty-fifty formula with US oil companies. At the encouragement of journalist Wanda Jablonski, the two like-minded men met at the 1959 Arab Petroleum Congress in Cairo; there they schemed to unite oil-exporting states: as one entity, they would consult on oil production rates, establish and force major companies to recognize the best (highest) price for crude produced in their countries, and show solidarity by requiring that members not accept special terms from an oil firm before seeking permission from the group to do so. They launched the Organization of Petroleum Exporting Countries (OPEC) the following year.[44]

With the Saudi royal family frayed on all sides, Aramco's ambassadors were left struggling to stay on the right side of the future until that future became clearer. Anxious about their own next steps, they kept Washington abreast of the latest developments inside the kingdom. They served as psychologists, in a way, relaying their impressions of the latest member of the royal family to rise to prominence. Tariki and Talal, whom they both surveyed, worried them, of course, and Faisal's handling of both garnered their satisfaction. They also eyed Tariki's successor. When Ahmed Yamani took over from Tariki, little was known about him, other than his loyalty to Faisal. Aramco's Arabian affairs informants compiled a report that cited Yamani's strong Muslim faith and anticommunist credentials, as well as his moderate reformist agenda, as reason for optimism about his tenure as Saudi Arabia's minister of petroleum. "Aramco friends find Yamani affable, kind, and sincere," one insider relayed. "His ability to comprehend both sides of a given issue and his initial willingness to please may make him appear a reasonable negotiator." The same surveillance produced favorable insight on Faisal. After a two-year period of struggle, Faisal earned enough support in his family to secure his position as prime minister—a position he held before battling his brother. With Saud frequently absent for medical reasons, Faisal consolidated that power over the course of 1963 and 1964, until he was made king in November 1964 (ushering Saud into exile). Washington welcomed the stability he brought to the crown, as well as his unfailing anticommunism and faith; here was the real "Muslim pope" that it had been looking for—a religious political leader who could unite Islamic societies against incursions by the Soviets and Nasser and reaffirm a moral alliance with the United States. "I beg of you, brothers, to look upon me as both brother and servant," Faisal uttered to his family in a manner that would have pleased Eisenhower. "'Majesty' is reserved to God alone and 'the throne' is the throne of the Heavens and Earth." For his part, Faisal saw opportunity to secure his personal power in the region and, through a persuasive theology, his dynasty's hold over oil revenues.[45]

While the ebb and flow of US-Saudi relations kept Aramco's Arabists guessing, the one constant anxiety—and the greatest bone of contention between them and Washington—was Israel. Each new gesture of support for the Jewish state that the White House delivered thrust William Eddy and his Arabist allies into a new round of condemnations. Eddy remained the most strident critic of Washington's Israel policy. As he had already demonstrated in the early 1950s, Aramco's chief lobbyist had absolutely no patience for American attempts to integrate Israel into a broader regional plan of development: it was not only unfeasible but, in his mind, unfair, considering the money and people pouring into the nascent state while Palestinians suffered on the margins. His pen was indeed biting. Throughout the 1950s he voiced his opinions in essays that filtered through networks of friends and colleagues and the press. When, in the mid-1950s, Ben-Gurion declared Jerusalem the capital of Israel, Eddy distributed a position paper demanding that "Greater Jerusalem" "be regarded as a province [neither] of pan-Arabia or of pan-Israel." It "belongs to the three faiths, Christendom, Islam and Judaism," he declared, "all of whom would be served if the area were removed completely from the police power of any one nation or sect." Eddy's personal crusade intensified in the late 1950s and early 1960s, as did his bitterness. His correspondence and writings certainly displayed a tinge of anti-Semitism that was not uncommon among the American intelligentsia at mid-century. At the same time, the primary lens through which he viewed developments was anti-Zionism of a variety he shared even with some American Jews. He lent his support to Rabbi Elmer Berger of the anti-Zionist American Council for Judaism, centered in the American Reform Jewish community, and commented on published material in *Commentary*, the organ of the centrist American Jewish Committee, through which Blaustein worked to advance Jewish and human rights. When *Commentary* essayists painted Israel as the "one element of stability" in the region, worthy of special attention from the United States, Eddy was quick to offer a rejoinder in the form of a letter to the editor. His was a complex view of Jews and Israel, which as a territory he and his wife (who was even more anti-Zionist than he) had loved visiting in the 1930s and romanticized as a glimpse into biblical times.[46]

When it came to opposing the state of Israel itself, however, he was unequivocal. In his writings he painted it as an imperial force with a theocratic bent that would constantly crave more land, squeezing out its non-Jewish inhabitants and commandeering its scant natural resources—water, maybe oil. He was especially relentless in his defense of Palestinian refugees, who faced increasingly stiff odds of community survival. On one occasion, when well-known Reverend Daniel Poling told tourists in Beirut that it was a "pity the Palestinian refugees refused to go back to their homes in Israel," Eddy erupted, excoriating the minister for his naïveté and heavy Jewish bias, which overlooked the degree to which Israel was intolerant. "Muslims and Christians will never be permitted equal rights in Israel," he wrote in a blistering editorial titled "Israel: The Bastion of Democracy?" "It would be well if Dr. Poling and his fellow Zionist-stooges would re-read the brutal Law of Israel and compare it to the hospitality of other countries in the Near East where Christians and Muslims, Jews and Gentiles, live together in peace." He finished with one other qualifier: "The Arab economic boycott of Israel is only a mild response to this sectarian, 100% boycott by Israel of all her neighbors, the real and permanent barrier to peace in the Near East."[47]

Eddy's political reaction entailed more than sharp use of his pen. Throughout the lingering Palestinian refugee crisis that intensified in the early 1960s and the concomitant struggle by Israel to annex the Jordan River and control its precious water supply, he triangulated between Washington, Dhahran, and the United Nations to foster aid and development on a scale that illustrated the commitment he still possessed for his civil religion of crude—his ideological charge to foster a Christian-Muslim moral alliance and uplift Arab societies through the technological and financial benefits of petroleum. Besides placing himself in the middle of talks between Washington and the United Nations Relief and Works Agency for Palestine Refugees in the Near East, which sought more UN and US intervention, Eddy took it upon himself to get Aramco invested. At his insistence, the company's Donations Committee poured tens of thousands of dollars into programs of aid that included the Committee for the Refugee Villages, coordinated out of the Anglican Church in Jerusalem, which sought funds for reroofing Palestinian homes. Eddy's involvement in this project paralleled another initiative Aramco undertook at the time. As the Palestinian refugee crisis increased, the company struck a financial arrangement with Musa al-Alami, a Palestinian entrepreneur who had built self-sufficient villages for Palestinian refugees near Jericho—replications of the Jewish kibbutzim that now dotted Israel's hinterlands. Aramco supplied Alami with drilling equipment to dig wells for water; upon retrieving it (shocking skeptics who doubted water existed there), Alami irrigated the soil. Over the course of a few years he and his villages grew crops that were then sold to Aramco for use in the company camps. The partnership waned in the early 1960s as Nasser's nationalist movement prohibited both parties' free trade. But the project was illustrative of the spirit of progress—under dire circumstances—that still drove Aramco and inspired Eddy, even as his own spirit grew less buoyant with time.[48]

By the middle of 1962, Eddy's heart as well as spirit was failing him. As he continued to write about history and current events at his home in Beirut, evidences of a struggling Palestine and Middle East were all around him. That same year, David Rockefeller and his wife visited several refugee camps in the Jordan River's West Bank and southern Lebanon, not far from Eddy's home. As Rockefeller later recalled, they were "appalled at the atrocious conditions under which the refugees lived, with little or no prospect that the situation would improve." Eddy surely knew by now that his beloved native region had been transformed, jarringly and permanently. A land once traversed by idealistic American missionaries like his parents and marked by intellectual curiosity and great hopes for social and economic progress all around had succumbed—in his romanticized view of things—to the bald, selfish interests of crass political regimes. The romanticism of the region had always skewed his view of global current events (and inflamed his political passions), but that had kept him energized in his work for Aramco and Washington, and as he struggled with weakening health, it gave him comfort.[49]

On May 3, 1962, his heart gave out, slipping him into a coma. He was taken to the hospital at the American University of Beirut, the institution founded by his parents' generation of missionaries. There he died. A short time later he was memorialized at All Saints Anglican Church on Beirut's coast, then buried just to the south in Sidon, his place of birth, in the cemetery of a church that centered an old village his parents had helped rescue from a violent Turkish landholder in the 1890s. As his body was laid to rest in ground populated by deceased Arabs, American flags flew at half-staff at Hobart College in upstate New York and at the US embassy in Jeddah, Saudi Arabia, marking other junctions in his completed sojourn.[50]

By the mid-1960s, the entanglements of Israel and its Arab neighbors and of God and black gold faced a reckoning. Inside Aramco, Eddy's colleagues carried on the commission they had signed onto in the 1940s and, to a surprising degree, managed to extend the morale groups and moral communities they had begun constructing then. The potential for crisis itself seemed to fuel their drive to strengthen the project of ecumenism across religious and political boundaries. They too, however, would have to confront their own shattered illusions. War would force that process upon them, even as it would provide further reason for wildcatters far away in the Canadian West to rejoice.

Looming larger in the Aramco orb at the time of Eddy's death was Tom Barger, another devotee of the civil religion of crude who, during the stormy 1960s, gave the sprawling enterprise—at least its American managers and employees—a sense of stability and purpose. While Eddy spent the 1950s networking his way through the United States and Middle East, Barger had stayed in Arabia, climbing the company's ranks. In 1958, after serving as Aramco's liaison to the Saudi crown, he was named vice president of government relations. In 1961, the geologist became Aramco's chief executive officer. No one was surprised by his ascent—upon his arrival in the kingdom in the 1930s, he immediately impressed his superiors. "This companion of yours will not be here more than a couple of years before becoming a real boss, because he is a first-rate man," Ibn Saud told Barger's partner. "It is evident that he is one of those excellent men who undertake to do things properly." "If ever a man deserved his promotions," Barger's fellow government relations man William Mulligan remarked, "Barger did. He earned them with his wit and energy." And during his term at the head of Aramco, Barger earned his colleagues' trust as well. "Although he dealt frequently with Saudi royalty," Mulligan noted, he "never lost the common touch. He was available to employees with grievances and to members of the public accustomed to relatively easy access to those in positions of power, but he was no easy mark, no pushover for a sob story."[51]

That combination of traits stood him in good stead as the captain of a corporation that had to endure so much political turmoil during his tenure. Barger was fully aware of the challenges Aramco faced as Arab nationalism and anti-Western pressures mounted. He had been committed to the "enlightened blend of corporate self-interest and social responsibility" that Aramco's Arab affairs and government relations people had endorsed from the very beginning. His commitment was heartfelt, and now as CEO he sought to translate it into stated policies. The bottom line for him, of course, remained the protection of corporate solidity. In the twelve planning papers he drafted over the course of a few years, he highlighted Aramco's primary function: "to preserve the Concession and optimize the returns to the Shareholders over the term of the Concession." Neglect that imperative, and Aramco's stay in the kingdom would be short. But he also insisted that the company become ever more committed to the full range of developmental strategies it had begun implementing in the 1940s. His goal was "to spread the economic benefits of the enterprise as widely through the local population as possible" and "direct the purchasing power of Aramco and employees to the development and support of services generally available to the public." Barger recognized that even if Aramco was to cross the thresholds he laid out, it might not be enough to keep the operation stable as dissent in the Middle East grew—even with its best display of corporate benevolence, Aramco's remaining stay might be short. But he was determined to try to forestall that outcome. Besides, his team had dealt with cracks in the business (labor troubles, racial politics, sectarian tension) before, and it had also survived the Saud-Faisal civil war. Tough circumstances, in other words, did not have to be fatal.[52]

Once again Barger looked to the ecumenical encounter that he and the "relations men" had instituted in the late 1940s and 1950s as a way to bolster consensus inside the company community. Like Mulligan, Barger was a serious Catholic who accepted the task of constructing moral community as a sacred task, not simply a good business strategy. Barger, in fact, was not just a regular communicant; he was also an acolyte who helped administer traditional ceremonies in Latin. He and his wife, Kathleen, and their family attended "welfare services" (code for worship) at Our Lady of Fatima Parish in Dhahran, which was governed by the conservative Capuchin Order. Beyond their parish walls, Barger and Mulligan helped the Holy Name Society, a Catholic fraternal order for laity that nurtured devotion in the Aramco compound and carried out annual spiritual retreats headed by Father John Nolan. Nolan was assistant secretary of the Catholic Near East Welfare Association (CNEWA), covering missionary and charitable activities across the Mediterranean region. The Bargers joined Nolan in positions of leadership within the CNEWA. Kathleen was head of its Dhahran office and, as a profile from the 1960s highlighted, "raised close to $25,000 through charity teas and fashion shows [and] the sale of Jerusalem candles and other handicrafts made by women in the community," money subsequently used to purchase living essentials for refugee children and adults. For the scale of her impact, the Catholic Church conferred upon her the honorific title "Lady of the Holy Sepulcher," the only Catholic chivalric order that admitted women as well as men. Tom's leadership in the Catholic Church and its humanitarian outlets, meanwhile, earned him a papal knighthood. He was invested as knight commander of the Order of St. Gregory the Great in 1962.[53]

The Bargers were just as animated in their religious outreach beyond Aramco's borders and just as vital in casting their fellow parishioners' gaze on global happenings in the region. No issue earned their attention more than the Palestinian refugee crisis. Like the Eddys, who were close friends, the Bargers followed the politics of Palestine intently and committed their resources to Arabs whose lives were ruined as a result. Kathleen toured Palestinian villages to supply goods, then returned to give firsthand accounts to audiences in Aramco's communities. Her husband did the same. They also helped coordinate trips to the Holy Land, including a 1966 pilgrimage of seventy-five people from the Aramco Catholic community, who traveled from Dhahran to Damascus and Amman to Jerusalem (only the Arab section). They could not enter Israel—that would have prevented their legal return to Saudi Arabia—but they glimpsed it from afar, a fitting reminder that their occupations and the disruptions of the day forced them to choose sides.[54]

Barger and Mulligan were also instrumental in maintaining the underground religious culture spawned in the 1940s. By the mid-1960s, Aramco's morale groups were functioning with impressive efficiency, with thousands of workers now practicing their faiths in one of the three main bodies. Through the soft diplomacy of the company's deacons, other gains were made. In 1961, three new morale groups—Mormon, Unitarian, and Christian Scientist—were allowed to form in the American camp. According to a report, "They were too small to justify resident Teachers, but some were given other assistance (shipments, annual visitors expenses) which Aramco gives the three recognized groups." Restrictions were still in place for other religious identities: Jews were still strictly prohibited in the kingdom, and Shiite Muslims and members of Zoroastrianism, Sikhism, "Paganism," and the Baha'i faith went unrecognized in the Aramco fold. But for the growing majority of Aramco's American workers, the canopy of religious inclusion seemed to be broadening in favorable ways. They were also pleased to learn in 1965 that the Saudi Arabian ministry of interior agreed to designate land in al-Khobar for a Christian cemetery and that Christian marriages in Saudi Arabia were allowed. At last, all cradle-to-the-grave ministries in Aramco's Protestant and Catholic folds could be conducted without fear of reprisal.[55]

By many measures, then, as of 1966, with morale groups flourishing and Aramco's devout pilgrimaging, the ecumenism that Aramco's cultural attachés had planted in the 1940s appeared rooted. Under Barger's leadership, goals stated a decade earlier—to educate Saudi workers and enable them to climb the corporate ladder and to improve the quality of life for all laborers—were finally being realized. "Tom believed his greatest accomplishments were in education and home ownership," a friend recalled. Statistics indicate as much. Between 1953 and 1963, the proportion of skilled Saudi workers at Aramco rose from 9 to 57 percent, and the trend accelerated during Barger's watch. By the 1960s, Aramco's home-ownership program was committing millions of dollars annually to the provision of interest-free, heavily subsidized loans, as well as to the acquisition of land that was then turned over to prospective home owners for free. Once a dusty "Bakersfield" of Arabia, Dhahran was beginning to look like a miniature San Diego, with ranch houses arranged in cul-de-sacs and paved roads heading in every direction, including to new schools and playgrounds where suburbanized children studied and played. Under the terms of an agreement with the government, Aramco spent the late 1950s and 1960s constructing schools throughout eastern Saudi Arabia for boys and girls of all ages, which upon completion were turned over to the state's public system. Aramco was required to maintain the schools and continue to pay for the operating costs. By the end of the 1970s, it had completed fifty-eight of them.[56]

But in 1967, the suburban bubble burst with the Six-Day War. June of that year brought the explosion, its effects permanent. With Arab nationalism spreading and Nasser wooing its neighbors—including Jordan—to his side, Israel grew increasingly anxious, certain that war was imminent. Rather than wait, it took the initiative. On Monday, June 5, 1967, Israel's fighter jets carried out a surprise attack on airfields in Jordan, Egypt, and Syria, destroying an estimated five hundred Arab aircraft in total. Next, the Israeli army attacked the Egyptian front; within three days it had forced 5,000 Egyptian soldiers to surrender, smashed the Egyptian army, and secured control of the Sinai Peninsula. Israelis also captured the Old City of Jerusalem, as well as the West Bank. On Friday, June 9, Israel stormed the Golan Heights and forced Syrian soldiers to retreat. Golan was now Israel's too. On

June 11, a cease-fire was signed. By then Israel had lost 1,000 lives, the stunned Arab combatants 20,000. In addition to possessing ancient holy sites always held dear by Jews and expanding its territory, Israel now possessed petroleum. With the capture of the Sinai came control of oil fields that could produce at least 65 percent of all the country's requirements. If unconventionally, the blessings of crude had finally arrived.[57]

Arab response to the war was equally swift, but only in the political realm. While Nasser scrambled to recover his reputation and rally his allies around the prospect of future fights, nations aligned with OPEC for the first time recognized the "oil weapon" they now wielded. In reaction to Western support for Israel, several Arab producing states banned oil shipments to the United States, the United Kingdom, and West Germany. More ominous signs of reprisal arose in other quarters. In the days leading up to June 5, 1967, one Aramco official admitted that as Israelis and Arabs tumbled toward war, it was almost certain that Aramco would be nationalized—"if not today, then tomorrow," he worried. He saw things clearly, and so did Ahmed Yamani, who began to make moves in that direction. On June 7, he ordered Aramco to stop shipping oil to the United States and Britain. At the same time, he and the Faisal government sent support to Jordan and Nasser's Egypt, which felt the heaviest aftereffects of the war. Nasser was now viewed not as a threat but as an ally—suggesting a new era in pan-Arab relations. Amid all the tectonic shifts, Yamani openly pondered nationalizing Aramco. Aramco's liaisons were exceedingly concerned and, during a visit by US government officials to Dhahran, lobbied hard for Washington to reconsider its commitments to Israel. Those concerns fell on deaf ears. Despite the threat, Yamani and the monarch refrained from drastic action—it would be imprudent, they thought, to add further economic and political uncertainty to the kingdom at that time. But that did not stop them from taking steps toward the inevitable. The first one would occur in 1968, when Yamani was appointed to Aramco's Executive Committee. The man Aramco's spies deemed "affable, kind, and sincere" was about to begin plotting radical change from inside.[58]

For the Bargers and the commonwealth they had helped construct, the effects of June 1967 were even more pronounced. On June 6, as word of the Israeli campaign spread over the radio, Arab workers at

Ras Tanura started strike action. Once again the underside of labor politics bubbled to the surface, sparking a new wave of violence that at one point forced Aramco families to flee to a secured school gymnasium for protection. On June 7, protest broke out in Dhahran. There, four hundred rioters attacked Aramco's vast corporate and residential facilities, as well as US government offices. Hundreds of American personnel were forced to evacuate. Aramco's managers held their breath, praying that the bedlam would subside and some sort of familiar status quo return. But they knew that was unlikely. Tom Barger worried about his family and business and also about his church, which, as he articulated in a letter to Father John Nolan, was in a state of "chaos." His own position at Aramco seemed destined for a change as well, as increased Saudi leadership in the managerial ranks was about to push him out. He would ride the wave of transition with greater equanimity than William Eddy but never shy away from opining bitterly about the state of affairs. In early 1968 he wrote a letter to US Senator Milton Young, his friend, in which he laid out the reasons for the ongoing crisis in the Middle East. Because of "the overwhelming weight of Zionist propaganda and pressure in the United States," he warned, "the possibility of a reasoned appraisal by Americans of their interest in the Middle East" was virtually zero. Barger blamed current conditions on poor Arab leadership too, but his primary plea was for Washington to shake free of Zionist bondage and, for the sake of Israel itself, now truly hated by Arabs, shift course. The "situation in the Middle East is relatively quiet as of the moment," he said, but "the ingredients for another explosion here are all at hand. Should another one be touched off, American involvement is likely to be much greater and far more costly than at any time in the past. Whatever the outcome, the United States is bound to be the loser."[59]

As the Six-Day War ended, a strikingly different tone settled over Alberta, Canada, some 7,000 miles away. Among evangelicals like Ernest Manning, the Israeli victory triggered an air of expectation. The short, devastating battle appeared to them as divine; surely, they believed, prophecy was being fulfilled, with Christ's return and the messianic age now on the near horizon. It was equally enlivening for Manning's partners in oil. After three years of negotiations and grueling work to construct a viable plant, Great Canadian Oil Sands was ready to be christened, its alternative to Middle Eastern crude about to be unleashed. "This venture combines drama (man against nature), daring (the risk of large financial resources), and science," Sun proudly announced to its stockholders in advance of GCOS's official opening. Created to change the world, the GCOS was also a world's creation: over the course of thirty-six months, a multinational multitude of scientists, engineers, and equipment operators had shaped a mass of international supplies into an enormous complex able to extract "one of the world's largest single energy resources." GCOS's hardworking laborers and their hard-won victories, Sun stressed, stood as a "tribute to man's inventiveness and determination [to overcome] the obstacles of nature" and a signal that the "dawn of a new age" had arrived.[60]

GCOS's official opening in late September and early October 1967 projected that same technological—and theological—wonder. The three-day affair brought dignitaries from New York, Philadelphia, Chicago, and Toronto and began with dinner at a posh Edmonton ballroom. While dining, they watched a documentary produced for the occasion called *Athabasca*, which tracked the development of the oil sands through the lives of two men. The first was a Siberian immigrant and fur trapper who had lived in the Fort McMurray area for years and now watched as GCOS's arrival transformed his daily life. Through the trapper's eyes, film viewers were to see the project unfold as a benevolent effort to harness earth's bounty and civilize an uncivilized realm. The second individual, on which cameras lingered longest, was the industrialist in charge of the harnessing: J. Howard Pew. Pew was filmed commanding the company's posh Philadelphia headquarters. Amid the excitement of the GCOS venture, *Athabasca*'s producers hoped that viewers would appreciate a man whose entrustment of nature's bounties gave meaning to his life and whose faith in God made the search for black gold sacred. The following day Pew himself, along with the four hundred guests and one-hundred-member press corps, flew to Fort McMurray. Once landed, they wound their way in buses through the housing and civic buildings and over the bridge that Sun had built for the town, before arriving at the GCOS plant site. Several luminaries, including Pew, Clarence Thayer, and Premier Ernest Manning, presided over the ceremony that followed. After the singing of "O Canada" and an invocation by a local pastor, each of them hailed the GCOS as Alberta's and petroleum's step into a new epoch. Following his own extended remarks, Manning pressed the ignition button on an excavator, marking the conclusion of the formal event.[61]

Immediately, R. G. LeTourneau's machines, along with other hulking bucketwheel excavators and shovels, started to burrow into muskeg, glacial boulders, and clay in an effort to reach some of the 600 billion barrels of oil contained in the estimated 30,000 square miles of Athabasca loam. By late 1967, LeTourneau's machines had stamped their presence on Alberta's bleakest but richest terrain. So too had his church and corporate peers, whose religious networking and political maneuvers had guided an ambitious continental enterprise into being.[62]

BY THE END of 1967, with Alberta's and Saudi Arabia's petroleum industries adjusting course, it seemed an appropriate time for some of their leading voices to contemplate retirement. They did so on different terms, reflecting the volatile global swings of the moment and the end of a Cold War flourish of transnational engagement.

When Ernest Manning decided not to run for reelection in 1968, he had served as provincial head for twenty-five years. The Social Credit Party, now in its fourth decade of power, celebrated Manning's career as premier and preacher. Then it hailed the election of his heir, Harry Strom, "a devoted Christian who serves Jesus Christ even as he performs his duties to province and country," as one journalist proclaimed. Strom was a populist in Manning's mold, with family ties to Prairie Bible Institute and the mission field and to his predecessor's worldview. One of Strom's first trips after becoming premier was to Washington, DC, to hear Manning keynote Richard Nixon's Presidential Prayer Breakfast, an event assisted by Billy Graham and J. Howard Pew. That same year Strom told Pew he wanted to help GCOS any way he could. He reduced the royalties GCOS was required to pay Albertans, easing the company's burdens but stirring the wrath of opponents, who said the act was an "outrageous concession to a subsidiary of a giant multi-national corporation." Meanwhile, Manning started a political consulting firm with his son, Preston, then in 1970 accepted appointment to the Canadian Senate. Petroleum-fueled prairie populism was headed to Ottawa.[63]

The months that followed the Fort McMurray celebration marked a period of power shifts for Pew, Sun, and the conservative revolution to which they were wedded. Pew retired from his position on Sun's executive board, which prompted a series of company tributes, including one at which Howard's nephew John (Jno.) G. Pew gifted him with a rare first edition of the 1611 Folio English Bible. The patriarch's formal duties with Sun were now complete, but the company's giant was not yet ready to retreat quietly. Quite the opposite—as 1968 unfolded he once again voiced and acted on his strong theological and political opinions. With another election season approaching, Pew stepped up his own personal campaign, answering calls from conservative strategists to help Richard Nixon get elected. Nelson Rockefeller's decision to attempt another run for the GOP nomination gave Pew extra incentive. "I do know much about Nelson Rockefeller," he wrote a fellow lobbyist, and "he would be the worst man that I can think of for President of this Country of ours. To put a Republican in as President like Nelson Rockefeller, who supports all of the evils that have brought this Country to its knees, would be the most tragic thing that could happen to our Country." Pew vented some more. "If we must continue these evil Democratic principles, let the Democrats destroy us. I have always voted the Republican Ticket, but if Rockefeller is our candidate, I shall either vote the Democratic Ticket or go fishing." Rockefeller failed, again, and Pew could rest easy. A few months after Nixon defeated Democrat Hubert Humphrey in November, the retired oilman joined Republican masterminds at Nixon's prayer breakfast in Washington to offer supplications on behalf of the new "silent majority."[64]

Quietly, behind the scenes, Pew also directed money northward to Alberta. His funds were channeled into Social Credit's effort to win crucial seats in the legislature—an act that elicited Preston Manning's written appreciation. It was Pew, though, who was most outspoken in his praise of the Mannings, Preston's father in particular. During his annual talk at Sun's employee Christmas party in late December 1968, Pew gave workers a history of Christianity, from the days of the Apostle Paul through the Reformations of Martin Luther and John Calvin to the drafting of the Westminster Confession of Faith in 1646. It was the confession, Pew told his audience, which carefully laid out the fundamentals of faith in an infallible Bible and immutable God and of evangelical witness through study, supplication, and proselytization. This was the faith Pew maintained—and, by intimation, the one he hoped his employees would accept. He concluded by quoting his favorite sermon by Ernest Manning, one of the "greatest sermons" he had ever heard: "Genuine spiritual recovery is possible only where Christian people personally become involved with Christ in His death, personally become involved with Christ in His resurrection, and personally become involved as a living member of His Body, the Church, in which He Himself is the Head." Pew echoed Manning's call for Christians to stand up for the Bible, stand firm against sin, and guide their church and country back to the cross of Jesus.[65]

Pew and Manning's allies in the oil sector and the church were about to enjoy even wider opportunities to proclaim their truths and spread their wildcat doctrine on a continental stage. Even though Pew was entering the twilight of his life, and Manning, a new stage of his political career, the apparatus of oil and religious politicking they helped construct in the Cold War years was only gaining steam. Amid the tumult of the 1970s, with energy crises and culture wars battering the American public and demoralizing the nation and with US major oil and its attending spirit of capitalism and Christianity suffocating under the mounting weight of international politics, wildcat Christians would seize the day and its end-times feel and preach revival the old-fashioned way.

# CHAPTER ELEVEN

# Approaching Armageddon

D avid Rockefeller had known there would be trouble when he received an honorary doctorate at his alma mater's commencement ceremony, but it pained him just the same. The lifetime achievement should have been a sublime affair. Instead, it was showered with protest.

The root of the strife rested in David's cash donation to the Harvard Divinity School. John D. Rockefeller Jr. had been happy with Harvard president Nathan Pusey's efforts to revitalize its ministerial training program. So when in 1967 Pusey requested $2.5 million to build a new dormitory and dining hall for the divinity school, David gladly agreed to contribute $750,000, with his family putting up the rest. Harvard would name the building in Junior's honor. Scheduled for groundbreaking in 1969, Rockefeller Hall turned into a flash point at a time when Harvard was already frayed politically. Pusey was trapped. While faculty and students had hailed him in the 1950s for publicly denouncing red-baiting Senator Joseph McCarthy, by the late 1960s they were disparaging him as a stodgy, churchgoing "patrician pighead." Pusey's plight worsened. Anti-Vietnam protestors demanded he bar the Reserve Officer Training Corps (ROTC) from campus, but he refused. Tensions came to a head in April 1969 when Pusey asked police to empty the administration building, which militants had commandeered. The police, dressed in riot gear, injured 45 and arrested 197. In response, striking students shut down the school. Rockefeller Hall further enflamed the culture clash. Several divinity students demanded that Pusey reject "tainted" Rockefeller money and simultaneously lobbied for a face-to-face meeting with the banker.[1]

The showdown took place at Chase's office on June 10, 1969, two days before Harvard's commencement. A few students queried, diplomatically, whether David's funds could be diverted to the poor. But two outspoken seminarians declared that any Rockefeller gift would morally bankrupt Harvard; ill-gotten by way of earth's exploitation, such oil money also perpetuated human suffering the world over. Rockefeller religion itself, they intimated, was false. One accuser, David would recount, was "a graduate student in religion, reeking with self-righteousness, [who] asserted that Father was ... 'no real Christian at all,' who had given money away only to purge his conscience." David could barely speak, anger bubbling. "I can't think of a moment in Father's life when his actions were not motivated and shaped by his deep religious beliefs and concern for his fellowman. This was unfair to him and my family, and a most disagreeable encounter for me." He stewed as he traveled that night to Cambridge.[2]

He grew more uncomfortable as he sat on stage. Pusey had informed Rockefeller that Students for a Democratic Society (SDS) planned to demonstrate, and he felt obliged to allow them to do so. On cue, as he stepped forward to receive his degree, an SDS activist jumped on his chair and with a loudspeaker harangued the recipient: "David Rockefeller needs ROTC to protect his empire, including racist South Africa, which his money maintains"; "Harvard is used by the very rich to attack the very poor"; "Our interests as students do not lie in this tea party with these criminals, these Puseys ... and Rockefellers." Rockefeller stood awkwardly as a smattering of cheers and applause broke out in agreement with the dissident. The incident was unpleasant, he would admit, but he was most dismayed that a strident, ideological few who cared little for civility had tarnished a solemn ceremony at a university whose civility his family had long sought to uphold. It would take a while for his memory of the event to fade, far more time than it took to erect Rockefeller Hall, which opened the following year.[3]

David Rockefeller's was a typical dilemma in the late-1960s and early-1970s heyday of the New Left. As a conspicuous representative of American business prowess and global capitalism, though, he stood out among a host of easy targets for radicals who clamored to tear down the establishment. The US oil industry as a whole bore this stigma and heavy burden of guilt as it weathered the uproarious period. With OPEC flexing its muscle in retribution for US support of Israel, oil-triggered environmental disasters occurring regularly, lines at the gas pump and stagflation increasing, and the public glaring at them again as the ultimate perpetrators of society-wrecking greed, the champions of petroleum became the cursed, forced to endure another paradigm-shifting season. One did not have to be religious to theologize this chaos in apocalyptic terms. Such thinking was everywhere by the early 1970s, and America's grappling with the dark reality of "peak oil" and lost leverage in the world of crude drove much of it.

In this fractious age, major oil companies and the Rockefeller civil religion of crude experienced a difficult brush with international geopolitical transformations. For nonwhite citizens of global oil patches, the bloom of the "American Century" was long gone, the United States' desperate grip on oil a sign only of withering moral authority. In a series of political quakes, oil-producing states outside the West began to reshape the international petroleum sector according to their interests. Meanwhile, in the domestic sphere, the vision that the Rockefellers advanced of boundless spiritual, human, and material uplift through the modernizing power of petroleum met with protest. Sharing a sense of injustice with their counterparts around the world, civil rights advocates and environmentalists hammered the large oil companies. But the civil religion of crude did not simply crack under that pressure; it also began to collapse upon itself.

In contrast to the increasingly frayed major oil sector, independent oilers seized upon the national crisis to make notable political gains. They did so by marketing a message claiming that America's last chance for redemption—from secularization and bad governance, economic and cultural fragmentation, oil-hungry Muslims and Arab sheikhs—was now. Linking premillennialist theology with peak-oil theory, which predicted the swift decline of remaining US oil reserves in the 1970s, and distributing diatribes prophesying that human time (just like oil's time) was scarily short, they beseeched citizens to turn in another direction before it was too late. Assured of their privilege in the new postindustrial society and awarded further legal and economic protections by Washington, oil-patch church folk threw their clout behind a revolution meant to end altogether the era of big government and big oil.

WHEN DAVID ROCKEFELLER stepped forward to receive his honorary doctorate, he stepped into several lines of political attack, the most trenchant of which revolved around race. The petroleum-rich banking "empire" he helped govern in "racist South Africa" was one source of his troubles. Yet that one charge was merely the tip of the spear for antioil combatants. Rockefeller's Harvard appearance occurred in the thick of a wider assault on US oil's Jim Crow order. Inspired by global anticolonial movements and America's own civil rights movement, preachers, parishioners, and a black oilman turned their wrath against petroleum's apartheid.

The overwhelming whiteness of the oil business had never gone unchallenged. Under provisions of Franklin Roosevelt's Executive Order No. 9346 in 1943, which outlawed workplace discrimination by federal contractors, and the Fair Employment Practice Committee (FEPC), created to ensure compliance with that law, African American activists had filed twenty complaints against oil firms benefiting from government largesse. The most significant targeted a Shell Oil refinery in Houston and resulted in improved contractual conditions for nonwhite employees trapped in third-tier jobs. But gains were short-lived. In the immediate postwar period, oil companies regained the right to forestall labor activism, and the US Congress abolished the FEPC, leaving black oil workers without recourse. But after the *Brown v. Board of Education* decision of 1954, with the nation's highest court now backing broad desegregation measures, the National Association for the Advancement of Colored People (NAACP) renewed attacks on oil for its bald and blatant—the most blatant in US industry—Jim Crow infrastructure. Specifically, it injected new life into the nondiscrimination clause of Executive Order 9346 (which remained law) by testing its application in petroleum. Besides directing local chapters to monitor refineries and depots, it solicited workers to file grievances so that action could be taken against unions and corporations. In 1954 three black oil workers at Shell sued the Congress of Industrial Organizations–affiliated Oil Workers International Union (OWIU) for segregating its locals and failing to ensure equal employment rights for blacks. The NAACP threatened to report the failures to the President's Committee on Government Contracts, President Dwight Eisenhower's scaled-down version of the FEPC. The OWIU promised it would ameliorate the conditions and going forward secure the rights and compensations of all workers, regardless of race. In a more ambitious case in 1955, the NAACP pooled and filed discrimination charges on behalf of thirty-one black employees of oil companies in Texas City, Texas; Baton Rouge and Lake Charles, Louisiana; and El Dorado, Arkansas. Once again, the rebuked parties pledged to do better at dismantling Jim Crow inside their ranks.[4]

The NAACP won other victories as well, though never without a cost. By 1956 its labor relations director could tell a conference of black oil workers that the "first significant breakthrough in the Jim Crow pattern within the Southern oil refining industry has occurred at the Magnolia Petroleum Company, Beaumont Refinery." Blacks were now moving into positions once reserved for whites. Meanwhile, black employees at the Shell and Phillips refineries in Houston were being promoted, and the Oil, Chemical, and Atomic Workers Union was negotiating trade union contracts that eliminated the "Separate Line of Progression," which limited employed blacks to unskilled jobs in all–African American labor departments. Yet the fight for racial justice would be ongoing and bloodying. Local nonwhite crusaders faced white backlash that could be severe. On that count, one plaintiff in the NAACP's suit against the oil company in El Dorado, Arkansas, asked to be removed from the case. "I am called trouble maker by my coworkers all because I did not understand," he complained. "I will have no part of this and let my family pay for it later on. They have plenty of ways of getting rid of me." Whereas factory-floor pushback often stalled reform, the evolution of the oil industry raised additional challenges. At the moment the NAACP was fighting for fairer labor practices in petroleum, technological revolutions were making many jobs obsolete. The brief heyday of oil's industrial union was drawing to a close because the business called for more engineers and technicians than roughnecks and refinery workers—more white-collar and fewer blue-collar types. This put more pressure on black workers. Last hired, they were the first fired and, regardless of civil rights inroads, faced poorer employment prospects in 1960 than they had in 1950.[5]

That downward trend would continue to plague the industry in the 1960s, prompting heightened efforts by other allies to broaden the campaign against oil's racial injustice. Civil rights leaders demanded vigilance backed by religious conviction. Pastors and parishioners answered that call and throughout the 1960s assumed the responsibility of holding oil companies accountable for their abiding prejudices. While the struggle inside refineries continued, these activists took the fight for rights to the pump, where they demanded equal treatment as clients and consumers.[6]

Pastors had always been part of the crusade against petroleum's Jim Crow order. As presidents of NAACP chapters, ministers often found themselves on the front line of the early coordinated action against local oil firms. A popular local reverend, for instance, oversaw the Texas City branch of the NAACP, which spearheaded its attack on the refineries and labor unions that populated the oil hub. But as the Southern Christian Leadership Conference (SCLC), Martin Luther King Jr.'s alliance of black ministers, gained momentum in the early 1960s, so too did the clerical class's role in the war with crude. Their weapon of choice was the boycott.[7]

The Pure Oil Company was an early target. In 1965, an activist aligned with the SCLC threatened Pure with recourse after he stopped for gas at one of its stations and saw "white only" signs posted on its washroom doors. "After more than seven months since the Civil Rights Bill has been passed, I would say this type of race discrimination is most humiliating, to say the least," he berated Pure's executives in a letter copied to King. "I do not wish to spend my money where I can't be treated like a human being." He demanded change, as well as reimbursement for charges on his Pure Oil credit card. Were Pure's head office not compliant, he stated, "I will have no other alternative than to 1) turn in my Pure Oil credit card, 2) encourage all my friends to do so, 3) and ask for a national boycott of all Pure Oil Service Stations and products." He promised that with the SCLC's help, he would ensure that Pure encountered staggering financial blowback.[8]

Pure's confrontation with the angered black consumer was not unusual at the time—King's allies carried out numerous corporate boycotts of this sort—but it still illustrated the uniquely vulnerable political position oil companies occupied. Their decades-long campaign to sell themselves and their industry as the ultimate American free enterprise was now the very weapon activists could use to expose their racial sins. If your industry is so liberty loving and *pure*, prove it, oil's dissenters shouted to the executives and managers they confronted. And if hypocrisy could be revealed in the nation's most illustrious industry, civil rights campaigners reasoned, imagine the demand for redress that would reverberate through every corporate sector and prick the conscience of every citizen of hydrocarbon society.

Reverend Leon Sullivan pioneered the boycott tactics that activists would inflict on oil. Much like Booker T. Washington, Sullivan saw capitalism as the primary means of racial uplift, provided it operated on truly free market principles, with rights and freedoms—and consumer power—reserved for no one. After studying at Union Theological Seminary and Columbia University in New York (where he earned a master's in Religion), he moved to Philadelphia. In 1950 he became pastor of Zion Baptist Church, a congregation of 600, which during his thirty-eight-year tenure would grow to 6,000. There he devised a philosophy of community-based self-help and nonviolent protest. He created several institutions that focused on the former: while his Zion Investment Association provided a cooperative mechanism for black citizens to invest in profit-making ventures, his Opportunities Industrialization Center supplied training in technical and life skills that would allow them to acquire jobs. In 1960 he consolidated his philosophy and Philadelphia's black clergy in a loose body called the "400 Ministers," which adopted the mantra "Selective Patronage." Sullivan mobilized his movement against racially biased businesses. "There was never a formal organization," he explained. "Strangely, its disorganization was its greatest strength." Members would rotate into the "primary committee," which would pinpoint area companies to expose and disable, and then the 400 Ministers would leap into action. Over the course of the early 1960s, they did so often and effectively.[9]

Sun Oil, headquartered in Philadelphia, was one of the first companies on the receiving end of Sullivan's corporate civil rights drive. Early in the 1960s, 400 Ministers concluded that Sun's hiring record was abysmal. Blacks remained on the outside looking in, while the company's refining town of Marcus Hook and service stations remained glaringly white. Sullivan's group demanded the company hire or promote more African Americans—thirty in thirty days, to be precise. If the company did not comply, Sullivan promised a boycott. Sun hired seven black workers, but the gesture fell far short of meeting Sullivan's expectations, and the boycott was launched. "No more Sunoco till your preacher says so!" Sullivan's brotherhood barnstormed. The prohibition dragged on for ten weeks, inflicting serious losses. According to a report, one Sun service station went out of business after its sales "dropped from thirty thousand gallons per month to fourteen thousand." Sun finally pledged to hire "25 Negro girls in clerical, three drivers and one salesman." Sullivan's strategy had worked. Soon he was helping the SCLC adopt it. Sun, meanwhile, became a parable for business. One management consultant included its story in his how-to book (in this case, how-not-to) for corporations. He told his company audiences that it was time they reckon with black boycotts because they were proving successful and because no company could expect to avoid the tactic.[10]

Among those whose tactics aligned with Sullivan's was African American oil mogul Jake Simmons. Throughout his Cold War sojourns on behalf of oil-fueled economic development, he had never lost sight of the injustices in his business. His sensitivities to them were deep-seated and sharpened by years of constant striving to overcome. "You were always racially conscious in my home," Simmons's son once said. "He [Jake] believed that the way for black people to compete in the world was that we could never be 'as good'—we had to be better." Simmons was relentless in preaching his self-help gospel. But like Sullivan, he also practiced it in the context of the black church and politics. The dutiful way he had shielded black families from white vigilantes in 1930s East Texas, sponsored their moves to Oklahoma, and fought school segregation signaled early on the heavy lifting he would do for racial justice throughout the remainder of his life. During the 1950s he had grown even more agitated by the racism of his corporate regime and country and more eager to enlist in the fight. At that time he became heavily involved in politics, determined to destabilize Oklahoma's white-dominant Democratic Party. He ran in several local elections, including for Muskogee's city council, but due to the white bias entrenched in its at-large electoral system (which allowed all citizens to vote for representatives in each district, giving the white majority a distinct advantage), he lost.[11]

He had more acute influence as the famous face of the state's black electorate. His adversary was the state's oil-rich Senator Robert Kerr. Beloved by fellow wildcatters and white Baptists for his conservative views of church, state, and the market, Kerr was resented by black voters for his casual racism. Kerr made no bones about his belief that black citizens were beneath him and easily manipulated. "I have a great deal of respect for you men," he told Simmons in a meeting during Kerr's reelection campaign in 1954, "but frankly, any nigra vote I need I'm gonna buy." Simmons fumed at Kerr's racial politicking during the campaign and decided to lend his stature to Kerr's Democratic opponent. In response, Kerr railed against Simmons, telling an audience of black voters, "I hear you've got a Negro here who carries water on both sides." Kerr painted Simmons as a "wealthy political mercenary" with only self-interest in mind; Simmons did not budge—he was too powerful to be taken down easily. But he also felt the effects of Kerr's subsequent win. Kerr, in a quest for revenge, Simmons believed, killed his first big chance with Phillips Oil to explore Liberia in the mid-1950s.[12]

By the time the black wildcatter arrived in Africa in the mid-1960s, he was more willing than ever to channel his money and experiences from oil into civil rights initiatives. Although Simmons refrained from criticizing US race relations during the 1963 trade mission that led to his work in Nigeria's and Ghana's emerging oil fields, he did not shy away from dialoguing about racial dynamics or absorbing the lessons he saw emerging from the continent's anticolonial movements. His subsequent labor in Africa alerted him to the strong critiques of white Western imperialism gestating there. While working in Ghana he grew close to an African American in Accra with the unlikely name Robert E. Lee. This Lee and his wife were part of the growing community of black expats in Ghana who gave up their US citizenship and renounced ties to US capitalist society. To what extent Lee's strident anticolonialism and anti-Americanism rubbed off on Simmons is unknown, but over time Simmons demonstrated a greater commitment to social justice. While continuing to broker oil deals, he took it upon himself to liaise between multinational oil companies and Ghana's government and serve as a protector against colonizing power. "Jake was somebody the Ghanaians felt they could trust and he would not do the wrong thing by them," one of Simmons's competitors admitted. "He acted ex officio, sort of as their adviser." By 1969, he had earned hundreds of thousands of dollars and made Ghana's political class— and several oil companies—rich. Back on US soil, he funneled his foreign profits into church and civic organizations geared to race reform, backed the boycott movement, and as president of the Oklahoma State Conference of the NAACP oversaw some of the most important backroom decisions and maneuvers involved in the campaign.[13]

By then, the civil rights circles in which he moved were immersed in another stage of the boycott movement, one that would turn the spirit of the Rockefellers' civil religion of crude against itself. David Rockefeller would feel the effects, as would the executives of other multinational oil corporations. To many Americans, killing Jim Crow in crude now necessitated a collective effort to punish US oil companies' global ventures in political zones governed by hate. Whereas earlier the major corporations felt free to direct their economic ambitions and developmental strategies toward foreign terrains ruled by oppressive regimes, continuing to do so risked alienating the consumers whose dollars propelled their advance.

Rumblings of this crusade began around the time Rockefeller visited Harvard in 1969. As the vestiges of colonialism began to disappear, activists zeroed in on those African nations where the combination of Western influence and racial political structures still existed. Topping their list were South Africa and Portuguese-held Angola. Major oil companies that operated there were singled out as accomplices in apartheid. Between 1969 and 1970, the Chicago Alliance Against Standard Oil—comprised of several women's, student, and black-power organizations—conducted a strike against Esso (Jersey Standard) at the company's stockholders meeting. Here was a company, the alliance fumed, that netted profits "of over one billion dollars (1,049,000,000) in 1969 by draining the resources of the Third World [and] denying the majority of its workers the right to unionize." The alliance also carried out an advertising blitz that used the Esso Tiger to embarrass its master. "The

ESSO Tiger . . . paw in paw with white racist militarism in Southern Africa," read one such ad. "Keep the Tiger Out of Your Tank." Mobil, also under assault, defended its presence in South Africa, echoing sentiments that its peers held. "As a major international oil company," it swore publicly, Mobil has "interests in more than 100 countries," some of which are run by undemocratic regimes that "we as Americans do not endorse." "Whatever our own view," it underscored, Mobil and other US oil companies in these countries "have tended historically to contribute to constructive change." Mobil cited the 1,000 nonwhites on its payroll "who are paid equally for the same work as whites" as evidence it was doing right and encouraging South Africans to do the same.[14]

Oil's dissenters saw little substance in those claims, and between the summers of 1970 and 1971 they ratcheted up their campaigning. In July 1970, the Ohio Conference of the United Church of Christ (UCC), a member of the National Council of Churches (NCC), formally resolved that as a major economic player in Portugal's African colonies, Gulf Oil "provides support for the suppression of the African national liberation movements." The denomination asked its 230,000 members to discontinue use of Gulf products until the company discontinued African operations "that cause human suppression and suffering." The stand received wide press coverage. In a private demand that went public, Gulf's president pressed UCC's president for "an immediate retraction of the resolution." The giant corporation was determined to nip the controversy in the bud—even if that meant taking on a church. But only built-up resentments and louder endorsements for the UCC followed. The loudest came from the American Committee on Africa (ACOA), the large (with 21,000 members circa 1963) interracial human rights organization with strong interfaith priorities and commitments to fighting African apartheid and supporting the continent's independence movements. In addition to calling on its members to boycott Gulf, the ACOA pledged the UCC legal assistance. The NCC-affiliated United Presbyterian Church, one of the largest denominations in the country, also joined the fight—in December 1970, a special task force approved a scheme to protest Gulf from within. The force urged church boards and agencies to "buy or retain Gulf stock [then] assign proxies to the Task Force [and] send representatives to the stockholders meeting."[15]

The tactic succeeded, if only at fomenting further public unrest. On April 27, 1971, representatives of the Presbyterian task force arrived at Gulf's annual meeting in Atlanta with 20,000 shares in hand, enough to force four of its proposals onto the agenda and nominate candidates for the board of directors. The meeting was raucous. "There were pickets present outside and fifty or sixty students and other protestors actually in the stockholders' meeting," a Presbyterian activist reported. "There were catcalls" on both sides, and they "tended to be disruptive, although the meeting was completed without undue disorder." The Presbyterians' resolutions for Gulf to sever itself from racist colonial governments were defeated in a vote, as were their candidates, which included the leader of the Popular Liberation Movement for Angola and black communist activist Angela Davis. But they did raise the profile of the entire crusade. The attention was not uniformly positive. Conservative columnist James J. Kilpatrick, a former champion of segregation, chastised the activists for "climbing into a political bed" with "terrorist gangs that are trained, armed and equipped by the Communists" and ignoring Gulf's "enlightened and humane program [of] jobs, income, medical care and education." Some unhappy Presbyterians chimed in, voicing displeasure with their denomination's liberal voices. One wrote Gulf's president promising to rally parishioners in defense of the oil corporation. "I hope you will not mistakenly believe that all Presbyterians agree with the Church leaders," he said. Another complained to J. Howard Pew, who responded by articulating his own strong opposition and a statement of hope "that the Church will be brought back to its proper mission—the proclaiming of the Gospel and the saving of souls."[16]

In the coming months, activists escalated the fight against oil companies operating in southern Africa. With the backing of ACOA, leaders like Leon Sullivan used their advanced standing in the corporate world to make their opinions known. By 1971, Sullivan was a new appointee on the executive board of General Motors (GM), and in that capacity he promised he would insist that GM and Gulf "move from South Africa to elsewhere in Africa" where, he stated, "black people are not treated like dogs." At the institutional level, the United Presbyterian Church joined the ACOA in contacting colleges around the country that owned Gulf stock, asking that they divest. Lobbying Washington was on their docket as well. Impassioned individuals, meanwhile, continued ground-level action. One Gulf stockholder—a grandmother from California—traveled to Africa to observe Gulf's operations firsthand. She returned with a less than glowing report. While Gulf had indeed assisted "the black government in Nigeria with the 'transition from colonialism to self-determination,'" its "Angolan efforts," she wrote in 1973, were "ludicrous and feeble." There she saw workers living in "one-room dormitories" while Gulf's white managerial class lived "in a world of golf courses, swimming pools and luxurious homes with well-stocked liquor cabinets." She implored Gulf to change its ways.[17]

Gulf did not change, but by the mid-1970s, with condemnation still echoing through the pews and press, it did find itself on another plane. As most corporations with international footprints were prone to do, the company insisted that as a "corporate citizen" of its host countries, it was committed to remaining completely "nonpartisan" and focused solely on improving the economic conditions of the people. What was the benefit of leaving locals out of work? "You don't help a man by taking his livelihood from him," an official with another company complained. David Rockefeller agreed, and that was his stated reason—despite the Harvard critics—for keeping Chase in South Africa. "I never hesitated to meet with . . . rulers whose despotic and dictatorial style I personally despised," he would write defensively. "Even though I was totally unsympathetic to these regimes, I believed the bank should work with them." In Gulf's case, Angola's war of independence in 1975 forced its hand. The company cut off its operation and withdrew. Once the Portuguese had been defeated and an independent government installed, Gulf returned, this time to aid postcolonial reconstruction and to a position of favor in the eyes of civil rights advocates. In 1976 the corporation sent a hefty check to the SCLC as a gesture of support (and rapprochement). Relations between the two promptly improved. SCLC president Ralph Abernathy expressed his appreciation to Gulf's president: "We want Gulf to know how pleased we are with your assistance in stabilizing the economy of Angola," he wrote. "We are positive that such efforts as yours will help all the people of Angola to achieve democracy in the long run. Once again, thank you for your generous contribution."[18]

FOR MANY ANGRY church folk and other activists, to attack the racist complicities of crude was to attack its abysmal environmental record as well. Gulf officials knew charges of negligence in the treatment of vulnerable ecosystems were waiting for them when they arrived at the Atlanta stockholders meeting on August 27, 1971, not simply charges of negligence in their dealings with apartheid regimes. They and their peers in other companies also knew they had plenty to contend with, as the ecological crisis their business had precipitated was quite literally erupting, and journalistic accounts of petrohavoc were moving Americans to action.[19]

From the late 1960s to the mid-1970s, it seemed like news of water set ablaze by oil and creatures suffocated in ebony goop would not abate. On March 18, 1967, one of the industry's first supertankers, bowels filled with BP product, neared the terminus of its trip from Kuwait to Wales. "I saw this huge ship sailing and I thought he's in rather close, I hope he knows what he's doing," recalled a resident who was peering off a cliff near Cornwall, England. The captain of the *Torrey Canyon* did not. The ship hit a reef, splitting open its holding tanks and precipitating the worst oil spill in British history; within twenty-four hours, it spread twenty miles. Newspapers on both sides of the Atlantic painted the *Torrey* as a tragic threshold. One after another suggested humans were now facing an apocalypse, if not a cosmic event then certainly a terrestrial one. It was painfully evident, the *New York Times* editorialized, that "there is no escape from the destructiveness of our industrial society." The *Times*'s *Sunday Magazine* ran a story titled "The Oil Around Us," with a searing takeaway: "petroleum has become a devil in our civilization ... creating a survival issue both for sea life and for man himself." Two years later, annihilation hit closer to home for Americans. In January 1969, a Union Oil rig off the shore of Santa Barbara, California, blew out, spewing 3 million barrels of crude into the channel and onto a fourteen-mile stretch of beach. The California Fish and Game Department, joined by area residents, rushed to rescue oil-soaked, beach-bound birds, 3,500 of which perished. The media arrived to document the grief Santa Barbara citizens displayed as they tried to save nature from the man-made calamity. No one arrived to save nature a few months later, in June, when the Cuyahoga River caught fire in Cleveland. Oil leakage from refineries combusted the polluted stream. This had occurred before; stock images from a 1952 river fire, in fact, graced the pages of *Time* magazine's account of the 1969 blaze, as if there were no point in distinguishing the events.[20]

With the Cleveland river fire of 1969, America's first Petrolia—the economic region bounded by the production zone of Pennsylvania's Oil Creek to the east and the refining zone of Rockefeller's Cleveland to the west—was reminded again of the damage the resource could do to its environs. Since the 1860s, reformers had always been first on the scene of petroleum's bloody disasters to lament the resulting death and try to make things better. But the industry had never witnessed the resolve of the reform-minded citizens of the 1970s, who after hearing about and seeing the oil spills decided they had had enough. As one scholar asserts, the images were especially powerful motivators. The portraits of oil-soaked birds, victims of technology and oil dependence, "paired with . . . volunteers bathing the animal[s]," evoked a new motif with moral weight, one of American consumers "seeking salvation from oil sin through efforts to save the helpless." "Not only was it man's fault that they suffered," the *Boston Globe* editorialized a few years later, "but we can look at their sad plight and see in it our own fate." Yet the actual words people wrote about the petrochemical catastrophes mattered too, and for reformers inside and outside the church, no two writers were more important than Rachel Carson and Lynn White.[21]

The former had passed away before the oil crises of 1969, but her ideas acquired traction in their wake. Carson was in many ways a product of Pennsylvania's Petrolia, and a mirror of Ida Tarbell. Her grandfather was a Presbyterian minister, while her mother had attended a United Presbyterian seminary before marrying Robert Carson, an equally devout Presbyterian. The two moved to Springdale, Pennsylvania, a town on the Allegheny River downstream from Franklin and Oil City, onetime terminuses for the barges that transported crude down French and Oil Creeks for shipping via the larger stream. Rachel grew up in Springdale and attended church with her family, immersing herself in its Calvinist natural theology, which called on Christians to appreciate God's handiwork in nature, as well as in her mother's love of nature, which she considered "divine obligation." Carson's worldview shifted away from Protestant orthodoxy as she studied to become a marine biologist. She became convinced that evolutionary theory was at the heart of the planetary story, so much so that she would later face accusations from conservatives that she was "two parts evolutionist, one part fallen Presbyterian," which she would reply was true. "I accept the theory of evolution as the most logical one that has ever been put forward to explain the development of living creatures on this earth," she said, before announcing there was "absolutely no conflict between a belief in evolution and a belief in God as the creator." Much like Tarbell, Carson's deistic lens allowed her to process the scientific and the spiritual in dual ledgers, with little sense that the two could or should clash. Nor did she have the patience to debate the point much—there were other theological crises weighing on humanity. By the late 1950s, as she watched Cold War technology and the whims of a plastic society overrun ecology, she determined to use convicting prose to warn people about the impending cataclysm.[22]

*Silent Spring* was published in 1962. It excoriated the chemical industry for its deadly synthetic pesticides. "As crude a weapon as the cave man's club, the chemical barrage has been hurled against the fabric of life," she wrote. "It is our alarming misfortune that so primitive a science has armed itself with the most modern and terrible weapons, and that in turning them against the insects it has also turned them against the earth." Carson urged the public to wake up to the physical and moral cancers chemicals and technology were unleashing on the bodies of society. Here her thinking departed from Tarbell's. Whereas Tarbell had seen the devastation oil wreaked on her valley as a sign of an enlightened economic system corrupted by a few men, Carson saw the origins of the ecological crisis in the very system itself—in the advent of industries like the one Frank Tarbell helped propel and in the "biologic change" they induced. The Calvinist in her did not go away completely; the jeremiad tone she used to describe a fallen humanity was a residue of her Presbyterian Sunday School. But the religion she now preached encouraged its practitioners to reverse the downfall by spiritually communing again with nature, Carson's first order, and ensuring that the springs were no longer silent or silenced.[23]

While oilmen would contend with Carson's treatise on the streets and in the popular press, they would have to counter historian Lynn Townsend White Jr.'s in the church and the classroom. Born in 1907, less than a month before Carson, White was, like his contemporary, raised in a home of theologically astute parents. White's father, as his son would describe him, was a "liberal Calvinist professor of Christian ethics" who conditioned his son to see the world through that theological lens. After graduating from Stanford University in 1928, White attended Union Theological Seminary in New York, where he studied with prominent theologian and public intellectual Reinhold Niebuhr. White would complete a PhD in history at Harvard University before eventually landing on the faculty of the University of California, Los Angeles. A medievalist, he was nevertheless drawn to contemporary debates about industry, technology, and environment—and their religious dimensions—and ready to contextualize them in the long cycles of time. His 1967 article "The Historical Roots of Our Ecological Crisis" quickly became a classic in environmentalist circles. Prior to the nineteenth century, he argued, technology had been "lower-class [and] action-oriented," science the realm of the "aristocratic [and] intellectual." The ecological crisis, White asserted, emerged from the period of industrial ferment that followed, when science and technology fused into one human quest to mechanize and modernize the world. According to White, Judeo-Christian religion legitimated this revolution. Its suppression of pagan notions of nature as an organic whole, in which humanity was just one equal part, justified technological conquest and "made it possible to exploit nature in a mood of indifference to the feelings of natural objects." White concluded that what was occurring around him in smog-suffused Los Angeles was the outgrowth of a mood and mode of modernity whose calamitous effects were sanctified by America's dominant faith. "Christianity bears a huge burden of guilt," he arraigned. "We shall continue to have a worsening ecological crisis until we reject the Christian axiom that nature has no reason for existence save to serve man."[24]

Armed with the charged writings of Carson, White, and other thinkers, a new class of environmental activists took to the streets and seminary classrooms to reverse the fearsome trends. Some marched on platforms drained of any explicit religion, while many others walked the middle path, rejecting orthodoxies of the church without abandoning the spiritual life. Influenced by Buddhism and transcendentalist concepts of an ecosystem impregnated with the divine and wedded to the cosmos (concepts not unlike what Henry Williams taught at his spiritualist colony off Santa Barbara's once pristine shores in the 1890s), they approached their protest as a priestly calling. It was time, they said, to remove man from the philosophical center of the universe, drain anthropocentrism from human presupposition, and—as Carson advocated—let the waters and fowl speak again as equals in the universe. Answering White's prompts, meanwhile, professors of theology began ironing out new ecological belief systems that reintroduced sacramental and holistic emphases of land care and personal devotion.[25]

Signs of collective impact came with the first Earth Day in April 1970. After touring the oil disaster at Santa Barbara, Wisconsin senator Gaylord Nelson had devised a plan. "If we could tap into the environmental concerns of the general public, and infuse the student anti-war energy into the environmental cause," he thought, "we could generate a demonstration that would force the issue onto the national political agenda." On April 22, 1970, 20 million Americans showed their support for environmental protection by way of their feet, chants, and song. Grassroots momentum extended up to Washington and produced a slew of bipartisan initiatives. On the heels of the Santa Barbara spill, the House Subcommittee on Minerals, Materials, and Fuels held hearings to consider banning offshore drilling in the Santa Barbara Channel. Drilling there was suspended for a time, and policies were put in place requiring offshore platform operators to pay hefty penalties and cleanup costs for any spill they incurred. President Richard Nixon, meanwhile, signed the National Environmental Policy Act and the Endangered Species Act, resulting in creation of the Environmental Protection Agency and the National Oceanic and Atmospheric Administration. The president's bold actions gave legitimacy to pro-environment activists and a significant boost to their causes in the public eye. Nixon himself acknowledged in his 1970 State of the Union address, "The question of the seventies, is: shall we surrender to our surroundings, or shall we make our peace with nature and begin to make reparations for the damage we have done to our air, to our land, and to our water?"[26]

Amid the popular and presidential outcries, the petroleum industry was placed in a difficult political spot. During the period of intense environmentalist action between 1969 and 1973, oil executives hewed to a cautious approach, wanting to voice support for the emerging Nixon consensus without entirely sacrificing their interests. Sun Oil was fairly typical in the way it walked that tightrope. On one hand, it defended its record. Speaking before the Subcommittee on Minerals, Materials, and Fuels in 1969, Executive Vice President R. E. Foss pleaded with Washington not to ban offshore oil production in the Santa Barbara Channel. Sun did not want its platforms there to stand idle. The wreckage caused by Union's offshore platform was an anomaly, Foss argued. Oil was being drilled in many sensitive zones with no negative consequences for nature. "Many of us who have been around the nation's oil areas," he observed, "have seen oil being pumped from beneath an egret rookery on Avery Island, La., a horticultural show place, and have watched fish being caught in quantity from drilling rigs in the Gulf." Foss was more forceful in a second claim: that an offshore drilling ban would weaken national security. "Imagine the dangers we would face," he said, "if we allowed ourselves to become too dependent on imported oil." "It is imperative," he added, "that we not only keep up our pace, but that we quicken it if we are to find the tremendous reserves our Country needs to maintain a safe level of self-sufficiency." Where were these new reserves coming from? he asked rhetorically. From the sea— proven grounds like the Santa Barbara Channel. Foss insisted that the area could be mined responsibly. Remember, he paused: "Oilmen do have a heart and a concern for the protection of wildlife." After demonstrating the safety of its offshore structures, Sun was eventually allowed to resume drilling.[27]

Internally, though, Sun took the lessons of the day to heart and started implementing structural changes. At the very same moment that the oil disasters were precipitating environmental action, Sun was undergoing a leadership change. With J. Howard Pew now absent from boardroom politics altogether, Sun's chairman, Robert Dunlop, and president, Robert Sharbaugh, tweaked its mission by stressing corporate citizenship over libertarian values. "While the company is primarily an economic organization," the company's annual report for 1970 read, "it is also a social institution." In accordance with that slight shift in emphasis, Dunlop and Sharbaugh formed the Corporate Committee on Environmental Conservation, charged with recalibrating the company's handling of sensitive ecospheres, adopting biodegradable materials for its containers, and foolproofing its technologies of exploration, drilling, and spill prevention. Meanwhile, it exuded a progressive public spirit. When Earth Day 1970 was announced, Sharbaugh told Sun's stockholders that the company was offering full support for its sit-ins, exhibits, and marches. "Our objective," he stated, "is not simply to abide by the law, but to do the most effective job we can of protecting the environment while successfully functioning as a competitive petroleum enterprise."[28]

Sun's political allies reinforced the political suppleness its new leaders encouraged. While some conservatives of Pew's ilk fretted over Washington's rapid extension of control over land and resources—another landgrab, they complained—most recognized the need for a nuanced approach. Levelheadedness and a clear cost-benefit analysis conducted by all invested parties were required at this sensitive juncture, they argued. Make no mistake, one commentator in the *National Review* reminded readers: the environmental movement was one that the political Right had to come to terms with, for both existential and politically pragmatic reasons. The "violation of the land, the violation of the natural environment generally, is felt without even the possibility of argument to be the quintessence of evil," the editorial acknowledged, and conservation is "likely to be a powerful, indeed an overriding *spiritual* issue, which it would be political suicide to concede to the Left."[29]

WHATEVER PUBLIC RELATIONS equanimity oil companies could muster during the early days of the environmental movement foundered on the shoals of the energy crisis that beset the nation at mid-decade. Charges of avarice voiced against the oil industry earlier in the century now resurfaced as a wholesale condemnation of its presence in modern society. Major corporations with immense international footprints suffered the heaviest opprobrium. The gospels of global outreach they once touted rang hollow. Some of the very architects of international oil now deemed the commodity, rather than a liquid from the gods, the devil's waste, responsible for the subjugation of entire peoples, the perpetuation of unequal systems of power, and a crumbling world order.

That sentiment gained traction as the Middle East returned to a season of grisly enmity. After the humiliations of the Six Day War, oil-producing Arab states had started pressuring Western oil companies with threats of nationalization. By the early 1970s, they possessed a political weapon of immense proportions, and they knew it. In the 1950s, geophysicist M. King Hubbert had theorized that US oil production would peak by the early 1970s and then fall off precipitously, rendering the nation vulnerable to foreign reserves. At least in an immediate context, he seemed largely correct. By the time Richard Nixon assumed the presidency in January 1969, domestic production was on the decline; worse yet, reserves were dropping too. Demand now almost equaled available supply, and the surplus that the industry had maintained for twenty years was virtually drained. All this meant one thing: unparalleled dependence on North African and Middle Eastern oil. To add an exclamation point, at this very juncture Saudi Arabia could boast the highest petroleum output of any country, assuming the lofty title once reserved for Texas. It was now the "swing producer of the entire world." "The moment has come," Saudi oil czar Ahmed Yamani uttered quietly in 1973, at a moment when he and King Faisal were deciding to brandish their weapon. "We are masters of our own commodity."[30]

Other Middle Eastern leaders, such as Muammar Qaddafi, were anxious to play the role of master. After orchestrating a military coup in 1969, the new Libyan lord fashioned himself the heir of Gamal Nasser (who died in 1970) and in that vein set out to extend OPEC's authority. He issued threats with the fatalistic abandon of a bedouin chief. "We lived without oil for 5,000 years, and we could live without it again," he told the world, making it clear he was unafraid of war. He was particularly animated in his hatred of US oil interests. "We tell America in a loud voice today," he announced in 1973, "that she needs a sharp slap in the face." By 1972 he had already proved as good as his word. Besides nationalizing 51 percent of Western oil companies at work on his terrain, including Armand Hammer's Occidental Petroleum, he expropriated altogether the independent oil operations of Texan Bunker Hunt, son of H. L. Hunt. Qaddafi boasted that by annexing Hunt he had landed "a big hard blow" on America's "cold insolent face." Qaddafi's message was starting to get through to US diplomats, if not with the brute force he craved. A US ambassador familiar with evolving sentiments in Libya warned Washington that the great game of oil had changed for good. "Asserting control over a vital source of energy would permit Middle Eastern states to regain the power position vis-à-vis the

West, which this area lost long ago." The diplomat's caution received only a lukewarm response.[31]

That was no longer the case after the Yom Kippur War of October 1973. With emerging voices such as Qaddafi's hardening the resolve of the Arab Middle East, conflict seemed inevitable. On October 6, 1973, Syria and Egypt attacked Israel, whose military personnel were observing Yom Kippur, the holiest day in Judaism. Applying the stealth Israel had exercised six years earlier, Syrian and Egyptian forces—soon fortified by materials and men from Iraq, Libya, Algeria, Jordan, and Saudi Arabia—stormed Israeli troops in the Sinai and Golan Heights. As the struggle heated up, the superpowers started doling out aid—the Soviet Union to its Arab allies, the United States to Israel. One week into the conflict, though, Israel was in trouble. "For several days it was touch and go, and the very survival of the state of Israel was at stake," oilman Zvi Alexander would recall. "It was a time of uncertainty, grief and disillusionment." Gradually, as the war entered its third week, Israel's military started recovering lost terrain and pushing into Egypt. The reversal pleased but also worried US Secretary of State Henry Kissinger; for the sake of maintaining some rapport with Saudi Arabia, he thought the best result (as he told Secretary of Defense James Schlesinger) "would be if Israel came out a little ahead but got bloodied in the process, and if the U.S. stayed clean." Kissinger helped guarantee that type of ending when he publicly endorsed a UN peace effort, promising Arab nations to take seriously the political anxieties on which they acted at the outset of war and now harbored as war drew to a close and the redrawing of national boundaries began. As of October 26, the conflict was over.[32]

The war ended, but the upheaval did not. Though more victor than vanquished, Israel was in a severely weakened position. Upset with the unpreparedness of their leaders, Israelis demanded changes, resulting in the resignation of Prime Minister Golda Meir and her cabinet. Israelis were also psychologically scarred by the awareness that their military prowess could no longer guarantee their security. That sense of exposure also redoubled Israel's worries about energy, a conundrum it had appeared to resolve when it seized Egypt's Abud Rudeis fields in the Sinai Peninsula during the Six Day War. After peace was restored in late 1973, Israel was forced to return the lucrative site. Meanwhile, as punishment for Israel's alignment with the United States, Israeli oil companies were exiled from Arab-friendly African producing nations in which they had been active since the early 1960s. Once again Jewish oilmen were forced to poke at their nation's barren soil. As before, their hopes would fade with each new dry hole, reaffirming the two major takeaways from the Yom Kippur War. First, as Zvi Alexander stated matter-of-factly, oil-rich Arabs were the unquestioned "kings of the world." Second, the Jewish state's existential struggle with crude would never see relief. Shortly before battle raged, Meir had delivered a quip at a state dinner that summed up a universal feeling among fellow Jews: "Let me tell you something that we Israelis have against Moses. . . . He took us 40 years through the desert in order to bring us to the one spot in the Middle East that has no oil."[33]

Even if still relatively rich in oil, the United States shared Alexander and Meir's darkened outlook. The Yom Kippur maelstrom rocked it in unexpected ways. Kissinger had hoped to straddle competing interests by supporting Israel while staying the course with Saudi Arabia. Yet the political dance was delicate. Three days into the conflict, Saudi Arabia agreed to OPEC's plan for payback by way of an oil embargo on the United States and all other supporters of Israel. Aramco president Frank Jungers was placed in the supremely awkward position of implementing a policy meant to punish his home country. "We were given day-by-day instruction of what the boycott order was," he later wrote. "And we [obeyed] in order not to give them [the chance of nationalization]. We had no choice." The embargo continued well after the ceasefire, raising tensions between the United States and Saudi Arabia. "It is clear," Kissinger opined, "that if pressures continue . . . the U.S. will have to consider what countermeasures it may have to take." Should Americans resort to "countermeasures," Ahmed Yamani retorted, Arab producers would blow up their own oil fields. A retired Tom Barger published an op-ed that advised a reduction in heated rhetoric, lest a decades-long bilateral endeavor combust into dust. Despite Barger's pleas, the embargo would last until March 1974. Only after the United States committed to ironing out postwar "disengagement" details between Israel and its Arab neighbors did OPEC lift its ban.[34]

By then, Americans were in a fit of panic. Although they could not appreciate it fully at the time, the energy crisis had vaulted them into a period of shattering transformation. The United States now had to confront the stark reality of economic globalization—multilateral flows of commodities, commerce, financial interests, and political power that smashed the bilateral clarities of the early Cold War period. Globalization left Washington scrambling to reclaim its footing as a superpower and reorient its diplomacy according to the demands of a new world order's dizzying "interdependencies." Simmering homegrown quandaries made matters worse. Within months of the oil embargo, economists came to recognize the strange brew of fiscal poisons—slow economic growth, high unemployment, and rising inflation—into which the country was now plunged. "The disease of the times is no longer simply inflation nor economic stagnation," the *New York Times* warned. "It is stagflation." Then there was Watergate. At the same moment Richard Nixon was compelled to address pressing energy questions, he was also fighting failure on raw political grounds. When, on October 20, 1973—even as the Yom Kippur battle climaxed—he fired special prosecutor Archibald Cox rather than comply with a court order to turn over the Oval Office's tape recordings, calls for his impeachment escalated. Regardless of whether they grasped the extent of the ruptures their society now faced, Americans had good reason to believe its fabric was coming undone.[35]

Over the next few years, the oil industry served as an object of scorn and reproach—and an outlet for citizens' mounting anxiety. As fuel prices skyrocketed and gas lines lengthened in 1973 and 1974, citizens fumed. Nixon's advisors fretted: "No issue has such a potential for producing social instability of the magnitude of the depression as does the energy crisis," one pollster submitted. "Considerable public fear and indignation, cries of industry conspiracy and government ineptitude, and possibly real hardships, appear imminent," another insider added. As complaints poured into the White House, it became evident that Americans were in the throes of an existential crisis. Residents of a North Carolina town wrote to tell Nixon, "People are spending every waking hour worrying over the gasoline situation." They were not alone. National polls showed that a vast majority of Americans believed the oil crisis was the nation's most critical problem. "What is worse than 'Watergate' and all the various charges against the President?" asked a New Jersey man. "Answer—the gas crisis in Bergen County."[36]

At the pumps, in the streets, and in the media, meanwhile, people expressed their emotions with additional heat. A rallying spirit did prevail in some quarters. Rideshares became popular, even fashionable. The ultimate model operated out of Riverside Church's Interchurch Center on Manhattan's Upper West Side. Several of the center's clerical leaders organized a commuters' co-op in the early 1960s. When the energy crisis occurred, it was already operating three large station wagons that whisked thirty dues-paying members from New Jersey to Manhattan. During the oil embargo they listened to the news and bonded. "I have found a Christian community in a car pool," one member admitted. Even oil companies tried to rally at the grass roots. Sun Oil started a bicycle sales and service division and implemented the program in several fueling stations along the East Coast. Still, the overriding sentiment was one of exasperation and anger. One pump attendant had customers threaten to "kill me or burn down the station." "They're out of their minds, they're turning sick," the co-owner of a Sun Oil station in Brooklyn attested. Upset with their pump attendants and with government mishandling of matters, customers' greatest ire was reserved for US oil companies themselves, major companies in particular. In the dark days of early 1974, rumors circulated that the petroleum giants had manufactured the crisis and quarantined filled tankers offshore in order to raise gas prices. Roughly three-quarters of all Americans believed the conspiracy to be real.[37]

It was not only the average American who believed that. US congressmen wrote Nixon words of populist protest. "Our energy 'crisis' is deliberately contrived by the major oil companies," one midwestern senator declared. Another leveled the same charge: "There is little doubt that the so-called gasoline shortage in the Midwest is just a big, lousy gimmick foisted on consumers to bilk them for billions in increased gasoline prices." Several different congressional hearings backed up those words with action. One, the Subcommittee on Multinational Corporations, headed by Senator Frank Church, produced a multivolume summation of US major oil's global profits and shady government partnerships. We must "uncover the trail that led the United States into dependency on Arab sheikhdoms for so much of its oil," Church offered when describing his task. "We must re-examine the premise that what's good for the oil companies is good for the United States." He demanded transparency: "In a democracy, important questions of policy with respect to a vital commodity like oil, the life blood of an industrial society, cannot be left to private companies acting in accord with private interests and a closed circle of government officials." Meanwhile, Democratic senators Henry "Scoop" Jackson and Hubert Humphrey accused oil firms of a "contrived effort" to limit supplies and asked the Federal Trade Commission (FTC) to investigate. Sitting before the FTC panel to plead their case was a humiliating experience for oil executives. "The contrivance theory is absolute nonsense," Gulf's president insisted. "We have not cheated or misled anyone and if any member of the subcommittee has proof of any such acts by Texaco," its CEO doubled down, "we would like to be presented with such proof." A month later, the FTC's report asserted that the eight largest oil companies in the United States had suppressed supplies in order to heighten profits. And as the oil firms' annual reports for 1973 emerged, they did indeed list record-setting profits, making the Texaco executive's stand a shaky one. In truth, though, his defense contained merit: although oil's gross profits were enormous, net windfalls after costs and losses revealed a below-average return for the US oil industry. But politicians won the day. US major oil was guilty of obscene profits, Jackson announced in headline-grabbing fashion.[38]

Meanwhile, headier critics asked fellow citizens to pause and consider the possibility that oil was not so much the cause of the nation's problems as a symptom of deeper moral flaws. In a rerun of the 1920s, the US oil industry was once again called to task for its greed, gluttony, and pride. Yet, in the 1970s climate of profound insecurity, blame for such deadly sins extended to the nation as a whole. Referencing recent images of the earth taken by astronauts, scientists pointed out the "whiskey-brown smog" hovering over Los Angeles, "where 4 million cars vomit unburned hydrocarbons." The visual limned a society trapped in its overwhelming desire for mastery and more—more freeways, more suburban paradises, more fuel for fancier cars in which people could dash around at higher speeds in pursuit of the next thing. Was that not greed, pride, and gluttony as well, critics pondered?[39]

There was another unique dimension to the collective confessionals of oil and society in the mid-1970s: foreign leaders were eager to help Americans self-flagellate. When President Nixon complained to Shah Pahlavi of Iran about OPEC's anti-American maneuvers, the shah responded with a litany of moral lessons. "They [industrial nations like the United States] will have to realize that the era of their terrific progress and even more terrific income and wealth based on cheap oil is finished." "Eventually they will have to tighten their belts," he continued; "those children of well-to-do families who have plenty to eat at every meal, who have their cars, and who act almost as terrorists and throw bombs here and there, they will have to rethink all these aspects of the advanced industrial world. And they will have to work harder." The shah would soon learn painful lessons of his own, but his stinging indictment was in keeping with prevailing moods. Other international voices cast broader aspersions on oil-rich nations for birthing a beast. Blame did fall on American shoulders, they argued: by so aggressively drawing bile from the earth's bowels, Americans had also let its demons escape. But others were implicated in the great game that paralyzed the world. That was Juan Pablo Perez Alfonzo's take. The former oil minister of Venezuela was dismayed by the geopolitical struggles petroleum instigated in the 1970s, as well as their impact on his own nation. By 1976 he was distraught at the way oil riches had corrupted his society's values. "I may be the father of OPEC," he confessed, "but now sometimes I feel like renouncing my offspring." The ancients, he said, used to call oil "the devil's excrement." Looking out on his nation and his world, he concluded they were right.[40]

Many Americans felt the same as they looked out on their own country in 1976, their nation's two-hundredth birthday. On the heels of Watergate, the rights revolution, *Roe v. Wade*, and the energy crisis, the bicentennial raised more anxiety than jubilation. How does a divided nation pay tribute to itself? How does a fractured nation pretend to be whole? Pretending was impossible. "I must say to you that the state of our Union is not good," President Gerald Ford told the nation during his State of the Union address in 1975. Little had changed by the following year. That was evident in the very planning of bicentennial celebrations as, on account of government debt and political polarization, American citizens typically settled on lower-key festivities. Sensing the promotional opportunity—and, in the case of corporate oil, penance, perhaps—the business community stepped up to sponsor events and sell their "kitsch." Gulf Oil gave generously to the American Revolution Bicentennial Administration, ostensibly to boost national morale. But that corporate giving only intensified critiques of an industry and now a nation that seemed morally bankrupt. At a time when Americans wanted to muster their patriotism, the most they could summon was ambivalence.[41]

Even Hollywood was there to frame the crisis in such terms and tie it to a root cause. In 1976, it released a new version of the movie *King Kong* with a revised plot. A large oil company's expedition team and its rapacious executive replace the film crew antagonists of the 1933 original. They head to an Indian island shrouded in dark clouds, a place they are convinced contains oil. They discover crude, but of a low grade, so they scour for another prize and find it in a softhearted giant ape. The resident Kong quickly falls for Dwan, a former actress whose sea rescue by the explorers draws her into their scheme. Against his and Dwan's wishes, Kong is seized and transported to New York—the oil firm reasons that if it cannot make money off crude, it will do so by marketing Kong as a freak show; in an age of diminishing opportunities for the industry, why not diversify? Kong eventually flees captivity, storming his way to the South Tower of the World Trade Center, which he climbs, Dwan in hand. There the ape fights off military aircraft, but the hail of bullets is too much. Kong plummets to the ground, where he perishes, with Dwan comforting him until his last breath and paparazzi surrounding him, wanting the best shot for the next day's daily. Beast and beauty, untrammeled tropics and well-trod New York streets: oil and its iniquitous habits, the parable reads, destroys everyone and everything in its path, leaving only the callous to reap rewards in the carnage.

THE BICENTENNIAL YEAR may have been bittersweet for much of the nation, but it was a good one for wildcat religion and its chief protagonists: evangelicals. Economic busts had always proved as enlivening as booms for churchly citizens of the oil patch—theirs was a crisis worldview that assumed hardship in the here and now and looked to cataclysms as signs of an impending end time with heaven on the horizon. But they never let their gaze toward that future forestall their labor on behalf of present self-interest. And by 1976, their agenda was rapacious to say the least. While they expanded their megachurches and media apparatus, they also lobbied Washington in support of tax breaks and Israel, consolidating political action committees in a quest to push their project of cultural conquest to new heights.

Dubbed "The Year of the Evangelical" by pollster George Gallup Jr., 1976 did indeed signal the annexation of the mainstream by the movement and by the larger cult of wildcat religiosity to which it was beholden. *Newsweek* was colorful in accounting for the ascent. There was the recent spate of high-profile conversion experiences, ranging from former Black Panther Eldridge Cleaver to former Nixon aide Charles Colson, which left uninitiated Americans scrambling to learn more about the "born-again" experience. Colson's popular book of the same year, titled *Born Again*, told them that even hardened criminals such as himself could accept heavenly forgiveness. The presidential election campaign of a born-again Baptist merely drove home the point that individuals committed to Christ were assuming author-ity and—as witnessed in Jimmy Carter's forthrightness—willing to attribute their success to the "Lord, their Savior." There were plenty of statistics to back up the anecdotes. By the late 1970s, the circula-tion of Billy Graham's newspaper, *Decision*, was roughly 24 million, while *Christianity Today* outpaced its liberal rival, *Christian Century*, by five subscribers to one. Other popular evangelical leaders such as Bill Bright, founder of Campus Crusade for Christ, an evangel-ical campus ministry, were boasting jaw-dropping numbers of their own. Bright aspired to "take the gospel to every person on the globe"; by the late 1970s the campaign had almost raised its stated goal of $1 billion in support. Church membership totals told the truth too. By the late 1970s, Carter's Southern Baptist Convention was surpassing the 13 million mark, while the Pentecostal Assemblies of God was posting a decennial growth rate of over 30 percent. Polls, meanwhile, showed that "thirty million Americans considered themselves reborn evangelical Christians, and another twenty million styled themselves evangelical in belief and sympathy."[42]

Several cultural factors contributed to the born-again phenome-non. One historian asserts that the years running between the early 1970s and 1990s were defined by the splintering of national identity and purpose, with earlier emphases on social and institutional bonds giving way to personal "choice, agency, performance, and desire." "Viewed by its acts of mind, the last quarter of the century was an era of disaggregation, a great age of fracture." A highly decentralized and personalized evangelical movement had many specialized outlets to offer Americans as they wrestled with these ruptures. To a populace still feeling burned by Watergate, Graham's closest allies proposed clear back-to-the-Bible steps toward renewal; for those caught up in the 1970s search for self-discovery, wholeness, and free expression, neo-Pentecostal strands of born-again faith provided emotive worship and individual access to healing, holiness, and an enchanted world of signs and wonders. Young campus activists could look to a social-justice wing of the church to right society's ills, while citizens consumed with current events and doomsday scenarios could turn to a burgeoning apocalyptic literature to make sense of a fragmenting world order. One expert on evangelicalism rightly stresses the degree to which a malleable "born-again Christianity provided alternatively a language, a medium, and a foil by which millions of Americans came to terms with political and cultural changes."[43]

That impressive sway did not operate separately from the oil contagion; to the contrary, petroleum powered a good deal of it. Thanks to men such as J. Howard Pew, by 1970 the decades-long process of funding alternative cultural institutions through which wildcat religion could affect society was bearing fruit. One obvious expression of this occurred on July 4, 1970, when Pew and Billy Graham oversaw "Honor America Day," which brought 350,000 people to the Washington Mall in a show of Christian patriotism and traditional values. The celebration was both a launch of the born-again sensation of the 1970s and the capstone of the oilman's career. A year later, on November 27, 1971, Pew died quietly at his home on the outskirts of Philadelphia. As he had done at Sid Richardson's memorial a decade prior, Graham offered a benediction at Pew's funeral. That was only fitting. Pew had had nailed to his Sun office walls two portraits "of his most admired Americans": one was of Herbert Hoover, the other of Graham. In the days that followed, the popular press would mix praise with censure when eulogizing the oiler. Pew was "ultraconservative in his politics, economics, and religion," the *New York Times* averred. But he also designed the "purchase plan for Sun Oil employes [*sic*] under which they acquired more than 2.5 million shares of Sun stock." And, the *Times* added, he was a prolific giver, donating millions to medicine, education, and humanitarianism. Upon his death, the remaining $100 million of his wealth was funneled into Pew's Freedom Trust, a substantial portion of the $900 million that comprised the entire Pew family trusts at that time.[44]

By the time he died, Pew's renown as God's bankroller had already been passed on to other oilmen. A symbolic follow-up event to Honor America Day was the weeklong religious rock festival—a Jesus-centered Woodstock—held in Dallas during the summer of 1972. Planned by Bill Bright, "Explo 72" drew over 100,000 youth to a downtown Dallas site where they learned from scripture and swayed and shook to the sounds of the era's greatest "born-again" musicians. Explo 72 tapped the support of Dallas's megachurch, W. A. Criswell–pastored First Baptist, home to the Murchison and Hunt families, wealthy by-products of the 1930s East Texas oil boom. Standing in for his aging father (who would pass away in 1975) was Nelson Bunker Hunt. Besides endorsing the fundamentals of faith preached by Criswell and Graham, Hunt also liked what Bright was doing to inculcate religious values in the silent majority's rising youth, which is why his petrofunds poured into Campus Crusade's loftiest projects, including its program of global outreach. By the mid-1970s, Bunker Hunt and his pet causes were being aided by other masters of Texas crude, including T. Cullen Davis and Eddie Chiles, both of whom considered the state's other star Baptist preacher, Fort Worth–based evangelist James Robison, their spiritual mentor. Altogether, these Baptist lights would ensure that Pew's passions for God and black gold continued to shape the religious impulses of an aroused American society.[45]

Pew's Presbyterians and Hunt's Baptists would be joined by a full spectrum of petrofunded evangelicals, including Pentecostals, whose charismatic ministries did even more to bridge denominational (and Protestant-Catholic) interests in the oil patch. Oral Roberts was charismatic Christianity's lynchpin. He knew all about oil. A product of Ada, Oklahoma, he had grown up surrounded by the derricks and wells of the Beebe and Fitts oil fields. There, during the Depression, the tuberculosis-stricken seventeen-year-old attended a Pentecostal revival service where a preacher laid healing hands on him. "I felt the healing power of the Lord," he would recall. It was "like electricity." Roberts determined to preach the same message of wholeness. By the 1960s, he was the state's most famous export, his healing services—at which he physically anointed broken bodies with oil—a national phenomenon. Political connections grew organically. Centered in Tulsa, Roberts hobnobbed with members of the city's Petroleum Club and befriended Robert Kerr, who arranged Roberts's visit with John F. Kennedy in 1961. "My meeting with the President . . . was something that I will always deeply treasure," he told Kerr. "I want to thank you for your personal influence, interest and intervention on my behalf that made this possible." By the mid-1970s, Roberts's college, television program, medical center, and office building in Tulsa shined as symbols of a prosperity gospel that promised favor to those who believed in God's miracles. The shimmer was supplied by funds from earnest followers—and independent oil's philanthropies. One was the H. E. and L. E. Mabee Foundation, charged with distributing the fortune of John E. Mabee, a rags-to-riches wildcatter who hit gushers at Burkburnett, Texas, in 1919. Mabee endorsed those who shared his risk-defying faith, and Roberts fit the bill. Thanks to the backing of oil barons, the born-again movement could look forward to ever-increasing outlets for mainstream impact.[46]

Yet money was not the only thing that bound them together; an ideological agenda did as well. As already demonstrated in prior decades, when they set their mind to building a united cultural and political front, the constituents of wildcat religion were difficult to resist. It was hardly different in the 1970s, and where so, only in terms of scale. Their regional aspirations now became national ones. The project of constructing an alternative apparatus of popular influence gained steam at this very moment, as the prevailing airs of crisis and the crease of political opportunity encouraged those in oil-patch pews and petroleum boardrooms to think big.

One facet of their project was intellectual and focused on the provision of "Bible-based" pedagogy for citizens who wanted to understand the ecological and energy crises of the day—and to rebut progressive environmentalists. The spectrum of analysis would range in emphasis, with some acolytes toeing a stronger, fundamentalist line of thought and others embracing openness to new ideas and concerns. Yet, in the creation of parallel curricula, evangelicalism's sages would hold tight to a few convictions: that the environment was God's creation meant for man to govern; that the environmental catastrophes were a tragedy and perhaps a sign of human mismanagement, but not of an innately flawed dominionist theology and capitalist worldview; and that the energy problems arising from political upheaval in the Middle East were both the harbinger of the end times prophesied in scripture and the destructive by-product of a government that refused to focus on America first—its independent oilmen, their industry, and the continent's rich resources. The treatises these sages scribed were popular—very popular.

Among the most widely disseminated treatments were those that tied current energy concerns to Armageddon, the culminating human battle between good and evil before God's day of judgment, and the apocalypse, the destruction of the world that would usher in God's kingdom. The most prominent producers of this literature were Hal Lindsey and John Walvoord. A graduate of Dallas Theological Seminary (DTS), a divinity school heavily committed to premillennialist eschatology and beholden to Texas oil wealth, Lindsey published his manifesto, *The Late Great Planet Earth*, in 1970. In it he urged believers to train their eyes on the Middle East and become well versed in its politics, because clues would emerge out of those environs about the Lord's return. Violent energy politics served as added fodder as he tried to scare readers into thinking their reckoning with Jesus was nigh. In his rendering of current events, biblical end-times teachings and theories of peak oil came together in a doomsday ideology that presupposed a fatal end to petroleum and the hydrocarbon society on which it depended. Lindsey scared a lot of people: by the end of the decade he had sold 10 million copies of his book, making it the decade's bestselling work of nonfiction. Walvoord was Lindsey's teacher. The DTS professor's 1974 best-selling text, *Armageddon: Oil and the Middle East Crisis*, wove oil and the prophecies of the Old and New Testaments into one chronology of worldly (and otherworldly) time. It also channeled opprobrium against environmentalists and their allies in Washington who had made the United States dependent on non-Christian others. "Immediately after the new energy crisis in 1973," Walvoord cogitated, "the entire world began with new determination to increase oil discovery and production." But such determination failed the United States, he complained, because US politicians were weak. "Self-sufficiency seemed only a political slogan as the U.S. continued to play into the hands of the oil exporters." Were strong-willed wildcatters able once again to tap freely the bountiful oil pools just off the Gulf Coast and in Alaska, underneath southwestern soil, and in the shale deposits of Colorado and Wyoming, he asserted, Americans would reclaim confidence in their Christian nation. This was the splendor promised by God and black gold, and it was time, in his mind, for politicians to take it seriously.[47]

Other evangelical authors gently steered Christians to reevaluate their ecological understanding. Rachel Carson and Lynn White loomed large in their imaginations. The most important writer was Francis Schaeffer, whose *Pollution and the Death of Man*, published in 1970, was designed to counter White especially. Schaeffer was anxious to fortify the Calvinist tradition against the transcendentalist impulses that White had legitimated for the environmental movement. Why was White's approach wrong? Schaeffer asked rhetorically. For one thing, it romanticized nature. "If everything is one, and a part of one essence with no basic distinction, how does one explain nature when it is destructive?" he pondered. More disconcerting for him was that White's "pantheistic stand" lowered humans to a place of subservience. Even "the rats and cows are finally given preference to man himself," he complained. Schaeffer's was an unabashedly anthropocentric worldview that said humans occupied the highest standing in the natural order; other than God, they were the center of the universe. He wanted to argue *for* not just *against*, however, and on that score he pointed to Reformed doctrines of creation and incarnation, and their valuing of earthly matter with transcendent worth, as the seeds of—not antithesis to—proper earth care. Much like Rachel Carson's mother, who conversed with nature in order to learn of God's plan for every plant and species, Schaeffer outlined a doctrine that in his mind enhanced both humans' and nature's placement in the cosmos. He did so to buck another worrisome trend for him: secularism, or as he called it, "secular humanism." If the new-age tendencies of the environmental movement upset him, the heightened stress some of its activists placed on science did too. Schaeffer's advocacy was meant to raise humanity over nature and simultaneously accentuate the divine mysteries and enchantments of the world that modern science, in his opinion, was trying to negate. Not entirely unlike oil's mystics of old—men like Lyman Stewart—he wanted to encourage God's people to perceive and probe the earth's bountiful garden with ears—and noses—to the ground, senses raised, and a synergy that balanced the extraction of natural resources with a call to stewardship.[48]

Upon publication, Schaeffer's text generated not just discussion within evangelical circles but policy pledges. In response, members of the National Association of Evangelicals formally resolved that "those who thoughtlessly destroy a God-ordained balance of nature are guilty of sin against God's creation" and promised their cooperation with "any responsible effort to solve environmental problems, and . . . willingness to support all proven solutions developed by competent authorities." It was a gesture most independent oil operators like the Pews could sign on to—dominion with a soft, smart touch. In varying degrees, champions of the wildcat ethic had always advocated such a conservationist ethic, provided it was administered at local and state levels. As the 1970s transitioned into the 1980s, Schaeffer's ethic would be tested and twisted by the less patient earth-care philosophies of apocalyptic environmentalism, but the underlying precepts of both strands would remain entrenched in the evangelical mind: that God designed nature for human use and that man was in charge.[49]

Schaeffer's appeal to his wildcat constituency only grew as his scholarship expanded and his son formalized ties between oildom's pews and boardrooms. Between 1976 and 1979, Schaeffer published two more major books, both of which were turned into films for viewing in church auditoriums around the country. His first production was the book and film series titled *How Should We Then Live?* (1976). As Schaeffer's son and production manager Frank recalls, the project argued that "the best of Western culture, art, freedom, and democracy could be traced to a Christian foundation. And that foundation was under attack from humanist and secularist ideas and elites. In consequence, we were losing our freedoms because there were no longer absolutes that we could all agree on to guarantee them." The last two episodes of the series focused on the 1973 Supreme Court ruling in *Roe v. Wade*, which legalized abortion. Here was the ultimate proof, Schaeffer warned, that the Christian West was in steep decline. He fleshed out that point in *Whatever Happened to the Human Race?* (1979). More graphic in its political application, this sequel implored Bible believers to combat emerging medical trends of euthanasia, infanticide, and abortion. The Christian's charge, now, was to fight for the "right to life." Through these projects the evangelical apologist laid the intellectual groundwork for the culture wars that would intensify in the coming years. Both film series received backing from several business sectors, but the biggest donations came from partners in independent oil, including the Pew Foundation and even more so the Hunt brothers—William, Lamar, and especially Bunker. It was up to Frank to secure those deals, a task for which a seasoned Christian fund-raiser coached him. "Look," he was told, "they know you're there for the money. . . . But you have to *play the game* that you're there for *them!*" "Ask the Hunt boys about their family. Remember, they know more than you do about money, so no bullshit, tell the truth if they ask for budget details!" Frank followed through and won the Hunts' support. Oilmen and churchmen were aligned for another stage in the fight for their fuel and family values.[50]

That the next stage of wildcat oil's culture war would be effectively orchestrated had something to do with quiet developments in domestic politics. Two in particular stood out. In 1975, President Gerald Ford signed a tax bill that repealed the depletion allowance for *major* oil companies. Although the allowance had been trimmed from the long-standing 27.5 percent rate to 22 percent in 1969, the oilman's cherished tax break had remained largely in place. After its sixty years of existence, though, Ford unceremoniously killed it, leaving petroleum lobbyists outraged. "The new rules point to less freedom of action and probably fewer opportunities to take the big risk and reap the big reward," an industry journal surmised. That was unfortunate, it added, because "the blunt situation is this: Oil is the only fuel that can keep America going for the foreseeable future." Yet independent oilmen could also rest easy—with some pride, even—that they were exempt from the repeal, their privileges protected. For the first time, the very label "independent" was written into tax law, signaling a special standing for those wildcatters who had long battled the big companies for government recognition and help. More than a symbol of Americanism, small producers could now present themselves to the nation as a special class of entrepreneurs who would explore and drill the nation out of the energy crisis.[51]

That class received another boost in a near-simultaneous ruling. In 1975, Sun Oil petitioned the Federal Election Commission (FEC) to allow "company employees . . . to authorize automatic deductions from their paychecks" for political purposes overseen by the Sun Political Action Committee (SunPAC). Organized labor already enjoyed that privilege; Sun demanded the same. Business activists had secured the right to form corporate political action committees (PACs) in 1971, but Sun wanted to clarify the terms of PAC-FEC registration and, transparently, legitimize corporate lobbying. It also wanted a say in the 1976 election, hence its urgency. In a 4–2 ruling, the FEC granted Sun authorization to collect voluntary contributions from "shareholders and employees and distribute the money among candidates as it saw fit." As the *New York Times* reported, the allowance had major implications. In giving SunPAC fund-raising freedoms, the FEC "also gave a green light to hundreds of other corporations and business associations to do likewise," clearing the way "for corporations to invest millions of dollars . . . in the political-campaigns of candidates regarded [as] 'friendly to business.'" The FEC ruling truly marked a watershed in corporate conservatism's—and by extension, social conservatism's—march to power. Had he lived to see his company's victory, J. Howard Pew would have been pleased and no doubt eager to roll up his sleeves and work the political trenches.[52]

THE UNIFYING WORK that Francis Schaeffer did for evangelicals and his oil backers amid the born-again boom of the late 1970s stood in stark contrast to the realities of the Rockefeller family and its allies in oil, the church, and politics. As the heart of the 1970s unfolded and internal and political pressures tore at the cosmopolitan and catholic projects they had assumed in the wake of World War II, the Rockefeller brothers grew disillusioned with their founding visions. To make matters worse, they weathered a period of intrafamily struggle, pitting not only personalities against one another but, more importantly, ideologies and generational outlooks as well.

At the center of the Rockefeller "civil war" stood John and Nelson. When the latter returned to the Rockefeller family office in January 1977 to resume management of the philanthropies, he did so as a spent individual, broken from the infighting of the Republican Party and the demise of his career. After Watergate, Nelson had been selected as Gerald Ford's vice president, an honor that he cherished on its own but also viewed as a stepping-stone to the presidency in 1976, should Ford decide not to run. Rockefeller served the White House well. None of that mattered. In the fall of 1975, Ford decided to vie for the GOP ticket—but without Nelson as his running mate. "I have been talking with my political advisers," Rockefeller recalled Ford telling him at a meeting in October, "and they feel that your presence on the ticket would be a liability in the nomination." Ford said he considered Nelson a friend but asked that he withdraw. It was a double blow for Rockefeller—no more vice presidency, no chance at the presidency. Ford's advisors believed he needed someone farther to the right, Senator Bob Dole, to deal with GOP contender Ronald Reagan's conservative base. In the end, Ford beat Reagan in a close leadership race before losing a tight election to Jimmy Carter. Ford later admitted that Nelson's presence on the ticket would have helped the cause. That was cold comfort for Rockefeller, who tried stoically to support the GOP campaign of 1976. But he was changed. "Ford's decision devastated Nelson," his brother David would write. "He lost all interest in politics, letting his network of political friends and allies languish. Thwarted when the greatest political prize seemed within his grasp, he had become an angry and deeply bitter man."[53]

That was a recipe for family tensions. Other dynastic strains plagued them as well. After Winthrop Rockefeller's death from cancer in 1973, the remaining four Rockefeller brothers began to fight over the future of the Rockefeller Brothers Fund (RBF) and the family's estate in Pocantico, New York. John, long committed to the philanthropic side of Rockefeller influence, desired a progressive path for the family institutions. Over the course of the late 1960s and early 1970s, he had devoted his energies and personal monies (upward of 60 percent of his annual income) to his charitable agencies, including the Population Council, and to learning from young people—Black Panthers, SDS radicals, Ivy League students—in order to decipher their critiques of society. He found what they had to say convincing. Environmentalism, anticolonialism, and the ideologies of the very sort of activists that protested his brother's Harvard honorary degree in 1969 rubbed off on him. He admitted as much in his 1973 book *The Second American Revolution: Some Personal Observations*. In a mode of self-reflection, Rockefeller called for his generation—his establishment—to start looking at the world through their children's eyes. It was up to "moderates," he declared, to guide the nation toward human understanding and cooperation on the critical issues of the day: "No one can say with authority how far this process has gone and how far it will go. I can only say with certainty that the crucial role of the moderates begins with the personal decision to become involved in the humanistic revolution, to play a part in the great drama of our time." At the heart of his message was expressed support for environmental initiatives that contained echoes of Rachel Carson. More regulation and conservation, more human awareness of nature's fragility, more incentive to "develop new technologies that will allow us to live in harmony with nature while still enjoying the benefits of a modern industrial state": these were now the determining factors, John believed, of humankind's survival.[54]

John Rockefeller's treatise generated further agitation among his brothers, with the exception of Laurance, whose environmental and entrepreneurial initiatives more closely aligned with John's. Nelson's views had turned especially conservative over time. Further fueling dissension was the family's own generational divide. When he endorsed a "second American revolution," John spoke for his children and their cousins. Many of the fourth generation of Rockefellers were coming of age just as the environmental and energy crises and human rights campaigns of the day were exploding onto the public scene. The sons and daughters of the five brothers had a growing sense that their clan was on the wrong side of the issues and on the wrong side of history.

They aired their opinions in Peter Collier and David Horowitz's 1976 bestseller *The Rockefellers: An American Dynasty*. The exposé revealed little that was new about the first three generations of Rockefellers. Its "aha" portion came in its study of the fourth generation, which relied on interviews with the cousins themselves. In page after page the authors detailed estrangement among the younger set—"Rockefeller" was a name they wanted to escape. The testimony from Marion, Laurance's daughter, was indicative. A back-to-nature devotee of Henry David Thoreau who spent weekends with her husband (a Berkeley English graduate student) in an old caboose in the California hills, Marion revealed her disdain for her heritage via the recounting of a dream about her extended family "gliding" down a road "in very expensive clothes" with beauty all around. But the peace was broken by the sight of people "in the pastures on both sides" peering at the Rockefellers "with envy and curiosity." "I feel embarrassed and want to tell them something," Marion remembered. "Somehow I manage to get away from my family. Then, the next thing I know, I'm in the field with the regular people, watching the Rockefellers on parade. I feel glad that I'm not one of *them*." Marion also told her inquisitors she hoped to make the Rockefeller fortune "extinct": "I hope the social revolution will come soon and take away from us the necessity of having to deal with it." The inquisitors admitted that Marion was extreme in her desire to break with the family but insisted that her testimony revealed her cousins' mentality as a whole. "Most of the fourth Rockefeller generation have spent long years with psychiatrists in their efforts to grapple with the money and the family, the taint and the promise." Most want to "experience the Horatio Alger myth in reverse. To some degree they are all princes and princesses yearning to be paupers."[55]

By 1977, then, the Rockefeller brothers were succumbing to the decade's fragmentation and rifts. The denouement transpired over the following year as Nelson and John vied for power within the RBF. When Nelson returned to the family office, he assumed leadership of the enterprise and pushed his agenda, which included forcing non–family members off the board; he wanted to return the agency to the old days, when its primary purpose was to manage the family's philanthropic goals. One board member's resignation in protest, subsequently reported in the press, brought the conflict into the open, adding embarrassment to an already tense circumstance. Nelson charged ahead, insisting that the board accept his other proposals, which included large grants for causes of his choosing, a tactic John especially denounced— RBF allotments had to be managed fairly and squarely, with popular consent, he argued in moralistic tones. The final blow to family unity occurred when Nelson proposed to overhaul Rockefeller philanthropy in its entirety, centered on creation of the Rockefeller Trust Company, to be headed by a board of directors, a chairman, and a chief executive officer. Nelson wanted to adopt a corporate model that would "charge clients for services rendered" and rationalize and reduce the heavy costs of office operations. He also proposed that he be the company's first chairman and CEO and that only family members with "proven capacity in the outside world" be eligible for the board. That measure meant his brother John would have no place in the pack. The proposal set off a firestorm. At a large family gathering, the cousins expressed outrage and, according to David, "attacked Nelson for the imperious manner in which he was trying to seize control of the office. Nelson responded in kind. It was a tense and unpleasant evening for everyone present." The next morning, David joined Laurance and John in asking that Nelson compromise, accept the cousins' wishes that he be chairman but not CEO, and "democratize" the entire enterprise. Nelson fumed. Negative energy carried over into 1978, as John fought his counterpart over plans for the future of the family's largest properties and in letters to Nelson expressed disappointment. "You have always indicated to me that there were two things you wanted to accomplish in your lifetime," he wrote on one occasion. One was to become US president, the other to lead the family in the rich traditions of "Father and Grandfather." "Obviously you have failed in the first of these objectives, and you are in danger of failing in the second, unless you modify your behavior."[56]

John and Nelson's feud came to a swift and tragic end. On July 9, 1978, John was on his way home from lunch with David and Peggy Rockefeller when a car driven by a distracted teen veered off the road, glanced off a tree, and hit his oncoming vehicle. Both John and the boy died instantly. Six months later, on January 26, 1979, Nelson and Happy Rockefeller, along with Laurance and his wife, Mary Rockefeller, attended a benefit event for the Buckley School in Manhattan. At the reception that followed, guests noted Nelson's pallid skin color and wondered if he was alright. Dinner later raised more questions, as Happy and her children worried at the sight of Nelson's hand "constantly roaming his chest." Nelson left them to meet with his young secretary, Megan Marshack. At around 10:00 p.m. he suffered a heart attack and died.[57]

The deaths of John and Nelson Rockefeller in quick succession drew to a close an era not just for the family but for their mission as well. Nelson's death in particular accentuated the darkness of the moment for those who had adhered to the type of creed that he and his peers in big religion and big oil had advocated since Henry Luce's time. "In the final months of his life," David would recall, "Nelson struck me as a very unhappy man. He was fatalistic about many things and seemed to have lost the will to live." His troubled mood was health related—his heart was failing, yet he refused to see a doctor—but also the by-product of a broader dissatisfaction as he contemplated his political journey. "Nelson hoped to translate his successes in New York into enduring national power," his brother eulogized, but "in this he failed." Nelson, David continued in a hagiographical retrospective, "would have been a magnificent president."[58]

As it happened, David was visiting the sultan of Oman in Muscat at the time of Nelson's death and had to keep his meeting with royalty short in order to board a plane for New York. As the fog of oil-fed unrest was settling over the Middle East again, David was anxious to shore up friendships and partnerships.

The fog grew more ominous at that precise moment. While the Rockefellers were burying one of their own, over 30,000 oil workers were striking in Iran. Angered by poor working and economic conditions, which contrasted sharply with the extravagances of their leader, Shah Pahlavi, the laborers began their protest in late December 1978. Despite the government's attempts to quell the revolt by sending troops into the oil fields, the strike lasted thirty-three days, grinding the Iranian economy to a halt and throwing the global oil market into another fit of panic. On January 19, 1979, the shah was forced to flee to Egypt, leaving a collapsed regime behind. In succeeding weeks, fundamentalist cleric Ayatollah Khomeini cobbled together a provisional government, then a political party, one that could quell workers' dissent and channel protest against the system into an Islamic revolution. The exiled shah, a reminder of secular, capitalist corruption, became an instant target. Rockefeller, with the help of Henry Kissinger—now a Chase consultant—decided to help. Stating that the former Iranian ruler had been "a friend of the United States for 37 years," the two persuaded President Jimmy Carter to bring the exiled politician to America. He arrived in October.[59]

The diplomatic favor turned the political heat on David Rockefeller—his bank, journalists surmised, would do anything to protect one of its longtime clients and his ill-gotten fortune—and also on the American president, whose own trials were escalating. As the Iran crisis continued to intensify, Jimmy Carter struggled with yet another energy crisis at home. The two were related. Both were products of the unrest generated by the disgruntled citizens of a global oil patch. And both were also emblems of a threshold at which American society stood: as was becoming evident in Iran and around the Middle East, the confidence of Nelson Rockefeller's generation of Americans, a self-assurance generated in no small part by the nation's oil dominance and sense of divine destiny, was not simply collapsing on itself; it was being co-opted and molded into an alternative dogma of God and oil.[60]

# CHAPTER TWELVE

# The End of the
# American Century

W hen Jimmy Carter addressed the nation on July 15, 1979, his speech betrayed the insecurities and somberness of the day. Seated at a large wooden bureau before drab yellow drapes, the president looked warily into the television camera. He cupped his hands, then began to talk, shakily at first, as if weighted down by the burden he now bore as commander in chief—a priest responsible for chastising his parishioners. His cadence accelerated slightly as he moved into the heart of his message, occasionally showing some emotion with a pitched voice and the slight pounding of his fists. But the entire performance was one of restraint.

Indeed, restraint and the need for soul-searching were central themes of his address. Carter was supposed to be making another plea for people to support his energy conservation agenda, but in the lead-up to the televised event, he changed his mind. "As I was preparing to speak," he said, "I began to ask myself the same question that I now know has been troubling many of you. Why have we not been able to get together as a nation to resolve our serious energy problem?" He continued to psychologize. "It's clear that the true problems of our Nation are much deeper—deeper than gasoline lines or energy shortages, deeper even than inflation or recession," he said, before singling out the culprit. "It is a crisis of confidence. It is a crisis that strikes at the very heart and soul and spirit of our national will. We can see this crisis in the growing doubt about the meaning of our own lives and in the loss of a unity of purpose for our Nation."

Carter struggled to end his elegy on an upbeat note. The president acknowledged the breadth of the decade's gloom, with "a growing disrespect for government and for churches and for schools, the news media, and other institutions" seemingly omnipresent. "This is not a message of happiness or reassurance, but it is the truth and it is a warning." He admitted to partial blame for the condition, promising he would do more to guide citizens to a better future—but only if they recognized their crisis of morals. "We are at a turning point in our history," he lectured. "There are two paths to choose. One is a path . . . that leads to fragmentation and self-interest"; the other holds the promise of "true freedom for our Nation and ourselves. We can take the first steps down that path as we begin to solve our energy problem." Carter closed with an attempt to inspire hope. "I have seen the strength of America in the inexhaustible resources of our people. In the days to come, let us renew that strength in the struggle for an energy secure nation. Let us commit ourselves together to a rebirth of the American spirit. Working together with our common faith we cannot fail." With that, the stiff-lipped parson-politician bid his flock good night.[1]

Jimmy Carter's own advisors would dub this "crisis-of-confidence" keynote his "malaise" speech. The press would use the latter label to underscore the disquiet threaded through the televised talk. But both sentiments captured the mood of the country. Anxious about the existential threats undercutting their energy sources and standing in the world, Americans were paralyzed by the fear that they possessed neither the ability nor the courage to right their condition.

The malaise was particularly trenchant among US oil's internationalists—those clustered in large corporate constituencies who once believed that the twin pillars of ecumenism and transnational petroleum would frame the American Century and usher in a better age. Amid the chaos of the late 1970s and 1980s, however, their buoyant dreams of a petrofueled Pax Americana died a thousand painful deaths. Veterans of Aramco's Arabist class experienced that declension firsthand. As they retreated permanently, they watched the transfer to Saudi control of oil production and projects of economic development begun under their command. With nationalization of Aramco complete, the Saudis set out to frame their possession of petroleum in familiar sacred discourse—but as Allah's blessing, not that of an American God. Other oil-producing Muslim countries would adopt a similar outlook, cognizant they were now living on oil time—borrowed time—and impelled to keep their rigs pumping while the pumping was good. The civil religion of crude once evangelized by Western missionaries, oil hunters, and high-minded capitalists was now theirs; the US gospel of oil's manifest destiny had been co-opted and primed to legitimate their own global interests.

Up front, at least, the 1980s were "morning in America" for producers and parishioners of the oil patch. The phalanx of religious, corporate, and political organizations that they created had produced a high point in the election of Ronald Reagan. In exchange for their support, Reagan gave them what they wanted: a return to yesteryear, when their sacrosanct rule of capture was guaranteed. And he gave them formal power, illustrated by the appointment of James Watt, an apocalyptic-minded Pentecostal, as interior secretary. With this maneuver, which hastened a fire sale of federal land for oil resource development, Reagan signaled the death of the liberal vision held by Harold Ickes, Franklin D. Roosevelt, and the Rockefellers. Yet the wildcatters' win was a Pyrrhic victory at best. As the 1980s unfolded and they labored to ensure their predilections were protected, the cycles of oil once again turned against them. Collapsing oil prices and insurmountable debt twisted their lofty ventures into bundles of failure and figments of the past. Even as their enterprise began to rebound at decade's end, their mission had seemed to change, as did that of the United States as a whole, which now entered war in the Middle East as a desperate measure to protect oil supplies over which it had once enjoyed supremacy. Troops marching and wells aflame in foreign fields; ghost towns, broken churches, and rusted-out rigs in North America's oildom; more ecological disaster of an unimaginable scale: these signs suggested that when Americans entered the 1990s, they left their global bailiwick behind.

WHEN JIMMY CARTER spoke on July 15, 1979, he thought he could solve the energy problem and shift the political tide in his favor. Yet his last stitch of optimism would be no match for the backlashes he faced in the Islamic Middle East and from hard-liners on his own soil. While he asked Americans to solemnly contemplate an oil-free horizon, a maverick politician emerged who promised to restore power to the oil patch and confidence to the nation.

Carter's speech was the outgrowth of a two-year political whirlwind that began when his administration deemed "energy" the White House's number one issue. On April 18, 1977, dressed in a cardigan sweater and promising to lower his thermostat, the president outlined why the United States had succumbed to foreign-bred and homegrown uncertainty and how to escape its clutches. Borrowing from philosopher William James, he told his television audience that the challenge ahead would require a momentous effort amounting to the "moral equivalent of war." On that note, the general sought to rally his troops and prepare them for a season of sacrifice. He laid out ten principles on which his administration would act in order to forestall future catastrophes. They included more aggressive conservation controls, reduced dependency on foreign oil, development of alternative energy supplies, and a commitment by the citizenry to limit its energy use overall. "The energy crisis has not yet overwhelmed us," he affirmed, "but it will if we do not act quickly." He finished with a nod to patriotism, an appropriate gesture in any declaration of battle. "If you will join me so that we can work together . . . we will again prove that our great Nation can lead the world into an age of peace, independence, and freedom."[2]

In the months that followed this clarion call, Carter won a few victories but generally lost the war. The subsequent passage of the National Energy Act (1978) meant that concrete policies would implement several features of Carter's ten-point plan. "Today we can rightfully claim that we have a conscious national policy for dealing with the energy problems of the present and also to help us deal with them in the future," he announced when signing the act. With this legislative event, he beamed, Americans could face "the future with new tools and also with a new resolve." Environmentalists praised the measures. With the passage of the Energy Act, installation of solar panels on the roof of the White House, and subsequent moves to protect western lands from mining and oil extraction, Carter seemed to be on their side. For too long, Carter asserted on more than one occasion, humans had "despoiled God's earth"; it was time to reverse course. Earth Day creator Gaylord Nelson concurred and for that reason later called Carter "the greatest environmental president the country ever had."[3]

Carter's favorable impact on energy extended beyond North American lands. His most impressive presidential accomplishment occurred two months before the passage of the National Energy Act. At Carter's encouragement, Egyptian president Anwar Sadat and Israeli prime minister Menachem Begin visited each other's capitals with the intent to start a dialogue. After their 1977 exchange, Carter invited both to Camp David, Maryland, where over thirteen days in September 1978 they mulled over a treaty that would end enmities stretching back to 1967. On the summit's final day, Sadat and Begin reached an accord. The final "Framework for Peace in the Middle East" included terms for self-governance by Palestinians living in the West Bank and Gaza, the return of the entire Sinai Peninsula to Egypt's control, and a template for future accords between Israel and its Arab neighbors. Carter was overjoyed. While he knew caution was required—the agreement did not sit well with other Arab nations, which chastised Sadat for acting alone—Carter had reason to gleam. His diplomacy not only brought two antagonistic nations together but also brought a measure of calm to an energy hotbed that had caused so much global stress. He celebrated the signing of the final treaty on the White House lawn in March 1979 in a manner he knew well—with tokens of faith. "Let us now reward all the children of Abraham who hunger for a comprehensive peace in the Middle East. Let us now enjoy the adventure of becoming fully human, fully neighbors, even brothers and sisters. We pray God, we pray God together, that these dreams will come true. I believe they will."[4]

Carter's moral campaigns to win peace with Jewish and Muslim nations and nature itself may have been well received in principle. Yet, in practical political terms, they entangled him in an increasingly dense web of competing agendas. Average Americans, it turned out, were more difficult to marshal around energy reform than he expected and harbored less than his desired quotient of self-sacrifice. With new oil fields coming online—Alaska, the North Sea—the United States entered 1978 with renewed prospects for abundant oil, creating a perception that, at the least, the cardigan-clad president's petition for frugality was overstated. In a 1978 article titled "The Wrong War? The Case Against a National Energy Policy," Michigan congressman David Stockman rebuked Carter for overplaying the energy crisis and his authority. "Rather than institute a politically imposed and bureaucratically managed ... regime of domestic-energy autarky," Stockman argued, "we need do little more than decontrol domestic energy prices, dismantle the energy bureaucracy, and allow the U.S. economy to equilibrate at the world level. Energy supply and demand will take care of itself." Stockman was not alone in his opinions and opposition to Carter. Due to the proliferation of political action committees in the second half of the decade, any attempt to muster unity was nearly impossible. "You had interest groups against interest groups," recollected James Schlesinger, Carter's secretary of energy, the first to hold that title. "You couldn't put a consensus together. It was distressing." In the wake of Watergate, no matter their particular ideology, few Americans were much interested in presidential proclamations anyway. The lack of hearing and listening among the populace left Carter and his advisors rueful. "The response was less close to William James' moral equivalent of war," Schlesinger wisecracked when discussing Carter's inability to connect with the citizenry, "than to the political equivalent of the Chinese water torture."[5]

Unsurprisingly, Middle Eastern politics had its way of raising new hurdles too, and by 1979 they were difficult to see past. While stability returned for the time being to Israel and its immediate neighbors, the region's other oil powerhouse combusted into civil war. By 1978, Iran was in disarray because of a malady that former oil minister Juan Pablo Perez Alfonzo had identified in Venezuela. Though rich in oil resources (by the late 1970s, Iran was second only to Saudi Arabia as the largest oil producer in the world), Iran could not handle its influx of petrodollars. Oil wealth poured into the hands of a few and was wasted on mismanaged modernization programs and lost through corruption. Meanwhile, farmers flocked to cities for work in industry, leaving the nation's agricultural output in decline. Inflation followed, with living costs in urban centers like Tehran skyrocketing. Iran's transportation infrastructure and electricity grid were stressed to the point of collapse. All these conditions bred malcontents—many of them also animated by a religious fundamentalism that connected the nation's problems to the encroaching evils of Western secular influences. Led by the exiled Ayatollah Khomeini, Iran's Shiite abolitionists wrapped all these complaints in one ideology of revolution, with Shah Pahlavi as the principal foe. Despite mounting opposition, the shah remained unwavering in his quest to modernize the state and willingness to quell discontent with force. As late as fall 1978, he continued to implement a "liberalization program" that expanded freedoms of the press, of assembly, and of the academy. But even he sensed that the people had little interest in what he was doing—and that severe trouble was brewing. "We are melting away like snow in water," he acknowledged.[6]

The oil workers who went on strike in late 1978 and early 1979 forced the issue. As thousands of them stormed the streets to protest poor economic conditions, the shah scrambled to get production up and running again; the nation was an oil exporter, with 4.5 million barrels out of 5.5 million barrels produced daily headed to open seas. Without that income, his regime would collapse. As a last-gasp measure, he instituted martial law, but that hardly settled matters. Thrust into the violence, Western petroleum personnel, some dodging bombs and bullets, evacuated. In Washington, meanwhile, the White House failed to see through the fog of Iran's populist uprising. Incoming information was scant, trust in the shah unwavering, and Carter too preoccupied with other diplomatic issues (such as the Israel-Egypt accord) to notice the severity of the threat. By mid-January 1979, he could no longer look away. With rumors about his ill health swirling, the shah decided he could not salvage the Pahlavi dynasty. He boarded a plane, carrying a scoop of Persian soil, and fled the country.[7]

A short time later, Khomeini landed in Tehran, a hero to his revolutionaries and ready to challenge the government of Prime Minister Shahpour Bakhtiar, to whom the shah had transferred power. Bakhtiar had orchestrated Khomeini's return, thinking a secular-religious partnership (like Italy's with the Vatican) would bolster his government, but upon landing the cleric made clear he intended to lead in his own way. "I appoint the government," he exclaimed. Khomeini designated Mehdi Bazargan the country's new prime minister. Bazargan had been Prime Minister Mohammad Mosaddegh's choice to lead Iran's nationalized oil industry in 1951. Khomeini was not fond of

Mosaddegh's secular nationalism, but he also knew the importance of good petroleum management: oil was to be the essential partner to his religious leadership. The cleric told Iranians that obeying Bazargan was mandatory. "Opposing this government means opposing the *sharia* of Islam.... Revolt against God's government is a revolt against God." Bakhtiar bitterly resented Khomeini's pronouncements. "As a Muslim," he stated, "I had not heard that jihad refers to one Muslim against other Muslims," citing Khomeini's ultimatums. "I will not give permission to Ayatollah Khomeini to form an interim government." But, his authority tenuous, Bakhtiar was no match for the Shiite scholar and his oil-smart right-hand man. On February 11, while Bakhtiar fled, Khomeini's insurgents assumed control of the government, media outlets, and Pahlavi family palaces. Americans learned of these final events' historic significance in their press the next day: oil-rich Iran was now a theocracy.[8]

Carter did not need the press to tell him that history was being made. He joined other experts in the West in pondering, with icy fear, how religious fundamentalism had wedded itself to fierce nationalism. Would the revolution spread through the region? In the short term, meanwhile, Carter now had another energy crisis to solve. During the stretch of time that Iranian oil exports were offline—from December 1978 through to the fall of 1979—another panic set in. Although the actual oil shortage was not severe, markets and consumers reacted with exaggerated fear of a 1973 repeat and the belief that all 1978's gains were at an end. And as their anxieties grew, other oil exporters took advantage of the situation to increase prices and their profits, sending the global system into another fit of dizzying disorientation.[9]

So, despite a few victories early in his presidency, Carter approached the end of his first term contending with another round of even more disastrous energy circumstances. Oil was not the only concern, of course. The Three Mile Island accident of March 1979, precipitated by mechanical failure in the Three Mile Island Nuclear Generating Station, near Harrisburg, Pennsylvania, which resulted in the release of nuclear reactor coolant, kept Americans on edge for an entire week. Once hailed as a clean alternative to carbon, nuclear power now seemed to the government and a wary public too dangerous, placing yet further pressure on the president to find a conventional solution. All these political tensions wearied him as he sought to rearticulate his wishes for an energy-independent, morally conscious nation.

Carter decided he would revisit those themes in what would become the "malaise" speech, originally planned for July 5, 1979. Carter's team started preparing months in advance for this sequel to the televised speech given by the punctilious president on April 18, 1977. The president's advisors scuffled over the sentiments they believed the president should convey. Some were outright against the idea of giving a speech. As lines at gas pumps grew, three of Carter's speechwriters were blunt. "*We strongly advise against another televised energy speech*," they said in a memo. "People want action on energy. They do not want Presidential preaching or the Administration piously saying, 'We told you so, but you didn't listen to us.'" But one key counselor said the opposite: Americans needed to be reminded of the "affluenza" that ailed them. Patrick Caddell was a Harvard-trained Catholic intellectual who, in addition to serving as Carter's pollster, devoured contemporary academic writings by the likes of Robert Bellah and Christopher Lasch, which lamented the "culture of narcissism" (Lasch's phrase) that pervaded modern society and prevented it from placing the common good over the individual and regaining a spiritual and moral core. Caddell was taken with their theology and laid out his thoughts in a seventy-five-page memo for the president. The idealist challenged Carter to inspire people with a message of moral depth. Echoing Bellah, he insisted that Americans needed to come together for one purpose and to restore the nation's singular calling as a city on a hill. Carter was instantly taken with Caddell's ideational scheme, convinced it was—in his words—"a masterpiece."[10]

As July 5 approached, Carter retreated to Camp David where, after further deliberation, he decided to postpone his talk so that he could dig deeper into Caddell's words. Some members of his team tried, one last time, to steer him away from the pollster's philosophy. "Instead of scolding the public we should play to their better instincts," Vice President Walter Mondale told Carter in a memo. Gerald Rafshoon, Carter's public relations advisor, issued stronger criticism: "I frankly think that if we give the speech that Caddell has proposed, it will be counterproductive to what we are trying to do. It could even be a disaster." "People don't want to hear you *talk* about their problems and they certainly don't want to hear you *whine* about them," he told the president. "They want to perceive you beginning to *solve* the problems, *inspire* confidence by your actions, and *lead*. You inspire confidence by being *confident*." Caddell's speech, he insisted, sent "all the opposite signals." But Carter did not budge. After consulting with a hastily assembled Camp David gathering of 150 local leaders in business, labor, civil service, and the church, he became more convinced that Caddell's preference to prick Americans' conscience with requisites of confession was the right one. Carter took those words with him into the Oval Office on July 15.[11]

Caddell's detractors proved right. The public reacted well to Carter's homily initially, but when the president proceeded to fire and reorganize most of his staff two days later, average Americans once again sensed his leadership was lacking. Criticism and mockery of the speech itself now cropped up in print. The conservative *National Review* published scathing critiques of Carter's July 15 performance: one compared the president to fictional fundamentalist preacher Elmer Gantry; another declared "gasoline" Carter's "Vietnam." An editorial in the *Wall Street Journal* lambasted him for his decision to chastise the country for its lack of commitment to the nation's institutions, community values, and patriotic self-sacrifice. "It is the kind of indictment clergymen use to lash their congregations with on Sunday mornings and it is appropriate in that setting of spiritual redemption. But it is highly inappropriate coming from the man who is supposed to be managing the affairs of the United States government." Rafshoon's prediction was coming true: trade in tentativeness and the returns will be poor—perhaps even disastrous.[12]

Ronald Reagan did not need Carter's consultant to tell him that. By fall of 1979, Carter's energy agenda was losing steam, and resentment was escalating. One outlet for discontent came by way of the Citizen Labor Energy Coalition, which held a protest on October 17, the six-year anniversary of the OPEC embargo. Dubbed "Big Oil Day," it featured countrywide demonstrations against high gasoline and heating bills. A few weeks later, on November 4, Iranian radicals seized more than fifty American diplomats and personnel at the US embassy in Tehran, beginning a 444-day hostage crisis that would sink Carter's White House to its nadir. On November 13, Reagan announced a third run at the GOP's nomination. "The crisis we face is not the result of any failure of the American spirit," he cheered his audience. "It is a failure of our leaders." The "lost confidence" spoken of by Carter was not theirs but his. "If you ever had any doubt of the government's inability to provide for the needs of the people, just look at the utter fiasco we now call 'the energy crisis.'" Reagan promised to address the problem another way: not by cutting back or asking citizens to sacrifice but—echoing Congressman Stockman—by freeing the market. "[We] must remove government obstacles to energy production. And, we must make use of those technological advantages we still possess. It is no program simply to say 'use less energy.'" Malaise had no place in Reagan's lexicon, and he told battered Americans it should have no place in theirs either.[13]

While the hostage crisis continued, limiting a guilt-ridden Carter in his campaigning for a second term, Reagan spent the 1980 election cycle traveling the country, preaching energy abundance and American greatness. In mid-July, at the Republican National Convention in Detroit, Reagan (running on a platform of "Let's Make America Great Again") easily won the GOP nomination for president and then chose former Texas oilman, US congressman and diplomat, and director of central intelligence George H. W. Bush as his running mate. One month later Reagan traveled to Dallas to speak at the Southern Baptist Convention's National Affairs Briefing, designed to allow pastors to hear politicians' positions on key issues. "We need to return to the God of our pilgrim fathers, to the faith of our praying mothers, to the God who can save us," Dallas's most recognizable pastor, W. A. Criswell, proclaimed at the two-day convention. But Fort Worth Baptist firebrand James Robison and Reagan mouthed the most memorable words. Prior to the rally, Robison had warned religious leaders that only 30 percent of "God-professing people" voted, compared to 95 percent of labor union members, 98 percent of liquor industry boosters, and all the "radicals" and "gays." He repeated the warning at the briefing. "Not voting is a sin against Almighty God! I'm sick and tired of hearing about all the radicals and the perverts and the leftists and the Communists coming out of the closet! It's time for God's people to come out of the closet!" Reagan followed Robison to the podium. The pastor had coached the candidate beforehand on how to speak to Baptists without compromising their commitment to church-state separation. Robison suggested that Reagan begin by acknowledging, "You can't endorse me, but I endorse you." Reagan followed the cue to a tee and won the crowd.[14]

Over the course of the next three months, Reagan continued to stoke the oil-patch crowd's passion as he talked freely about family and fuel values. The nation would be great again, the Republican guaranteed, as soon as Washington's bureaucrats took a back seat and let rugged wild-catters open up new frontiers of extractive wealth and God-fearing pioneers raise their children in communities calibrated to the morals of an honorable past. Reagan conveyed a version of that message the day before the election. "Americans, who have always known that excessive bureaucracy is the enemy of excellence and compassion," he declared, "seek a vision of a society that frees the energies and ingenuity of our people while it extends compassion to the lonely, the desperate, and the forgotten." Exuding an audacity that contrasted sharply with his opponent's modesty, the Republican outlined his policy goals of less government, fewer taxes, and more freedom for enterprising individuals to prime the pump of economic growth. But his primary appeal was to Americans' emotional side. He asked them simple questions: Were they more confident in the economy, more secure as a country, more proud of their nation than they were when Jimmy Carter took office? "And," he added, "are you happier today than when Mr. Carter became President of the United States?" He sensed they were not and asked them to do something about it. Washington was in need of fixing. "Let us resolve tonight," he concluded, "that young Americans . . . will always find there a city of hope in a country that is free. And let us resolve they will say of our day and of our generation that we did keep faith with our god . . . [and] did protect and pass on lovingly that shining city on a hill." The next day, Reagan swept the electoral map to victory, inaugurating an era he would call "morning in America."[15]

If the months following Reagan's election marked dawn for America's domestic oil patch, they signified dusk for the nation's global dominance in oil. While Reagan's revolutionaries reveled in the burst of religious fervor and economic freedoms, Muslims in the Middle East pursued petroleum power with equal passion. Awash in unprecedented liquid wealth, they crafted metaphors of their own manifest destinies, which urged them to drill with purpose. Their narratives of oil-enriched Islam turned the tables on a sagging American confidence and forced proponents of Pax Americana to concede their loss and begin reframing the histories that brought them to this point of unexpected reversal.

That shift had already begun in the 1970s. While Ayatollah Khomeini was beginning to threaten Iran's royalty with a fundamentalist Shiite ideology, other Muslim nations were beginning to do the same through the specific theological lenses of their Sunni faith. The 1973 Yom Kippur War was the turning point. In one sense the war allowed Arab nationalists such as Anwar Sadat and Syrian president Hafez al-Assad to reclaim the legitimacy they and their movement had lost during the 1967 war and continue the pan-Arab project begun by Gamal Nasser. Yet the real benefactors of the 1973 war were Arab oil producers whose successful embargo emboldened them to accelerate projects of petroleum-sponsored economic and social development within the context of re-enlivened Islam. Prior to 1973, Arab nationalism had squelched the political centrality of religion, allowing Islam to flourish only in local and sectarian contexts. After 1973, with Saudi Arabia and the conservative doctrines of its Wahhabi royalty ascendant, the balance of power shifted. Oil-rich Wahhabi leaders were now in a position to carry out an ambitious program of proselytization and consolidation among the world's Sunnis. Muslim evangelizers did not simply want to propagate their faith and draw the diaspora into their fold; they wanted to shore up its ultimate authority within the kingdom and region by making it the principal guarantor of the state's rapid wealth accumulation and modernization. While Saudi royalty made religious obedience central to acquisition of government subsidies and access to an emerging market, one historian notes, it also constructed a "huge empire of charity and good works . . . [seeking] to legitimize a prosperity it claimed was manna from heaven, blessing the peninsula where the Prophet Mohammed had received his Revelation." Saudis embraced their windfalls as signs of a shining destiny to lead a global religion.[16]

Scholars have used the contested label "petro-Islam" to capture the essence of this emerging theological-economic-political matrix—or "theopetrocracy." "Petro-Islam," a student of Arab politics explains, "proceeds from the premise that it is not merely an accident that oil is concentrated in the thinly populated Arabian countries ... and that this apparent irony of fate is indeed a grace and a blessing from God ... that should be solemnly acknowledged and lived up to." The notion that Allah had entrusted this resource to their custody impelled Muslim Arabs to craft societies that embraced modern technologies and capital while resisting modernity's cultural pitfalls—the disintegration of traditional family values, moral standards, and modesty. Because of the sheer volume of its oil fields and unmatched status as home to Islam's holiest sites, as well as its familiarity with a Western-capitalist order, Saudi Arabia stood as the "city on the hill" of this theology of exceptionalism. During the late 1970s, it won favor with a global Muslim citizenry by channeling petrodollars into philanthropic agencies such as the Muslim World League, which supported the construction of mosques and the distribution of millions of free Korans. At the same time, it opened its borders to immigration from Muslim countries, joining other oil-producing gulf states in welcoming oil workers from Pakistan, India, Egypt, Palestine, Lebanon, Syria, and other parts of Africa and Southeast Asia. In 1975, the gulf oil states harbored 1.2 million immigrants; as of 1985, 5.15 million. These migrants sent their paychecks home (Pakistani workers transferred $3 billion home in 1983 alone) and at the same time served as conduits for dispersing the teachings of conservative Islam across national boundaries. When they returned home, they did so with cash in hand, a desire (and capacity) for finer lifestyles, and also an intensified religious devotion. In turn, their values and monies contributed to the construction of civic complexes replete with shopping malls and suburban neighborhoods, all encircling glittering new mosques. Through the mechanisms of petrocapitalism, in other words, the Saudi Arabian dream began to go global.[17]

The transformation was profound for all the societies now immersed in this arising order. Even as they operated under the shadow of Saudi Arabia, smaller petroleum kingdoms such as Oman were transformed and helped transform the system in equally striking ways. British oil prospectors had worked Oman's terrain since the early twentieth century, but not until the 1970s did its oil industry make major leaps. Large finds during the early half of the decade brought more oil online and more wealth into the kingdom. "Thereafter," a British diplomat and witness to the growth recalls through Anglophile eyes, "oil provided the propellant for the abrupt emergence of Oman from the darkness of the Middle Ages into the light of the 20th century." The dramatic growth thrust Omani society into a different theological as well as technological state—indeed, into a different teleology. "The problem is a problem of time," Oman's minister of education Yahya bin Mahfoudh al-Mantheri explained in a published interview in 1985, titled "Oman Rushing into Modern Times Before Oil Money Runs Out." "Oman in 1970 was nothing. As we say in Oman, we are running, not walking, to get our infrastructure built." Resting, like Saudi Arabia, on a strong foundation of traditionalist Islam, Omani society approached the 1980s with a drive both to catch up to its larger peers in the advancement of its technologies and economy and to appropriate its surprising wealth in spiritual terms as a miraculous interlude in the unfolding of divine purpose. Al-Mantheri knew that oil and oil wealth were impermanent and finite, and Omanis as a whole sensed that their new material reality was geared to the short-term blessings of messianic time. Like their counterparts in Saudi Arabia, they processed that exigency by rededicating their lives to Allah and cultivating profits and capitalist landscapes at a quicker pace, before his gift dried up.[18]

No one entity did more to frame and facilitate petro-Islam's sense of exceptionalism than Aramco, which became a Saudi national enterprise. Aramco's journey through the 1970s and into the 1980s offered further proof that the societies in the region were not merely undergoing breakneck transformations but being launched into new dispensations of oil wealth under their command. The corporate transitions for the Saudi-American firm happened fast and furiously, all to the liking of Saudi minister of oil Ahmed Yamani, who had long dreamed of its nationalization. The first advance occurred in the tumultuous 1973. That year of Middle Eastern unrest saw Aramco award the monarch a 25 percent share. The following year, the king gained a 60 percent share and asked the company to begin implementing a plan for Aramco's complete takeover by the Saudi government. In 1976—at the same time it became the first firm in the world to produce over 3 billion barrels of crude in one year—Aramco ironed out a final deal with Yamani and the king. As of 1980, with a purchase of 100 percent of Aramco stock, Saudi Arabia would gain full control of the company. Yamani's adept boardroom diplomacy meant that American ownership was over and the corporate ghosts of Rockefeller officially exorcised.[19]

Like Aramco's corporate trajectory, its shift in discourses of development indicated that Muslim Arabs were taking control of their commodity. For many of its earnest managers and emissaries, the US venture in Saudi Arabia had served as the ultimate test case of modernization in the "third world," with Westerners in the lead. But by the late 1960s, men such as Tom Barger and William Mulligan were coming to realize that their aspirations—their narratives of Aramco's past and future— had to give way to others articulated by Saudis themselves. Considering the heated politics of the day, it was no longer propitious for a foreign company to talk in paternalistic terms about uplifting Middle Eastern society; nor could Aramco's managers be as forward with the king's court in advocating westernized values and agendas. By the late 1970s, with Yamani at the controls, his face the international symbol of Arabs' rising state power, the oil company literally began to rewrite its history. Prominent motifs and metaphors of courageous oilmen from America plumbing the Arabian desert to help backward bedouin tribesmen advance gave way to stories about kingly and religious duty. The annals of Aramco now foregrounded an honorable, God-fearing Ibn Saud and his court as the true agents of a modern transfiguration that Allah had intended for his people.[20]

Aramco's new homegrown agendas began to flourish as the Saudi Arabian takeover of Aramco transpired. In the wake of the Yom Kippur War, Aramco shifted into a high gear of operational expansion. As evidenced in the construction of worker camps, the overall growth of the multisite complex was momentous. According to a 1976 development plan, in Aramco's more established centers at Dhahran, Abqaiq, and Ras Tanura, the number of family camp residents was projected to increase by 68 percent, 57 percent, and 83 percent, respectively, with new camps at Udhailiya and Safaniya seeing increases of 850 percent and 630 percent. By year's end in 1975, 6,975 total family residents were reported; by 1980, the number was projected at 12,950. Immigrant workers, meanwhile, poured in, inundating Aramco's housing sites for single men, whose overall population was planned to grow from 5,500 to 10,000. The quality of housing Aramco now supplied changed too. The white-only enclaves of the 1950s and 1960s gave way to sprawling residential-service-entertainment districts: swimming pools, air-conditioned theaters, and elegant mosques now awaited the modern oil laborer. Compared to the early days, Aramco officials noted, "our new employees are coming from a greatly improved environment and they expect more." Their profiles were indeed different. By the late 1970s, Saudi Arabian and Muslim-Arab students trained at the region's top engineering and science schools—American University of Beirut (AUB) or Saudi Arabia's own University of Petroleum and Minerals (accredited in 1975 and subsequently renamed for King Fahd)—or at other international institutions were sharpening their skills in advanced programs, then settling at Aramco to lead it into the next phase of global dominance. Cosmopolitans in their appreciation of modernity's finer things, they expected to be treated as such by their employer.[21]

Those in charge of treating workers with sensitivity to the finer things, moreover, comprised a very different managerial class, one whose ambitions for developing Saudi Arabia's economy grew out of their own nationalist commitments. Capping a process of recruitment of Saudi nationals begun in the late 1950s and early 1960s, by the 1980s Saudis would hold (as corporate literature boasted) "nearly all of the company's top management positions, 76 percent of the supervisory positions, 77 percent of the industrial jobs and about 60 percent of the professional positions—testament to the company's commitment to nurturing leadership from within." The ultimate illustration of that commitment came via the hiring in 1983 of Ali I. Al-Naimi as Aramco's first Saudi president. The product of a bedouin tribe and trained in Aramco's company school before attaining advanced degrees in geology and business (on Aramco's dime) at several top American universities, Al-Naimi had a compelling life story, celebrated by the company as testimony to corporate responsibility and Saudi ambition. Al-Naimi was a symbolic first. But he was also the substantive head of a vast team of Saudi experts who managed all the company's developmental initiatives, including agricultural test farms and marine biology labs, computer labs and hospitals, and a host of sponsored educational centers and smaller service industries. Aramco's vast domain was now governed for the people *by* the people.[22]

Aramco spent the early 1980s selling that message through its new promotional campaign, which emphasized Saudi Arabia's self-orchestrated fate. The campaign itself relied on reworked chronicles of Aramco's role in the development of the country. One communiqué, titled "The Change Agent," tacked a slightly different course from the corporate histories of earlier days, with the corporate brass now placed third in the chain of causation. The company may have jump-started change, it began, but "it was through its workforce that the chain reaction spread from the corporation to its employees, to their families, to their friends, and into towns and villages." Grassroots encounters rather than top-down planning, in other words, had driven the Aramco experiment. Moreover, the king, who "wanted a better life for his people," not Aramco's men, had inspired the entire venture. Thus it was time for Aramco's leaders to honor a past in which Saudi princes and people were cast as partners in "one of the outstanding jobs of social engineering in this phase of the history of the world."[23]

"Partnership" with Saudi princes and people, with Allah in the lead: that was the principal takeaway that Saudi Aramco and the government wanted Muslim employees, Saudi citizens, and US investors to internalize as they observed the company's progressions in the 1980s. To celebrate the fifty-year anniversary of the company in 1983, Ahmed Yamani used Aramco's press to wax eloquent on its past and future. Thanks belonged to the king, he declared, for recruiting oilmen to his kingdom and acting out God-given generosity for his subjects. Folding Western notions of linear progress into the messianic timetable his fellow Muslims embraced, Yamani highlighted the fruits that the king's leadership of the oil project had produced for Saudis and "the people of other lands." That "hard-won achievement's most striking feature," he measured, was "Saudi Arabia's admirable ability to conjoin history's noblest faith with the latest innovations of Western technology, without permitting either to dominate or interfere with the other. The secret lies, no doubt, in the fact that Islam is a religion of development and construction." Yamani thanked Aramco's American experts—"pioneers in the understanding and operation of the mysteries of the petroleum industry"—who patiently transferred their knowledge to their hosts, allowing the latter to construct a contemporary society. As "we pass from one historic era into another," his tribute closed, "I cannot help but praise the spirit of diligence, dedication, and effort that pervades the Aramco work force—Americans, Saudis and other nationalities. I pray God Almighty to continue to bless this peaceful country and . . . to spare it the pitfalls of falsehood and error. God is the grantor of success."[24]

While Yamani's words pervaded the corporate press, Saudi Arabia's US embassy sold the same message to the American public through advertisement campaigns that spoke of two nations and one set of values. "Saudi Arabia's concern for the day-to-day welfare of people is conditioned by two enduring traditions," one magazine ad proclaimed: "Our religion. And our commitment to family." "Islam preaches equality and the rights of the individual. It is a religion of peace and tolerance. Our faith in God is a way of life." Aided by photographs of schoolchildren and young engineers, the ad eased into its second point. "For us, the family has always been a close, mutually reinforcing entity, as well as basic and central to society. . . . [E]ven while Saudi Arabia has more than 25 percent of the world's proven oil reserves, our single most important natural resource is our people. They are our hope. And our future." These shared faith, fuel, and family values enabled Saudi Arabia and the United States to continue to act in unison. "Today," the blurb read, "Saudi Arabia looks forward to even more fulfilled dreams with the United States." Saudi Aramco's marketers mixed boilerplate with a history of brotherhood that men such as William Eddy had always longed for and managed, to a degree, to achieve.[25]

But by the time Yamani and Saudi royalty began seizing control of Aramco, Eddy's old contemporaries were finding their company's period of traded authority difficult to navigate. Amid the turbulence of Middle Eastern politics, they retreated altogether, some more reluctantly than others, some against their will. Beyond the Aramco compound, those associated with the Arabist community that had built institutions such as AUB and rallied for Washington support of the Muslim Middle East turned into targets of violence. The first punctuating occurrence came in 1976 when a disgruntled Palestinian engineering student, who had been expelled from the university along with 103 other militant protestors the previous year, reappeared on campus brandishing a pistol and a grenade. He killed the school's dean of engineering, as well as its dean of students, Robert Najemi, a US citizen of Lebanese birth.

Najemi's death hit the Aramco Catholic community particularly hard. A devout Catholic, he also supported John Nolan of the Catholic Near East Welfare Association, with whom the Mulligans and the Bargers were close. This was not the last violence AUB saw. In 1984, two men gunned down Malcolm Kerr, AUB president and professor of Middle Eastern studies and the son of missionaries who had taught at AUB for forty years. Islamic Jihad, a Shiite militia (precursor to Hezbollah) that violently protested American and Western presence in Lebanon during the country's civil war in the early 1980s, took credit for the murder. One of Aramco's very own was terrorized too. In July 1982, Shiite militants with ties to Iran kidnapped AUB president David Dodge (Kerr's predecessor), a former Aramco employee and the fourth generation of Dodges to guide the school. He was held captive for a year. No longer an island in the desert, Aramco's compounds felt the mounting crises acutely. As the Iranian Revolution flared, along with it attacks on US embassies in Iran, Libya, and Pakistan, and pro-Iranian rioting in Qatif, near Ras Tanura in Saudi Arabia, Aramco's managers ramped up security of company camps. Fear was rampant, a journalist reported. "Six junior Aramco employees quit in recent weeks because of the anti-American climate in the Mideast, and the compound is rife with rumor of many more resignations." "People here are nervous," a company official admitted. "That's only natural."[26]

Fears of physical violence were pervasive, but just as worrisome to Aramco's American constituency were the threats to their liberties and religious freedom that simmered beneath the surface. Those were the anxieties that burdened William Mulligan as he spent his last days at Aramco in the late 1970s and monitored the company's transitions in the 1980s from afar. After Tom Barger left Aramco in 1969, Mulligan both maintained his leadership position within Aramco's public relations sector and assumed seniority within the community's underground Catholic Church. Like the Bargers, he and his wife, Shirley, were honored for their exceptional service to the church with bestowal of the honorific titles of knight commander and lady commander of the Holy Sepulcher. By the late 1970s, Mulligan's Catholic brethren believed they had much to be thankful for: despite operating in the shadows, the Catholic morale groups had built an impressive network, with twenty-four "clerics" shepherding the almost 10,000 Aramco workers who attended weekly services in the company's main camps.[27]

Yet new tensions with the monarchy were emerging. Late in 1977, with Christmas approaching, Saudi royalty indicated it was going to prohibit Aramco's Christians from celebrating the event. US Ambassador John West intervened and managed to win some concessions, but in return Saudi officials said he was to guarantee that all Christian services would be held "without publicity or fanfare" and that "there would be no major expansion of Christian activities," intimating that a scaling back of religious activity might be next. On-the-ground experiences suggested as much. Starting in 1977, with intensification as the 1980s progressed, Aramco's morale groups were monitored and in cases infiltrated by Saudi "religious police"; on a few occasions, clerics were called in for questioning—a process that sometimes involved brief imprisonment, then perhaps expulsion from the kingdom. One Aramco veteran would later recall to Mulligan, "The holding of religious services got sticky in the 1980s, and to lower profile, Friday masses were transferred to the gym tucked away in a school in Dhahran Hills." Still, he noted, "self-proclaimed mutawa [religious police] were not deterred and on one occasion, a group actually entered the chapel when mass was in progress. The parishioners quickly turned it into a 'meeting' and fortunately there were no religious objects on display, so life went on." By this point, Christmas services were banned and heavier restrictions placed on incoming "teachers," with visas much harder to come by. All morale groups felt the suppression. When a prominent Protestant speaker, who had visited Aramco in the late 1960s, began making plans to worship with the evangelical group at Dhahran, he was answered with a somber note. Due to his credentials, it was clear he would be denied entry. "The situation has changed much since 1967," an Aramco representative explained, "and even now the restrictions are constantly tightening. Aramco is just in the last stages of becoming Saudi Aramco, being completely Saudi owned and having cut all ties to the United States. This too, adds to the tightening restrictions."[28]

Squeezed out by shifting leadership in Aramco and cognizant that political exigencies were bringing their experiment in the civil religion of crude to an end, Mulligan returned to the United States and like

Barger continued to measure their former home's transitions. President of the parish council at his New Hampshire church, Mulligan championed a progressive catholicity that shunned sectarianism of any kind—be it the kind forced upon Aramco's Christian communities by an increasingly rigid Islamic state or the type exacerbated by Catholics, Protestants, and Jews prejudiced against Middle Eastern Muslims. Like Barger, Mulligan used his pen to combat the deterioration of the Arabist dreams. His rebuttal of an overly zealous Catholic survey of Christianity in the gulf states was typical in its curtness: "Perhaps I should be grateful, that Father Tescaroli doesn't carry his fervor as far as did St. Francis Xavier who told a Muslim that God takes no pleasure in infidels, still less in their prayers." He also acted with his feet, joining a civil rights organization for Arab Americans. Even as he would grow increasingly defensive about the Aramco enterprise he had been wedded to for so long, Mulligan also became more self-critical of it amid the explosive—and now seemingly unsolvable—terrors of the 1980s. Mulligan had been one of Aramco's most important media boosters; yet by the time he passed away in 1992, his view of affairs had—not unlike William Eddy's—grown bleak.[29]

Barger's may have too, if with slightly less edge. During the 1970s and 1980s, even with deteriorating health, Barger penned opinion pieces from his San Diego home that appeared in national newspapers, hoping to forestall knee-jerk American reactions against Muslim oil-producing countries. He also delivered talks that implored people to strive for understanding across the Christian-Muslim, Western–Middle Eastern divide. He presented one of his most important talks at the Annual National Security Affairs Conference in Washington, DC, in 1980. Barger walked audience members through the intricacies of Islam and Middle Eastern oil, wanting them to grasp the depth of belief that informed the people he considered his brethren and the complex theological and political entanglements that made the region so delicate. His point: when it came to quelling tensions in the Middle East, Americans needed to let genuine curiosity about other peoples' heritages and practical consideration of their present feed a spirit of encounter. "Knowledge of history, customs and religion is no substitute for common sense and exercise of the imagination," he asserted, "an exercise our narcissistic tendencies seem to inhibit."[30]

It was a message his fellow Arabists had been preaching since the 1930s and one he kept preaching to his grave. Barger died on June 30, 1986, at the age of seventy-seven. Aramco veterans and eulogies from both sides of the ocean poured in. All of them labeled the man the lynchpin of an oil venture and cultural endeavor of epic proportions. At his funeral there were singing, testimonials, and a procession of the assembled knight commanders and lady commanders in full uniform. That sense of nobility shined through the sermon, which reflected on Barger as a diplomat of goodwill. According to one witness who journeyed from Dhahran, the homily stressed Tom's respect for Muslim Arabs and reported that his "proudest moment was when he learned Ali Naimi became president of Aramco, some fifteen years after his retirement." For all the ruptures he had witnessed as Aramco's chief and as a distant advocate during the 1970s and 1980s, Barger seemed pleased that the Muslim man chosen to take over his oil company came from the ranks of the bedouins who had helped him acclimatize after his arrival in the 1930s and nurtured his love of the desert land and bewitching wanderings "out in the blue."[31]

WHILE BARGER AND Mulligan's grand oil venture drew to a close, America's other oil cabal achieved its apex of authority. With Ronald Reagan in the White House, independents and their allies in the church were certain that their businesses and ministries were about to prosper. Armed with access to the nation's highest office, they influenced policy and, more importantly, consolidated an oil-patch culture of conservative educational, economic, and family values whose evolution over time now seemed complete. For its earnest proponents, the pinnacle of wildcat religion's national authority would be sweet but also short and incomplete.

When Reagan assumed control of the White House in January 1981, America's wildcatters rejoiced. In electing him to the nation's top office, they believed they were about to witness the rollback of government in their homes, schools, religious institutions, and oil fields; the promises of liberty that Barry Goldwater had lobbed in 1964 to court their vote, it seemed, were being realized. Scholars have written at length about the Reagan coalition of conservatives that secured his revolution. They have dug deep into the activities of the Religious Right, whose anger with society's leftward turn on social issues like abortion, gender equality, and homosexuality propelled them into the political realm. Yet, as witnessed in the seamless blend of oil-patch politicking practiced by Baptist and Pentecostal chieftains James Robison and Oral Roberts, John Walvoord and Bunker Hunt, and their allies in the pulpits, seminaries, and boardrooms of oildom, the advance of progressive energy and environmental policies under Richard Nixon and Jimmy Carter catalyzed the backlash too. In Reagan they identified a biblical king who would lead his followers back into Petrolia's promised land.[32]

Reagan took his conservative constituents' social and environmental values seriously and, on that score, rewarded them with key administrative posts. One appointee was C. Everett Koop. A Presbyterian layman with close ties to Francis Schaeffer (Koop had narrated one of his documentaries), Koop was also a respected doctor, which is why Reagan named him surgeon general, a position that would place him in the middle of the abortion controversy. The other reward came via James Watt's appointment as secretary of the interior. Watt was a Pentecostal who shared John Walvoord's premillennialist beliefs and deep suspicion of Washington. His professional experience as president of the Mountain States Legal Foundation, based in Denver, had plunged him into combat with environmentalists, a fight he seemed to relish. His legal work with the foundation also saw him litigate on behalf of oil, mining, and energy business interests against the US Department of the Interior. Watt was a warrior for the wildcat way, confronting Washington in a no-holds-barred manner, demanding it leave western capitalists' lands alone. "We will mine more, drill more, and cut more timber," he pledged. Watt encased that pledge in an end-times fervor that said the world's impending end justified the rush of extractive activity.[33]

Watt signaled his theological convictions at the very outset of his tenure and never hid them from public light. In his testimony before the House Interior Committee in February 1981, he noted the "delicate balance the Secretary of the Interior must have: to be steward for the natural resources for this generation as well as future generations." On that point he added his own doubts about the future, which made the balance he sought to strike even more delicate. "I do not know how many future generations we can count on before the Lord returns;

whatever it is we have to manage with a skill to leave the resources needed for future generations." Later that spring Watt reiterated his wish to use his position in Washington to honor his god by managing the nation's natural resources with resolve to maximize economic returns. "My responsibility is to follow the Scriptures which call upon us to occupy the land until Jesus returns." Watt acted—rather than just speaking—in the spirit of the wildcatters who had fought the New Deal order by confronting an interior secretary of a different ilk. He promised to transfer custodianship of the oil patch from Harold Ickes's successors to the people who had long worked it as theirs. During his first months in office he leased federal land for strip mining and eased restrictions for offshore oil drilling and exploration. "I don't believe government should stand in the way of the free market," he explained, "and I'm here to do what I can to make sure it doesn't."[34]

Watt may have stood out for his brashness, but he was not alone in his attempts to champion a free market ideal of land management. Reagan in fact siphoned critical political support from the anti-environmentalist Sagebrush Rebellion of the 1970s, which rejected Washington's claims to western lands. Beyond the Sagebrush backlash operated a wider range of counter-environmentalist individuals and agendas that would help spark the more moderate-sounding Wise Use movement of the 1980s and 1990s. Wise Use would continue to demonize environmentalism as un-American, partly by discrediting it (as one Idaho Republican did) as "a cloudy mixture of New Age mysticism, Native American folklore, and primitive earth worship—pantheism" that violated Christian American values. But it would also connect wider flows of alternative philosophies of land care to particular policies. Some of its think tank activists contended that the best way to guarantee responsible resource management was to bolster private ownership; local landowners, not distant bureaucrats, they argued, understood how best to use land. A number of counter-environmentalist intellectuals, meanwhile, authored books that highlighted nature's resilience and human technology's ability to innovate society past crisis. Watt, in other words, was a maverick in his posture but not entirely in his thinking.[35]

Still, his political authority meant that his posture mattered a great deal, which is why he quickly became a lightning rod of controversy.

The only other person who came close to that unfavorable position was Anne Gorsuch, whom Watt sponsored to head the Environmental Protection Agency (EPA). Gorsuch assumed the post and then turned it into a weapon against itself, trimming the agency's workforce from 14,075 to 10,396, gutting its influence and morale. After clashing with Congress in 1983 over her questionable dealings with a government program that contracted companies to clean up abandoned waste sites, Gorsuch would be forced to resign. Watt would share that fate. Not long into his administration it became clear that Reagan's choice for interior secretary was a weak one. Watt's ill-timed provocations and relentless attacks on the people who staffed offices under his authority wore on Reagan's friends and foes alike. Conservative journalist George Will considered Watt a serious liability, if for no other reason than that he was inspiring environmentalists to act. "He speaks almost too clearly, indifferent to the bureaucratic art of constructing whole paragraphs perfectly devoid of substance," Will jabbed. "His cocksureness, his thirst for conflict, his tone-deafness regarding his own shrillness, have invigorated environmental groups." Even major oilmen despaired at the negative impact of Reagan's outspokenly anti-environmentalist interior secretary on their profile. "Jim Watt has done more to harm our industry than any other government official in recent history," complained Socal (soon to be Chevron) chairman George Keller. "You couldn't carry on a conversation with him without getting aggravated." When Watt told a racist joke at a public hearing in 1983, Reagan jumped at the chance to fire him and hire a replacement who could promulgate the same politics with tact.[36]

Watt's forced departure neither killed his reputation nor muted his type of rhetoric in the oil patch. "I never use the words Democrats and Republicans," Watt once jibed. "It's liberals and Americans." That discourse shaded the politics of God and black gold throughout the mid-1980s, as residents of North America's oil-production zones took advantage of doors opened by Reagan's friendly administration. That included an effort to expand their educational institutions as a means of offsetting liberalism's perceived encroachment in their classrooms. Within evangelical circles especially, the 1980s witnessed dramatic growth of an alternative pedagogy that covered everything from environmental studies to history and geology. Gradations in temperament were present. Some evangelicals built on the work of Schaeffer and other earth care thinkers, who implored Christians to embrace an "ecotheology" of social justice and "creation stewardship" while still adhering to Schaeffer's fundamental belief in the supremacy of God and man. Such broader-minded initiatives filtered through the oil-saturated Southwest, but Watt's tougher philosophy sank deeper roots there. During the 1980s, oil-patch Christians became more determined to counter the very understandings of time, history, and science on which environmentalists' arguments rested.[37]

The oil patch's staunchest fundamentalists took the lead in that counteraction. Longview, Texas—once the center of the East Texas boom—served as an epicenter. By the early 1980s, Longview residents Mel and Norma Gabler were using their nonprofit firm, Educational Research Analysts, to influence Texas schoolboard politics. After working with Esso (Exxon) for thirty-nine years, Mel retired to focus all his time and energies on studying educational textbooks used by the Texas public school system, reporting liberal biases and threatening school officials with lawsuits. "Textbooks were indoctrinating children with a philosophy of humanism that was alien to mainstream America," he complained—and also promoting evolutionary science and understandings of history that negated Bible principles, moral absolutes, and the privileged standing of Christianity in the nation's development. Not far from the Gablers, meanwhile, was LeTourneau College, the creation of R. G. LeTourneau, whose move to the area in the 1940s was meant to strengthen connections to the oil industry. By the 1980s, the school's science, technology, and engineering programs were attracting hundreds of students (the college's total enrollment in 1980 was 1,000), with young men and women studying to be pilots, mechanics, and petroleum geologists *and* better God-fearing Christians. The curriculum LeTourneau offered was "unapologetically Christian" and unwavering in its prioritization of faith over secular science. In the view of its administrators and instructors, a student's acquisition of the technical skills needed to succeed in industry did not require relegating belief in the Bible to the margins. Center God and the Bible in your vocation, they countered, and watch your careers thrive. It was an increasingly popular formula. In 1989, LeTourneau College became LeTourneau University, offering four- and two-year degree programs and satellite campuses in Tyler and soon Dallas and Houston. With extended reach, the school could service the state's most important industry—petroleum—with greater efficiency.[38]

LeTourneau's was a familiar push among Texans and Oklahomans to underscore the fundamentals of their faith while advancing the technologies of the region's oil sector. At this time emerging tensions between new, sophisticated methods and theories of petroleum geology and biblical orthodoxy resulted in some evangelicals' embrace of an alternative premise: "creation science." Whereas in the 1920s Christian oil geologists such as University of Oklahoma professor Charles Gould could still straddle a middle line between geology and their traditional faith in the Bible, after the 1930s rapid technical advancements such as seismology and carbon dating made that posture more difficult to maintain. The earth, it now appeared, was millions of years old, its rock formations a product of evolution over millennia. "This oil geology has opened up the depths of the earth in a way that we never dreamed of twenty years ago," one Christian scholar acknowledged after visiting the East Texas oil fields on the eve of World War II. The observation encouraged him to shift his thinking slightly and allow room for geological theories of sequential fossiliferous rock formation. Many postwar scientists with faith commitments had similar experiences but continued to hold the intellectual stance Gould had maintained. Members of the religious-based American Scientific Affiliation (ASA) published textbooks that asserted Genesis and geology could be "harmonized" through steadying "faith in supernatural revelation." It was true, one Christian scientist admitted, that the "accredited geological interpretation" of earth's origins was highly incompatible with a Christian worldview—but not entirely. In advancing a "progressive creation" scheme, which underscored the development of an old earth over time, he carved out room for modern geology's latest findings. Meanwhile, he also took geology's mainstream experts to task for practicing their own degree of blind trust. No matter how sophisticated their science may be, he exclaimed, surefire answers about world beginnings were not possible: "any theory of Origins must involve some faith," he said. "The proponents of [the generally accredited geological interpretation] manifest an astonishing amount of pure faith and muster an unusually small array of facts in proportion."[39]

Other evangelical geology hounds, however, were less willing than the ASA to compromise with new geological science. The most important was Henry Morris. "Consistency with Scripture is more important than temporary harmony with a continually changing science," he chastised the ASA; no amount of compromise with secular scientists was acceptable. He wore that conviction openly. Educated in engineering at Rice University and the University of Minnesota before teaching at Virginia Polytechnic University, the Texan came to his claims for a strict creationism with plenty of applied knowledge in hand. He was convinced that intellectual trends in his line of work were dangerous: theories of an old earth, evolution, and gradual progressions of fossilization were evidence, in his view, not of clearer thinking but of humanity's secular drift. In 1961, he co-authored *The Genesis Flood*, which argued that earth was created in six days, that earth itself was only a few thousand years old, and that a cataclysmic flood was responsible for the rearrangement of earth's fossil record. Morris's section on geology was particularly pointed. Due to almost unanimous rejection of the Genesis account of creation and Noah's Flood, he admitted, Christians faced a "serious dilemma." Nevertheless, he asserted, "evidences of full divine inspiration of Scripture are far weightier than the evidences for any fact of science." Drawing on his engineering expertise, he argued that "fossil-bearing strata were . . . laid down in large measure during the Flood, with the apparent sequences attributed not to evolution but rather to hydrodynamic selectivity, ecological habitats, and differential mobility and strength of the various creatures." On one matter he could agree with his ASA equals: that the new science itself operated on faith in the unseen. More than that, he contended, evolutionists who were corrupting it were acting out of "moral and emotional decision[s]" and seeking "intellectual justification for escape from personal responsibility to [their] Creator and escape from the 'way of the Cross' as the necessary and sufficient means of [their] personal redemption."[40]

The publication of *The Genesis Flood* sparked a "creationist revival" (as one historian puts it) that proliferated among evangelicals over the coming decades. Morris himself became a celebrity—he eventually oversaw the Creation Research Institute in California and traveled widely to tout the legitimacy of its creation science. His tours took him back to Oklahoma and Texas, with stops at colleges such as LeTourneau. At one point in the 1970s he was even asked to join LeTourneau's faculty as dean of its engineering school. He declined the offer but not the invitations that followed for him and his team of creationists to visit Longview to teach their doctrine. Few Christians within the petroleum guild would accept his theories entirely; in private and public universities, the advances of science and technology would continue to be pursued with a spirit of discovery that stretched thinking beyond literalist interpretations of Genesis. Yet, by the mid-1980s, evangelicals in the oil patch—including those who staffed its most technically advanced industrial posts—could glean assurance from the trickle-down sentiments of Morris and the ASA that the work of drilling through miles of subsurface sediment and strata to reach fossils of prehistoric lineage did not necessitate their abandonment of their faith. Even if new methods of reading the earth could help people better understand its material properties and find more abundant oil quicker, they could not answer ultimate questions—such as why the universe exists. "This will always be a matter of speculation—or faith," a contemporary geologist concedes. "The Lord acts in mysterious ways" was a mantra early oil hunters believed and that later oil hunters could still consider gospel truth.[41]

Favorable energy policies and educational restructurings all affirmed wildcatters' new standing at the top of the oil order, as did the economics of the Reagan moment. On account of Arab oil embargoes and foreign unpredictability, the early Reagan years witnessed a momentous boom in domestic exploration. Rig counts climbed dramatically in Texas, from an estimated low of 600 in the late 1970s to over 4,000 by the end of 1981. With crude prices hovering around ten times historic levels, small producers could afford to explore with enormous range. Expensive but efficient technologies of drilling and extraction, previously ruled out for their costliness, were now put to work in the quest to harvest nature's more difficult oil terrains, including those once deemed depleted, dry, or impractical. "Across the state of Texas," one historian writes, "the fundamental configurations of drilling deals were simply transformed. 'It's time,' independents told one another, 'to drill!'" Once again, it seemed, the Texas wildcatter's moment in the sun was now.[42]

The euphoria filtered through company boardrooms and church pews alike. Sun Oil executives, buoyed as company profits rose at a steeper pitch, cheered at the progress they seemed to have made in human and public relations. Leveled with charges of environmental negligence and racial prejudice in the 1960s and 1970s, Sun spent the booming early 1980s attempting to put all those accusations to rest. Besides continuing to improve environmental protection procedures in its drilling operations, it also asked a former nemesis to address employees. In November 1983, Reverend Leon Sullivan, former leader of the Philadelphia boycott movement that challenged Sun's racist hiring practices, delivered a speech to Sun managers that praised their support of his ministry. Since his breakout on a national stage, the black minister had continued to sell his economic uplift program—Opportunities Industrialization Center (OIC)—as the way to improve the lot of America's lower-class minorities and by extension remedy the world's injustices. "The most important need for the amelioration of human problems of the developing world," he told Sun employees, "will be the efforts of the people themselves in 'self-help', augmented by the greatest possible support from industrialized countries." As a result of the programs OIC was implementing with Sun's help, Sullivan reported, "billions of dollars are being earned in new incomes by successful trainees from the OIC, and hundreds of millions of dollars are being paid to the government in new tax revenues." Sullivan was particularly excited about OIC's investment in Africa, where "'self-help' training schemes" were instilling market skills in people and raising prospects for Africa's fledgling nations. "Either the people will be prepared from the bottom up, or there will be no hope of competing equitably with the Western World, either now or tomorrow," he predicted. Sullivan finished with a doxology: "With great enterprises like Sun oil . . . and others helping lead the way, I believe with God's help, together, we can build a better and more humane world for impoverished people everywhere." Sullivan's was praise for a wildcat ethic that the Pews had instilled in their corporate family generations before, an ethic now drained, in appearance at least, of its explicit racisms.[43]

The same elation with ascendant wildcat capitalism seemingly freed of its lingering sins also reverberated throughout the oil patch's public. During the early 1980s boom, numerous apostles of the philosophy delivered the message that "Christian principles" were the key "to getting ahead." One motivational speaker characterized Texans' good fortune in simple terms: it was "the payoff . . . for cowboy Christian values—hard work, faith in God, honesty in all deeds." His listeners learned that the will to work and a desire to believe—in self-attainment, in market returns, in family as the bedrock, and in God—were all one needed to make Reagan-era capitalism work in one's favor. The apostle essentially granted oildom's citizens permission to redouble their faith in the core attributes they had always considered tested and true.[44]

That exact doctrine informed the oil patch's booming churches as well. During the early 1980s—much like their predecessors in Beaumont, Texas, circa 1901—church folk came to see their latest windfall as a sign of God's grace. The experience of Grandview Assembly of God Church in Elk City, Oklahoma, was typical. By 1982, this small town on the western edge of the state was bursting, all thanks to discovery of a major oil and gas field. During the first two years of the decade, Elk City's population grew from 8,000 to 30,000. As one local recalled, "Land in the oil and gas-rich Anadarko Basin was being leased by homesteaders to investors and feverishly worked by roughnecks and 'oilies' who drifted into Elk City in search of fortune." With the excitement all around, residents Marie and Ecca "Ecc" Roberts decided to build a church. Ecc said he had "received a vision from God" in which he was called to plant a parish and let Christ "do many wonderful and miraculous things." The Robertses called on Mark Little, a young Pentecostal evangelist who knew oil country (he had been raised in Borger, Texas, where his father worked for Phillips Petroleum Company), to be their pastor. Mark and Sandra Little arrived in Elk City in 1982, where a congregation of forty awaited their guidance into the era of expectation the Robertses envisioned.[45]

Mark Little helped his church make great strides in that direction. Within six months, the small fellowship of oil and gas workers that started with 17 members meeting in a funeral home had grown to 230, who now packed a community hall outfitted with folding chairs from Walmart. Little said he was "living a pastor's dream." So the church board decided to take a chance and acquire a loan to build an eight-hundred-seat auditorium. Men and women in the congregation volunteered their labor in order to offset costs. Awed by the commitment of

Christian verve, Little quoted Nehemiah 4:6 to describe what he began to witness among his parishioners: "For the people worked with all their heart." Grandview's congregants, one churchman wrote, "had a mind-set to work and complete the task to which God had called them."[46]

GRANDVIEW'S BLITZ WOULD be short-lived, its reversal of fortunes a micro-scale illustration of macro-level pivots in oil—turns without full recovery. Even as transitions in the Middle East signaled the end of US dominance in one petroleum context, by the mid-1980s downturns in the independent oil sector precipitated further worries of a system in decline. Residents of the continent's oil patches would recover, but only in spiritual terms, by confessing their sins and rechristening their efforts to "occupy" the earth and spread the gospel before the Lord's return.

The collapse was not expected—not with such severity, at least. It began incrementally with 1982's drop in world oil prices. Declining petroleum use in the slowing economies of the United States and Europe and a corresponding surfeit in oil supplies triggered downward pricing. "Oil glut! . . . is here," the *New York Times* declared; "the world temporarily floats in a glut of oil," *Time* echoed. All producers felt the pinch, but production continued. The crash of 1986, however, brought all remaining activity to a halt. Saudi Arabia and OPEC precipitated the collapse. Although Saudi Arabia wanted to institute proration systems to mesh oil supply with demand and ease pressures on global markets, its partners refused to abide. It could only balance Persian Gulf output with world market demand by cutting its own production—but the more it did so, the more its OPEC allies increased their output, in gleeful spite. Exasperated, the Saudis opened their valves late in 1985, flooding the market, and in January 1986 the international price of crude plummeted. In the twelve months that followed, oil fell from a high of $30 per barrel to under $10. US production stopped. Whereas in 1982 more than 4,500 rigs were in operation in the United States, by July 1986 only 663 remained alive. Oil equipment sales sank from $40 billion to $9 billion. Drilling derricks were dismantled and sold for scrap.[47]

Every corner of the petroleum realm suffered. US major companies lost billions of dollars as expensive recovery ventures became unviable, so they slashed their budgets and laid off staff in the tens of thousands. Even Saudi Aramco felt the pain. In response to the collapsing prices, it jettisoned 17,000 members of its workforce between 1982 and 1987. But due to the scale of their operations, Aramco and major oil companies could wait out the troubles. Despite the dislocations, they were able to refocus on long-term recovery and operational plans.[48]

The independents had no such cushion. Their world quite literally disintegrated. Numerous regional banks that had counted on exploration loans for solidity went under; panicked by what they were witnessing, most remaining lending agencies called in their loans from oil producers. Handcuffed by these maneuvers and severely overstretched, the producers declared bankruptcy. They did not have long-term adjustment schemes (nor could they): their only agenda was short-term survival, and the vast majority of them lacked the means to carry it out. In West Texas, suburban tracts in Midland and Odessa emptied out, returning split-levels to the tumbleweed and jackrabbits that had ruled the area before oil clans arrived. "Houses were just being evacuated," an observer recalled. "It was a crazy time." The devastation was just as conspicuous in major oil cities like Houston. After a decade of opulent living, the oil capital was driven to its nadir. A journalist later summarized the calamitous effects: "The colossal fall in oil prices . . . not only sapped Houston's wildcat spirit, but undermined Houston's economic foundations. Houston lost more than 225,000 jobs, about one in eight, and [the] unemployment rate climbed above 9 percent. . . . Office vacancies soared above 20 percent. Office rents plunged." Family life was shuttered there as well. Lending agencies went bankrupt, leaving mortgage options in short supply; construction ground to a halt, and over 200,000 homes remained vacant.[49]

The independent-reliant oil economy that collapsed in Texas failed elsewhere, devastating all the continent's oil patches. No state suffered as swift a drop in oil rig activity as Oklahoma. Whereas in 1982 eight hundred rigs were operational, by 1986 that number was well below one hundred. Louisiana, meanwhile, lost 9 percent of its workforce, a greater decline than the United States realized during the Great Depression. These two states, along with Texas, faced equally daunting futures in government. Fully dependent on oil and gas royalties and taxes for their revenue streams, the three states now confronted shortfalls that thrust them into bankruptcy mode. The Texas state government, one report offers, "crumbled with a $2.9-billion deficit in July, 1986, on the way to a $5.8-billion shortfall." Oklahoma was next, its low point arriving "in June, 1987, with a projected $565-million deficit. Then Louisiana hit bottom May 12, 1988, when the state had an accumulated deficit of $1.3 billion and failed to meet its payroll."[50]

Canada's oil patches teetered too. Alberta in particular suffered heavily, with unemployment rates rocketing to historic levels (11 percent), housing prices plummeting, and the provincial gross domestic product contracting by 3 percent. There was no more striking example of Alberta's topsy-turvy oil sector than the Great Canadian Oil Sands (GCOS), which had limped into the 1980s reporting poor returns on its costly venture. Further pressuring Alberta energy was the federal government. After his convincing electoral win in 1980, Prime Minister Pierre Trudeau asserted a new federalism that imposed greater Ottawa oversight on the provinces. Trudeau was particularly anxious to neutralize Alberta and Quebec, both formidable opponents of the federalist mandate. In the case of the latter, he wanted to shore up the constitution in order to prevent the French province's withdrawal from the union, an ongoing concern. In the case of the former, he wished to exercise more control over Alberta's oil industry and distribute its wealth equally throughout the country. Instituted in 1980, the National Energy Program (NEP) legitimated federal intervention in Alberta's energy sector, and GCOS—now called Suncor—felt the pinch. The NEP installed price controls, created tax incentives to steer oil exploration beyond the established Alberta oil sands area, and created Petro-Canada, a national oil corporation. Suncor officials, Alberta's oil executives, and oil-dependent citizens revolted, chanting in populist rhythms for Ottawa to leave them alone ("Let the Eastern Bastards Freeze in the Dark!" became a popular bumper sticker). But to no avail—their domain was now under Ottawa's control. Meanwhile, Suncor suffered other setbacks. Even as production of the sands continued—with several technological advances expediting the process and inflating the profits—Suncor slogged through a period that included a massive, debilitating fire in its compressor plant, a six-month labor dispute, and the sudden death of its president in a plane crash.[51]

Economic and political trials of the type that paralyzed the continent's petroleum-producing communities naturally produced cultural ones. As swift financial decline swept over them, the specter of lost identity did too. In the Texas and Oklahoma panhandles, there was a sense that the boomtowns of yesteryear were about to be abandoned completely, left for ghosts to inhabit. By the mid-1980s, the once illustrious company town of Texon was not even a shell of its former self. Smooth streets that Estha Briscoe roller-skated on in the 1920s were now rough and barren. In 1986, Texon closed its post office, leaving its citizens—less than one hundred total—to drive elsewhere to mail their missives. Borger, Texas, due north, was much larger and able to withstand the discomforts of the oil crisis, but not without a cost. Thanks to Phillips Oil's petrochemical plant, the hometown of Pastor Mark Little remained a viable community, albeit a declining one. After a fall in population in the 1970s, Borger steadied during the 1980s at a figure of 15,000 before entering another period of decline; over the course of the next three decades, its population would sink to 13,000, a far cry from the roughly 21,000 people who inhabited it when Little called it home. As populations plummeted, institutions folded. Joining local banks in financial collapse were schools, municipal governments, and community centers. As cultural institutions folded, individuals were left to scrape by for alternative career and life paths on their own, burdened with regret for having spent too much and saved too little when the times were good. Another popular bumper sticker of the times playfully—poignantly—expressed the prevailing sentiment of the day: "Lord, Give Me One More Boom—This Time I Promise Not to Blow It Away."[52]

As the experience of Pastor Little's Grandview congregation illustrates, churches were hardly spared from the crash. Yet, despite the turmoil around them, Grandview's members pressed on with their building program. While the women cooked dinners, the men swung hammers. By 1984, Grandview's edifice stood atop the oil patch as a wondrous sign of God's goodness, or so Pastor Little wanted to believe. Yet behind the impressive facade trouble stewed: after the collapse in oil, Little could only watch as his membership roll shrank. Over one month, twenty-five oil-worker families left Little's church, and in no time over two-thirds of its members were gone. He fretted about how church debts would be paid and the religious community maintained. Adding to his anxiety was the physical and psychological stress afflicting many of those members who stayed in Elk City. "Satan seemed to be attacking on all fronts," parishioners recounted. At one point Little locked himself in his house, brooding over his prospects, wondering how he would survive. He stayed sequestered for three days.[53]

But then he emerged and challenged his people to pray for miracles. In yet another pattern familiar to generations of oil-patch residents, Grandview church folk answered their pastor's plea, daring doom to deliver another blow. The more powerful narrative of collective salvation that emerged from their tribulation would be memorialized in the annals of time. As church historians would recount, revival started with their pastor's own reckoning with God. In the midst of his despondency, Little "knelt to pray at one of the pulpit chairs in the sanctuary." He "cried out for God to empower him and lead him to rise to the occasion," then "felt his spirit literally rising out of his body." From high above ground he saw the burdens with which Grandview was saddled, then a towering Jesus, who "was so much bigger and greater than every difficulty and circumstance piled onto the church." His epiphany emboldened him. Even as church membership continued to decline, he urged his followers to finish their cathedral. After more arduous labor, they did, leaving only the purchase of church pews—at a cost of $23,000—unaddressed. But how to raise such a sum in the face of broken careers? Little asked families in his church to dig deep into their remaining savings—this was their chance to claim victory over the darkness wrought by unpredictable crude. Families across the area responded, and as they gave generously, sacrificially, they also readily testified to the workings of the miraculous in their own lives. One family drained its bank account to purchase half a pew. Another couple—Tammy and Rick Ackerman—donated funds in gratitude for Grandview's influence on them. When their young son was suffering from seizures, the church had prayed for him, and over time (and with the help of specialists) he was healed. This all while Rick, a "fisherman" who retrieved oil equipment lost during drilling operations, endured a year without work. The couple petitioned God with specifics: a three-week job for Rick that paid $25,000—or they would leave town. Three days later, they would testify, Rick received an offer of employment that paid $28,000 for twenty-one days of labor. As a love offering, they sent money Little's way.[54]

With miracles seeming to flow freely, Grandview climbed out of its debt. Appeals to the supernatural and a willingness to pray prosperity into being, even when the odds were stiff, appeared to work; by 1986, as further economic crisis enveloped the community, Grandview was on surer financial footing, drawing oildom's lost souls into its fashionable auditorium to inspire with tales of redemption and praise for the Lord. Little's church had not only survived the storm, he announced, but emerged from its season of trial stronger than ever before. Such was the compelling logic—and magical thinking—of the wildcat way: in bad times as well as good, God's mysterious deliverance of grace was more than sufficient for all.[55]

Countless other veterans of the oil patch internalized that same personal gospel and reaffirmed their wildcat ethic by way of large-scale evangelism that swept through the area in the mid-1980s. Whereas preachers such as Little sought to reach locals, more famous evangelists considered it their duty to draw together the multitudes of hurting people. One such evangelist was Arthur Blessitt, and one such hurting person, George W. Bush. Blessitt was a peripatetic preacher known worldwide for dragging a twelve-foot-tall, one-wheeled cross with him wherever he ministered. By 1984 he had lugged his crucifix 36,000 miles in sixty countries on six continents. His appearance in Midland, Texas, that year was no accident; sought out as someone who could heal a broken community, he came to West Texas to minister to the spiritual needs of unemployed and unmoored oilmen and their families. Jim Sale, Bush's friend and a local oilman, was among those who welcomed that antidote and its messenger. Bush, for his part, was ready to grab onto something spiritual. Although he had grown up in a near-idyllic Midland—where, he would recall, his weekly schedule included high school football on Fridays and church on Sundays—by the time he reached middle age he was consumed with other things, most notably his small oil exploration company. By the mid-1980s he was facing extraordinary pressure that came with life in the boom-bust vocation he had learned from his father. Under heavy debt and unable to draw his own salary, Bush struggled to stay afloat, while at home the stresses of work tore at his marriage. On an April day in 1984, at Sale's urging, Bush met Blessitt to talk about God. The minister wasted no time in asking his standard question: "If you died this moment, do you have the assurance you would go to heaven?" Bush blurted, "No," then gave in to Blessitt's message. Holding hands, the two men prayed the sinner's prayer. Thrilled with the outcome, Blessitt wrote in his journal words evangelicals would remember for years: "A good and powerful day. Led Vice President Bush's son to Jesus today. George Bush Jr.!! This is great. Glory to God."[56]

Bush's process of regeneration was not yet complete. As he himself would recount, his "rededication" to Christ became real under Billy Graham's counsel at a gathering at the Bush family compound in Kennebunkport, Maine, in 1985. "He [Graham] led me to . . . a new walk where I would recommit my heart to Jesus Christ." Bush experienced yet a third generative moment. In 1986, while celebrating his fortieth birthday, he imbibed too much. The next day he decided he would quit drinking and turned to a men's Bible study group for mentoring. During the next few years he continued to "mature" as a Christian: he gave up smoking, prayed regularly, and read devotional literature before going to bed. Forced toward a spiritual accounting by the devastating conditions of the collapsing oil patch and inspired by Blessitt and Graham to embrace a quintessentially oil-patch faith, Bush emerged from his tribulation more fully committed to a religion that promised him personal atonement, a better life on terms set by him and his God, and the spiritual strength to survive.[57]

Grandview Church's collective experience and Bush's personal one mirrored those of countless other oil-dependent citizens and institutions during the 1980s. In their businesses, households, communities, and churches, residents of oildom felt overwhelmed by tragic discord but still certain that their best response was to double down on the doctrines of personal healing, self-fulfillment, and divine calling that had long operated in their land. Their remedy did nothing to solve the actual oil crisis itself. Wildcatters would never fully recover from the 1980s crash as they had from previous boom-bust cycles. "It is not an easy task to describe the psychological as well as the economic consequences of this shock," one historian concludes, "other than to suggest that fallout from the crude price crash has influenced in large or small ways every subsequent development affecting independent producers down to the present." Yet, in their local domains, where apparitions of the possible had always superseded the tangibles of difficult reality, their unwavering trust in miracles and a Christ who changed hearts connected them to a long history of redemption by fire and to the familiar and comfortable rationales of oil's early days.[58]

FOR ALL THEIR attempts to process the disruptions of the 1980s, small and big oil alike approached the 1990s in an altered state. While the crash of 1986 upended their operations, a subsequent sequence of petroleum-fueled political developments further accentuated US oilers' sense of lost control. They also repositioned America in a dizzying matrix of religious-political antagonisms.

The foreign policy challenges George W. Bush's father faced provided one sign that a new epoch of global encounters with God and black gold had begun. In July 1989, President George H. W. Bush met with Saudi Arabia's King Fahd to underscore the "friendship of the two countries" based on a half century of shared interests and "bonds of trust and understanding." The reasons for the meeting extended beyond niceties, of course; its purpose was to reaffirm a military accord, which both the Bush and Fahd administrations deemed necessary in light of new rumblings in Middle Eastern petroleum politics. That alliance was tested a short time later when, in August 1990, Saddam Hussein's Iraq invaded Kuwait. Hussein's objective was straightforward: to capture Kuwait's oil fields and become the petroleum king of the Middle East. Bush and his Saudi allies recognized the threat. Should Kuwait fall to Iraq, Saudi Arabia could be next, resulting in the collapse of one oil kingdom and the rise of another, one hostile to US interests. "This will not stand, this aggression against Kuwait," Bush announced. "Our jobs, our way of life, our own freedom and the freedom of friendly countries around the world would all suffer if control of the world's great oil reserves fell into the hands of Saddam Hussein."[59]

United with Saudi Arabia and a host of Western nations, Bush and the US military answered Hussein's challenge. Between August 1990 and January 1991, US forces poured into Saudi Arabia, shoring up the kingdom's defense against possible invasion and preparing for an offensive against the Hussein regime. Then, on January 16, Operation Desert Storm began. Already battered by US air assaults, Iraqi ground forces now faced the onslaught of coalition tanks and infantry, as US-led troops moved into Kuwait, liberated its oil fields, then headed toward Iraq. One hundred hours after it began, the war was over. But the apparent US victory did not negate the fact that the geopolitics of oil had been permanently altered. For the first time, Washington had been forced to deploy an oil-centered foreign policy from a position of vulnerability rather than strength. Fully reliant on a goodwill partnership with Saudi Arabia, the White House approached the conflict with the firepower of a superpower but awareness that it now depended on others for protection of America's oil-fueled way of life. The days of shaping the Middle East in its image were over. Sensing their society's new weakness in the post–Cold War world, many citizens of America's oil patch turned their theological furor away from a defeated communist regime toward Muslims—in this instance, Saddam Hussein. Hussein's warlike machinations and aspiration to rebuild the "ancient evil city of Babylon," they believed, were proof he was the Antichrist. Arab oil producers who challenged their nation's hegemony and the security of the Israeli state had long worried these Americans. But for the first time they ascribed "evil empire" status once reserved for the Soviets to the Muslim other.[60]

While the Gulf War affirmed the nation's new course in global oil politics, another crisis reminded Americans of their increased vulnerabilities at home. On March 24, 1989, the supertanker *Exxon Valdez* entered Alaska's Prince William Sound after unmooring at the Valdez Marine Terminal with a hull full of crude oil. At 12:04 a.m., the ship bottomed on a reef, spilling its contents into the sea. All told, 11 million gallons of oil emptied into the pristine waters, fouling more than 1,000 miles of coastline and killing hundreds of thousands of animals. Exxon was forced to pay billions of dollars in cleanup costs and fines, but the damage was incalculable. Over a decade removed from the environmental crises of the 1960s and 1970s, Americans were once again thrust into the politics of energy and environment. This time the ugly shock of oil stirred a righteous wrath that would have longer-lasting political consequences.[61]

In the months that followed the *Exxon Valdez* crisis, a new coalition of environmental activists formed, one that included old nemeses.

Among their leading spokespersons was Bill McKibben, a self-described "Methodist Sunday School teacher" whose breakout book, *The End of Nature*, published in the same year as the Valdez affair, cast him into the public eye. In his best-selling text McKibben warned of a growing threat to earth that combined all previous known environmental perils into one overarching menace: global warming. Oil was very much to blame, he explained. "When we drill into an oil field, we tap into a vast reservoir of organic matter that has been in storage for millennia. We unbury it. When we burn that oil ... we release its carbon into the atmosphere in the form of carbon dioxide." McKibben listed statistics showing that the amount of carbon dioxide humans had released into the air had increased 25 percent over the last century. We "will almost certainly double it in the next," he added; "we have more than doubled the level of methane; we have added a soup of other gases. *We have substantially altered the earth's atmosphere.*" McKibben's was a prophetic rallying cry for Americans to look past their selfish interests and comforts—and past themselves altogether—to help a world in frantic need. If carbon use and foul air had defined the American Century, he wanted the next one hundred years to be defined by a united human effort to occupy the earth with sensitivity to nature's vulnerability and the need for its collective care.[62]

McKibben's carbon-free gospel quickly spread, drawing morally charged citizens into the public realm. On April 22, 1990, 200 million people in 141 nations marched in the twentieth annual Earth Day. Aided by new marketing tools, the celebration marked a milestone for the movement and vaulted it onto an international stage. Behind the scenes, meanwhile, two former competitors—one named Pew, the other Rockefeller—joined the same cause. In 1990, the Pew Foundation outlined the dawn of a new era. After a "two-year overhaul," during which "it replaced 95 percent of its staff and hired a team of specialists with impressive academic credentials to oversee its programs," *New York Times* reporters explained, the foundation, now the "second-most generous philanthropy in the country," was steering a new course away from the conservative causes championed by its former self. "Pew intends to make a major effort to help our disadvantaged population," the foundation's president explained, before admitting that this "might surprise some people accustomed to think of the old Pew as reactionary and secretive in its early years." Other than helping America's underclasses through social and economic programs, the revamped Pew Foundation with a younger generation at its helm designated its monies for energy conservation and the environment. In the spirit of the day, the trust that J. Howard Pew started with oil money fifty years prior wanted to get on the other side of history.[63]

And in that respect, it wanted to be on the same side as the Rockefellers. Since the late 1970s, the fourth generation of the Rockefeller family had gravitated toward progressive causes, none more important than the environment. In 1977, Steven Rockefeller, son of Nelson Rockefeller, joined the board of the Rockefeller Brothers Fund and began shaping its next steps in the causes of environmental conservation and preservation. Like McKibben, his future colleague, he did so in the framework of faith. After graduating with an MDiv from Union Theological Seminary and a PhD in religion from Columbia University in New York, Rockefeller accepted a professorship in religion at Middlebury College. There he taught world religions and continued to participate in global religious and environmental activism. In 1990, as global concern with energy swirled, he organized a four-day symposium on religion and the environment at his home school, titled "Spirit and Nature: Religion, Ethics, and Environmental Crisis." When introducing it, Rockefeller paid tribute to the faithful thinkers who had come before—Rachel Carson, Lynn White Jr., and other theologians he encountered at seminary, as well as those with whom he now rubbed shoulders, McKibben among them. Accepting these intellectuals' lead was essential, Rockefeller implored, if humanity was to exit an era of waste and pollution and embrace a new "planetary vision that joins democracy, ecology, and moral faith." He insisted that faith be central to the charge. "The global environmental crisis, which threatens not only the future of human civilization but all life on earth, is fundamentally a moral and religious problem," he proclaimed. "It calls upon us to exercise our human freedom with a renewed sense of humility and responsibility."[64]

Much like his great grandfather, Steven Rockefeller wore his theology openly and leaned on it as a guide to his life. Yet the theology itself could hardly be more different. The civilization the younger Rockefeller dreamed of was drained of his ancestor's petrocapitalist impudence and Baptist assurance that the future was America's to guide, exploit, and control. Steven Rockefeller's theology preferred that Americans fall in line, bond with the world as one, and approach a new millennium eager to commune with nature rather than capture it.

# God and Black Gold in the New Millennium

*Let Asher be blessed with children.*
*Let him be acceptable to his brethren,*
*and let him dip his foot in oil.*

—DEUTERONOMY 33:24

O n the shores of the Congo River in the mid-1920s, future esteemed scholar of American history and culture Perry Miller had an "epiphany." While unloading drums of oil from a barge, petroleum products encircling him, he saw his nation and its "meaning" in fresh light, as the materialization of the Puritan "errand," the sort of spiritual quest for terrestrial supremacy that had inspired America's earliest Christians to penetrate the dark frontier to save it from resident evil and provide a spiritual light for those they left behind in secular Europe. Like the Puritans of old, Miller surmised, the United States seemed eternally driven by a theological imperative to be the world's beacon of progress and assert itself as the way forward, out of the proverbial wilderness toward an enlightened tomorrow. In the physical form of oil drums pervading the jungles of Africa, Miller identified the psychic desires of a restless nation and the very essence of its soul.[1]

In the 1940s and 1950s, Miller would bank his illustrious career as a Pulitzer Prize–winning Harvard professor on that historical understanding of America's Puritan errand to the world, even as many of his contemporaries in government, business, academia, and the church were recreating it by propelling their nation's oil-fueled influence abroad. However much (or little) Miller's notions resonated or even registered with them, the architects of oil's civil religion of crude certainly operated out of the longings he identified. Committed to their social gospel of economic and technological development, convinced that their petroleum quests and philanthropic missions were one and the same, they pressed forward onto distant shores, eager to save global humanity with a redemptive message of benevolent faith, capitalism, and crude. But by the start of the new millennium, that errand had crumbled, as had the twin pillars of American exceptionalism imagined by Henry Luce in the 1940s: big, inclusive, ecumenical religion coupled with big, integrated, major oil had succumbed to forces both of its making and beyond its control.

War's fallout in the Middle East certainly raised insurmountable challenges to the ideals of Luce and the Rockefellers and those who had joined Aramco's Arabists in building bridges of peace based on shared monotheism and the modern applications of petroleum. Ironies abounded, of course: the very commitment to Saudi Arabia promoted so forcefully by William Eddy's allies had compelled a former oilman, the first to hold the US presidency, to take action in 1990 against Saddam Hussein. Operation Desert Storm's swift victory seemed to announce the beginning of a new world order, with US global authority restored. Yet the lack of definitive conclusions to the Gulf War (signaled by Hussein's staying in power) in fact contributed to a world system that was anything but stable or US controlled, causing George W. Bush, the second oilman to hold the presidency, to finish what his father started. In the wake of the 9/11 attacks on the World Trade Center and the Pentagon, planned and carried out by a Saudi rebel with ties to oil wealth, the latter Bush's foreign policy advisors seized the opportunity to flex military muscle in the Middle East in order to prop up Israel, buttress Saudi Arabia, weaken Syria, isolate Iran, and destroy Hussein. Even with that conclusion finally achieved, stability in the area and long-term global authority for the United States remained elusive. Eddy's beloved region, and all it stood for to him and his missionary parents, was but a vague shadow of yesteryear.[2]

Between those two advances by an American government anxious to protect US access to Middle Eastern oil occurred other related turns in the global life and faith of crude. Several forces further worked against US petroleum's return to its pre-1990s sense of certainty—and by extension, its sense of moral mission to the world. The First Gulf War unleashed a torrent of economic and political impulses that splintered the world order. Globalization of markets increased exponentially, and the dizzying proliferation and decentering of capital flows triggered in the 1970s accelerated. As one analyst asserts, the "'global village,' a speculative concept in the 1960s, was now becoming a reality," and the "oil and gas industry was caught up in these revolutions." Within this climate emerged old and new players, all of whom made US dominance in petroleum a thing of the past. On one hand, a new Russia, loosened from communist restraints, reentered the oil markets with a boom; as it had done a century before when Baku roared as a refining center, the Russian oil industry, helped by its reach into the Caspian Sea region, became a juggernaut with which Western oil companies once again had to wrestle. On the other hand, an emerging China began vying for control of the world's oil production centers and markets. Together these two nations helped inject another component in the race for crude: large, state-run, national oil companies (Gazprom and Lukoil in Russia; CNPC, CNOOC, and Sinopec in China). In an effort to stay competitive with these private-public conglomerates, established majors in the West scrambled to combine forces. Starting with Amoco and BP in December 1998 and culminating with the Exxon-Mobil merger the following year, the "Seven Sisters" of mid-century oil dominance broke with their histories to form supermajors—"behemoths," as the *New York Times* bluntly described them. No longer would the singular companies of the twentieth century work to define their corporate cultures and civic visions in singular terms. The phantoms of Standard Oil and John D. Rockefeller were officially vanquished.[3]

More sequences of crisis further undermined the Rockefeller legacy and the civil religion of crude at the turn of the twenty-first century. With greater violence than ever before, major oil companies faced backlash in former colonized regions of the world. No nation saw more bloodletting of this sort than Nigeria, no province of that country more than the Niger Delta, a region Jake Simmons had helped open up to Western oil in the 1960s. During the late 1990s and 2000s, as Nigeria fractured politically and suffered endemic corruption related to the "oil curse" (overreliance on this one resource), the offshore oil platforms of companies such as BP and Gulf became bull's-eyes for retribution and rebellion. In March 2003, oil companies evacuated their workers, shutting down a third of Nigeria's production. Things worsened. In January 2006, four foreign oil workers were kidnapped from an offshore platform, while at another facility gunmen associated with the Movement for the Emancipation of the Niger Delta killed twenty-two people. Coursing through these acts of terror was a politicized and radicalized Islam, epitomized by Osama bin Laden and Al-Qaeda (the inspiration for the March 2003 attack in Nigeria).[4]

By then, of course, Bin Laden's oil-laden terrorism had left its profound mark on American society and global politics. Its targeting of US sites in Africa—and its destruction of the Twin Towers—of course precipitated much of the US military action that followed in Iraq, Afghanistan, and the Middle East. "The lesson of 9/11," George W. Bush would later rationalize, "was that if we waited for a danger to fully materialize, we would have waited too long." On that premise, together with a belief held by many in Congress that Hussein possessed weapons of mass destruction, he invaded Iraq in March 2003. Amid the action, Bin Laden and Al-Qaeda adopted a new strategy. In 2004, they called for the targeting of Western-owned oil infrastructures in the Middle East as a way to carry out "economic jihad" against the United States. In 2005, Bin Laden's deputy announced that his recruits should "'focus their attacks on the stolen oil of the Muslims' in order to 'save this resource'" for future use by the newly established Islamic Caliphate. The call would be heeded and later adopted (and adapted) by the Islamic State of Iraq and the Levant, or ISIS. What Ahmed Yamani had started in the 1970s, Bin Laden intended to finish, but with fundamentalist intent, spurning anything "civil" that Yamani and the Saudi government—in keeping with their Aramco roots—had advocated while wielding their own theology in the takeover of their land's valuable resource. If Bin Laden had his way, Saudi Arabia would no longer concede to the sacred designs of any foreign power—be it a satanic America or an apostate, Western-compromised Saudi royalty. In Bin Laden's scenario, it was time for Allah's true and purest believers—warrior Wahhabists—to reverse the power dynamics of faith and petroleum in their favor, decidedly and permanently.[5]

While external transformations changed US major oil's engagement with the world, domestic and industry politics contributed to its fragmentation and failing at home. Once again the public lambasted America's largest oil companies for greedily consolidating their monopolies. During the formation of oil's supermajors in the late 1990s and early 2000s, reverberations of the 1910s could be felt as the Federal Trade Commission weighed the mergers of several old Standard entities. Ultimately, it became clear that the political climate had changed from that of Theodore Roosevelt's day; even wary citizens seemed to concede that big companies needed to get bigger to compete in widening global oil markets. Still—big oil heard its detractors, who became louder as other controversies emerged. The scandal surrounding Enron Corporation in the early 2000s topped them all. The pioneering energy company, based in Houston, was the seventh-largest company in the nation before it declared bankruptcy in late 2001; involving $40 billion in debt, the failure was the largest of its kind in US history. Enron executives had seized a moment of government deregulation at the turn of the twenty-first century to carry out a bonanza of speculation in a range of sectors, under ruses and false pretenses, and with a penchant to doctor the books. In the postbankruptcy filing phase, Americans learned just how far a massive corporation would go to bend rules for profits. Once again the muckrakers took aim, calling for the United States to "break the tyranny of oil" and bring about the "end of the oil age."[6]

Battered and bruised by the sweep of scandal and high-profile mergers, the social vision of major oil and its religious allies failed in the early 2000s—though not entirely. There would be more quiet demonstrations of the American civil religion of crude. In the wake of 9/11, national supplications calling for Christians, Jews, and Muslims to bind together in search of unity and relief from terrorism were heard in the nation's halls of power, resurrecting the four-faith consensus that Dwight Eisenhower—at Aramco's urging—had celebrated in the

1950s. Oil companies themselves continued to promote ecumenism in their global operations in an effort to be effective producers, diplomats, and partners with foreign states and peoples. Christian oilmen-turned-politicians, such as Exxon chief executive–turned–secretary of state Rex Tillerson, would take that message with them into political office. Meanwhile, oil leaders outside the political limelight would continue to preach it all the harder to their wary and cynical public, alongside messages that mirrored major oil's founding convictions. "I make it my job to educate the public ... about how the oil industry produces the lifeblood of civilization," one current advocate of big oil explains, "and about how we should value the industry and above all value its freedom to produce." Oil is more than a commodity, he sermonizes, in an effort to win over Americans. It is the "single most vital industry in the world" and has transformed each sector of human life. It is an enriching and essential—and moral—life source of society, he proclaims, echoing 1920s advertising guru Bruce Barton. "It is the juice of the fountain of eternal youth. It is health. It is comfort. It is success." It is the bedrock of a modernity tethered to dreams of progress and the values of human oneness needed to get there.[7]

Still, by the first decade of the twenty-first century, the US oil industry had ceded much of its control over this message to other agents on a global stage. By then, the exceptionalism in God and black gold that Luce proclaimed for his carbon-rich country was no longer America's alone to enjoy or to sell. America is now on the receiving end of global ricochets it set in motion generations ago. The mechanisms of petro-capitalism that Eddy and the Rockefellers sold abroad at mid-century as keys to development of an enlightened and technologically modern global order have since reproduced remarkably similar oil patches around the world, where acts of summoning subsurface wealth and living and worshipping assume striking uniformity. On landscapes where pumps and derricks encircle mosques, praying to a higher being for a higher power makes perfect sense. So does framing the health and wealth oil provides as a miraculous interlude in humanity's march across time. Meanwhile, the world the Rockefeller oil empire helped create is now bending back on North Americans. Amid the current boomerangs of God and black gold, waves of workers are streaming from Nigeria to Texas, South Asia to Alberta. Gathered in their faith communities, worshipping in a range of dialects, Nigerian Christians in Houston and South Asian Muslims in Fort McMurray testify to oil's global, transformative reach in their own theological idioms, in ways that Eddy and Luce would recognize if not fully comprehend.[8]

While the civil religion of crude that Eddy and Luce envisioned is now spent as an American phenomenon, the strong conviction they exhibited when looking out onto the world in an effort to transform it has increasingly found its outlet in the carbon-free gospel that Bill McKibben began to preach in the late 1980s and early 1990s. Since then, the movement against the US oil industry has unfolded in waves. At its crest between the last years of the George W. Bush presidency and first years of the Barack Obama presidency, the carbon-free gospel gained wide traction, due in no small part to the legacy of some of oil's own high-profile families.

One of the galvanizing messages for the antioil environmental campaign came by way of the award-winning 2006 documentary *An Inconvenient Truth*. Written by and starring former vice president Al Gore, the film set out a weighty, moral critique of carbon society and a warning about global warming—of the kind one might expect from a seminarian. Gore's enrollment at Vanderbilt University Divinity School in the early 1970s, where he studied on a Rockefeller Foundation scholarship designed to train and facilitate leadership in "secular" careers, allowed him to wrestle with spiritual issues and social injustices that challenged his religious beliefs, among the most important being environmental degradation. "The search for truths about this ungodly (environmental) crisis and the search for truths about myself have been the same search all along," he would later write. Of his evolving faith, he explained that it was "rooted in the unshakable belief in God as creator and sustainer, a deeply personal interpretation of the relationship with Christ, and an awareness of a constant and holy spiritual presence in all people, all life, all things." "God is in us as human beings," he charged; so "why do our children believe that the Kingdom of God is up, somewhere in the ethereal reaches of space, far removed from this planet? Are we still . . . looking everywhere except in the real world?" On the basis of his social gospel—one that clearly evokes John D. Rockefeller Jr. and Harry Emerson Fosdick—Gore set out to upend the world of crude.[9]

With Gore providing some of the inspiration and McKibben the leadership—and with the Rockefellers' backing—the carbon-free crusade took dramatic leaps in the political realm as well. The battle over the Keystone Pipeline, which climaxed between 2011 and 2013, galvanized the movement. McKibben and his movement 350.org provided much of the organizational glue. This Methodist muckraker was convinced that the plan to process and move a million barrels a day of Alberta's oil sands to the Gulf of Mexico was a game changer—and possibly "game over for the climate." During 2011 and 2012, he led nonviolent protests in Washington, DC, for which he spent three days in prison. His July 2012 essay in *Rolling Stone*, "Global Warming's Terrifying New Math," tore through social media and led one pundit to name him "Nature's Prophet." In September 2013, he stepped up his rhetoric (promising, metaphorically, "a call to arms") and his ambition by coordinating the People's Climate March, which drew 300,000 to New York City. With each step forward, McKibben deliberately reached back into the repositories of scripture and back-to-the-land spirituality of the kind that once inspired Ida Tarbell and Rachel Carson.[10]

His followers loved him for it. Though an admirer of Job, McKibben was bestowed with the title "New Noah" by some of 350.org's Bible-believing constituents. "It's his job to warn us that we have 'grieved the Lord in his heart' and that the flood waters will rise again if we don't get back to working within our 'original contract' and reverse climate change," one of them wrote, while criticizing the Keystone. "The proposed pipeline," she continued, is evidence that our "modern, technocratic, myth-spinning machine" is "strangling God's world." As the Keystone battle heated up, Catholic nuns, Mennonites, Quakers, evangelical youth, and indigenous communities marched in opposition to the steel strand. In other moments they traveled to Nebraska and Texas to chain themselves to bulldozers and pray on pipe. One subversive stated it simply: "Many people see the pipeline as a political or an economic issue, but I see it as a moral issue." Invoking Charles Finney, another promised a "power shift": "If Christians and other people of faith . . . rise up and demand that our nation turn away from the planet-threatening actions that have fed global warming, it will launch an irresistible force for change," the activist proclaimed. "We need a faith of revival on behalf of the world as God intends, a planet where life not simply survives but thrives, a creation where God is at the center and delights in it." McKibben intended for the fires of revival to burn bright.[11]

As the Keystone Pipeline battle played out—leading ultimately to its delayed construction in 2015, though not its abandonment— McKibben's allies led protests on related fronts. With the Alberta oil sands financially viable once again and its corporate heads promising to channel its oil through the Keystone, it became a target for green activists, including the Rockefellers. By the time the Keystone fight flared, Steven Rockefeller and his siblings, and especially their children, had already demonstrated their resolve to roll back the oil empire their ancestor had birthed. Among those caught in the crosshairs was ExxonMobil, which the Rockefellers began criticizing for inaction on climate change at shareholders meetings in 2003. In 2008, the Rockefellers, whose remaining stock in the company was small, nevertheless used the power of their name to chastise the supermajor publicly for failing to invest in "high-profile renewable energy ventures, like BP's solar business or Shell's wind energy play." For the environment's sake and for the health of the nation going forward, Rockefeller activists announced, the company needed to change its ways immediately. "There's a crisis building, and you're part of it," one Rockefeller told ExxonMobil powerbrokers. "ExxonMobil needs to reconnect with the forward-looking and entrepreneurial vision of my great-grandfather," he added. The crisis was not just economic and philosophical; it was ethical, which the scientific and journalistic studies of climate change and global warming that Rockefeller monies now funded were quick to point out. That moral campaigning extended north to Alberta in the early 2010s. There, by way of the Rockefeller Brothers Fund, Rockefellers joined a host of "green 'salvationist' billionaires" (as one perturbed conservative Canadian journalist labeled them) in an anti-oil-sands campaign that used media and publicity to decry the "tar sands" as environmentally dangerous. Besides tearing up thousands of square miles to plunder the soil of its natural properties, the oil sands industry was—in critics' minds—also generating carbon emissions at staggering rates just to get at the oil deposits it so coveted. Joining the "green" lobby against the venture that J. Howard Pew had created was the Pew

Charitable Trusts. The philanthropic legacies of the Pews and Rockefellers, families that were once bitter adversaries, now banded together
to fight the specters of unbridled corporate oil.[12]

Were he privy again to his philanthropy's civic engagement, J. Howard Pew would likely be shaken by the prospect of a Rockefeller-Pew
assault on his beloved creation; yet with other contemporary developments, he would likely express satisfaction. If major oil and the civil
religion of crude largely succumbed to the dynamics of global change
in the post-1990s, leaving carbon-free activists to ratchet up a social
gospel of protest, wildcatters—as they were known to do—survived,
barely, until their next moment of rebirth eventually arrived.

Revival flashed on multiple fronts, thanks in no small part to the
same economic dynamics that dismantled John D. Rockefeller's dream.
While major US oil companies were scrambling to reorganize in the
dizzying global oil realm, their perennially embattled nemeses—the
independents of the West—were scrambling to find a new niche. As
illustrated by the heated efforts of China's CNOOC to buy Unocal
(Union) in 2005, independents were hardly sheltered from the oil wars
playing out beyond US borders. Once again—just as they had done
in the 1920s in order to save Lyman Stewart's firm from Shell Oil—
Union supporters emerged in the press and in Washington to thwart a
foreign giant. The Chinese withdrew their $18.5 billion takeover bid,
and Unocal remained in American hands—but those of supermajor
ExxonMobil, whose aggressive plan for conquest worked. Subjected to
the coercions of globalization, amid fresh cries of peak oil and predictions of the end of the oil age in the early 2000s, independents nevertheless found new outlets to assert themselves. In the early 1980s,
a Houston-based independent oilman and gas producer by the name
of George Mitchell had started studying the Barnett Shale geological
region bordering Dallas, certain that its layers of shale rock contained
trapped gas and oil. For two decades he tried to perfect a method to
find and release those hidden treasures, ignoring mocking critics along
the way. Finally he succeeded in developing hydraulic fracturing, which
uses water pressure to crack open pathways through the concrete-like
layers and free their contents. By 2001, Mitchell had "cracked the code"
of next-wave oil exploration that could diminish fears of peak oil: with
the Barnett Shale boom, domestic energy exploration came alive again,

as did proclamations of US oil's sustainability. Mitchell's peers raced to apply his technology, along with another new technology, horizontal drilling, to shale fields in Louisiana, Arkansas, Oklahoma, New York, Pennsylvania—and in North Dakota, whose subsequent boom, inaugurated in 2006, thrust it to the center of energy production.[13]

With economic gains came another stage of politicking in defense of wildcat Christianity's fuel and family values. To be sure, even as the geopolitical tumult of the 1990s consumed their attention, independent oilmen, along with their clerical and lay allies in the pews of the oil patch, had hardly stayed quiet on the political front; quite the opposite, of course. Even if the likes of J. Howard Pew, Bunker Hunt, Ignatius O'Shaughnessy, and their generation of bankrollers were no longer present, plenty of other fiercely libertarian oilers were more than ready to step up and continue building the movement that had propelled the wildcat wing of the GOP to power. None would be more important than Charles and David Koch. Heirs to their father Fred's oil fortune, they also harbored his extreme hatred for collectivism in any guise, a hatred generated by his encounters with Soviet communism and his unceasing professional fight with major oil companies, who consistently tried to run him out of the refinery business. With the Koch brothers' financial backing and organizational support, wildcat politicking only intensified after Ronald Reagan and George H. W. Bush left Washington. The consolidation of a GOP Right in the 1990s, during Bill Clinton's presidency, occurred thanks in no small part to their influence and institution building, which set the stage for the fiery politics of the 2000s and the Kochs' attempt—as one writer puts it—to "remake the political landscape" for good.[14]

That political landscape truly started taking shape during the George W. Bush years of the 2000s, before assuming clear definition during and immediately following the Barack Obama presidency. By 2006, deep into the Bush presidency and the ongoing uncertainty in the Middle East and the war on terror, centrist Republicans were joining liberal and left-wing critics in decrying the takeover of the Republican Party by antiestablishment oilers and church folk. One pointed criticism came from the always-incisive political commentator (and former Republican strategist) Kevin Phillips. In 2006, he published *American Theocracy: The Peril and Politics of Radical Religion, Oil, and Borrowed Money in the*

*21st Century*. While largely glancing over historical trends that had in fact fused his triumvirate of political dynamics together, his book spared no condemnatory words in singling out each component's plague on his former party. "The pitfalls of American petro-politics, radical religion, and debt finance have to be addressed in a present-day context," he declared. "They are real perils, not an abstract problem in political evolution." Phillips's words of warning about a "petroleum-defined national security," "crusading, simplistic Christianity," and "reckless credit-feeding financial complex" would reverberate—and amplify—in the years that followed their publication.[15]

That is because many of the impulses and crusaders Phillips singled out as fuel for the GOP Right entered the Obama years ready—and eager—to combust. In 2009, on the heels of Obama's inauguration and in the face of his proposals for Washington to restructure a broken mortgage-lending system and stimulate a broken economy, former Wall Street trader and CNBC contributor Rick Santelli (following the lead of the preceding guest, angry free market purist Wilbur Ross) ranted against big government and called for a modern-day "tea party" to unite patriots against the threat of tyranny. The spontaneous charge gave rise to the Tea Party movement, whose machinations over the coming years would further entrench the GOP in the wildcat camp. While conspicuous oil backers such as the Kochs—Ross's close friends—would intensify their propagation of the ideology of independence and quietly fund Tea Party causes, lesser-known (but even more fervent) Christian oilmen such as West Texas's Tim Dunn would wield their considerable clout in an attempt to push "the Republican Party into the arms of God" and keep Washington at bay. Meanwhile, preachers and parishioners across oil's heartland would march in defense of their desire for full control of their capital, land, and communities. Alaska governor (child of the oil patch and Pentecostalism) Sarah Palin would be their champion. She secured that standing the year prior while sparring with Joe Biden in the vice presidential debate of 2008 by speaking the language of wildcat Christianity, encapsulated in the simplest of phrases. "Drill, baby, drill," she declared, demanding Washington honor the wishes of her constituents, who "are so hungry for those domestic sources of energy to be tapped into." A defense of the wildcatter's coveted rule of capture, hers was also an appeal to her people's wish to act alone, be it on the oil field or before their God—on their rigs and platforms or in their schools and pews.[16]

Even though her political star soon set, Palin's chant only gained traction in the culture wars that followed. By 2015, with another presidential election in the air, versions of the populist refrain seemed everywhere, as did the structures of philanthropy and political lobbying that oil-rich independents had helped take to another level of impact. A *New York Times* special article in October of that year offered insight into Republican fund-raising efforts, pointing to the fact that "just 158 families have provided nearly half of the early money for efforts to capture the White House." The typical profile of these families: self-made types and boomers in oil and gas. In the crucial giving sector of energy, the article explained, many of the givers were "latter-day wildcatters, early to capitalize on the new drilling technologies and high energy prices that made it economical to exploit shale formations in North Dakota, Ohio, Pennsylvania, and Texas." "Others," meanwhile, "made fortunes supplying those wildcatters with pipelines, trucks and equipment for 'fracking.'" To what degree the "latter-day wildcatters" shaped the 2016 election is unclear. But if indications from the presidency of Donald Trump are factored in, it may be safe to say their influence was significant. With an evangelical Oklahoman at the helm of the Environmental Protection Agency, the Trump administration would begin its season of authority by rolling back regulation of the oil patch and extending oilers' freedoms to stretch the limits of their continental hunt in the West, in Alaska, and into the sea. In the spirit of James Watt—and in the face of Harold Ickes, Watt's New Deal counterpart—Trump has promised to restore custodianship of the oil-rich West to a rank and file that has long worked it as theirs.[17]

With each policy move of this sort has come more protest and more pointed journalistic treatments of the current era. Borrowing from the lexicon of Upton Sinclair, liberal scribes have labored to expose the "dark money" and hidden conspiracies of oil-fueled power behind "the radical Right," whose machinations have put "democracy in chains" and thrust America backward into another Gilded Age. In their quest for impact, they have tended to glance over the long history of emotionally and morally charged crude politics that has created our current tensions. By doing so, they gloss over existential struggles of an earlier day, when it was wildcat oilmen of Lyman Stewart, William Buckley, and Ignatius O'Shaughnessy's ilk who saw their democratic freedoms placed in chains by the Rockefeller corporate juggernaut and who—desperate to keep family businesses alive—cried foul. And they also downplay the cycles of giving—generous and never completely hidden—that Koch and O'Shaughnessy, his onetime partner, the Pews, and their peers carried out over generations in an effort to prop up institutions that promised to preach, teach, and sustain a "living gospel truth" of personal faith and freedom. Still, in their sense of urgency, contemporary critics have effectively conjured up a suspicion that wildcatters and wildcat Christianity have won.[18]

There is some truth in that conclusion. From the very outset, wildcatters were attuned to the jarring fluctuations of their modernizing industry and society. More so than their competitors in major oil, who believed they could stem the tides of capitalist carnage by imposition of their will, producers of the Pews' class responded to the revolutions of their day by accepting the spasms as an existential—and spiritual—reality. Battered by oil's bloody cut-throat system, yet determined to follow their calling, they clung to a personal trust in the supernatural, which came with a transaction. Place your faith in a higher being and honor his rules for holy living, the logic read, and ride the capricious offerings of earth and the markets to heavenly fulfillment—no matter the heavy human (and ecological) costs. Place your trust in a God who giveth and taketh suddenly, but who is always there, and watch (and feel) the pain of oil's boom-bust cycles and ever-present maladies melt away in the face of his saving grace. Our current age, in which the fluctuations of economy have intensified on a global stage and during which the inequalities of capitalist society have calcified, has only emboldened that ethic all the more. Its promises of spiritual and, in unpredictable moments, financial returns on the magical, miraculous workings of oil, its allowances for stark enigmas and contradictions in the modern condition—between hope and futility, empowerment and despair, hyperwealth and utter poverty—and its panic to drill, find, and sell redemption before the Messiah returns have proved more than prescient and resilient. In the battle of sparring spirits of capitalism and eschatology, oil's generations-old warrior class and its end-times thinking have indeed shown themselves to be a conquering lot.[19]

Christianity and crude's warrior class have experienced victories in other respects as well. In the late nineteenth century, when the business of petroleum was just beginning to expand, social scientists theorized that as modern capitalism and society advanced, both would become increasingly rationalized and secularized and trapped in an "iron cage" of calculation, efficiency, and control. Yet that teleology has not played out entirely as they predicted. As witnessed in a wildcat Christianity that continues to define America's oil patches and Washington politically, the enchantments early oilers identified in their industrial labor and their working of the land, fusing sacred and mundane aspirations, are as strong today as they were in Patillo Higgins's day. The iron cage of advanced modernity, it turns out, is much more porous than initially allowed, the progressions of secularization neither as linear nor as overpowering as theorists first surmised. That the entanglements of the sacred and the secular—not the latter's sheer triumph over the former—continue to define contemporary society is abundantly evident in the sprawling institutional apparatus of oil-funded churches, philanthropies, missionary enterprises, and parachurch ministries that to this day rely on crude profits for the chance to spread their influence. And they are evinced in the ideological and structural support these religious institutions offer oil in return—whether through their preaching or political lobbying or by way of their partnerships in local (now national) governance. Blending human designs for earthly conquest and aspirations for heavenly splendor, the apparatus of modern-day wildcat oil is a sprawling, integrated system of belief and action, pragmatism and metaphysical longing that defies containment or models of its demise.

Yet to state unequivocally that wildcatters have won is also to disregard the profound losses that they and the oil patch continue to shoulder in the late modern era. The heavy costs of oil dependency—present at the very beginnings of Pennsylvania's Petrolia—are just as burdensome today. In America's oil extraction and refining zones, petroleum still scars the human body and natural environments, molds social relations, and determines the daily activities and local cultures of the resource's rank and file. Sarah Palin may have asked Washington to let oil-patch people drill, drill, drill; yet in the wake of her 2008 pronouncement, oil-patch people were reminded that the black stuff could also be a hellacious curse. In the spring of 2010, off Louisiana's gulf coast, BP's

*Deepwater Horizon* erupted in a blowout that would discharge 5 million barrels of oil into the Gulf of Mexico, the largest marine oil spill in the industry's entire history. Mocking chants of "spill, baby, spill" and "kill, baby, kill" resounded through the political chambers of those who wanted to disparage Palin's wildcat gospel. Yet, despite this and other oil-borne apocalypses, in petroleum-saturated places such as Louisiana, very little leeway is allowed for those who decry the wildcatting way. There, amid greasy muck and the toxic refining fires of "Cancer Alley," with crude's decaying influences all around them, Louisianans—like their counterparts across oil time and space—continue to hold firm to the doctrines handed down to them from yesteryear. Their theological answer to their troubles has been to pray—for their oil fields, for their employed (and unemployed) roughnecks and engineers, and for deliverance from the inevitable casualties that life in crude brings. Their political answer has sounded a familiar chord as well. Amid oil and petrochemicals' destruction and a lethal environment that is killing them, Louisianans' frustration has been directed at the federal government, big oil companies, and global internationalists—the Eddys, Rockefellers, and Roosevelts of today—who, in their estimation, created the problem by meddling in their business and attempting to bend it to false, man-made dreams. Louisianans have responded by preaching all the harder the wildcat gospel, which says good Christians should be allowed to chase fortune and shoulder the calamities of this world on their terms, with only God determining their fates. It is a familiar refrain, one that Pennsylvanians in the 1860s, Texans in the 1930s, and Oklahomans and Albertans in the 1980s would recognize.[20]

Heavy losses and biting costs continue to plague faithful wildcat producers as well. The work of John Brown and Zion Oil & Gas testifies to that by-product of Christianity and crude's power. In 1981, Brown listened to a preacher named Jim Spillman expound on "the oil of Israel." "By faith," he later testified, "God used Jim Spillman first in my life to deposit the vision for the oil in my heart." Brown visited Israel in 1983, at which point he decided to follow the lead of earlier American independents and invest in oil exploration in the Holy Land. If it was there that Asher "dipped his foot in oil," could they not do the same? Brown was not alone in following this charge. Other evangelical oilmen such as Harold "Hayseed" Stephens and Andrew SoRelle were at that same moment pursuing their own prophecies. A Baptist oilman from Houston, SoRelle predicted in 1982 that Israel was about to hit it big: "I know Israel will get oil. It is time to bless Israel." With the Israeli government's permission, SoRelle set off into the Sinai Desert to prospect for crude. When that venture failed, he shifted north toward Haifa, where the tribe of Asher—his biblical oil guide—had been known to settle. SoRelle's subsequent wells would come up dry. Hayseed Stephens's plans would stall too. But he kept preaching: "The greatest oil field on Earth is under the southwest corner of the Dead Sea," he told fellow believers, whom he addressed individually in fund-raising letters as "Dear End Time Servant." Stephens promised his company, Ness ("miracle" in Hebrew) Energy International, would tap Israel's subterranean crude and in the process "drain the oil fields of the Persian Gulf, prompt Arab countries to attack Israel, and at last touch off the great battle that would usher in the last days." Church people would heartily invest in Ness, eventually to the tune of tens of millions of dollars. "I didn't have any doubt that Ness was a plan of God," one investor later testified. "He raised up Hayseed Stephens to find Israel's oil." "When they hit oil and the stock goes sky-high, that means Armageddon is around the corner." Stephens's supporters seemed unfazed by his continued failings in the hunt for crude. John Brown seemed unfazed by his contemporary's failure too and pressed on with remarkable patience. Over the course of the next seventeen years, he pursued and gained government permissions, tested technologies, and raised funds from the Christian flock. In 2000 he started pursuing Israel's hidden treasure in the valley he believed one day would serve as the battleground of Armageddon.[21]

Zion Oil continues to pursue Israel's oil and the end times today, though with diminishing expectation. With his map of Israel's ancient tribes in hand, backed by "modern science and good business practice," Brown and Zion entered 2018 reporting slow but steady progress and noting the success of one of the company's wildcat wells. "I am ecstatic to see clear evidence of hydrocarbons," a Zion executive admitted in spring 2018, before asking for caution. "At this time we cannot comment on the commerciality or ability to successfully produce the well. We ask that our shareholders continue to pray for safe and successful drilling, logging, and testing operations, and for God's wisdom for management as we make key decisions in the following days and weeks." Zion officials could not entirely quell investors' enthusiasm, though, or their prayers for a gusher. "I'm going to keep investing for as long as it takes," one middle-aged woman of modest income vouched, convinced her money would not only result in personal dividends but provide energy independence to the Holy Land and quicken the Lord's return. Alas, Zion's caution was wise. By early summer of 2018, it became clear that the company's Megiddo-Jezreel No. 1 would not be the producing well people were praying for. Making matters worse for John Brown's company, at this very same juncture the US Securities and Exchange Commission (SEC) subpoenaed Zion, "informing Zion of the existence of a non-public, fact-finding inquiry." "The investigation and the subpoena do not mean that we have concluded that [Zion] or anyone else has violated the law," the filing stated, but a few questions about Zion's money handling needed answers. By late fall of 2018, with rumblings of complaint among some of its shareholders adding urgency, Zion was struggling to survive the "string of serious blows" and "growing existential threat." Even still, its officials continue to assure their company's investors that aside from "significant costs and management's attention," the SEC investigation will not prevent them from charging forward in the search for God's people's lifeblood. With echoes of Patillo Higgins and Gladys City Oil, Brown and Zion Oil are determined to assume more risks, drill more holes, and shape our times, with Jesus by their side.[22]

# Acknowledgments

I started writing this book decades ago; I just didn't know it at the time. While growing up in Edmonton, Alberta, during the 1980s, I sensed the pangs of the province's oil-dependent economy adjusting to the shocks of falling global oil prices and the bust that followed. I didn't understand petroleum economics—but I didn't need to in order to intuit these were dark times. They were made all the darker by the Cold War politicking of the Reagan years and by the preaching I heard in churches my family attended, which said we were living in the last days. Sunday worship left me pondering threats to civilization: while oil-producing Muslim Arabs appeared intent on dictating world oil prices (and killing Albertans' livelihoods), they also appeared intent on destroying Israel, God's chosen nation (so I was told). Equally dire, I was warned, was the fact that our federal government, led by Prime Minister Pierre Trudeau, was secularizing society and imposing federal oversight on our economy by creating a national energy plan and national oil company, Petro-Canada. Rather than protecting the Alberta oil industry, Trudeau seemed determined to exploit it for the benefit of the eastern Canadian consumer and, in foreign policy, let the Saudis have their way. But worry not, I was reassured: should this indeed be the end, all would be fine once the rapture happened and I, as a "born again" believer, had been whisked up to the heavens to be with my Lord.

I consciously started writing this book eight years ago. I am indebted to so many people and institutions for making the process a rewarding one. Immediate thanks go to my agent, Geri Thoma, for helping me hone the book proposal and stay the course, and to Lara Heimert, who masterfully (and patiently) guided the project to completion. It has been a tremendous privilege to work with Lara, as well as with Katie Lambright, Melissa Raymond, Stephanie Summerhays, Kait Howard, and the team at Basic Books. The sage editorial advice Brian Distelberg offered on the first full draft of the book and that Roger Labrie and Jennifer Kelland offered in the book's last stages of development is indicative of the extraordinary attention Basic pays to its authors, and I feel fortunate to have benefited from it. A good friend and a talented editor, Steven Miller, helped with critical insight throughout the entire process. I would also like to thank Paul Harvey and Thomas Andrews, who commented on the manuscript at a critical phase, as well as Timothy Gloege, Matthew Sutton, and Nathan Citina, who at other junctures offered access to and advice on sources and prose. I am also appreciative of oil historians Brian Black and Karen Merrill, who took time late in the game to ensure that the manuscript was error-free. I alone am responsible for any errors that remain.

There are many other people who helped me navigate earlier stages of writing. First and foremost, I would like to thank the several archivists who fielded my requests for resources and helped me make my way through boxes of catalogued (and at times uncatalogued) archival sources. I enjoyed visiting the repositories cited in the notes—and that is because of the people I met there who were eager to dig into the files with me. Of critical importance to me was the opportunity to lecture on and workshop sections (often rough) of this manuscript. After presenting preliminary research in symposia at Cambridge University and the Bruce Center for American Studies at Keele University (England) in 2011 and in a lecture at King's College, London, in 2013, I had the chance to talk about the project in a number of forums. Special thanks go to Baylor University, Valparaiso University, the University of Missouri, Kansas City, the Huntington Library, Claremont Graduate School, Canadian Mennonite University, Pacific Lutheran University, Washington State University, the University of Alabama, and the University of Mississippi for lecture invitations. I also had the privilege of testing portions of my manuscript at several seminars. Thanks are extended to the American History Seminar, Princeton University; Seminar on the Study of Fundamentalism, Yale University; Labor History Seminar, Newberry Library; Institute for Religion, Culture, and Public Life, Columbia University; Dordt College; Wheaton College; History Seminar at Vanderbilt University; the Department of Religion and the Miller Center for Democracy at the University of Virginia; the Cambridge American History Seminar, Cambridge University; the Center for the Study of Religion and American Culture; the Heidelberg Center for American Studies, Heidelberg University; the Department of History, Bielefeld University; and the Obama Institute for Transnational American Studies, University of Mainz. The generous and engaged scholars who were instrumental in coordinating these visits and in offering trenchant feedback—and who deserve special thanks—include Uta Balbier, Brian Balogh, Courtney Bender, Manfred Berg, Peter Boag, Bettina Brandt, Chris Cantwell, Heath Carter, Seth Dowland, Leon Fink, Andrew Finstuen, Kathleen Flake, Brian Froese, Gary Gerstle, Philip Goff, Darren Grem, Matthew Hedstrom, William Hitchcock, Sarah Igo, Thomas Kidd, Kevin Kruse, Melvyn Leffler, Katie Lofton, Emma Long, Mark McCarthy, Andrew Preston, Axel R. Schäfer, Anja Schuler, Bruce Schulman, Josef Sorett, Jan Stievermann, Matthew Sutton, Grant Wacker, Robert Wuthnow, John Young, and Julian Zelizer.

This book would not have happened without considerable financial and scholarly support from other institutions and individuals. My research was facilitated by fellowships and grants from the following institutions, none of which necessarily espouse or are accountable for the views expressed in this book: the Hagley Museum and Library; Wardlaw Research Fellowship—Texas Collection at Baylor University; Purdue Research Foundation at Purdue University; International Council for Canadian Studies (on behalf of Foreign Affairs and International Trade, Canada, Canadian Embassy, Washington, DC); Rockefeller Archive Center; American Philosophical Society; National Endowment for the Humanities; and American Council of Learned Societies. Extended leave time for writing was facilitated by a National Endowment for the Humanities Public Scholar Fellowship and a Bill & Rita Clements Senior Research Fellowship at the Clements Center for Southwest Studies, Southern Methodist University (SMU). My semester at SMU was invaluable, as it allowed me (and Debra) to comb the Everette DeGolyer papers, visit local archives, and gain a firmer grasp of all things Texas crude. More importantly, it gave me the chance to work with many talented scholars and friends, especially Andrew Graybill, Ruth Ann Elmore, Neil Foley, Kate Carte, Jeff Engel, Mark Chancey, Paul Conrad, Paula Lupkin, Tyina Steptoe, and Ted Campbell. The manuscript workshop that the center facilitated was both instructive and enjoyable, and I owe much to all of those at SMU who participated in it.

I also owe much to so many supportive colleagues. While at Washington University in St. Louis, I benefited from a welcoming and engaged environment in the Department of History and especially in the John C. Danforth Center on Religion and Politics. The seminars, conferences, and countless conversations I enjoyed with colleagues at the center—along with the generous support it provided—were edifying and essential as my writing continued to take shape. I am grateful for the opportunity to have worked with Senator John Danforth, Director Marie Griffith, Mark Jordan, Debra Kennard, Rachel Lindsey, Lerone Martin, Laurie Maffly-Kipp, Sheri Pena, Leigh Schmidt, Tiffany Stanley, Mark Valeri, and Abram Van Engen. My thanks go to Molly Prothero as well, who provided research assistance during my time at the center, as well as to center fellows Anne Blankenship, Emily Johnson, Ronit Stahl, and Lauren Turek, who helped me rethink and reframe the project during my stay in St. Louis. The Department of History at the University of Notre Dame has provided me all the opportunity I have needed to bring the book to completion. Special thanks go to Jon Coleman, Kathy Cummings, Patrick Griffin, John McGreevy, Mark Noll, Linda Przybyszewski, and Thomas Tweed for easing my transition to Notre Dame and providing feedback on sections of my work at critical stages along the way. Special thanks are also extended to graduate students and faculty members of the weekly Colloquium on Religion and History, as well as to postdoctoral fellows Peter Cajka, Maggie Elmore, Daniel Silliman, and Ben Wetzel. I have enjoyed working with a number of talented graduate students who have provided help, feedback, and encouragement (and demonstrated patience) these past few years. Philip Byers and Suzanna Krivulskaya offered extensive, expert help with research and related book matters—thank you. Thanks also go to Jessica Brockmole, Mauricio Castro, Anna Fett, Lauren Hamblen, Anna Holdorf, Sejoo Kim, and Hannah Peckham, as well as to those in my twentieth-century US history class who provided a thoughtful critique of my written drafts, including James Breen, Heather Lane, John Nelson, Nick Roberts, and Augusto Rocha Ramirez.

I have many good friends and family members to thank for all the warm encouragement and hospitality they supplied over the past few years, especially David Atkinson, Glenn Cook, Heidi Cook, Jennifer Foray, Ilona Francois, Lee Francois, Clarissa Gaff, Will Gray, Carrie Janney, Brian Kelly, Ruby Kidd, Corinna Klassen, Spencer Lucas, George Marsden, Lucie Marsden, Sarah Mullen, Wayne Orobko, Fran Preston, Kristen Coke Sutton, Bill Svelmoe, Lisa Svelmoe, Charity Tabol, and Kristin Van Engen. I look forward to many good times—better times—ahead. Tetyana, Michael, Gabriel, Everett, and Mackenzie Klassen and Greg, Janelle, Alana, Nolan, and Addison Dochuk provided much-needed Canadian escapes from the dull days of writing. Martha Dochuk and Rene Cochrane were unfailing in their encouragement and in their readiness to help me flee the office to dine at a local restaurant. My deepest thank you goes to Debra, who has lived with my oil fixations for far too long. I love you.

# Cast of Characters and Corporations

## Core Characters, Organizations, and (Where Applicable) Abbreviations Used in Text and Notes

### Individuals

Abdulaziz ibn Saud (King Ibn Saud): founder and first monarch of Saudi Arabia, 1932–1953

Abdulaziz Al Saud, Faisal bin (King Faisal): Saud's brother and king of Saudi Arabia, 1964–1975

Abdulaziz Al Saud, Saud bin (King Saud): Ibn Saud's son and king of Saudi Arabia, 1953–1964

Archbold, John: Standard Oil executive and John D. Rockefeller confidant

Bard, Thomas (TRB): Founding chief executive of Union Oil and California statesman

Barger, Thomas (TB): Oil geologist and onetime president of Aramco

Blaustein, Jacob (JB): Jewish oilman, human rights activist, and corporate booster for Israel

Carroll, George: Baptist oilman, Baylor University donor, and civic leader in Beaumont, Texas

Carson, Rachel: Environmental writer and activist

Crane, Charles: Presbyterian layman, Arabist, and philanthropist

Cullen, Hugh (HRC): East Texas wildcat oilman and prominent donor to conservative causes

Cummins, William (WC): Methodist itinerant preacher and amateur geologist

DeGolyer, Everette Lee: Leading petroleum geologist of the early twentieth century

Eddy, William (WAE): Arabist diplomat, American envoy in Middle East, and Aramco ally

Fosdick, Harry Emerson (HEF): Progressive minister and Rockefeller ally and advisor

Fosdick, Raymond (RF): Progressive activist and Rockefeller Foundation executive

Fuller, Charles (CEF): Radio evangelist, oilman, and voice of the "new evangelicalism"

Gates, Frederick (FTG): Baptist minister and philanthropic advisor to the Rockefeller family

Graham, Billy (WFG): America's preeminent evangelist of the twentieth century

Hankamer, Earl (ECH): Baptist oilman from Houston and supporter of Billy Graham

Higgins, Patillo: Early oil hunter in South Texas dubbed the "Prophet of Spindletop"

Hunt, H. L.: Wildcatter from East Texas and prominent conservative activist and donor

Ickes, Harold: Secretary of the interior under Franklin D. Roosevelt

Jablonski, Wanda: Leading oil journalist of the mid-twentieth century

Kerr, Robert (RK): Oklahoma governor and senator and independent oilman

LeTourneau, R. G. (RGLT): Heavy-equipment manufacturer and evangelical philanthropist

Manning, Ernest (ECM): Alberta premier and evangelical leader

Mulligan, William (WEM): Ardent Arabist and public relations liaison for Aramco

O'Shaughnessy, Ignatius (IOS): Catholic wildcat oilman and philanthropist

Ockenga, Harold (HO): Prominent evangelical minister and partner of Charles Fuller

Pew, J. Edgar (JEP): Nephew of Sun Oil's founder and Sun's chief executive in the Southwest

Pew, J. Howard (JHP): Son of Sun Oil's founder and Sun Oil's second president

Pew, Joseph N., Jr. (JNP): Son of Sun Oil's founder, Sun Oil executive, and Republican operative

Rentz, George (GSR): Student of Islam and the Middle East and Aramco public relations man

Richardson, Sid: Wildcatter who struck it rich in East Texas and prominent conservative donor

Rockefeller, David: Third-generation Rockefeller and president of Chase Bank

Rockefeller, John D., Jr. (JDRJr): Son of Standard's founder, churchman, and philanthropist

Rockefeller, John D., Sr. (JDR): Founder of the Standard Oil Company

Rockefeller, John D., III: Third-generation Rockefeller active in Rockefeller philanthropy

Rockefeller, Nelson (NAR): Third-generation Rockefeller active in philanthropy and politics

Simmons, Jake: African American oilman and civil rights activist from Oklahoma

Sonneborn, Rudolf: Prominent Jewish oilman, Zionist, and Israeli statesman

Stewart, Lyman (LS): Pennsylvania wildcatter, founder of Union Oil, and leading churchman

Stewart, Milton (MS): Pennsylvania wildcatter and brother of Lyman Stewart

Stewart, William (WLS): Son of Lyman Stewart and eventual president of Union Oil

Sullivan, Leon (RLS): Reverend, civil rights activist, and corporate leader

Tariki, Abdullah: Saudi Arabia's first oil minister

Tarbell, Ida (IT): Muckraking journalist responsible for challenging Standard Oil

Yamani, Ahmed: Saudi Arabia oil minister in charge of nationalizing Aramco

## Institutions and Organizations

American Board of Commissioners for Foreign Missions (ABCFM)

American Committee on Africa (ACOA)

American Friends of the Middle East (AFME)

American International Association for Economic and Social Development (AIA)

American Jewish Committee (AJC)

American Petroleum Institute (API)

American University of Beirut (AUB)

Catholic Near East Welfare Association (CNEWA)

Chase International Investment Corporation (CIIC)

Council for Latin America (CLA)

Fair Employment Practice Commitee (FEPC)

Federal Council of Churches (FCC)

Federal Trade Commission (FTC)

Great Canadian Oil Sands (GCOS)

Independent Petroleum Association of America (IPAA)

International Basic Economy Corporation (IBEC)

International Labor Organization (ILO)

Jungle Aviation and Radio Service (JAARS)

Missionary Aviation Fellowship (MAF)

National Association for the Advancement of Colored People (NAACP)

National Association of Evangelicals (NAE)

National Baptist Convention (NBC)

National Council of Churches (NCC)

National Energy Program (NEP)

Office of the Coordinator of Inter-American Affairs (OCIAA)

Office of Strategic Services (OSS)

Oil, Chemical, and Atomic Workers Union (OCAW)

Oil Workers International Union (OWIU)

Organization of Petroleum Exporting Countries (OPEC)

Psychological Strategy Board (PSB)

Rockefeller Brothers Fund (RBF)

Southern Baptist Convention (SBC)

Southern Christian Leadership Conference (SCLC)

Summer Institute of Linguistics (SIL)

Texas Independent Producers and Royalty Owners Association (TIPRO)

Texas Railroad Commission (TRC)

United Church of Christ (UCC)

United Nations Educational, Scientific and Cultural Organization (UNESCO)

United States Geological Survey (USGS)

United States Information Agency (USIA)

Voice of America (VOA)

World Council of Churches (WCC)

## Chronology of Oil Corporations

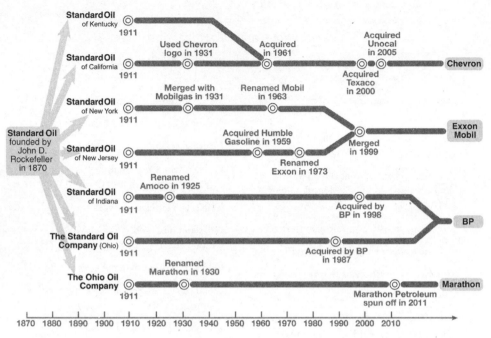

CREDIT: SUZANNA KRIVULSKAYA

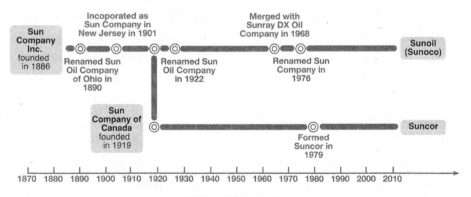

CREDIT: SUZANNA KRIVULSKAYA

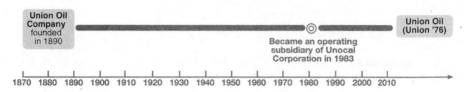

CREDIT: SUZANNA KRIVULSKAYA

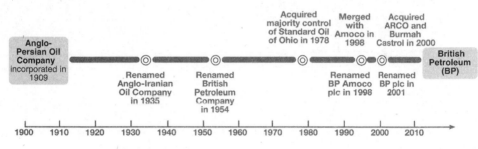

CREDIT: SUZANNA KRIVULSKAYA

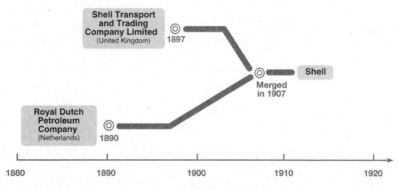

CREDIT: SUZANNA KRIVULSKAYA

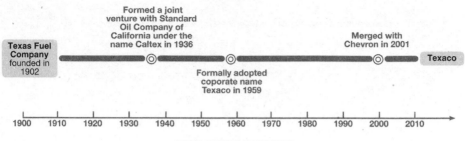

CREDIT: SUZANNA KRIVULSKAYA

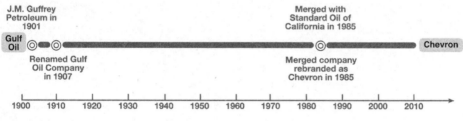

CREDIT: SUZANNA KRIVULSKAYA

# Notes

## Abbreviations

### Newspapers

| | | | |
|---|---|---|---|
| AC | Atlanta Constitution | NPN | National Petroleum News |
| ADN | Aberdeen Daily News | NR | National Review |
| BS | Baptist Standard | NYH | New York Herald |
| BW | Businessweek | NYP | New York Post |
| CH | Calgary Herald | NYT | New York Times |
| CP | Canadian Petroleum | NYTr | New York Tribune |
| CT | Christianity Today | OGJ | Oil and Gas Journal |
| CTT | Courier Times Telegraph | OW | Oil Weekly |
| DMN | Dallas Morning News | PG | Petroleum Gazette |
| ES | Evening Standard | PR | Philadelphia Record |
| FNT | Fort Worth Evening News Telegram | PW | Petroleum Week |
| | | SD | Sunday Dispatch |
| GDN | Galveston Daily News | SEP | Saturday Evening Post |
| HC | Houston Chronicle | SFE | San Francisco Examiner |
| HM | Harper's Magazine | TA | The Atlantic |
| HP | Houston Post | TG | The Guardian |
| HT | Henderson Times | TM | Texas Monthly |
| KDN | Kilgore Daily News | TMT | Tyler Morning Telegraph |
| LAE | Los Angeles Examiner | TW | Tulsa World |
| LAH | Los Angeles Herald | WP | Washington Post |
| LAT | Los Angeles Times | WSJ | Wall Street Journal |
| LDN | Longview Daily News | | |

## Archives and Collections Consulted and Cited and (Where Applicable) Abbreviations Used in Notes

ALC    Allegheny College, Pelletier Library Special Collections, Meadville, Pennsylvania
        ITC    Ida Tarbell Collection

APA    Alberta Provincial Archives, Edmonton, Alberta
        ECM    Premier Ernest C. Manning Papers
        HSP    Premier Harry Strom Papers
        WAP    Premier William Aberhart Papers

ARC    Amistad Research Center, Tulane University, New Orleans, Louisiana
        ACOA    Records of the American Committee on Africa

BIOL    Biola University Archives, La Mirada, California
        LSP    Lyman Stewart Papers

BUTC    Baylor University, the Texas Collection, Waco, Texas
        PPNP    President Pat Neff Papers
        TC    Texas Collection

CHL    Central Michigan University, Clark Historical Library, Mt. Pleasant, Michigan
        RMB    R. Mortimer Buck Papers

CSA    California State Archives, Sacramento, California
        EW    Governor Earl Warren Papers

CTA    Cameron Townsend Archives, Waxhaw, North Carolina

CUBL    Columbia University, Butler Library, New York, New York
        BOI    Benedum and the Oil Industry Oral History Collection

CUL    Cornell University Library, Rare and Manuscript Collections, Ithaca, New York
        CHB    Charles Hazen Blood Collection
        RFP    Raymond Family Papers
        SFC    Shelton Family Collection

DPL    Dallas Public Library, Dallas, Texas
        BAP    Bruce Alger Papers
        SJCS    San Jacinto Company Stock Records

DWM    Drake Well Museum Library, Titusville, Pennsylvania
        GBF    George H. Bissell File
        LJM    Louis J. Mackey Collection
        SFM    Steadman Family Material

EPLA    Dwight D. Eisenhower Presidential Library and Archives, Abilene, Kansas
        DEWF    Dwight D. Eisenhower, Papers as President of the United States, Ann Whitman File
        DEWH    Dwight D. Eisenhower, Records as President, White House Central Files
                CF    Confidential File
                OF    Official File
        DH    Dulles-Herter Series
        DS    Diary Series

EUA    Emory University, Manuscript, Archives, and Rare Book Library, Atlanta, Georgia
- LHS    Leon Howard Sullivan Papers
- SCLC    Southern Christian Leadership Conference Records
- ZCM    Zerah Coston Monks Papers

FDRL    Franklin D. Roosevelt Presidential Library, Hyde Park, New York
- POF    President's Official File

FSA    Fuller Theological Seminary Archives and Special Collections, Pasadena, California
- CFC    Charles E. Fuller and Grace Payton Fuller Collection

GULL    Georgetown University, Lavinger Library Special Collections, Washington, DC
- GSR    George S. Rentz Papers
- JAM    Joseph A. Mahon Papers
- RTC    Richard T. Crane Papers
- WEM    William E. Mulligan Papers

HLM    Hagley Library and Museum, Wilmington, Delaware
- JHP    J. Howard Pew Papers
- PFP    Pew Family Papers
- SOC    Sun Oil Corporate Records

JBU    John Brown University Special Collections, Siloam Springs, Arkansas
- JBSF    John Brown University Standing File

JCPL    Jimmy Carter Presidential Library, Atlanta, Georgia
- Henrik Hertzberg Papers
- Jimmy Carter–Walter Mondale Campaign Committee, 1976
  - Issues Office Files
- President Jimmy Carter—Office of the Cabinet Secretary
  - Paula Schneider's Subject Files
  - Jack Watson's Subject Files
- President Jimmy Carter—Office of the Chief of Staff Files
  - Stephen Selig's Subject Files
- President Jimmy Carter—White House Central Files
- RSO    Records of the Speechwriter's Office
- SF    Speechwriter's Chronological Files

JHU    Johns Hopkins University, Sheridan Libraries/Milton S. Eisenhower Library, Baltimore, Maryland
- LJB    Louis and Jacob Blaustein Papers

LAC    Library and Archives Canada, Ottawa, Canada
- WLM    Diaries of William Lyon Mackenzie King

LOC    Library of Congress, Washington, DC
- JKP    John F. Kennedy Papers Collection
- NACP    Papers of the National Association for the Advancement of Colored People
- SCLC    Records of the Southern Christian Leadership Conference
- WGM    Woody Guthrie Manuscript Collection

LOMC  Lambton Oil Museum of Canada
       LOCC  Lambton Oil Records of Canada

LUA  LeTourneau University Archives, Longview, Texas

LUL  Lehigh University, Fairchild-Martindale Library, Bethlehem, Pennsylvania
       HBP  Harvey Bassler Papers

MHSR  Montana Historical Society Research Library and Archives
       RAB  Robert A. Bell Papers

MNHS  Minnesota Historical Society, St. Paul, Minnesota
       IOSP  Ignatius Aloysius O'Shaughnessy Papers

NARA  National Archives and Records Administration, United States, Washington, DC
       JFK  John F. Kennedy Presidential Papers

NASC  National Archives of Scotland, Edinburgh
       DFP  Dundonald Family Papers

NHHS  New Haven Colony Historical Society, Whitney Library, New Haven, Connecticut
       MCS  Marion C. Sheridan Papers

OMC  Oil Museum of Canada, Petrolia, Ontario
       FWD  Fred Winnett Diary

PUFL  Princeton University, Seely G. Mudd Library, Princeton, New Jersey
       KTP  Karl Twitchell Papers
       RBFP  Raymond B. Fosdick Papers
       WEP  William Eddy Papers

RAC  Rockefeller Archive Center, Tarrytown, New York
       FGP  Frederick Gates Papers
       JJrPP  John D. Rockefeller Jr., Personal Papers
       LRSM  Laura R. Spellman Papers
       NER  Near East Relief Records
       RFC  Rockefeller Family Collection
       WOI  William O. Inglis Interview of John D. Rockefeller

RUFL  Rice University, Woodson Research Center, Fondren Library, Houston, Texas
       WHP  William H. Hamman Papers

SMUD  Southern Methodist University, DeGolyer Library, Dallas, Texas
       ELD  Everett L. DeGolyer Collection
       ELDP  Everett L. DeGolyer Pamphlet Collection
             Ellis W. Shuler Papers

STUA   St. Thomas University Archives, St. Paul, Minnesota
       IAOS   Ignatius Aloysius O'Shaughnessy Papers

TLM   Harry S. Truman Presidential Library, Independence, Missouri
       Clark M. Clifford Papers
       Edwin W. Pauley Papers
       George C. McGhee Papers
       President Harry S. Truman Papers, President's Secretary Files
       OLC   Oscar L. Chapman Papers

TSA   Texas State Archives, Austin
       ASG   Governor Allan Shivers Records
       BJP   Governor Beauford Jester Papers
       JVA   Governor James V. Allred Records
       WOD   Governor W. Lee O'Daniel Records

UCSC   University of Chicago Special Collections, Chicago, Illinois
       FTG   Frederick T. Gates Papers
       WRH   William Rainey Harper Papers

UOCA   University of Oklahoma, Carl Albert Archives, Norman
       RSK   Robert S. Kerr Papers

UOW   University of Oklahoma, Western History Collection,
Petroleum Industry Papers, Norman
       CNG   Charles Newtown Gould Papers
       CWH   Charles W. Hamilton Papers

UTBC   University of Texas at Austin, Briscoe Center for American History, Austin
       ECB   Eugene C. Barker Texas History Collection
       EMHC ExxonMobil Historical Collection
       LMIT   Labor Movement in Texas Collection
       OHTO Oral History of Texas Oil Industry
       SGC   Shadegg/Goldwater Collection
       TIPRO Texas Independent Producers and Royalty Owner Records/
                Oral History Collection
       UNSD United North and South Development Company
       WBS   Walter Benona Sharp Papers
       WFC   William Fletcher Cummins Papers
       Wesley Gibson Gish Papers

UWA   University of Wyoming, American Heritage Center, Laramie
       JJC   John J. Carter Papers

UWC   University of Warwick, Modern Records Centre, Warwick, United Kingdom
       BPR   British Petroleum Records

WGA    Wheaton College, Billy Graham Archives, Wheaton, Illinois
      BGEA   Billy Graham Evangelistic Association
      ECH   Earl C. Hankamer Papers
      RLCW  Records of the Lausanne Committee for World Evangelization
             Collection

WRLA   Walter Reuther Library and Archives, Detroit, Michigan
      HOC   Harry O'Connor Collection
      IWW   International Workers of the World Collection

YUL     Yale University Library, New Haven, Connecticut
      BSP   Benjamin Silliman Papers

## Prologue: The Strange Career of Patillo Higgins

1. Patillo Higgins, interviewed by W. A. Owens, July 25, 1952 (Tape No. 21), transcript p. 4, Box 3k21, OHTO, UTBC; Robert W. McDaniel with Henry C. Dethloff, *Patillo Higgins and the Search for Texas Oil* (College Station: Texas A&M University Press, 1989), 65. See also Darren Dochuk, "Blessed by Oil, Cursed with Crude: God and Black Gold in the American Southwest," *Journal of American History* 99 (June 2012): 51–61.

2. McDaniel with Dethloff, *Patillo Higgins and the Search for Texas Oil*, 63–66.

3. McDaniel with Dethloff, *Patillo Higgins and the Search for Texas Oil*, 63–66, 74–75.

4. McDaniel with Dethloff, *Patillo Higgins and the Search for Texas Oil*, 15–16; Christine Moor Sanders, *Spindletop: The Untold Story* (Beaumont, TX: Tejas Sanders, 2000), 45.

5. Quoted in Sanders, *Spindletop*, 46; quoted in McDaniel with Dethloff, *Patillo Higgins and the Search for Texas Oil*, 23.

6. McDaniel with Dethloff, *Patillo Higgins and the Search for Texas Oil*, 30–31.

7. McDaniel with Dethloff, *Patillo Higgins and the Search for Texas Oil*, 35.

8. Quoted in McDaniel with Dethloff, *Patillo Higgins and the Search for Texas Oil*, 37–38; Higgins, interviewed by W. A. Owens, July 25, 1952 (Tape No. 20), transcript p. 16–17, Box 3k21, OHTO, UTBC.

9. Higgins, interviewed by W. A. Owens, July 25, 1952; McDaniel with Dethloff, *Patillo Higgins and the Search for Texas Oil*, 54.

10. Quoted in Sanders, *Spindletop*, 84.

11. McDaniel with Dethloff, *Patillo Higgins and the Search for Texas Oil*, 57, 60–61.

12. McDaniel with Dethloff, *Patillo Higgins and the Search for Texas Oil*, 63–64.

## Introduction

1. Henry Luce, "Oil," American Petroleum Institute, Tulsa, Oklahoma, January 11, 1941, Folder 72, Box 7, RSK, UOCA.

2. My notion of "sparring spirits of capitalism" is shaped by a plethora of outstanding studies of Christianity and capitalism, the most important of which are fully cited in my bibliography. Historians John Corrigan, Timothy Gloege, Darren Grem, Sarah Hammond, James Hudnut-Beumler, Kevin Kruse, Chris Lehmann, Kathryn Lofton, Bethany Moreton, and Amanda Porterfield are among those who prove how deeply and thoroughly Protestant and capitalist conceptions of modern life are imbricated. These historians have been particularly effective in tracing the "neoliberal" strain of capitalist logic that courses through evangelical Protestantism, orients it toward fiercely laissez-faire modes of consumer and

corporate capitalism, and defines and empowers it in the dizzyingly decentralized and deregulated free markets of our time. My hope is that this book will contribute to this vibrant conversation by connecting the neoliberal strain witnessed in modern evangelicalism to the unique fantasies and functions of one particular commodity, in order to underscore the distinctive and essential features of extractive capitalism as a mode ripe for evangelicalism's fiscal values, and by mapping out the long and continual history of a Christian capitalist ethic that defies overbearing calculation and order and harbors a remarkable capacity—indeed hunger—for risk. Here, too, I am indebted to the rich literature in the history of capitalism, in particular the exemplary works of Sven Beckert, Angus Burgin, Louis Hyman, Meg Jacobs, Jonathan Levy, Julia Ott, and others whose scholarship has opened up fresh understanding of commodity and capital flows on a global scale and the making of modern market systems, if with limited attention to matters of religion.

3. Much has been written of late about the dynamic work that liberal Protestantism and its attending civil religion of social, political, and international engagement performed in the early and mid-twentieth century. Missionaries and diplomats, librarians and editors, educators and NGOs: the degree to which these agents of mainline Protestantism answered Henry Luce's clarion call to transform the world, we now know, was expansive and effective, if also fraught with subtler imperial prejudices. My intended contribution to this conversation is twofold: to trace in longer progression how the Rockefellers and their allies in oil tied dreams of ecumenism and internationalism to the prospects of one particular commodity, their dogmas and dreams for modernity to one particular material form; and to map out the extent to which oil money and interests blended seamlessly into their philanthropic principles and aims to remake the globe in their image. Oil money is not the only money that has determined the course of American charitable activity on behalf of religious, humanitarian, and political causes in the modern era, but it is hard to argue against the fact that it has—until recently—been the most critical lifeblood of that expansive action. And as the battle between the Rockefellers and the Stewarts and Pews strikingly shows, many of the most important pivots in the life of modern American Christianity and culture have in fact revolved around the politics of giving as much as around the politics of wealth acquisition. My study of the Rockefeller-led civil religion of crude is informed by several stellar books about the liberal mainline and "tri-faith" moment at midcentury and the processes of secularization that emerged in its shadow, including those written by Elesha Coffman, Mark Edwards, Matthew Hedstrom, David Hollinger, Kevin Schultz, Ian Tyrrell, and Wendy Wall, as well as those authored by students of philanthropy such as Lucy Bernholz, Chiara Cordelli, Rob Reich, Judith Sealander, and Olivier Zunz.

In my attempt to fold liberal international religion into broader narratives of modernization and global development—a field populated by several skilled scholars, most of whom have not yet sufficiently embedded institutions, ideas, and individuals of faith into their narratives, I have leaned heavily on the work of Chad Parker, Nathan Citino, David Ekladh, Daniel Immerwahr, and Emily Rosenberg. I am indebted to Heather Curtis and Francis Bonenfant-Juwong for helping me see more clearly ties between faith and modernization and development strategies in the Middle East. I have also leaned on several scholars whose work on the Middle East charts the seamless blend of religious and political goals that shaped American engagement there, including Caitlin Carenen, Christine Heyrman, William Inboden, Robert Kaplan, Ussama Makdisi, Melani McAlister, Michael Oren, Heather Sharkey, Karine Walther, and Hugh Wilford.

4. I am indebted to a sprawling literature on modern evangelicalism and evangelical culture produced by the likes of Joel Carpenter, Paul Harvey, Amy Johnson Frykholm, George Marsden, Steven Miller, and Randall Stephens. While evangelicalism is a key component

and protagonist of wildcat Christianity, the latter category speaks to wider permutations of religious experience, identity, and belonging tied to the peculiar capitalist structures, notions of and encounters with land and its resources, and concepts of time and space nurtured in the extraction zones of the oil patch—arrangements and forces that Catholics encounter and process as well. In this regard, I am also interested in the degree to which my subjects' encounters with the soil and its subsurface materials suggest an environmental ethic that was more syncretic, esoteric, and dynamic than most histories of evangelicalism and environment suggest. While the Calvinist call to exercise dominion of the earth stands at the center of Protestant concepts of environmental care, many of the amateur oil sleuths and geologists who populate my story also harbored romanticist and spiritualist impulses to commune and dialogue with the organic material they surveyed, as if they were one with it. In my reading of wildcat Christianity and its engagement with nature, I draw insights from the work of Catherine Albanese, Patrick Allitt, Mark Fiege, David Montgomery, Mark Stoll, and experts in the history of spiritualism such as Ann Braude and Leigh Schmidt.

5. Much has been written, of course, about the rise of evangelical conservatism and the Christian Right, including by historians such as Seth Dowland, Daniel Williams, Neil Young, and Matthew Sutton. My aim here is to place "quotidian" concerns with energy, land-use, and environmental policies at the heart of the story, an aspect of the culture wars that has not yet received sustained or sufficient attention.

6. Scholarship on the history of oil is extensive and constantly evolving, and I relied on it in order to make sense of the industry, its economic development, and its effects on culture. I am indebted to the oil histories—both local and international in scope—written by several authors cited in the bibliography, in particular Brian Black, Rachel Bronson, Paul Chastko, Brian Frehner, Lawrence Goodwyn, Meg Jacobs, Toby Craig Jones, Diana Olien, Roger Olien, Karen Merrill, Houston Faust Mount II, Gerald Nash, David Painter, Chad Parker, Tyler Priest, Paul Sabin, Robert Vitalis, Bobby Weaver, and Steve Weinberg. Key popular historical and journalistic accounts of oil with which this book engages include those by Anthony Cave Brown, Brian Burrough, Ron Chernow, Kevin Phillips, Kirkpatrick Sale, Anthony Sampson, and, of course, Daniel Yergin. With the exception of Phillips and especially Chernow, whose biographical account of John D. Rockefeller richly integrates the oilman's faith in a broader account of his oil enterprise, these core scholarly and popular texts tend to cordon off or ignore altogether the role of religion in the construction and flourishing of the modern oil industry. While some structural elements of the history of oil are downplayed or neglected in these pages (refining/downstream facets of the industry, as well as natural gas and petrochemicals, for example), I trust that the book's more general takeaways for oil historians will include a reimagined outline of how institutional and theological structures of religion helped facilitate the evolution of the industry, inspire its executives, engineers, and workers, fuel and shape its political objectives, and influence substantive policy outcomes and petroleum projects of global breadth.

Recent scholarship in what might be broadly defined as energy humanities—historical, cultural studies, and anthropological works on oil written by Ross Barrett, Andrew Behrends, Matthew Huber, Bob Johnson, Stephanie LeMenager, David Nye, Stephen Reyna, Michael Ross, Gunther Schlee, Matthew Schneider-Mayerson, and Daniel Worden, for instance, as well as by Kate Brown (nuclear), Andrew Needham (electricity), and Peter Shulman (coal)—is rich with new insights into the cultural as well as political heavy lifting energy does in modern society. What is striking, Imre Szeman and Dominic Boyer write in the introduction to their provocative anthology, is the degree to which energy and "the energy riches of the past two centuries have influenced our relationships to our bodies, molded human social relations, and impacted the imperatives of even those varied activities we group together under the term 'culture.'" Energy regimes such as oil quite simply dictate the terms by which societies—particularly communities in proximity to the source—work, live, play, raise families, imagine their futures, view the world, and vote. To that I would add a missing piece in the current literature: energy regimes also frame social and cultural contexts that forge the way societies—particularly communities proximate to the source—worship, gather in and map out sacred spaces, embrace certain theologies to explain the here and now and life beyond, and prepare the saints for tragedy, triumph, and the end times. See Imre Szeman and Dominic Boyer, eds., *Energy Humanities: An Anthology* (Baltimore: Johns Hopkins University Press, 2017), 2.

The paucity of studies in modern US religion that delve deep into the structural, ideational, and allegorical ties between religion and material forms of energy and energy production is equally pronounced. For a few exceptions to this rule, see works by Richard Callahan Jr., Kathryn Lofton, Chad Seales, Jared Roll, and Deborah Weiner, all of whom have helped me make sense of how visions of the holy were, at the very onset of the industrial era, grafted onto America's understanding of its manifest destiny and the essential role energy (carbon-based especially) played in it, and in return how the experiences of life in taxing and violent carbon-producing communities patterned a particular type of lived religion, in which "whole gospels" of spiritual and physical healing and the mysteries of the divine were embraced.

7. Paul T. Anderson et al., *There Will Be Blood* (Hollywood, CA: Paramount Home Entertainment, 2008).

8. Quoted in Owen P. White, "Drilling for Trouble," *Collier's*, June 27, 1931, 14.

9. I am informed, here, by the work of Timothy Mitchell and Thomas Andrews, whose framing concepts of "carbon democracy" (Mitchell) and "workscapes" (Andrews) outline the parameters (and restraints) of work life, democratic action, and power that workers, citizens, and the rank and file possess in carbon-based societies. Mitchell's study of the unique limits of freedom (freedom of labor protest, for instance) in oil as opposed to coal regimes is particularly instructive and something I have adopted in my own reading of labor activism (or the lack thereof) in the petroleum industry. At the same time, it should be remembered that for many workers across regions and times, "workscapes" were also "sacrospaces" (see Tom Tweed), where labor ideology and theology, work practices and lived religion fused into one human ecology, sometimes to promote labor activism, at other times to forestall it. My considerations of faith and labor are informed by the work of Heath Carter, Elizabeth Fones-Wolf, Ken Fones-Wolf, Janine Giordano Drake, Richard Callahan, and Jarod Roll.

10. For further insight into conservative religion and technology, see Timothy E. W. Gloege, *Guaranteed Pure: The Moody Bible Institute, Business, and the Making of Modern Evangelicalism* (Chapel Hill: University of North Carolina Press, 2015); B. M. Pietsch, *Dispensational Modernism* (New York: Oxford University Press, 2015). On the temporality and "messianic" notion of oil time, see Mandana E. Limbert, *In the Time of Oil: Piety, Memory, and Social Life in an Omani Town* (Stanford, CA: Stanford University Press, 2010), 9, 11.

# Chapter One: Rules of Capture

1. Robert Martin Krivoshey, "'Going Through the Eye of the Needle': The Life of Oil Man Fundamentalist Lyman Stewart, 1840–1923" (PhD diss., University of Chicago, 1973), 15–16. For focused treatment of Lyman Stewart and his role in the construction of a fundamentalist movement, see Darren Dochuk, "Fighting for the Fundamentals: Lyman Stewart and the Protestant Politics of Oil," in *Faithful Republic: Religion and Politics in Modern America*, ed. Andrew Preston, Bruce Schulman, and Julian Zelizer (Philadelphia: University of Pennsylvania Press, 2015), 41–55.

2. Krivoshey, "'Going Through the Eye,'" 19–21; LS to WBS, March 4, 1911, LSP, BIOL; Earl M. Welty and Frank J. Taylor, *The 76 Bonanza: The Fabulous Life and Times of the Union Oil Company of California* (Menlo Park, CA: Lane Magazine and Book Company, 1966), 49.

3. LS to US Department of the Interior, Department of Pensions, October 4, 1913; LS to Lyman (grandson), November 9, 1918, LSP, BIOL.

4. Krivoshey, "'Going Through the Eye,'" 23, 31; LS to Mrs. Stella Andrews Lahey, July 19, 1912; LS to Frank Crowell, April 27, 1922, LSP, BIOL.

5. Heidi Scott, "Whale Oil Culture, Consumerism, and Modern Conservation," in *Oil Culture*, ed. Ross Barrett and Daniel Worden (Minneapolis: University of Minnesota Press, 2014), 5–6; Brian Black, *Petrolia: The Landscape of America's First Oil Boom* (Baltimore: Johns Hopkins University Press, 2000), 16–17, 20–21; Paul H. Giddens, *The Birth of the Oil Industry* (New York: MacMillan, 1938), 19–20; Daniel Yergin, *The Prize: The Epic Quest for Oil, Money, and Power* (New York: Simon & Schuster, 1991), 23.

6. J. D. B. DeBow, "Statistical View of the United States: Compendium of the Seventh Census" (Washington, DC: Beverley Tucker, Senate Printer, 1854); "2010 Census of Population and Housing, Population and Housing Unit Counts, CPH-2-5" (US Government Printing Office, Washington, DC: US Census Bureau. 2012), 20–26, 1. On this revolution in business, see Alfred Chandler, *The Visible Hand: The Managerial Revolution in American Business* (Cambridge, MA: Belknap Press of Harvard University Press, 1977).

7. *NYH*, February 27, 1858; Kathryn T. Long, *The Revival of 1857–58: Interpreting an American Religious Awakening* (New York: Oxford University Press, 1998), 26, 36, 51, 144–150.

8. "Oil Region Characters," *PG*, April 8, 1897; "George H. Bissell Biography Certified by Grandson, Pelham St. George Bissell, 1927," GBF, DWM; Mike Byfield, "150th Anniversary: Ontario Celebrates the World's First Commercial Oilwell," April 2008, LOCC, LOMC. Numerous other members of Bissell's generation shared his Yankee Protestant roots, nervous vim, and obsession with oil, as well as his ties to elite colleges such as Dartmouth and the revivalistic religion of the day. See, for instance, Charles Blood, Aaron Raymond Russell, and George W. Shelton, whose correspondence (filed in CHB, CUL; SFC, CUL; and RFP, CUL) reveals a similar course of action in business, education, social reform, and the church.

9. B. Silliman Jr., *Report on the Rock Oil, or Petroleum, from Venango Co., Pennsylvania* (New Haven, CT: J. H. Benham's Steam Power Press, 1855), 3–4; Yergin, *The Prize*, 22, 25.

10. Yergin, *The Prize*, 25. On Kier, see "Samuel Kier—Medicine Man & Refiner," Oil 150, February 23, 2007, www.oil150.com/essays/article?article_id=68 (accessed March 22, 2016); "They Done Sam Kier Wrong!," *Our Sun: Magazine of Sun Oil Company* (summer 1963): 23–25, Mr. J. N. Pew Jr. Folder, Box 10, SOC, HLM.

11. George H. Bissell biography certified by grandson, Pelham St. George Bissell, 1927; George H. Bissell Diary, 1858, January 3, GBF, DWM.

12. "Many Things," undated newspaper clipping, GBF, DWM; Paul H. Giddens, *The American Petroleum Industry: Its Beginnings in Pennsylvania!* (Erie: Newcomen Society in North America, 1953), 8; Yergin, *The Prize*, 27–28.

13. News of Titusville discovery, dateline September 8, 1859, Titusville, Pennsylvania, *NYTr*, September 13, 1859; Thomas Gale, *Rock Oil, the Wonder of the Nineteenth Century in Pennsylvania and Elsewhere* (1860), ELDP, SMUD; Robert James Forbes, *More Studies in Early Petroleum History, 1860–1880* (Leiden: E. J. Brill, 1959), 141–143; George Bissell to Ophelia Bissell, November 4, 1859, GBF, DWM; Yergin, *The Prize*, 28.

14. Yergin, *The Prize*, 30; quoted in George Richard Crooks, *The Life of Bishop Matthew Simpson of the Methodist Episcopal Church* (New York: Harper 7 Brothers, Franklin Square,

1891), 373; Giddens, *American Petroleum Industry*, 28. There is some uncertainty as to the precise year of Bishop Simpson's sermon before Lincoln.

15. John Schmidt, *Growing Up in the Oil Patch* (Toronto, ON: Natural Heritage, 1989), 7; "Striking Ile, as Sung by Christy's Minstrels," in George Christy, *George Christy's Essence of Old Kentucky Containing a Choice Collection of New and Popular Songs, Interludes, Dialogues, Funny Speeches, Darkey Jokes, and Plantation Wit* (New York: Dick & Fitzgerald, Publishers, 1862), 65; Mary Sennholz, *Faith and Freedom: The Journal of a Great American, J. Howard Pew* (Grove City, PA: Grove City College, 1975), 4–5. On this region's "burned over" religiosity, see Whitney R. Cross, *The Burned-Over District: The Social and Intellectual History of Enthusiastic Religion in Western New York, 1800–1850* (Ithaca, NY: Cornell University Press, 1965).

16. Ernest C. Miller, *John Wilkes Booth in the Pennsylvania Oil Region* (Meadville, PA: Crawford County Historical Society, 1987), 13–15, 18, 21, 64–65, 69, 71; oral interview transcripts for A. W. Smiley, 1; O. B. Steele, 1; Jerry Allen, 1, LJM, DWM; Richard O'Connor, *The Oil Barons: Men of Greed and Grandeur* (London: Hart-Davis MacGibbon, 1972), 17.

17. Donna Howell, "Entrepreneur George Bissell," *Investor's Business Daily*, October 25, 2004; Giddens, *Early Days of Oil*, 46–47; typescript history of George H. Bissell, 3–4, GBF, DWM.

18. "Notes to Correspondence Between Zerah Coston Monks and Hannah Tabitha Rohrer," 1–2, 13–14, 17, Folder 2, Box 1; Zerah Coston Monks to "Hattie" Rohrer, February 26, May 27, July 16, July 29, 1865; Rorher to Monks, April 20, 1865; microfilmed letters, ZCM, EUA.

19. David Murray, "Petroleum: Its History and Properties," read before the Albany Institute, December 16, 1862, 3–4; unknown, "The Canadian Native Oil; Its Story, Its Uses, and Its Profits" (London: Ashby & Co., 1862), 5–6; William J. Buck, *Early Accounts of Petroleum in the United States* (Titusville, PA: Bloss & Cogswell, 1876), 4; Edwin C. Bell, "The Late Joseph Carver Robinson," *PG* 17 (1912), 10; Joseph Carver Robinson, *A Dream: An Epic Poem* (Boston: J. C. Robinson, Publisher, 1889), 35.

20. "The History and Destiny of Coal," *Christian Review* 21 (April 1856): 282; "Petroleum, Old and New," *Merchants' Magazine and Commercial Review* 47 (July 1862): 26. For more extensive treatment of the differences between oil and coal, see Paul Sabin, "A Dive into Nature's Great *Grab-Bag*': Nature, Gender and Capitalism in the Early Pennsylvania Oil Industry," *Pennsylvania History: A Journal of Mid-Atlantic Studies* 66 (autumn 1999): 487–488.

21. Rev. S. J. M. Eaton, *Petroleum: A History of the Oil Region of Venango County, Pennsylvania* (Philadelphia: J. P. Skelly & Co., 1866), 20–21, 22, 43–44.

22. Quoted in Giddens, *Birth of the Oil Industry*, 87.

23. Charles A. Whiteshot, *The Oil Well Driller: A History of the World's Greatest Enterprise, the Oil Industry* (Oil City, PA: Oil Region Alliance, 2006), 380, 382; Yergin, *The Prize*, 30; Allan Nevins, *John D. Rockefeller: The Heroic Age of American Enterprise* (New York: Charles Scribner's Sons, 1940), 1:199.

24. Whiteshot, *Oil Well Driller*, 380; Gary May, *Hard Oiler! The Story of Early Canadians' Quest for Oil at Home and Abroad* (Toronto: Dundurn Press, 1998), 67.

25. William Wright, *The Oil Region of Pennsylvania* (New York: Harper & Brothers, 1865), 107–109; "Oil Fires of the Past," *Harper's*, August 1, 1908, 31; "The Recent Conflagration in Philadelphia," *Harper's*, February 25, 1865, 117–118.

26. B. Franklin, "After Petroleum," *Harper's*, December 1864, 59. For fuller description and analysis, see Black, *Petrolia*, 64–67; Amasa M. Eaton, "A Visit to the Oil Regions of Pennsylvania," 195, 200, ELDP, SMUD; John Schmidt, *Growing Up in the Oil Patch* (Toronto: Natural Heritage, 1989), 9.

27. Giddens, *Early Days of Oil*, 60; Joseph J. Millard, *The Wickedest Man: The True Story of Ben Hogan* (New York: Gold Medal, 1954), 98–99; Charles Almanzo Babcock, *Venango County, Pennsylvania: Her Pioneers and People, Embracing a General History of the County* (Chicago: J. H. Beers & Company, 1919), 143; Susan Hutchison Tassin, *Pennsylvania Ghost Towns: Uncovering the Hidden Past* (Mechanicsburg, PA: Stackpole Books, 2007), n.p.

28. Giddens, *Early Days of Oil*, 46–47; "Petroleum Centre" in GBF, DWM.

29. Letters addressed "Dear Sir," from George H. Bissell, April 13 and May 15, 1867; typescript history of George H. Bissell, 3–4, GBF, DWM.

30. "Petroleum, Old and New," 26.

31. Brian Frehner, *Finding Oil: The Nature of Petroleum Geology, 1859–1920* (Lincoln: University of Nebraska Press, 2011), 6–7.

32. Andrew Hervey Caughey, *Memoir of the Rev. S. J. M. Eaton* (Erie, PA: Dispatch Publishing Company, Limited, 1890), 200; Eaton, *Petroleum*, v–xi, 257–258.

33. Frehner, *Finding Oil*, 6–7; Wright, *The Oil Region of Pennsylvania*, 62–63; Eaton, *Petroleum*, 88–89; Giddens, *The American Petroleum Industry*, 9.

34. J. M. Peebles, *The Practical of Spiritualism: A Biographical Sketch of Abraham James: Historic Description of His Oil-Well Discoveries in Pleasantville, Pa., Through Spirit Direction* (Chicago: Horton & Leonard, 1868), 19, 36–37, DWM; Rochelle Raineri Zuck, "The Wizard of Oil: Abraham James, the Harmonial Wells, and the Psychometric History of the Oil Industry," in *Oil Culture*, ed. Ross Barrett and Daniel Worden (Minneapolis: University of Minnesota Press, 2014), 26–29.

35. Joseph Eastburn Winner, *Oil on the Brain* (New York: H. De Marsan, 1865), ELDP, SMUD.

36. John D. Rockefeller, *Some Random Reminiscences of Men and Events* (New York: Doubleday, Page & Company, 1909), 5.

37. Ron Chernow, *Titan: The Life of John D. Rockefeller, Sr.* (New York: Vintage Books, 1998), 80; Yergin, *The Prize*, 35.

38. John D. Rockefeller interview, WOI, RAC, 555, 1264; Chernow, *Titan*, 88, 283; quoted in John T. Flynn, *God's Gold: The Story of Rockefeller and His Times* (New York: Harcourt, Brace and Company, 1932), 401. For comparison with these other titans, see Charles R. Morris, *The Tycoons: How Andrew Carnegie, John D. Rockefeller, Jay Gould, and J. P. Morgan Invented the American Supereconomy* (New York: Time Books–Henry Holt and Company, 2005).

39. John D. Rockefeller interview, WOI, RAC, 1682; Steve Weinberg, *Taking On the Trust: The Epic Battle of Ida Tarbell and John D. Rockefeller* (New York: W. W. Norton), 64, 65.

40. John K. Winkler, *John D.: A Portrait in Oils* (Toronto: Blue Ribbon Books, 1929), 62; Hildegarde Dolson, *The Great Oildorado* (New York: Random House, 1959), 60. Considering the anecdotal nature of the original sources, the veracity of these tales, which Chernow also recounts, warrants some skepticism.

41. Weinberg, *Taking On the Trust*, 66–67, 288–289, 292. A full portrait of Flagler, his faith, and his partnership with Rockefeller is drawn in Edward Akin, *Flagler: Rockefeller Partner and Florida Baron* (Gainesville: University of Florida Press, 1991).

42. Chernow, *Titan*, 134, 136; John D. Rockefeller interview, WOI, RAC, 23, 141, 17–18; Weinberg, *Taking On the Trust*, 76.

43. John D. Rockefeller interview, WOI, RAC, 76, 42, 299, 195; Chernow, *Titan*, 153–154.

44. John D. Rockefeller interview, WOI, RAC, 102.

45. August W. Giebelhaus, *Business and Government in the Oil Industry: A Case Study of Sun Oil, 1876–1945* (Greenwich, CT: JAI Press, 1980), 2; Paul Sabin, *Crude Politics: The California Oil Market, 1900–1940* (Berkeley: University of California Press, 2005), 15–16.

46. John D. Rockefeller interview, WOI, RAC, 96, 98, 145, 155, 1064.

47. LS to Mrs. Stella Andrews Lahey, July 19, 1912; LS to Dr. Frank Crowell, April 27, 1922; LS to children, September 4, 1914, LSP, BIOL; Krivoshey, "'Going Through the Eye,'" 22; Welty and Taylor, *The 76 Bonanza*, 93.

48. LS to William, May, and Fred, September 4, 1914, LSP, BIOL; B. M. Pietsch, "Lyman Stewart and Early Fundamentalism," *Church History* 82 (September 2013): 619.

49. LS to L. H. Severance, June 8, 1909, LSP, BIOL.

50. Matthew Josephson, *The Robber Barons: The Great American Capitalists, 1861–1901* (New York: Harcourt Brace and World, Inc., 1943), 160; quoted in Yergin, *The Prize*, 41.

51. John D. Rockefeller interview, WOI, RAC, 134; Yergin, *The Prize*, 41–42.

52. Austin Leigh Moore, *John D. Archbold and the Early Development of Standard Oil* (New York: Macmillan, 1930), 17, 48–49; Yergin, *The Prize*, 98–99; quoted in Chernow, *Titan*, 139, also see 164–165.

53. Quoted in Weinberg, *Taking On the Trust*, 83; Whiteshot, *The Oil Well Driller*, 642–643; Yergin, *The Prize*, 43, 81; Chandler, *The Visible Hand*, 326.

54. Yergin, *The Prize*, 43.

55. Wright, *The Oil Region of Pennsylvania*, 55–57.

56. Samuel P. Bates, Robert C. Brown, and John Brandt Mansfield, *History of Crawford County, Pennsylvania* (Chicago: Warner, Beers & Co., 1885), 482; Herbert Charles Bell, *History of Venango County, Pennsylvania* (Chicago: Brown, Runk & Co., 1890), 490. Not atypical, for instance, were the fortunes of First Baptist Church in Oil City, a congregation that grew from 3 members at its founding in 1863 to 796 members by 1888. Oil City's Trinity Methodist, which counted 440 members as of 1890, and St. Joseph Catholic Church, which grew from 30 members in 1860 to 2,000 in 1890, boasted similarly fantastic gains. Bursting at the seams, these churches and their counterparts dominated the landscape and culture of Oil City, which in 1890 reported a population of 11,000. The account of the oilman in Pithole is drawn from George Van Lew Diary, DWM.

57. See, for instance, the image of Pithole, provided in Giddens, *Early Days of Oil*, 63. On the importance of hilltops and graveyards in early oil, see Frehner, *Finding Oil*, 38–39.

58. Ann Zabroski, "Altar at Pithole Dedicated," *Titusville Herald*, August 24, 1959; note of captain's commission; "Half a Century in Gospel Ministry," unknown, undated newspaper clipping; Margo Mong, "Life in the Valley," *Oilfield Barker*, n.d., 7, SFM, DWM.

59. Steadman biography transcript; David L. Taylor, "The Preacher of Pithole, Penn.," *Pure Oil News*, 12–14, SFM, DWM.

60. Giddens, *Early Days of Oil*, 15.

61. Emily Arnold McCully, *Ida M. Tarbell: The Woman Who Challenged Big Business— and Won!* (Boston: Clarion Books, 2014), 16–17.

62. McCully, *Ida M. Tarbell*, 15, 20; Ida M. Tarbell, *All in the Day's Work: An Autobiography* (Champaign: University of Illinois Press, 2003), 5–6.

63. History and initial goal of Chautauqua Institution, available at "Chautauqua Movement History," Colorado Chautauqua Association, www.chautauqua.com/about-us/history/chautauqua-movement-history (accessed September 3, 2016); see also Weinberg, *Taking On the Trust*, 109–110.

64. McCully, *Ida M. Tarbell*, 21, 25.

65. Weinberg, *Taking On the Trust*, 111; McCully, *Ida M. Tarbell*, 30; Tarbell, *All in the Day's Work*, 32.

66. Weinberg, *Taking On the Trust*, 69, 71; Tarbell, *All in the Day's Work*, 28–29, 30.

67. McCully, *Ida M. Tarbell*, 23, 32, 45, 49; Tarbell, *All in the Day's Work*, 35, 41, 42, 55–57.

68. Tarbell, *All in the Day's Work*, 72–76, 79; Weinberg, *Taking On the Trust*, 110, 115.

69. Tarbell, *All in the Day's Work*, 84, 45.

70. McCully, *Ida M. Tarbell*, 72; quoted in Kathleen Brady, *Ida Tarbell: Portrait of a Muckraker* (Pittsburgh, PA: University of Pittsburgh Press, 1989), 23; Ida M. Tarbell, *The History of the Standard Oil Company: Briefer Version*, ed. David M. Chalmers (New York: Harper & Row, 1966), xvi.

71. Ida Tarbell, "My Religion," 1–2, 3, "IMT: Autobiography" Folder, Box 53:4, ITC, ALC.

72. Peter B. Doran, *Breaking Rockefeller: The Incredible Story of the Ambitious Rivals Who Toppled an Oil Empire* (New York: Viking, 2016), 9.

73. Tarbell, *The History of the Standard Oil Company*, 22; Max Weber, *The Protestant Ethic and the Spirit of Capitalism and Other Writings* (New York: Penguin Twentieth-Century Classics, 2002 [1930]), 68–69.

74. LS to J. L. Severance, January 11, 1915, and LS to J. W. Baer, July 2, 1913, LSP, BIOL; W. H. Hutchinson, *Oil, Land and Politics: The California Career of Thomas R. Bard* (Norman: University of Oklahoma Press, 1965); Krivoshey, "'Going Through the Eye,'" 32–34.

75. Welty and Taylor, *The 76 Bonanza*, 59.

## Chapter Two: Worlds of Wonder

1. Krivoshey, "'Going Through the Eye,'" 37–38.

2. Krivoshey, "'Going Through the Eye,'" 39–40, 51, 59; LS to MS, April 12, 1884, LSP, BIOL.

3. LS to MS, September 30, 1884, LSP, BIOL.

4. Krivoshey, "'Going Through the Eye,'" 53, 58, 68, 74.

5. Krivoshey, "'Going Through the Eye,'" 77–78; LS to children, September 4, 1914, LSP, BIOL; Welty and Taylor, *The 76 Bonanza*, 93.

6. Alexander Von Millern, *All About Petroleum and the Great Oil Districts of Crawford and Venango Counties, PA* (New York: William Skelly, 1865), 77–78, 38–39, 40, ELDP, SMUD.

7. Benjamin Silliman, *A Description of the Recently Discovered Petroleum Region in California with a Report on the Same* (New York: n.p., 1864), 12–13; Benjamin Silliman, "Professor Silliman's Report upon the Oil Property of the Philadelphia and California Petroleum Company, of Philadelphia" (1865) and "Prospectus of the Anticlinal Rock Oil Co." (1865), ELDP, SMUD; Benjamin Silliman Jr. to Susan Huldah Forbes Silliman, December 21, 1864, BSP, YUL; George E. Webb, "Benjamin Silliman's Visit to California: A Letter to His Wife, 1864," *Southern California Quarterly* 59 (winter 1977): 365–378.

8. At one time, the Philadelphia and California Petroleum Company also assumed the name Pacific Petroleum Company of New York. On its work in California, see *Prospectus of the Pacific Petroleum Company of New York* (New York: John W. Amerman, 1865), 3, 14; "Oil and Gas Production: History in California," *Oil & Gas History*, State of California, ftp://ftp.consrv.ca.gov/pub/oil/history/History_of_Calif.pdf (accessed November 1, 2016).

9. David Murray, "Petroleum: Its History and Properties," 9; Byfield, "150th Anniversary"; "The Oil Question," *NYT*, January 28, 1865; *The Canadian Native Oil: Its Story, Its Uses, and Its Profits* (London: Ashby & Co, 1862), 49–50.

10. "Note Book (1853)," Folder 9, Box 1; "Memorandum Book (1864)," Folder 7, Box 1; "Diary—1965," Folder 5, Box 1 (for instance, entries dated June 3–8, 1865); and "Ida Oil Well Company, Treasury Book, 1866," Folder 6, Box 1, RMB, CHL.

11. C. A. Warner, *Texas Oil & Gas Since 1843* (1939; rpt. Ingleside, TX: Copano Bay Press, 2007), 21–24; "Biographical Sketch of General William H. Hamman," "Biographical Sketch" Folder, Box 1, WHP, RUFL.

12. Albert Henry Redford, *Life and Times of H. H. Kavanaugh, D.D.* (Nashville, 1884), 57; S. W. Geiser, "Benjamin Taylor Kavanaugh, and the Discovery of East Texas Oil," *Field & Lab* 12 (June 1944): 49, 50–53; W. H. C. Folsom, *Fifty Years in the Northwest: Reminiscences, Incidents and Notes* (Pioneer Press, 1888), 384.

13. Isabella Margaret Elizabeth Blandin, *History of Shearn Church, 1837–1907* (Houston, TX: Shearn Auxiliary of Women's Home Mission Society, 1908), 75; Redford, *Life and Times of H. H. Kavanaugh, D.D.*, 60–61; Geiser, "Benjamin Taylor Kavanaugh and the Discovery of East Texas Oil," 50.

14. Elisabeth Stiles, "Life and Reminiscences of W. F. Cummins" (unpublished manuscript, 1922), 12–13, 22–23, "W. F. Cummins, Life and Reminiscences of, by E. Stiles" Folder, WFC, UTBC.

15. Stiles, "Life and Reminiscences of W. F. Cummins," 26–27, 34, 47–48.

16. Stiles, "Life and Reminiscences of W. F. Cummins," 48, 51–54, 61, 72, 83, 145, 149–150, 155–159.

17. Ann Braude, *Radical Spirits: Spiritualism and Women's Rights in Nineteenth-Century America*, 2nd ed. (Bloomington: Indiana University Press, 2001), xiv, 4; Leigh Eric Schmidt, *Restless Souls: The Making of American Spirituality* (San Francisco: HarperSanFrancisco, 2005), 12–13; Molly McGarry, *Ghosts of Futures Past: Spiritualism and the Cultural Politics of Nineteenth-Century America* (Berkeley: University of California Press, 2008), 61; Mark Twain, "The New Wildcat Religion," *The Golden Era*, March 4, 1866, http://www.twain quotes.com/Era/18660304.html (accessed December 21, 2018).

18. McGarry, *Ghosts of Futures Past*, 62–64; Frank Podmore, *Modern Spiritualism: A History and a Criticism* (London: Methuen & Co., 1902), 15; Richard Benson, *The Valley: A Hundred Years in the Life of a Family* (London: Bloomsbury, 2014), 4–6; Cornish Mining World Heritage, last edited September 18, 2018, www.cornish-mining.org.uk/delving -deeper/cornish-mining-north-america (accessed September 25, 2018).

19. R. A. Bell to John N. Larson, October 8, 1913, and John N. Larson to R. A. Bell, January 8, 1914, Folder 8, Box 6; R. A. Bell to *The Progressive Thinker*, August 17, 1911, and August 21, 1913, Folder 11, Box 8; D. D. Bryant to R. A. Bell, May 29, 1912, and R. A. Bell to D. D. Bryant, July 4, 1916, Folder 17, Box 2; "Petroleum: The Magic Wealth Producer," Folder 9, Box 14; R. A. Bell to D. D. Bryant, August 17, 1911, and July 4, 1916, Folder 11, Box 8; undated letter clip, Folder 17, Box 14, RAB, MHSR.

20. B. T. Kavanaugh, *The Electric Theory of Astronomy* (Cincinnati, OH: Cranston & Stowe, 1886), 186–187. On the prevalence of spiritualism in 1890s Texas and Texas populism, see Joseph L. Locke, *Making the Bible Belt: Texas Prohibitionists and the Politicization of Southern Religion* (New York: Oxford University Press, 2017), 18–20.

21. Stiles, "Life and Reminiscences of W. F. Cummins," 62–63, 64, 87–89, 197–199.

22. Ann Brenoff, "History of High Spirits," *LAT*, June 17, 2007; Ralph Arnold, "Geology and Oil Resources of the Summerland District, Santa Barbara County, California" (Washington, DC: Government Printing Office, 1907), 9–10, 11; Mark Mau and Henry Edmundson, "First Steps Offshore," last edited July 21, 2015, Engineering and Technology History Wiki, http://ethw.org/First_Steps_Offshore (accessed May 27, 2017).

23. Dana Goodyear, "Drill and Spill," *New Yorker*, May 26, 2015, www.newyorker .com/news/news-desk/santa-barbara-oil-drill-and-spill (accessed May 27, 2017); Arnold, "Geology and Oil Resources of the Summerland District, 16–17; "Offshore Petroleum History," American Oil & Gas Historical Society, http://aoghs.org/offshore-history /offshore-oil-history (accessed May 27, 2017).

24. Yergin, *The Prize*, 24–25, 56–58. On Hecker, Lukasiewicz, and early European oil, see Julien Hirszhaut, *The Jewish Oil Magnates of Galicia*, Part I: *The Jewish Oil Magnates: A History, 1853–1945* (Montreal: McGill-Queen's University Press, 2015), esp. chap. 3;

Marija Wakounig and Karlo Ruzicic-Kessler, eds., *From the Industrial Revolution to World War II in East Central Europe* (Zürich: LIT Verlag Münster, 2011), 62; Alison Fleig Frank, *Oil Empire: Visions of Prosperity in Austrian Galicia* (Cambridge, MA: Harvard University Press, 2009), 3–4 (quote), 55–58.

25. Quoted in Yergin, *The Prize*, 59, 63; Abraham Valentine Williams Jackson, *From Constantinople to the Home of Omar Khayyam* (New York: Macmillan Company, 1911), 25.

26. R. Hrair Dekmejian and Hovann H. Simonian, *Troubled Waters: The Geopolitics of the Caspian Region* (London: I. B. Tauris & Company, 2003), 16.

27. Dekmejian and Simonian, *Troubled Waters*, 71, 73, 116. The merger placed 60 percent of company control in the hands of the Dutch corporate group and 40 percent under British authority.

28. At this relatively early stage of international development, oil might be compared more fairly to the earlier workings of cotton, which, prior to the 1860s and its firmer attachments to state and empire building, Sven Beckert accentuates, was very much dictated by cotton merchants' networking and global exchange. See Sven Beckert, *Empire of Cotton: A Global History* (New York: Alfred A. Knopf, 2014), 345.

29. Quoted in Beckert, *Empire of Cotton*, 6, xiv; Barbara Freese, *Coal: A Human History* (New York: Penguin Books, 2003), 10, 12.

30. Doran, *Breaking Rockefeller*, 37–38; Piotr Wrobel, "The Jews of Galicia Under Austrian-Polish Rule, 1867–1918," *The Galitzianer* 8, no. 2: 1; Hirszhaut, *The Jewish Oil Magnates of Galicia*, 13; Norman Davies, *God's Playground: A History of Poland*, Vol. 2: *1795 to the Present* (New York: Oxford University Press, 2005), 106–108; Rosa Lehmann, *Symbiosis and Ambivalence: Poles and Jews in a Small Galician Town* (New York: Berghahn Books, 2001), 33; Frank, *Oil Empire*, 11. On Lukasiewicz, see the biographical account in Ludwik Tomanek, *Ignacy Łukasiewicz twórca przemysłu naftowego w Polsce, wielki inicjator—wielki jałmużnik: w 75-tą rocznicę zapalenia pierwszej lampy naftowej* (Druk. Tow. Św. Michała Archanioła, 1928). For further assessment of Kessler and Dutch oil exploration in Indonesia, see J. Ph. Poley, *Eroica: The Quest for Oil in Indonesia, 1850–1898* (New York: Springer, 2000).

31. John J. Carter to John D. Archbold, May 14, 1907; John J. Carter to Hon. John L. McKinney, May 20, 1907; John Carter to Rev. J. M. Dunn, May 27, 1907, Folder 2, Box 1, JJC, UWA.

32. May, *Hard Oiler!*, 133–134, 184–185; Fred Winnett diary entry, September 12, 1898, FWD, OMC; Christina Burr, "Some Adventures of the Boys: Enniskillen Township's 'Foreign Drillers,' Imperialism, and Colonial Discourse, 1873–1923," unpublished manuscript, OMC.

33. Josiah Strong, *Our Country: Its Possible Future and Its Present Crisis* (New York: Baker & Taylor, 1885), 28; Rev. R. A. Jaffray, "The First Report of the Dutch East Indies Mission of the Christian and Missionary Alliance, 1928–1929," *The Pioneer: A Missionary Newsletter Concerning the Work of the Alliance Mission in Borneo and the Adjacent Islands of the Dutch East Indies* 1 (June 1930): 8–16.

34. "Compendium of the History and Abstract of Titles (10th) Earl of Dundonald and of Succession of Thomas Barnes, 11th Earl, in lands of La Brea, Trinidad," GD20/3/42; "Memorandum on Trinidad Asphalt," August 5, 1899, GD20/3/35; T. Daniel to Lady Dundonald, June 1897, June 22, 1898, November 22, 1898, and December 7, 1898, all GD20/3/21, DFP, NASC.

35. George R. Gibson, "Great American Industries IV: 'A Lampful of Oil,'" *Harper's*, January 1886, 253; Nevins, *John D. Rockefeller*, 2:22; John T. Kilham, "The Oil Wells of the

United States" (address to Onondaga Academy of Science, Syracuse, New York, November 21, 1902), 8–9; John J. McLaurin, *Sketches in Crude Oil: Some Accidents and Incidents of the Petroleum Development in All Parts of the Globe* (Harrisburg, PA: published by author, 1896), 364–365, 367. See also Francis N. Thorpe, "The Dominant Idea of American Democracy," *Harper's*, November 1896, 838–843.

36. McLaurin, *Sketches in Crude Oil*, 74.

37. O'Connor, *Oil Barons*, 53, 55; Yergin, *The Prize*, 97–98; Nevins, *John D. Rockefeller*, 4–5, 9–10; Henry Demarest Lloyd, *Wealth Against Commonwealth* (New York: Harper & Brothers, 1894), 44–45.

38. O'Connor, *Oil Barons*, 64; Irvine H. Anderson Jr., *The Standard-Vacuum Oil Co. and United States East Asian Policy, 1933–1941* (Princeton, NJ: Princeton University Press, 1975), 16, 203; Nevins, *John D. Rockefeller*, 25–26; Yergin, *The Prize*, 130–131.

39. McLaurin, *Sketches in Crude Oil*, 369.

40. Quoted in Chernow, *Titan*, 342–343.

41. Clarice Stasz, *The Rockefeller Women: Dynasty of Piety, Privacy, and Service* (New York: St. Martin's Press, 1995), 67, 84, 114.

42. Nevins, *John D. Rockefeller*, 206–207, 211, 214; quoted in John E. Harr and Peter J. Johnson, *The Rockefeller Century* (New York: Charles Scribner's Sons, 1988), 1, 14, 15; descriptions of Rockefeller's and Harper's characters drawn from Frederick Gates autobiography, unpublished manuscript in RAC; see also Frederick Gates, *Chapters in My Life* (New York: Free Press, 1977). On Rockefeller's hesitancy, see John D. Rockefeller to Harper, January 15, 1889, WRH, UCSC.

43. Harr and Johnson, *Rockefeller Century*, 1, 15; Thomas W. Goodspeed, *The History of the University of Chicago, 1891–1906* (Chicago: University of Chicago Press, 1916), 66–67; quoted in Chernow, *Titan*, 325–326.

44. Quoted in Chernow, *Titan*, 321; quoted in Harr and Johnson, *Rockefeller Century*, 22; quoted in Raymond B. Fosdick, *The Story of the Rockefeller Foundation* (New York: Harper & Publishers, 1952), 7.

45. Krivoshey, "'Going Through the Eye,'" 111–112, 118–120; R. E. Crowder, *Los Angeles City Oil Field: California Division of Oil and Gas, Summary of Operations* 47, no. 1 (1961): 68–70; LS to C. P. Collins, June 23, 1893, LSP.

46. Krivoshey, "'Going Through the Eye,'" 79, 88–89, 92; LS to TB, September 6, 1899; LS to TB, September 6, 1899, LSP, BIOL.

47. LS to C. P. Collins, October 7, 1895; MS to LS, August 17, 1891, LSP, BIOL; quoted in Krivoshey, "'Going Through the Eye,'" 133–134, 139, 144, 146, 148.

48. LS to TB, September 6, 1899, LSP, BIOL; Krivoshey, "'Going Through the Eye,'" 152–153, 160.

49. Krivoshey, "'Going Through the Eye,'" 147.

50. Quoted in Welty and Taylor, *The 76 Bonanza*, 114; Pietsch, "Lyman Stewart and Early Fundamentalism," 630.

51. Pietsch, "Lyman Stewart and Early Fundamentalism," 625; Melanie McAlister, *The Kingdom of God Has No Borders: A Global History of American Evangelicals* (New York: Oxford University Press, 2018), 71.

52. Gloege, *Guaranteed Pure*, 2, 8, 104, 206.

53. For brief snapshot of the Corsicana discovery, see "First Texas Oil Boom," American Oil & Gas Historical Society, http://aoghs.org/petroleum-pioneers/texas-oil-boom (accessed June 2, 2017).

54. Quoted in Sanders, *Spindletop*, 110–111.

## Chapter Three: Dawn of the Gusher Age

1. Quoted in Sanders, *Spindletop*, 110–111; "Day at Beaumont," *GDN*, January 21, 1901, available at www.wtblock.com/WtblockJr/aday.htm (accessed January 2, 2017); Ruth Sheldon Knowles, *The Greatest Gamblers: The Epic of American Oil Exploration*, 2nd ed. (Norman: University of Oklahoma Press, 1978), 40.

2. "Beaumont Is Booming," *GDN*, reprinted in Sanders, *Spindletop*, 117; Knowles, *The Greatest Gamblers*, 38–39.

3. Quoted in Giebelhaus, *Business and Government*, 42.

4. JEP to JNP, April 8, 1904, "Beaumont, TX" Folder, Box 212, SOC, HLM.

5. Bobby D. Weaver, *Oilfield Trash: Life and Labor in the Oil Patch* (College Station: Texas A&M University Press, 2010), 6; *J. Edgar Pew, His Life and Times, 1870–1946* (Philadelphia: Sun Oil Company, 1947), 1; Samuel W. Tait Jr., *The Wildcatters: An Informal History of Oil-Hunting in America* (Princeton, NJ: Princeton University Press, 1946), 123. On field totals for 1902, see Robert Wooster and Christine Moor Sanders, "Spindletop Oilfield," Texas State Historical Association, June 15, 2010, modified July 26, 2016, https://tshaonline.org/handbook/online/articles/dos03 (accessed August 10, 2017).

6. William Joseph Philp, interview by William A. Owens, July 17, 1953 (Tape No. 110), 6; James William Kinnear, interview by William A. Owens, July 24, 1953 (Tape No. 108), 3, Box 3k21, OHTO, UTBC; Weaver, *Oilfield Trash*, 9–11.

7. An estimated 20,000 of these newcomers worked on Spindletop. Weaver, *Oilfield Trash*, 14; Mody C. Boatright and William A. Owens, *Tales from the Derrick Floor: A People's History of the Oil Industry* (New York: Doubleday & Company, 1970), 42, 181; James Anthony Clark, *Spindletop* (New York: Random House, 1952), 99.

8. O'Connor, *Oil Barons*, 79; Knowles, *The Greatest Gamblers*, 9, 37.

9. Quoted in Boatright and Owens, *Tales from the Derrick Floor*, 76, 187–188.

10. "Beaumont Is Booming"; Knowles, *The Greatest Gamblers*, 38–39; O'Connor, *Oil Barons*, 81, 86–87; R. T. Hill, "The Beaumont Oil Field," *Journal of the Franklin Institute* (August–October 1902): n.p.

11. O'Connor, *Oil Barons*, 67, 78.

12. Harold F. Williamson et al., *The Age of Energy, 1899–1959*, Vol. 2, *The American Petroleum Industry* (Evanston, IL: Northwestern University Press, 1963), 4–7; J. Edgar Pew, undated address to the American Society of Civil Engineers, Dallas, Texas, 1–4, "J. Edgar Pew Special Articles" Folder, SOC, HLM.

13. Travis L. Summerlin, "Cranfill, James Britton Buchanan Boone," Texas State Historical Association, June 12, 2010, https://tshaonline.org/handbook/online/articles/fcr07 (accessed June 2, 2017).

14. Giebelhaus, *Business and Government*, 43; letter from San Jacinto Oil Company, September 15, 1902, as well as returned stock options, for instance, Chas. M. Spinning to E. F. Allen, July 31, 1903; Office of J. W. Conger to Mr. J. B. Cranfill, March 2, 1903; J. B. Edmonson to Rev. J. B. Cranfill, May 5, 1903; Rev. H. T. Crand to W. V. Newlin, Esq., July 7, 1903, Folder 1, Box 1, SJCS, DPL.

15. Summerlin, "Cranfill."

16. Myrna I. Santiago, *The Ecology of Oil: Environment, Labor, and the Mexican Revolution, 1900–1938* (New York: Cambridge University Press, 2006), 6.

17. Bob Johnson, *Carbon Nation: Fossil Fuels in the Making of American Culture* (Lawrence: University Press of Kansas, 2014), 100. The transportation of oil, controlled by the Teamsters, would be an exception to the rule in the scale of its collective labor and relative openness to nonwhite haulers.

18. Neil Foley, *The White Scourge: Mexicans, Blacks, and Poor Whites in Texas Cotton Culture* (Berkeley: University of California Press, 1997), 4, 7; Robert Wuthnow, *Rough Country: How Texas Became America's Most Powerful Bible-Belt State* (Princeton, NJ: Princeton University Press, 2014), 68–69, 164; "At the Stake," *Arkansas Gazette*, February 21, 1892. For details, see E. R. Bills, *The 1910 Slocum Massacre: An Act of Genocide in East Texas* (Charleston, SC: History Press, 2014), esp. ch. 1.

19. Stiles, "Life and Reminiscences of W. F. Cummins," 62–63, 64, 87–89, WFC, UTBC.

20. Paul Harvey, "Religion, Race, and Culture in the American South," Oxford Research Encyclopedia of Religion, http://religion.oxfordre.com/view/10.1093/acrefore/9780199340378.001.0001/acrefore-9780199340378-e-7 (accessed July 10, 2017); Wuthnow, *Rough Country*, 164–165.

21. Ruth A. Allen, *Chapters in the History of Organized Labor in Texas* (Austin: University of Texas, 1912), 173, 208; Weaver, *Oilfield Trash*, 8; John Loos, *Oil on Stream! A History of Interstate Oil Pipe Line Company, 1909–1959* (Baton Rouge: Louisiana State University Press, 1959), 13; Philp interview (Tape No. 109), 28; Higgins interview (Tape No. 20), 11; Kinnear interview (Tape No. 108), 11, OHTO, UTBC; Carl B. King and Howard W. Risher Jr., "The Negro in the Petroleum Industry," Industrial Research Unit, *Wharton School of Finance and Commerce* (University of Pennsylvania, distributed by University of Pennsylvania Press, 1969), 26.

22. Loos, *Oil on Stream!*, 23; Kinnear interview (Tape No. 108), 6, OHTO, UTBC; Boatright and Owens, *Tales from the Derrick Floor*, 69.

23. Weaver, *Oilfield Trash*, 12; Kinnear interview (Tape No. 108), 6, OHTO, UTBC.

24. Edith Blumhofer, *Restoring the Faith: The Assemblies of God, Pentecostalism, and American Culture* (Champaign: University of Illinois Press, 1993), 53–54; Jarod Roll, "Faith Powers and Gambling Spirits in Late Gilded Age Metal Mining," in *Between the Pew and the Picket Line: Christianity and the American Working Class*, ed. Christopher D. Cantwell, Heath W. Carter, and Janine Giordano Drake (Champaign: University of Illinois Press, 2016), 77.

25. Gaston Espinosa, *William J. Seymour and the Origins of Global Pentecostalism: A Biography and Documentary History* (Durham, NC: Duke University Press, 2014), 55–57.

26. Philp interview (Tape No. 109), 17, OHTO, UTBC; Clark, *Spindletop*, 95.

27. Philp interview (Tape No. 109), 17–18, OHTO, UTBC.

28. Philp interview (Tape No. 109), 30, OHTO, UTBC.

29. Philp interview (Tape No. 109), 8, 13–14; Philp interview (Tape No. 110), 19, 21–22, OHTO, UTBC; Boatright and Owens, *Tales from the Derrick Floor*, 109.

30. William R. Estep, *And God Gave the Increase: The Centennial History of the First Baptist Church of Beaumont, Texas, 1872–1972* (Fort Worth, TX: Centennial Historical Committee, 1972), 70–74; O'Connor, *Oil Barons*, 80; Boatright and Owens, *Tales from the Derrick Floor*, 92; Philp interview (Tape No. 109), 21–22, OHTO, UTBC.

31. Judith Linsley and Ellen Rienstra, "Carroll, George Washington," Texas State Historical Association, June 12, 2010, https://tshaonline.org/handbook/online/articles/fcacb (accessed June 4, 2017); Kinnear interview (Tape No. 108), 3–4, OHTO, UTBC.

32. Quoted in Sanders, *Spindletop*, 147.

33. Higgins interview (Tape No. 21), 15, Box 3k21, OHTO, UTBC; "The Contributions of F. L. Carroll and George W. Carroll and Members of Their Families to Baylor University, Presented by John B. Fisher, an Ardent Admirer and Appreciative Beneficiary on the Occasion of the Annual Meeting of the Baylor Historical Society, 1949," TC, BUTC.

34. O'Connor, *Oil Barons*, 78.

35. Knowles, *The Greatest Gamblers*, 40; Boatright and Owens, *Tales from the Derrick Floor*, 187.

36. Sarah Ruth Hammond and Darren Dochuk, eds., *God's Businessmen: Entrepreneurial Evangelicals in Depression and War* (Chicago: University of Chicago Press, 2017), 16; Philp interview (Tape No. 109), 4, 10, Box 3k21, OHTO, UTBC.

37. O'Connor, *Oil Barons*, 78; Higgins interview (Tape No. 21), 7, 9–10, OHTO, UTBC.

38. McDaniel with Dethloff, *Patillo Higgins and the Search for Texas Oil*, 79–80. By 1908, Higgins was credited with surveying at least nine proven oil fields along the Gulf Coast.

39. McDaniel with Dethloff, *Patillo Higgins and the Search for Texas Oil*, 115.

40. "J. N. Pew: A Biographical Sketch," *Our Sun: 75th Anniversary Issue* (1961): 11, "Sun Oil—75th Anniversary, 1961" Folder, Box 55, SOC, HLM.

41. "J. N. Pew: A Biographical Sketch," 12, 17; Giebelhaus, *Business and Government*, 25–26, 28, 35.

42. Giebelhaus, *Business and Government*, 34–35; "1901–1912: Spindletop and the Rise of Sun," *Our Sun: 75th Anniversary Issue* (1961), 20, "Sun Oil—75th Anniversary, 1961" Folder, Box 55, SOC, HLM.

43. "1901–1912: Spindletop and the Rise of Sun," 20; quoted in Giebelhaus, *Business and Government*, 43.

44. O'Connor, *Oil Barons*, 75–78, 85; Knowles, *The Greatest Gamblers*, 41; Yergin, *The Prize*, 93; Giebelhaus, *Business and Government*, 34–35.

45. JEP to JNP, July 9, 18, and 26, 1902, "Beaumont, Texas—J. E. Pew—July 1902" Folder, Box 210; JEP to JNP, January 19 and 20, 1903, "Beaumont, Texas—J. E. Pew—Jan. 1903" Folder, Box 211; JEP to JNP, January 15, 1904, "Beaumont, Texas—J. E. Pew—Jan. 1904" Folder, Box 212; JEP to JNP, October 8, 1902, "Beaumont, Texas—J. E. Pew—Oct. 1902" Folder, Box 210; JEP to JNP, April 24, 1903, Beaumont, Texas—J. E. Pew—Apr. 1903" Folder, Box 211; JEP to JNP, March 6, 1903, "Beaumont, Texas—J. E. Pew—Mar. 1903" Folder, Box 211, SOC, HLM.

46. JEP to JNP, August 1, 1902, "Beaumont, Texas—J. E. Pew—July 1902" Folder, Box 210; "All from the Beaumont Enterprise," Folder 9, Company History Box, SOC, HLM.

47. McDaniel with Dethloff, *Patillo Higgins and the Search for Texas Oil*, 69; JEP to JNP, November 8, 1902, "Beaumont, Texas—J. E. Pew—Nov. 1902" Folder, Box 210; JEP to JNP, April 8, 1904, "Beaumont, Texas—J. E. Pew—Apr. 1904" Folder, Box 212, SOC, HLM.

48. JEP to JNP, April 8, 21, 23, and 25, 1904, "Beaumont, Texas—J. E. Pew—Apr. 1904" Folder, Box 212; JEP to JNP, March 31, 1904, "Beaumont, Texas—J. E. Pew—Mar. 1904" Folder, Box 212, SOC, HLM.

49. JEP to JNP, February 1, 1904, "Beaumont, Texas—J. E. Pew—Feb. 1904" Folder, Box 212, SOC; S. G. Burnett to JEP, January 18, 1917, and records of Pew's tithing, in "Central Presbyterian Church, Beaumont" Folder, Box 36, PFP, HLM.

50. Boatright and Owens, *Tales from the Derrick Floor*, 207; Weaver, *Oilfield Trash*, 27.

51. Giebelhaus, *Business and Government*, 40, 57; O'Connor, *Oil Barons*, 82–83.

52. Krivoshey, "'Going Through the Eye,'" 177.

53. Krivoshey, "'Going Through the Eye,'" 177, 187; Welty and Taylor, *The 76 Bonanza*, 139; LS to I. E. Blake, January 17, 1900; LS to Milton Stewart, December 13, 1900; LS to F. H. Rindge, June 22, 1901, LSP, BIOL.

54. Knowles, *The Greatest Gamblers*, 47–49, 48 (quote).

55. WLS to LS, September 12, 1901; Welty and Taylor, *The 76 Bonanza*, 139.

56. Krivoshey, "'Going Through the Eye,'" 201; Yergin, *The Prize*, 82.

57. LS to Edmont Doble, May 20, 1901; LS to P. D. McConnell, August 26, 1901, LSP, BIOL.

58. LS to children, September 4, 1914, LSP, BIOL; Pietsch, "Lyman Stewart and Early Fundamentalism," 625; estimate of Stewart's incoming requests drawn from Krivoshey, "'Going Through the Eye,'" 363.

59. LS to J. W. Baer, September 21, 1910; LS to MS, December 30, 1914; LS to Rev. George T. B. Davies, August 17, 1911; LS to MS, December 30, 1914; LS to Rev. George T. B. Davies, August 17, 1911, LSP, BIOL; quoted in Krivoshey, "'Going Through the Eye,'" 163, 168.

60. Quoted in Yergin, *The Prize*, 80–81. Statistics demonstrating Standard's relative slide and the growth of Texaco, Gulf, Union, and Sun Oil, as well as the similar profiles of the latter two, provided in several tables listed by Giebelhaus, *Business and Government*, 287–292.

61. Giebelhaus, *Business and Government*, 59–61; "The Story of Sun," *Our Sun: 75th Anniversary Issue*, 30–33, "Sun Oil—75th Anniversary, 1961" Folder, Box 55, SOC, HLM.

62. McDaniel with Dethloff, *Patillo Higgins and the Search for Texas Oil*, 93, 123–124, 133.

63. McDaniel with Dethloff, *Patillo Higgins and the Search for Texas Oil*, 98.

## Chapter Four: Trust Busting

1. Quoted in Weinberg, *Taking On the Trust*, 229; Ida Tarbell, "John D. Rockefeller: A Character Study, Part II," *McClure's Magazine*, August 1905, 391–392, 394, 396; Euclid Baptist Church bulletin, Tarbell notes, and church layout, October 11, 1903, in "IMT: All in the Day's Work: John D. Rockefeller" Folder, Box 53:4, ITC, ALC.

2. Quoted in Tarbell, "John D. Rockefeller," 395, 387, 386.

3. Weinberg, *Taking On the Trust*, 229; Brady, *Ida Tarbell*, 143–144.

4. Quoted in Weinberg, *Taking On the Trust*, 132, 138, 232–233.

5. Brady, *Ida Tarbell*, 52; Weinberg, *Taking On the Trust*, 132, 138; Tarbell, "My Religion," manuscript draft in "IMT: Autobiography" Folder, Box 53:4, ITC, ALC.

6. Tarbell, "My Religion," 2, 3, 5, ITC, ALC.

7. Tarbell, "My Religion," 6–7, 8, ITC, ALC.

8. Weinberg, *Taking On the Trust*, 3, 207.

9. Quoted in Weinberg, *Taking On the Trust*, 148, 159.

10. Weinberg, *Taking On the Trust*, 161; Tarbell, *The History of the Standard Oil Company*, xiii.

11. "Interview with Mr. Rogers," notes in "IMT: All in the Day's Work: Henry Rogers" Folder, Box 53:4, ITC, ALC; Doran, *Breaking Rockefeller*, 183.

12. Quoted in Doran, *Breaking Rockefeller*, 184–185; Brady, *Ida Tarbell*, 150; S. S. McClure to Ida Tarbell, April 6, 1903, General Correspondence, ITC, ALC.

13. Notes in "IMT: All in the Day's Work: Henry Rogers" Folder and "IMT: All in the Day's Work: John Rockefeller" Folder, Box 53:4, ITC, ALC.

14. Tarbell, *The History of the Standard Oil Company*, xvi; Tarbell, "My Religion," manuscript draft, 6–7, 8, "IMT: Autobiography" Folder, Box 53:4, ITC, ALC.

15. Walter Rauschenbusch, *Christianizing the Social Order* (New York: Macmillan, 1912), 366–367; "Gladden Again on Tainted Money," *LAH*, November 19, 1905; Gladden in Janette Thomas Greenwood, *The Gilded Age: A History in Documents* (New York: Oxford University Press, 2000), 26.

16. Thorstein Veblen, *The Theory of the Leisure Class: An Economic Study of American Institutions and a Social Critique of Conspicuous Consumption* (New York: Macmillan Company, 1899), 38; Harper in Flynn, *God's Gold*, 308.

17. LS to Mrs. H. M. N. Armstrong, May 2, 1911; LS to MS, July 3, 1911, LSP, BIOL.

18. Krivoshey, "'Going Through the Eye,'" 142, 177, 189, 197; LS to MS, April 26, 1901; WLS to LS, January 28, 1903, LSP, BIOL.

19. LS to WLS, July 18, 1905; Luther Conant Jr. to LS, October 17, 1907; LS to Union Oil Company, October 23, 1907, LSP, BIOL.

20. LS to MS, November 11, 1901; LS to Ida Tarbell, February 14, 1913, LSP, BIOL; Tarbell, *The History of the Standard Oil Company*, 20–21.

21. Quoted in Yergin, *The Prize*, 108.

22. Yergin, *The Prize*, 109; "Bryan Says Lawyers Aid Public Abuses," *NYT*, May 29, 1911, 3; Tarbell, *All in the Day's Work*, 253.

23. Independent producer quoted in Frank B. Kellogg, "Results of the Standard Oil Decision," *American Review of Reviews* 45 (January–June 1912), 728.

24. "Says Company Will Go On," *NYT*, May 16, 1911, 4; Yergin, *The Prize*, 110; quoted in Nevins, *John D. Rockefeller*, 605.

25. Yergin, *The Prize*, 113; Judith Sealander, *Private Wealth and Public Life: Foundation Philanthropy and the Reshaping of American Social Policy from the Progressive Era to the New Deal* (Baltimore: Johns Hopkins University Press, 1997), 221.

26. Rockefeller, *Some Random Reminiscences of Men and Events*, 14, 63, 65; JDR to H. C. Folger, April 22, 1909, "Standard Oil Company: Rockefeller Letters 4-22-1909" Folder, and February 19, 1909, "Standard Oil Company: Rockefeller Letters 2-19-1909" Folder, EMHC, UTBC.

27. Nevins, *John D. Rockefeller*, 604; Yergin, *The Prize*, 217.

28. Quoted in Nevins, *John D. Rockefeller*, 291; FTG to Dr. E. Benjamin Andrews, January 2, 1908, Folder 2, Box 1, FGP, RAC; Harr and Johnson, *Rockefeller Century*, 82.

29. JDR to Rev. D. L. Moody, September 26, 1897, and George Rogers to Rev. D. L. Moody, January 10, 1898, Moody-JDR Correspondence, N-Religious Interests, RFC; "Gates' Letter to Rockefeller," April 17, 1905, in Folder 5, Box 1, FGP, RAC.

30. D. T. Hinkley, "Industrial Betterment," *Social Gospel* 35 (January 1901): 13; "Engineering and the Millennium," *Methodist Review* 96 (January–February 1914): 42, 44.

31. Starr Murphy to JDRJr, May 17, 1906; FTG to JDR, May 10, 1905; James B. Ely to JDR, August 22, 1906; Starr Murphy to JDR, April 5, 1907, and June 1, 1908; Arthur J. Smith to JDR, April 9, 1909, Folder 364, Box 46, N-Religious Interests, RFC, RAC.

32. John Mott to JDR, June 8, 1911; John Mott to JDR, June 26, 1911; FTG to John Mott, July 21, 1913, Folder 365, Box 46, N-Religious Interests, RFC, RAC.

33. Daniel Gorman, *International Cooperation in the Early Twentieth Century* (New York: Bloomsbury Academic, 2017), 105–107. See Heather Curtis, *Holy Humanitarians: American Evangelicals and Global Aid* (Cambridge, MA: Harvard University Press, 2018).

34. "A Report and Message from Near East Relief to the Religious Bodies New York City 1924," Box 137, Vol. 1, NER; "Comments on NER by American Visitors to Region," "Near East Relief 1921–1923," Folder 100, Box 8, LRSM, RAC; James Barton, "Near East Foundation: A Twentieth Century Concept of Practical Philanthropy" (1931), Folder 35, Box 129, NER, RAC; Fosdick, *The Story of the Rockefeller Foundation*, 11, 15.

35. Sealander, *Private Wealth and Public Life*, 220, 223; Fosdick, *The Story of the Rockefeller Foundation*, 20.

36. Sealander, *Private Wealth and Public Life*, 2.

37. Raymond Fosdick, *John D. Rockefeller Jr.: A Portrait* (New York: Harper & Brothers, 1956), 11; Harr and Johnson, *Rockefeller Century*, 41, 87, 46, 49.

38. Quoted in Harr and Johnson, *Rockefeller Century*, 53.

39. Fosdick, *John D. Rockefeller Jr.*, 111–112; quoted in Harr and Johnson, *Rockefeller Century*, 61, 86.

40. Quoted in Fosdick, *The Story of the Rockefeller Foundation*, 33, 21–22.

41. John D. Rockefeller Jr., "The Christian Church: What of Its Future?," *SEP*, February 9, 1918, 3–4; Harr and Johnson, *Rockefeller Century*, 174.

42. "Committee on Cooperation in Latin America," November 18, 1915, and N. S. Richardson to Starr Murphy, November 26, 1915, Folder 371, Box 47, N-Religious Interests, RFC, RAC; Charles E. Harvey, "John D. Rockefeller Jr., and the Interchurch World Movement of 1919–1920: A Different Angle on the Ecumenical Movement," *Church History* 51, no. 2 (June 1982): 198; Harr and Johnson, *Rockefeller Century*, 176; Interchurch Movement initiative quoted in Fosdick, *John D. Rockefeller Jr.*, 207; see, for instance, W. A. Sunday to "Dear Friend John," July [n.d.], 1917, and JDR to Miss A. Adams, July 10, 1917, and JDR to William B. Miller, July 14, 1917, Folder 742, Box 91, N-Religious Interests, RFC, RAC.

43. William R. Hutchison, *The Modernist Impulse in American Protestantism* (Durham, NC: Duke University Press, 1992), 275; Gertrude Samuels, "Fosdick at 75—Still a Rebel," *NYT Sunday Magazine*, May 24, 1953, 3; Fosdick, "Shall the Fundamentalists Win?"

44. JDRJr. to Fosdick, January 13, 1933, Folder 558, Box 72, N-Religious Interests, RFC, RAC.

45. Krivoshey, "'Going Through the Eye,'" 207.

46. George M. Marsden, *Fundamentalism and American Culture: The Shaping of Twentieth-Century Evangelicalism, 1870–1925* (New York: Oxford University Press, 1980), 119; Gloege, *Guaranteed Pure*, 170–171, 188.

47. LS to MS, July 20, 1911, LSP, BIOL.

48. LS to MS, September 24, 1909, LSP, BIOL. Analysis here leans heavily on the insights of Gloege, *Guaranteed Pure*, 176–177.

49. James O. Henry, "Black Oil & Souls to Win," *The King's Business* (February 1958): 11–41; LS to Mrs. H. E. Butters, August 26, 1911; LS to MS, July 26, 1911, LSP, BIOL.

50. Pietsch, "Lyman Stewart and Early Fundamentalism," 619, 628; Krivoshey, "'Going Through the Eye,'" 363; Herbert Faulkner West, ed., *The Autobiography of Robert Watchorn* (Oklahoma City: Robert Watchorn Charities, Ltd., 1959), 164.

51. Stanley White to LS, March 15, 1909; LS to C. H. Stimson, July 17, 1913; LS to T. C. Horton, February 5, 1918, LSP, BIOL; Krivoshey, "'Going Through the Eye,'" 222; "Western Securities," *LAT*, January 25, 1925; Joseph Ezekiel Pogue, *The Economics of Petroleum* (New York: John Wiley & Sons, 1921), 73.

52. Fosdick, *The Story of the Rockefeller Foundation*, 81; Wallace Buttrick to Roger S. Greene, November 13, 1916, Folder 10, Box 1, FGP, RAC.

53. "The China Medical Board" (undated), 1, 8, Folder 10, Box 1, FGP, RAC; Fosdick, *The Story of the Rockefeller Foundation*, 84–84; David Rockefeller, *David Rockefeller Memoirs* (New York: Random House, 2002), 243–244.

54. Joel A. Carpenter, ed., "Introduction," *Fundamentalism in American Religion, 1880–1950* (New York: Garland Publishing, 1988), 3–6; Charles Trumbull, "Victorious Life Conferences in the Far East," *Sunday School Times*, May 1, 1920, 245–246; W. H. Griffith Thomas, "Modernism in China," *Princeton Theological Review* 19 (October 1921): 630–631, 669, 671.

55. Harry Emerson Fosdick, *The Living of These Days: The Autobiography of Harry Emerson Fosdick* (New York: Harper Chapel Books, 1967), 179–180; Miller, *Harry Emerson Fosdick*, 106–108; Harold Sheridan to Marion Sheridan, July 14, 1912, March 25, 1915, and April 25, 1915, Folder H, Box 79, MCS, NHHS.

56. William R. Hutchison, "Modernism and Missions: The Liberal Search for an Exportable Christianity, 1875–1935," in *The Missionary Enterprise in China and America*, ed. John K. Fairbank (Cambridge, MA: Harvard University Press, 1974), 126–131; Robert Moats Miller, *Harry Emerson Fosdick: Preacher, Pastor, Prophet* (New York: Oxford University Press, 1985), 106–109.

57. Harry Emerson Fosdick, "Shall the Fundamentalists Win?," *Christian Work* 102 (June 10, 1922): 718–719, 721–722; Fosdick, *The Living of These Days*, 145.

58. The critique of Fosdick's sermon was eventually published in pamphlet form: Clarence E. Macartney, *Shall Unbelief Win? A Reply to Dr. Fosdick* (Philadelphia: Wilbur Hanf, 1922). Harr and Johnson, *Rockefeller Century*, 178–179; Fosdick, *The Living of These Days*, 179–180; Miller, *Harry Emerson Fosdick*, 106–108; Harry Emerson Fosdick to John D. Rockefeller Jr., October 11, 1934, Folder 558, Box 72, N-Religious Interests, RFC, RAC.

59. Welty and Taylor, *The 76 Bonanza*, 180.

60. *SFE*, December 20, 1921; *LAE*, March 22, 1922.

61. Welty and Taylor, *The 76 Bonanza*, 187; *PW*, October 1923.

## Chapter Five: American Plans

1. Thomas Andrews, *Killing for Coal: America's Deadliest Labor War* (Cambridge, MA: Harvard University Press, 2010), 1, 4; Harr and Johnson, *Rockefeller Century*, 129; quoted in F. A. McGregor, *The Fall and Rise of Mackenzie King* (Toronto: Macmillan, 1962), 96; "Battle Is Raging at Bayonne, N.J." and "Police in Fight with Striking Workmen," *ADN*, July 21, 1915, 1.

2. "Nitro Blows Up Home of Oil Man," *TW*, October 30, 1917, 1, 6.

3. "Nitro Blows Up Home of Oil Man," 6; "Grilling Fails Cause Powers Change[s] Story," *TW*, October 31, 1917, 1; "IWW Members Flogged, Tarred, and Feathered," *TW*, November 10, 1917, 1; "Bleeding Backs Given Coat of Tar," *AC*, November 11, 1917, 6; "The 'Knights of Liberty' Mob and the IWW Prisoners at Tulsa, Okla.," published by the National Civil Liberties Bureau, February 1918; Nigel Anthony Sellars, *Oil, Wheat, and Wobblies: The Industrial Workers of the World in Oklahoma, 1905–1930* (Norman: University of Oklahoma Press, 1998), 108–109.

4. Sellars, *Oil, Wheat, and Wobblies*, 108. Note: this stems from a report done by an investigator hired by the IWW. Its accuracy seems corroborated by state officials, though police claimed they could not identify the robed and hooded men in attendance at this terrorizing event.

5. "Dynamite Bomb for J. D. Archbold," *NYT*, November 22, 1915, 1.

6. Donald E. Winters, *The Soul of the Wobblies: The IWW, Religion, and American Culture in the Progressive Era, 1905–1917* (New York: Praeger, 1985), 133. The history of this age of bombs and riots in New York is told in Beverly Gage, *The Day Wall Street Exploded: A Story of America in Its First Age of Terror* (New York: Oxford University Press, 2009).

7. On nineteenth-century workers' commitment to a "radical Jesus," see David Burns, *The Life and Death of the Radical Jesus* (New York: Oxford University Press, 2013), and Heath W. Carter, *Union Made: Working People and the Rise of Social Christianity in Chicago* (New York: Oxford University Press, 2015), 4; quoted in Winters, *The Soul of the Wobblies*, 133; Stanislaus Cullen, "The Proletaire," *Industrial Worker*, July 23, 1910, 2; Walker P. Smith, "The God of Our Masters," *Industrial Worker*, July 2, 1910. See Richard J. Callahan Jr., *Work and Faith in the Kentucky Coal Fields: Subject to Dust* (Bloomington, IN: Indiana University Press, 2008), esp. 176–179, for discussion of labor and religion in the 1930s.

8. William D. Haywood, *The Autobiography of Big Bill Haywood* (New York: International Publishers, 1929), 181; Sellars, *Oil, Wheat, and Wobblies*, 15; Winter, *The Soul of the Wobblies*, 4, 19.

9. Emma Goldman, *Living My Life: Two Volumes in One* (New York: Alfred A. Knopf, 1931), 523; "Militia to Quell Bayonne Rioters: 1 Dead, Many Hurt," *NYT*, July 22, 1915, 1; Tannenbaum quoted and accounted for in Matthew G. Yeager, *Frank Tannenbaum: The Making of a Convict Criminologist* (New York: Routledge, 2016), 9, 20, 22–23.

10. "Militia to Quell Bayonne Rioters," 1; Frank Tannenbaum, *The Labor Movement* (New York: G. P. Putnam's Sons, 1921), 92; "Sheriff Captures Police for Strike," *NYT*, July 27, 1915, 1; "10,000 Oil Workers Get Wage Increase," *NYT*, November 29, 1916, 1.

11. Harvey O'Connor, *History of Oil Workers Intl. Union (CIO)* (Denver: Published by the Oil Workers Intl. Union, A. B. Hirschfeld Press, 1950), 4; Grady L. Mullennix, "A History of the Labor Movement in the Oil Industry" (MS thesis, North Texas State Teachers College, 1942), 10; Allen, *Chapters in the History of Organized Labor in Texas*, 222.

12. Allen, *Chapters in the History of Organized Labor in Texas*, 222–223.

13. Yergin, *The Prize*, 12; Stiles, "Life and Reminiscences of W. F. Cummins," 177, WFC, UTBC; Everette L. DeGolyer, memorandum, "Instructions for Geologic and Topographic Work of the Cia. Mex. De Petroleo, 'El Aguila,' S.A.," March 16, 1912, Folder 5347, Box 114, ELD, SMUD; Howard F. Cline, *The United States and Mexico* (Cambridge, MA: Harvard University Press, 1961), 211, 418; Linda B. Hall, *Oil, Banks, and Politics: The United States and Postrevolutionary Mexico, 1917–1924* (Austin: University of Texas Press, 1995), 13.

14. O'Connor, *History of Oil Workers Intl. Union*, 5–6, 11; James C. Maroney, "The Texas Louisiana Oil Field Strike of 1917," in *Essays in Southern Labor History* (Westport, CT: Greenwood Press, 1976), 163.

15. Maroney, "The Texas-Louisiana Oil Field Strike of 1917," 164; Sellars, *Oil, Wheat, and Wobblies*, 9–10.

16. "Pastor Scores IWW Enemies," *Daily Republican*, January 1, 1923, and George P. West, "Bishop Scores Syndicalist Law," undated newspaper clip, both in "Scrapbook on Criminal Syndicalism" Folder, Box 151, HOC, WRLA; Oscar Ameringer and A. C. Walker quoted in James R. Green, *Grassroots Socialism: Radical Movements in the Southwest, 1895–1943* (Baton Rouge: Louisiana State University Press, 1978), 153, 308.

17. Winter, *The Soul of the Wobblies*, 6, 11, 38; E. J. Hobsbawm, *Primitive Rebels: Studies in Archaic Forms of Social Movement in the 19th and 20th Centuries* (Manchester, UK: Manchester University Press, 1959), 57.

18. Melvyn Dubofsky, *We Shall Be All* (New York: Quadrangle Press, 1969), 154; James Jones, *From Here to Eternity* (New York: Charles Scribner's Sons, 1952), 640.

19. "IWW Members Flogged, Tarred, and Feathered," 1.

20. Patrick Renshaw, *The Wobblies: The Story of Syndicalism in the United States* (New York: Doubleday and Co., 1967), 238.

21. O'Connor, *History of Oil Workers Intl. Union*, 13, 15; R. H. Stickel to Alvin H. Scaff, August 17, 1936, "Classified Files on Labor: Occupations: Oil Workers: Correspondence, 1936–1941" Folder, and "Oil Workers Union: Membership," "Classified Files on Labor: Occupations: Oil Workers: Contract, 1936" Folder, both in Box 2E308, LMIT, UTBC.

22. Stickel to Scaff, August 17, 1936, "Classified Files on Labor: Occupations: Oil Workers: Correspondence, 1936–1941" Folder, Box 2E308, LMIT, UTBC; O'Connor, *History of Oil Workers Intl. Union*, 18.

23. Quoted in Jonathan H. Rees, *Representation and Rebellion: The Rockefeller Plan at the Colorado Fuel and Iron Company, 1914–1942* (Boulder: University of Colorado Press, 2015), 5.

24. Rees, *Representation and Rebellion*, 2, 24; "The Colorado Industrial Plan and Memorandum of Agreement," 1916, 63; Rockefeller quoted in Harr and Johnson, *Rockefeller Century*, 181.

25. Frederick Gates, "Capital and Labor," 1, Folder 9, Box 1, FGP. Although unsigned, the essay was presumably authored by Gates.

26. Frederick T. Gates, "The Struggle for Industrial Freedom," May 20, 1914, as quoted in Raymond Fosdick draft, Folder 507, Box 58, RG 2, JJrPP, RAC.

27. For a sample of William Lyon Mackenzie King's social gospel sentiments and church affiliation, see diary entry, March 7, 1915, WLM, LAC; Harr and Johnson, *Rockefeller Century*, 130–131, King quote, 133; Rockefeller quoted in McGregor, *The Fall and Rise of Mackenzie King*, 190.

28. William Lyon Mackenzie King, diary entry, February 20, 1915, WLM, LAC; Harr and Johnson, *Rockefeller Century*, 140–141, 144.

29. "Raymond B. Fosdick Dies at 89; Headed Rockefeller Foundation," *NYT*, July 19, 1972, 41; Harr and Johnson, *Rockefeller Century*, 160.

30. RF to W. L. Mackenzie King, September 19, 1919, and W. L. Mackenzie King to RF, October 13, 1919, Folder 3, Box 22, RBFP, PUFL; quoted in Harr and Johnson, *Rockefeller Century*, 182, 183. On Riverside Church's welcoming of this doctrine, RF to JDRJr., February 5, 1931, Folder 3, Box 22, RBFP, PUFL.

31. Harr and Johnson, *Rockefeller Century*, 183.

32. "Information for Employees," Carter Oil Company, 1–2, 3–5, "Labor—1954" Folder, Box 81, HOC, WRLA.

33. Benedum-Trees corporate compound at Trees City is documented in BOI, CUBL. For overview, see also Henry Alexander Wiencek, "Oil City: The Social, Economic and Environmental Anatomy of North Louisiana's Oil Boomtowns, 1901–1935" (PhD diss., University of Texas, 2017), 91–92; Weaver, *Oilfield Trash*, 84, 112; "Oil Towns Yesterday," *The Lamp*, January 1947, 13, "Oil Magazines" Folder, Box 2G190, WBS, UTBC.

34. Timothy Mitchell, *Carbon Democracy: Political Power in the Age of Oil* (New York: Verso, 2013), 8; "C.I.O. Drive Gaining Oil Workers Are Told," undated clipping (1937), and "C.I.O. Oil Union to Start Drive in East Texas," unknown newspaper clipping (November 2, 1937); "A Report on the Texas State Federation of Labor Convention and an Interpretation of the Condition of the Federation" (May 1937), "Subject, Classified Files on Labor" Folder, Box 2E208, LMIT, UTBC.

35. Estha Briscoe Stowe, *Oil Field Child* (Fort Worth: Texas Christian University Press, 1989), xv, 5, 8, 42.

36. Stowe, *Oil Field Child*, 90, 94, 100.

37. Stowe, *Oil Field Child*, 49, 88–89.

38. The Spikes episode and quotation are drawn from Wiencek, "Oil City," 89–90.

39. Robert S. Lynd, "Crude-Oil Religion," *HM*, September 1922, 427, 429, 431.

40. Giebelhaus, *Business and Government*, 60.

41. JEP to B. C. Dale, February 13, 1920, and J. H. Williams to JEP, March 16, 1920, "YMCA in the Oil Fields" Folder, Box 34; JEP to Herbert M. Harrison, "American Petroleum Institute 1919–1928" Folder, Box 40; E. J. Gorman to JEP, July 11, 1933, Folder 71, Box 79, SOC, HLM; Giebelhaus, *Business and Government*, 91, 92.

42. "An Album of Sun Memories," *Our Sun: 75th Anniversary Issue*, "Sun Oil—75th Anniversary, 1961" Folder, Box 55, SOC, HLM.

43. M. N. Sweeney to JEP, June 13, 1919, and JEP to JHP, June 14, 1919, "Oil Fields Store" Folder, Box 34; R. Ray McGrew to JEP, August 20, 1919; W. B. Pyron to JEP, March 21, 1919; "Statement of Receipts and Disbursements, YMCA Fund, June 5, 1919

to April 7, 1920"; "Night School at Olden YMCA"; "Report of Activities for March, 1920"; JEP to "Gentlemen," April 8, 1920, "YMCA in the Oil Fields" Folder, Box 34, SOC, HLM.

44. Davis background and quote drawn from Luling Foundation overview, available at "Edgar B. Davis," Luling Foundation, www.lulingfoundation.org/about/edgar-b-davis (accessed October 2, 2017); Davis paraphrased at "Davis, Edgar Byram," Texas State Historical Association, June 12, 2010, https://tshaonline.org/handbook/online/articles /fda36 (accessed October 2, 2017); quotes from John Nova Lomax, "Edgar Byram Davis, Luling's Wildcatter and Philanthropist," *TM*, www.texasmonthly.com/energy /edgar-byram-davis-lulings-wildcatter-philanthropist (accessed October 2, 2017); album in UNSD, UTBC.

45. Nova Lomax, "Edgar Byram Davis, Luling's Wildcatter and Philanthropist"; Chuck Parsons, *Luling: Images of America* (Charleston, SC: Arcadia Publishing, 2009), 101; quoted in Gene Fowler, *Mavericks: A Gallery of Texas Characters* (Austin: University of Texas Press, 2008), 137.

46. E. J. Gorman to JEP, July 11, 1933, Folder 71, Box 79, SOC, HLM; Larry J. Frazier, "Adjustments and Responses of Southern Baptist Churches in East Texas to the East Texas Oil Boom of the 1930s" (PhD diss., Baylor University, 2002), 232.

47. Yergin, *The Prize*, 208–209.

48. Yergin, *The Prize*, 209.

49. "Deny Agreement to Fix Oil Prices," *NYT*, December 23, 1922, 20; "Standard Explains Gasoline Advance," *NYT*, July 2, 1922, 25; La Follette in Yergin, *The Prize*, 211.

50. Entry for June 20, 1917, in *The Cabinet Diaries of Josephus Daniels, 1913–1921* (Lincoln: University of Nebraska Press, 1963), 167.

51. "Oil Towns Re-create the Old West," *NYT*, June 24, 1923, SM11.

52. For statistics on guardians, see Molly Stephey, "The Osage Murders: Oil Wealth, Betrayal and the FBI's First Big Case," NMAI, March 1, 2011, http://blog.nmai.si.edu /main/2011/03/the-osage-murders-oil-wealth-betrayal-and-the-fbis-first-big-case.html (accessed October 1, 2017); Gertrude Bonnin, Charles H. Fabens, and Matthew K. Sniffen, *Oklahoma's Poor Rich Indians: An Orgy of Graft and Exploitation of the Five Civilized Tribes—Legalized Robbery* (Philadelphia: Office of the Indian Rights Association, 1924), 5, 6; "Osage Oil Leases Under the Hammer," *NYT*, March 17, 1924, 27; Associated Press, "Advance for AMS of Sunday, Jan. 27," TC, BUTC; "Courts End Osage Indian 'Reign of Terror,'" *NYT*, January 17, 1926, XX4; "Hale Found Guilty of Osage Murder," *NYT*, January 27, 1929, 20. For a full account, see David Grann, *Killers of the Flower Moon: The Osage Murders and the Birth of the FBI* (New York: Doubleday, 2017).

53. Daniels in O'Connor, *Oil Barons*, 246; "Teapot Dome Casts a Broad Shadow," *NYT*, January 27, 1924, XX1.

54. "Teapot Dome Casts a Broad Shadow," XX1; Yergin, *The Prize*, 214–216.

55. Lauren Coodley, *Upton Sinclair: California Socialist, Celebrity Intellectual* (Lincoln: University of Nebraska Press, 2013), 43–44, 46, 90, 92; Mary Craig, *Southern Belle* (Jackson: University of Mississippi Press, 1999), 301.

56. Upton Sinclair, *Oil!* (New York: Penguin Books, 2007), 177, 488.

57. Sinclair, *Oil!*, 150, 159, 183, 221, 299, 380, 439, 496, 539.

58. "Socialist Doctrine," *NYT*, May 8, 1927, 22.

59. Sinclair, *Oil!*, 548.

60. Yergin, *The Prize*, 216–217.

61. R. L. Welch to JEP, August 5, 1919; R. L. Welch to JEP, June 17, 1919, "American Petroleum Institute 1919–1928" Folder, Box 40, SOC, HLM; Giebelhaus, *Business and Government*, 127.

62. Giebelhaus, *Business and Government*, 125, 126; "Announcement of Semi-annual API Standardization Conference," June 15–17, 1927, "American Petroleum Institute–August 1926–April 1927" Folder, Box 41; JEP to JHP, September 17, 1927, "J. Howard Pew—May 1927–June 1928" Folder, Box 22, SOC, HLM; "API Past Living Presidents," *NPN*, October 30, 1946, 53.

63. Giebelhaus, *Business and Government*, 130, 131, 135; "Investigators Warn President of Waning Oil Supply for Future," *NYT*, September 6, 1926, 1; JHP to Mark Requa, November 20, 1925, A, "Administrative" Folder, Box 23; JHP to JEP, June 1, 1927; JEP to JHP, May 26, 1927, "J. Howard Pew May 1927–June 1928" Folder, Box 22, SOC, HLM.

64. Giebelhaus, *Business and Government*, 128; JHP to JEP, May 23, 1924, "J. Howard Pew November 1923–May 1924" Folder, Box 22; JEP to C. D. Keene, June 25, 1924; JEP to R. L. Welch, May 19, 1924; JEP to Hollis S. Reavis, May 20, 1924, "American Petroleum Institute 1924–26" Folder, Box 40, SOC, HLM.

65. "Report: General Committee on Code of Ethics," "API-Cte on Code of Ethics in Oil Industry" Folder, Box 38; "P.R. Report of Activities," addressed to Mr. W. R. Boyd Jr., "The Oil Industry To-Day," and "The Open Road?," "API Public Relations" Folder, Box 42, SOC, HLM.

66. JEP to Hollis S. Reavis, May 20, 1924, "American Petroleum Institute 1924–26" Folder, Box 40; see clips titled "Important Development in Business Methods to Be Applied in Production and Marketing of Petroleum," "Washington's Early Adventures in New Historic View," "Panama and Suez Canals in Close Race for World Leadership," and "Petroleum No Longer Used to Perform Miracles in Far East" in "Tulsa Relations" Folder, Box 42, SOC, HLM. The phrase "lifeblood of the nation" first entered the American lexicon around this time. One historian attributes it to a 1933 statement by Harold Ickes, Franklin D. Roosevelt's secretary of the interior. See Sebastian Herbstreuth, *Oil and American Identity: A Culture of Dependency and the Impact on US Foreign Policy* (New York: I. B. Tauris, 2016), 36.

67. Barton, "The Magic of Gasoline," quoted in Kendall Beaton, *Enterprise in Oil: A History of Shell in the United States* (New York: Appleton-Century-Crofts, Inc., 1957), 267–268.

68. Ross Barrett, "Picturing a Crude Past: Primitivism, Public Art, and Corporate Oil Promotion in the United States," in *Oil Culture*, ed. Ross Barrett and Daniel Worden (Minneapolis: University of Minnesota Press, 2014), 60; signs and Shell service quoted in Yergin, *The Prize*, 210.

69. "Information for Employees," Carter Oil Company, 31; sampling of themes found in a partially compete series of *The Lamp* stem from a survey of issues produced in the 1940s, available in "Oil Magazines" Folder, Box 2G190, WBS; "Gulf-Grams" and *The Orange Disc* clippings, undated (likely from late 1920s or early 1930s), "Gulf Oil, Labor" Folder, Box 76, HOC, WRLA; "Torch Bearers" section appears in issues of Indiana Standard's (Amoco) *Torch and Oval* magazine, Folder 4–7, Box 2.75, LJB, JHU.

70. On the popularity of *The Lamp*, see "*The Lamp* Bids Farewell," ExxonMobil, http://corporate.exxonmobil.com/en/company/multimedia/the-lamp/the-lamp-bids-farewell (accessed November 1, 2017).

71. Lynd, "Crude-Oil Religion," 434.

72. Lynd, "Crude-Oil Religion," 434; "Done in Oil," *Survey* 49 (November 1, 1922), 136–146; Charles E. Harvey, "Robert S. Lynd, John D. Rockefeller Jr., and Middletown," *Indiana Magazine of History* 79 (December 1983): 331–332.

## Chapter Six: Fightin' Oil

1. Roger M. Olien and Diana Davids Hinton, *Wildcatters: Texas Independent Oilmen* (College Station: Texas A&M University Press, 2007), 36; Yergin, *The Prize*, 245.

2. James A. Clark, *The Last Boom* (Fredericksburg, TX: Shearer Publishing, 1984), 4, 31–32; Yergin, *The Prize*, 245; Dennis McCarthy, "Prominent Neighbors: Daisy Bradford," *CTT*, January 29, 1933, 5, Clippings File, TC, BUTC.

3. Mrs. H. C. Miller interview, Box 2A20, OHTO, UTBC, also in Boatright and Owens, *Tales from the Derrick Floor*, 57–58; Lucile Silvey Beard, "The History of the East Texas Oil Field" (MA thesis, Hardin-Simmons University, 1938), 35.

4. Harry Harter, *East Texas Oil Parade* (San Antonio, TX: Naylor Company, 1934), 70–73; Ruel McDaniel, *Some Ran Hot* (Dallas, TX: Regional Press, 1939), 9; Olien and Davids Hinton, *Wildcatters*, 56–57.

5. McCarthy, "Prominent Neighbors"; Clark, *The Last Boom*, 67; Brad Mills, "East Texas Ranks High," *OW* 81, no. 4 (February 17, 1936), 17–25; "A Decade of East Texas," *OW* 99, no. 5 (October 7, 1940); David F. Prindle, *Petroleum Politics and the Texas Railroad Commission* (Austin: University of Texas Press, 1981), 21.

6. Guthrie letter, no title, Box 1, Folder 4, Box 1, WGM, LOC.

7. Guthrie letter; Lawrence Goodwyn, *Texas Oil, American Dreams*, 34–36, 38; Carl Coke Rister, *Oil! Titan of the Southwest* (Norman: University of Oklahoma Press, 1949), 306–311; Bryan Burrough, *The Big Rich: The Rise and Fall of the Greatest Texas Oil Fortunes* (New York: Penguin Press, 2009), 75; Lawrence Goodwyn, "East Texas: Thirty Years Later," *TIPRO Reporter* (March–April 1960), 11–15; Weaver, *Oilfield Trash*, 95; Mrs. E. H. Spear, interviewed by Bobby H. Johnson, Box 2A23, OHTO, UTBC; Department of Commerce, Bureau of the Census, *Abstract of the Fifteenth Census of the United States* ([Washington, DC]: US Department of Commerce, Bureau of the Census, 1933), 16, 42, 49, 507–509; Department of Commerce, Bureau of the Census, *Fifteenth Census of the United States: 1930*, Vol. 3: *Population* ([Washington, DC]: US Department of Commerce, Bureau of the Census, 1932), 1036, 1037, 1047, 1050; Department of Commerce, Bureau of the Census, *Sixteenth Census of the United States: 1940*, Vol. 2: *Population* ([Washington, DC]: US Department of Commerce, Bureau of the Census, 1943), 869, 870, 880, 883; Department of Commerce, Bureau of the Census, *Sixteenth Census of the United States: 1940*, Vol. 1: *Population* ([Washington, DC]: US Department of Commerce, Bureau of the Census, 1942), 42, 1042.

8. "Kilgore Continues to Grow Rapidly as Oil Boom Unabated," *TMT*, May 2, 1931, 2; press clipping, March 23, 1933, Clippings File, TC, BUTC; Weaver, *Oilfield Trash*, 95; L. D. Winfrey, interviewed by Mrs. Robert A. Montgomery, August 2, 1959, and N. L. Field, interviewed by Bobby H. Johnson, August 20, 1970, Box 2A23, OHTO, UTBC.

9. Terry G. Jordan, John L. Bean Jr., and William M. Holmes, *Texas: A Geography* (Boulder, CO: Westview Press, 1984), 91; Scot McFarlane, "The Oil Boom's Roots in East Texas Cotton Farming," *TM*, November 1, 2017, www.texasmonthly.com/energy/oil-booms-roots-east-texas-cotton-farming (accessed December 14, 2018). See also Wallace Scot McFarlane, "Oil on the Farm: The East Texas Oil Boom and the Origins of an Energy Economy," *Journal of Southern History* 83 (November 2017): 853–888.

10. Harter, *East Texas Oil Parade*, 76; Frehner, *Finding Oil*, 7–9; O. W. Killam interview, Box 2A20, OHTO, UTBC; Boatright and Owens, *Tales from the Derrick Floor*, 19–20.

11. Frehner, *Finding Oil*, 23; Boatright and Owens, *Tales from the Derrick Floor*, 16, 20–26.

12. Goodwyn, *Texas Oil, American Dreams*, 36–37; Olien and Davids Hinton, *Wildcatters*, 58–59.

13. Henrietta M. Larson and Kenneth Wiggins Porter, *History of Humble Oil and Refining Company* (New York: Harper and Brothers, 1959), 355–362; Bob Duncan, *The Dicky Bird Was Singing: Men, Women and Black Gold* (New York: Rinehart & Co., 1952), 5; Burrough, *The Big Rich*, 73–75; Yergin, *The Prize*, 248.

14. "Church Lot Well Comes in Producer," unknown newspaper clipping, March 25, 1931, Clippings File, Box 3L425, ECB, UTBC.

15. "Church Lot Well Comes in Producer"; Wuthnow, *Rough Country*, 208.

16. E. P. Alldredge, *Southern Baptist Handbook, 1930* (Nashville: Sunday School Board of the Southern Baptist Convention, 1930), 206, 303, 304; *Southern Baptist Handbook, 1940* (Nashville: Sunday School Board of the Southern Baptist Convention, 1940), 280, 320; Frazier, "Adjustments and Responses of Southern Baptist Churches," 4; "Dr. Porter M. Bailes Celebrates Third Anniversary as Pastor of First Baptist Church Here Today," *CTT,* May 1, 1932, 8. White Protestant educational institutions of various affiliations benefitted from Depression-era oil money; for some smaller institutions, that influx determined their very survival. A case in point is John Brown University, whose key donors included Murray Sells, founder of Sells Petroleum Company, whose drilling near Longview made him rich, and Jesse H. Jones, whose stocks in Humble Oil supplemented his fortune and allowed him to give generously. John Brown Sr., "A Statement to the Board of the John Brown Schools," June 23, 1941, "John Brown Correspondence" Folder; "A Tribute," *John Brown University Bulletin,* July 1951, "Bulletin" Folder, JBSF, JBU. See Oral Memoirs of Joseph Martin Dawson, Baylor University Program for Oral History, 112, TC, BUTC; James A. Clark, *Marrs McLean: A Biography* (Houston, TX: Clark Book Co., Inc., 1969), 130–131; Pat M. Neff, "The Building of a Bigger and Better Baylor University," n.d., "Purpose and Magnitude" Folder, Box 2E224J, PPNP, BUTC.

17. Bill C. Malone, "'Sing Me Back Home': Growing Up in the South and Writing the History of Its Music," in *Shapers of Southern History: Autobiographical Reflections*, ed. John B. Boles (Athens: University of Georgia Press, 2004), 93, 98–99.

18. Wuthnow, *Rough Country*, 208.

19. "Black Mammy's Neighbors Jubilant as Oil Enriches Her," *DMN*, March 21, 1931. See also "Oil Institute Staff Enjoys Ranch Party," *DMN*, December 11, 1932, Clippings File, TC, BUTC.

20. "Joy and Woe Curiously Mingle Where Oil Flows, Is Opinion of Man Who Went thru Etex Boom," *Tyler Journal*, March 3, 1933, Clippings File, TC, BUTC; Edward J. Robinson, *Show Us How You Do It: Marshall Keeble and the Rise of Black Churches of Christ in the United States, 1914–1968* (Tuscaloosa: University of Alabama Press, 2008), 63.

21. Jonathan D. Greenberg, *Staking a Claim: Jake Simmons and the Making of an African-American Oil Dynasty* (New York: Penguin Books, 1990), 78–80, 103–104.

22. Greenberg, *Staking a Claim*, 107; Jake Simmons Jr. (1901–1981), Encyclopedia of Oklahoma History & Culture (Oklahoma Historical Society), https://www.okhistory.org/publications/enc/entry.php?entry-SI004 (accessed December 12, 2018).

23. "Joy and Woe Curiously Mingle Where Oil Flows."

24. "Refinery Blast Kills 2, Injures 10," unknown newspaper clipping, June 30, 1934; "Oil Changes Southwest Map," unknown newspaper clipping, May 26, 1930, Clippings File, TC, BUTC.

25. John R. Abernathy, *"Catch 'em Alive Jack": The Life and Adventures of an American Pioneer*. Reprint with introduction by Jon T. Coleman (Lincoln: University of Nebraska Press, 2006), 218–223, 224.

26. Abernathy, *"Catch 'em Alive Jack,"* 224.

27. Limbert, *In the Time of Oil*, 9–10; Reinhart Hoselleck, *The Practice of Conceptual History: Timing History, Spacing Concept* (Palo Alto, CA: Stanford University Press, 2002), 120.

28. Fred Barlow, "A Brief Biography of Dr. John R. Rice, Giant of Evangelism," *Sword of the Lord* (September 22, 2006); Robert L. Sumner, *Man Sent from God: A Biography of Dr. John R. Rice* (Grand Rapids, MI: Eerdmans Publishing Company, 1959); E. C. Fuqua, "The Norris-Wallace Debate: A Reply to 'The Fundamentalist,'" *Bible Banner* 13 (July/August 1944), 75–75; W. E. Brightwell, "The Man Who Came Back," *Gospel Advocate* 79 (May 6, 1937): 425.

29. "Explosion at Consolidated School New London, Tex.: Report on Investigation of Explosion at Consolidated School, New London, Tex., March 18, 1937" (presented by Mr. Connally to US Congress, April 14, 1937), 1, 4–5, LOC; Frazier, "Adjustments and Responses of Southern Baptist Churches," 220–221, 226–227.

30. "Explosion at Consolidated School New London," 9; Frazier, "Adjustments and Responses of Southern Baptist Churches," 220–221; "Walter Cronkite Remembers," http://nlsd.net/Recollections05.htm (accessed February 15, 2014).

31. See School of Landrecies letter, March 23, 1937; Governor Allred to Prof. Antonio G. Alvarado et al., April 9, 1937; letter from embassy, Tokyo, April 16, 1937, New London School Explosion, "General Correspondence 1937" File, Box 1985/024-22, JVA, TSA; Frazier, "Adjustments and Responses of Southern Baptist Churches," 224–228; quoted in White, "Drilling for Trouble," 14; "Text of Memorial Address by Rev. Jackson," *KDN*, March 29, 1937, 3; quoted in Roger M. Olien and Diana Davids Olien, *Oil and Ideology: The Cultural Creation of the American Petroleum Industry* (Chapel Hill: University of North Carolina Press, 2000), 192; "An Unprecedented Horror," *BS*, March 25, 1937, 3; W. T. Bratton, "New London Tragedy," *BS*, April 1, 1937, 5; "America Still Is . . . America," *HT*, March 25, 1937, 2.

32. Yergin, *The Prize*, 250; William R. Childs, *The Texas Railroad Commission: Understanding Regulation in America to the Mid-Twentieth Century* (College Station: Texas A&M University Press, 2005), 315–316.

33. Harter, *East Texas Oil Parade*, 103, 120–123; untitled press release from Henderson, Texas, October 31, 1932; untitled press release from Longview, Texas, November 2, 1932, Clippings File, TC, BUTC.

34. "Tyler Editor Sees Oil Theft with Own Eyes," *CTT*, May 1, 1932; "Investigation Launched: Millions of Barrels and Three Score Persons Are Involved in Giant Fraud," *DMN*, May 2, 1932, Clippings File, TC, BUTC.

35. "Methodists Told Church Can Help End Depression," *DMN*, November 13, 1931; *LDN*, February 8, 1931, 5; "Oilfield Memorial Baptist Church," *KDN*, November 7, 1931, 4. For an overview, see also Frazier, "Adjustments and Responses of Southern Baptist Churches," 229–230.

36. Cyclone Davis, *Memoir* (Sherman, TX: Courier Press, 1935), 45; Donald W. Whisenhut, "The Bard in the Depression: Texas Style," *Journal of Popular Culture* 2 (1968): 370–372.

37. McDaniel, *Some Ran Hot*, 15; Norman Emanuel Nordhauser, "The Quest for Stability: Domestic Oil Policy, 1919–1935" (PhD diss., Stanford University, 1970), 98; Gerald D. Nash, *United States Oil Policy, 1890–1964: Business and Government in Twentieth Century America* (Pittsburg, PA: University of Pittsburgh Press, 1968), 115.

38. Alan Brinkley, *Voices of Protest: Huey Long, Father Coughlin, and the Great Depression* (New York: Vintage Books, 1982), 24–25; "Thirty Pieces of Silver," *TMT*, October 18, 1932, Clippings File, TC, BUTC. W. Lee "Pappy" O'Daniel especially knew how to speak the language of Huey Long and evangelical populism. "As your servant," the latter liked to say, "I am happy to stand at the helm of this ship of Texas in turbulent waters . . . so we may

sail peacefully to that Port of Happiness and Prosperity for the Great Masses of Common Citizens," ever "bearing in mind, that all these noble ambitions and desires cannot materialize without the Blessings and generosity of the Creator of all things." Governor W. Lee O'Daniel Radio Broadcast, August 6, 1939, Radio Broadcast Transcript, August 6, 1939 Folder, Box 2001/18-64, WOD, TSA.

39. William L. Svelmoe, "The General and the Gringo: W. Cameron Townsend as Lazaro Cardenas's 'Man in America,'" in *The Foreign Missionary Enterprise at Home: Explorations in North American Cultural History*, ed. Daniel H. Bays and Grant Wacker (Tuscaloosa: University of Alabama Press, 2003), 172–173, 176–178; Janet Benge and Geoff Benge, *Cameron Townsend: Good News in Every Language* (Seattle: YWAM Publishing, 2000), 84, 131; William Cameron Townsend, *Lazaro Cardenas: Mexican Democrat* (Ann Arbor, MI: George Wahr Publishing Co., 1952), 291–292; Josephus Daniels, *Shirt-Sleeve Diplomat* (Chapel Hill: University of North Carolina Press, 1947), 255–256.

40. Townsend, *Lazaro Cardenas*, 291, 165; W. C. Townsend, "Mexico Confiscates the Oil Industry," Townsend to Cardenas, September 1938, TA #902284; "Report of Mr. and Mrs. W. C. Townsend for the Year Sept. 1937–Sept. 1938," TA #02283; William Cameron Townsend, *The Truth About Mexico's Oil*, #42593, CTA.

41. Olien and Davids Hinton, *Wildcatters*, 108–109; Goodwyn, *Texas Oil, American Dreams*, 41, 62–63. See untitled, unknown newspaper clipping, Austin, June 22, 1932, Clippings File, TC, BUTC.

42. Prindle, *Petroleum Politics and the Texas Railroad Commission*, 49; Olien and Davids Hinton, *Wildcatters*, 74; Duncan, *The Dicky Bird Was Singing*, 6; Goodwyn, *Texas Oil, American Dreams*, 55.

43. For federal election results in Texas see, for instance, "Presidential Elections, 1900–1956," Texas Almanac, https://texasalmanac.com/topics/elections/presidential-elections-1900-%E2%80%93-1956 (accessed December 2, 2018).

44. Yergin, *The Prize*, 254–255; Goodwyn, *Texas Oil, American Dreams*, 48–49; Harold L. Ickes, *Fightin' Oil* (New York: Alfred A. Knopf, 1943), 142.

45. Ickes, *Fightin' Oil*, 50.

46. "Texans Defeat Oil Dictator Bill at This Session," unknown newspaper clipping, San Antonio, June 14, 1934, Clippings File, TC, BUTC.

47. "Sun Oil," *Fortune* 23 (February 1941): 114; Annual Report of the Sun Oil Company, 1936, SOC, HLM; "Bolt from the Sun," *Time*, October 24, 1932, 49.

48. O'Connor, *History of Oil Workers Int'l Union*, 34, 36; Tyler Priest and Michael Botson, "Bucking the Odds: Organized Labor in Gulf Coast Oil Refining," *Journal of American History* 99 (June 2012): 105; "C.I.O. Drive Gaining Oil Workers Are Told," undated, unknown newspaper clipping (1937); "C.I.O. Oil Union to Start Drive in East Texas," unknown newspaper clipping, November 2, 1937; "A Report on the Texas State Federation of Labor Convention and an Interpretation of the Condition of the Federation."

49. Giebelhaus, *Business and Government*, 159–160; Annual Report of the Sun Oil Company, 1932, SOC, HLM.

50. "Thirty Pieces of Silver"; Giebelhaus, *Business and Government*, 199.

51. Giebelhaus, *Business and Government*, 205.

52. Darren Grem, *The Blessings of Business: How Corporations Shaped Conservative Christianity* (New York: Oxford University Press, 2016), 28; "Joseph Pew's Explanation: A Hope for Cleaner Politics," *PR*, November 24, 1944, 8, and Clifton P. Anderson to Joseph N. Pew Jr., November 24, 1944, "J. N. Pew Political-A, 1944–1961" Folder, Box 33, PFP, HLM.

53. J. Howard Pew, "The Oil Industry: A Living Monument to the American System of Free Enterprise," 14, address to API, November 16, 1938, Speeches and Remarks by

J. Howard Pew, Book 1, Box 153, SOC, HLM; Waldemar A. Nielsen, *Golden Donors: A New Anatomy of the Great Foundations* (New Brunswick, NJ: Transaction Publishers, 2002), 169.

54. "Testimony of J. Howard Pew," September 19, 1934, US Congress, House, *Petroleum Investigation: Hearings Before a Sub Committee of the Committee on Interstate and Foreign Commerce*, 73rd Congress Part 1 (Washington, DC: US Government Printing Office, 1934), 378; Olien and Davids Olien, *Oil and Ideology*, 204; Giebelhaus, *Business and Government*, 219.

55. Pew, "The Oil Industry," 10, 13–14; Giebelhaus, *Business and Government*, 211.

56. Harold L. Ickes, *The Secret Diary of Harold L. Ickes*, Vol. 1: *The First Thousand Days, 1933–1936* (New York: Simon & Schuster, 1953), 81; "Mr. Pew at Valley Forge," *Time*, May 6, 1940, 18; Giebelhaus, *Business and Government*, 231.

57. Ickes, *Fightin' Oil*, 7.

58. Ickes, *Fightin' Oil*, 71; Giebelhaus, *Business and Government*, 267–268; "Return of Oil Control to Free Initiative Asked," *Journal of Commerce*, May 27, 1944, clipping in "J. Edgar Pew's Speeches—API" Folder, Box 18, SOC, HLM; "Letter of Sun Oil President Probes Meaning of Vague Phrases in Anglo-American Pact," *NPN*, August 23, 1944, 9–10; "Pew Denounces Oil Pact as a Vicious Cartel," *NPN*, October 25, 1944, 3.

59. Quoted in Yergin, *The Prize*, 403, 406–407; Arthur M. Johnson, *The Challenge of Change: The Sun Oil Company, 1945–1977* (Columbus: Ohio State University Press, 1983), 26–27; Nash, *United States Oil Policy*, 177–178.

60. Giebelhaus, *Business and Government*, 249–262; "Sun Ship's 30 Years," *Our Sun* 12, no. 2 (July/August 1946): 4–6; "Sun Shipbuilding," *Fortune* 23, no. 12 (February 1941): 54; "Billionth Gallon," *Our Sun* 11, no. 1 (February 1945): 15; memos dated March 17, 1941, and March 31, 1941, Box 5, JHP, HLM.

# Chapter Seven: Holy Grounds

1. William A. Eddy, *F.D.R. Meets Ibn Saud* (Washington, DC: America-Mideast Educational & Training Services, 1954), 11, 14, 17–18, 22.

2. Quoted in Thomas W. Lippman, *Arabian Knight: Colonel Bill Eddy USMC and the Rise of American Power in the Middle East* (Vista, CA: Selwa Press, 2008), 128, 130, 133, 135; Eddy, *F.D.R. Meets Ibn Saud*, 19–20, 23, 27.

3. Lippman, *Arabian Knight*, 143–144; Eddy, *F.D.R. Meets Ibn Saud*, 32–33, 36.

4. Eddy, *F.D.R. Meets Ibn Saud*, 35.

5. Quoted in Ussama Makdisi, *Faith Misplaced: The Broken Promise of U.S.-Arab Relations: 1820–2001* (New York: PublicAffairs, 2010), 21, 49; quoted in Ussama Makdisi, "Reclaiming the Land of the Bible: Missionaries, Secularism, and Evangelical Modernity," *American Historical Review* 102 (June 1997): 689.

6. Robert D. Kaplan, *The Arabists: The Romance of an American Elite* (New York: Free Press, 1995), 1; Thomas S. Kidd, *American Christians and Islam: Evangelical Culture and Muslims from the Colonial Period to the Age of Terrorism* (Princeton, NJ: Princeton University Press, 2009), 66, 72; Lewis R. Scudder III, *The Arabian Mission's Story: In Search of Abraham's Other Son* (Grand Rapids, MI: William B. Eerdmans, 1998), 256–257 and "Missionary Appointments and Distribution by Station" appendix, n.p. Estimate of those treated annually circa 1924 comes from John Van Ess, "Christian Missions in the Persian Gulf," ARC142644, BPR, UWC.

7. Quoted in Kaplan, *The Arabists*, 67–68; Makdisi, *Faith Misplaced*, 106–108.

8. Ismail I. Nawwab, Peter C. Speers, and Paul F. Hoye, eds., *Aramco and Its World: Arabia and the Middle East* (Washington, DC: Arabian American Oil Company, 1980),

184–185; Robert Coughlan, "Mystery Billionaire," *Life*, November 27, 1950, 81–107; Churchill quoted and paraphrased in Yergin, *The Prize*, 12.

9. "Mr. William D'Arcy and Iranian Oil," undated, unknown newspaper clipping; "Oil: Man Who Started It All in Persia," *SD*, May 6, 1951; Ian Coster, "D'Arcy—A Portrait in Oil," *ES*, January 12, 1932; "Temple Flame Led Him to Persia's Oil Millions," newspaper clippings in ARC29404, BPR, UWC; Nawwab, Speers, and Hoye, *Aramco and Its World*, 185.

10. R. W. Ferrier, *The History of the British Petroleum Company*, Vol. 1: *The Developing Years, 1901–1932* (Cambridge, UK: Cambridge University Press, 1982), 280; G. B. Reynolds to Messrs The Concessions Syndicate and attached medical report, February 5, 1909, and March 28, 1909, ARC78751; M. Y. Young, "The Re-organization of the Company's Medical Services in Persia," 2, 13, 1930, ARC68938; Dr. D. C. Rennie to Dr. M. Y. Young, September 15, 1927, September 30, 1927, and October 7, 1927, and M. Y. Young to D. C. Rennie, October 13, 1927, and November 10, 1927, ARC62400; "Missions" note and John Van Ess correspondence with Arnold Wilson, ARC142644, BPR, UWC; John Van Ess, *Meet the Arab* (New York: John Day Company, 1943), 138; Ferrier, *The History of the British Petroleum Company*, 309.

11. Van Ess, "Christian Missions in the Persian Gulf."

12. Quoted in Scudder, *The Arabian Mission's Story*, 77; Ferrier, *The History of the British Petroleum Company*, chap. 10., esp. 397–398, 401, 425, 451, 659. As a whole, APOC's labor force increased from 6,784 in 1919 to 31,246 in 1930.

13. Nawwab, Speers, and Hoye, *Aramco and Its World*, 187–188; John M. Blair, *The Control of Oil* (New York, 1977), 80–90. On St. Sarkis, see "St. Sarkis," ACCUK, www.accc.org.uk/st-sarkis (accessed October 3, 2017).

14. Quoted in Kaplan, *The Arabists*, 56–57; Anthony Cave Brown, *Oil, God, and Gold: The Story of Aramco and the Saudi Kings* (Boston: Houghton Mifflin, 1999), 23–23, 33; Elizabeth Monroe, *Philby of Arabia* (London: Ithaca Press, 1998), 40, 45; John Philby, *Arabian Oil Ventures* (Washington, DC: Middle East Institute, 1964), 74, 176.

15. Norman E. Saul, *The Life and Times of Charles R. Crane, 1858–1939: American Businessman, Philanthropist, and a Founder of Russian Studies in America* (Lanham, MD: Lexington Books, 2013), 223; Scudder, *The Arabian Mission's Story*, 72; Brown, *Oil, God, and Gold*, 22, 28–29; Michael B. Oren, *Power, Faith, and Fantasy: America in the Middle East, 1776 to the Present* (New York: W. W. Norton, 2011), 412; Charles R. Crane to John O. Crane, March 6, 1932, Folder 6, Box 12, RTC, GULL.

16. Quoted in Brown, *Oil, God, and Gold*, 31–33, 52–53; K. S. Twitchell, "Sa'udi Arabian Oil Started by Philanthropic Sentiment," *Oil Forum* (1947): 291–292, clipping in Folder 1-23, Box 2.19, LJB, JHU; Oren, *Power, Faith, and Fantasy*, 411–413; Scudder, *The Arabian Mission's Story*, 19. Twitchell's Arabian surveys and reporting are accessed in Folders 5–7, Box 7, KTP, PUFL.

17. Frehner, *Finding Oil*, 144, 172, 165.

18. Charles Gould sermon notes for "Geology and the Bible," June 17, 24, 1928, Folder 18, Box 26, CNG, UOW; Pat M. Neff, "The Building of a Bigger and Better Baylor University," Baylor University, Box 2E224J, PPNP, BUTC.

19. Ray Fairchild, "Yemen Oil Hunt—a Gift from the Gods," in *The Oil Finders: A Collection of Stories About Exploration*, ed. Allen G. Hatley Jr. (Tulsa, OK: American Association of Petroleum Geologists, 1992), 127, ARC221244, BPR, UWC; Harvey Bassler, "Adventures on the Upper Amazon," *The Lamp*, April 1926, 19, 24; Lee Edson, "The Collector," *The Lamp* (winter 1952): 13–14; "Bassler, Harvey" biography; James Shelhamer, "Science Gained Valued Legacy from Area Man," unknown newspaper clipping, Bassler Standing File; Harvey Bassler, "General Summary of Work Done to Date in Eastern

Peru and Recommendations for Future Work," April 17, 1926, "Summary of Work Done" Folder, Box 1; Bassler diary entry, October 24, 1922, "Journals" Folder, Box 4; "Harvey Bassler's Peruvian Anecdotes: A Geologist's Largely Non-geological Observations in Northeastern Peru," 170–174, "Peruvian Anecdotes" Folder, Box 6; Bassler to Samuel Mosser in "Samuel Mosser" Folder, Box 9, HBP, LUL. At the end of his career, Bassler would donate 16,000 of his rock and fossil samples to Lehigh University, his alma mater, and to other repositories a collection of 10,000 amphibians, including 6,000 snakes, which would eventually be housed in the American Museum of Natural History in New York.

20. J. Edgar Pew, "The Fifth Dimension in the Oil Industry," American Association of Petroleum Geologists Annual Meeting, April 3, 1941, "J. Edgar Pew's Speeches—API" Folder, Box 18, SOC, HLM.

21. Miguel Tinker Salas, *The Enduring Legacy: Oil, Culture, and Society in Venezuela* (Durham, NC: Duke University Press, 2009), 6–8; Giebelhaus, *Business and Government*, 86; "Pioneering Petroleum Progress: A 75th Anniversary Address by Robert G. Dunlop, President, Sun Oil Company," 5, "Sun Oil—75th Anniversary 1961" Folder, Box 55, SOC, HLM.

22. Sir Arnold T. Wilson, "A Voyage Up the Persian Gulf," *APOC Magazine*, October 1924, 3, ARC175252; J. R. Bourchier, "Out in the Blue," *APOC Magazine*, April 1925, 25, ARC175256, BPR, UWC; Thomas C. Barger, *Out in the Blue: Letters from Arabia, 1937–1940* (Vista, CA: Selwa Press, 2000), 62.

23. Barger, *Out in the Blue*, 30, 59, 68, 80, 206.

24. Wallace Stegner, *Discovery! The Search for Arabian Oil* (Vista, CA: Selwa Press, 2007), 35; Brown, *Oil, God, and Gold*, 70; Nawwab, Speers, and Hoye, *Aramco and Its World*, 196–197; Yergin, *The Prize*, 292, 295, 297, 300.

25. Scudder, *The Arabian Mission's Story*, 19–21.

26. Nawwab, Speers, and Hoye, *Aramco and Its World*, 197, 200; Barger, *Out in the Blue*, 165–166; Kyle L. Pakka, ed., *The Energy Within: A Photo History of the People of Saudi Aramco* (Dammam, Saudi Arabia: Saudi Aramco, 2006), 25; Brown, *Oil, God, and Gold*, 77.

27. Scudder, *The Arabian Mission's Story*, 388; Kaplan, *The Arabists*, 72, 73–74.

28. Quoted in Lippman, *Arabian Knight*, 39–40.

29. Lippman, *Arabian Knight*, 40–43; William Eddy, "First Sunday Chapel Service, St. John's Chapel, September 18, 1937," Folder 24, Box 14, WEP, PUFL; David A. Hollinger, *Protestants Abroad: How Missionaries Tried to Change the World but Changed America* (Princeton, NJ: Princeton University Press, 2017), 124.

30. Francis B. Sayre to WAE, December 14, 1938, and February 8, 1939, Folder 5, Box 8; "The Power of God and the Secular World," 2, Folder 8, Box 15, WEP, PUFL.

31. Henry Luce, "The American Century," *Life*, February 17, 1941, 64, 65; David Ekbladh, *The Great American Mission: Modernization and the Construction of an American World Order* (Princeton, NJ: Princeton University Press, 2010), 69; Henry Luce, "Oil," delivered at American Petroleum Institute, Tulsa, Oklahoma, January 11, 1941, Folder 72, Box 7, RSK, UOCA.

32. Robert E. Herzstein, *Henry R. Luce, Time, and the American Crusade in Asia* (New York: Cambridge University Press, 2005), 21; Ekbladh, *The Great American Mission*, 6.

33. Harr and Johnson, *Rockefeller Century*, 358, 362–363, 393.

34. JDRJr. to the Northern Baptist Convention, March 7, 1935, Folder 61, Box 9; "Mr. Rockefeller and His Money," *Watchman-Examiner*, November 28, 1935; JDR to JDRJr., December 5, 1935, Folder 61, Box 9; Fosdick article, *New York Times Magazine*, May 24, 1953, and JDRJr to HEF, January 28, 1947, Folder 558, Box 72, RFC, RAC; Adlai E. Stevenson, "A Man Brave in Spirit, a Man of Wide-Ranging Enthusiasm," *NYT*, April 14, 1963, 329.

35. Harr and Johnson, *Rockefeller Century*, 306–307. On the conundrums of Rockefeller's faith and Kissinger's eulogy, see also Mark D. Tooley, "Nelson Rockefeller as Social Gospel Christian," *First Things*, May 20, 2015, www.firstthings.com/web-exclusives/2015/05/nelson -rockefeller-as-social-gospel-christian (accessed December 2, 2017).

36. Quoted in Harr and Johnson, *Rockefeller Century*, 435–436, 439–442, 483–485, 518–520; Darlene Rivas, *Missionary Capitalist: Nelson Rockefeller in Venezuela* (Chapel Hill: University of North Carolina Press, 2002), 18–19.

37. Rivas, *Missionary Capitalist*, 21–22.

38. Quoted in Rivas, *Missionary Capitalist*, 23–24.

39. Gisela Cramer and Ursula Prutsch, "Nelson A. Rockefeller's Office of Inter-American Affairs (1940–1946) and Record Group 229," *Hispanic American Historical Review* 86 (November 2006): 785–806; Franklin D. Roosevelt, "Executive Order 8840 Establishing the Office of Coordinator of Inter-American Affairs," American Presidency Project, July 30, 1941, www.presidency.ucsb.edu/ws/index.php?pid=16152#axzz1kZmKEFYg (accessed December 7, 2017).

40. "C. L. Harding Declares Middle East Oil Is Essential to Meet World Demand in Future," *Oildom*, undated clipping, Folder 1-23, Box 2.19, LJB, JHU; quoted in Chad H. Parker, *Making the Desert Modern: Americans, Arabs, and Oil on the Saudi Frontier, 1933– 1973* (Amherst: University of Massachusetts Press, 2015), 2; Brown, *Oil, God, and Gold*, 112; Everette Lee DeGolyer, "Preliminary Report of the Technical Oil Mission to the Middle East: Report by DeGolyer," 1944, Folder 2315, Box 19, ELD, SMUD; Yergin, *The Prize*, 393; "Near East's Oil Reserve Said Huge," *DMN*, March 23, 1944; Irvine H. Anderson, *Aramco, the United States and Saudi Arabia: A Study of the Dynamics of Foreign Oil Policy, 1933–1950* (Princeton, NJ: Princeton University Press, 1981), 20, 120.

41. Eddy, "The Power of God and the Secular World"; Lippman, *Arabian Knight*, 61, 72, 75.

42. Cordell Hull to Franklin D. Roosevelt, "Memorandum for the President," May 31, 1944, OF 5552, POF, FDRL.

43. Nathan J. Citino, *From Arab Nationalism to OPEC: Eisenhower, King Saud, and the Making of U.S.-Saudi Relations* (Bloomington: Indiana University Press, 2002), 6; Ekbladh, *The Great American Mission*, 4, 8–9.

44. Harr and Johnson, *Rockefeller Century*, 433–434, 443; "Truman Inaugural Address, January 20, 1949," Harry S. Truman Presidential Library & Museum, www.trumanlibrary .org/whistlestop/50yr_archive/inagural20jan1949.htm (accessed December 8, 2017); Ekbladh, *The Great American Mission*, 9, 128–129, 141; quoted in Salas, *The Enduring Legacy*, 174.

45. John R. Suman, "Middle Eastern Oil and Its Importance to the World," speech, Dallas, Texas, October 5, 1948, "Exxon Corporation: Subject Files: Corporate Public Affairs: Speeches, Addresses and Statements" Folder; "Suman, John R.," Box 2.207/L13D, EMHC, UTBC; Parker, *Making the Desert Modern*, 5, 37.

46. Lippman, *Arabian Knight*, 176, 203, 235; WE resignation, October 10, 1947, Folder 6, Box 8, WEP, PUFL.

47. Lippman, *Arabian Knight*, 238–240; Brown, *Oil, God, and Gold*, 138, 140; Parker, *Making the Desert Modern*, 16.

48. Parker, *Making the Desert Modern*, 15; WE to Mr. J. T. Duce, April 5, 1949, Box 1, Folder 18; "Government Relations: How It Is Organized and What It Does," Folder 1, Box 7, WEM, GULL.

49. Stegner, *Discovery!*, 217, 219; "Interview with Mr. W. Mulligan," November 18, 1985, 20, Folder 4, Box 8, WEM, GULL.

50. "George Rentz, Noted Arabist, Dies; Lauded as a Pioneering Aramco Figure," *Arabian Sun*, February 1988, Folder 1, Box 2, GSR, GULL; quoted in Robert Vitalis, *America's Kingdom: Mythmaking on the Saudi Oil Frontier* (Brooklyn, NY: Verso, 2009), 57, 98, 133; Parker, *Making the Desert Modern*, 15; Mulligan biography available at "William E. Mulligan," Aramco Expats, www.aramcoexpats.com/obituaries/william-e-mulligan (accessed December 2, 2017).

51. Parker, *Making the Desert Modern*, 15; Michael Sheldon Cheney, *Big Oilman from Arabia* (London: Heinemann, 1958), 35–36; quoted in Brown, *Oil, God, and Gold*, 139, 140.

52. Mulligan interview, Folder 4, Box 8, WEM, GULL.

53. Quoted in Nathan J. Citino, *Envisioning the Arab Future: Modernization in U.S.-Arab Relations, 1945–1967* (New York: Cambridge University Press, 2017), 114; Parker, *Making the Desert Modern*, 97; Mulligan interview, Folder 4, Box 8, WEM, GULL.

54. "George Rentz, Noted Arabist, Dies," Folder 91, Box 2; on scholarly ambitions, see GSR to W. Wendell Cleland, March 23, 1949, Folder 4, Box 1, and GSR to Dr. S. M. Stern, February 2, 1954, Folder 9, Box 1, GSR, GULL; "Mulligan Speech Notes," Folder 22, Box 8; "Muhammad," Folder 6, Box 8, WEM, GULL; Pakka, *The Energy Within*, 56; Parker, *Making the Desert Modern*, 16.

55. Quoted in Brown, *Oil, God, and Gold*, 59; Parker, *Making the Desert Modern*, 20; "Muhammad"; Grant C. Butler, *Kings and Camels: An American in Saudi Arabia* (New York: Devin-Adair Company, 1960), 14–15.

56. Quoted in Anderson, *Aramco*, 108, 113; Alfonzo quoted at "Chapter 22, Fifty-Fifty: The New Deal in Oil," Erenow, https://erenow.com/modern/theepicquestforoilmoneyand power/23.html (accessed October 23, 2017). See also Mulligan interview, 28, Folder 4, Box 8, WEM, GULL.

57. Quoted in Butler, *Kings and Camels*, 9, 23, 30, 35–36, 42–43.

58. WEM to Elmer Douglas, undated, 1962, Folder 21, Box 7; memorandum, Tom Barger, September 23, 1948; memorandum re: employee-directed morale groups, February 13, 1962; minutes of meeting on religious services, October 30, 1950, Folder 21, Box 7, WEM, GULL.

59. Memorandum, Mr. J. Macpherson, January 24, 1949; minutes of meeting on religious services, October 30, 1950, Folder 21, Box 7, WEM, GULL.

60. "Religious Services" chronology; "Review of Morale Groups"; TB and E. C. Singelyn to Cardinal P. Fumasoni Biondi, January 25, 1950, "Review of Morale Groups"; TB to Father Dennis of Dublin, November 30, 1955; employee-directed morale groups, February 13, 1962, Folder 21, Box 7, WEM, GULL.

61. Minutes of meeting on religious services, October 30, 1950, Folder 21, Box 7, WEM, GULL.

62. Parker, *Making the Desert Modern*, 16.

63. William A. Eddy, "The Impact of an American Private Company on a Middle East Community," Folder 19, Box 15, WEP, GULL.

64. Parker, *Making the Desert Modern*, 22; Vitalis, *America's Kingdom*, 93–97; "Aramco Industrial Relations Brief," Folder 1, Box 7, WEM, GULL.

65. Quoted in Vitalis, *America's Kingdom*, xxxvi, 99; Mulligan biographical sketch of Rentz, Folder 53, Box 1, WEM, GULL.

66. Vitalis, *America's Kingdom*, 24, 102–104.

67. Quoted in Vitalis, *America's Kingdom*, 101, 102–105, 148–149; WE, "Saudi Arabs as Supervisors," 1955, Folder 1, Box 7, WEM, GULL.

68. Oren, *Power, Faith, and Fantasy*, 484, 487–488; Lippman, *Arabian Knight*, 430–432.

69. Quoted in Brown, *Oil, God, and Gold*, 193.

70. Lippman, *Arabian Knight*, 248; quoted in Parker, *Making the Desert Modern*, 51–52.

71. "Conference on President's Point IV Proposals for the Near East," January 29, 1951, Folder 11, Box 11, WEP, GULL.

72. "Conference on President's Point IV Proposals for the Near East."

73. Wolfgang Saxon, "Rudolf Sonneborn Dies at 87; a Zionist Leader in the U.S.," *NYT*, June 4, 1986; "Sonneborn, Rudolf Goldschmidt," Encyclopaedia Judaica, 2007, www .encyclopedia.com/religion/encyclopedias-almanacs-transcripts-and-maps/sonneborn -rudolf-goldschmidt (accessed January 12, 2018); "The Story of American Oil," 4, 12, and "Jacob Blaustein: The Story of an American Citizen," 7, in *Amoco Oval*, September-October 1958, Folder 322, Box 2.14; "Memo—JB Conference with President Truman," September 22, 1950, and "Memo—Meeting JB with Sec. George C. McGhee," August 3, 1950, Folder 3-68, Box 2.111, LJB, JHU.

74. Helen Fuller, "Plot Against Palestine," unknown newspaper clipping; Jacob S. Ardon, "Israel Oil Law Aim Is a Race Against Time," *Oil Forum*, August 1952, clipping; Frances Gunther, "Israel Hopes for Oil," *World and Press* clipping, October 10, 1952, "Israel—1956" Folder, Box 67; Max W. Ball and Douglas Ball, "Oil Prospects of Israel," Folder 1481, Box 1.74, LJB, JHU.

75. Quoted in Lippman, *Arabian Knight*, 251–252.

76. Eddy, "The Impact of an American Private Company on a Middle East Community"; William A. Eddy, "How Arabs See the West Today," address at the Middle East Institute, December 19, 1950, Folder 16, Box 15, WEP, GULL.

## Chapter Eight: Wildcat Redemption

1. Daniel P. Fuller, *Give the Winds a Mighty Voice: The Story of Charles E. Fuller* (Waco, TX: Word Books, 1972), 113–122, 140; Joel A. Carpenter, *Revive Us Again: The Reawakening of American Fundamentalism* (New York: Oxford University Press, 1999), 24.

2. George Marsden, *Reforming Fundamentalism: Fuller Seminary and the New Evangelicalism* (Grand Rapids, MI: William B. Eerdmans Publishing Company, 1987), 53; Harold Ockenga to Charles Fuller, March 7, 1947; Harold Ockenga to Charles Fuller, March 12, 1947, CFC, FSA.

3. CEF to HO, March 7, 1947, CFC; Marsden, *Reforming Fundamentalism*, 53–54, 62–63, 66–67; Fuller, *Give the Winds a Mighty Voice*, 211.

4. CF to HO, December 29, 1949; HO to CF, May 24, 1948; CF to HO, January 5, 1951, CFC, FSA; Garth M. Rosell, *The Surprising Work of God: Harold Ockenga, Billy Graham, and the Rebirth of Evangelicalism* (Grand Rapids, MI: Baker, 2008), 203.

5. For further treatment of the rise of the new evangelicalism and wildcat oil in the 1940s and 1950s, see also Darren Dochuk, "Prairie Fire: The New Evangelicalism and the Politics of Oil, Money, and Moral Geography," in *American Evangelicals and the 1960s*, ed. Axel Schaefer (Madison: University of Wisconsin Press, 2013), 39–60.

6. "Special 75th Anniversary Issue," *Our Sun* (1961): 30, Box 55, SOC, HLM.

7. Quoted in Nielsen, *Golden Donors*, 169.

8. Anniversary Prayer, "Anniversaries—Sun and Oil Industry" Folder, Box 639; "Pioneering Petroleum Progress: A 75th Anniversary Address by Robert G. Dunlop, President, Sun Oil Company," 7, 9–11, 14, "Sun Oil—75th Anniversary 1961" Folder, Box 55, SOC, HLM.

9. "Special 75th Anniversary Issue," 30–31, 40.

10. Nielsen, *Golden Donors*, 172–173. Prior to 1947, the Pew children distributed their donations on a personal basis, principally to the Presbyterian Church and medical, educational, and cultural institutions in the Philadelphia area.

11. Nielsen, *Golden Donors*, 174.

12. Grem, *The Blessings of Business*, 71; Glenn Fowler, "H. E. Kershner, 98, a Long-time Worker in Children's Causes," *NYT*, January 3, 1990, www.nytimes.com/1990/01/03/obituaries/h-e-kershner-98-a-longtime-worker-in-children-s-causes.html (accessed January 2, 2018).

13. George H. Nash, "Simply Superlative," *National Review Online*, February 28, 2008, https://web.archive.org/web/20080303043521/http://article.nationalreview.com/print/?q=YmZkMTRmN2MyZjcwYWVhYWI4YjhkNjE5YTA5NmY3ODg (accessed January 2, 2018); Douglas Reed, "Odyssey of an Oilman," in *W.F.B.: An Appreciation by His Family and Friends*, ed. Priscilla L. Buckley and William F. Buckley Jr. (New York: privately printed, 1979), 154; John Belding Wirt to JHP, June 28, 1954, "Yale Law Lecture Committee," and JHP to John Belding Wirt, July 2, 1954, "Yale School Lectures" Folder, Box 40, JHP, HLM; Nicole Hoplin and Ron Robinson, *Funding Fathers: The Unsung Heroes of the Conservative Movement* (Washington, DC: Regnery Publishing, 2008), 72.

14. Doug Hennes, *That Great Heart: The Life of I. A. O'Shaughnessy Oilman and Philanthropist* (Edina, MN: Beaver's Pond Press, 2014), 44; "Notes from John Lindley, Virginia Kunz Interview with Msgr. Terrence Murphy," "Terrence Murphy Interview" Folder, Box 7; Larry O'Shaughnessy interview, "Interview with Larry O'Shaughnessy" Folder, Box 7; "O'Shaughnessy Foundation History," "O'Shaughnessy Foundation History" Folder, Box 8; Richard W. Conklin, "Ignatius A. O'Shaughnessy," *Notre Dame Magazine*, February 1974, 41, IAOS, STUA.

15. See correspondence, particularly John A. Hastings to Ignatius Aloysius O'Shaughnessy, January 12, 1946, Folder 8, Box 1, IAOS, STUA; minutes for Petroleum Industry Council for National Defense, December 8, 1941, 7, "Petroleum Industry Council for National Defense" Folder, Box 12, IOSP, MNHS.

16. "Mr. I. A. O'Shaughnessy's Speech on the Occasion of the Laying of the Cornerstone of the Fine Arts Building," May 1952, "O'Shaughnessy Hall of Liberal + Fine Arts" Folder, Box 2, IAOS, STUA. O'Shaughnessy's "intellectual weapons" quote is drawn from US Steel executive Irving S. Olds. Father Theodore Hesburgh to JHP, June 13, 1955, "U" Folder, Box 45, JHP, HLM.

17. Grem, *The Blessings of Business*, 71–72.

18. Quoted in Rosell, *The Surprising Work of God*, 97–98; "Annual Report of the 'Committee on Christian Liberty,'" minutes of the Meeting of the Board of Administration, National Association of Evangelicals, Tuesday, April 19, 1949, Chicago, Illinois, National Association of Evangelicals Master Minutes 1940s–50s, Box 30, National Association of Evangelicals. See also Darren Dochuk, "Moving Mountains: The Business of Evangelicalism and Extraction in a Liberal Age," in *What's Good for Business: Business and American Politics Since World War II*, ed. Kim Phillips-Fein and Julian E. Zelizer (New York: Oxford University Press, 2012), 78–79.

19. Olien and Davids Hinton, *Wildcatters*, 87–89, 92–93, 101.

20. CEF to HO, August 29, 1952, CFC, FSA.

21. CEF to HO, August 29, 1952, CFC, FSA.

22. HO to CEF, June 3, 1954; HO to CEF, June 11, 1954; CEF to HO, August 4, 1955; HO to CEF, August 8, 1955, CFC, FSA.

23. Yergin, *The Prize*, 410–416, 425–428.

24. Olien and Davids Hinton, *Wildcatters*, 108; "Testimony of H. B. Fell Before Subcommittee of the Senate Labor Committee, Washington, D.C., May 23, 1950," Folder 40, Box 3, Speeches Series, RSK, UOCA.

25. "Testimony of H. B. Fell Before Subcommittee of the Senate Labor Committee, Washington, DC, May 23, 1950."

26. Nash, *United States Oil Policy*, 228–232.

27. Olien and Davids Hinton, *Wildcatters*, 108; "Special 75th Anniversary Issue," 30–31.

28. "Independents Encompass the Globe," mid-November 1957, unknown newspaper clipping in Box 67, "Independents Abroad" Folder; Harry Gilroy, "Oil Crews Probe Sands of Israel," *NYT* clipping; "Israeli Oil Search Gets Under Way," unknown newspaper clipping, "Israel—1956" Folder, Box 67, HOC, WRLA; Buckley and Buckley, *W.F.B.*, 165; Russell B. Brown to Jacob Blaustein, March 25, 1954, and Jacob Blaustein to Russell B. Brown, March 27, 1954, Folder 3-58, Box 2.111, LJB, JHU.

29. Olien and Davids Hinton, *Wildcatters*, 108–109; Lawrence Goodwyn, *Texas Oil, American Dreams: A Study of the Texas Independent Producers and Royalty Owners Association* (Austin: Texas State Historical Association, 1996), 62–63.

30. Goodwyn, *Texas Oil*, 429; Daniel Yergin, *The Quest: Energy, Security, and the Remaking of the Modern World* (New York: Penguin Press, 2011), 244; John S. Ezell, *Innovations in Energy: The Story of Kerr-McGee* (Norman: University of Oklahoma Press, 1970), 152–169.

31. Nash, *United States Oil Policy*, 228–232; "Truman Vetoes Kerr Gas Bill," *Ludington Daily News*, April 17, 1950, 1.

32. C. M. Lea to Robert Kerr, November 9, 1954, Folder 22, and Mrs. Annie Allen to Robert Kerr, April 28, 1951, Folder 13, Box 2, Topical Series, RSK, UOCA.

33. Robert Kerr, "America Unlimited," American Petroleum Institute, November 10, 1949, Folder 23, Box 3, Speeches Series, RSK. Also Robert Kerr, "Oil for American Defense," February 20, 1949, Folder 90, Box 2, Speeches Series, RSK, UOCA.

34. Robert Kerr, "Always Bearing Our Witness as Christian Citizens," May 20, 1949, Folder 7, Box 3, Speech Series, RSK, UOCA.

35. Paul Chastko, *Developing Alberta's Oil Sands: From Karl Clark to Kyoto* (Calgary, AB: University of Calgary Press, 2004), 71; David H. Breen, *Alberta's Petroleum Industry and the Conservation Board* (Edmonton, AB: University of Alberta Press, 1993), 245–246; Ted Byfield, *Alberta in the 20th Century: Leduc, Manning, and the Age of Prosperity, 1946–1963* (Edmonton, AB: United Western Communications, 2001), 8–9, 13–14; Earle Gray, *The Great Canadian Oil Patch*, 2nd ed. (Edmonton, AB: June Warren Publishing, 2004), 140; Mark Lisac, "Leduc First Gush of Alberta Oil Wealth," *Ottawa Citizen*, February 7, 1987, A22.

36. See, for instance, Buckley and Buckley, *W.F.B.*, 165.

37. Malcolm Gordon Taylor, "The Social Credit Movement in Alberta" (MA thesis, University of California, n.d.), 6–7, 82. On Aberhart and Manning, see Lloyd Mackey, *Like Father, Like Son: Ernest Manning and Preston Manning* (Toronto: ECW Press, 1997), 20.

38. Ernest Manning biographical profile (untitled), 2–3, File 1821, WAP and ECM, APA. See Harry Roye to ECM, September 5, 1946, File 1179, ECM. Manning was a close associate of Fuller's. The two men cochaired the "Christ for America" campaign of 1951. See Horace F. Dean to Peter Elliott, November 20, 1951, File 1828, ECM, APA.

39. Taylor, "The Social Credit Movement in Alberta", 6–7. On Manning's popularity with evangelicals and in the United States, see Bob Jones to Ernest Manning, July 5, 1946, File 1179; "Hon. Ernest Charles Manning—Edmonton Constituency," File 1821; "Address of Ernest C. Manning, 39th National Gideon Convention, Montreal, June 15th to 18th, 1950," File 1826, ECM, APA.

40. Lisac, "Leduc First Gush of Alberta Oil Wealth," A22; Byfield, *Alberta in the 20th Century*, 8–9, 13–14; Gray, *The Great Canadian Oil Patch*, 140.

41. "Broadcast on Provincial Affairs, by Ernest C. Manning, Alberta Series No. 7: Our Minerals and Forests," File 1824, ECM, APA.

42. "Broadcast on Provincial Affairs, by Ernest C. Manning, Premier of Alberta: Alberta Series No. 14, Government Insurance: Breaking Monopoly—Not Creating Monopoly," File 1824; remarks by J. R. White, Association of Professional Engineers of Alberta, Annual Meeting, Calgary, Alberta, March 27, 1954, File 1826; Ernest Manning speech, undated, File 1825, ECM, APA.

43. Ernest C. Manning, "Christian Statesmanship," *Decision Magazine* (February 1962): 6. On Hubbert and peak oil, see Kenneth S. Deffeyes, *Hubbert's Peak: The Impending World Oil Shortage* (Princeton, NJ: Princeton University Press, 2008).

44. Ernest Manning speech to Interstate Oil Compact Commission, September 1–3, 1952, File 1825; Charles E. Simons to ECM, August 20, 1954, File 1821; Peter Elliott to John W. Wagner, September 3, 1954, File 1821, ECM, APA. See, for instance, Olin Culberson, Railroad Commission of Texas, Austin, to ECM, September 30, 1952, File 1825, ECM, APA.

45. In the 1950s, *Ladies Home Journal* published a profile of America's ten richest men, six of whom worked in oil: Sid Richardson, John D. Rockefeller III, Joseph Pew, Paul Mellon, Howard Hughes, and Clint Murchison. Two other oilmen received honorable mention: H. L. Hunt and Hugh Roy Cullen. Graham knew at least five of them. Margaret Parton, "Who Are America's 10 Richest Men?," *Ladies Home Journal*, April 1957, 72.

46. Don Graham, *Cowboys and Cadillacs: How Hollywood Looks at Texas* (Austin: Texas Monthly Press, 1983), 60–61.

47. "Hollywood Bowl Jammed with 20,000 for Premier of Billy Graham's Film," *FNT*, October 2, 1951; "16,000 Attend Premier of 'Mr. Texas,'" *FNT*, October 10, 1951; Erskine Johnson, "Flock of Film Actors Are Seen in New Graham Film," *Los Angeles Daily News*, March 2, 1953. See poster advertising "Billy Graham in Oiltown, U.S.A., World Premier—Sam Houston Coliseum," clippings file, BGEA, WGA.

48. "Graham Movie Jams Coliseum," *HC*, March 4, 1953.

49. Barbara Elmore, "The Story of Oilman Earl Hankamer: Sharing the Wealth," *Baylor Business Review*, April 10, 2008; "'Oil Town' Story of Two-Fisted Sinner," *HP*, June 2, 1952, 3. On Hankamer's leadership in Graham's Houston revival, see, for instance, "Contract No. 2486" and "Post Card" by George Fuermann, *HP*, April 1, 1952, Folder 1, ECH, WGA.

50. Charles A. Riggs to ECH, June 10, 1953; Dick Ross to ECH, May 15, 1952; Dick Ross to ECH, May 20, 1952; Dick Ross to ECH, June 11, 1952, Folder 1, ECH, WGA; "'Oil Town' Story of Two-Fisted Sinner," 3.

51. "Oil Town, U.S.A.!" brochure, Folder 2; John K. Gurwell, "Houstonian Sees His Home in Graham Film," unknown newspaper clipping, Folder 1, ECH, WGA.

52. Bety Haniotis, "Graham Movie Jams Coliseum," *HC*, March 4, 1953; John K. Gurwell, "Houston Welcomes Back Billy Graham," *Houston News*, March 4, 1953.

53. Lindsy Escoe Pack, "The Political Aspects of the Texas Tidelands Controversy" (PhD diss., Texas A&M University, 1979), iii; on Ickes and his commentary, see Tidelands Oil Controversy Folder, Box 101, and on oil corporations with significant leases in the gulf, see Tidelands Controversy Folder, Box 102, OLC, TLM.

54. *Supreme Court Reporter* 67, 1659; Price Daniel to Beauford Jester, May 14, 1947, Box 371, BJP, TSA; Pack, "The Political Aspects of the Texas Tidelands Controversy," 37–39, 43; *NYT*, November 4, 1945, 23, 48.

55. Address of Governor Earl Warren, Fort Worth, Texas, October 21, 1948, F3640:649, EW, CSA.

56. *NYT*, October 22, 1948, 21; Drew Pearson, "Ike Eisenhower and Texas Oil," *DMN*, May 9, 1952; Joseph Crespino, *Strom Thurmond's America* (New York: Hill and Wang, 2012), 79. On questions about Cullen and oil's role in the campaign, see Kari Frederickson,

*The Dixiecrat Revolt and the End of the Solid South, 1932–1968* (Chapel Hill: University of North Carolina Press, 2001), 168–170; "Ike Is Wooing Dixie with Tidelands Oil," *NYP*, April 25, 1952, 2.

57. HRC to RSK, February 15, 1952, F17, Box 2, Topical Series, RSK, UOCA; Tyler Priest, *The Offshore Imperative: Shell Oil's Search for Petroleum in Postwar America* (College Station: Texas A&M Press, 2007), 54–55; Goodwyn, *Texas Oil, American Dreams*, 69.

58. Burrough, *The Big Rich*, 212; reports of Women Investors Research Institute in Folder 13, Box 3, BAP, DPL; see, for instance, "Oil the Yardstick of American Progress," Plymouth Oil Company advertisement, *OGJ*, undated, 94, and "Address of Walter S. Hallanan, Sinton, Texas, April 6, 1950," in "Oil & Gas—Clippings & Publications, 1950" Folder, Box 1977 081-235, ASG, TSA.

59. Burrough, *The Big Rich*, 212. See, for instance, Women Investors Research Institute reports in Folder 13, Box 3, BAP, DPL.

60. Steven P. Miller, *Billy Graham and the Rise of the Republican South* (Philadelphia: University of Pennsylvania Press, 2009), 70; Nancy Gibbs and Michael Duffy, *The Preacher and the Presidents: Billy Graham in the White House* (New York: Center Street, 2007), 31–34.

61. "Ike Is Wooing Dixie with Tidelands Oil," 2, 17.

62. Pearson, "Ike Eisenhower and Texas Oil"; "Cullen Raps Ike's Right on Amendment," *DMN*, February 20, 1954; "Hugh Roy Cullen, Philanthropist and Oil Operator, Dies," *DMN*, July 5, 1957.

63. WFG to ECH, November 10, 1952; ECH to WFG, November 12, 1952; WFG to ECH, December 14, 1953, Folder 1; Billy Graham Greater Houston Crusade Bulletin, April 1965, Folder 2, EHP, WGA.

64. Parton, "Who Are America's 10 Richest Men?," 72–73, 173–179; "Billy Graham, with Strong Ties to Dallas, Considered Himself 'Half-Texan,'" *DMN*, February 21, 2018, www.dallasnews.com/life/faith/2018/02/21/billy-graham-strong-ties-dallas-considered -half-texan (accessed March 21, 2018); quoted in Marshall Frady, *Billy Graham: A Parable of American Righteousness* (New York: Simon & Schuster, 2006), 232.

## Chapter Nine: The Great Game

1. Parton "Who Are America's 10 Richest Men?," 72–73, 173–179.

2. "Text of Billy Graham's Sermon Opening His Crusade in Madison Square Garden," *NYT*, May 16, 1957, 22; "Crusade's Impact," *Time*, July 8, 1957, 57.

3. Morris Kaplan, "Graham Crusade Extended Again," *NYT*, August 4, 1957, 64; George Dugan, "Graham Crusade Termed a Record," *NYT*, August 30, 1957.

4. "Catholic Guild Will Observe Petroleum Sunday by Attending Mass to Pray for Oil Industry," pamphlet clipping, "Religion" Folder, Box 78, HOC, WRLA.

5. Priest and Botson, "Bucking the Odds," 100, 103, 106; Clyde Johnson, "CIO Oil Workers' Organizing Campaign in Texas, 1942–1943," in *Essays in Southern Labor History: Selected Papers, Southern Labor History Conference, 1976*, ed. Gary Fink and Merl E. Reed (Westwood, CT: Greenwood Press, 1977), 177; "Help Humble Help You; Vote OWIU!," "Labor—1954" Folder, Box 81, HOC, WRLA.

6. Priest and Botson, "Bucking the Odds," 107–108; Carl B. King and Howard W. Risher Jr., *The Negro in the Petroleum Industry* (Philadelphia: University of Pennsylvania Press, 1969), 20–21, 27.

7. Quoted in James L. Anderson, "The Oil Workers International Union Strike of 1948," January 10, 1949, University of California, Berkeley, 2–3, 12; "Union-Busting Repudiated,"

and "America's Iron Curtain" photograph, unknown newspaper clipping, "California Strike—1948" Folder, Box 87, HOC, WRLA.

8. Milton Plumb, "Oilmen Top Fund Contributors to Manion's Anti-union Lobby," *AFL-CIO News*, undated newspaper clipping; "Oil Should Gird Now to Battle Socialistic Control," *NPN*, August 29, 1951, 23; "Arm Public with Facts to Halt Socialism," *NPN*, September 26, 1951, 27, propaganda, "Socialism" Folder, Box 78, HOC, WRLA.

9. "Capitalism Gets a Boost," *PW*, August 10, 1956, 30; "Like to Meet a Capitalist?," unknown newspaper clipping, 1948, and "Union Oil Owners Get 5.4% of 1948 Sales Dollars," "Industry—1954" Folder, Box 80, HOC, WRLA.

10. "Will They Inherit Socialism?," Gabriel Oil Co. ad, propaganda, "Socialism" Folder, Box 78; Frank Breese, "Public Relations Keyed to 'Citizen of the West' Theme," *NPN*, August 24, 1949, 11, and Leonard Castle, "Institutional Ads Help to Sell Oil Industry Company Products," *NPN*, May 31, 1950, 9, "Advertising General—1954" Folder, Box 80, HOC, WRLA.

11. On women entering (slowly and in modest proportions compared to other industrial sectors), see, for instance, "Women in Oil Jobs," "Exxon Corporation, Subject Files: Corporate Public Affairs: Reprints, 1945–1952" Folder, Box 2.207-G105, EMHC, UTBC; see also "Women in the Oil Patch, Beginnings to 1946," Alberta, http://www.history.alberta .ca/energyheritage/oil/the-waterton-and-the-turner-valley-eras-1890s-1946/women-in -the-oil-patch-beginnings-to-1946.aspx (accessed December 2, 2018), and Robbie Rice Gries, *Anomalies: Pioneering Women in Petroleum Geology: 1917–2017* (n.p.: Robbie Rice Gries, 2018). Keith K. King, "Advance for AMS of Sunday," November 30, 1952, Clippings File, TC, BUTC.

12. "22 Oil Unions Show the Way," 5, unknown newspaper clipping; "Excerpt from President O. A. Knight's '22nd State of the Union' Address," "Labor—1954" Folder, Box 81; "Oil Union Leader Sees Industry Wages Doubled in Five Years," Federated Press clipping, January 20, 1956; "Oil's Expanding Job Market," Oil Industry Information Bulletin, 1954, 3–4, 6, "Labor" Folder, Box 77, HOC, WRLA; King and Risher, *The Negro in the Petroleum Industry*, 20–21, 27.

13. "International Ladies Auxiliary," "International Ladies Auxiliary" Folder, Box 89; "White Union Members Must Ask Fair Deal for Negroes," unknown newspaper clipping, "Labor—1954" Folder, Box 81, HOC, WRLA; Priest and Botson, "Bucking the Odds," 107–108; King and Risher, *The Negro in the Petroleum Industry*, 20–21, 27.

14. Johnson, "CIO Oil Workers' Organizing Campaign in Texas, 1942–1943, 176–178; Richard Geddes and Loyd Haskins to O. A. Knight, October 30, 1952; "Oil Industry Challenged to Help Bring About World Peace," *Oil, Chemical and Atomic Union News*, May 21, 1956, "International Labor Organization" Folder, Box 67, HOC, WRLA.

15. "Where Are We Going, Daddy?," advertisement, *Oil Daily*, January 23, 1953, "Religion" Folder, Box 78, HOC, WRLA.

16. Wendy L. Wall, *Inventing the "American Way": The Politics of Consensus from the New Deal to the Civil Rights Movement* (New York: Oxford University Press, 2009), 10.

17. For a full account of Eisenhower's speech and the framing of a Judeo-Christian America, see Kevin Kruse, *One Nation Under God: How Corporate America Invented Christian America* (New York: Basic Books, 2015), 67–68, and the entirety of chapter 3.

18. Kruse, *One Nation Under God*, 69, 75, 76–78, 82, 92; Public Laws 84-851 and 84-140.

19. "Leading Industrials 1948–1958," "DDE Dictation July 1959 (2)" Folder, Box 49; see, for example, Dwight Eisenhower to Sid Richardson, July 16, 1959, "DDE Dictation July 1959 (1)" Folder, Box 49, and Dwight Eisenhower to Mrs. John D. Rockefeller Jr., May 11, 1960, "DDE Dictation May 1960" Folder, Box 49, DS, DEWF, EPLA; Kruse, *One Nation Under God*, 69.

20. Robert Engler, "How to Influence People," *New Republic*, September 26, 1955, 21, 25, 34, New Republic Series, "Oil and Politics, 1955" Folder, Box 77, HOC, WRLA.

21. Jacob Blaustein, "Freedom and Fear," 45th Annual Meeting of the American Jewish Committee, January 26, 1942, Folder 1497, Box 1.74, LJB, JHU; "NCCEM's Professional Impact in 1966," and Willmar Thorkelson, "O'Shaughnessy Give Award," *Minneapolis Star*, June 11, 1971, clipping in "N-Miscellaneous" Folder, Box 7, IOSP, MNHS.

22. Jonathan P. Herzog, *The Spiritual-Industrial Complex: America's Religious Battle Against Communism in the Early Cold War* (New York: Oxford University Press, 2011); Robert Kerr, "The Church and the Peace of the World," Tulsa, Oklahoma, September 13, 1954, Folder 5, "Speeches" Box 6; Robert Kerr, address to American Petroleum Institute, November 11, 1957, Folder 46, "Speeches" Box 6, RSK, UOCA.

23. Justin Hart, *Empire of Ideas: The Origins of Public Diplomacy and the Transformation of U.S. Foreign Policy* (New York: Oxford University Press, 2013), 5; "Local Matters of Interest to Kuwait Oil Company," ARC106872, BPR, UWC.

24. Hollinger, *Protestants Abroad*, 135.

25. William Inboden, *Religion and American Foreign Policy, 1945–1960: The Soul of Containment* (New York: Cambridge University Press, 2008), 289–292; report on Operations of International Information Administration, March 3 to July 31, 1953, March 31, 1954, United States Information Agency, Box 99, CF, DEWH, EPLA; Nicholas J. Cull, *The Cold War and the United States Information Agency: American Propaganda and Public Diplomacy, 1945–1989* (New York: Cambridge University Press, 2008), 87–88, 93.

26. Kenneth Osgood, *Total Cold War: Eisenhower's Secret Propaganda Battle at Home and Abroad* (Lawrence: University Press of Kansas, 2006), 314; James R. Vaughan, *The Failure of American and British Propaganda in the Arab Middle East, 1945–1957: Unconquerable Minds* (Houndmills, UK: Palgrave Macmillan, 2005), 33; Bayard Dodge to Dwight G. Eisenhower, September 24, 1953, OF 144-B-4 Islamic and Moslem Religion, Box 619, OF, DEWH, EPLA.

27. Wanda Jablonski, "King Saud: Our Best Friend in the Middle East," *PW*, January 25, 1957, 6–7; Wanda Jablonski, "This Is No 'Arabian Nights' Potentate," *PW*, February 8, 1957, 16–18; Dwight D. Eisenhower, *The Papers of Dwight David Eisenhower*, Vol. 14: *The Presidency: The Middle Way*, ed. Louis Galambos and Daun van Ee (Baltimore: Johns Hopkins University Press, 1996), 2441; Oren, *Power, Faith, and Fantasy*, 514; Citino, *From Arab Nationalism to OPEC*, 128.

28. Louis Galambos and Daun van Ee, eds., *The Papers of Dwight David Eisenhower: The Presidency: Keeping the Peace* (Baltimore: Johns Hopkins University Press, 2001), 18:384. On King Saud's visit, see "The Return of the King—Saud Visits the U.S.," Association for Diplomatic Studies & Training, http://adst.org/2015/11/return-of-the-king-saud-visits-the-us (accessed January 2, 2018). On Saud and the UN banquet, see www.kingsaud.org/history/subarticle/king-saud-speech-to-the-american-people-during-his-visit/12 (accessed January 2, 2018). For the joint statement, see "Joint Statement Following Discussions with King Saud of Saudi Arabia, February 8, 1957," American Presidency Project, https://www.presidency.ucsb.edu/documents/joint-statement-following-discussions-with-king-saud-saudi-arabia (accessed January 2, 2018).

29. W. H. Lawrence, "President and Wife Doff Shoes at Rites Dedicating Mosque," *NYT*, June 29, 1957, 1; "Eisenhower's 1957 Speech at Islamic Center of Washington," American Presidency Project, https://www.presidency.ucsb.edu/documents/remarks-ceremonies-opening-the-islamic-center (accessed December 2, 2018); memorandum for files, August 9, 1957, reaction to president's Islamic Center address, August 1957, "August 1957—Memo on Appts." Folder (1), Box 26, DS, DEWH, EPLA; memorandum for the president, John

Foster Dulles to Dwight D. Eisenhower, June 19, 1957, "Dulles, John Foster June '57" Folder, Box 8, DS, DEWF, EPLA; quoted in Inboden, *Religion and American Foreign Policy, 1945–1960*, 291–293.

30. Inboden, *Religion and American Foreign Policy, 1945–1960*, 293.

31. "Graham Outlines Needs," *New York Crusade News*, January 1957, 1, 3, Folder 422, Box 53, N-Religious Interests, RFC; Leonard M. Fanning to JHP, August 26, 1959, Folder A, Box 66, JHP, HLM; Rockefeller, *David Rockefeller Memoirs*, 190.

32. Richard Norton Smith, *On His Own Terms: A Life of Nelson Rockefeller* (New York: Random House, 2014), 338.

33. For background on the Special Studies Project, see "The Special Studies Project," Rockefeller Brothers Fund, www.rbf.org/75/special-studies-project (accessed January 3, 2018); *Prospect for America: The Rockefeller Panel Reports* (Garden City, NY: Doubleday & Company, 1961), 15, 24, 464.

34. Rockefeller, *David Rockefeller Memoirs*, 21.

35. Rockefeller, *David Rockefeller Memoirs*, 173.

36. C. W. Hamilton, "Africa (Mostly a Travel Log)," 4–5, "Africa 1958" Folder, Box 2, CWH, UOW; "5th World Petroleum Congress Preliminary Program," May 30–June 5, 1959, and official banquet seating arrangement, "World Petroleum Congress 1959" Folder, Box 66, JHP, HLM; "News from the AFL-CIO," September 3, 1962, 2, "International Labor Organization" Folder, Box 67, HOC, WRLA.

37. Quoted Greenberg, *Staking a Claim*, 183–184.

38. Andrew Zimmerman, *Alabama in Africa: Booker T. Washington, the German Empire, and the Globalization of the New South* (Princeton, NJ: Princeton University Press, 2010), 1; Greenberg, *Staking a Claim*, 187.

39. Greenberg, *Staking a Claim*, 8, 136–137.

40. *Report of the 1963 Trade Mission to Kenya, Tanganyika, Uganda* (Washington, DC: US Government Printing Office, 1963), 4, 8; quoted in Greenberg, *Staking a Claim*, 185–186.

41. Quoted in Greenberg, *Staking a Claim*, 186–187.

42. Quoted in Greenberg, *Staking a Claim*, 189–191, 195, 197, 208; "How They Won the West—and More," *BW*, January 28, 1967, 178.

43. Yergin, *The Prize*, 529; "Independents Encompass the Globe," *International Oilman*, Mid-November 1957, 401.

44. Quoted in Rockefeller, *David Rockefeller Memoirs*, 133, 201, 425–427. The underside of David Rockefeller's work in Brazil receives treatment in "David Rockefeller & a Dark Legacy in Brasil—a Critical Obituary," Brasil Wire, www.brasilwire.com/david-rockefeller -legacy-in-brasil (accessed January 2, 2018).

45. Rockefeller, *David Rockefeller Memoirs*, 201; Timothy Naftali, ed., *The Presidential Recordings: John F. Kennedy: The Great Crises* (New York: W. W. Norton, 2001), 1:8–9. On the role of Rockefeller-aligned business groups' involvement in Brazilian politics, see Jan Knippers Black, *United States Penetration of Brazil* (Manchester, UK: Manchester University Press, 1977).

46. "Change Comes to the Chaco," *The Lamp* (summer 1964): 20–24, TC, BUTC.

47. Wanda M. Jablonski, "Oil Men Dodge Arrows in Venezuelan Jungle," *PW*, February 21, 1958, 88, 90.

48. Grem, *The Blessings of Business*, 100; quoted in Hugh Steven, *Yours to Finish the Task: The Memoirs of W. Cameron Townsend, Part Four: 1947–1982* (Wheaton, IL: Hugh Steven, 2004), 120, 167. Townsend and Nelson Rockefeller's parallel Cold War political efforts in Latin America are documented (with more than a hint of "gotcha journalism") in Gerald Colby with Charlotte Dennett, *Nelson Rockefeller and Evangelism in the Age of Oil* (New York: Harper Collins, 1995).

49. Steven, *Yours to Finish the Task*, 214, 229, 231; "Go Ye and Preach the Gospel," *Life*, January 30, 1956, 10.

50. "Shifting of Load from Traction," *NOW*, February 1, 1962, 2; "Steel to Illustrate a Spiritual Truth," reprinted in *NOW*, September 1971, 1; "Invasion," *NOW*, December 8, 1944, 1; "R.G. Talks," *NOW*, September 15, 1961, 2; "The Wildcat and the Black Dog," *NOW*, September 15, 1961, 2–3, LUA.

51. R. G. LeTourneau, *Mover of Men and Mountains: The Autobiography of R. G. LeTourneau* (Upper Saddle River, NJ: Prentice Hall, 1960), 242, 245; "The Wildcat and the Black Dog," 2–3.

52. LeTourneau, *Mover of Men and Mountains*, 258.

53. Details of this arrangement are charted in LeTourneau's correspondence. See James C. LeTourneau to Mr. M. C. Gleter, August 24, 1961, "Mobile Oil Company Del Peru, 1961" Folder, Box JFE; Roy LeTourneau to RGLT, December 21, 1959, "Letters from Roy LeTourneau—1959" Folder, Box B5G; Roy LeTourneau to Sterling Stephens, July 1, 1960, "Letters from Peru—1960" Folder, Box B5G, LUA. For a summary of the project, see also "Peru," *NOW*, February 1, 1962, 3; "Feeding the Billions," *NOW*, September 15, 1961, 1; LeTourneau, *Mover of Men and Mountains*, 258–259; quoted in Grem, *The Blessings of Business*, 103–104.

54. Quoted in Grem, *The Blessings of Business*, 104.

55. Quoted in Kruse, *One Nation Under God*, 86.

56. "North American Oil Sands: History of Development, Prospects for the Future," 8; quoted in "Profiles in Pioneering," *Our Sun*, 2; Chastko, *Developing Alberta's Oil Sands*, 87, 105.

# Chapter Ten: Power Shifts

1. "Alberta Premier Lauds Athabasca Oil Project," *Sunoco News* (August 1964), Folder 18, Box 641, SOC, HLM. For further treatment of Sun Oil, wildcat Christianity, and the Alberta oil sands, see Dochuk, "Blessed by Oil, Cursed with Crude," and Darren Dochuk, "Extracted Truths: The Politics of God and Black Gold on a Global Stage," in *Outside In: The Transnational Circuitry of US History*, ed. Andrew Preston and Doug Rossinow (New York: Oxford University Press, 2016), 153–181.

2. "Athabasca Special Report: One Year to Completion," *CP* (September 1966), 43–45, Folder 16, Box 641; "Tar Sand and Oil Mining," *Engineering and Mining Journal* (December 1967), Folder 16, Box 641, SOC, HLM; Mark Humphries, "North American Oil Sands: History of Development, Prospects for the Future," *CRS Report for Congress*, January 17, 2008, 8–9; Chastko, *Developing Alberta's Oil Sands*, 87, 105; "Abasand," Alberta, www.history.alberta.ca/energyheritage/sands/unlocking-the-potential/abasand/default.aspx (accessed January 3, 2018).

3. Chastko, *Developing Alberta's Oil Sands*, 31–32, 34–35, 45, 59, 87–89, 105; "North American Oil Sands," 8–9; "Profiles in Pioneering," 2; Honourable N. E. Tanner, "Government Policy Regarding Oil-Sand Leases and Royalties," *Proceedings: Athabasca Oil Sands Conference* (Edmonton, AB: King's Printer, 1951), 176.

4. "Profiles in Pioneering," 2.

5. Chastko, *Developing Alberta's Oil Sands*, 92–94, 97–98; Alberta Technical Committee, "Report to the Minister of Mines and Minerals and the Oil and Gas Conservation Board: With Respect to an Experiment Proposed by Richfield Oil Corporation Involving an Underground Nuclear Explosion Beneath the McMurray Oil Sands with the Objective of Determining the Feasibility of Recovering the Oil with the Aid of the Heat

Released from Such an Explosion" (Edmonton, AB: Government Printer, 1959), ECM, APA; Breen, *Alberta's Petroleum Industry and the Conservation Board*, 450; R. G. Rollin to President Dwight Eisenhower, July 2, 1959, "DDE Dictation July 1959 (2)" Folder, Box 49, DS, DEWF, EPLA; "Report of the United Stated Delegation to the United States–Canadian Discussion of Petroleum Policies and Programs," Ottawa, December 13–14, 1962, President John F. Kennedy's Office Files, 1961–1963, Part 4: Subjects: Oil Imports, JFK, NARA; Stephen J. Randall, *United States Foreign Oil Policy Since World War II: For Profits and Security* (Montreal: McGill-Queen's University Press, 2005), 282, 320.

6. "Pioneering Petroleum Progress"; "Good Citizen," *Longview Morning Journal*, April 29, 1961, newspaper clipping; "Sun Oil Employees Observe Anniversary," unknown newspaper clipping, "Sun Oil—75th Anniversary 1961" Folder, Box 55, SOC, HLM.

7. Graham D. Taylor, "Sun Oil Company and Great Canadian Oil Sands Ltd.: The Financing and Management of a 'Pioneer' Enterprise, 1962–1974," *Journal of Canadian Studies* 20 (1985): 104; Johnson, *Challenge of Change*, 283.

8. Manning, "Christian Statesmanship," 6; "Suncor, Inc.: An Account of the First Seventy Years," 7–8, 32–33, "Subsidiaries, 1987" Folder, Box 605, SOC, HLM.

9. Chastko, *Developing Alberta's Oil Sands*, 108–110; see logbook for "Sunoco Trip #2," Sept. 18–19, 1963, Loose File, Box 35, SOC, HLM; "New Oil Sands Project May Have Fast Start," *The Albertan*, November 26, 1963.

10. Chastko, *Developing Alberta's Oil Sands*, 113, 117; ECM to D. J. Wilkins, March 9, 1964, "Athabasca Tar Sands Project, Great Canadian Oil Sands Correspondence, 1963–1964" Folder, Box 35, SOC, HLM.

11. W. H. Rea to Robert G. Dunlop, September 2, 1964, and Sun memo titled "Investment in GCOS by Albertans," March 30, 1964; "Memorandum," March 1964, "Athabasca Tar Sands Project, Great Canadian Oil Sands Correspondence, 1963–1964" Folder, Box 35, SOC, HLM.

12. "Notes Re Meeting in Sun Aircraft—Quebec City on April 2, 1964—Athabasca Project," "Athabasca Tar Sands Project, Great Canadian Oil Sands Correspondence, 1963–1964" Folder, Box 35, Series 6, SOC, HLM; "Memorandum," Premier of Alberta—Honorable Ernest C. Manning, December 21, 1964; JHP to ECM, January 4, February 23, and March 15, 1965; ECM to JHP, March 29, April 2, and June 11, 1965, "C-P 1965" Folder, Box 231, JHP, HLM; Mackey, *Like Father, Like Son*, 126, 130–131.

13. Chastko, *Developing Alberta's Oil Sands*, 112; "Athabasca Special Report: One Year to Completion," 43–45; "Tar Sand and Oil Mining"; Humphries, "North American Oil Sands," 8–9.

14. The Eisenhower text is at "Veto of Bill to Amend the Natural Gas Act," American Presidency Project, www.presidency.ucsb.edu/ws/index.php?pid=10736 (accessed January 5, 2018); the Richardson response is at Ben H. Procter, "Richardson, Sid Williams," Texas State Historical Association, June 15, 2010, https://tshaonline.org/handbook/online/articles/fri08 (accessed January 5, 2018); quoted in Yergin, *The Prize*, 535–536, 538.

15. Alan J. Lichtman, *White Protestant Nation: The Rise of the American Conservative Movement* (New York: Atlantic Monthly Press, 2008), 213; JHP to Maurice A. Gale, November 20, 1956, "G" Folder, Box, JHP, HLM.

16. On Morgenthau and depletion allowance, see American Presidency Project, https://www.presidency.ucsb.edu/documents/message-congress-tax-evasion-prevention (accessed January 22, 2018); Harvey O'Connor, *The Empire of Oil* (New York: Monthly Review Press, 1955), 209–210.

17. Edward H. Miller, *Nut Country: Right-Wing Dallas and the Birth of the Southern Strategy* (Chicago: University of Chicago Press, 2015), 86. On Kennedy's stand on depletion allowance, see "Letter of Senator John F. Kennedy to Gerald C. Mann on Oil

Depletion Allowance," American Presidency Project, www.presidency.ucsb.edu/node
/274556 (accessed February 2, 2018); David R. Jones, "H. L. Hunt: Magnate with Mission," *NYT*, August 17, 1964, H-1.

18. Harry Hurt, III, "Welcome, Mr. Kennedy, to Dallas," *TM* (April 1981): 240–241,
248.

19. Quoted in Hennes, *That Great Heart*, 94, 96.

20. Quoted in Robert Alan Goldberg, *Barry Goldwater* (New Haven, CT: Yale University Press, 1995), 92–93, 95–96, 138–143; quoted in Daniel McCarthy, "Rediscovering the
Beginnings of Conservatism: A Review of *Flying High: Remembering Barry Goldwater*, by
William F. Buckley Jr.," *Intercollegiate Review*, fall 2008, https://home.isi.org/rediscovering
-beginnings-conservatism-review-iflying-high-remembering-barry-goldwateri-william-f
(accessed January 5, 2018).

21. Quoted in Goldberg, *Barry Goldwater*, 138; Lisa McGirr, *Suburban Warriors: The
Origins of the New American Right* (Princeton, NJ: Princeton University Press, 2001);
quoted in Darren Dochuk, *From Bible Belt to Sunbelt: Plain-Folk Religion, Grassroots Pol-
itics, and the Rise of Evangelical Conservatism* (New York: Norton, 2011), 228; Mrs. John
Stenbeck to Denison Kitchel, October 1, 1964, Box 3H510; "Text of a Speech by Senator
Barry Goldwater Before Notre Dame University Student Body," February 6, 1962, Box 3J3,
SGC, UTBC.

22. Dean Burch to JHP, March 28, 1967, "Political" Folder, Box 91, JHP, HLM. Pew
addressed his membership in the John Birch Society in a 1966 press release, in answer to
California Governor Pat Brown's charge, and in a 1970 memo to R. G. Dunlop, in which
he claimed, "Some, for example, have delighted in calling me a Bircher. But they are wrong.
It is true that when Mr. Welsh [*sic*] began publishing his magazine, American Opinion, I
saw in it a medium for helping to spread understanding of the devious contortions of communism, and I agreed to serve on the editorial board. Later, Mr. Welsh [*sic*] organized the
John Birch Society, and the magazine came to be used as the Birch Society organ. I severed
my association after that because freedom to me is indivisible and universally to be sought
for all men. And for that reason I chose not to have an affiliation with the Birch Society
itself." "Statement of J. Howard Pew, Chairman of Sun Oil Company, October 11, 1966,"
"Newspaper and Magazine Articles; J. Howard Pew, 1932–1969" Folder, Box 152; JHP to
R. G. Dunlop, January 28, 1970, "J. Howard Pew Receipt of William Penn Award" Folder,
Box 155, SOC, HLM; "Goldwater Gets H. L. Hunt Backing," *NYT*, November 1, 1964;
Alfred S. Regnery, *Upstream: The Ascendance of American Conservatism* (New York: Thresh-
old Editions, 2008), 189–191; Joe Shell obituary, *Bakersfield Californian*, April 9, 2008.

23. Lichtman, *White Protestant Nation*, 246–347.

24. Smith, *On His Own Terms*, 445; quoted in Goldberg, *Barry Goldwater*, 189, 193–194.

25. For the Rockefeller speech, see "Remarks on Extremism at the 1964 Republican
National Convention," Rockefeller Archive Center, http://rockarch.org/inownwords
/nar1964text.php (accessed January 10, 2018); quoted in Smith, *On His Own Terms*, 452.

26. Lichtman, *White Protestant Nation*, 263; Steven V. Roberts, "Ronald Reagan Is Giving 'Em Heck," *NYT*, October 25, 1970.

27. On the "Middle East mess" that Eisenhower left Kennedy, see Rachel Bronson,
*Thicker Than Oil: America's Uneasy Partnership with Saudi Arabia* (Oxford, UK: Oxford University Press, 2006), 77.

28. Rockefeller, *David Rockefeller Memoirs*, 264–265, 267.

29. Rockefeller, *David Rockefeller Memoirs*, 266; Smith, *On His Own Terms*, 290; "Presentation to Gov. Nelson Rockefeller—JDA Campaign NYC—Tues 9/22/59" and Nelson
Rockefeller, "Potential for Peace," Folder F5-19, Box 2.67, LJB, JHU.

30. Rockefeller, *David Rockefeller Memoirs*, 267.

31. Ernest Aschner, "Can Oil and Israel Mix? An Economic Opportunity for the New State," *Commentary*, November 1, 1948, 444–445.

32. Zvi Alexander, *Oil: Israel's Covert Efforts to Secure Oil Supplies* (Jerusalem: Gefen Publishing House, 2004), 12; "Israel Worries as Oil Capital Wanes," *PW*, December 28, 1956, 23.

33. Alexander, *Oil*, 18, 20–21.

34. Quoted in Alexander, *Oil*, 30.

35. Quoted in Alexander, *Oil*, 22–23, 30–31.

36. Quoted in Alexander, *Oil*, 35, 45.

37. Memo from Meir Sherman to JB, January 30, 1956, "Outline of Oral Presentation to Allen on January 25, 1956"; Meir Sherman to JB, June 4, 1956, Folder F5-19, Box 2.67, LJB, JHU; Uri Bialer, *Oil and the Arab-Israeli Conflict, 1948–63* (London: Palgrave -Macmillan, 1999), 199–202.

38. JB to Lyndon B. Johnson, February 22, 1964, 2; "Presentation of American Liberties Medallion to Secretary of State Dean Rusk," April 30, 1964; "Conference President Kennedy/JB," April 15, 1961; "Various Comments by Jacob Blaustein to President Kennedy During April 30, 1962 Conference," April 30, 1962, Folder 5-80, Box 2.18, LJB, JHU. For additional context, see Nancy Turck, "The Middle East: The Arab Boycott of Israel," *Foreign Affairs* 55 (April 1977): 472–493.

39. Quoted in Oren, *Power, Faith, and Fantasy*, 521, 523; Bronson, *Thicker Than Oil*, 78; Parker, *Making the Desert Modern*, 122. Blaustein also maintained correspondence with UN Secretary-General Dag Hammarskjold, with lobbying for Israeli interests always in play. See, for instance, written exchanges in Folder 3-34, Box 2.111, LJB, JHU.

40. Quoted in Rockefeller, *David Rockefeller Memoirs*, 267–268.

41. Rockefeller, *David Rockefeller Memoirs*, 268.

42. GSR to WEM, February 18, 1957, Folder 12, Box 1; GSR to Garry Owen, March 4, 1958, Folder 13, Box 1, GSR, GULL; Miles Copeland quoted in Lippman, *Arabian Knight*, 286.

43. Brown, *Oil, God, and Gold*, 251–253.

44. Brown, *Oil, God, and Gold*, 246–247; Yergin, *The Prize*, 415; Anna Rubino, *Queen of the Oil Club: The Intrepid Wanda Jablonski and the Power of Information* (Boston: Beacon Press, 2008), 10.

45. See biographical sketch, signed by John R. Jones, March 24, 1962, Folder 67, Box 1, WEM, GULL; Bronson, *Thicker Than Oil*, 84; Citino, *From Arab Nationalism to OPEC*, 160; Parker, *Making the Desert Modern*, 123; Faisal quoted in Roger Owen, *State Power and Politics in the Making of the Modern Middle East*, 2nd ed. (New York: Routledge, 2000), 47.

46. Lippman, *Arabian Knight*, 278–280; William Eddy, "To the Editor of *Commentary*," *Commentary*, January 1955, 87, clipping, Folder 8, Box 14, WEP, PUFL.

47. William Eddy, "Israel: Bastion of Democracy?," Folder 10, Box 14, WEP, PUFL.

48. See, for instance, John H. Davis to Senator William J. Fulbright, May 24, 1960; William Eddy to Chairman, Aramco Donations Committee, April 11, 1961; Harry McDonald to K. S. Shyvers, May 10, 1961, Folder 9, Box 9, WEM, GULL; Citino, *Envisioning the Arab Future*, 109–111.

49. Rockefeller, *David Rockefeller Memoirs*, 266.

50. Lippman, *Arabian Knight*, 292–293.

51. "Thomas C. Barger," obituary, clipping; Barger tribute by William E. Mulligan, 1–2, Folder 5, Box 1, WEM, GULL.

52. Quoted in Brown, *Oil, God, and Gold*, 260–261; Thomas C. Barger, "Planning Guides for Aramco as Corporation," Folder 6, Box 1, JAM, GULL.

53. Barger tribute by William E. Mulligan, 5; Father Ron Jansch to WEM, February 28, 1992; First Annual Retreat at Udhailiyah, March 27–29, 1963, Folder 20, Box 7; "His Fair Lady," 15, and "Employe [*sic*] #60: The Story of Tom Barger," *Aramco World Magazine*, September–October, 1969, Folder 6, Box 6, WEM, GULL.

54. "His Fair Lady," 15; untitled travel report, Folder 20, Box 7, WEM, GULL.

55. "Religious Services" and statement on "Bahai Sect," Folder 21, Box 7, WEM, GULL.

56. Letter to John J. Kelberer, July 7, 1986, Folder 5, Box 1, WEM, GULL; Nawwab, Speers, and Hoye, *Aramco and Its World*, 230–231.

57. Bronson, *Thicker Than Oil*, 98–103; Samantha Gross, "The 1967 War and the 'Oil Weapon,'" *Brookings*, June 5, 2017, https://www.brookings.edu/blog/markaz/2017/06/05/the-1967-war-and-the-oil-weapon (accessed December 3, 2018).

58. Quoted in Parker, *Making the Desert Modern*, 23; Bronson, *Thicker Than Oil*, 101–103; Brown, *Oil, God, and Gold*, 261.

59. Parker, *Making the Desert Modern*, 124; TB to John G. Nolan, July 12, 1967, Folder 21, Box 7; TB to Milton R. Young, February 19, 1968, Folder 4, Box 1, WEM, GULL.

60. "GCOS: The Way It Works," *Our Sun* (autumn 1967): 30, Box 34; "Athabasca Press Conference Proposal," "Athabasca Tar Sands Project, Great Canadian Oil Sands, 1963–1964" Folder, Box 35, SOC, HLM; "Athabasca Special Report: One Year to Completion," 43–45.

61. "Information Booklet, Athabasca Plant Opening Activities, September 29–30, October 1, 1967, Great Canadian Oil Sands Limited"; "Film Tells Athabasca Story," unknown newspaper clipping, Folder 18, Box 641, SOC, HLM.

62. Chastko, *Developing Alberta's Oil Sands*, 112; "Athabasca Special Report: One Year to Completion," 43–45; "Tar Sand and Oil Mining"; Humphries, "North American Oil Sands," 8–9.

63. "Meet Alberta's New Premier," *Power for Living* (May 3, 1970): 7, attached to correspondence between W. S. Woods Jr. and Robert Dunlop, July 21, 1970; Robert Dunlop to Honorable Harry Strom, June 12, 1970; F. O'Sullivan to Robert Dunlop, July 9, 1970; "Notley Raps Royalty Reduction," July 2, 1970, unknown newspaper clipping, "Great Canadian Oil Sands, Ltd., 1970" Folder, Box 36, SOC, HLM. The depth of Strom's religious commitments and breadth of his religious and corporate connections are well documented in Boxes 100 and 101 of HSP, APA.

64. Joseph P. Kamp to JHP, October 17, 1968; JHP to James S. Kemper, May 9, 1968, "K-O, 1968" Folder, Box 234, JHP, HLM.

65. "Remarks by Jno. G. Pew on Occasion of Dinner in Honor of J. Howard Pew," October 1966, "J. N. Pew, Speeches 1947–66" Folder, Box 54; "Talk by J. Howard Pew, Sun Oil Company Employees' Christmas Party," December 24, 1968, Speeches and Remarks by J. Howard Pew, Book 3, Box 153, SOC, HLM; Preston Manning to JHP, November 22, 1968, "K-O, 1968" Folder, Box 234, JHP, HLM.

## Chapter Eleven: Approaching Armageddon

1. Andrew L. Yarrow, "Nathan Pusey, Harvard President Through Growth and Turmoil Alike, Dies at 94," *NYT*, November 15, 2001; Rockefeller, *David Rockefeller Memoirs*, 332, 333.

2. Rockefeller, *David Rockefeller Memoirs*, 333.

3. Rockefeller, *David Rockefeller Memoirs*, 334.

4. King and Risher, *The Negro in the Petroleum Industry*, 30–31; memorandum to Walter White from Herbert Hill," September 3, 1954; memo on "Liability of Union for Racial

Discrimination in Bargaining," June 22, 1954; "NLRB Gests Specific Job Bias Charges Against 4 Oil Companies, 4 Unions," June 1, 1955, press release, "Labor Cases—Oil Industries, 1954–55" Folder, Box 119, Part 13, Series A, NACP, LOC.

5. "Memorandum to Mr. Moon from Muriel S. Outlaw," April 9, 1956, "Labor Complaints—Oil Refining Industry (Texas) 1956" Folder, Box 69, Part 13, Supplement; Willie Lee to Herbert Hill, June 8, 1955, "Labor Cases—Oil Industries, 1954–55" Folder, Box 119, Part 13, Series A, NACP, LOC; King and Risher, *The Negro in the Petroleum Industry*, 35.

6. William A. Miller to Roy Wilkins, December 13, 1961, "Labor—Oil, Chemical, and Atomic Workers Int'l Union 1956, 1961" Folder, Box 118, Part 13, Supplement, NACP, LOC.

7. Herbert Hill to Reverend J. H. Scott, January 5, 1955, "Labor Cases—Oil Industries, 1954–55" Folder, Box 119, Part 13, Series A, NACP, LOC.

8. Tharen Stevens to the Pure Oil Company, February 9, 1965, Folder 14:15, Box 14, Series 1, SCLC, LOC.

9. Paul Lewis, "Leon Sullivan, 78, Dies; Fought Apartheid," *NYT*, April 26, 2001; quoted in Eric Augenbraun, "'Stand on Your Feet, Black Boy!': Leon Sullivan, Black Power, Job Training, and the War on Poverty" (MA thesis, University of Pennsylvania, 2010), 30.

10. Quoted in Jennifer Alice Delton, *Racial Integration in Corporate America, 1940–1990* (New York: Cambridge University Press, 2009), 37; Augenbraun, "'Stand on Your Feet,'" 33.

11. Quoted in Greenberg, *Staking a Claim*, 131, 163.

12. Quoted in Greenberg, *Staking a Claim*, 170–172, 177.

13. Greenberg, *Staking a Claim*, 207–209; John Morsell to J. J. Simmons, December 12, 1962, File 001473 016 0246 0003, Papers of the NAACP, Part 21: NAACP Relations with the Modern Civil Rights Movement; Gloster B. Current to J. J. Simmons, April 23, 1963, File 001471 011 0274, Papers of the NAACP, Part 20: White Resistance and Reprisals, 1956–1965, NACP, LOC (accessed through ProQuest History Vault, https://proquest .libguides.com/historyvault/NAACP); Greenberg, *Staking a Claim*, 211–212.

14. "Perspectives, Not Solutions," Folder 17, Box 106; "Support the Strike Demands with Action," Folder 6, Box 109; "Mobil's Presence in South Africa," ACOA, ARC.

15. Betty Medsger, "Gulf Oil Threatening Suit Against Religious Group," *WP*, August 25, 1970; "News—Presbyterian Office of Information," December 23, 1970, "Presbyterian Church Gulf Oil Controversy 1970–1971" Folder, Box B141, JHP, HLM; "Staff Report," undated, Folder 10, Box 3; "Resolution on ACOA Support for the Ohio Conference of the United Church of Christ," September 14, 1970, Folder 45, Box 1, ACOA, ARC.

16. James J. Kilpatrick, "Of Presbyterians and Terrorists, June 27, 1971," unknown newspaper clipping; Roger Hull to E. D. Brockett, February 5, 1971; Hal Lainson to JHP, June 28, 1971; JHP to Hal Lainson, July 16, 1971, "Presbyterian Church Gulf Oil Controversy 1970–1971" Folder, Box B141, JHP, HLM; memorandum to executive committee from John Coventry Smith, April 28, 1970, Folder 6, Box 109, ACOA, ARC.

17. Minutes of the steering committee meeting, February 17, 1971, Folder 3, Box 4 (001544-006-0165 p. 15); Jack Anderson, "Gulf, Angola & Grandma," *NYP*, October 20, 1973, clipping, Folder 31, Box 2 (001544-005-0715 p. 16), ACOA, ARC.

18. "Position Paper on Angola," Gulf Oil Corporation; Ray Vicker, "Some U.S. Firms Ignore Urgings to Leave, Instead Seek to Upgrade Status of Blacks," *WSJ*, September 22, 1971, clipping, "Presbyterian Church Gulf Oil Controversy 1970–1971" Folder, Box B141, JHP, HLM; Rockefeller, *David Rockefeller Memoirs*, 222; David Binder, "Gulf Oil Cuts Off Angola Operation," *NYT*, December 23, 1975; Ralph Abernathy to James Lee, n.d., 1976, Folder 8, Box 191, SCLC, EUA.

19. Memorandum to executive committee from John Coventry Smith, April 28, 1970, Folder 6, Box 109, ACOA, ARC.

20. Adam Vaughan, "Torrey Canyon Disaster—the UK's Worst-Ever Oil Spill 50 Years On," *TG*, March 18, 2017; "Death by Oil," *NYT*, April 21, 1967, 38; Robert Rienow and Leona Train Rienow, "The Oil Around Us," *NYT Sunday Magazine*, June 4, 1967, SM13; "Oil Slick Spreads, but Leak Slows," *NYT*, February 1, 1969, 32; Gladwin Hill, "Slick Off California Coast Revives Oil Deal Disputes," *NYT*, February 2, 1969, 1; Jennifer Latson, "The Burning River That Sparked a Revolution," *Time*, June 22, 2015, http://time .com/3921976/cuyahoga-fire (accessed December 2, 2018).

21. Kathryn Morse, "There Will Be Birds: Images of Oil Disasters in the Nineteenth and Twentieth Centuries," *Journal of American History* 99 (June 2012): 129.

22. Lisa H. Sideris, "The Secular and Religious Sources of Rachel Carson's Sense of Wonder," 233–235, 241–242; Paul Brooks, *The House of Life: Rachel Carson at Work* (Boston: Houghton Mifflin, 1972), 9.

23. Rachel Carson, *Silent Spring* (Boston: Houghton Mifflin, 1987), 297; Robert H. Nelson, "*Silent Spring* as Secular Religion," in *Silent Spring at 50*, ed. Roger Meiners, Pierre Desrochers, and Andrew Morriss (Washington, DC: Cato Institute, 2012), 81, 88–89; Carson, *Silent Spring*, 219–220.

24. Lynn T. White Jr., "History and Horseshoe Nails," in *The Historian's Workshop: Original Essays by Sixteen Historians*, ed. L. P. Curtis Jr. (New York: Alfred A. Knopf, 1970), 60; Lynn White, "The Historical Roots of Our Ecological Crisis," *Science* 155 (March 10, 1967), 1204–1205, 1206–1207.

25. Steven Rockefeller, "Faith and Community in an Ecological Age," in *Spirit and Nature: Why the Environment Is a Religious Issue*, ed. Steven C. Rockefeller and John C. Elder (Boston: Beacon Press, 1992), 166.

26. See "Introduction: The Earth Day Story and Gaylord Nelson," Gaylord Nelson and Earth Day, www.nelsonearthday.net/earth-day (accessed January 3, 2018); Shelby Grad, "The Environmental Disaster That Changed California—and Started the Movement Against Offshore Oil Drilling," *LAT*, April 28, 2017, www.latimes.com/local/lanow /la-me-santa-barbara-spill-20170428-htmlstory.html (accessed February 2, 2018). For the Nixon speech, see "Annual Message to the Congress on the State of the Union, January 22, 1970," American Presidency Project, https://www.presidency.ucsb.edu/documents /annual-message-the-congress-the-state-the-union-2 (accessed February 2, 2018).

27. Sun Oil Company news release and "Statement of R. E. Foss Before Subcommittee on Minerals, Materials and Fuels of the Senate Committee on Interior and Insular Affairs," May 20, 1969, 2–3, "JGP—Corresp Apr 1969–Dec 1969" Folder, Box B52, SOC, HLM; Johnson, *The Challenge of Change*, 275.

28. Quoted in Johnson, *The Challenge of Change*, 270–271, 399–400.

29. Quoted in Patrick Allitt, *A Climate of Crisis: America in the Age of Environmentalism* (New York: Penguin Press, 2014), 73.

30. Quoted in Yergin, *The Prize*, 567, 594, 606.

31. Raymond H. Anderson, "Libya's Premier Crusades Against Tea Break and the Oil-Rich Life," *NYT*, January 3, 1972, 14; Henry Tanner, "Libyan Chief, Citing U.S. Aid to Israel, Seizes Oil Concern," *NYT*, June 12, 1973, 93; quoted in Yergin, *The Prize*, 585, 587.

32. Bronson, *Thicker Than Oil*, 117–119; Alexander, *Oil*, 207.

33. Alexander, *Oil*, 207; "Mrs. Meir Says Moses Made Israel Oil-Poor," *NYT*, June 11, 1973, 3.

34. Quoted in Bronson, *Thicker Than Oil*, 118–119, 121–122.

35. Daniel J. Sargent, *A Superpower Transformed: The Remaking of American Foreign Relations in the 1970s* (New York: Oxford University Press, 2015), 10–11; "Looking

Toward Summit," *NYT*, September 4, 1974, 57; quoted in Meg Jacobs, *Panic at the Pump: The Energy Crisis and the Transformation of American Politics in the 1970s* (New York: Hill and Wang, 2016), 58–59.

36. Quoted in Jacobs, *Panic at the Pump*, 5–6, 59, 79.

37. Quoted in Mark Fiege, *The Republic of Nature: An Environmental History of the United States* (Seattle: University of Washington Press, 2012), 381, 387, 394–395; Jacobs, *Panic at the Pump*, 79.

38. Quoted in Jacobs, *Panic at the Pump*, 44–45; quoted in Anthony Sampson, *The Seven Sisters: The Great Oil Companies and the World They Shaped* (New York: Viking Press, 1975), 273, 275.

39. David Perlman, "American the Beautiful?," *Look*, November 4, 1969, 25–26; Amorty B. Lovins, letter to the editor, *NYT*, June 8, 1973.

40. Quoted in Yergin, *The Prize*, 626; "Founder of OPEC Dead," *NYT*, September 5, 1979, 7; Richard Gott, "A Society Nurtured by Devil's Excrement," *TG*, November 19, 1976, 4.

41. Christopher Capozzola, "'It Makes You Want to Believe in the Country': Celebrating the Bicentennial in an Age of Limits" in *America in the Seventies*, ed. Beth Bailey and David Farber (Lawrence: University of Kansas Press, 2004), 29, 39.

42. Kenneth L. Woodward, "Born Again!," *Newsweek*, October 25, 1976, 68–78; "Back to That Oldtime Religion," *Time*, December 26, 1976, 52–58; Grant Wacker, "Searching for Norman Rockwell: Popular Evangelicalism in Contemporary America," in *The Evangelical Tradition in America*, ed. Leonard I. Sweet (Macon, GA: Mercer University Press, 1997), 291–293.

43. Daniel T. Rodgers, *Age of Fracture* (Cambridge, MA: Belknap Press of Harvard University Press, 2011), 3; Steven P. Miller, *The Age of Evangelicalism: America's Born-Again Years* (New York: Oxford University Press, 2014), 4–5.

44. Dochuk, *From Bible Belt to Sunbelt*, 333–334; Mary Sennholz, *Faith and Freedom: A Biographical Sketch of a Great American John Howard Pew* (Grove City, PA: Grove City College, 1975), 37; "J. Howard Pew of Sun Oil Dies," *NYT*, November 28, 1971. On Pew's final donation, see www.philanthropyroundtable.org/almanac/hall_of_fame/j._howard_pew (accessed February 8, 2018).

45. Wacker, "Searching for Norman Rockwell," 292; "'Here's Life' Receives $60.4 million in Pledges," *DMN*, May 22, 1979; Helen Parmley, "Robison Case Gets Attention of Racehorse," *DMN*, March 15, 1979; William Martin, "God's Angry Man," *TM*, April 1981, 152.

46. Quoted in David Edwin Harrell Jr., *Oral Roberts: An American Life* (Bloomington: Indiana University Press, 1985), 3, 7, 12, 279; Oral Roberts to RSK, July 26, 1961, Folder 22, Box 15, RSK, UOCA; Nielsen, *Golden Donors*, 355–358.

47. Hal Lindsey, *The Late Great Planet Earth* (New York: Zondervan, 1970); John F. Walvoord, *Armageddon: Oil and the Middle East Crisis*, rev. ed. (Grand Rapids, MI: Zondervan Publishing, 1974), 46–47.

48. Francis A. Schaeffer and Udo Middelmann, *Pollution and the Death of Man* (Wheaton, IL: Tyndale House, 2011), 33, 35; Katharine K. Wilkinson, *Between God and Green: How Evangelicals Are Cultivating a Middle Ground on Climate Change* (New York: Oxford University Press, 2012), 16.

49. Quoted in Wilkinson, *Between God and Green*, 16.

50. Frank Schaeffer, *Crazy for God: How I Grew Up as One of the Elect, Helped Found the Religious Right, and Lived to Take All (or Almost All) of It Back* (New York: Da Capo Press, 2008), 41, 43.

51. William D. Smith, "In Texas, Anger over the Oil Depletion Allowance," *NYT*, April 20, 1975, 1.

52. Johnson, *The Challenge of Change*, 405; Gordon Adams, *The Iron Triangle: The Politics of Defense Contracting* (New Brunswick, NJ: Transaction Publishers, 1989), 108; Warren Weaver Jr., "Elections Panel to Allow Companies to Raise Funds," *NYT*, November 19, 1975, 1.

53. Quoted in Smith, *On His Own Terms*, 676–677; Rockefeller, *David Rockefeller Memoirs*, 337.

54. Rockefeller, *David Rockefeller Memoirs*, 336, 339; John D. Rockefeller III, *The Second American Revolution: Some Personal Observations* (New York: Harper & Row, 1973), 57, 67.

55. Quoted in Peter Collier and David Horowitz, *The Rockefellers: An American Dynasty* (New York: Holt, Rinehart and Winston, 1976), 504–505.

56. Quoted in Rockefeller, *David Rockefeller Memoirs*, 342–346, 349–350.

57. Rockefeller, *David Rockefeller Memoirs*, 351; quoted in Smith, *On His Own Terms*, 708–709.

58. Rockefeller, *David Rockefeller Memoirs*, 355.

59. Rockefeller, *David Rockefeller Memoirs*, 354.

60. Dan Morgan, "Chase Manhattan's Ties to the Shah," *WP*, November 16, 1979.

## Chapter Twelve: The End of the American Century

1. Jimmy Carter, "Address to the Nation on Energy, April 18, 1977," American Presidency Project, https://www.presidency.ucsb.edu/documents/address-the-nation-energy (accessed February 2, 2018).

2. As recounted and quoted in Yergin, *The Prize*, 662–663; Carter, "Address to the Nation on Energy."

3. Jimmy Carter, "National Energy Bills Remarks on Signing," American Presidency Project, https://www.presidency.ucsb.edu/documents/national-energy-bills-remarks-sign-ing-hr-4018-hr-5263-hr-5037-hr-5146-and-hr-5289-into-law (accessed February 2, 2018); quoted in Randall Balmer, *Redeemer: The Life of Jimmy Carter* (New York: Basic Books, 2014), 155.

4. "Camp David: An Outpouring of Prayer," *CT*, October 6, 1978, 48; quoted in Balmer, *Redeemer*, 86; "Remarks of President Carter at the Egyptian-Israeli Peace Treaty Signing Ceremony," American Presidency Project, https://www.presidency.ucsb.edu/documents/remarks-president-carter-president-anwar-al-sadat-egypt-and-prime-minister-menahem-begin (accessed February 3, 2018).

5. David Stockman, "The Wrong War? The Case Against a National Energy Policy," *Public Interest* 53 (fall 1978): 44; quoted in Yergin, *The Prize*, 663–665.

6. See Michael L. Ross, *The Oil Curse: How Petroleum Wealth Shapes the Development of Nations* (Princeton, NJ: Princeton University Press, 2013); quoted in Yergin, *The Prize*, 674–675, 678.

7. Quoted in Yergin, *The Prize*, 679–680, 681.

8. Quoted in Yergin, *The Prize*, 681–682; quoted in Baqer Moin, *Khomeini: Life of the Ayatollah* (New York: Thomas Dunne Books, 2000), 204; Dan Geist, "'A Darker Horizon': The Assassination of Shapour Bakhtiar," *Frontline*, August 6, 2011, www.pbs.org/wgbh/pages/frontline/tehranbureau/2011/08/a-darker-horizon-the-assassination-of-shapour-bakhtiar.html (accessed February 2, 2018); "The Khomeini Era: Iran Becomes a Theocracy," *Time*, February 12, 1979.

9. Yergin, *The Prize*, 685–686.

10. Achsah Nesmith, Walter Shapiro, and Gordon Stewart to Gerald Rafshoon and Hendrik Hertzberg, memorandum, "Energy Speech," June 29, 1979, 7/15/79, Proposed

Remarks on Energy [2] Folder, Box 50, SF-RSO, JCPL; Patrick Caddell, memorandum to the President, July 12, 1979, 7/15/79, Proposed Remarks on Energy [2] Folder, Box 50, SF-RSO, JCPL; quoted in Daniel Horowitz, *Jimmy Carter and the Energy Crisis of the 1970s: The "Crisis of Confidence" Speech of July 15, 1979: A Brief History with Documents* (Boston: Bedford–St. Martin's, 2005), 20.

11. Walter Mondale quoted in Horowitz, *Jimmy Carter and the Energy Crisis of the 1970s*, 95; Gerald Rafshoon to Jimmy Carter, memorandum, July 10, 1979, 7/15/79, Address to the Nation—Energy/Crisis of Confidence Folder [1], Box 50, SF-RSO, JCPL.

12. Quoted in Horowitz, *Jimmy Carter and the Energy Crisis of the 1970s*, 25; "Carter on the *Titanic*," *NR*, July 27, 1979, B105; "Gantry on Energy," *NR*, August 3, 1979, 953–956; "The Real Jimmy Carter," *WSJ*, July 17, 1979, 18.

13. Quoted in Jacobs, *Panic at the Pump*, 242, 244–245.

14. Helen Parmley, "Reagan Reaps Bible, Cap," *DMN*, August 23, 1980; "'Here's Life' Receives $60.4 Million in Pledges," *DMN*, May 22, 1979; Parmley, "Robison Case Gets Attention of Racehorse"; see also Dochuk, *From Bible Belt to Sunbelt*, 392–393.

15. Ronald Reagan, "A Vision for Tomorrow," American Presidency Project, November 3, 1980, https://www.presidency.ucsb.edu/documents/election-eve-address-vision-for-america (accessed February 3, 2018).

16. Gilles Kepel, *Jihad: The Trail of Political Islam* (London: I. B. Tauris, 2002), 70.

17. Quoted in Nazih N. Ayubi, *Over-stating the Arab State: Politics and Society in the Middle East* (London: I. B. Tauris, 1995), 232–233; Louis M. Wolfrum, "The Change Agent," Folder 2, Box 7, WEM; Kepel, *Jihad*, 70–72.

18. Sir Terence Clark, "Oman: A Century of Oil Exploration and Development," *Asian Affairs* 39 (November 2008): 399; Limbert, *In the Time of Oil*, 9, 11.

19. Pakka, *The Energy Within*, 81. In actuality, the king would not sign the agreement officially ending Aramco's concession in the kingdom until 1990. See Parker, *Making the Desert Modern*, 126.

20. Parker, *Making the Desert Modern*, 123.

21. "Development Plans for Aramco Communities," June 1976, 11, 14, 20–21, Folder 37, Box 1, JAM, GULL; quoted in Pakka, *The Energy Within*, 74, 90–93.

22. Quoted in Pakka, *The Energy Within*, 88, 103, 106, 108, 110.

23. Louis M. Wolfrum, "The Change Agent," May 9, 1979, Folder 2, Box 7, WEM, GULL.

24. Ahmed Zaki Yamani, "Aramco: Fifty Years of Achievement," *Arabian Sun*, May 25, 1983, Folder 67, Box 1, WEM, GULL.

25. "Now, New Dreams to Share," Folder 2, Box 7, WEM, GULL.

26. "Gunman Shot After 2 Slain," *Desert Sun*, February 17, 1976, A2; Msgr. John G. Nolan to WEM, February 20, 1976, Folder 21, Box 7, WEM; Farid Farid, "Steve Kerr and His Mother Talk About the Legacy of His Father's Assassination," *New Yorker*, June 16, 2016, www.newyorker.com/news/news-desk/steve-kerr-and-his-mother-talk-about-the-legacy-of-his-fathers-assassination (accessed February 5, 2018); Margalit Fox, "David Dodge, an Early Lebanon Hostage, Dies at 86," *NYT*, January 30, 2009; Walter S. Mossberg, "A Desert 'America' Is Governed by Fear of Mideast Turmoil," *WSJ*, undated newspaper clipping, Folder 2, Box 7, WEM, GULL.

27. WEM to Father Timon Costello, June 27, 1985; "Summary: R. C. Group of Dhahran," Folder 21, Box 7, WEM, GULL.

28. Memo of Ambassador West's meeting with HRH Prince Nayyef, November 29, 1977; see for instance, note beginning "In December 1982," letter beginning with "Dear Friends, I always knew," and "Private," October 31; Mary Horton to WEM, February 7, 1992; letter from Xavier House to WEM, February 11, 1980, Folder 21, Box 7, WEM,

GULL; Tom Houston to Miki Stewart, October 16, 1989, and Miki Stewart to Tom Houston, November 20, 1989, Folder 3, Box 312, RLCW, WGA.

29. WEM to Father Timon Costello, June 27, 1985, and WEM to John G. Nolan, May 21, 1978, Folder 21, Box 7, WEM, GULL. On civil rights work, see "William E. Mulligan," Aramco Expats, www.aramcoexpats.com/obituaries/william-e-mulligan (accessed March 2, 2018).

30. Thomas C. Barger, "Suppose We Seized Arab Oil Fields," *LAT*, April 13, 1975, Part XI, 1; Thomas Barger, "Communicating in the Middle East" (presented at the Seventh Annual National Security Affairs Conference, Washington, DC, July 21–23, 1980), 5, Folder 6, Box 1, WEM, GULL.

31. WEM to John J. Kelberer, July 7, 1986, Folder 5, Box 1, WEM, GULL.

32. James Morton Turner, "'The Specter of Environmentalism': Wilderness, Environmental Politics, and the Evolution of the New Right," *Journal of American History* 96 (June 2009): 132.

33. Quoted in Allitt, *A Climate of Crisis*, 162.

34. James Watt, testimony before the House Interior Committee, February 5, 1981, quoted in Timothy P. Weber, "Happily at the Edge of the Abyss: Popular Premillennialism in America," *Ex Auditu: An International Journal of Theological Interpretation of Scripture* 6 (1990): 93. See also David Douglass, "God, the World and James Watt," *Christianity and Crisis* 41 (October 5, 1981): 258, 269–270; Colman McCarthy, "James Watt and the Puritan Ethic," *WP*, May 24, 1981. For further detail and context, see Briefing by the Secretary of the Interior, hearings of House Committee on Interior and Insular Affairs, 97th Congress, February 5, 1981 (Washington, DC: US Government Printing Office, 1981); Energy and Natural Resources, 97th Congress, January 7–8, 1981 (Washington, DC: US Government Printing Office, 1981). D. Michael Lindsay, *Faith in the Halls of Power: How Evangelicals Joined the American Elite* (New York: Oxford University Press, 2008), 19; Turner, "'The Specter of Environmentalism,'" 134; Robert H. Nelson, *The New Holy Wars: Economic Religion Versus Environmental Religion in Contemporary America* (State College: Pennsylvania State University Press, 2010), xviii–xix; quoted in Allitt, *A Climate of Crisis*, 162.

35. Quoted in Allitt, *A Climate of Crisis*, 172, 181–183.

36. Douglas Martin, "Anne Gorsuch Burford, 62, Reagan E.P.A. Chief, Dies," *NYT*, July 22, 2004; Brady Dennis and Christ Mooney, "Neil Gorsuch's Mother Once Ran the EPA. It Didn't Go Well," *WP*, February 1, 2017; quoted in "The Legacy of James Watt," *Time*, October 24, 1983, 31; quoted in Allitt, *A Climate of Crisis*, 163–164.

37. Wilkinson, *Between God and Green*, 17.

38. Joe Holley, "Textbook Activist Mel Gabler, 89," *WP*, December 23, 2004, B8; Melissa Marie Deckman, *School Board Battles: The Christian Right in Local Politics* (Washington, DC: Georgetown University Press, 2004), 13. For a brief timeline of LeTourneau University, see Ken Durham, "LeTourneau University," Texas State Historical Association, June 15, 2010, https://tshaonline.org/handbook/online/articles/kbl09 (accessed February 4, 2018).

39. Allitt, *A Climate of Crisis*, 165; quoted in Ronald L. Numbers, *The Creationists: From Scientific Creationism to Intelligent Design* (Cambridge, MA: Harvard University Press, 2006), 145; quoted in Mark Alan Kalthoff, "The New Evangelical Engagement with Science: The American Scientific Affiliation, Origin to 1963" (PhD diss., Indiana University, 1998), 375–376.

40. Quoted in Kalthoff, "The New Evangelical Engagement with Science," 385; John C. Whitcomb and Henry M. Morris, *The Genesis Flood: The Biblical Record and Its Scientific Implications* (Philipsburg, NJ: Presbyterian and Reformed Publishing, 1961), 117–118, 327, 328–330.

41. Numbers, *The Creationists*, 234–235, 329; David R. Montgomery, *The Rocks Don't Lie: A Geologist Investigates Noah's Flood* (New York: W. W. Norton, 2012), 254. Montgomery's concession does not signal his endorsement of the creation science approach.

42. Goodwin, *Texas Oil, American Dreams*, 157, 160–161.

43. "Speech Given by Reverend Leon Sullivan," November 16, 1983, 5–7, 9, Folder 20, Box 85, LHS, EUA.

44. Quoted in Grem, *Blessings of Business*, 212–213; Mimi Swartz, "Myth-o-Maniacs," *TM*, February 1993, 140–145.

45. Quoted in Bob Burke and Marcia Shottenkirk, *From Boom to Bust and Back: The Story of Elk City, Oklahoma and Grandview Church* (Oklahoma City, OK: Commonwealth Press, 2006), 12, 15, 18, 45–46.

46. Quoted in Burke and Shottenkirk, *From Boom to Bust and Back*, 48–49.

47. Robert Hershey Jr., "How the Oil Glut Is Changing Business," *NYT*, June 21, 1981, https://www.nytimes.com/1981/06/21/business/how-the-oil-glut-is-changing-business.html (accessed December 2, 2018); Byron Christopher, "Problems for Oil Producers," *Time*, January 19, 2008; quoted in Goodwin, *Texas Oil, American Dreams*, 170–171; Collin Eaton, "1980s Oil Bust Left a Lasting Mark," *HC*, August 31, 2016, www.chron.com/local/history/economy-business/article/The-1980s-oil-bust-left-lasting-mark-on-Houston-9195222.php (accessed February 5, 2018).

48. Goodwin, *Texas Oil, American Dreams*, 171–172; Pakka, *The Energy Within*, 109.

49. Nigel Duara, "In West Texas Oil Boomtowns, 'The End Is Near,'" *LAT*, March 3, 2015, www.latimes.com/nation/la-na-texas-oil-20150303-story.html (accessed February 3, 2018); Eaton, "1980s Oil Bust Left a Lasting Mark."

50. Jason P. Brown, "The Response of Employment to Changes in Oil and Gas Exploration," *Economic Review* (second quarter 2015): 67; David Maraniss, "Texas, Oklahoma and Louisiana Make Slow Comeback from '86 Oil Bust," *LAT*, November 18, 1990, http://articles.latimes.com/1990-11-18/news/mn-6593_1_oil-prices (accessed February 3, 2018).

51. Chris Varcoe, "Varcoe: Miserable Alberta Recession No Match for '80s Upheaval," *CH*, April 5, 2016, http://calgaryherald.com/business/energy/varcoe-miserable-alberta-recession-no-match-for-80s-upheaval (accessed February 23, 2018); "Alberta's Housing Sector Is Hurting, but It's No 1980s Flashback: Feds," *Canadian Press*, May 2, 2015, www.nationalobserver.com/2015/05/02/news/albertas-housing-sector-hurting-its-no-1980s-flashback-feds (accessed February 22, 2018); Chastko, *Developing Alberta's Oil Sands*, 174, 181–182, 184; "The Oil Sands Story (1960s, 1970s & 1980s)," Suncor, www.suncor.com/about-us/history/the-oil-sands-story (accessed February 21, 2018).

52. Jane Spraggins Wilson, "Texon, TX," Texas State Historical Association, June 15, 2010, https://tshaonline.org/handbook/online/articles/hnt15 (accessed February 23, 2018); Eaton, "1980s Oil Bust Left a Lasting Mark"; Maraniss, "Texas, Oklahoma and Louisiana Make Slow Comeback from '86 Oil Bust."

53. Quoted in Burke and Shottenkirk, *From Boom to Bust and Back*, 48–49, 67–68.

54. Burke and Shottenkirk, *From Boom to Bust and Back*, 80–81, 86.

55. Quoted in Burke and Shottenkirk, *From Boom to Bust and Back*, 90–91.

56. George W. Bush, *Decision Points* (New York: Crown Publishers, 2010), 6, 30. For Blessitt's take on this encounter, see "Praying with George W. Bush," Official Website of Arthur Blessitt, http://www.blessitt.com/praying-with-george-w-bush (accessed December 2, 2018). Also see David Aikman, *A Man of Faith: The Spiritual Journey of George W. Bush* (Nashville: W Publishing Group, 2004), 42, 70–71; Alan Cooperman, "Openly Religious, to a Point: Bush Leaves the Specifics of His Faith to Speculation," *WP*, September 16, 2004. For further treatment, see also Darren Dochuk, "There Will Be Oil: Presidents, Wildcat Religion, and the Culture Wars of Pipeline Politics," in *Recasting the Presidency*,

ed. Brian Balogh and Bruce Schulman (Philadelphia: University of Pennsylvania Press, 2015), 93–107.

57. George W. Bush, *A Charge to Keep* (New York: William Morrow, 1999): 18–19, 136, 206; Tony Carnes, "A Presidential Hopeful's Progress," *CT* 44 (October 2, 2000); Howard Fineman et al., "Bush and God: How Faith Changed His Life and Shapes His Presidency," *Newsweek* 141 (March 10, 2003), 25; Aikman, *Man of Faith*, 45, 75–76.

58. Goodwin, *Texas Oil, American Dreams*, 171.

59. "A Dream Fulfilled," Saudi Aramco advertisement, Folder 2, Box 7, WEM; Yergin, *The Prize*, 12.

60. Kevin Phillips, *American Theocracy: The Peril and Politics of Radical Religion, Oil, and Borrowed Money in the 21st Century* (New York: Penguin Books, 2006), xxi, 81.

61. Alan Taylor, "The Exxon Valdez Oil Spill: 25 Years Ago Today," *TA*, March 24, 2014.

62. Bill McKibben, *Oil and Honey: The Education of an Unlikely Activist* (New York: Times Books, 2014), 71; Bill McKibben, *The End of Nature*, rpt. ed. (New York: Anchor Books, 1989, 1997), 10–11. For further treatment, see also Darren Dochuk, "Crude Awakenings in the Age of Oil," in *Faith in the New Millennium: The Future of Religion and American Politics*, ed. Matthew Avery Sutton and Darren Dochuk (New York: Oxford University Press, 2016), 110–131.

63. "The Business of Earth Day," *NYT*, November 12, 1989; Kathleen Teltsch, "2-d Largest Philanthropy Widens Role," *NYT*, August 27, 1990, A14.

64. Steven C. Rockefeller and John C. Elder, eds., *Spirit and Nature: Why the Environment Is a Religious Issue* (Boston: Beacon Press, 1992), 1, 4, 10.

## Epilogue: God and Black Gold in the New Millennium

1. Amy Kaplan, "'Left Alone with America': The Absence of Empire in the Study of American Culture," in *Cultures of United States Imperialism*, ed. Amy Kaplan and Donald E. Pease (Durham, NC: Duke University Press, 1993), 9. It is highly unlikely that Miller actually traveled to the Congo or unloaded drums of petroleum along its legendary waterway. As those closest to him would later deduce, the vision was one he concocted in his head. Rivka Maizlish, "Rethinking the Origin of American Studies (with Help from Perry Miller)," S-USIH, November 13, 2013, https://s-usih.org/2013/11/rethinking-the-origin-of-american-studies-with-help-from-perry-miller (accessed June 2, 2018).

2. Yergin, *The Quest*, 10; Mark Thomas Edwards, "The 1990s—a Historiographical Survey," in *The Routledge History of the Twentieth-Century United States*, ed. Jerald Podair and Darren Dochuk (New York: Routledge, 2018), 101–102.

3. Yergin, *The Quest*, 13, 93, 96–97.

4. Yergin, *The Quest*, 135–137.

5. Bush, *Decision Points*, 229, 240; Yergin, *The Quest*, 290.

6. Yergin, *The Quest*, 97; Richard A. Oppel Jr. with Kurt Eichenwald, "Enron's Collapse: The Overview; Arthur Anderson Fires an Executive for Enron Orders," *NYT*, January 16, 2002; "The End of the Oil Age," *The Economist*, October 23, 2003.

7. Alex Epstein, "Why We Should Love the Oil Companies (Straight Talk from an Industry Outsider)," MasterResource, June 15, 2012, www.masterresource.org/energy-education/love-oil-companies-educate (accessed June 12, 2018).

8. For context on foreign workers in North American oil, see, for instance, Moira Herbst, "U.S. Oil, Imported Workers," *Businessweek*, August 4, 2008.

9. Al Gore and David Guggenheim, *An Inconvenient Truth* (Los Angeles, CA: Lawrence Bender Productions, 2006); Julia Lieblich, "Born-Again Gore Takes Open-Minded Tack," *Register-Guard*, July 10, 2000, 3A.

10. McKibben, *Oil and Honey*, 13–14, 71, 105.

11. "Why Bill McKibben Is the New Noah," *Sojourners*, August 8, 2012; Rosie Marie Berger, "For God So Loved the World," *Sojourners*, May 2013.

12. Marc Gunther, "ExxonMobil Braces for Rockefeller Showdown," *Fortune Magazine*, May 27, 2008; Reeves Wiedeman, "The Rockefellers vs. the Company That Made Them Rockefellers," *New York Magazine*, January 7, 2018; Peter Foster, "Peter Foster: Green Billionaires Undermining Canada," *Financial Post*, August 8, 2014, http://business.financial post.com/2014/08/08/peter-foster-green-billionaires-undermining-canada (accessed October 22, 2014); Vivian Krause, "U.S. Foundations Against the Oil Sands," *Business Financial Post*, October 14, 2010.

13. Yergin, *The Quest*, 204–205, 233, 325–327; Ben White, "Chinese Drop Bid to Buy U.S. Oil Firm," *WP*, August 3, 2005; Diana Davids Hinton, "The Seventeen-Year Overnight Wonder: George Mitchell and Unlocking the Barnett Shale," in "Oil in American History: A Special Issue," ed. Brian C. Black, Karen R. Merrill, and Tyler Priest, *Journal of American History* (June 2012): 229–235.

14. Daniel Schulman, *Sons of Wichita: How the Koch Brothers Became America's Most Powerful and Private Dynasty* (New York: Grand Central, 2014), 5.

15. Phillips, *American Theocracy*, xii–xiii.

16. Jane Mayer, *Dark Money: The Hidden History of the Billionaires Behind the Rise of the Radical Right* (New York: Doubleday, 2016), 166–167; here I am borrowing from R. G. Ratcliffe, "The Power Issue: Tim Dunn Is Pushing the Republican Party into the Arms of God," *TM*, December 2018, https://www.texasmonthly.com/politics/power-issue -tim-dunn-pushing-republican-party-arms-god (accessed December 15, 2018).

17. Nicholas Confessore, Sarah Cohen, and Karen Yourish, "Buying Power," *NYT*, October 10, 2015.

18. See, for instance, Mayer, *Dark Money*, and Nancy MacLean, *Democracy in Chains: The Deep History of the Radical Right's Stealth Plan for America* (New York: Penguin, 2017). This is not to discount Mayer's stellar account of dark money—hidden, unlimited, and undisclosed financial donations funneled by corporations and individuals into nonprofit organizations for the purpose of shifting American elections and political policies toward the libertarian Right—but merely to highlight the degree to which such funneling has long fueled the wildcat Right, often in clear view.

19. Charles Postel, *The Populist Vision* (New York: Oxford University Press, 2007), 22; Drew Pendergrass, "The Televangelist-in-Chief: Trump and the Prosperity Gospel," *Harvard Political Review*, November 12, 2017; Jean Comaroff and John L. Comaroff, "Millennial Capitalism: First Thoughts on a Second Coming," in *Millennial Capitalism and the Culture of Neoliberalism*, ed. Jean Comaroff and John L. Comaroff (Durham, NC: Duke University Press, 2001), 23–25.

20. Imre Szeman and Dominic Boyer, "Introduction: On the Energy Humanities," in *Energy Humanities: An Anthology*, ed. Imre Szeman and Dominic Boyer (Baltimore: Johns Hopkins University Press, 2017), 2; see, for instance, Derek Hawkins, "Oklahoma Gov. Mary Fallin Says All Faiths, Not Just Christians, Should Observe 'Oilfield Prayer Day,'" *WP*, October 11; "Louisiana Lawmakers Propose Prayer to Stop Oil Disaster," *CNN*, June 20, 2010, www.cnn.com/2010/US/06/20/gulf.oil.spill/index.html (accessed August 23, 2018). See Arlie Russell Hochschild, *Strangers in Their Own Land: Anger and Mourning on the American Right* (New York: New Press, 2016).

21. See "A Scripture. A Vision. A Calling.," Zion Oil & Gas, www.zionoil.com/vision/vision-statement/founders-page (accessed August 22, 2018); "A Petroleum Engineer and Oil Company Founder Says the . . . ," UPI, November 9, 1982, www.upi.com/Archives/1982/11/09/A-petroleum-engineer-and-oil-company-founder-says-the/1192405666000 (accessed August 22, 2018); Mariah Blake, "Let There Be Light Crude," *Mother Jones* (January/February 2008).

22. Benjamin Glatt, "Evangelical Firm Encounters Oil in Jezreel," *Jerusalem Post*, February 14, 2018; Jeff Mosier, "As Dallas' Zion Oil and Gas Drills in the Valley of Armageddon, Its Believers Are Praying for a Gusher," *Dallas News*, August 2017, https://www.dallas news.com/business/energy/2017/08/03/dallas-oil-firm-thousands-investors-pray-gusher-biblical-site-armageddon-israel (accessed August 23, 2018); quoted in Lison Joseph, "SEC Investigating Zion Oil and Gas, the Faith-Based Dallas Company That Drills Exclusively in Israel," *Dallas News*, July 12, 2018, https://www.dallasnews.com/business/energy/2018/07/12/sec-investigating-zion-oil-gas-faith-based-dallas-company-drills-exclusively-israel (accessed August 23, 2018); quoted in Jeff Mosier, "Dallas' Faith-Based Oil Company Hit a Dry Hole in Israel and Is Running Out of Money," *Dallas News*, November 26, 2018, https://www.dallasnews.com/business/energy/2018/11/26/dallas-faith-based-oil-company-hit-dry-hole-israel-running-money (accessed December 18, 2018).

# Selected Bibliography

## Books

Allitt, Patrick. *A Climate of Crisis: America in the Age of Environmentalism.* New York: Penguin, 2014.

Andrews, Thomas. *Killing for Coal: America's Deadliest Labor War.* Cambridge, MA: Harvard University Press, 2010.

Barrett, Ross, and Daniel Worden, eds. *Oil Culture.* Minneapolis: University of Minnesota Press, 2014.

Beckert, Sven. *Empire of Cotton: A Global History.* New York: Alfred A. Knopf, 2014.

Beeth, Howard, and Cary D. Wintz, eds. *Black Dixie: Afro-Texan History and Culture in Houston.* College Station: Texas A&M University Press, 1992.

Behrends, Andrea, Stephen P. Reyna, and Gunther Schlee, eds. *Crude Domination: An Anthropology of Oil.* New York: Berghahn Books, 2011.

Berman, Edward H. *The Influence of the Carnegie, Ford, and Rockefeller Foundations on American Foreign Policy: The Ideology of Philanthropy.* Albany: State University of New York Press, 1983.

Black, Brian. *Crude Reality: Petroleum in World History.* New York: Rowman & Littlefield, 2012.

———. *Petrolia: The Landscape of America's First Oil Boom.* Baltimore: Johns Hopkins University Press, 2000.

Blum, Edward J. *Reforging the White Republic: Race, Religion, and American Nationalism, 1865–1898.* Baton Rouge: Louisiana State University Press, 2005.

Boatright, Mody C., and William A. Owens. *Tales from the Derrick Floor: A People's History of the Oil Industry.* Garden City, NY: Doubleday, 1970.

Bowman, Matthew. *The Urban Pulpit: New York City and the Fate of Liberal Evangelicalism.* New York: Oxford University Press, 2014.

Bromley, Simon. *American Hegemony and World Oil: The Industry, the State System and the World Economy.* University Park: Pennsylvania State University Press, 1991.

Bronson, Rachel. *Thicker Than Oil: America's Uneasy Partnership with Saudi Arabia.* Oxford: Oxford University Press, 2006.

Brown, Anthony Cave. *Oil, God, and Gold: The Story of Aramco and the Saudi Kings.* New York: Houghton Mifflin Company, 1999.

Brown, Kate. *Plutopia: Nuclear Families, Atomic Cities, and the Great Soviet and American Plutonium Disasters.* New York: Oxford University Press, 2013.

Bullard, Robert D. *Invisible Houston: The Black Experience in Boom and Bust.* College Station: Texas A&M University Press, 1987.

Burgin, Angus. *The Great Persuasion: Reinventing Free Markets Since the Depression.* Cambridge, MA: Harvard University Press, 2012.

Burrough, Brian. *The Big Rich: The Rise and Fall of the Greatest Texas Oil Fortunes.* New York: Penguin Press, 2009.

Callahan, Richard J. Jr. *Work and Faith in the Kentucky Coal Fields: Subject to Dust.* Bloomington: Indiana University Press, 2008.

Carenen, Caitlin. *The Fervent Embrace: Liberal Protestants, Evangelicals, and Israel.* New York: New York University Press, 2012.

Carter, Heath W. *Union Made: Working People and the Rise of Social Christianity in Chicago.* New York: Oxford University Press, 2015.

Chastko, Paul. *Developing Alberta's Oil Sands: From Karl Clark to Kyoto.* Calgary, AB: University of Calgary Press, 2004.

Chernow, Ron. *Titan: The Life of John D. Rockefeller, Sr.* New York: Vintage Books, 1998.

Childs, William R. *The Texas Railroad Commission: Understanding Regulation in America to the Mid-Twentieth Century.* College Station: Texas A&M University Press, 2005.

Citino, Nathan J. *Envisioning the Arab Future: Modernization in U.S.-Arab Relations, 1945–1967.* Cambridge: Cambridge University Press, 2017.

———. *From Arab Nationalism to OPEC: Eisenhower, King Saud, and the Making of U.S.-Saudi Relations.* Bloomington: Indiana University Press, 2002.

Coffman, Elesha J. *The Christian Century and the Rise of the Protestant Mainline.* New York: Oxford University Press, 2013.

Cohen, Lizabeth. *A Consumer's Republic: The Politics of Mass Consumption in Postwar America.* New York: Vintage Press, 2003.

———. *Making a New Deal: Industrial Workers in Chicago, 1919–1939.* 2nd ed. New York: Cambridge University Press, 2014.

Conroy-Krutz, Emily. *Christian Imperialism: Converting the World in the Early American Republic.* Ithaca, NY: Cornell University Press, 2015.

Corrigan, John. *Business of the Heart: Religion and Emotion in the Nineteenth Century.* Berkeley: University of California Press, 2002.

Cowie, Jefferson. *Stayin' Alive: The 1970s and the Last Days of the Working Class.* New York: New Press, 2012.

Curtis, Heather. *Holy Humanitarians: American Evangelicals and Global Aid.* Cambridge, MA: Harvard University Press, 2018.

Davis, Margaret Leslie. *Dark Side of Fortune: Triumph and Scandal in the Life of Oil Tycoon Edward L. Doheny.* Berkeley: University of California Press, 2001.

Deffeyes, Kenneth S. *Hubbert's Peak: The Impending World Oil Shortage.* Princeton, NJ: Princeton University Press, 2008.

Dowland, Seth. *Family Values and the Rise of the Christian Right.* Philadelphia: University of Pennsylvania Press, 2015.

Dubofsky, Melvyn. *We Shall Be All: A History of the Industrial Workers of the World.* Urbana: University of Illinois Press, 1988.

Dudziak, Mary L. *Cold War Civil Rights: Race and the Image of American Democracy.* Princeton, NJ: Princeton University Press, 2000.

Ekbladh, David. *The Great American Mission: Modernization and the*

*Construction of an American World Order*. Princeton, NJ: Princeton University Press, 2010.

Engel, Jeffrey A. *When the World Seemed New: George H. W. Bush and the End of the Cold War*. Boston: Houghton Mifflin Harcourt, 2017.

Fiege, Mark. *The Republic of Nature: An Environmental History of the United States*. Seattle: University of Washington Press, 2012.

Fones-Wolf, Elizabeth, and Ken Fones-Wolf. *Struggle for the Soul of the Postwar South: White Evangelical Protestants and Operation Dixie*. Urbana: University of Illinois Press, 2015.

Fosdick, Raymond B. *The Story of the Rockefeller Foundation*. New York: Harper & Brothers, 1952.

Frank, Alison Fleig. *Oil Empire: Visions of Prosperity in Austrian Galicia*. Cambridge, MA: Harvard University Press, 2005.

Franklin, Jimmie Lewis. *Journey Toward Hope: A History of Blacks in Oklahoma*. Norman: University of Oklahoma Press, 1982.

Frehner, Brian. *Finding Oil: The Nature of Petroleum Geology, 1859–1920*. Lincoln: University of Nebraska Press, 2011.

Fried, Richard M. *The Man Everybody Knew: Bruce Barton and the Making of Modern America*. Chicago: Ivan R. Dee, 2005.

Frykholm, Amy Johnson. *Rapture Culture: Left Behind in America*. New York: Oxford University Press, 2004.

Giebelhaus, August W. *Business and Government in the Oil Industry: A Case Study of Sun Oil, 1876–1945*. Greenwich, CT: JAI Press, 1980.

Gloege, Timothy E. W. *Guaranteed Pure: The Moody Bible Institute, Business, and the Making of Modern Evangelicalism*. Chapel Hill: University of North Carolina Press, 2015.

Gold, Russell. *The Boom: How Fracking Ignited the American Energy Revolution and Changed the World*. New York: Simon & Schuster, 2014.

Goodwyn, Lawrence. *Texas Oil, American Dreams: A Study of the Texas Independent Producers and Royalty Owners Association*. Austin: Texas State Historical Association, 1996.

Graham, Don. *Cowboys and Cadillacs: How Hollywood Looks at Texas*. Austin: Texas Monthly, 1983.

Greenberg, Jonathan D. *Staking a Claim: Jake Simmons and the Making of an African-American Oil Dynasty*. New York: Plume, 1991.

Grem, Darren. *The Blessings of Business: How Corporations Shaped Conservative Christianity*. New York: Oxford University Press, 2016.

Hammond, Sarah Ruth, and Darren Dochuk, ed. *God's Businessmen: Entrepreneurial Evangelicals in Depression and War*. Chicago: University of Chicago Press, 2017.

Harr, John Ensor, and Peter J. Johnson. *The Rockefeller Century*. New York: Charles Scribner's Sons, 1988.

Harvey, David. *A Brief History of Neoliberalism*. New York: Oxford University Press, 2005.

Harvey, Paul. *Freedom's Coming: Religious Culture and the Shaping of the South from the Civil War Through the Civil Rights Era*. Chapel Hill: University of North Carolina Press, 2005.

———. *Redeeming the South: Religious Cultures and Racial Identities Among Southern Baptists, 1865–1925*. Chapel Hill: University of North Carolina Press, 1997.

Hays, Samuel P. *Conservation and the Gospel of Efficiency: The Progressive Conservation Movement, 1890–1920*. Cambridge, MA: Harvard University Press, 1959.

Hedstrom, Matthew S. *The Rise of Liberal Religion: Book Culture and American Spirituality in the Twentieth*

*Century*. New York: Oxford University Press, 2012.

Hertog, Steffen. *Princes, Brokers, and Bureaucrats: Oil and the State in Saudi Arabia*. Ithaca, NY: Cornell University Press, 2010.

Herzstein, Robert E. *Henry R. Luce, Time, and the American Crusade in Asia*. New York: Cambridge University Press, 2005.

Heyrman, Christine Leigh. *American Apostles: When Evangelicals Entered the World of Islam*. New York: Hill and Wang, 2015.

Hochschild, Arlie Russell. *Strangers in Their Own Land: Anger and Mourning on the American Right*. New York: New Press, 2016.

Hoganson, Kristin L. *Consumers' Imperium: The Global Production of American Domesticity, 1865–1920*. Chapel Hill: University of North Carolina Press, 2007.

Hollinger, David A. *Protestants Abroad: How Missionaries Tried to Change the World but Changed America*. Princeton, NJ: Princeton University Press, 2017.

Huber, Matthew T. *Lifeblood: Oil, Freedom, and the Forces of Capital*. Minneapolis: University of Minnesota Press, 2013.

Hudnut-Beumler, James. *In Pursuit of the Almighty's Dollar: A History of Money and American Protestantism*. Chapel Hill: University of North Carolina Press, 2007.

Hutchison, William R. *Errand to the World: American Protestant Thought and Foreign Missions*. Chicago: University of Chicago Press, 1987.

———. *The Modernist Impulse in American Protestantism*. Durham, NC: Duke University Press, 1992.

Hyman, Louis. *Debtor Nation: The History of America in Red Ink*. New York: Oxford University Press, 2011.

Immerwahr, Daniel. *Thinking Small: The United States and the Lure of Community Development*. Cambridge, MA: Harvard University Press, 2015.

Inboden, William. *Religion and American Foreign Policy, 1945–1960: The Soul of Containment*. New York: Cambridge University Press, 2008.

Ise, John. *The United States Oil Policy*. New Haven, CT: Yale University Press, 1926.

Isenberg, Andrew C. *Mining California: An Ecological History*. New York: Hill and Wang, 2005.

Jacobs, Meg. *Panic at the Pump: The Energy Crisis and the Transformation of American Politics in the 1970s*. New York: Hill and Wang, 2017.

———. *Pocketbook Politics: Economic Citizenship in Twentieth-Century America*. Princeton, NJ: Princeton University Press, 2005.

Jacobsen, Matthew Frye. *Barbarian Virtues: The United States Encounters Foreign Peoples at Home and Abroad, 1876–1917*. New York: Hill and Wang, 2000.

Jacoby, Neil H. *Multinational Oil: A Study in Industrial Dynamics*. New York: Macmillan, 1974.

Jakle, John A., and Keith A. Sculle. *The Gas Station in America*. Baltimore: Johns Hopkins University Press, 1994.

Johnson, Arthur M. *The Challenge of Change: The Sun Oil Company, 1945–1977*. Columbus: Ohio State University Press, 1983.

Johnson, Bob. *Carbon Nation: Fossil Fuels in the Making of American Culture*. Lawrence: University Press of Kansas, 2014.

Jones, Toby Craig. *Desert Kingdom: How Oil and Water Forged Modern Saudi Arabia*. Cambridge, MA: Harvard University Press, 2010.

Kaplan, Amy, and Donald E. Pease, eds. *Cultures of United States Imperialism*. Durham, NC: Duke University Press, 1994.

Kaplan, Robert D. *The Arabists: The Romance of an American Elite*. New York: Free Press, 1995.

Karl, Terry Lynn. *The Paradox of Plenty: Oil Booms and Petro-States*. Berkeley: University of California Press, 1997.

Klein, Christina. *Cold War Orientalism: Asia in the Middlebrow Imagination, 1945-1961*. Berkeley: University of California Press, 2003.

Knowles, Ruth Sheldon. *The Greatest Gamblers: The Epic of American Oil Exploration*. Norman: University of Oklahoma Press, 1978.

Kruse, Kevin. *One Nation Under God: How Corporate America Invented Christian America*. New York: Basic Books, 2015.

Kuklick, Bruce. *Puritans in Babylon: The Ancient Near East and American Intellectual Life, 1880–1930*. Princeton, NJ: Princeton University Press, 1996.

Lears, T. J. Jackson. *No Place of Grace: Antimodernism and the Transformation of American Culture, 1880–1920*. New York: Pantheon Books, 1981.

Lehmann, Chris. *The Money Cult: Capitalism, Christianity, and the Unmaking of the American Dream*. Brooklyn, NY: Melville House, 2016.

LeMenager, Stephanie. *Living Oil: Petroleum Culture in the American Century*. New York: Oxford University Press, 2014.

Levy, Jonathan. *Freaks of Fortune: The Emerging World of Capitalism and Risk in America*. Cambridge, MA: Harvard University Press, 2012.

Lichtman, Allan J. *White Protestant Nation: The Rise of the American Conservative Movement*. New York: Atlantic Monthly Press, 2008.

Limbert, Mandana E. *In the Time of Oil: Piety, Memory, and Social Life in an Omani Town*. Stanford, CA: Stanford University Press, 2010.

Lind, Michael. *Made in Texas: George W. Bush and the Southern Takeover of American Politics*. New York: Basic Books, 2003.

Lofton, Kathryn. *Consuming Religion*. Chicago: University of Chicago Press, 2017.

Long, Kathryn. *The Revival of 1857–58: Interpreting an American Religious Awakening*. New York: Oxford University Press, 1998.

Maas, Peter. *Crude World: The Violent Twilight of Oil*. New York: Vintage Books, 2009.

MacLean, Nancy. *Democracy in Chains: The Deep History of the Radical Right's Stealth Plan for America*. New York: Viking, 2017.

Makdisi, Ussama. *Artillery of Heaven: American Missionaries and the Failed Conversion of the Middle East*. Ithaca, NY: Cornell University Press, 2008.

———. *Faith Misplaced: The Broken Promise of U.S.-Arab Relations, 1820–2001*. New York: Public Affairs, 2010.

Malm, Andreas. *Fossil Capital: The Rise of Steam Power and the Roots of Global Warming*. Brooklyn, NY: Verso, 2016.

Marsden, George M. *Fundamentalism and American Culture*. 2nd ed. New York: Oxford University Press, 2006.

Mayer, Jane. *Dark Money: The Hidden History of the Billionaires Behind the Rise of the Radical Right*. New York: Doubleday, 2016.

McAlister, Melani. *Epic Encounters: Culture, Media, and U.S. Interests in the Middle East Since 1945*. Upd. ed. Berkeley: University of California Press, 2005.

———. *The Kingdom of God Has No Borders: A Global History of American Evangelicals*. New York: Oxford University Press, 2018.

McDaniel, Robert W., and Henry C. Dethlof. *Patillo Higgins and the*

*Search for Texas Oil.* College Station: Texas A&M Press, 1989.

Merchant, Carolyn. *Ecological Revolutions: Nature, Gender, and Science in New England.* Chapel Hill: University of North Carolina Press, 1989.

Miller, Edward H. *Nut Country: Right-Wing Dallas and the Birth of the Southern Strategy.* Chicago: University of Chicago Press, 2015.

Mitchell, Timothy. *Carbon Democracy: Political Power in the Age of Oil.* New York: Verso, 2013.

Monroe, Elizabeth. *Philby of Arabia.* Reading, UK: Garnet Publishing, 1998.

Montgomery, David R. *The Rocks Don't Lie: A Geologist Investigates Noah's Flood.* New York: W. W. Norton, 2012.

Moreton, Bethany. *To Serve God and Wal-Mart: The Making of Christian Free Enterprise.* Cambridge, MA: Harvard University Press, 2010.

Morris, Charles R. *The Tycoons: How Andrew Carnegie, John D. Rockefeller, Jay Gould, and J. P. Morgan Invented the American Supereconomy.* New York: Holt, 2006.

Mount, Houston Faust, II. *Oilfield Revolutionary: The Career of Everette Lee DeGolyer.* College Station: Texas A&M University Press, 2014.

Nash, Gerald D. *State Government and Economic Development: A History of Administrative Policies in California, 1849–1933.* Berkeley: Institute of Governmental Studies, University of California, 1964.

———. *United States Oil Policy, 1890–1964: Business and Government in Twentieth Century America.* Pittsburgh: University of Pittsburgh Press, 1968.

Nash, Roderick. *Wilderness and the American Mind.* 3rd ed. New Haven, CT: Yale University Press, 1982.

Needham, Andrew. *Power Lines: Phoenix and the Making of the Modern*

*Southwest.* Princeton, NJ: Princeton University Press, 2016.

Nevins, Allan. *John D. Rockefeller: The Heroic Age of American Enterprise.* New York: Charles Scribner's Sons, 1940.

Nielsen, Waldemar A. *Golden Donors: A New Anatomy of the Great Foundations.* New Brunswick, NJ: Transaction Publishers, 2002.

Noll, Mark, ed. *God and Mammon: Protestants, Money, and the Market, 1790–1860.* New York: Oxford University Press, 2001.

Numbers, Ronald L. *The Creationists: From Scientific Creationism to Intelligent Design.* Expanded ed. Cambridge, MA: Harvard University Press, 2006.

Nye, David E. *Consuming Power: A Social History of American Energies.* Boston: MIT Press, 1999.

O'Connor, Harvey. *History of Oil Workers Int'l Union (CIO).* Denver: Published by the Oil Workers Intl. Union, A. B. Hirschfeld Press, 1950.

———. *The Oil Barons: Men of Greed and Grandeur.* Boston: Little, Brown and Company, 1971.

Olien, Roger M. *Oil and Ideology: The Cultural Creation of the American Petroleum Industry.* Chapel Hill: University of North Carolina Press, 2000.

Olien, Roger M., and Diana Davids Hinton. *Wildcatters: Texas Independent Oilmen.* College Station: Texas A&M University Press, 2007.

Oren, Michael B. *Power, Faith, and Fantasy: America in the Middle East, 1776 to the Present.* New York: W. W. Norton, 2011.

Ott, Julia C. *When Wall Street Met Main Street: The Quest for an Investors' Democracy.* Cambridge, MA: Harvard University Press, 2014.

Painter, David. *Oil and the American Century.* Baltimore: Johns Hopkins University Press, 1986.

Parker, Chad H. *Making the Desert Modern: Americans, Arabs, and Oil on the Saudi Frontier, 1933–1973*. Amherst: University of Massachusetts Press, 2015.

Phillips, Kevin. *American Theocracy: The Peril and Politics of Radical Religion, Oil, and Borrowed Money in the 21st Century*. New York: Penguin Books, 2006.

Pietsch, B. M. *Dispensational Modernism*. New York: Oxford University Press, 2015.

Piketty, Thomas. *Capital in the Twenty-First Century*. Cambridge, MA: Harvard University Press, 2014.

Porterfield, Amanda. *Corporate Spirit: Religion and the Rise of the Modern Corporation*. New York: Oxford University Press, 2018.

Porterfield, Amanda, John Corrigan, and Darren Grem, eds. *The Business Turn in American Religious History*. New York: Oxford University Press, 2017.

Postel, Charles. *The Populist Vision*. New York: Oxford University Press, 2009.

Pratt, Mary Louise. *Imperial Eyes: Travel Writing and Transculturation*. 2nd ed. New York: Routledge, 2008.

Preston, Andrew. *Sword of the Spirit, Shield of Faith: Religion in American War and Diplomacy*. New York: Knopf, 2012.

Priest, Tyler. *The Offshore Imperative: Shell Oil's Search for Petroleum in Postwar America*. College Station: Texas A&M University Press, 2007.

Prindle, David F. *Petroleum Politics and the Texas Railroad Commission*. Austin: University of Texas Press, 1981.

Pruitt, Bernadette. *The Other Great Migration: The Movement of Rural African Americans to Houston, 1900–1941*. College Station: Texas A&M University Press, 2013.

Randall, Stephen J. *United States Foreign Oil Policy Since World War II: For Profits and Security*. Montreal: McGill-Queen's University Press, 2005.

Rigueur, Leah Wright. *The Loneliness of the Black Republican: Pragmatic Politics and the Pursuit of Power*. Princeton, NJ: Princeton University Press, 2015.

Rister, Carl Coke. *Oil! Titan of the Southwest*. Norman: University of Oklahoma Press, 1949.

Roberts, Paul. *The End of Oil: On the Edge of a Perilous New World*. New York: Mariner Books, 2005.

Rockefeller, David. *Memoirs*. New York: Random House, 2003.

Rodgers, Daniel T. *Age of Fracture*. Cambridge, MA: Belknap Press of Harvard University Press, 2011.

Roll, Jarod. *Spirit of Rebellion: Labor and Religion in the New Cotton South*. Urbana: University of Illinois Press, 2010.

Rosenberg, Emily S. *Financial Missionaries to the World: The Politics and Culture of Dollar Diplomacy, 1900–1930*. Cambridge, MA: Harvard University Press, 1999.

Ross, Michael L. *The Oil Curse: How Petroleum Wealth Shapes the Development of Nations*. Princeton, NJ: Princeton University Press, 2012.

Rubino, Anna. *Queen of the Oil Club: The Intrepid Wanda Jablonski and the Power of Information*. Boston: Beacon Press, 2008.

Sabato, Larry J. *PAC Power: Inside the World of Political Action Committees*. New York: W. W. Norton, 1984.

Sabin, Paul. *Crude Politics: The California Oil Market, 1900–1940*. Berkeley: University of California Press, 2005.

Sale, Kirkpatrick. *Power Shift: The Rise of the Southern Rim and Its Challenges to the Eastern Establishment*. New York: Random House, 1975.

Sampson, Anthony. *The Seven Sisters: The Great Oil Companies and the World They Shaped*. New York: Bantam Books, 1975.

Santiago, Myrna. *Ecology of Oil: Environment, Labor, and the Mexican Revolution, 1900–1938*. Cambridge: Cambridge University Press, 2006.

Sargent, Daniel J. *A Superpower Transformed: The Remaking of American Foreign Relations in the 1970s*. New York: Oxford University Press, 2015.

Schatzker, Valerie. *The Jewish Oil Magnates of Galicia*, Part I: *The Jewish Oil Magnates: A History, 1853–1945*. Montreal: McGill-Queen's University Press, 2015.

Schlossstein, Steven. *The End of the American Century*. New York: Congdon & Weed, 1989.

Schmidt, Leigh Eric. *Restless Souls: The Making of American Spirituality*. 2nd ed. Berkeley: University of California Press, 2012.

Schneider-Mayerson, Matthew. *Peak Oil: Apocalyptic Environmentalism and Libertarian Political Culture*. Chicago: University of Chicago Press, 2015.

Schulman, Daniel. *Sons of Wichita: How the Koch Brothers Became America's Most Powerful and Private Dynasty*. New York: Grand Central, 2014.

Schultz, Kevin M. *Tri-Faith America: How Catholics and Jews Held Postwar America to Its Protestant Promise*. New York: Oxford University Press, 2011.

Sealander, Judith. *Private Wealth and Public Life: Foundation Philanthropy and the Reshaping of American Social Policy from the Progressive Era to the New Deal*. Baltimore: Johns Hopkins University Press, 1997.

Sharkey, Heather J. *American Evangelicals in Egypt: Missionary Encounters in an Age of Empire*. Princeton, NJ: Princeton University Press, 2008.

Shelley, Toby. *Oil: Politics, Poverty and the Planet*. New York: Palgrave Macmillan, 2005.

Sherill, Robert. *The Oil Follies of 1970–1980: How the Petroleum Industry Stole the Show (and Much More Besides)*. New York: Anchor Press, 1983.

Shulman, Peter A. *Coal and Empire: The Birth of Energy Security in Industrial America*. Baltimore: Johns Hopkins University Press, 2015.

Sinclair, Upton. *Oil!* Berkeley: University of California Press, 1997.

Singh, Devin. *Divine Currency: The Theological Power of Money in the West*. Stanford, CA: Stanford University Press, 2018.

Sklar, Martin J. *The Corporate Reconstruction of American Capitalism, 1890–1916: The Market, the Law, and Politics*. Cambridge: Cambridge University Press, 1988.

Skowronek, Stephen. *Building a New American State: The Expansion of National Administrative Capacities, 1877–1920*. New York: Cambridge University Press, 1982.

Smith, Richard Norton. *On His Own Terms: A Life of Nelson Rockefeller*. New York: Random House, 2014.

Stasz, Clarice. *The Rockefeller Women: Dynasty of Piety, Privacy, and Service*. New York: St. Martin's Press, 1995.

Stein, Judith. *Pivotal Decade: How the United States Traded Factories for Finance in the Seventies*. New Haven, CT: Yale University Press, 2010.

Stephens, Randall J., and Karl W. Giberson. *The Anointed: Evangelical Truth in a Secular Age*. Cambridge, MA: Belknap Press of Harvard University Press, 2011.

Stoll, Mark R. *Inherit the Holy Mountain: Religion and the Rise of American Environmentalism*. New York: Oxford University Press, 2015.

———. *Protestantism, Capitalism, and Nature in America*. Albuquerque: University of New Mexico Press, 1997.

Sutton, Matthew Avery. *American Apocalypse: A History of Modern*

*Evangelicalism.* Cambridge, MA: Belknap Press of Harvard University Press, 2017.

Tait, Samuel W. Jr. *The Wildcatters: An Informal History of Oil-Hunting in America.* Princeton, NJ: Princeton University Press, 1946.

Tweed, Thomas A. *Crossing and Dwelling: A Theory of Religion.* Cambridge, MA: Harvard University Press, 2006.

Tyrrell, Ian. *Reforming the World: The Creation of America's Moral Empire.* Princeton, NJ: Princeton University Press, 2010.

Vitalis, Robert. *America's Kingdom: Mythmaking on the Saudi Oil Frontier.* Brooklyn, NY: Verso, 2009.

Wall, Wendy L. *Inventing the "American Way": The Politics of Consensus from the New Deal to the Civil Rights Movement.* New York: Oxford University Press, 2008.

Walther, Karine V. *Sacred Interests: The United States and the Islamic World, 1821–1921.* Chapel Hill: University of North Carolina Press, 2015.

Waterhouse, Benjamin C. *Lobbying America: The Politics of Business from Nixon to NAFTA.* Princeton, NJ: Princeton University Press, 2014.

Weaver, Bobby D. *Oilfield Trash: Life and Labor in the Oil Patch.* College Station: Texas A&M University Press, 2010.

Weinberg, Steve. *Taking On the Trust: The Epic Battle of Ida Tarbell and John D. Rockefeller.* New York: W. W. Norton, 2009.

Weiner, Deborah R. *Coalfield Jews: An Appalachian History.* Champaign: University of Illinois Press, 2006.

Wilford, Hugh. *America's Great Game: The CIA's Secret Arabists and the Shaping of the Modern Middle East.* New York: Basic Books, 2013.

Williams, Daniel K. *God's Only Party: The Making of the Christian Right.* New York: Oxford University Press, 2010.

Worster, Donald. *Rivers of Empire: Water, Aridity, and the Growth of the American West.* New York: Pantheon, 1985.

Wuthnow, Robert. *Rough Country: How Texas Became America's Most Powerful Bible-Belt State.* Princeton, NJ: Princeton University Press, 2014.

Yergin, Daniel. *The Prize: The Epic Quest for Oil, Money, and Power.* New York: Simon & Schuster, 1991.

——. *The Quest: Energy, Security, and the Remaking of the Modern World.* New York: Penguin Books, 2012.

Zimmerman, Andrew. *Alabama in Africa: Booker T. Washington, the German Empire, and the Globalization of the New South.* Princeton, NJ: Princeton University Press, 2010.

Zunz, Olivier. *Philanthropy in America: A History.* Princeton, NJ: Princeton University Press, 2012.

## Journal Articles, Chapters in Books, and Dissertations

Bonenfant-Juwong, Francis. "'Ever-Widening Circles': Private Voluntary Development, Colonialism, and Palestinian Arabs, 1930–1960." PhD diss., University of Notre Dame, 2018.

Callahan, Richard J. Jr., Kathryn Lofton, and Chad E. Seales. "Allegories of Progress: Industrial Religion in the United States." *Journal of the American Academy of Religion* 78 (March 2010): 1–39.

Frazier, Larry J. "Adjustments and Responses of Southern Baptist Churches in East Texas to the East

Texas Oil Boom of the 1930s." PhD diss., Baylor University, 2002.

Kalthoff, Mark Alan. "The New Evangelical Engagement with Science: The American Scientific Affiliation, Origin to 1963." PhD diss., Indiana University, 1998.

Kim, Nami. "A Mission to the 'Graveyard of Empires'? Necolonialism and the Contemporary Evangelical Missions of the Global South." *Missions Studies: Journal of the International Association for Mission Studies* 27, no. 1 (2010): 3–23.

Krivoshey, Robert Martin. "'Going Through the Eye of the Needle': The Life of Oil Man Fundamentalist Lyman Stewart, 1840–1923." PhD diss., University of Chicago, 1973.

McFarlane, Wallace Scot. "Oil on the Farm: The East Texas Oil Boom and the Origins of an Energy Economy." *Journal of Southern History* 83 (November 2017): 853–888.

Pietsch, B. M. "Lyman Stewart and Early Fundamentalism." *Church History* 82 (September 2013): 617–646.

Quam-Wickham, Nancy. "Petroleocrats and Proletarians: Work, Class, and Politics in the California Oil Industry, 1917–1925." PhD diss., University of California, Berkeley, 1994.

Roll, Jarod. "Faith Powers and Gambling Spirits in Late Gilded Age Metal Mining." In *The Pew and the Picket Line: Christianity and the American Working Class*, edited by Christopher D. Cantwell, Heath W. Carter, and Janine Giordano Drake, 74–95. Urbana: University of Illinois Press, 2016.

Sabin, Paul. "'A Dive into Nature's Great Grab-Bag': Nature, Gender, and Capitalism in the Early Pennsylvania Oil Industry." *Pennsylvania History: A Journal of Mid-Atlantic Studies* 66, no. 4 (autumn 1999): 472–505.

Viehe, Fred W. "Black Gold Suburbs: The Influence of the Extractive Industry on the Suburbanization of Los Angeles, 1890–1930." *Journal of Urban History* 8, no. 1 (November 1981): 3–26.

Wiencek, Henry Alexander. "Oil City: The Social, Economic and Environmental Anatomy of North Louisiana's Oil Boomtowns, 1901–1935." PhD diss., University of Texas, 2017.

# Index

**Darren Dochuk** is associate professor of history at the University of Notre Dame. He is author of *From Bible Belt to Sunbelt*, which received the John H. Dunning Prize from the American Historical Association (best first or second book in American history) and the Ellis W. Hawley Prize from the Organization of American Historians (best book in post–Civil War political history), and was based on a dissertation that was awarded the Allan Nevins Prize from the Society of American Historians (best dissertation in American history). He has also edited several other books in American religious history. Born and raised in Edmonton, Alberta—Canada's oil capital—he now lives in South Bend, Indiana.